# Principles of Microeconomics 3e

SENIOR CONTRIBUTING AUTHORS

**DAVID SHAPIRO, PENNSYLVANIA STATE UNIVERSITY**
**DANIEL MACDONALD, CALIFORNIA STATE UNIVERSITY, SAN BERNADINO**
**STEVEN A. GREENLAW, UNIVERSITY OF MARY WASHINGTON**

ISBN: 978-1-711471-50-1

**OpenStax**
Rice University
6100 Main Street MS-375
Houston, Texas 77005

To learn more about OpenStax, visit https://openstax.org.
Individual print copies and bulk orders can be purchased through our website.



| | |
|---|---|
| **HARDCOVER BOOK ISBN-13** | **978-1-711471-49-5** |
| **B&W PAPERBACK BOOK ISBN-13** | **978-1-711471-50-1** |
| **DIGITAL VERSION ISBN-13** | **978-1-951693-65-7** |
| **ORIGINAL PUBLICATION YEAR** | **2022** |
| 1 2 3 4 5 6 7 8 9 10 JAY 22 | |

Printed by

XanEdu

17177 Laurel Park Dr., Suite 233
Livonia, MI 48152
800-562-2147
www.xanedu.com

# OpenStax

OpenStax provides free, peer-reviewed, openly licensed textbooks for introductory college and Advanced Placement® courses and low-cost, personalized courseware that helps students learn. A nonprofit ed tech initiative based at Rice University, we're committed to helping students access the tools they need to complete their courses and meet their educational goals.

# Rice University

OpenStax, OpenStax CNX, and OpenStax Tutor are initiatives of Rice University. As a leading research university with a distinctive commitment to undergraduate education, Rice University aspires to path-breaking research, unsurpassed teaching, and contributions to the betterment of our world. It seeks to fulfill this mission by cultivating a diverse community of learning and discovery that produces leaders across the spectrum of human endeavor.

# Philanthropic Support

OpenStax is grateful for the generous philanthropic partners who advance our mission to improve educational access and learning for everyone. To see the impact of our supporter community and our most updated list of partners, please visit openstax.org/impact.

| | |
|---|---|
| Arnold Ventures | Burt and Deedee McMurtry |
| Chan Zuckerberg Initiative | Michelson 20MM Foundation |
| Chegg, Inc. | National Science Foundation |
| Arthur and Carlyse Ciocca Charitable Foundation | The Open Society Foundations |
| Digital Promise | Jumee Yhu and David E. Park III |
| Ann and John Doerr | Brian D. Patterson USA-International Foundation |
| Bill & Melinda Gates Foundation | The Bill and Stephanie Sick Fund |
| Girard Foundation | Steven L. Smith & Diana T. Go |
| Google Inc. | Stand Together |
| The William and Flora Hewlett Foundation | Robin and Sandy Stuart Foundation |
| The Hewlett-Packard Company | The Stuart Family Foundation |
| Intel Inc. | Tammy and Guillermo Treviño |
| Rusty and John Jaggers | Valhalla Charitable Foundation |
| The Calvin K. Kazanjian Economics Foundation | White Star Education Foundation |
| Charles Koch Foundation | Schmidt Futures |
| Leon Lowenstein Foundation, Inc. | William Marsh Rice University |
| The Maxfield Foundation | |

# CONTENTS

**CHAPTER 5**

# Elasticity  111



**CHAPTER 6**

# Consumer Choices  137



**CHAPTER 7**

# Production, Costs, and Industry Structure  157

**CHAPTER 20**

# Globalization and Protectionism     471

# Preface

Welcome to *Principles of Microeconomics 3e* (Third Edition), an OpenStax resource. This textbook was written to increase student access to high-quality learning materials, maintaining highest standards of academic rigor at little to no cost.

## About OpenStax

OpenStax is part of Rice University, which is a 501(c)(3) nonprofit charitable corporation. As an educational initiative, it's our mission to transform learning so that education works for every student. Through our partnerships with philanthropic organizations and our alliance with other educational resource companies, we're breaking down the most common barriers to learning. Because we believe that everyone should and can have access to knowledge.

## About OpenStax Resources

### Customization

*Principles of Microeconomics 3e* is licensed under a Creative Commons Attribution 4.0 International (CC BY) license, which means that you can distribute, remix, and build upon the content, as long as you provide attribution to OpenStax and its content contributors.

Because our books are openly licensed, you are free to use the entire book or select only the sections that are most relevant to the needs of your course. Feel free to remix the content by assigning your students certain chapters and sections in your syllabus, in the order that you prefer. You can even provide a direct link in your syllabus to the sections in the web view of your book.

Instructors also have the option of creating a customized version of their OpenStax book. Visit the Instructor Resources section of your book page on OpenStax.org for more information.

### Art attribution

In *Principles of Microeconomics 3e*, most art contains attribution to its title, creator or rights holder, host platform, and license within the caption. Because the art is openly licensed, anyone may reuse the art as long as they provide the same attribution to its original source. To maximize readability and content flow, some art does not include attribution in the text. If you reuse art from this text that does not have attribution provided, use the following attribution: Copyright Rice University, OpenStax, under CC-BY 4.0 license.

### Errata

All OpenStax textbooks undergo a rigorous review process. However, like any professional-grade textbook, errors sometimes occur. In addition, economic data and related developments change frequently, and portions of the textbook may become out of date. Since our books are web based, we can make updates periodically when deemed pedagogically necessary. If you have a correction to suggest, submit it through the link on your book page on OpenStax.org. Subject matter experts review all errata suggestions. OpenStax is committed to remaining transparent about all updates, so you will also find a list of past and pending errata changes on your book page on OpenStax.org.

### Format

You can access this textbook for free in web view or PDF through OpenStax.org, and for a low cost in print.

## About *Principles of Microeconomics 3e*

*Principles of Microeconomics 3e* aligns to the topics and objectives of most introductory microeconomics courses. The text uses conversational language and ample illustrations to explore economic theories, and provides a wide array of examples using both fictional and real-world scenarios. The third edition has been carefully and thoroughly updated to reflect current data and understanding, as well as to provide a deeper background in diverse contributors and their impacts on economic thought and analysis.

### Coverage and scope

In response to faculty feedback and to ease transition to a new edition, Principles of Microeconomics 3e retains the organization of the previous editions. The book covers the breadth of economics topics and also provides the necessary depth to ensure the course is manageable for instructors and students alike. We strove to balance theory and application, as well as the amount of calculation and mathematical examples.

The book is organized into five main parts:

- **What is Economics?** The first two chapters introduce students to the study of economics with a focus on making choices in a world of scarce resources.
- **Supply and Demand**, Chapters 3 and 4, introduces and explains the first analytical model in economics—supply, demand, and equilibrium—before showing applications in the markets for labor and finance.
- **The Fundamentals of Microeconomic Theory**, Chapters 5 through 10, begins the microeconomics portion of the text, presenting the theories of consumer behavior, production and costs, and the different models of market structure, including some simple game theory.
- **Microeconomic Policy Issues**, Chapters 11 through 18, covers the range of topics in applied micro, framed around the concepts of public goods and positive and negative externalities. Students explore competition and antitrust policies, environmental problems, poverty, income inequality, and other labor market issues. The text also covers information, risk and financial markets, and public economy.
- **International Economics**, Chapters 19 and 20, introduces the international dimensions of economics, including international trade and protectionism.

### Changes to the third edition

The revision process incorporated extensive feedback from faculty who have used the book in their courses. They advised that the third edition changes focus on currency updates, integration of newer perspectives and more diverse contributors, and relevance to students' lives and careers.

**Current data and analysis:** The authors have updated dozens of explanations, graphs, and tables containing financial, demographic, employment, and related economic data. The corresponding discussions provide context and interpretations of the data, including descriptions of change over time, cause-and-effect relationships, and balanced analysis of policies and opinions.

**Diverse perspectives and contributors:** The third edition highlights the research and views of a broader group of economists. These include people from across the spectrum of economic thought, with a particular focus on those who take what are often considered non-traditional views of economic policy and government action. Examples include:

- Chapter 1: Esther Duflo, Abhijit Banerjee, and Michael Kremer regarding experimental analysis in development economics.
- Chapter 4: Walter Williams and Thomas Sowell regarding the downsides of minimum wages.
- Chapter 13: Carlota Perez regarding employment shifts resulting from innovation; Mariana Mazzucato regarding government involvement in innovation; Elinor Ostrom and the "non-tragedy of the commons."
- Chapter 14: William A. Darity Jr. on employment discrimination and market forces; Phyllis Ann Wallace and the EEOC.

**Relevance and engagement:** In order to show the importance and application of economics in students' lives and careers, the third edition directly addresses and expands topics likely to connect to various industries, issues, groups, and events. Brief references and deeply explored socio-political examples have been updated to showcase the critical—and sometimes unnoticed—ties between economic developments and topics relevant to students. Examples include education spending, the value of college degrees, discrimination, environmental policies, immigration policies, entrepreneurship and innovation, healthcare and insurance, and general financial literacy. Finally, the COVID-19 pandemic is referenced frequently to demonstrate its deep and evolving impacts on financial data, employment, and other aspects of the economy.

**FRED Data and Graphs:** As in previous editions, the authors have included and referenced data from the Federal Reserve Economic Data (FRED). In some cases, interactive FRED graphs are embedded directly in the web view of the book; students may magnify and focus on specific time periods, analyze individual data points, and otherwise manipulate the graphs from within the OpenStax reading experience. In others cases (and in the PDF), links to the direct source of the FRED data are provided, and students are encouraged to explore the information and the overall FRED resources more thoroughly. Note that other data sources, such as the Bureau of Labor Statistics, U.S. Census Bureau, and World Bank, usually include links in the captions or credits; instructors and students can also explore those sites for more detailed investigations of the topics at hand.

Updated art

*Principles of Microeconomics 3e* includes updated and redesigned art to clarify concepts and provide opportunities for graphical interpretation. Many graphs are shown with accompanying data tables and explanations of the drivers and consequences of change.

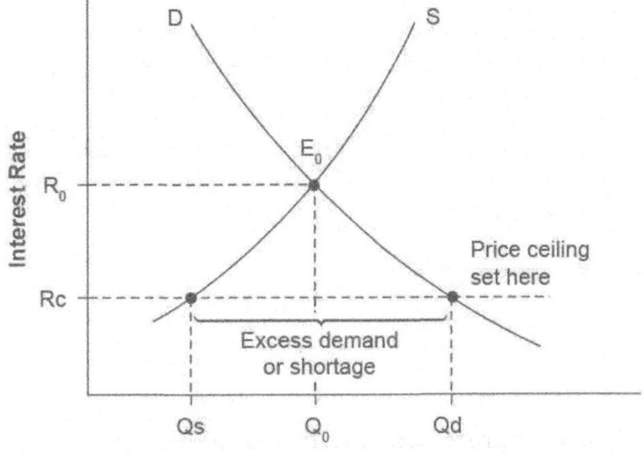

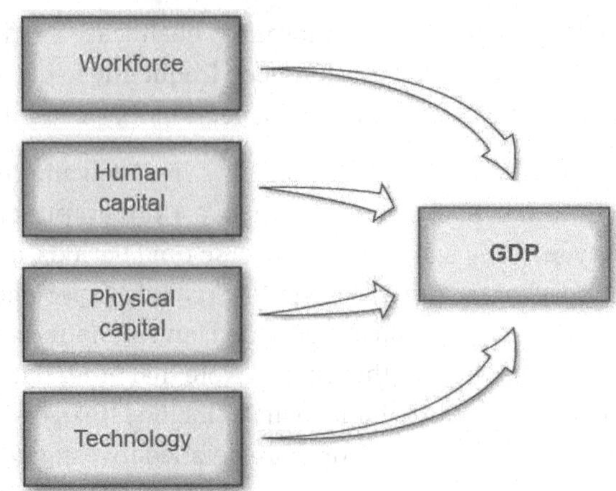

(a) Aggregate production function with GDP as its output

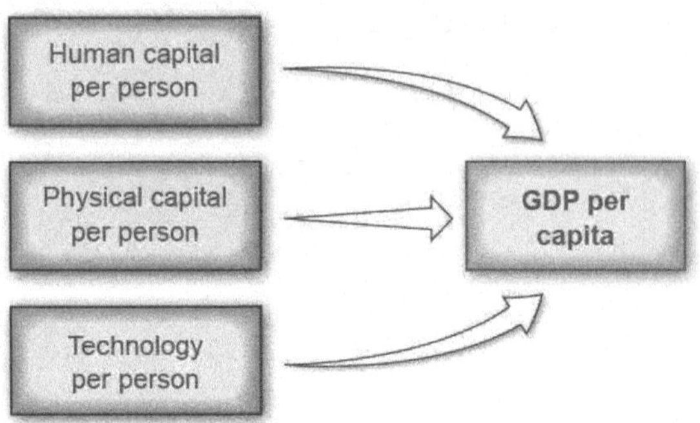

(b) Aggregate production function with GDP per capita as its output

Pedagogical foundation

The narrative explanations and analysis presented in *Principles of Microeconomics 3e* have been carefully crafted to provide a solid basis in economic concepts, flexibly approach skills and assess understanding, and deepen students' engagement with the course materials. You will also find features that promote economic inquiry and explorations, including:

- **Bring It Home:** These explorations include a brief case study, specific to each chapter, which connects the chapter's main topic to the real world. It is broken up into two parts: the first at the beginning of the chapter (in the Intro module) and the second at chapter's end, when students have learned what's necessary to understand the case and "bring home" the chapter's core concepts.
- **Work It Out:** These worked examples progress through an analytical or computational problem, and guide students step-by-step to find out how its solution is derived.
- **Clear It Up:** These boxes are deeper explanations of something in the main body of the text. Each CIU starts with a question. The rest of the feature explains the answer.

Questions for each level of learning

*Principles of Microeconomics 3e* offers flexibility in practice and assessment, and provides a range of opportunities to check understanding and encourage deeper thinking and application.

- **Self-Checks** are analytical self-assessment questions that appear at the end of each module. They "click to reveal" an answer in the web view so students can check their understanding before moving on to the next module. Self-Check questions are not simple look-up questions. They push the student to think beyond what is said in the text. Self-Check questions are designed for formative (rather than summative) assessment. The questions and answers are explained so that students feel like they are being walked through the problem.

- **Review Question** are simple recall questions from the chapter and are in open-response format (not multiple choice or true/false). The answers can be looked up in the text.
- **Critical Thinking Questions** are higher-level, conceptual questions ask students to demonstrate their understanding by applying what they have learned in different contexts.
- **Problems** are exercises give students additional practice working with the analytic and computational concepts in the module.

## About the Authors

### Senior contributing authors

**David Shapiro, Pennsylvania State University**

David Shapiro is Professor Emeritus of Economics, Demography, and Women's, Gender, and Sexuality Studies at the Pennsylvania State University. He received a BA in Economics and Political Science from the University of Michigan, and an MA as well as a PhD in Economics from Princeton University. He began his academic career at Ohio State University in 1971, and moved to Penn State in 1980. His early research focused on women and youth in the United States labor market. Following a 1978-79 stint as a Fulbright professor at the University of Kinshasa in the Democratic Republic of the Congo, his research shifted focus to fertility in Kinshasa and more broadly, in sub-Saharan Africa. He has also received the top prize for teaching at both Ohio State and Penn State.

**Daniel MacDonald, California State University, San Bernardino**

Professor Daniel MacDonald is the Chair of the Economics Department at California State University, San Bernardino. He earned his BA in mathematics and economics from Seton Hall University in 2007 and his economics PhD from the University of Massachusetts Amherst in 2013. Macdonald conducts economic research in labor economics, public policy (housing), and the economic history of the U.S. Consulting. He is also the author of the weekly Inland Empire Economic Update newsletter (https://dpmacdonald.substack.com/), which he started in 2021.

**Steven A. Greenlaw, Professor Emeritus at University of Mary Washington**

Steven Greenlaw taught principles of economics for 39 years. In 1999, he received the Grellet C. Simpson Award for Excellence in Undergraduate Teaching at the University of Mary Washington. He is the author of Doing Economics: A Guide to Doing and Understanding Economic Research, as well as a variety of articles on economics pedagogy and instructional technology, published in the *Journal of Economic Education*, the *International Review of Economic Education*, and other outlets. He wrote the module on Quantitative Writing for *Starting Point: Teaching and Learning Economics*, the web portal on best practices in teaching economics. Steven Greenlaw lives in Alexandria, Virginia with his wife Kathy. Since retiring from full-time teaching, he has been doing faculty development work and other writing projects.

### Contributing authors

Eric Dodge, Hanover College
Cynthia Gamez, University of Texas at El Paso
Andres Jauregui, Columbus State University
Diane Keenan, Cerritos College
Amyaz Moledina, The College of Wooster
Craig Richardson, Winston-Salem State University
Ralph Sonenshine, American University

### Reviewers

Bryan Aguiar, Northwest Arkansas Community College

Basil Al Hashimi, Mesa Community College
Jennifer Ball, Washburn University
Emil Berendt, Mount St. Mary's University
Zena Buser, Adams State University
Douglas Campbell, The University of Memphis
Sanjukta Chaudhuri, University of Wisconsin-Eau Claire
Xueyu Cheng, Alabama State University
Robert Cunningham, Alma College
Rosa Lea Danielson, College of DuPage
Steven Deloach, Elon University
Debbie Evercloud, University of Colorado Denver
Sal Figueras, Hudson County Community College
Reza Ghorashi, Stockton University
Robert Gillette, University of Kentucky
George Jones, University of Wisconsin-Rock County
Charles Kroncke, College of Mount St. Joseph
Teresa Laughlin, Palomar Community College
Carlos Liard-Muriente, Central Connecticut State University
Heather Luea, Kansas State University
Charles Meyrick, Housatonic Community College
William Mosher, Nashua Community College
Michael Netta, Hudson County Community College
Nick Noble, Miami University
Joe Nowakowski, Muskingum University
Shawn Osell, University of Wisconsin, Superior
Mark Owens, Middle Tennessee State University
Sonia Pereira, Barnard College
Brian Peterson, Central College
Jennifer Platania, Elon University
Robert Rycroft, University of Mary Washington
Adrienne Sachse, Florida State College at Jacksonville
Hans Schumann, Texas A&M University
Gina Shamshak, Goucher College
Chris Warburton, John Jay College of Criminal Justice, CUNY
Mark Witte, Northwestern University
Chiou-nan Yeh, Alabama State University

## Additional Resources

### Student and instructor resources

We've compiled additional resources for both students and instructors, including Getting Started Guides, an instructor's manual, test bank, and image slides. Instructor resources require a verified instructor account, which you can apply for when you log in or create your account on OpenStax.org. Take advantage of these resources to supplement your OpenStax book.

- **Premium Course Shells:** These robust course cartridges are preloaded with assessments, activities, discussion prompts, readings, and other assignable material. They are logically organized to match the way you manage your course, with pre-lecture, synchronous, and post-lecture experiences. Activities and assessments are designed so that the answers are not easily found via online searches. These offerings are provided for D2L, Canvas, and Blackboard, and may require support from campus instructional technology or related teams to import and integrate.

- **Enhanced Lecture PowerPoint Slides:** These lecture slides include selected graphics from the text, key concepts and definitions, examples, and discussion questions.
- **Test Bank:** The test bank contains multiple choice, short answer, and essay questions for each chapter of the textbook. Since many instructors use these questions in graded assignments, we ask that you not post these questions and the answers on any publicly available websites.
- **Instructor Solution Guide:** The instructor solutions guide contains the instructor-facing answers to the problems and exercises within the textbook.
- **Video Guide:** This video guide is a collection of videos recommended by instructors and grouped topically by OpenStax textbook chapters.
- **Polling Questions:** Spark discussion and support in-class learning and engagement using this set of polling questions. Survey students' understanding by a raise of hands or by pairing these questions with your polling technology; 3–4 questions are provided for each chapter.

## Academic integrity

Academic integrity builds trust, understanding, equity, and genuine learning. While students may encounter significant challenges in their courses and their lives, doing their own work and maintaining a high degree of authenticity will result in meaningful outcomes that will extend far beyond their college career. Faculty, administrators, resource providers, and students should work together to maintain a fair and positive experience.

We realize that students benefit when academic integrity ground rules are established early in the course. To that end, OpenStax has created an interactive to aid with academic integrity discussions in your course.

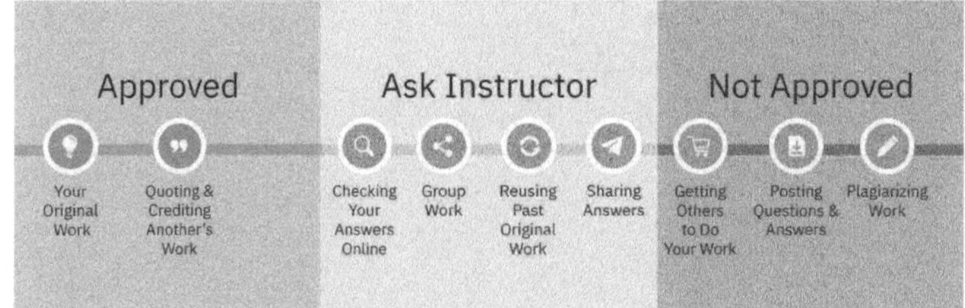


Visit our academic integrity slider (https://view.genial.ly/61e08a7af6db870d591078c1/interactive-image-defining-academic-integrity-interactive-slider). Click and drag icons along the continuum to align these practices with your institution and course policies. You may then include the graphic on your syllabus, present it in your first course meeting, or create a handout for students.

At OpenStax we are also developing resources supporting authentic learning experiences and assessment. Please visit this book's page for updates. For an in-depth review of academic integrity strategies, we highly recommend visiting the International Center of Academic Integrity (ICAI) website at https://academicintegrity.org/ (https://academicintegrity.org/).

## Community hubs

OpenStax partners with the Institute for the Study of Knowledge Management in Education (ISKME) to offer Community Hubs on OER Commons—a platform for instructors to share community-created resources that support OpenStax books, free of charge. Through our Community Hubs, instructors can upload their own materials or download resources to use in their own courses, including additional ancillaries, teaching material, multimedia, and relevant course content. We encourage instructors to join the hubs for the subjects most relevant to your teaching and research as an opportunity both to enrich your courses and to engage with other faculty. To reach the Community Hubs, visit www.oercommons.org/hubs/openstax (http://www.oercommons.org/hubs/openstax).

## Technology partners

As allies in making high-quality learning materials accessible, our technology partners offer optional low-cost tools that are integrated with OpenStax books. To access the technology options for your text, visit your book page on OpenStax.org.

# Welcome to Economics!

**FIGURE 1.1 Do You Use Facebook?** Economics is greatly impacted by how well information travels through society. Today, social media giants Twitter, Facebook, and Instagram are major forces on the information super highway. (Credit: modification of "Social Media Mixed Icons - Banner" by Blogtrepreneur/Flickr, CC BY 2.0)

**CHAPTER OBJECTIVES**

In this chapter, you will learn about:

- What Is Economics, and Why Is It Important?
- Microeconomics and Macroeconomics
- How Economists Use Theories and Models to Understand Economic Issues
- How Economies Can Be Organized: An Overview of Economic Systems

## Introduction

### BRING IT HOME

### Information Overload in the Information Age

To post or not to post? Every day we are faced with a myriad of decisions, from what to have for breakfast, to which show to stream, to the more complex—"Should I double major and add possibly another semester of study to my education?" Our response to these choices depends on the information we have available at any given moment. Economists call this "imperfect" because we rarely have all the data we need to make perfect decisions. Despite the lack of perfect information, we still make hundreds of decisions a day.

Streams, sponsors, and social media are altering the process by which we make choices, how we spend our time, which movies we see, which products we buy, and more. Whether they read the reviews or just check the ratings, it's unlikely for Americans to make many significant decisions without these information streams.

As you will see in this course, what happens in economics is affected by how well and how fast information disseminates through a society, such as how quickly information travels through Facebook. "Economists love nothing better than when deep and liquid markets operate under conditions of perfect information," says Jessica Irvine, National Economics Editor for News Corp Australia.

This leads us to the topic of this chapter, an introduction to the world of making decisions, processing information, and understanding behavior in markets —the world of economics. Each chapter in this book will start with a discussion about current (or sometimes past) events and revisit it at chapter's end—to "bring home" the concepts in play.

---

What is economics and why should you spend your time learning it? After all, there are other disciplines you could be studying, and other ways you could be spending your time. As the Bring it Home feature just mentioned, making choices is at the heart of what economists study, and your decision to take this course is as much as economic decision as anything else.

Economics is probably not what you think. It is not primarily about money or finance. It is not primarily about business. It is not mathematics. What is it then? It is both a subject area and a way of viewing the world.

## 1.1 What Is Economics, and Why Is It Important?

**LEARNING OBJECTIVES**

By the end of this section, you will be able to:

- Discuss the importance of studying economics
- Explain the relationship between production and division of labor
- Evaluate the significance of scarcity

**Economics** is the study of how humans make decisions in the face of scarcity. These can be individual decisions, family decisions, business decisions or societal decisions. If you look around carefully, you will see that scarcity is a fact of life. **Scarcity** means that human wants for goods, services and resources exceed what is available. Resources, such as labor, tools, land, and raw materials are necessary to produce the goods and services we want but they exist in limited supply. Of course, the ultimate scarce resource is time- everyone, rich or poor, has just 24 expendable hours in the day to earn income to acquire goods and services, for leisure time, or for sleep. At any point in time, there is only a finite amount of resources available.

Think about it this way: In 2015 the labor force in the United States contained over 158 million workers, according to the U.S. Bureau of Labor Statistics. The total land area was 3,794,101 square miles. While these are certainly large numbers, they are not infinite. Because these resources are limited, so are the numbers of goods and services we produce with them. Combine this with the fact that human wants seem to be virtually infinite, and you can see why scarcity is a problem.

### Introduction to FRED

Data is very important in economics because it describes and measures the issues and problems that economics seek to understand. A variety of government agencies publish economic and social data. For this course, we will generally use data from the St. Louis Federal Reserve Bank's FRED database. FRED is very user friendly. It allows you to display data in tables or charts, and you can easily download it into spreadsheet form if you want to use the data for other purposes. The FRED website (https://openstax.org/l/FRED/) includes data on nearly 400,000 domestic and international variables over time, in the following broad categories:

- Money, Banking & Finance
- Population, Employment, & Labor Markets (including Income Distribution)
- National Accounts (Gross Domestic Product & its components), Flow of Funds, and International Accounts
- Production & Business Activity (including Business Cycles)
- Prices & Inflation (including the Consumer Price Index, the Producer Price Index, and the Employment Cost Index)
- International Data from other nations
- U.S. Regional Data
- Academic Data (including Penn World Tables & NBER Macrohistory database)

For more information about how to use FRED, see the variety of videos (https://openstax.org/l/FRED_intro) on

YouTube starting with this introduction.

**FIGURE 1.2 Scarcity of Resources** People experiencing homelessness are a stark reminder that scarcity of resources is real. (Credit: "Pittsburgh Homeless" by "daveyinn"/Flickr Creative Commons, CC BY 2.0)

If you still do not believe that scarcity is a problem, consider the following: Does everyone require food to eat? Does everyone need a decent place to live? Does everyone have access to healthcare? In every country in the world, there are people who are hungry, homeless (for example, those who call park benches their beds, as Figure 1.2 shows), and in need of healthcare, just to focus on a few critical goods and services. Why is this the case? It is because of scarcity. Let's delve into the concept of scarcity a little deeper, because it is crucial to understanding economics.

## The Problem of Scarcity

Think about all the things you consume: food, shelter, clothing, transportation, healthcare, and entertainment. How do you acquire those items? You do not produce them yourself. You buy them. How do you afford the things you buy? You work for pay. If you do not, someone else does on your behalf. Yet most of us never have enough income to buy all the things we want. This is because of scarcity. So how do we solve it?

## 🔗 LINK IT UP

Visit this website (http://openstax.org/l/drought) to read about how the United States is dealing with scarcity in resources.

---

Every society, at every level, must make choices about how to use its resources. Families must decide whether to spend their money on a new car or a fancy vacation. Towns must choose whether to put more of the budget into police and fire protection or into the school system. Nations must decide whether to devote more funds to national defense or to protecting the environment. In most cases, there just isn't enough money in the budget to do everything. How do we use our limited resources the best way possible, that is, to obtain the most goods and services we can? There are a couple of options. First, we could each produce everything we each consume. Alternatively, we could each produce some of what we want to consume, and "trade" for the rest of what we want. Let's explore these options. Why do we not each just produce all of the things we consume? Think back to pioneer days, when individuals knew how to do so much more than we do today, from building their homes, to growing their crops, to hunting for food, to repairing their equipment. Most of us do not know how to do all—or any—of those things, but it is not because we could not learn. Rather, we do not have to. The reason why is something called *the division and specialization of labor*, a production innovation first put forth by Adam Smith (Figure 1.3) in his book, *The Wealth of Nations*.

**FIGURE 1.3 Adam Smith** Adam Smith introduced the idea of dividing labor into discrete tasks. (Credit: "Adam Smith" by Cadell and Davies (1811), John Horsburgh (1828), or R.C. Bell (1872)/Wikimedia Commons, Public Domain)

## The Division of and Specialization of Labor

The formal study of economics began when Adam Smith (1723–1790) published his famous book *The Wealth of Nations* in 1776. Many authors had written on economics in the centuries before Smith, but he was the first to address the subject in a comprehensive way. In the first chapter, Smith introduces the concept of **division of labor**, which means that the way one produces a good or service is divided into a number of tasks that different workers perform, instead of all the tasks being done by the same person.

To illustrate division of labor, Smith counted how many tasks went into making a pin: drawing out a piece of wire, cutting it to the right length, straightening it, putting a head on one end and a point on the other, and packaging pins for sale, to name just a few. Smith counted 18 distinct tasks that different people performed—all for a pin, believe it or not!

Modern businesses divide tasks as well. Even a relatively simple business like a restaurant divides the task of serving meals into a range of jobs like top chef, sous chefs, less-skilled kitchen help, servers to wait on the tables, a greeter at the door, janitors to clean up, and a business manager to handle paychecks and bills—not to mention the economic connections a restaurant has with suppliers of food, furniture, kitchen equipment, and the building where it is located. A complex business like a large manufacturing factory, such as the shoe factory (Figure 1.4), or a hospital can have hundreds of job classifications.

**FIGURE 1.4 Division of Labor** Workers on an assembly line are an example of the divisions of labor. (Credit: "Red Wing Shoe Factory Tour" by Nina Hale/Flickr Creative Commons, CC BY 2.0)

## Why the Division of Labor Increases Production

When we divide and subdivide the tasks involved with producing a good or service, workers and businesses can produce a greater quantity of output. In his observations of pin factories, Smith noticed that one worker alone might make 20 pins in a day, but that a small business of 10 workers (some of whom would need to complete two or three of the 18 tasks involved with pin-making), could make 48,000 pins in a day. How can a group of workers, each specializing in certain tasks, produce so much more than the same number of workers who try to produce the entire good or service by themselves? Smith offered three reasons.

First, **specialization** in a particular small job allows workers to focus on the parts of the production process where they have an advantage. (In later chapters, we will develop this idea by discussing comparative advantage.) People have different skills, talents, and interests, so they will be better at some jobs than at others. The particular advantages may be based on educational choices, which are in turn shaped by interests and talents. Only those with medical degrees qualify to become doctors, for instance. For some goods, geography affects specialization. For example, it is easier to be a wheat farmer in North Dakota than in Florida, but easier to run a tourist hotel in Florida than in North Dakota. If you live in or near a big city, it is easier to attract enough customers to operate a successful dry cleaning business or movie theater than if you live in a sparsely populated rural area. Whatever the reason, if people specialize in the production of what they do best, they will be more effective than if they produce a combination of things, some of which they are good at and some of which they are not.

Second, workers who specialize in certain tasks often learn to produce more quickly and with higher quality. This pattern holds true for many workers, including assembly line laborers who build cars, stylists who cut hair, and doctors who perform heart surgery. In fact, specialized workers often know their jobs well enough to suggest innovative ways to do their work faster and better.

A similar pattern often operates within businesses. In many cases, a business that focuses on one or a few products (sometimes called its "core competency") is more successful than firms that try to make a wide range of products.

Third, specialization allows businesses to take advantage of **economies of scale**, which means that for many goods, as the level of production increases, the average cost of producing each individual unit declines. For example, if a factory produces only 100 cars per year, each car will be quite expensive to make on average. However, if a factory produces 50,000 cars each year, then it can set up an assembly line with huge machines and workers performing specialized tasks, and the average cost of production per car will be lower. The ultimate result of workers who can focus on their preferences and talents, learn to do their specialized jobs better, and work in larger organizations is that society as a whole can produce and consume far more than if each person tried to produce all of their own goods and services. The division and specialization of labor has been a force against the problem of scarcity.

## Trade and Markets

Specialization only makes sense, though, if workers can use the pay they receive for doing their jobs to purchase the other goods and services that they need. In short, specialization requires trade.

You do not have to know anything about electronics or sound systems to play music—you just buy an iPod or MP3 player, download the music, and listen. You do not have to know anything about artificial fibers or the construction of sewing machines if you need a jacket—you just buy the jacket and wear it. You do not need to know anything about internal combustion engines to operate a car—you just get in and drive. Instead of trying to acquire all the knowledge and skills involved in producing all of the goods and services that you wish to consume, the market allows you to learn a specialized set of skills and then use the pay you receive to buy the goods and services you need or want. This is how our modern society has evolved into a strong economy.

## Why Study Economics?

**FIGURE 1.5 Esther Duflo, Abhijit Banerjee, and Michael Kremer** Esther Duflo, Abhijit Banerjee (both from Massachusetts Institute of Technology), and Michael Kremer (University of Chicago) were awarded the Nobel Prize for groundbreaking work in which they established experimental methods to understand poverty and outcomes of initiatives to address it. (Credit: modification of work by U.S. Embassy Sweden/Wikimedia Commons, CC BY 2.0; Financial Times/Wikimedia Commons, CC BY 2.0; U.S. Embassy Sweden/Flickr Creative Commons, CC BY 2.0)

Now that you have an overview on what economics studies, let's quickly discuss why you are right to study it. Economics is not primarily a collection of facts to memorize, although there are plenty of important concepts to learn. Instead, think of economics as a collection of questions to answer or puzzles to work. Most importantly, economics provides the tools to solve those puzzles.

Consider the complex and critical issue of education barriers on national and regional levels, which affect millions of people and result in widespread poverty and inequality. Governments, aid organizations, and wealthy individuals spend billions of dollars each year trying to address these issues. Nations announce the revitalization of their education programs; tech companies donate devices and infrastructure, and celebrities and charities build schools and sponsor students. Yet the problems remain, sometimes almost as pronounced as they were before the intervention. Why is that the case? In 2019, three economists—Esther Duflo, Abhijit Banerjee, and Michael Kremer—were awarded the Nobel Prize for their work to answer those questions. They worked diligently to break the widespread problems into smaller pieces, and experimented with small interventions to test success. The award citation credited their work with giving the world better tools and information to address poverty and improve education. Esther Duflo, who is the youngest person and second woman to win the Nobel Prize in Economics, said, "We believed that like the war on cancer, the war on poverty was not going to be won in one major battle, but in a series of small triumphs. . . . This work and the culture of learning that it fostered in governments has led to real improvement in the lives of hundreds of millions of poor people."

As you can see, economics affects far more than business. For example:

- Virtually every major problem facing the world today, from global warming, to world poverty, to the conflicts in Syria, Afghanistan, and Somalia, has an economic dimension. If you are going to be part of solving those problems, you need to be able to understand them. Economics is crucial.
- It is hard to overstate the importance of economics to good citizenship. You need to be able to vote intelligently on budgets, regulations, and laws in general. When the U.S. government came close to a standstill at the end of 2012 due to the "fiscal cliff," what were the issues? Did you know?
- A basic understanding of economics makes you a well-rounded thinker. When you read articles about economic issues, you will understand and be able to evaluate the writer's argument. When you hear

classmates, co-workers, or political candidates talking about economics, you will be able to distinguish between common sense and nonsense. You will find new ways of thinking about current events and about personal and business decisions, as well as current events and politics.

The study of economics does not dictate the answers, but it can illuminate the different choices.

## 1.2 Microeconomics and Macroeconomics

**LEARNING OBJECTIVES**

By the end of this section, you will be able to:

- Describe microeconomics
- Describe macroeconomics
- Contrast monetary policy and fiscal policy

Economics is concerned with the well-being of *all* people, including those with jobs and those without jobs, as well as those with high incomes and those with low incomes. Economics acknowledges that production of useful goods and services can create problems of environmental pollution. It explores the question of how investing in education helps to develop workers' skills. It probes questions like how to tell when big businesses or big labor unions are operating in a way that benefits society as a whole and when they are operating in a way that benefits their owners or members at the expense of others. It looks at how government spending, taxes, and regulations affect decisions about production and consumption.

It should be clear by now that economics covers considerable ground. We can divide that ground into two parts: **Microeconomics** focuses on the actions of individual agents within the economy, like households, workers, and businesses. **Macroeconomics** looks at the economy as a whole. It focuses on broad issues such as growth of production, the number of unemployed people, the inflationary increase in prices, government deficits, and levels of exports and imports. Microeconomics and macroeconomics are not separate subjects, but rather complementary perspectives on the overall subject of the economy.

To understand why both microeconomic and macroeconomic perspectives are useful, consider the problem of studying a biological ecosystem like a lake. One person who sets out to study the lake might focus on specific topics: certain kinds of algae or plant life; the characteristics of particular fish or snails; or the trees surrounding the lake. Another person might take an overall view and instead consider the lake's ecosystem from top to bottom; what eats what, how the system stays in a rough balance, and what environmental stresses affect this balance. Both approaches are useful, and both examine the same lake, but the viewpoints are different. In a similar way, both microeconomics and macroeconomics study the same economy, but each has a different viewpoint.

Whether you are scrutinizing lakes or economics, the micro and the macro insights should blend with each other. In studying a lake, the micro insights about particular plants and animals help to understand the overall food chain, while the macro insights about the overall food chain help to explain the environment in which individual plants and animals live.

In economics, the micro decisions of individual businesses are influenced by whether the macroeconomy is healthy. For example, firms will be more likely to hire workers if the overall economy is growing. In turn, macroeconomy's performance ultimately depends on the microeconomic decisions that individual households and businesses make.

### Microeconomics

What determines how households and individuals spend their budgets? What combination of goods and services will best fit their needs and wants, given the budget they have to spend? How do people decide whether to work, and if so, whether to work full time or part time? How do people decide how much to save for the future, or whether they should borrow to spend beyond their current means?

What determines the products, and how many of each, a firm will produce and sell? What determines the prices a firm will charge? What determines how a firm will produce its products? What determines how many workers it will hire? How will a firm finance its business? When will a firm decide to expand, downsize, or even close? In the microeconomics part of this book, we will learn about the theory of consumer behavior, the theory of the firm, how markets for labor and other resources work, and how markets sometimes fail to work properly.

### Macroeconomics

What determines the level of economic activity in a society? In other words, what determines how many goods and services a nation actually produces? What determines how many jobs are available in an economy? What determines a nation's standard of living? What causes the economy to speed up or slow down? What causes firms to hire more workers or to lay them off? Finally, what causes the economy to grow over the long term?

We can determine an economy's macroeconomic health by examining a number of goals: growth in the standard of living, low unemployment, and low inflation, to name the most important. How can we use government macroeconomic policy to pursue these goals? A nation's central bank conducts **monetary policy**, which involves policies that affect bank lending, interest rates, and financial capital markets. For the United States, this is the Federal Reserve. A nation's legislative body determines **fiscal policy**, which involves government spending and taxes. For the United States, this is the Congress and the executive branch, which originates the federal budget. These are the government's main tools. Americans tend to expect that government can fix whatever economic problems we encounter, but to what extent is that expectation realistic? These are just some of the issues that we will explore in the macroeconomic chapters of this book.

## 1.3 How Economists Use Theories and Models to Understand Economic Issues

**LEARNING OBJECTIVES**

By the end of this section, you will be able to:
- Interpret a circular flow diagram
- Explain the importance of economic theories and models
- Describe goods and services markets and labor markets

**FIGURE 1.6 John Maynard Keynes** One of the most influential economists in modern times was John Maynard Keynes. (Credit: "John Maynard Keynes" by IMF/Wikimedia Commons, Public Domain)

John Maynard Keynes (1883–1946), one of the greatest economists of the twentieth century, pointed out that economics is not just a subject area but also a way of thinking. Keynes (Figure 1.6) famously wrote in the introduction to a fellow economist's book: "[Economics] is a method rather than a doctrine, an apparatus of the mind, a technique of thinking, which helps its possessor to draw correct conclusions." In other words, economics teaches you how to think, not what to think.

### ⊘ LINK IT UP

Watch this video (http://openstax.org/l/Keynes) about John Maynard Keynes and his influence on economics.

---

Economists see the world through a different lens than anthropologists, biologists, classicists, or practitioners of any other discipline. They analyze issues and problems using economic theories that are based on particular assumptions about human behavior. These assumptions tend to be different than the assumptions an anthropologist or psychologist might use. A **theory** is a simplified representation of how two or more variables interact with each other. The purpose of a theory is to take a complex, real-world issue and simplify it down to its essentials. If done well, this enables the analyst to understand the issue and any problems around it. A good theory is simple enough to understand, while complex enough to capture the key features of the object or situation you are studying.

Sometimes economists use the term **model** instead of theory. Strictly speaking, a theory is a more abstract representation, while a model is a more applied or empirical representation. We use models to test theories, but for this course we will use the terms interchangeably.

For example, an architect who is planning a major office building will often build a physical model that sits on a tabletop to show how the entire city block will look after the new building is constructed. Companies often build models of their new products, which are more rough and unfinished than the final product, but can still demonstrate how the new product will work.

A good model to start with in economics is the **circular flow diagram** (Figure 1.7). It pictures the economy as consisting of two groups—households and firms—that interact in two markets: the **goods and services market** in which firms sell and households buy and the **labor market** in which households sell labor to business firms or other employees.

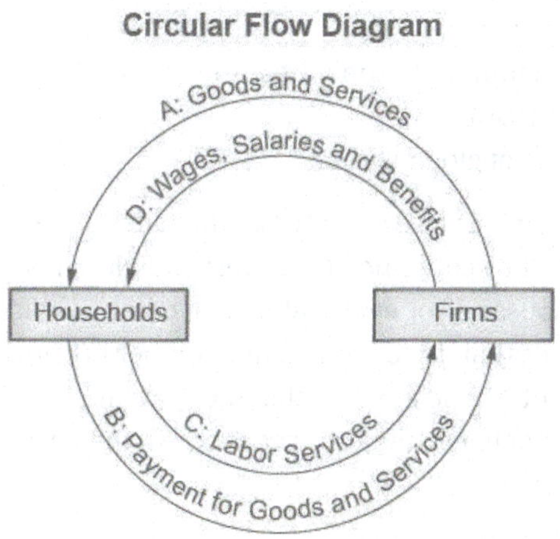

### Circular Flow Diagram



FIGURE 1.7 **The Circular Flow Diagram** The circular flow diagram shows how households and firms interact in the goods and services market, and in the labor market. The direction of the arrows shows that in the goods and services market, households receive goods and services and pay firms for them. In the labor market, households provide labor and receive payment from firms through wages, salaries, and benefits.

Firms produce and sell goods and services to households in the market for goods and services (or product market). Arrow "A" indicates this. Households pay for goods and services, which becomes the revenues to firms. Arrow "B" indicates this. Arrows A and B represent the two sides of the product market. Where do households obtain the income to buy goods and services? They provide the labor and other resources (e.g., land, capital, raw materials) firms need to produce goods and services in the market for inputs (or factors of production). Arrow "C" indicates this. In return, firms pay for the inputs (or resources) they use in the form of wages and other factor payments. Arrow "D" indicates this. Arrows "C" and "D" represent the two sides of the factor market.

Of course, in the real world, there are many different markets for goods and services and markets for many different types of labor. The circular flow diagram simplifies this to make the picture easier to grasp. In the diagram, firms produce goods and services, which they sell to households in return for revenues. The outer circle shows this, and represents the two sides of the product market (for example, the market for goods and services) in which households demand and firms supply. Households sell their labor as workers to firms in return for wages, salaries, and benefits. The inner circle shows this and represents the two sides of the labor market in which households supply and firms demand.

This version of the circular flow model is stripped down to the essentials, but it has enough features to explain how the product and labor markets work in the economy. We could easily add details to this basic model if we wanted to introduce more real-world elements, like financial markets, governments, and interactions with the rest of the globe (imports and exports).

Economists carry a set of theories in their heads like a carpenter carries around a toolkit. When they see an economic issue or problem, they go through the theories they know to see if they can find one that fits. Then they use the theory to derive insights about the issue or problem. Economists express theories as diagrams, graphs, or even as mathematical equations. (Do not worry. In this course, we will mostly use graphs.) Economists do not figure out the answer to the problem first and then draw the graph to illustrate. Rather, they use the graph of the theory to help them figure out the answer. Although at the introductory level, you can sometimes figure out the right answer without applying a model, if you keep studying economics, before too long you will run into issues and problems that you will need to graph to solve. We explain both micro and macroeconomics in terms of theories and models. The most well-known theories are probably those of supply and demand, but you will learn a number of others.

## 1.4 How To Organize Economies: An Overview of Economic Systems

### LEARNING OBJECTIVES

By the end of this section, you will be able to:
- Contrast traditional economies, command economies, and market economies
- Explain gross domestic product (GDP)
- Assess the importance and effects of globalization

Think about what a complex system a modern economy is. It includes all production of goods and services, all buying and selling, all employment. The economic life of every individual is interrelated, at least to a small extent, with the economic lives of thousands or even millions of other individuals. Who organizes and coordinates this system? Who ensures that, for example, the number of televisions a society provides is the same as the amount it needs and wants? Who ensures that the right number of employees work in the electronics industry? Who ensures that televisions are produced in the best way possible? How does it all get done?

There are at least three ways that societies organize an economy. The first is the **traditional economy**, which is the oldest economic system and is used in parts of Asia, Africa, and South America. Traditional economies organize their economic affairs the way they have always done (i.e., tradition). Occupations stay in the family. Most families are farmers who grow the crops using traditional methods. What you produce is what you consume. Because tradition drives the way of life, there is little economic progress or development.

**FIGURE 1.8 A Command Economy** Ancient Egypt was an example of a command economy. (Credit: "Pyramids at Giza" by Jay Bergesen/Flickr Creative Commons, CC BY 2.0)

Command economies are very different. In a **command economy**, economic effort is devoted to goals passed down from a ruler or ruling class. Ancient Egypt was a good example: a large part of economic life was devoted to building pyramids, like those in Figure 1.8, for the pharaohs. Medieval manor life is another example: the lord provided the land for growing crops and protection in the event of war. In return, vassals provided labor and soldiers to do the lord's bidding. In the last century, communism emphasized command economies.

In a command economy, the government decides what goods and services will be produced and what prices it will charge for them. The government decides what methods of production to use and sets wages for workers. The government provides many necessities like healthcare and education for free. Currently, Cuba and North Korea have command economies.

**FIGURE 1.9 A Market Economy** Nothing says "market" more than The New York Stock Exchange. (Credit: work by Erik Drost/Flickr Creative Commons, CC BY 2.0)

Although command economies have a very centralized structure for economic decisions, market economies have a very decentralized structure. A **market** is an institution that brings together buyers and sellers of goods or services, who may be either individuals or businesses. The New York Stock Exchange (Figure 1.9) is a prime example of a market which brings buyers and sellers together. In a **market economy**, decision-making is decentralized. Market economies are based on **private enterprise**: the private individuals or groups of private individuals own and operate the means of production (resources and businesses). Businesses supply goods and services based on demand. (In a command economy, by contrast, the government owns resources and businesses.) Supply of goods and services depends on what the demands are. A person's income is based on their ability to convert resources (especially labor) into something that society values. The more society values the person's output, the higher the income (think Lady Gaga or LeBron James). In this scenario, market forces, not governments, determine economic decisions.

Most economies in the real world are mixed. They combine elements of command and market (and even traditional) systems. The U.S. economy is positioned toward the market-oriented end of the spectrum. Many countries in Europe and Latin America, while primarily market-oriented, have a greater degree of government involvement in economic decisions than the U.S. economy. China and Russia, while over the past several decades have moved more in the direction of having a market-oriented system, remain closer to the command economy end of the spectrum. The Heritage Foundation provides perspective on countries' economic freedom, as the following Clear It Up feature discusses.

 ## CLEAR IT UP

### What countries are considered economically free?

Who is in control of economic decisions? Are people free to do what they want and to work where they want? Are businesses free to produce when they want and what they choose, and to hire and fire as they wish? Are banks free to choose who will receive loans, or does the government control these kinds of choices? Each year, researchers at the Heritage Foundation and the *Wall Street Journal* look at 50 different categories of economic freedom for countries around the world. They give each nation a score based on the extent of economic freedom in each category. Note that while the Heritage Foundation/WSJ index is widely cited by an array of scholars and publications, it should be regarded as only one viewpoint. Some experts indicate that the index's category choices and scores are politically biased. However, the index and others like it provide a useful resource for critical discussion of economic freedom.

The 2016 Heritage Foundation's Index of Economic Freedom report ranked 178 countries around the world: Table 1.1 lists some examples of the most free and the least free countries. Although technically not a separate country, Hong Kong has been granted a degree of autonomy such that, for purposes of measuring economic statistics, it is often treated as a separate country. Several additional countries were not ranked because of extreme instability that made judgments about economic freedom impossible. These countries include Afghanistan, Iraq, Libya, Syria, Somalia, and Yemen.

The assigned rankings are inevitably based on estimates, yet even these rough measures can be useful for discerning trends. In 2015, 101 of the 178 included countries shifted toward greater economic freedom, although 77 of the countries shifted toward less economic freedom. In recent decades, the overall trend has been a *higher level of economic freedom around the world*.

| Most Economic Freedom | Least Economic Freedom |
| --- | --- |
| 1. Hong Kong | 167. Timor-Leste |
| 2. Singapore | 168. Democratic Republic of Congo |
| 3. New Zealand | 169. Argentina |
| 4. Switzerland | 170. Equatorial Guinea |
| 5. Australia | 171. Iran |
| 6. Canada | 172. Republic of Congo |
| 7. Chile | 173. Eritrea |
| 8. Ireland | 174. Turkmenistan |
| 9. Estonia | 175. Zimbabwe |

**TABLE 1.1 Economic Freedoms, 2016** (Source: The Heritage Foundation, 2016 Index of Economic Freedom, Country

| Most Economic Freedom | Least Economic Freedom |
| --- | --- |
| 10. United Kingdom | 176. Venezuela |
| 11. United States | 177. Cuba |
| 12. Denmark | 178. North Korea |

**TABLE 1.1 Economic Freedoms, 2016** (Source: The Heritage Foundation, 2016 Index of Economic Freedom, Country Rankings, http://www.heritage.org/index/ranking)

## Regulations: The Rules of the Game

Markets and government regulations are always entangled. There is no such thing as an absolutely free market. Regulations always define the "rules of the game" in the economy. Economies that are primarily market-oriented have fewer regulations—ideally just enough to maintain an even playing field for participants. At a minimum, these laws govern matters like safeguarding private property against theft, protecting people from violence, enforcing legal contracts, preventing fraud, and collecting taxes. Conversely, even the most command-oriented economies operate using markets. How else would buying and selling occur? The government heavily regulates decisions of what to produce and prices to charge. Heavily regulated economies often have **underground economies** (or black markets), which are markets where the buyers and sellers make transactions without the government's approval.

The question of how to organize economic institutions is typically not a straightforward choice between all market or all government, but instead involves a balancing act over the appropriate combination of market freedom and government rules.

**FIGURE 1.10 Globalization** Cargo ships are one mode of transportation for shipping goods in the global economy. (Credit: "Cargo Ship" by Raul Valdez/Flickr Creative Commons, CC BY 2.0)

## The Rise of Globalization

Recent decades have seen a trend toward **globalization**, which is the expanding cultural, political, and economic connections between people around the world. One measure of this is the increased buying and selling of goods, services, and assets across national borders—in other words, international trade and financial capital flows.

Globalization has occurred for a number of reasons. Improvements in shipping, as illustrated by the container ship in Figure 1.10, and air cargo have driven down transportation costs. Innovations in computing and telecommunications have made it easier and cheaper to manage long-distance economic connections of production and sales. Many valuable products and services in the modern economy can take the form of information—for example: computer software; financial advice; travel planning; music, books and movies; and blueprints for designing a building. These products and many others can be transported over telephones and computer networks at ever-lower costs. Finally, international agreements and treaties between countries have encouraged greater trade.

Table 1.2 presents one measure of globalization. It shows the percentage of domestic economic production that was exported for a selection of countries from 2010 to 2015, according to an entity known as The World Bank. **Exports** are the goods and services that one produces domestically and sells abroad. **Imports** are the goods and services that one produces abroad and then sells domestically. **Gross domestic product (GDP)** measures the size of total production in an economy. Thus, the ratio of exports divided by GDP measures what share of a country's total economic production is sold in other countries.

| Country | 2010 | 2011 | 2012 | 2013 | 2014 | 2015 |
|---|---|---|---|---|---|---|
| **Higher Income Countries** | | | | | | |
| United States | 12.4 | 13.6 | 13.6 | 13.5 | 13.5 | 12.6 |
| Belgium | 76.2 | 81.4 | 82.2 | 82.8 | 84.0 | 84.4 |
| Canada | 29.1 | 30.7 | 30.0 | 30.1 | 31.7 | 31.5 |
| France | 26.0 | 27.8 | 28.1 | 28.3 | 29.0 | 30.0 |
| **Middle Income Countries** | | | | | | |
| Brazil | 10.9 | 11.9 | 12.6 | 12.6 | 11.2 | 13.0 |
| Mexico | 29.9 | 31.2 | 32.6 | 31.7 | 32.3 | 35.3 |
| South Korea | 49.4 | 55.7 | 56.3 | 53.9 | 50.3 | 45.9 |
| **Lower Income Countries** | | | | | | |
| Chad | 36.8 | 38.9 | 36.9 | 32.2 | 34.2 | 29.8 |
| China | 29.4 | 28.5 | 27.3 | 26.4 | 23.9 | 22.4 |
| India | 22.0 | 23.9 | 24.0 | 24.8 | 22.9 | - |
| Nigeria | 25.3 | 31.3 | 31.4 | 18.0 | 18.4 | - |

**TABLE 1.2 The Extent of Globalization (exports/GDP)**
(Source: http://databank.worldbank.org/data/)

In recent decades, the export/GDP ratio has generally risen, both worldwide and for the U.S. economy. Interestingly, the share of U.S. exports in proportion to the U.S. economy is well below the global average, in part because large economies like the United States can contain more of the division of labor inside their national borders. However, smaller economies like Belgium, Korea, and Canada need to trade across their borders with other countries to take full advantage of division of labor, specialization, and economies of scale. In this sense, the enormous U.S. economy is less affected by globalization than most other countries.

Table 1.2 indicates that many medium and low income countries around the world, like Mexico and China, have also experienced a surge of globalization in recent decades. If an astronaut in orbit could put on special glasses that make all economic transactions visible as brightly colored lines and look down at Earth, the astronaut would see the planet covered with connections.

Despite the rise in globalization over the last few decades, in recent years we've seen significant pushback against globalization from people across the world concerned about loss of jobs, loss of political sovereignty, and increased economic inequality. Prominent examples of this pushback include the 2016 vote in Great Britain to exit the European Union (i.e. Brexit), and the election of Donald J. Trump for President of the United States.

Hopefully, you now have an idea about economics. Before you move to any other chapter of study, be sure to read the very important appendix to this chapter called The Use of Mathematics in Principles of Economics. It is essential that you learn more about how to read and use models in economics.

 **BRING IT HOME**

## Information Overload in the Information Age

The world provides nearly instant access to a wealth of information. Consider that as recently as the late 1970s, the *Farmer's Almanac*, along with the Weather Bureau of the U.S. Department of Agriculture, were the primary sources American farmers used to determine when to plant and harvest their crops. Today, these decisions are driven by data. Farmers access detailed data streams driven by global positioning systems, historical rainfall patterns, and complex weather monitoring services. They combine this information with crop yield data and soil quality measurements from prior years. Maximizing production efficiently can mean the difference between a farm that remains profitable and one that may need to sell its land, and data helps eliminate guesswork.

Information helps us make decisions as simple as what to wear today to how many reporters the media should send to cover an event. Each of these decisions is an economic decision. After all, resources are scarce. If the media send ten reporters to cover an announcement, they are not available to cover other stories or complete other tasks. Information provides the necessary knowledge to make the best possible decisions on how to utilize scarce resources. Welcome to the world of economics!

## Key Terms

**circular flow diagram** a diagram that views the economy as consisting of households and firms interacting in a goods and services market and a labor market

**command economy** an economy where economic decisions are passed down from government authority and where the government owns the resources

**division of labor** the way in which different workers divide required tasks to produce a good or service

**economics** the study of how humans make choices under conditions of scarcity

**economies of scale** when the average cost of producing each individual unit declines as total output increases

**exports** products (goods and services) made domestically and sold abroad

**fiscal policy** economic policies that involve government spending and taxes

**globalization** the trend in which buying and selling in markets have increasingly crossed national borders

**goods and services market** a market in which firms are sellers of what they produce and households are buyers

**gross domestic product (GDP)** measure of the size of total production in an economy

**imports** products (goods and services) made abroad and then sold domestically

**labor market** the market in which households sell their labor as workers to business firms or other employers

**macroeconomics** the branch of economics that focuses on broad issues such as growth, unemployment, inflation, and trade balance

**market** interaction between potential buyers and sellers; a combination of demand and supply

**market economy** an economy where economic decisions are decentralized, private individuals own resources, and businesses supply goods and services based on demand

**microeconomics** the branch of economics that focuses on actions of particular agents within the economy, like households, workers, and business firms

**model** see theory

**monetary policy** policy that involves altering the level of interest rates, the availability of credit in the economy, and the extent of borrowing

**private enterprise** system where private individuals or groups of private individuals own and operate the means of production (resources and businesses)

**scarcity** when human wants for goods and services exceed the available supply

**specialization** when workers or firms focus on particular tasks for which they are well-suited within the overall production process

**theory** a representation of an object or situation that is simplified while including enough of the key features to help us understand the object or situation

**traditional economy** typically an agricultural economy where things are done the same as they have always been done

**underground economy** a market where the buyers and sellers make transactions in violation of one or more government regulations

## Key Concepts and Summary

### 1.1 What Is Economics, and Why Is It Important?

Economics seeks to solve the problem of scarcity, which is when human wants for goods and services exceed the available supply. A modern economy displays a division of labor, in which people earn income by specializing in what they produce and then use that income to purchase the products they need or want. The division of labor allows individuals and firms to specialize and to produce more for several reasons: a) It allows the agents to focus on areas of advantage due to natural factors and skill levels; b) It encourages the agents to learn and invent; c) It allows agents to take advantage of economies of scale. Division and specialization of labor only work when individuals can purchase what they do not produce in markets. Learning about economics helps you understand the major problems facing the world today, prepares you to be a good citizen, and helps you become a well-rounded thinker.

## 1.2 Microeconomics and Macroeconomics

Microeconomics and macroeconomics are two different perspectives on the economy. The microeconomic perspective focuses on parts of the economy: individuals, firms, and industries. The macroeconomic perspective looks at the economy as a whole, focusing on goals like growth in the standard of living, unemployment, and inflation. Macroeconomics has two types of policies for pursuing these goals: monetary policy and fiscal policy.

## 1.3 How Economists Use Theories and Models to Understand Economic Issues

Economists analyze problems differently than do other disciplinary experts. The main tools economists use are economic theories or models. A theory is not an illustration of the answer to a problem. Rather, a theory is a tool for determining the answer.

## 1.4 How To Organize Economies: An Overview of Economic Systems

We can organize societies as traditional, command, or market-oriented economies. Most societies are a mix. The last few decades have seen globalization evolve as a result of growth in commercial and financial networks that cross national borders, making businesses and workers from different economies increasingly interdependent.

## Self-Check Questions

1. What is scarcity? Can you think of two causes of scarcity?

2. Residents of the town of Smithfield like to consume hams, but each ham requires 10 people to produce it and takes a month. If the town has a total of 100 people, what is the maximum amount of ham the residents can consume in a month?

3. A consultant works for $200 per hour. She likes to eat vegetables, but is not very good at growing them. Why does it make more economic sense for her to spend her time at the consulting job and shop for her vegetables?

4. A computer systems engineer could paint her house, but it makes more sense for her to hire a painter to do it. Explain why.

5. What would be another example of a "system" in the real world that could serve as a metaphor for micro and macroeconomics?

6. Suppose we extend the circular flow model to add imports and exports. Copy the circular flow diagram onto a sheet of paper and then add a foreign country as a third agent. Draw a rough sketch of the flows of imports, exports, and the payments for each on your diagram.

7. What is an example of a problem in the world today, not mentioned in the chapter, that has an economic dimension?

8. The chapter defines *private enterprise* as a characteristic of market-oriented economies. What would *public enterprise* be? *Hint:* It is a characteristic of command economies.

9. Why might Belgium, France, Italy, and Sweden have a higher export to GDP ratio than the United States?

## Review Questions

10. Give the three reasons that explain why the division of labor increases an economy's level of production.

11. What are three reasons to study economics?

12. What is the difference between microeconomics and macroeconomics?

13. What are examples of individual economic agents?

14. What are the three main goals of macroeconomics?

15. How did John Maynard Keynes define economics?

16. Are households primarily buyers or sellers in the goods and services market? In the labor market?

17. Are firms primarily buyers or sellers in the goods and services market? In the labor market?

18. What are the three ways that societies can organize themselves economically?

19. What is globalization? How do you think it might have affected the economy over the past decade?

## Critical Thinking Questions

20. Suppose you have a team of two workers: one is a baker and one is a chef. Explain why the kitchen can produce more meals in a given period of time if each worker specializes in what they do best than if each worker tries to do everything from appetizer to dessert.

21. Why would division of labor without trade not work?

22. Can you think of any examples of *free* goods, that is, goods or services that are not scarce?

23. A balanced federal budget and a balance of trade are secondary goals of macroeconomics, while growth in the standard of living (for example) is a primary goal. Why do you think that is so?

24. Macroeconomics is an aggregate of what happens at the microeconomic level. Would it be possible for what happens at the macro level to differ from how economic agents would react to some stimulus at the micro level? *Hint:* Think about the behavior of crowds.

25. Why is it unfair or meaningless to criticize a theory as "unrealistic?"

26. Suppose, as an economist, you are asked to analyze an issue unlike anything you have ever done before. Also, suppose you do not have a specific model for analyzing that issue. What should you do? *Hint:* What would a carpenter do in a similar situation?

27. Why do you think that most modern countries' economies are a mix of command and market types?

28. Can you think of ways that globalization has helped you economically? Can you think of ways that it has not?

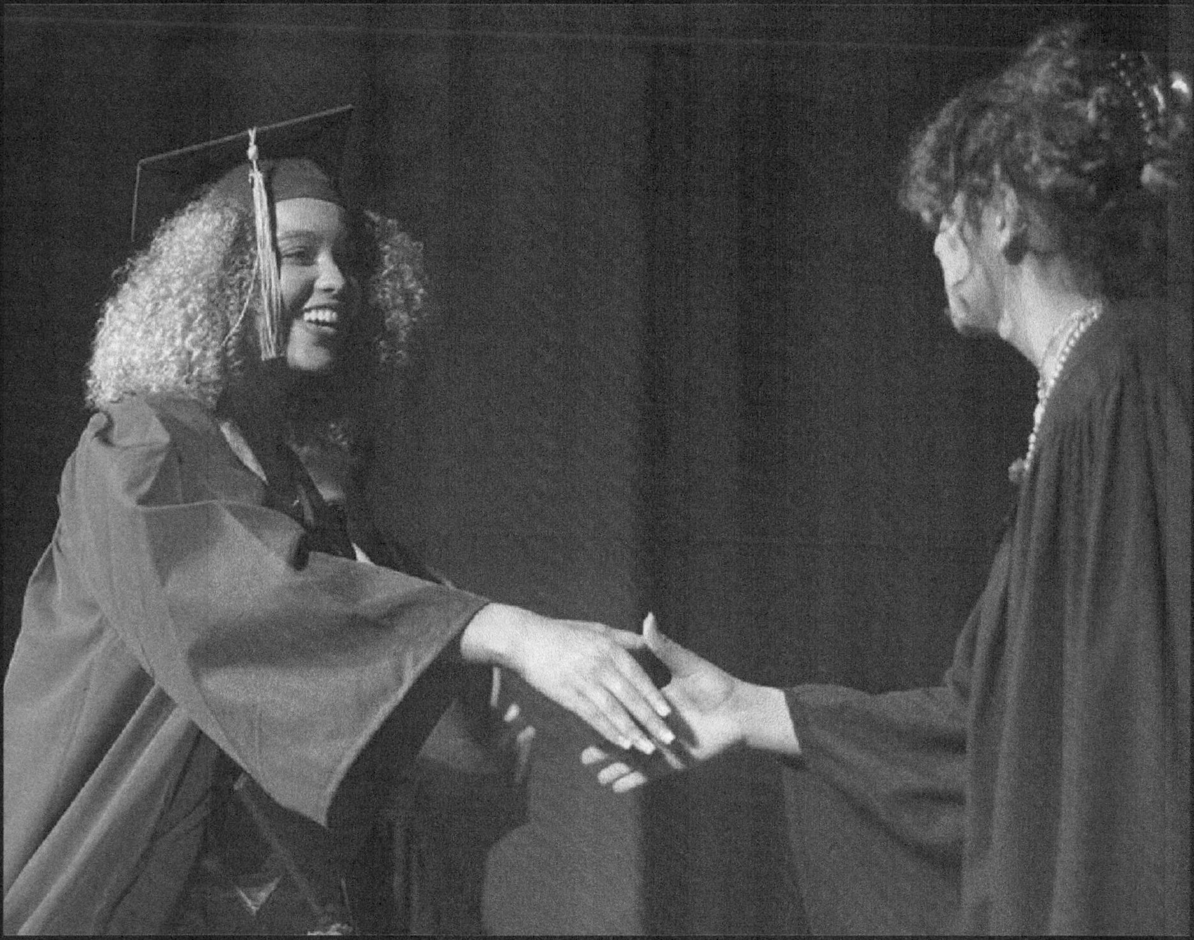

**FIGURE 2.1 Choices and Tradeoffs** In general, the higher the degree, the higher the salary, so why aren't more people pursuing higher degrees? The short answer: choices and tradeoffs. (Credit: modification of "College of DuPage Commencement 2018 107" by COD Newsroom/Flickr, CC BY 2.0)

**CHAPTER OBJECTIVES**

In this chapter, you will learn about:

- How Individuals Make Choices Based on Their Budget Constraint
- The Production Possibilities Frontier and Social Choices
- Confronting Objections to the Economic Approach

## Introduction to Choice in a World of Scarcity

### BRING IT HOME

#### Choices ... to What Degree?

Does your level of education impact earning? Let's look at some data from the Bureau of Labor Statistics (BLS). In 2020, among full-time wage and salary workers, median weekly earnings for those with a master's degree were $1,545. Multiply this average by 52 weeks, and you get average annual earnings of $80,340. Compare that to the median weekly earnings for full-time workers aged 25 and over with just a bachelor's degree: $1,305 weekly and $67,860 a year. What about those with no higher than a high school diploma in 2020? They earn an average of just $781 weekly and $40,612 over 12 months. In other words, data from the BLS indicates that receiving a bachelor's degree boosts earnings by 67% over what workers would have earned if they only obtained a high school diploma, and a master's degree yields average earnings that are nearly double those of workers with a high school diploma.

Given these statistics, we might expect many people to choose to go to college and at least earn a bachelor's degree. Assuming that people want to improve their material well-being, it seems like they would make those choices that provide them with the greatest opportunity to consume goods and services. As it turns out, the analysis is not nearly as simple as this. In fact, in 2019, the BLS reported that while just over 90% of the population aged 25 and over in the United States had a high school diploma, only 36% of those aged 25 and over had a bachelor's or higher degree, and only 13.5% had earned a master's or higher degree.

This brings us to the subject of this chapter: why people make the choices they make and how economists explain those choices.

---

You will learn quickly when you examine the relationship between economics and scarcity that choices involve tradeoffs. Every choice has a cost.

In 1968, the Rolling Stones recorded "You Can't Always Get What You Want." Economists chuckled, because they had been singing a similar tune for decades. English economist Lionel Robbins (1898–1984), in his *Essay on the Nature and Significance of Economic Science* in 1932, described not always getting what you want in this way:

> The time at our disposal is limited. There are only twenty-four hours in the day. We have to choose between the different uses to which they may be put. … Everywhere we turn, if we choose one thing we must relinquish others which, in different circumstances, we would wish not to have relinquished. Scarcity of means to satisfy given ends is an almost ubiquitous condition of human nature.

Because people live in a world of scarcity, they cannot have all the time, money, possessions, and experiences they wish. Neither can society.

This chapter will continue our discussion of scarcity and the economic way of thinking by first introducing three critical concepts: opportunity cost, marginal decision making, and diminishing returns. Later, it will consider whether the economic way of thinking accurately describes either how we *make* choices and how we *should* make them.

## 2.1 How Individuals Make Choices Based on Their Budget Constraint

### LEARNING OBJECTIVES

By the end of this section, you will be able to:
- Calculate and graph budget constraints
- Explain opportunity sets and opportunity costs
- Evaluate the law of diminishing marginal utility
- Explain how marginal analysis and utility influence choices

Consider the typical consumer's budget problem. Consumers have a limited amount of income to spend on the things they need and want. Suppose Alphonso has $10 in spending money each week that he can allocate between bus tickets for getting to work and the burgers that he eats for lunch. Burgers cost $2 each, and bus tickets are 50 cents each. We can see Alphonso's budget problem in Figure 2.2.

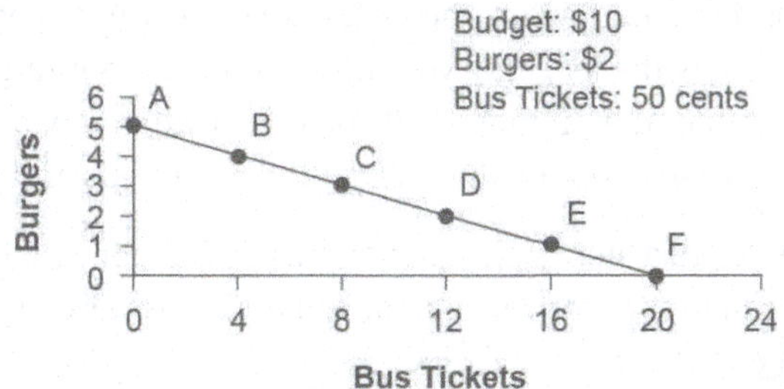


**FIGURE 2.2 The Budget Constraint: Alphonso's Consumption Choice Opportunity Frontier** Each point on the budget constraint represents a combination of burgers and bus tickets whose total cost adds up to Alphonso's budget of $10. The relative price of burgers and bus tickets determines the slope of the budget constraint. All along the budget set, giving up one burger means gaining four bus tickets.

The vertical axis in the figure shows burger purchases and the horizontal axis shows bus ticket purchases. If Alphonso spends all his money on burgers, he can afford five per week. ($10 per week/$2 per burger = 5 burgers per week.) However, if he does this, he will not be able to afford any bus tickets. Point A in the figure shows the choice (zero bus tickets and five burgers). Alternatively, if Alphonso spends all his money on bus tickets, he can afford 20 per week. ($10 per week/$0.50 per bus ticket = 20 bus tickets per week.) Then, however, he will not be able to afford any burgers. Point F shows this alternative choice (20 bus tickets and zero burgers).

If we connect all the points between A and F, we get Alphonso's **budget constraint**. This indicates all the combination of burgers and bus tickets Alphonso can afford, given the price of the two goods and his budget amount.

If Alphonso is like most people, he will choose some combination that includes both bus tickets and burgers. That is, he will choose some combination on the budget constraint that is between points A and F. Every point on (or inside) the constraint shows a combination of burgers and bus tickets that Alphonso can afford. Any point outside the constraint is not affordable, because it would cost more money than Alphonso has in his budget.

The budget constraint clearly shows the tradeoff Alphonso faces in choosing between burgers and bus tickets. Suppose he is currently at point D, where he can afford 12 bus tickets and two burgers. What would it cost Alphonso for one more burger? It would be natural to answer $2, but that's not the way economists think. Instead they ask, how many bus tickets would Alphonso have to give up to get one more burger, while staying within his budget? Since bus tickets cost 50 cents, Alphonso would have to give up four to afford one more burger. That is the true cost to Alphonso.

### The Concept of Opportunity Cost

Economists use the term **opportunity cost** to indicate what people must give up to obtain what they desire. The idea behind opportunity cost is that the cost of one item is the lost opportunity to do or consume something else. In short, opportunity cost is the value of the next best alternative. For Alphonso, the opportunity cost of a burger is the four bus tickets he would have to give up. He would decide whether or not to choose the burger depending on whether the value of the burger exceeds the value of the forgone alternative—in this case, bus tickets. Since people must choose, they inevitably face tradeoffs in which they have to give up things they desire to obtain other things they desire more.

### ⊘ LINK IT UP

View this website (http://openstax.org/l/linestanding) for an example of opportunity cost—paying someone else to wait in line for you.

A fundamental principle of economics is that every choice has an opportunity cost. If you sleep through your economics class, the opportunity cost is the learning you miss from not attending class. If you spend your income on video games, you cannot spend it on movies. If you choose to marry one person, you give up the opportunity to marry anyone else. In short, opportunity cost is all around us and part of human existence.

The following Work It Out feature shows a step-by-step analysis of a budget constraint calculation. Read through it to understand another important concept—slope—that we further explain in the appendix The Use of Mathematics in Principles of Economics.

WORK IT OUT

### Understanding Budget Constraints

Budget constraints are easy to understand if you apply a little math. The appendix The Use of Mathematics in Principles of Economics explains all the math you are likely to need in this book. Therefore, if math is not your strength, you might want to take a look at the appendix.

Step 1: The equation for any budget constraint is:

$$\text{Budget} = P_1 \times Q_1 + P_2 \times Q_2$$

where P and Q are the price and quantity of items purchased (which we assume here to be two items) and Budget is the amount of income one has to spend.

Step 2. Apply the budget constraint equation to the scenario. In Alphonso's case, this works out to be:

$$\text{Budget} = P_1 \times Q_1 + P_2 \times Q_2$$
$$\$10 \text{ budget} = \$2 \text{ per burger} \times \text{quantity of burgers} + \$0.50 \text{ per bus ticket} \times \text{quantity of bus tickets}$$
$$\$10 = \$2 \times Q_{burgers} + \$0.50 \times Q_{bus\ tickets}$$

Step 3. Using a little algebra, we can turn this into the familiar equation of a line:

$$y = b + mx$$

For Alphonso, this is:

$$\$10 = \$2 \times Q_{burgers} + \$0.50 \times Q_{bus\ tickets}$$

Step 4. Simplify the equation. Begin by multiplying both sides of the equation by 2:

$$2 \times 10 = 2 \times 2 \times Q_{burgers} + 2 \times 0.5 \times Q_{bus\ tickets}$$
$$20 = 4 \times Q_{burgers} + 1 \times Q_{bus\ tickets}$$

Step 5. Subtract one bus ticket from both sides:

$$20 - Q_{bus\ tickets} = 4 \times Q_{burgers}$$

Divide each side by 4 to yield the answer:

$$5 - 0.25 \times Q_{bus\ tickets} = Q_{burgers}$$

$$\text{or}$$

$$Q_{burgers} = 5 - 0.25 \times Q_{bus\ tickets}$$

Step 6. Notice that this equation fits the budget constraint in Figure 2.2. The vertical intercept is 5 and the slope is −0.25, just as the equation says. If you plug 20 bus tickets into the equation, you get 0 burgers. If you plug other numbers of bus tickets into the equation, you get the results (see Table 2.1), which are the points on Alphonso's budget constraint.

| Point | Quantity of Burgers (at $2) | Quantity of Bus Tickets (at 50 cents) |
|---|---|---|
| A | 5 | 0 |
| B | 4 | 4 |
| C | 3 | 8 |
| D | 2 | 12 |
| E | 1 | 16 |
| F | 0 | 20 |

**TABLE 2.1**

Step 7. Notice that the slope of a budget constraint always shows the opportunity cost of the good which is on the horizontal axis. For Alphonso, the slope is −0.25, indicating that for every bus ticket he buys, he must give up 1/4 burger. To phrase it differently, for every four tickets he buys, Alphonso must give up 1 burger.

There are two important observations here. First, the algebraic sign of the slope is negative, which means that the only way to get more of one good is to give up some of the other. Second, we define the slope as the price of bus tickets (whatever is on the horizontal axis in the graph) divided by the price of burgers (whatever is on the vertical axis), in this case $0.50/$2 = 0.25. If you want to determine the opportunity cost quickly, just divide the two prices.

## Identifying Opportunity Cost

In many cases, it is reasonable to refer to the opportunity cost as the price. If your cousin buys a new bicycle for $300, then $300 measures the amount of "other consumption" that he has forsaken. For practical purposes, there may be no special need to identify the specific alternative product or products that he could have bought with that $300, but sometimes the price as measured in dollars may not accurately capture the true opportunity cost. This problem can loom especially large when costs of time are involved.

For example, consider a boss who decides that all employees will attend a two-day retreat to "build team spirit." The out-of-pocket monetary cost of the event may involve hiring an outside consulting firm to run the retreat, as well as room and board for all participants. However, an opportunity cost exists as well: during the two days of the retreat, none of the employees are doing any other work.

Attending college is another case where the opportunity cost exceeds the monetary cost. The out-of-pocket costs of attending college include tuition, books, room and board, and other expenses. However, in addition, during the hours that you are attending class and studying, it is impossible to work at a paying job. Thus, college imposes both an out-of-pocket cost and an opportunity cost of lost earnings.

 **CLEAR IT UP**

### What is the opportunity cost associated with increased airport security measures?

After the terrorist plane hijackings on September 11, 2001, many steps were proposed to improve air travel safety. For example, the federal government could provide armed "sky marshals" who would travel inconspicuously with the rest of the passengers. The cost of having a sky marshal on every flight would be roughly $3 billion per year. Retrofitting all U.S. planes with reinforced cockpit doors to make it harder for terrorists to take over the plane would have a price tag of $450 million. Buying more sophisticated security equipment for airports, like three-dimensional baggage scanners and cameras linked to face recognition software, could cost another $2 billion.

However, the single biggest cost of greater airline security does not involve spending money. It is the opportunity cost of additional waiting time at the airport. According to the United States Department of Transportation (DOT), there were 895.5 million systemwide (domestic and international) scheduled service passengers in 2015. Since the 9/11 hijackings, security screening has become more intensive, and consequently, the procedure takes longer than in the past. Say that, on average, each air passenger spends an extra 30 minutes in the airport per trip. Economists commonly place a value on time to convert an opportunity cost in time into a monetary figure. Because many air travelers are relatively high-paid business people, conservative estimates set the average price of time for air travelers at $20 per hour. By these back-of-the-envelope calculations, the opportunity cost of delays in airports could be as much as 800 million × 0.5 hours × $20/hour, or $8 billion per year. Clearly, the opportunity costs of waiting time can be just as important as costs that involve direct spending.

---

In some cases, realizing the opportunity cost can alter behavior. Imagine, for example, that you spend $8 on lunch every day at work. You may know perfectly well that bringing a lunch from home would cost only $3 a day, so the opportunity cost of buying lunch at the restaurant is $5 each day (that is, the $8 buying lunch costs minus the $3 your lunch from home would cost). Five dollars each day does not seem to be that much. However, if you project what that adds up to in a year—250 days a year × $5 per day equals $1,250, the cost, perhaps, of a decent vacation. If you describe the opportunity cost as "a nice vacation" instead of "$5 a day," you might make different choices.

## Marginal Decision-Making and Diminishing Marginal Utility

The budget constraint framework helps to emphasize that most choices in the real world are not about getting all of one thing or all of another; that is, they are not about choosing either the point at one end of the budget constraint or else the point all the way at the other end. Instead, most choices involve **marginal analysis**, which means examining the benefits and costs of choosing a little more or a little less of a good. People naturally compare costs and benefits, but often we look at total costs and total benefits, when the optimal choice necessitates comparing how costs and benefits change from one option to another. You might think of marginal analysis as "change analysis." Marginal analysis is used throughout economics.

We now turn to the notion of **utility**. People desire goods and services for the satisfaction or utility those goods and services provide. Utility, as we will see in the chapter on Consumer Choices, is subjective but that does not make it less real. Economists typically assume that the more of some good one consumes (for example, slices of pizza), the more utility one obtains. At the same time, the utility a person receives from consuming the first unit of a good is typically more than the utility received from consuming the fifth or the tenth unit of that same good. When Alphonso chooses between burgers and bus tickets, for example, the first few bus rides that he chooses might provide him with a great deal of utility—perhaps they help him get to a job interview or a doctor's appointment. However, later bus rides might provide much less utility—they may only serve to kill time on a rainy day. Similarly, the first burger that Alphonso chooses to buy may be on a day when he missed breakfast and is ravenously hungry. However, if Alphonso has multiple burgers every day, the last few burgers may taste pretty boring. The general pattern that consumption of the first few units of any good tends to bring a higher level of utility to a person than consumption of later units is a common pattern. Economists refer to this pattern as the **law of diminishing marginal utility**, which means that as a person receives more of a good, the additional (or marginal) utility from each additional unit of the good declines. In other words, the first slice of pizza brings more satisfaction than the sixth.

The law of diminishing marginal utility explains why people and societies rarely make all-or-nothing choices. You would not say, "My favorite food is ice cream, so I will eat nothing but ice cream from now on." Instead, even if you get a very high level of utility from your favorite food, if you ate it exclusively, the additional or marginal utility from those last few servings would not be very high. Similarly, most workers do not say: "I enjoy leisure, so I'll never work." Instead, workers recognize that even though some leisure is very nice, a combination of all leisure and no income is not so attractive. The budget constraint framework suggests that when people make choices in a world of scarcity, they will use marginal analysis and think about whether they would prefer a little more or a little less.

A rational consumer would only purchase additional units of some product as long as the marginal utility exceeds the opportunity cost. Suppose Alphonso moves down his budget constraint from Point A to Point B to Point C and further. As he consumes more bus tickets, the marginal utility of bus tickets will diminish, while the opportunity cost, that is, the marginal utility of foregone burgers, will increase. Eventually, the opportunity cost will exceed the marginal utility of an additional bus ticket. If Alphonso is rational, he won't purchase more bus tickets once the marginal utility just equals the opportunity cost. While we can't (yet) say exactly how many bus tickets Alphonso will buy, that number is unlikely to be the most he can afford, 20.

### Sunk Costs

In the budget constraint framework, all decisions involve what will happen next: that is, what quantities of goods will you consume, how many hours will you work, or how much will you save. These decisions do not look back to past choices. Thus, the budget constraint framework assumes that **sunk costs**, which are costs that were incurred in the past and cannot be recovered, should not affect the current decision.

Consider the case of Selena, who pays $8 to see a movie, but after watching the film for 30 minutes, she knows that it is truly terrible. Should she stay and watch the rest of the movie because she paid for the ticket, or should she leave? The money she spent is a sunk cost, and unless the theater manager is sympathetic, Selena will not get a refund. However, staying in the movie still means paying an opportunity cost in time. Her choice is whether to spend the next 90 minutes suffering through a cinematic disaster or to do something—anything—else. The lesson of sunk costs is to forget about the money and time that is irretrievably gone and instead to focus on the marginal costs and benefits of current and future options.

For people and firms alike, dealing with sunk costs can be frustrating. It often means admitting an earlier error in judgment. Many firms, for example, find it hard to give up on a new product that is doing poorly because they spent so much money in creating and launching the product. However, the lesson of sunk costs is to ignore them and make decisions based on what will happen in the future.

### From a Model with Two Goods to One of Many Goods

The budget constraint diagram containing just two goods, like most models used in this book, is not realistic. After all, in a modern economy people choose from thousands of goods. However, thinking about a model with many goods is a straightforward extension of what we discussed here. Instead of drawing just one budget constraint, showing the tradeoff between two goods, you can draw multiple budget constraints, showing the possible tradeoffs between many different pairs of goods. In more advanced classes in economics, you would use mathematical equations that include many possible goods and services that can be purchased, together with their quantities and prices, and show how the total spending on all goods and services is limited to the overall budget available. The graph with two goods that we presented here clearly illustrates that every choice has an opportunity cost, which is the point that does carry over to the real world.

## 2.2 The Production Possibilities Frontier and Social Choices

**LEARNING OBJECTIVES**

By the end of this section, you will be able to:
- Interpret production possibilities frontier graphs
- Contrast a budget constraint and a production possibilities frontier
- Explain the relationship between a production possibilities frontier and the law of diminishing returns
- Contrast productive efficiency and allocative efficiency
- Define comparative advantage

Just as individuals cannot have everything they want and must instead make choices, society as a whole cannot have everything it might want, either. This section of the chapter will explain the constraints society faces, using a model called the **production possibilities frontier (PPF)**. There are more similarities than differences between individual choice and social choice. As you read this section, focus on the similarities.

Because society has limited resources (e.g., labor, land, capital, raw materials) at any point in time, there is a limit to the quantities of goods and services it can produce. Suppose a society desires two products, healthcare and education. The production possibilities frontier in Figure 2.3 illustrates this situation.

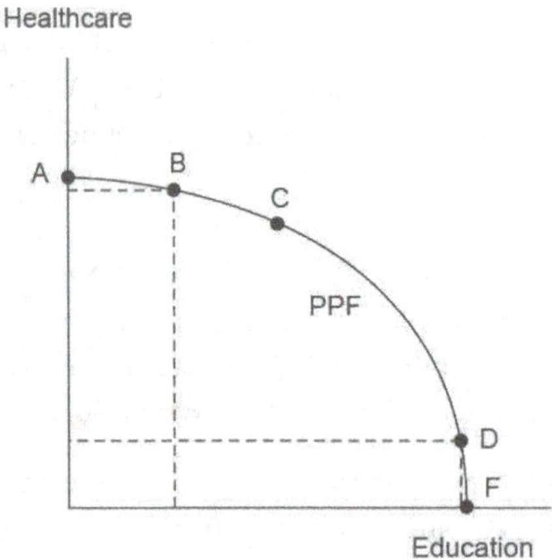


**FIGURE 2.3 A Healthcare vs. Education Production Possibilities Frontier** This production possibilities frontier shows a tradeoff between devoting social resources to healthcare and devoting them to education. At A all resources go to healthcare and at B, most go to healthcare. At D most resources go to education, and at F, all go to education.

Figure 2.3 shows healthcare on the vertical axis and education on the horizontal axis. If the society were to allocate all of its resources to healthcare, it could produce at point A. However, it would not have any resources to produce education. If it were to allocate all of its resources to education, it could produce at point F. Alternatively, the society could choose to produce any combination of healthcare and education on the production possibilities frontier. In effect, the production possibilities frontier plays the same role for society as the budget constraint plays for Alphonso. Society can choose any combination of the two goods on or inside the PPF. However, it does not have enough resources to produce outside the PPF.

Most importantly, the production possibilities frontier clearly shows the tradeoff between healthcare and education. Suppose society has chosen to operate at point B, and it is considering producing more education. Because the PPF is downward sloping from left to right, the only way society can obtain more education is by giving up some healthcare. That is the tradeoff society faces. Suppose it considers moving from point B to point C. What would the opportunity cost be for the additional education? The opportunity cost would be the healthcare society has to forgo. Just as with Alphonso's budget constraint, the **slope** of the production possibilities frontier shows the opportunity cost. By now you might be saying, "Hey, this PPF is sounding like the budget constraint." If so, read the following Clear It Up feature.

 **CLEAR IT UP**

### What's the difference between a budget constraint and a PPF?

There are two major differences between a budget constraint and a production possibilities frontier. The first is the fact that the budget constraint is a straight line. This is because its slope is given by the relative prices of the two goods, which from the point of view of an individual consumer, are fixed, so the slope doesn't change. In contrast, the PPF has a curved shape because of the law of the diminishing returns. Thus, the slope is different at various points on the PPF. The second major difference is the absence of specific numbers on the axes of the PPF. There are no specific numbers because we do not know the exact amount of resources this imaginary economy has, nor do we know how many resources it takes to produce healthcare and how many resources it takes to produce education. If this were a real world example, that data would be available.

Whether or not we have specific numbers, conceptually we can measure the opportunity cost of additional education as society moves from point B to point C on the PPF. We measure the additional education by the horizontal distance between B and C. The foregone healthcare is given by the vertical distance between B and C. The slope of the PPF between B and C is (approximately) the vertical distance (the "rise") over the horizontal distance (the "run"). This is the opportunity cost of the additional education.

## The PPF and the Law of Increasing Opportunity Cost

The budget constraints that we presented earlier in this chapter, showing individual choices about what quantities of goods to consume, were all straight lines. The reason for these straight lines was that the relative prices of the two goods in the **consumption budget constraint** determined the slope of the budget constraint. However, we drew the production possibilities frontier for healthcare and education as a curved line. Why does the PPF have a different shape?

To understand why the PPF is curved, start by considering point A at the top left-hand side of the PPF. At point A, all available resources are devoted to healthcare and none are left for education. This situation would be extreme and even ridiculous. For example, children are seeing a doctor every day, whether they are sick or not, but not attending school. People are having cosmetic surgery on every part of their bodies, but no high school or college education exists. Now imagine that some of these resources are diverted from healthcare to education, so that the economy is at point B instead of point A. Diverting some resources away from A to B causes relatively little reduction in health because the last few marginal dollars going into healthcare services are not producing much additional gain in health. However, putting those marginal dollars into education, which is completely without resources at point A, can produce relatively large gains. For this reason, the shape of the PPF from A to B is relatively flat, representing a relatively small drop-off in health and a relatively large gain in education.

Now consider the other end, at the lower right, of the production possibilities frontier. Imagine that society starts at choice D, which is devoting nearly all resources to education and very few to healthcare, and moves to point F, which is devoting *all* spending to education and none to healthcare. For the sake of concreteness, you can imagine that in the movement from D to F, the last few doctors must become high school science teachers, the last few nurses must become school librarians rather than dispensers of vaccinations, and the last few emergency rooms are turned into kindergartens. The gains to education from adding these last few resources to education are very small. However, the opportunity cost lost to health will be fairly large, and thus the slope of the PPF between D and F is steep, showing a large drop in health for only a small gain in education.

The lesson is not that society is likely to make an extreme choice like devoting no resources to education at point A or no resources to health at point F. Instead, the lesson is that the gains from committing additional marginal resources to education depend on how much is already being spent. If on the one hand, very few resources are currently committed to education, then an increase in resources used for education can bring relatively large gains. On the other hand, if a large number of resources are already committed to education, then committing additional resources will bring relatively smaller gains.

This pattern is common enough that economists have given it a name: **the law of increasing opportunity cost**, which holds that as production of a good or service increases, the marginal opportunity cost of producing it increases as well. This happens because some resources are better suited for producing certain goods and services instead of others. When government spends a certain amount more on reducing crime, for example, the original increase in opportunity cost of reducing crime could be relatively small. However, additional increases typically cause relatively larger increases in the opportunity cost of reducing crime, and paying for enough police and security to reduce crime to nothing at all would be a tremendously high opportunity cost.

The curvature of the production possibilities frontier shows that as we add more resources to education, moving from left to right along the horizontal axis, the original increase in opportunity cost is fairly small, but gradually increases. Thus, the slope of the PPF is relatively flat near the vertical-axis intercept. Conversely, as we add more resources to healthcare, moving from bottom to top on the vertical axis, the original declines in opportunity cost are fairly large, but again gradually diminish. Thus, the slope of the PPF is relatively steep near the horizontal-axis intercept. In this way, the law of increasing opportunity cost produces the outward-bending shape of the production possibilities frontier.

## Productive Efficiency and Allocative Efficiency

The study of economics does not presume to tell a society what choice it should make along its production possibilities frontier. In a market-oriented economy with a democratic government, the choice will involve a mixture of decisions by individuals, firms, and government. However, economics can point out that some choices are unambiguously better than others. This observation is based on the concept of efficiency. In everyday usage, efficiency refers to lack of waste. An inefficient machine operates at high cost, while an efficient machine operates at lower cost, because it is not wasting energy or materials. An inefficient organization operates with long delays and high costs, while an efficient organization meets schedules, is focused, and performs within budget.

The production possibilities frontier can illustrate two kinds of efficiency: productive efficiency and allocative efficiency. Figure 2.4 illustrates these ideas using a production possibilities frontier between healthcare and education.

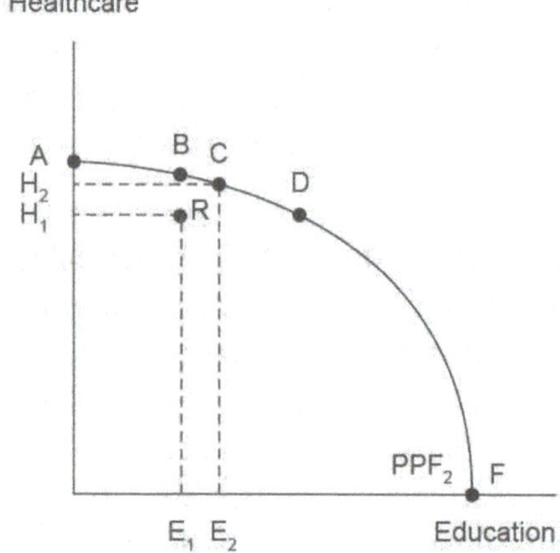


**FIGURE 2.4 Productive and Allocative Efficiency** Productive efficiency means it is impossible to produce more of one good without decreasing the quantity that is produced of another good. Thus, all choices along a given PPF like B, C, and D display productive efficiency, but R does not. Allocative efficiency means that the particular mix of goods being produced—that is, the specific choice along the production possibilities frontier—represents the allocation that society most desires.

**Productive efficiency** means that, given the available inputs and technology, it is impossible to produce more of one good without decreasing the quantity that is produced of another good. All choices on the PPF in Figure 2.4, including A, B, C, D, and F, display productive efficiency. As a firm moves from any one of these choices to any other, either healthcare increases and education decreases or vice versa. However, any choice inside the production possibilities frontier is productively inefficient and wasteful because it is possible to produce more of one good, the other good, or some combination of both goods.

For example, point R is productively inefficient because it is possible at choice C to have more of both goods: education on the horizontal axis is higher at point C than point R ($E_2$ is greater than $E_1$), and healthcare on the vertical axis is also higher at point C than point R ($H_2$ is great than $H_1$).

We can show the particular mix of goods and services produced—that is, the specific combination of selected healthcare and education along the production possibilities frontier—as a ray (line) from the origin to a specific point on the PPF. Output mixes that had more healthcare (and less education) would have a steeper ray, while those with more education (and less healthcare) would have a flatter ray.

**Allocative efficiency** means that the particular combination of goods and services on the production possibility curve that a society produces represents the combination that society most desires. How to determine what a society desires can be a controversial question, and is usually a discussion in political science, sociology, and philosophy classes as well as in economics. At its most basic, allocative efficiency means producers supply the quantity of each product that consumers demand. Only one of the productively efficient choices will be the allocatively efficient choice for society as a whole.

## Why Society Must Choose

In Welcome to Economics! we learned that every society faces the problem of scarcity, where limited resources conflict with unlimited needs and wants. The production possibilities curve illustrates the choices involved in this dilemma.

Every economy faces two situations in which it may be able to expand consumption of all goods. In the first case, a society may discover that it has been using its resources inefficiently, in which case by improving efficiency and producing on the production possibilities frontier, it can have more of all goods (or at least more of some and less of none). In the second case, as resources grow over a period of years (e.g., more labor and more capital), the economy grows. As it does, the production possibilities frontier for a society will tend to shift outward and society will be able to afford more of all goods. In addition, over time, improvements in technology can increase the level of production with given resources, and hence push out the PPF.

However, improvements in productive efficiency take time to discover and implement, and economic growth happens only gradually. Thus, a society must choose between tradeoffs in the present. For government, this process often involves trying to identify where additional spending could do the most good and where reductions in spending would do the least harm. At the individual and firm level, the market economy coordinates a process in which firms seek to produce goods and services in the quantity, quality, and price that people want. However, for both the government and the market economy in the short term, increases in production of one good typically mean offsetting decreases somewhere else in the economy.

## The PPF and Comparative Advantage

While every society must choose how much of each good or service it should produce, it does not need to produce every single good it consumes. Often how much of a good a country decides to produce depends on how expensive it is to produce it versus buying it from a different country. As we saw earlier, the curvature of a country's PPF gives us information about the tradeoff between devoting resources to producing one good versus another. In particular, its slope gives the opportunity cost of producing one more unit of the good in the x-axis in terms of the other good (in the y-axis). Countries tend to have different opportunity costs of producing a specific good, either because of different climates, geography, technology, or skills.

Suppose two countries, the US and Brazil, need to decide how much they will produce of two crops: sugar cane and wheat. Due to its climatic conditions, Brazil can produce quite a bit of sugar cane per acre but not much wheat. Conversely, the U.S. can produce large amounts of wheat per acre, but not much sugar cane. Clearly, Brazil has a lower opportunity cost of producing sugar cane (in terms of wheat) than the U.S. The reverse is also true: the U.S. has a lower opportunity cost of producing wheat than Brazil. We illustrate this by the PPFs of the two countries in Figure 2.5.

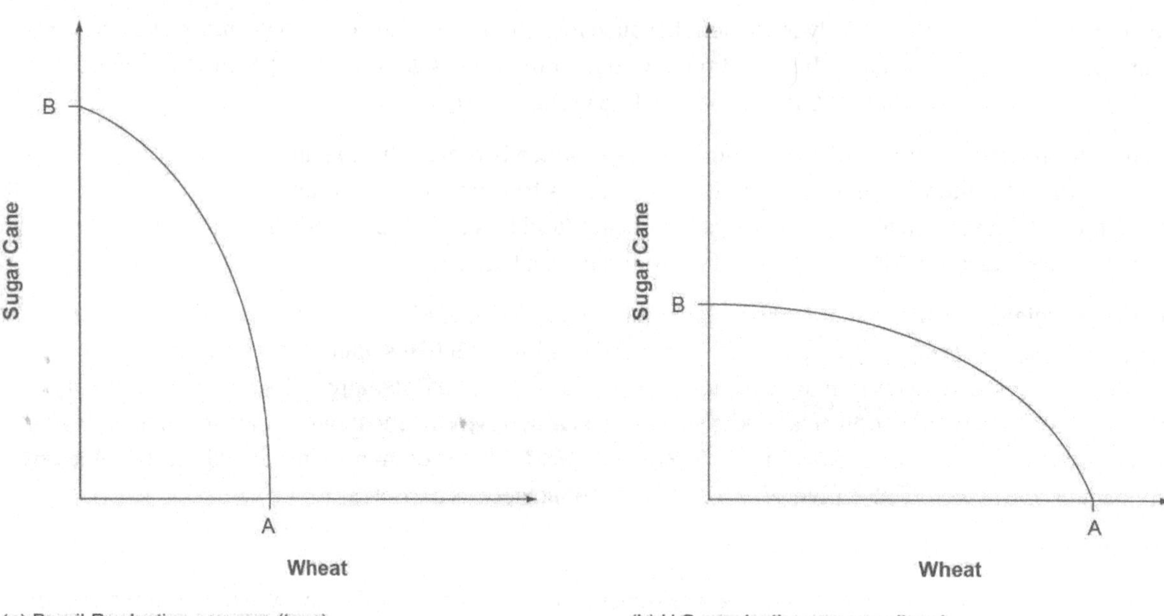


**FIGURE 2.5 Production Possibility Frontier for the U.S. and Brazil** The U.S. PPF is flatter than the Brazil PPF implying that the opportunity cost of wheat in terms of sugar cane is lower in the U.S. than in Brazil. Conversely, the opportunity cost of sugar cane is lower in Brazil. The U.S. has comparative advantage in wheat and Brazil has comparative advantage in sugar cane.

When a country can produce a good at a lower opportunity cost than another country, we say that this country has a **comparative advantage** in that good. Comparative advantage is not the same as absolute advantage, which is when a country can produce more of a good. In our example, Brazil has an absolute advantage in sugar cane and the U.S. has an absolute advantage in wheat. One can easily see this with a simple observation of the extreme production points in the PPFs of the two countries. If Brazil devoted all of its resources to producing wheat, it would be producing at point A. If however it had devoted all of its resources to producing sugar cane instead, it would be producing a much larger amount than the U.S., at point B.

The slope of the PPF gives the opportunity cost of producing an additional unit of wheat. While the slope is not constant throughout the PPFs, it is quite apparent that the PPF in Brazil is much steeper than in the U.S., and therefore the opportunity cost of wheat is generally higher in Brazil. In the chapter on International Trade you will learn that countries' differences in comparative advantage determine which goods they will choose to produce and trade. When countries engage in trade, they specialize in the production of the goods in which they have comparative advantage, and trade part of that production for goods in which they do not have comparative advantage. With trade, manufacturers produce goods where the opportunity cost is lowest, so total production increases, benefiting both trading parties.

## 2.3 Confronting Objections to the Economic Approach

**LEARNING OBJECTIVES**

By the end of this section, you will be able to:

- Analyze arguments against economic approaches to decision-making
- Interpret a tradeoff diagram
- Contrast normative statements and positive statements

It is one thing to understand the economic approach to decision-making and another thing to feel comfortable applying it. The sources of discomfort typically fall into two categories: that people do not act in the way that fits the economic way of thinking, and that even if people did act that way, they should try not to. Let's consider these arguments in turn.

## First Objection: People, Firms, and Society Do Not Act Like This

The economic approach to decision-making seems to require more information than most individuals possess and more careful decision-making than most individuals actually display. After all, do you or any of your friends draw a budget constraint and mutter to yourself about maximizing utility before you head to the shopping mall? Do members of the U.S. Congress contemplate production possibilities frontiers before they vote on the annual budget? The messy ways in which people and societies operate somehow doesn't look much like neat budget constraints or smoothly curving production possibilities frontiers.

However, the economics approach can be a useful way to analyze and understand the tradeoffs of economic decisions. To appreciate this point, imagine for a moment that you are playing basketball, dribbling to the right, and throwing a bounce-pass to the left to a teammate who is running toward the basket. A physicist or engineer could work out the correct speed and trajectory for the pass, given the different movements involved and the weight and bounciness of the ball. However, when you are playing basketball, you do not perform any of these calculations. You just pass the ball, and if you are a good player, you will do so with high accuracy.

Someone might argue: "The scientist's formula of the bounce-pass requires a far greater knowledge of physics and far more specific information about speeds of movement and weights than the basketball player actually has, so it must be an unrealistic description of how basketball passes actually occur." This reaction would be wrongheaded. The fact that a good player can throw the ball accurately because of practice and skill, without making a physics calculation, does not mean that the physics calculation is wrong.

Similarly, from an economic point of view, someone who shops for groceries every week has a great deal of practice with how to purchase the combination of goods that will provide that person with utility, even if the shopper does not phrase decisions in terms of a budget constraint. Government institutions may work imperfectly and slowly, but in general, a democratic form of government feels pressure from voters and social institutions to make the choices that are most widely preferred by people in that society. Thus, when thinking about the economic actions of groups of people, firms, and society, it is reasonable, as a first approximation, to analyze them with the tools of economic analysis. For more on this, read about behavioral economics in the chapter on Consumer Choices.

## Second Objection: People, Firms, and Society Should Not Act This Way

The economics approach portrays people as self-interested. For some critics of this approach, even if self-interest is an accurate description of how people behave, these behaviors are not moral. Instead, the critics argue that people should be taught to care more deeply about others. Economists offer several answers to these concerns.

First, economics is not a form of moral instruction. Rather, it seeks to describe economic behavior as it actually exists. Philosophers draw a distinction between **positive statements**, which describe the world as it is, and **normative statements**, which describe how the world should be. Positive statements are factual. They may be true or false, but we can test them, at least in principle. Normative statements are subjective questions of opinion. We cannot test them since we cannot prove opinions to be true or false. They just are opinions based on one's values. For example, an economist could analyze a proposed subway system in a certain city. If the expected benefits exceed the costs, he concludes that the project is worthy—an example of positive analysis. Another economist argues for extended unemployment compensation during the COVID-19 pandemic because a rich country like the United States should take care of its less fortunate citizens—an example of normative analysis.

Even if the line between positive and normative statements is not always crystal clear, economic analysis does try to remain rooted in the study of the actual people who inhabit the actual economy. Fortunately however, the assumption that individuals are purely self-interested is a simplification about human nature. In fact, we need to look no further than to Adam Smith, the very father of modern economics to find evidence of this. The opening sentence of his book, *The Theory of Moral Sentiments*, puts it very clearly: "How selfish soever man may be supposed, there are evidently some principles in his nature, which interest him in the fortune of others, and render their happiness necessary to him, though he derives nothing from it except the pleasure of seeing it." Clearly, individuals are both self-interested and altruistic.

Second, we can label self-interested behavior and profit-seeking with other names, such as personal choice and freedom. The ability to make personal choices about buying, working, and saving is an important personal freedom. Some people may choose high-pressure, high-paying jobs so that they can earn and spend considerable amounts of money on themselves. Others may allocate large portions of their earnings to charity or spend it on their friends and family. Others may devote themselves to a career that can require much time, energy, and expertise but does not offer high financial rewards, like being an elementary school teacher or a social worker. Still others may choose a job that does consume much of their time or provide a high level of income, but still leaves time for family, friends, and contemplation. Some people may prefer to work for a large company; others might want to start their own business. People's freedom to make their own economic choices has a moral value worth respecting.

  **CLEAR IT UP**

### Is a diagram by any other name the same?

When you study economics, you may feel buried under an avalanche of diagrams. Your goal should be to recognize the common underlying logic and pattern of the diagrams, not to memorize each one.

This chapter uses only one basic diagram, although we present it with different sets of labels. The consumption budget constraint and the production possibilities frontier for society, as a whole, are the same basic diagram. Figure 2.6 shows an individual budget constraint and a production possibilities frontier for two goods, Good 1 and Good 2. The tradeoff diagram always illustrates three basic themes: scarcity, tradeoffs, and economic efficiency.

The first theme is scarcity. It is not feasible to have unlimited amounts of both goods. Even if the budget constraint or a PPF shifts, scarcity remains—just at a different level. The second theme is tradeoffs. As depicted in the budget constraint or the production possibilities frontier, it is necessary to forgo some of one good to gain more of the other good. The details of this tradeoff vary. In a budget constraint we determine, the tradeoff is determined by the relative prices of the goods: that is, the relative price of two goods in the consumption choice budget constraint. These tradeoffs appear as a straight line. However, a curved line represents the tradeoffs in many production possibilities frontiers because the law of diminishing returns holds that as we add resources to an area, the marginal gains tend to diminish. Regardless of the specific shape, tradeoffs remain.

The third theme is economic efficiency, or getting the most benefit from scarce resources. All choices on the production possibilities frontier show productive efficiency because in such cases, there is no way to increase the quantity of one good without decreasing the quantity of the other. Similarly, when an individual makes a choice along a budget constraint, there is no way to increase the quantity of one good without decreasing the quantity of the other. The choice on a production possibilities set that is socially preferred, or the choice on an individual's budget constraint that is personally preferred, will display allocative efficiency.

The basic budget constraint/production possibilities frontier diagram will recur throughout this book. Some examples include using these tradeoff diagrams to analyze trade, environmental protection and economic output, equality of incomes and economic output, and the macroeconomic tradeoff between consumption and investment. Do not allow the different labels to confuse you. The budget constraint/production possibilities frontier diagram is always just a tool for thinking carefully about scarcity, tradeoffs, and efficiency in a particular situation.

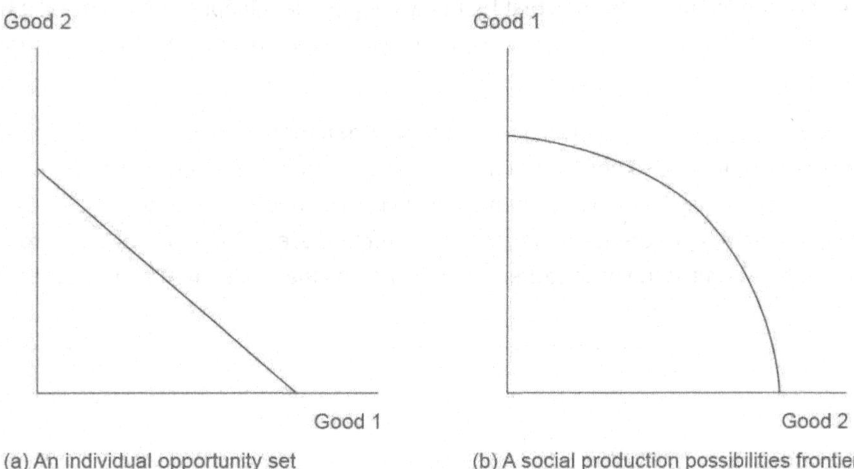


**FIGURE 2.6 The Tradeoff Diagram** Both the individual opportunity set (or budget constraint) and the social production possibilities frontier show the constraints under which individual consumers and society as a whole operate. Both diagrams show the tradeoff in choosing more of one good at the cost of less of the other.

Third, self-interested behavior can lead to positive social results. For example, when people work hard to make a living, they create economic output. Consumers who are looking for the best deals will encourage businesses to offer goods and services that meet their needs. Adam Smith, writing in *The Wealth of Nations*, named this property the **invisible hand**. In describing how consumers and producers interact in a market economy, Smith wrote:

> Every individual...generally, indeed, neither intends to promote the public interest, nor knows how much he is promoting it. By preferring the support of domestic to that of foreign industry, he intends only his own security; and by directing that industry in such a manner as its produce may be of the greatest value, he intends only his own gain. And he is in this, as in many other cases, led by an invisible hand to promote an end which was no part of his intention...By pursuing his own interest he frequently promotes that of the society more effectually than when he really intends to promote it.

The metaphor of the invisible hand suggests the remarkable possibility that broader social good can emerge from selfish individual actions.

Fourth, even people who focus on their own self-interest in the economic part of their life often set aside their own narrow self-interest in other parts of life. For example, you might focus on your own self-interest when asking your employer for a raise or negotiating to buy a car. Then you might turn around and focus on other people when you volunteer to read stories at the local library, help a friend move to a new apartment, or donate money to a charity. Self-interest is a reasonable starting point for analyzing many economic decisions, without needing to imply that people never do anything that is not in their own immediate self-interest.

##  BRING IT HOME

### Choices ... to What Degree?

What have we learned? We know that scarcity impacts all the choices we make. An economist might argue that people do not obtain a bachelor's or master's degree because they do not have the resources to make those choices or because their incomes are too low and/or the price of these degrees is too high. A bachelor's or a master's degree may not be available in their opportunity set.

The price of these degrees may be too high not only because the actual price, college tuition (and perhaps room and board), is too high. An economist might also say that for many people, the full opportunity cost of a bachelor's or a master's degree is too high. For these people, they are unwilling or unable to make the tradeoff of forfeiting years of working, and earning an income, to earn a degree.

Finally, the statistics we introduced at the start of the chapter reveal information about intertemporal choices. An economist might say that people choose not to obtain a college degree because they may have to borrow money to attend college, and the interest they have to pay on that loan in the future will affect their decisions today. Also, it could be that some people have a preference for current consumption over future consumption, so they choose to work now at a lower salary and consume now, rather than postponing that consumption until after they graduate college.

## Key Terms

**allocative efficiency** when the mix of goods produced represents the mix that society most desires

**budget constraint** all possible consumption combinations of goods that someone can afford, given the prices of goods, when all income is spent; the boundary of the opportunity set

**comparative advantage** when a country can produce a good at a lower cost in terms of other goods; or, when a country has a lower opportunity cost of production

**invisible hand** Adam Smith's concept that individuals' self-interested behavior can lead to positive social outcomes

**law of diminishing marginal utility** as we consume more of a good or service, the utility we get from additional units of the good or service tends to become smaller than what we received from earlier units

**law of diminishing returns** as we add additional increments of resources to producing a good or service, the marginal benefit from those additional increments will decline

**marginal analysis** examination of decisions on the margin, meaning a little more or a little less from the status quo

**normative statement** statement which describes how the world should be

**opportunity cost** measures cost by what we give up/forfeit in exchange; opportunity cost measures the value of the forgone alternative

**opportunity set** all possible combinations of consumption that someone can afford given the prices of goods and the individual's income

**positive statement** statement which describes the world as it is

**production possibilities frontier (PPF)** a diagram that shows the productively efficient combinations of two products that an economy can produce given the resources it has available.

**productive efficiency** when it is impossible to produce more of one good (or service) without decreasing the quantity produced of another good (or service)

**sunk costs** costs that we make in the past that we cannot recover

**utility** satisfaction, usefulness, or value one obtains from consuming goods and services

## Key Concepts and Summary

### 2.1 How Individuals Make Choices Based on Their Budget Constraint

Economists see the real world as one of scarcity: that is, a world in which people's desires exceed what is possible. As a result, economic behavior involves tradeoffs in which individuals, firms, and society must forgo something that they desire to obtain things that they desire more. Individuals face the tradeoff of what quantities of goods and services to consume. The budget constraint, which is the frontier of the opportunity set, illustrates the range of available choices. The relative price of the choices determines the slope of the budget constraint. Choices beyond the budget constraint are not affordable.

Opportunity cost measures cost by what we forgo in exchange. Sometimes we can measure opportunity cost in money, but it is often useful to consider time as well, or to measure it in terms of the actual resources that we must forfeit.

Most economic decisions and tradeoffs are not all-or-nothing. Instead, they involve marginal analysis, which means they are about decisions on the margin, involving a little more or a little less. The law of diminishing marginal utility points out that as a person receives more of something—whether it is a specific good or another resource—the additional marginal gains tend to become smaller. Because sunk costs occurred in the past and cannot be recovered, they should be disregarded in making current decisions.

### 2.2 The Production Possibilities Frontier and Social Choices

A production possibilities frontier defines the set of choices society faces for the combinations of goods and services it can produce given the resources and the technology that are available. The shape of the PPF is typically curved outward, rather than straight. Choices outside the PPF are unattainable and choices inside the

PPF are wasteful. Over time, a growing economy will tend to shift the PPF outwards.

The law of diminishing returns holds that as increments of additional resources are devoted to producing something, the marginal increase in output will become increasingly smaller. All choices along a production possibilities frontier display productive efficiency; that is, it is impossible to use society's resources to produce more of one good without decreasing production of the other good. The specific choice along a production possibilities frontier that reflects the mix of goods society prefers is the choice with allocative efficiency. The curvature of the PPF is likely to differ by country, which results in different countries having comparative advantage in different goods. Total production can increase if countries specialize in the goods in which they have comparative advantage and trade some of their production for the remaining goods.

## 2.3 Confronting Objections to the Economic Approach

The economic way of thinking provides a useful approach to understanding human behavior. Economists make the careful distinction between positive statements, which describe the world as it is, and normative statements, which describe how the world should be. Even when economics analyzes the gains and losses from various events or policies, and thus draws normative conclusions about how the world should be, the analysis of economics is rooted in a positive analysis of how people, firms, and governments actually behave, not how they should behave.

# Self-Check Questions

1.  Suppose Alphonso's town raised the price of bus tickets from $0.50 per trip to $1 per trip (while the price of burgers stayed at $2 and his budget remained $10 per week.) Draw Alphonso's new budget constraint. What happens to the opportunity cost of bus tickets?

2.  Return to the example in Figure 2.4. Suppose there is an improvement in medical technology that enables more healthcare with the same amount of resources. How would this affect the production possibilities curve and, in particular, how would it affect the opportunity cost of education?

3.  Could a nation be producing in a way that is allocatively efficient, but productively inefficient?

4.  What are the similarities between a consumer's budget constraint and society's production possibilities frontier, not just graphically but analytically?

5.  Individuals may not act in the rational, calculating way described by the economic model of decision making, measuring utility and costs at the margin, but can you make a case that they behave approximately that way?

6.  Would an op-ed piece in a newspaper urging the adoption of a particular economic policy be a positive or normative statement?

7.  Would a research study on the effects of soft drink consumption on children's cognitive development be a positive or normative statement?

# Review Questions

8.  Explain why scarcity leads to tradeoffs.

9.  Explain why individuals make choices that are directly on the budget constraint, rather than inside the budget constraint or outside it.

10.  What is comparative advantage?

11.  What does a production possibilities frontier illustrate?

12.  Why is a production possibilities frontier typically drawn as a curve, rather than a straight line?

13. Explain why societies cannot make a choice above their production possibilities frontier and should not make a choice below it.

14. What are diminishing marginal returns?

15. What is productive efficiency? Allocative efficiency?

16. What is the difference between a positive and a normative statement?

17. Is the economic model of decision-making intended as a literal description of how individuals, firms, and the governments actually make decisions?

18. What are four responses to the claim that people should not behave in the way described in this chapter?

## Critical Thinking Questions

19. Suppose Alphonso's town raises the price of bus tickets from $0.50 to $1 and the price of burgers rises from $2 to $4. Why is the opportunity cost of bus tickets unchanged? Suppose Alphonso's weekly spending money increases from $10 to $20. How is his budget constraint affected from all three changes? Explain.

20. During the Second World War, Germany's factories were decimated. It also suffered many human casualties, both soldiers and civilians. How did the war affect Germany's production possibilities curve?

21. It is clear that productive inefficiency is a waste since resources are used in a way that produces less goods and services than a nation is capable of. Why is allocative inefficiency also wasteful?

22. What assumptions about the economy must be true for the invisible hand to work? To what extent are those assumptions valid in the real world?

23. Do economists have any particular expertise at making normative arguments? In other words, they have expertise at making positive statements (i.e., what *will* happen) about some economic policy, for example, but do they have special expertise to judge whether or not the policy *should* be undertaken?

## Problems

Use this information to answer the following 4 questions: Jade has a weekly budget of $24, which she likes to spend on magazines and pies.

24. If the price of a magazine is $4 each, what is the maximum number of magazines she could buy in a week?

25. If the price of a pie is $12, what is the maximum number of pies she could buy in a week?

26. Draw Jade's budget constraint with pies on the horizontal axis and magazines on the vertical axis. What is the slope of the budget constraint?

27. What is Jade's opportunity cost of purchasing a pie?

# Demand and Supply 3

FIGURE 3.1 **Farmer's Market** Organic vegetables and fruits that are grown and sold within a specific geographical region should, in theory, cost less than conventional produce because the transportation costs are less. That is not, however, usually the case. (Credit: modification of "Old Farmers' Market" by NatalieMaynor/Flickr, CC BY 2.0)

**CHAPTER OBJECTIVES**

In this chapter, you will learn about:
- Demand, Supply, and Equilibrium in Markets for Goods and Services
- Shifts in Demand and Supply for Goods and Services
- Changes in Equilibrium Price and Quantity: The Four-Step Process
- Price Ceilings and Price Floors

## Introduction to Demand and Supply

### BRING IT HOME

#### Why Can We Not Get Enough of Organic Foods?

Organic food is increasingly popular, not just in the United States, but worldwide. At one time, consumers had to go to specialty stores or farmers' markets to find organic produce. Now it is available in most grocery stores. In short, organic has become part of the mainstream.

Ever wonder why organic food costs more than conventional food? Why, say, does an organic Fuji apple cost $2.75 a pound, while its conventional counterpart costs $1.72 a pound? The same price relationship is true for just about every organic product on the market. If many organic foods are locally grown, would they not take less time to get to market and therefore be cheaper? What are the forces that keep those prices from coming down? Turns out those forces have quite a bit to do with this chapter's topic: demand and supply.

---

An auction bidder pays thousands of dollars for a dress Whitney Houston wore. A collector spends a small fortune for a few drawings by John Lennon. People usually react to purchases like these in two ways: their jaw drops because they think these are high prices to pay for such goods or they think these are rare, desirable items and the amount paid seems right.

## ⊘ LINK IT UP

Visit this website (http://openstax.org/l/celebauction) to read a list of bizarre items that have been purchased for their ties to celebrities. These examples represent an interesting facet of demand and supply.

---

When economists talk about prices, they are less interested in making judgments than in gaining a practical understanding of what determines prices and why prices change. Consider a price most of us contend with weekly: that of a gallon of gas. Why was the average price of gasoline in the United States $3.16 per gallon in June of 2020? Why did the price for gasoline fall sharply to $2.42 per gallon by January of 2021? To explain these price movements, economists focus on the determinants of what gasoline buyers are willing to pay and what gasoline sellers are willing to accept.

As it turns out, the price of gasoline in June of any given year is nearly always higher than the price in January of that same year. Over recent decades, gasoline prices in midsummer have averaged about 10 cents per gallon more than their midwinter low. The likely reason is that people drive more in the summer, and are also willing to pay more for gas, but that does not explain how steeply gas prices fell. Other factors were at work during those 18 months, such as increases in supply and decreases in the demand for crude oil.

This chapter introduces the economic model of demand and supply—one of the most powerful models in all of economics. The discussion here begins by examining how demand and supply determine the price and the quantity sold in markets for goods and services, and how changes in demand and supply lead to changes in prices and quantities.

## 3.1 Demand, Supply, and Equilibrium in Markets for Goods and Services

### LEARNING OBJECTIVES

By the end of this section, you will be able to:
- Explain demand, quantity demanded, and the law of demand
- Explain supply, quantity supplied, and the law of supply
- Identify a demand curve and a supply curve
- Explain equilibrium, equilibrium price, and equilibrium quantity

First let's first focus on what economists mean by demand, what they mean by supply, and then how demand and supply interact in a market.

### Demand for Goods and Services

Economists use the term **demand** to refer to the amount of some good or service consumers are willing and able to purchase at each price. Demand is fundamentally based on needs and wants—if you have no need or want for something, you won't buy it. While a consumer may be able to differentiate between a need and a want, from an economist's perspective they are the same thing. Demand is also based on ability to pay. If you cannot pay for it, you have no effective demand. By this definition, a person who does not have a drivers license has no effective demand for a car.

What a buyer pays for a unit of the specific good or service is called **price**. The total number of units that consumers would purchase at that price is called the **quantity demanded.** A rise in price of a good or service almost always decreases the quantity demanded of that good or service. Conversely, a fall in price will increase the quantity demanded. When the price of a gallon of gasoline increases, for example, people look for ways to reduce their consumption by combining several errands, commuting by carpool or mass transit, or taking weekend or vacation trips closer to home. Economists call this inverse relationship between price and quantity demanded the **law of demand**. The law of demand assumes that all other variables that affect demand (which we explain in the next module) are held constant.

We can show an example from the market for gasoline in a table or a graph. Economist call a table that shows the quantity demanded at each price, such as Table 3.1, a **demand schedule**. In this case we measure price in dollars per gallon of gasoline. We measure the quantity demanded in millions of gallons over some time period (for example, per day or per year) and over some geographic area (like a state or a country). A **demand curve** shows the relationship between price and quantity demanded on a graph like Figure 3.2, with quantity on the horizontal axis and the price per gallon on the vertical axis. (Note that this is an exception to the normal rule in mathematics that the independent variable (x) goes on the horizontal axis and the dependent variable (y) goes on the vertical axis. Economics is not math.)

Table 3.1 shows the demand schedule and the graph in Figure 3.2 shows the demand curve. These are two ways to describe the same relationship between price and quantity demanded.

| Price (per gallon) | Quantity Demanded (millions of gallons) |
| --- | --- |
| $1.00 | 800 |
| $1.20 | 700 |
| $1.40 | 600 |
| $1.60 | 550 |
| $1.80 | 500 |
| $2.00 | 460 |
| $2.20 | 420 |

**TABLE 3.1** Price and Quantity Demanded of Gasoline

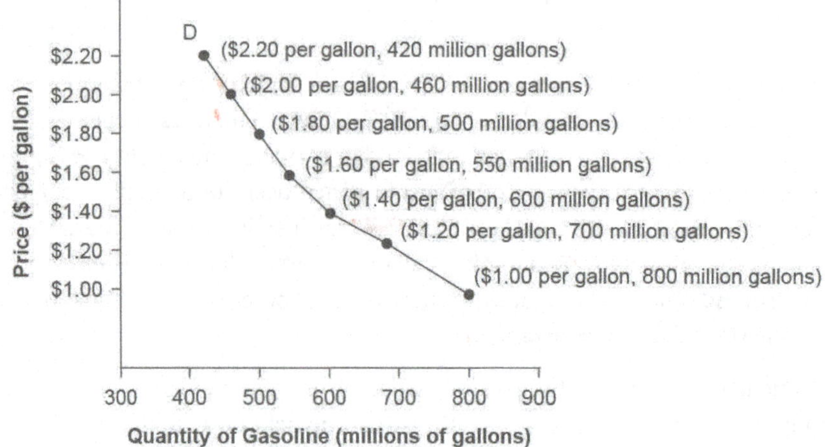



**FIGURE 3.2 A Demand Curve for Gasoline** The demand schedule shows that as price rises, quantity demanded decreases, and vice versa. We graph these points, and the line connecting them is the demand curve (D). The downward slope of the demand curve again illustrates the law of demand—the inverse relationship between prices and quantity demanded.

Demand curves will appear somewhat different for each product. They may appear relatively steep or flat, or they may be straight or curved. Nearly all demand curves share the fundamental similarity that they slope down from left to right. Demand curves embody the law of demand: As the price increases, the quantity demanded decreases, and conversely, as the price decreases, the quantity demanded increases.

Confused about these different types of demand? Read the next Clear It Up feature.

 **CLEAR IT UP**

### Is demand the same as quantity demanded?

In economic terminology, demand is not the same as quantity demanded. When economists talk about demand, they mean the relationship between a range of prices and the quantities demanded at those prices, as illustrated by a demand curve or a demand schedule. When economists talk about quantity demanded, they mean only a certain point on the demand curve, or one quantity on the demand schedule. In short, demand refers to the curve and quantity demanded refers to a (specific) point on the curve.

### Supply of Goods and Services

When economists talk about **supply**, they mean the amount of some good or service a producer is willing to supply at each price. Price is what the producer receives for selling one unit of a good or service. A rise in price almost always leads to an increase in the **quantity supplied** of that good or service, while a fall in price will decrease the quantity supplied. When the price of gasoline rises, for example, it encourages profit-seeking firms to take several actions: expand exploration for oil reserves; drill for more oil; invest in more pipelines and oil tankers to bring the oil to plants for refining into gasoline; build new oil refineries; purchase additional pipelines and trucks to ship the gasoline to gas stations; and open more gas stations or keep existing gas stations open longer hours. Economists call this positive relationship between price and quantity supplied—that a higher price leads to a higher quantity supplied and a lower price leads to a lower quantity supplied—the **law of supply**. The law of supply assumes that all other variables that affect supply (to be explained in the next module) are held constant.

Still unsure about the different types of supply? See the following Clear It Up feature.

## CLEAR IT UP

### Is supply the same as quantity supplied?

In economic terminology, supply is not the same as quantity supplied. When economists refer to supply, they mean the relationship between a range of prices and the quantities supplied at those prices, a relationship that we can illustrate with a supply curve or a supply schedule. When economists refer to quantity supplied, they mean only a certain point on the supply curve, or one quantity on the supply schedule. In short, supply refers to the curve and quantity supplied refers to a (specific) point on the curve.

Figure 3.3 illustrates the law of supply, again using the market for gasoline as an example. Like demand, we can illustrate supply using a table or a graph. A **supply schedule** is a table, like Table 3.2, that shows the quantity supplied at a range of different prices. Again, we measure price in dollars per gallon of gasoline and we measure quantity supplied in millions of gallons. A **supply curve** is a graphic illustration of the relationship between price, shown on the vertical axis, and quantity, shown on the horizontal axis. The supply schedule and the supply curve are just two different ways of showing the same information. Notice that the horizontal and vertical axes on the graph for the supply curve are the same as for the demand curve.

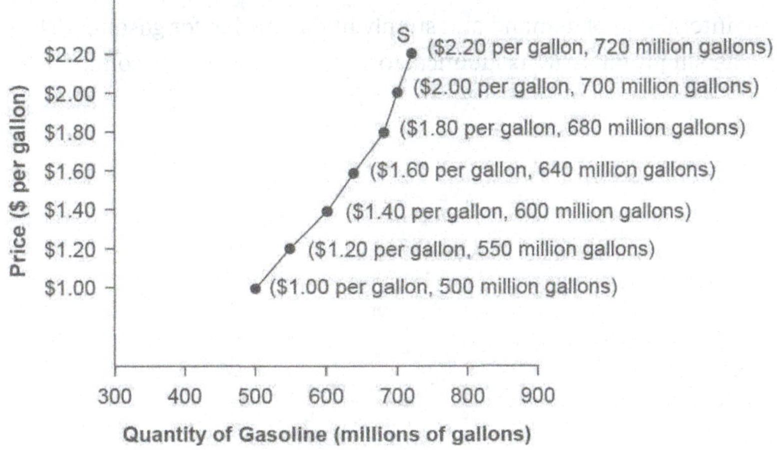


**FIGURE 3.3 A Supply Curve for Gasoline** The supply schedule is the table that shows quantity supplied of gasoline at each price. As price rises, quantity supplied also increases, and vice versa. The supply curve (S) is created by graphing the points from the supply schedule and then connecting them. The upward slope of the supply curve illustrates the law of supply—that a higher price leads to a higher quantity supplied, and vice versa.

| Price (per gallon) | Quantity Supplied (millions of gallons) |
|---|---|
| $1.00 | 500 |
| $1.20 | 550 |
| $1.40 | 600 |
| $1.60 | 640 |
| $1.80 | 680 |

**TABLE 3.2 Price and Supply of Gasoline**

| Price (per gallon) | Quantity Supplied (millions of gallons) |
| --- | --- |
| $2.00 | 700 |
| $2.20 | 720 |

**TABLE 3.2 Price and Supply of Gasoline**

The shape of supply curves will vary somewhat according to the product: steeper, flatter, straighter, or curved. Nearly all supply curves, however, share a basic similarity: they slope up from left to right and illustrate the law of supply: as the price rises, say, from $1.00 per gallon to $2.20 per gallon, the quantity supplied increases from 500 gallons to 720 gallons. Conversely, as the price falls, the quantity supplied decreases.

## Equilibrium—Where Demand and Supply Intersect

Because the graphs for demand and supply curves both have price on the vertical axis and quantity on the horizontal axis, the demand curve and supply curve for a particular good or service can appear on the same graph. Together, demand and supply determine the price and the quantity that will be bought and sold in a market.

Figure 3.4 illustrates the interaction of demand and supply in the market for gasoline. The demand curve (D) is identical to Figure 3.2. The supply curve (S) is identical to Figure 3.3. Table 3.3 contains the same information in tabular form.

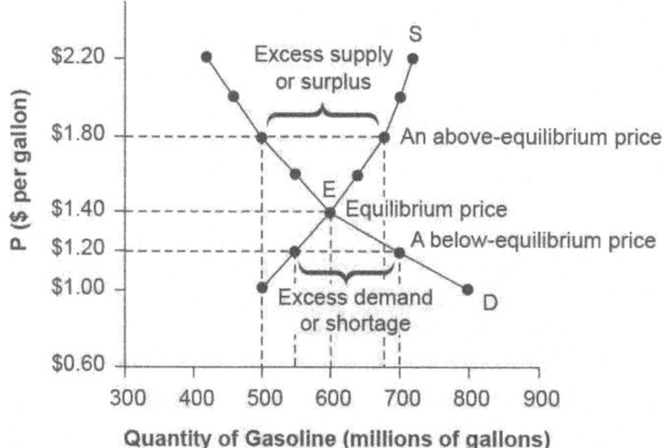


**FIGURE 3.4 Demand and Supply for Gasoline** The demand curve (D) and the supply curve (S) intersect at the equilibrium point E, with a price of $1.40 and a quantity of 600. The equilibrium price is the only price where quantity demanded is equal to quantity supplied. At a price above equilibrium like $1.80, quantity supplied exceeds the quantity demanded, so there is excess supply. At a price below equilibrium such as $1.20, quantity demanded exceeds quantity supplied, so there is excess demand.

| Price (per gallon) | Quantity demanded (millions of gallons) | Quantity supplied (millions of gallons) |
| --- | --- | --- |
| $1.00 | 800 | 500 |
| $1.20 | 700 | 550 |
| **$1.40** | **600** | **600** |

**TABLE 3.3 Price, Quantity Demanded, and Quantity Supplied**

| Price (per gallon) | Quantity demanded (millions of gallons) | Quantity supplied (millions of gallons) |
| --- | --- | --- |
| $1.60 | 550 | 640 |
| $1.80 | 500 | 680 |
| $2.00 | 460 | 700 |
| $2.20 | 420 | 720 |

**TABLE 3.3** Price, Quantity Demanded, and Quantity Supplied

Remember this: When two lines on a diagram cross, this intersection usually means something. The point where the supply curve (S) and the demand curve (D) cross, designated by point E in Figure 3.4, is called the **equilibrium**. The **equilibrium price** is the only price where the plans of consumers and the plans of producers agree—that is, where the amount of the product consumers want to buy (quantity demanded) is equal to the amount producers want to sell (quantity supplied). Economists call this common quantity the **equilibrium quantity**. At any other price, the quantity demanded does not equal the quantity supplied, so the market is not in equilibrium at that price.

In Figure 3.4, the equilibrium price is $1.40 per gallon of gasoline and the equilibrium quantity is 600 million gallons. If you had only the demand and supply schedules, and not the graph, you could find the equilibrium by looking for the price level on the tables where the quantity demanded and the quantity supplied are equal.

The word "equilibrium" means "balance." If a market is at its equilibrium price and quantity, then it has no reason to move away from that point. However, if a market is not at equilibrium, then economic pressures arise to move the market toward the equilibrium price and the equilibrium quantity.

Imagine, for example, that the price of a gallon of gasoline was above the equilibrium price—that is, instead of $1.40 per gallon, the price is $1.80 per gallon. The dashed horizontal line at the price of $1.80 in Figure 3.4 illustrates this above-equilibrium price. At this higher price, the quantity demanded drops from 600 to 500. This decline in quantity reflects how consumers react to the higher price by finding ways to use less gasoline.

Moreover, at this higher price of $1.80, the quantity of gasoline supplied rises from 600 to 680, as the higher price makes it more profitable for gasoline producers to expand their output. Now, consider how quantity demanded and quantity supplied are related at this above-equilibrium price. Quantity demanded has fallen to 500 gallons, while quantity supplied has risen to 680 gallons. In fact, at any above-equilibrium price, the quantity supplied exceeds the quantity demanded. We call this an **excess supply** or a **surplus**.

With a surplus, gasoline accumulates at gas stations, in tanker trucks, in pipelines, and at oil refineries. This accumulation puts pressure on gasoline sellers. If a surplus remains unsold, those firms involved in making and selling gasoline are not receiving enough cash to pay their workers and to cover their expenses. In this situation, some producers and sellers will want to cut prices, because it is better to sell at a lower price than not to sell at all. Once some sellers start cutting prices, others will follow to avoid losing sales. These price reductions in turn will stimulate a higher quantity demanded. Therefore, if the price is above the equilibrium level, incentives built into the structure of demand and supply will create pressures for the price to fall toward the equilibrium.

Now suppose that the price is below its equilibrium level at $1.20 per gallon, as the dashed horizontal line at this price in Figure 3.4 shows. At this lower price, the quantity demanded increases from 600 to 700 as drivers take longer trips, spend more minutes warming up the car in the driveway in wintertime, stop sharing rides to work, and buy larger cars that get fewer miles to the gallon. However, the below-equilibrium price reduces gasoline producers' incentives to produce and sell gasoline, and the quantity supplied falls from 600 to 550.

When the price is below equilibrium, there is **excess demand**, or a **shortage**—that is, at the given price the quantity demanded, which has been stimulated by the lower price, now exceeds the quantity supplied, which has been depressed by the lower price. In this situation, eager gasoline buyers mob the gas stations, only to find many stations running short of fuel. Oil companies and gas stations recognize that they have an opportunity to make higher profits by selling what gasoline they have at a higher price. As a result, the price rises toward the equilibrium level. Read Demand, Supply, and Efficiency for more discussion on the importance of the demand and supply model.

## 3.2 Shifts in Demand and Supply for Goods and Services

### LEARNING OBJECTIVES

By the end of this section, you will be able to:

- Identify factors that affect demand
- Graph demand curves and demand shifts
- Identify factors that affect supply
- Graph supply curves and supply shifts

The previous module explored how price affects the quantity demanded and the quantity supplied. The result was the demand curve and the supply curve. Price, however, is not the only factor that influences buyers' and sellers' decisions. For example, how is demand for vegetarian food affected if, say, health concerns cause more consumers to avoid eating meat? How is the supply of diamonds affected if diamond producers discover several new diamond mines? What are the major factors, in addition to the price, that influence demand or supply?

 **LINK IT UP**

Visit this website (https://openstax.org/l/toothfish) to read a brief note on how marketing strategies can influence supply and demand of products.

---

### What Factors Affect Demand?

We defined demand as the amount of some product a consumer is willing and able to purchase at each price. That suggests at least two factors that affect demand. Willingness to purchase suggests a desire, based on what economists call tastes and preferences. If you neither need nor want something, you will not buy it, and if you really like something, you will buy more of it than someone who does not share your strong preference for it. Ability to purchase suggests that income is important. Professors are usually able to afford better housing and transportation than students, because they have more income. Prices of related goods can affect demand also. If you need a new car, the price of a Honda may affect your demand for a Ford. Finally, the size or composition of the population can affect demand. The more children a family has, the greater their demand for clothing. The more driving-age children a family has, the greater their demand for car insurance, and the less for diapers and baby formula.

These factors matter for both individual and market demand as a whole. Exactly how do these various factors affect demand, and how do we show the effects graphically? To answer those questions, we need the *ceteris paribus* assumption.

### The *Ceteris Paribus* Assumption

A demand curve or a supply curve is a relationship between two, and only two, variables: quantity on the horizontal axis and price on the vertical axis. The assumption behind a demand curve or a supply curve is that no relevant economic factors, other than the product's price, are changing. Economists call this assumption **ceteris paribus**, a Latin phrase meaning "other things being equal." Any given demand or supply curve is based on the *ceteris paribus* assumption that all else is held equal. A demand curve or a supply curve is a relationship between two, and only two, variables when all other variables are kept constant. If all else is not held equal, then the laws of supply and demand will not necessarily hold, as the following Clear It Up feature shows.

 ## CLEAR IT UP

### When does *ceteris paribus* apply?

We typically apply *ceteris paribus* when we observe how changes in price affect demand or supply, but we can apply *ceteris paribus* more generally. In the real world, demand and supply depend on more factors than just price. For example, a consumer's demand depends on income and a producer's supply depends on the cost of producing the product. How can we analyze the effect on demand or supply if multiple factors are changing at the same time—say price rises and income falls? The answer is that we examine the changes one at a time, assuming the other factors are held constant.

For example, we can say that an increase in the price reduces the amount consumers will buy (assuming income, and anything else that affects demand, is unchanged). Additionally, a decrease in income reduces the amount consumers can afford to buy (assuming price, and anything else that affects demand, is unchanged). This is what the *ceteris paribus* assumption really means. In this particular case, after we analyze each factor separately, we can combine the results. The amount consumers buy falls for two reasons: first because of the higher price and second because of the lower income.

### How Does Income Affect Demand?

Let's use income as an example of how factors other than price affect demand. Figure 3.5 shows the initial demand for automobiles as $D_0$. At point Q, for example, if the price is $20,000 per car, the quantity of cars demanded is 18 million. $D_0$ also shows how the quantity of cars demanded would change as a result of a higher or lower price. For example, if the price of a car rose to $22,000, the quantity demanded would decrease to 17 million, at point R.

The original demand curve $D_0$, like every demand curve, is based on the *ceteris paribus* assumption that no other economically relevant factors change. Now imagine that the economy expands in a way that raises the incomes of many people, making cars more affordable. How will this affect demand? How can we show this graphically?

Return to Figure 3.5. The price of cars is still $20,000, but with higher incomes, the quantity demanded has now increased to 20 million cars, shown at point S. As a result of the higher income levels, the demand curve shifts to the right to the new demand curve $D_1$, indicating an increase in demand. Table 3.4 shows clearly that this increased demand would occur at every price, not just the original one.

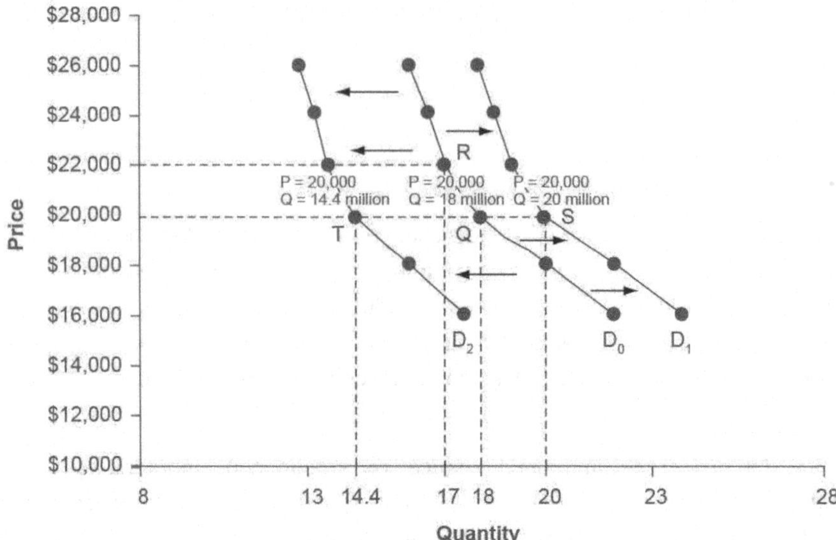



**FIGURE 3.5 Shifts in Demand: A Car Example** Increased demand means that at every given price, the quantity demanded is higher, so that the demand curve shifts to the right from $D_0$ to $D_1$. Decreased demand means that at every given price, the quantity demanded is lower, so that the demand curve shifts to the left from $D_0$ to $D_2$.

| Price | Decrease to $D_2$ | Original Quantity Demanded $D_0$ | Increase to $D_1$ |
|---|---|---|---|
| $16,000 | 17.6 million | 22.0 million | 24.0 million |
| $18,000 | 16.0 million | 20.0 million | 22.0 million |
| $20,000 | 14.4 million | 18.0 million | 20.0 million |
| $22,000 | 13.6 million | 17.0 million | 19.0 million |
| $24,000 | 13.2 million | 16.5 million | 18.5 million |
| $26,000 | 12.8 million | 16.0 million | 18.0 million |

**TABLE 3.4 Price and Demand Shifts: A Car Example**

Now, imagine that the economy slows down so that many people lose their jobs or work fewer hours, reducing their incomes. In this case, the decrease in income would lead to a lower quantity of cars demanded at every given price, and the original demand curve $D_0$ would shift left to $D_2$. The shift from $D_0$ to $D_2$ represents such a decrease in demand: At any given price level, the quantity demanded is now lower. In this example, a price of $20,000 means 18 million cars sold along the original demand curve, but only 14.4 million sold after demand fell.

When a demand curve shifts, it does not mean that the quantity demanded by every individual buyer changes by the same amount. In this example, not everyone would have higher or lower income and not everyone would buy or not buy an additional car. Instead, a shift in a demand curve captures a pattern for the market as a whole.

In the previous section, we argued that higher income causes greater demand at every price. This is true for most goods and services. For some—luxury cars, vacations in Europe, and fine jewelry—the effect of a rise in income can be especially pronounced. A product whose demand rises when income rises, and vice versa, is called a **normal good**. A few exceptions to this pattern do exist. As incomes rise, many people will buy fewer generic brand groceries and more name brand groceries. They are less likely to buy used cars and more likely to buy new cars. They will be less likely to rent an apartment and more likely to own a home. A product whose demand falls when income rises, and vice versa, is called an **inferior good**. In other words, when income increases, the demand curve shifts to the left.

## Other Factors That Shift Demand Curves

Income is not the only factor that causes a shift in demand. Other factors that change demand include tastes and preferences, the composition or size of the population, the prices of related goods, and even expectations. A change in any one of the underlying factors that determine what quantity people are willing to buy at a given price will cause a shift in demand. Graphically, the new demand curve lies either to the right (an increase) or to the left (a decrease) of the original demand curve. Let's look at these factors.

### Changing Tastes or Preferences

From 1980 to 2021, the per-person consumption of chicken by Americans rose from 47 pounds per year to 97 pounds per year, and consumption of beef fell from 76 pounds per year to 59 pounds per year, according to the U.S. Department of Agriculture (USDA). Changes like these are largely due to movements in taste, which change the quantity of a good demanded at every price: that is, they shift the demand curve for that good, rightward for chicken and leftward for beef.

### Changes in the Composition of the Population

The proportion of elderly citizens in the United States population is rising. It rose from 9.8% in 1970 to 12.6% in 2000, and will be a projected (by the U.S. Census Bureau) 20% of the population by 2030. A society with relatively more children, like the United States in the 1960s, will have greater demand for goods and services like tricycles and day care facilities. A society with relatively more elderly persons, as the United States is projected to have by 2030, has a higher demand for nursing homes and hearing aids. Similarly, changes in the size of the population can affect the demand for housing and many other goods. Each of these changes in demand will be shown as a shift in the demand curve.

### Changes in the Prices of Related Goods

Changes in the prices of related goods such as substitutes or complements also can affect the demand for a product. A **substitute** is a good or service that we can use in place of another good or service. As electronic books, like this one, become more available, you would expect to see a decrease in demand for traditional printed books. A lower price for a substitute decreases demand for the other product. For example, in recent years as the price of tablet computers has fallen, the quantity demanded has increased (because of the law of demand). Since people are purchasing tablets, there has been a decrease in demand for laptops, which we can show graphically as a leftward shift in the demand curve for laptops. A higher price for a substitute good has the reverse effect.

Other goods are **complements** for each other, meaning we often use the goods together, because consumption of one good tends to enhance consumption of the other. Examples include breakfast cereal and milk; notebooks and pens or pencils, golf balls and golf clubs; gasoline and sport utility vehicles; and the five-way combination of bacon, lettuce, tomato, mayonnaise, and bread. If the price of golf clubs rises, since the quantity demanded of golf clubs falls (because of the law of demand), demand for a complement good like golf balls decreases, too. Similarly, a higher price for skis would shift the demand curve for a complement good like ski resort trips to the left, while a lower price for a complement has the reverse effect.

### Changes in Expectations about Future Prices or Other Factors that Affect Demand

While it is clear that the price of a good affects the quantity demanded, it is also true that expectations about the future price (or expectations about tastes and preferences, income, and so on) can affect demand. For example, if people hear that a hurricane is coming, they may rush to the store to buy flashlight batteries and bottled water. If people learn that the price of a good like coffee is likely to rise in the future, they may head for the store to stock up on coffee now. We show these changes in demand as shifts in the curve. Therefore, a **shift in demand** happens when a change in some economic factor (other than price) causes a different quantity to be demanded at every price. The following Work It Out feature shows how this happens.



## Shift in Demand

A shift in demand means that at any price (and at every price), the quantity demanded will be different than it was before. Following is an example of a shift in demand due to an income increase.

Step 1. Draw the graph of a demand curve for a normal good like pizza. Pick a price (like $P_0$). Identify the corresponding $Q_0$. See an example in Figure 3.6.

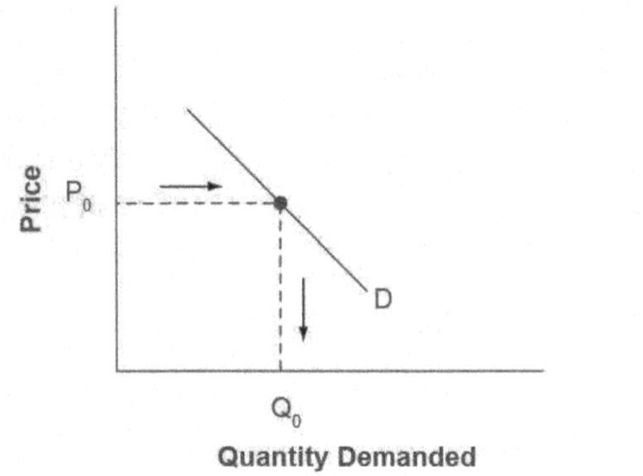


**FIGURE 3.6 Demand Curve** We can use the demand curve to identify how much consumers would buy at any given price.

Step 2. Suppose income increases. As a result of the change, are consumers going to buy more or less pizza? The answer is more. Draw a dotted horizontal line from the chosen price, through the original quantity demanded, to the new point with the new $Q_1$. Draw a dotted vertical line down to the horizontal axis and label the new $Q_1$. Figure 3.7 provides an example.

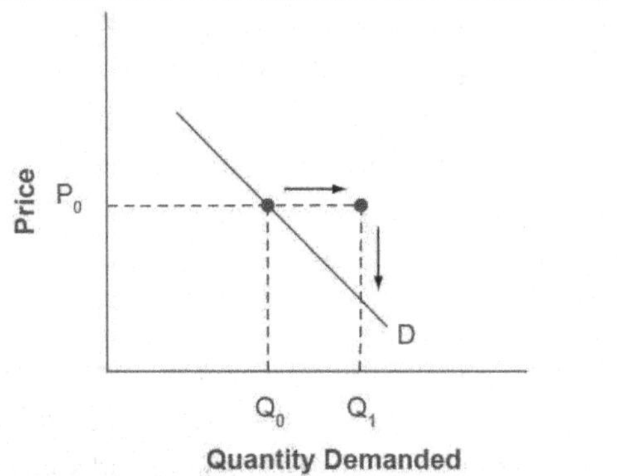


**FIGURE 3.7 Demand Curve with Income Increase** With an increase in income, consumers will purchase larger quantities, pushing demand to the right.

Step 3. Now, shift the curve through the new point. You will see that an increase in income causes an upward (or rightward) shift in the demand curve, so that at any price the quantities demanded will be higher, as Figure 3.8 illustrates.

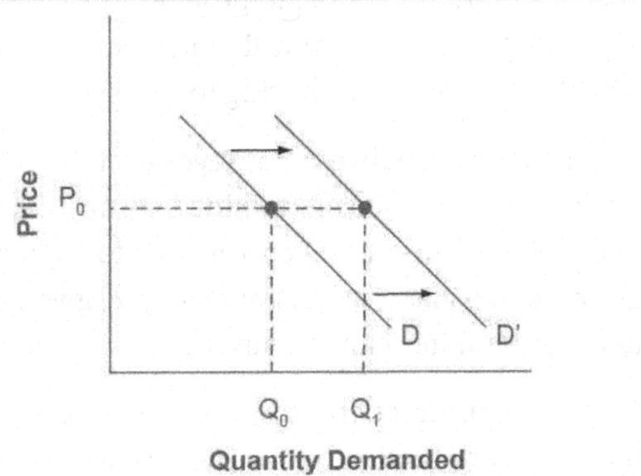


**FIGURE 3.8 Demand Curve Shifted Right** With an increase in income, consumers will purchase larger quantities, pushing demand to the right, and causing the demand curve to shift right.

## Summing Up Factors That Change Demand

Figure 3.9 summarizes six factors that can shift demand curves. The direction of the arrows indicates whether the demand curve shifts represent an increase in demand or a decrease in demand. Notice that a change in the price of the good or service itself is not listed among the factors that can shift a demand curve. A change in the price of a good or service causes a movement along a specific demand curve, and it typically leads to some change in the quantity demanded, but it does not shift the demand curve.

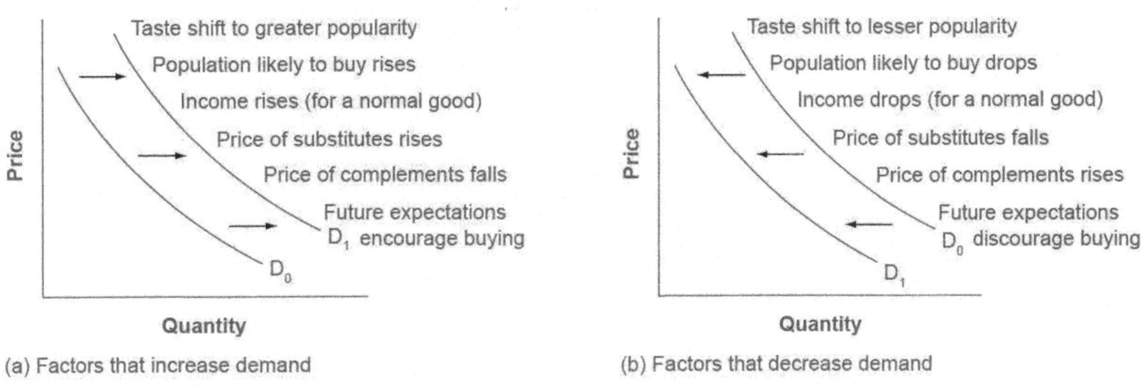


**FIGURE 3.9 Factors That Shift Demand Curves** (a) A list of factors that can cause an increase in demand from $D_0$ to $D_1$. (b) The same factors, if their direction is reversed, can cause a decrease in demand from $D_0$ to $D_1$.

When a demand curve shifts, it will then intersect with a given supply curve at a different equilibrium price and quantity. We are, however, getting ahead of our story. Before discussing how changes in demand can affect equilibrium price and quantity, we first need to discuss shifts in supply curves.

## How Production Costs Affect Supply

A supply curve shows how quantity supplied will change as the price rises and falls, assuming *ceteris paribus* so that no other economically relevant factors are changing. If other factors relevant to supply do change, then the entire supply curve will shift. Just as we described a shift in demand as a change in the quantity demanded at every price, a **shift in supply** means a change in the quantity supplied at every price.

In thinking about the factors that affect supply, remember what motivates firms: profits, which are the difference between revenues and costs. A firm produces goods and services using combinations of labor, materials, and machinery, or what we call **inputs** or **factors of production**. If a firm faces lower costs of production, while the prices for the good or service the firm produces remain unchanged, a firm's profits go up. When a firm's profits increase, it is more motivated to produce output, since the more it produces the more profit it will earn. When costs of production fall, a firm will tend to supply a larger quantity at any given price for its output. We can show this by the supply curve shifting to the right.

Take, for example, a messenger company that delivers packages around a city. The company may find that buying gasoline is one of its main costs. If the price of gasoline falls, then the company will find it can deliver messages more cheaply than before. Since lower costs correspond to higher profits, the messenger company may now supply more of its services at any given price. For example, given the lower gasoline prices, the company can now serve a greater area, and increase its supply.

Conversely, if a firm faces higher costs of production, then it will earn lower profits at any given selling price for its products. As a result, a higher cost of production typically causes a firm to supply a smaller quantity at any given price. In this case, the supply curve shifts to the left.

Consider the supply for cars, shown by curve $S_0$ in Figure 3.10. Point J indicates that if the price is $20,000, the quantity supplied will be 18 million cars. If the price rises to $22,000 per car, *ceteris paribus,* the quantity supplied will rise to 20 million cars, as point K on the $S_0$ curve shows. We can show the same information in table form, as in Table 3.5.

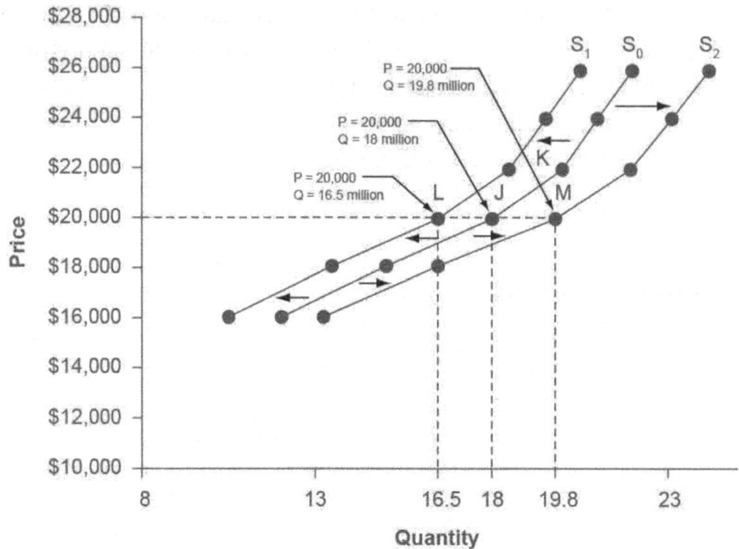


FIGURE 3.10 Shifts in Supply: A Car Example Decreased supply means that at every given price, the quantity supplied is lower, so that the supply curve shifts to the left, from $S_0$ to $S_1$. Increased supply means that at every given price, the quantity supplied is higher, so that the supply curve shifts to the right, from $S_0$ to $S_2$.

| Price | Decrease to $S_1$ | Original Quantity Supplied $S_0$ | Increase to $S_2$ |
| --- | --- | --- | --- |
| $16,000 | 10.5 million | 12.0 million | 13.2 million |
| $18,000 | 13.5 million | 15.0 million | 16.5 million |
| $20,000 | 16.5 million | 18.0 million | 19.8 million |
| $22,000 | 18.5 million | 20.0 million | 22.0 million |
| $24,000 | 19.5 million | 21.0 million | 23.1 million |
| $26,000 | 20.5 million | 22.0 million | 24.2 million |

TABLE 3.5 Price and Shifts in Supply: A Car Example

Now, imagine that the price of steel, an important ingredient in manufacturing cars, rises, so that producing a car has become more expensive. At any given price for selling cars, car manufacturers will react by supplying a lower quantity. We can show this graphically as a leftward shift of supply, from $S_0$ to $S_1$, which indicates that at any given price, the quantity supplied decreases. In this example, at a price of \$20,000, the quantity supplied decreases from 18 million on the original supply curve ($S_0$) to 16.5 million on the supply curve $S_1$, which is labeled as point L.

Conversely, if the price of steel decreases, producing a car becomes less expensive. At any given price for selling cars, car manufacturers can now expect to earn higher profits, so they will supply a higher quantity. The shift of supply to the right, from $S_0$ to $S_2$, means that at all prices, the quantity supplied has increased. In this example, at a price of \$20,000, the quantity supplied increases from 18 million on the original supply curve ($S_0$) to 19.8 million on the supply curve $S_2$, which is labeled M.

## Other Factors That Affect Supply

In the example above, we saw that changes in the prices of inputs in the production process will affect the cost of production and thus the supply. Several other things affect the cost of production, too, such as changes in weather or other natural conditions, new technologies for production, and some government policies.

Changes in weather and climate will affect the cost of production for many agricultural products. For example, in 2014 the Manchurian Plain in Northeastern China, which produces most of the country's wheat, corn, and soybeans, experienced its most severe drought in 50 years. A drought decreases the supply of agricultural products, which means that at any given price, a lower quantity will be supplied. Conversely, especially good weather would shift the supply curve to the right.

When a firm discovers a new technology that allows the firm to produce at a lower cost, the supply curve will shift to the right, as well. For instance, in the 1960s a major scientific effort nicknamed the Green Revolution focused on breeding improved seeds for basic crops like wheat and rice. By the early 1990s, more than two-thirds of the wheat and rice in low-income countries around the world used these Green Revolution seeds—and the harvest was twice as high per acre. A technological improvement that reduces costs of production will shift supply to the right, so that a greater quantity will be produced at any given price.

Government policies can affect the cost of production and the supply curve through taxes, regulations, and subsidies. For example, the U.S. government imposes a tax on alcoholic beverages that collects about \$8 billion per year from producers. Businesses treat taxes as costs. Higher costs decrease supply for the reasons we discussed above. Other examples of policy that can affect cost are the wide array of government regulations that require firms to spend money to provide a cleaner environment or a safer workplace. Complying with regulations increases costs.

A government subsidy, on the other hand, is the opposite of a tax. A subsidy occurs when the government pays a firm directly or reduces the firm's taxes if the firm carries out certain actions. From the firm's perspective, taxes or regulations are an additional cost of production that shifts supply to the left, leading the firm to produce a lower quantity at every given price. Government subsidies reduce the cost of production and increase supply at every given price, shifting supply to the right. The following Work It Out feature shows how this shift happens.



### Shift in Supply

We know that a supply curve shows the minimum price a firm will accept to produce a given quantity of output. What happens to the supply curve when the cost of production goes up? Following is an example of a shift in supply due to a production cost increase. (We'll introduce some other concepts regarding firm decision-making in

Chapters 7 and 8.)

Step 1. Draw a graph of a supply curve for pizza. Pick a quantity (like $Q_0$). If you draw a vertical line up from $Q_0$ to the supply curve, you will see the price the firm chooses. Figure 3.11 provides an example.

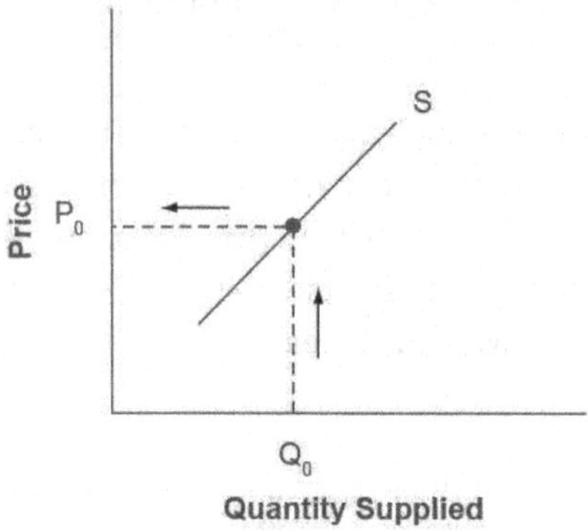


**FIGURE 3.11 Supply Curve** You can use a supply curve to show the minimum price a firm will accept to produce a given quantity of output.

Step 2. Why did the firm choose that price and not some other? One way to think about this is that the price is composed of two parts. The first part is the cost of producing pizzas at the margin; in this case, the cost of producing the pizza, including cost of ingredients (e.g., dough, sauce, cheese, and pepperoni), the cost of the pizza oven, the shop rent, and the workers' wages. The second part is the firm's desired profit, which is determined, among other factors, by the profit margins in that particular business. (Desired profit is not necessarily the same as economic profit, which will be explained in Chapter 7.) If you add these two parts together, you get the price the firm wishes to charge. The quantity Q0 and associated price P0 give you one point on the firm's supply curve, as Figure 3.12 illustrates.

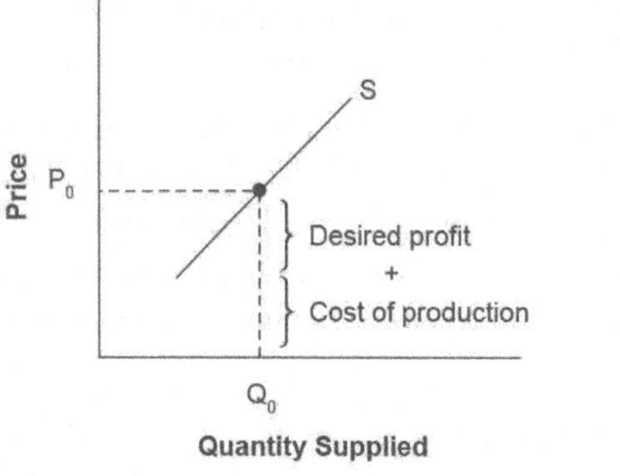


**FIGURE 3.12 Setting Prices** The cost of production and the desired profit equal the price a firm will set for a product.

Step 3. Now, suppose that the cost of production increases. Perhaps cheese has become more expensive by $0.75 per pizza. If that is true, the firm will want to raise its price by the amount of the increase in cost ($0.75). Draw this point on the supply curve directly above the initial point on the curve, but $0.75 higher, as Figure 3.13 shows.

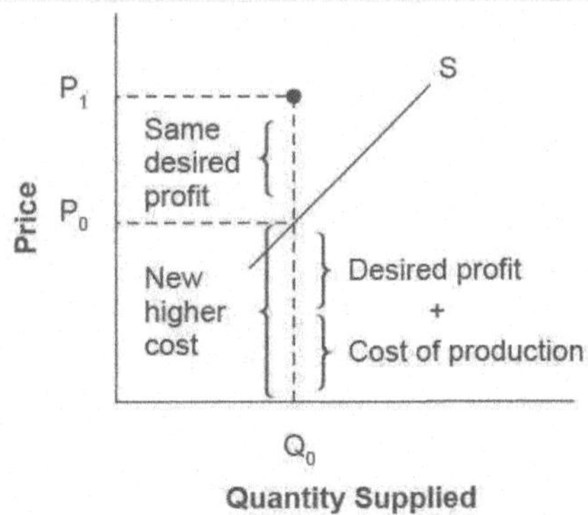



**FIGURE 3.13 Increasing Costs Leads to Increasing Price** Because the cost of production and the desired profit equal the price a firm will set for a product, if the cost of production increases, the price for the product will also need to increase.

Step 4. Shift the supply curve through this point. You will see that an increase in cost causes an upward (or a leftward) shift of the supply curve so that at any price, the quantities supplied will be smaller, as Figure 3.14 illustrates.

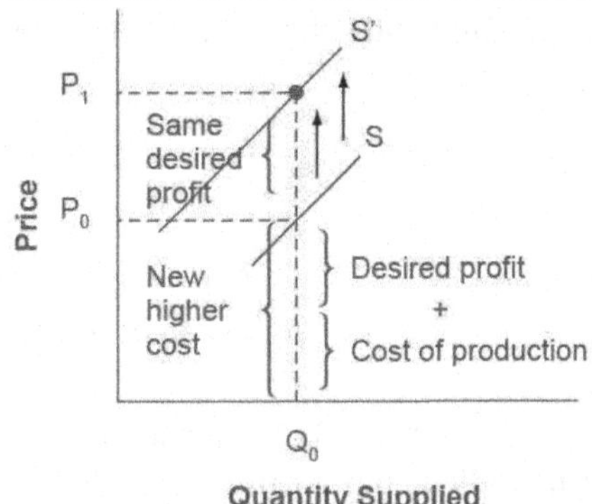



**FIGURE 3.14 Supply Curve Shifts** When the cost of production increases, the supply curve shifts upwardly to a new price level.

## Summing Up Factors That Change Supply

Changes in the cost of inputs, natural disasters, new technologies, and the impact of government decisions all affect the cost of production. In turn, these factors affect how much firms are willing to supply at any given price.

Figure 3.15 summarizes factors that change the supply of goods and services. Notice that a change in the price of the product itself is not among the factors that shift the supply curve. Although a change in price of a good or service typically causes a change in quantity supplied or a movement along the supply curve for that specific good or service, it does not cause the supply curve itself to shift.

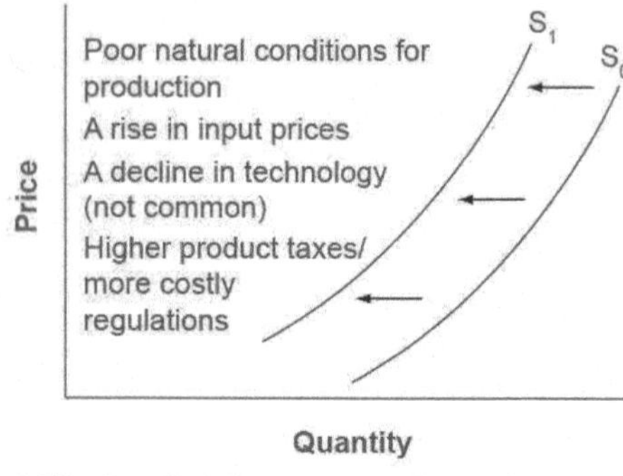



(a) Factors that increase supply          (b) Factors that decrease supply

**FIGURE 3.15 Factors That Shift Supply Curves** (a) A list of factors that can cause an increase in supply from $S_0$ to $S_1$. (b) The same factors, if their direction is reversed, can cause a decrease in supply from $S_0$ to $S_1$.

Because demand and supply curves appear on a two-dimensional diagram with only price and quantity on the axes, an unwary visitor to the land of economics might be fooled into believing that economics is about only four topics: demand, supply, price, and quantity. However, demand and supply are really "umbrella" concepts: demand covers all the factors that affect demand, and supply covers all the factors that affect supply. We include factors other than price that affect demand and supply by using shifts in the demand or the supply curve. In this way, the two-dimensional demand and supply model becomes a powerful tool for analyzing a wide range of economic circumstances.

## 3.3 Changes in Equilibrium Price and Quantity: The Four-Step Process

### LEARNING OBJECTIVES

By the end of this section, you will be able to:

- Identify equilibrium price and quantity through the four-step process
- Graph equilibrium price and quantity
- Contrast shifts of demand or supply and movements along a demand or supply curve
- Graph demand and supply curves, including equilibrium price and quantity, based on real-world examples

Let's begin this discussion with a single economic event. It might be an event that affects demand, like a change in income, population, tastes, prices of substitutes or complements, or expectations about future prices. It might be an event that affects supply, like a change in natural conditions, input prices, or technology, or government policies that affect production. How does this economic event affect equilibrium price and quantity? We will analyze this question using a four-step process.

Step 1. Draw a demand and supply model before the economic change took place. To establish the model requires four standard pieces of information: The law of demand, which tells us the slope of the demand curve is negative; the law of supply, which tells us that the slope of the supply curve is positive; the shift variables for demand; and the shift variables for supply. From this model, find the initial equilibrium values for price and quantity.

Step 2. Decide whether the economic change you are analyzing affects demand or supply. In other words, does the event refer to something in the list of demand factors or supply factors?

Step 3. Decide whether the effect on demand or supply causes the curve to shift to the right or to the left, and sketch the new demand or supply curve on the diagram. In other words, does the event increase or decrease the amount consumers want to buy or producers want to sell?

Step 4. Identify the new equilibrium and then compare the original equilibrium price and quantity to the new equilibrium price and quantity.

Let's consider one example that involves a shift in supply and one that involves a shift in demand. Then we will consider an example where both supply and demand shift.

## Good Weather for Salmon Fishing

Suppose that during the summer of 2015, weather conditions were excellent for commercial salmon fishing off the California coast. Heavy rains meant higher than normal levels of water in the rivers, which helps the salmon to breed. Slightly cooler ocean temperatures stimulated the growth of plankton, the microscopic organisms at the bottom of the ocean food chain, providing everything in the ocean with a hearty food supply. The ocean stayed calm during fishing season, so commercial fishing operations did not lose many days to bad weather. How did these climate conditions affect the quantity and price of salmon? Figure 3.16 illustrates the four-step approach, which we explain below, to work through this problem. Table 3.6 also provides the information to work the problem.

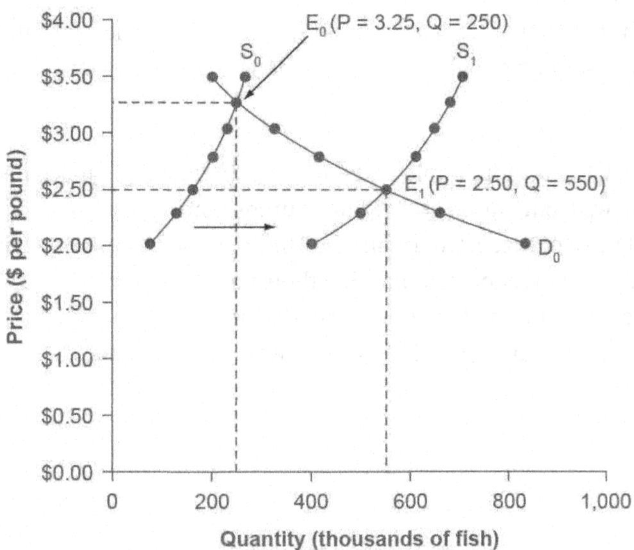


**FIGURE 3.16 Good Weather for Salmon Fishing: The Four-Step Process** Unusually good weather leads to changes in the price and quantity of salmon.

| Price per Pound | Quantity Supplied in 2014 | Quantity Supplied in 2015 | Quantity Demanded |
| --- | --- | --- | --- |
| $2.00 | 80 | 400 | 840 |
| $2.25 | 120 | 480 | 680 |
| $2.50 | 160 | 550 | 550 |
| $2.75 | 200 | 600 | 450 |
| $3.00 | 230 | 640 | 350 |
| $3.25 | 250 | 670 | 250 |
| $3.50 | 270 | 700 | 200 |

**TABLE 3.6 Salmon Fishing**

Step 1. Draw a demand and supply model to illustrate the market for salmon in the year before the good weather conditions began. The demand curve $D_0$ and the supply curve $S_0$ show that the original equilibrium price is \$3.25 per pound and the original equilibrium quantity is 250,000 fish. (This price per pound is what commercial buyers pay at the fishing docks. What consumers pay at the grocery is higher.)

Step 2. Did the economic event affect supply or demand? Good weather is an example of a natural condition that affects supply.

Step 3. Was the effect on supply an increase or a decrease? Good weather is a change in natural conditions that increases the quantity supplied at any given price. The supply curve shifts to the right, moving from the original supply curve $S_0$ to the new supply curve $S_1$, which Figure 3.16 and Table 3.6 show.

Step 4. Compare the new equilibrium price and quantity to the original equilibrium. At the new equilibrium $E_1$, the equilibrium price falls from \$3.25 to \$2.50, but the equilibrium quantity increases from 250,000 to 550,000 salmon. Notice that the equilibrium quantity demanded increased, even though the demand curve did not move.

In short, good weather conditions increased supply of the California commercial salmon. The result was a higher equilibrium quantity of salmon bought and sold in the market at a lower price.

## Newspapers and the Internet

According to the Pew Research Center for People and the Press, increasingly more people, especially younger people, are obtaining their news from online and digital sources. The majority of U.S. adults now own smartphones or tablets, and most of those Americans say they use them in part to access the news. From 2004 to 2012, the share of Americans who reported obtaining their news from digital sources increased from 24% to 39%. How has this affected consumption of print news media, and radio and television news? Figure 3.17 and the text below illustrates using the four-step analysis to answer this question.

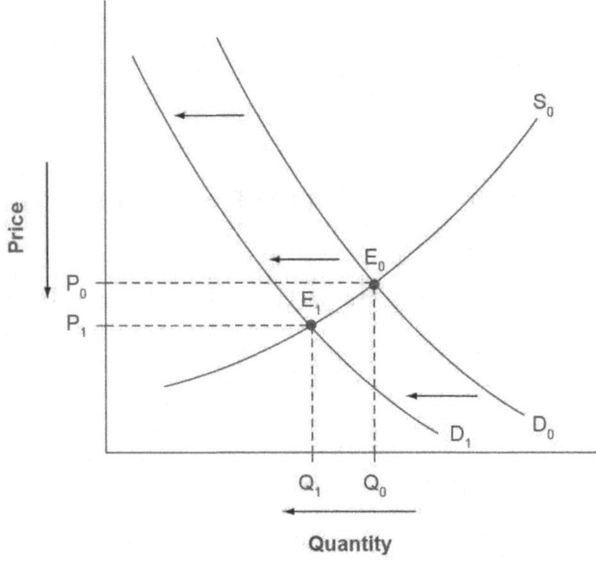


**FIGURE 3.17 The Print News Market: A Four-Step Analysis** A change in tastes from print news sources to digital sources results in a leftward shift in demand for the former. The result is a decrease in both equilibrium price and quantity.

Step 1. Develop a demand and supply model to think about what the market looked like before the event. The demand curve $D_0$ and the supply curve $S_0$ show the original relationships. In this case, we perform the analysis without specific numbers on the price and quantity axis.

Step 2. Did the described change affect supply or demand? A change in tastes, from traditional news sources (print, radio, and television) to digital sources, caused a change in demand for the former.

Step 3. Was the effect on demand positive or negative? A shift to digital news sources will tend to mean a lower quantity demanded of traditional news sources at every given price, causing the demand curve for print and other traditional news sources to shift to the left, from $D_0$ to $D_1$.

Step 4. Compare the new equilibrium price and quantity to the original equilibrium price. The new equilibrium ($E_1$) occurs at a lower quantity and a lower price than the original equilibrium ($E_0$).

The decline in print news reading predates 2004. Print newspaper circulation peaked in 1973 and has declined since then due to competition from television and radio news. In 1991, 55% of Americans indicated they received their news from print sources, while only 29% did so in 2012. Radio news has followed a similar path in recent decades, with the share of Americans obtaining their news from radio declining from 54% in 1991 to 33% in 2012. Television news has held its own in recent years, with a market share staying in the mid to upper fifties. What does this suggest for the future, given that two-thirds of Americans under 30 years old say they do not obtain their news from television at all?

## The Interconnections and Speed of Adjustment in Real Markets

In the real world, many factors that affect demand and supply can change all at once. For example, the demand for cars might increase because of rising incomes and population, and it might decrease because of rising gasoline prices (a complementary good). Likewise, the supply of cars might increase because of innovative new technologies that reduce the cost of car production, and it might decrease as a result of new government regulations requiring the installation of costly pollution-control technology.

Moreover, rising incomes and population or changes in gasoline prices will affect many markets, not just cars. How can an economist sort out all these interconnected events? The answer lies in the *ceteris paribus* assumption. Look at how each economic event affects each market, one event at a time, holding all else constant. Then combine the analyses to see the net effect.

## A Combined Example

The U.S. Postal Service is facing difficult challenges. Compensation for postal workers tends to increase most years due to cost-of-living increases. At the same time, increasingly more people are using email, text, and other digital message forms such as Facebook and Twitter to communicate with friends and others. What does this suggest about the continued viability of the Postal Service? Figure 3.18 and the text below illustrate this using the four-step analysis to answer this question.

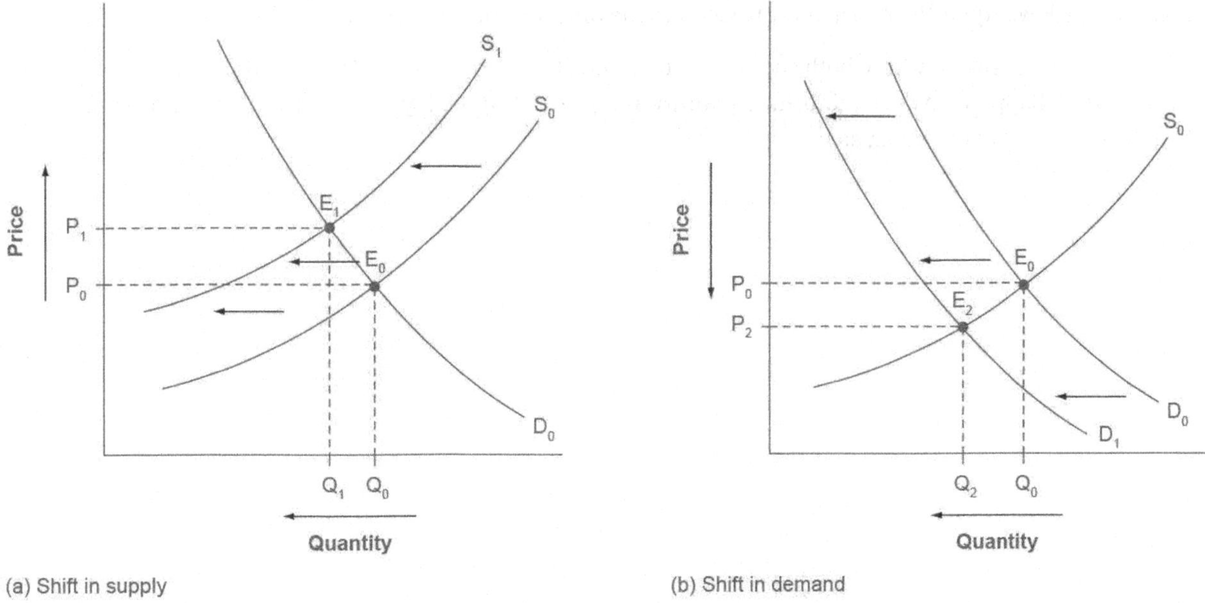


FIGURE 3.18 Higher Compensation for Postal Workers: A Four-Step Analysis (a) Higher labor compensation causes

a leftward shift in the supply curve, a decrease in the equilibrium quantity, and an increase in the equilibrium price. (b) A change in tastes away from Postal Services causes a leftward shift in the demand curve, a decrease in the equilibrium quantity, and a decrease in the equilibrium price.

Since this problem involves two disturbances, we need two four-step analyses, the first to analyze the effects of higher compensation for postal workers, the second to analyze the effects of many people switching from "snail mail" to email and other digital messages.

Figure 3.18 (a) shows the shift in supply discussed in the following steps.

Step 1. Draw a demand and supply model to illustrate what the market for the U.S. Postal Service looked like before this scenario starts. The demand curve $D_0$ and the supply curve $S_0$ show the original relationships.

Step 2. Did the described change affect supply or demand? Labor compensation is a cost of production. A change in production costs caused a change in supply for the Postal Service.

Step 3. Was the effect on supply positive or negative? Higher labor compensation leads to a lower quantity supplied of postal services at every given price, causing the supply curve for postal services to shift to the left, from $S_0$ to $S_1$.

Step 4. Compare the new equilibrium price and quantity to the original equilibrium price. The new equilibrium ($E_1$) occurs at a lower quantity and a higher price than the original equilibrium ($E_0$).

Figure 3.18 (b) shows the shift in demand in the following steps.

Step 1. Draw a demand and supply model to illustrate what the market for U.S. Postal Services looked like before this scenario starts. The demand curve $D_0$ and the supply curve $S_0$ show the original relationships. Note that this diagram is independent from the diagram in panel (a).

Step 2. Did the change described affect supply or demand? A change in tastes away from snail mail toward digital messages will cause a change in demand for the Postal Service.

Step 3. Was the effect on demand positive or negative? A change in tastes away from snailmail toward digital messages causes lower quantity demanded of postal services at every given price, causing the demand curve for postal services to shift to the left, from $D_0$ to $D_1$.

Step 4. Compare the new equilibrium price and quantity to the original equilibrium price. The new equilibrium ($E_2$) occurs at a lower quantity and a lower price than the original equilibrium ($E_0$).

The final step in a scenario where both supply and demand shift is to combine the two individual analyses to determine what happens to the equilibrium quantity and price. Graphically, we superimpose the previous two diagrams one on top of the other, as in Figure 3.19.

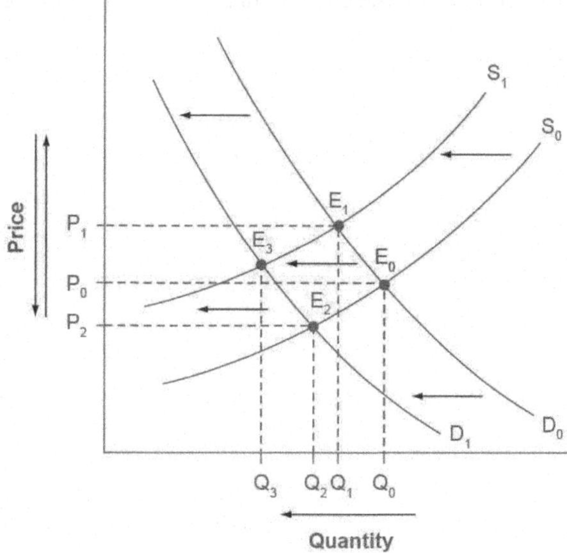


**FIGURE 3.19 Combined Effect of Decreased Demand and Decreased Supply** Supply and demand shifts cause changes in equilibrium price and quantity.

Following are the results:

Effect on Quantity: The effect of higher labor compensation on Postal Services because it raises the cost of production is to decrease the equilibrium quantity. The effect of a change in tastes away from snail mail is to decrease the equilibrium quantity. Since both shifts are to the left, the overall impact is a decrease in the equilibrium quantity of Postal Services ($Q_3$). This is easy to see graphically, since $Q_3$ is to the left of $Q_0$.

Effect on Price: The overall effect on price is more complicated. The effect of higher labor compensation on Postal Services, because it raises the cost of production, is to increase the equilibrium price. The effect of a change in tastes away from snail mail is to decrease the equilibrium price. Since the two effects are in opposite directions, unless we know the magnitudes of the two effects, the overall effect is unclear. This is not unusual. When both curves shift, typically we can determine the overall effect on price or on quantity, but not on both. In this case, we determined the overall effect on the equilibrium quantity, but not on the equilibrium price. In other cases, it might be the opposite.

The next Clear It Up feature focuses on the difference between shifts of supply or demand and movements along a curve.

 **CLEAR IT UP**

### What is the difference between shifts of demand or supply versus movements along a demand or supply curve?

One common mistake in applying the demand and supply framework is to confuse the shift of a demand or a supply curve with movement along a demand or supply curve. As an example, consider a problem that asks whether a drought will increase or decrease the equilibrium quantity and equilibrium price of wheat. Lee, a student in an introductory economics class, might reason:

"Well, it is clear that a drought reduces supply, so I will shift back the supply curve, as in the shift from the original supply curve $S_0$ to $S_1$ on the diagram (Shift 1). The equilibrium moves from $E_0$ to $E_1$, the equilibrium quantity is lower and the equilibrium price is higher. Then, a higher price makes farmers more likely to supply the good, so the supply curve shifts right, as shows the shift from $S_1$ to $S_2$, shows on the diagram (Shift 2), so that the equilibrium now moves from $E_1$ to $E_2$. The higher price, however, also reduces demand and so causes demand to shift back, like the shift from the original demand curve, $D_0$ to $D_1$ on the diagram (labeled Shift 3), and the equilibrium moves from $E_2$ to $E_3$."

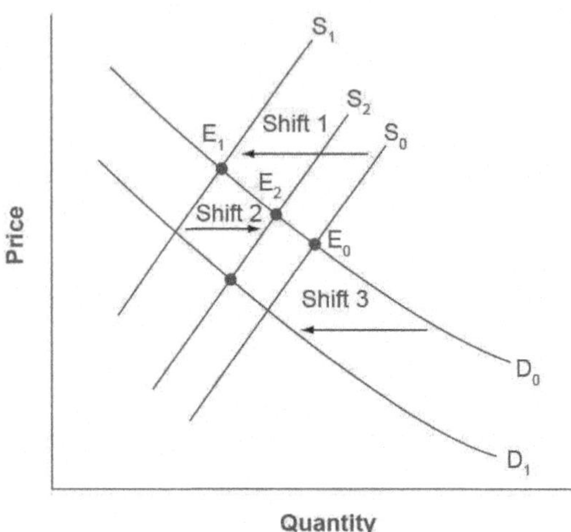


**FIGURE 3.20 Shifts of Demand or Supply versus Movements along a Demand or Supply Curve** A shift in one curve never causes a shift in the other curve. Rather, a shift in one curve causes a movement along the second curve.

At about this point, Lee suspects that this answer is headed down the wrong path. Think about what might be wrong with Lee's logic, and then read the answer that follows.

*Answer:* Lee's first step is correct: that is, a drought shifts back the supply curve of wheat and leads to a prediction of a lower equilibrium quantity and a higher equilibrium price. This corresponds to a movement along the original demand curve ($D_0$), from $E_0$ to $E_1$. The rest of Lee's argument is wrong, because it mixes up shifts in supply with quantity supplied, and shifts in demand with quantity demanded. A higher or lower price never shifts the supply curve, as suggested by the shift in supply from $S_1$ to $S_2$. Instead, a price change leads to a movement along a given supply curve. Similarly, a higher or lower price never shifts a demand curve, as suggested in the shift from $D_0$ to $D_1$. Instead, a price change leads to a movement along a given demand curve. Remember, a change in the price of a good never causes the demand or supply curve for that good to shift.

Think carefully about the timeline of events: What happens first, what happens next? What is cause, what is effect? If you keep the order right, you are more likely to get the analysis correct.

---

In the four-step analysis of how economic events affect equilibrium price and quantity, the movement from the old to the new equilibrium seems immediate. As a practical matter, however, prices and quantities often do not zoom straight to equilibrium. More realistically, when an economic event causes demand or supply to shift, prices and quantities set off in the general direction of equilibrium. Even as they are moving toward one new equilibrium, a subsequent change in demand or supply often pushes prices toward another equilibrium.

## 3.4 Price Ceilings and Price Floors

### LEARNING OBJECTIVES

By the end of this section, you will be able to:

- Explain price controls, price ceilings, and price floors
- Analyze demand and supply as a social adjustment mechanism

To this point in the chapter, we have been assuming that markets are free, that is, they operate with no government intervention. In this section, we will explore the outcomes, both anticipated and otherwise, when government does intervene in a market either to prevent the price of some good or service from rising "too high" or to prevent the price of some good or service from falling "too low".

Economists believe there are a small number of fundamental principles that explain how economic agents respond in different situations. Two of these principles, which we have already introduced, are the laws of demand and supply.

Governments can pass laws affecting market outcomes, but no law can negate these economic principles. Rather, the principles will become apparent in sometimes unexpected ways, which may undermine the intent of the government policy. This is one of the major conclusions of this section.

Controversy sometimes surrounds the prices and quantities established by demand and supply, especially for products that are considered necessities. In some cases, discontent over prices turns into public pressure on politicians, who may then pass legislation to prevent a certain price from climbing "too high" or falling "too low."

The demand and supply model shows how people and firms will react to the incentives that these laws provide to control prices, in ways that will often lead to undesirable consequences. Alternative policy tools can often achieve the desired goals of price control laws, while avoiding at least some of their costs and tradeoffs.

## Price Ceilings

Laws that governments enact to regulate prices are called **price controls**. Price controls come in two flavors. A **price ceiling** keeps a price from rising above a certain level (the "ceiling"), while a **price floor** keeps a price from falling below a given level (the "floor"). This section uses the demand and supply framework to analyze price ceilings. The next section discusses price floors.

A price ceiling is a legal maximum price that one pays for some good or service. A government imposes price ceilings in order to keep the price of some necessary good or service affordable. For example, in 2005 during Hurricane Katrina, the price of bottled water increased above $5 per gallon. As a result, many people called for price controls on bottled water to prevent the price from rising so high. In this particular case, the government did not impose a price ceiling, but there are other examples of where price ceilings did occur.

In many markets for goods and services, demanders outnumber suppliers. Consumers, who are also potential voters, sometimes unite behind a political proposal to hold down a certain price. In some cities, such as Albany, renters have pressed political leaders to pass rent control laws, a price ceiling that usually works by stating that landlords can raise rents by only a certain maximum percentage each year. Some of the best examples of rent control occur in urban areas such as New York, Washington D.C., or San Francisco.

Rent control becomes a politically hot topic when rents begin to rise rapidly. Everyone needs an affordable place to live. Perhaps a change in tastes makes a certain suburb or town a more popular place to live. Perhaps locally-based businesses expand, bringing higher incomes and more people into the area. Such changes can cause a change in the demand for rental housing, as Figure 3.21 illustrates. The original equilibrium ($E_0$) lies at the intersection of supply curve $S_0$ and demand curve $D_0$, corresponding to an equilibrium price of $500 and an equilibrium quantity of 15,000 units of rental housing. The effect of greater income or a change in tastes is to shift the demand curve for rental housing to the right, as the data in Table 3.7 shows and the shift from $D_0$ to $D_1$ on the graph. In this market, at the new equilibrium $E_1$, the price of a rental unit would rise to $600 and the equilibrium quantity would increase to 17,000 units.

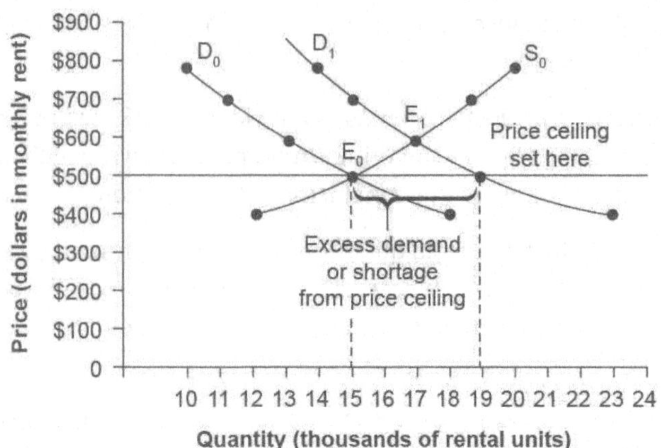


**FIGURE 3.21 A Price Ceiling Example—Rent Control** The original intersection of demand and supply occurs at $E_0$. If demand shifts from $D_0$ to $D_1$, the new equilibrium would be at $E_1$—unless a price ceiling prevents the price from rising. If the price is not permitted to rise, the quantity supplied remains at 15,000. However, after the change in demand, the quantity demanded rises to 19,000, resulting in a shortage.

| Price | Original Quantity Supplied | Original Quantity Demanded | New Quantity Demanded |
|---|---|---|---|
| $400 | 12,000 | 18,000 | 23,000 |
| $500 | 15,000 | 15,000 | 19,000 |
| $600 | 17,000 | 13,000 | 17,000 |
| $700 | 19,000 | 11,000 | 15,000 |
| $800 | 20,000 | 10,000 | 14,000 |

**TABLE 3.7 Rent Control**

Suppose that a city government passes a rent control law to keep the price at the original equilibrium of $500 for a typical apartment. In Figure 3.21, the horizontal line at the price of $500 shows the legally fixed maximum price set by the rent control law. However, the underlying forces that shifted the demand curve to the right are still there. At that price ($500), the quantity supplied remains at the same 15,000 rental units, but the quantity demanded is 19,000 rental units. In other words, the quantity demanded exceeds the quantity supplied, so there is a shortage of rental housing. One of the ironies of price ceilings is that while the price ceiling was intended to help renters, there are actually fewer apartments rented out under the price ceiling (15,000 rental units) than would be the case at the market rent of $600 (17,000 rental units).

Price ceilings do not simply benefit renters at the expense of landlords. Rather, some renters (or potential renters) lose their housing as landlords convert apartments to co-ops and condos. Even when the housing remains in the rental market, landlords tend to spend less on maintenance and on essentials like heating, cooling, hot water, and lighting. The first rule of economics is you do not get something for nothing—everything has an opportunity cost. Thus, if renters obtain "cheaper" housing than the market requires, they tend to also end up with lower quality housing.

Price ceilings are enacted in an attempt to keep prices low for those who need the product. However, when the market price is not allowed to rise to the equilibrium level, quantity demanded exceeds quantity supplied, and thus a shortage occurs. Those who manage to purchase the product at the lower price given by the price ceiling will benefit, but sellers of the product will suffer, along with those who are not able to purchase the product at all. Quality is also likely to deteriorate.

## Price Floors

A price floor is the lowest price that one can legally pay for some good or service. Perhaps the best-known example of a price floor is the minimum wage, which is based on the view that someone working full time should be able to afford a basic standard of living. The federal minimum wage in 2022 was $7.25 per hour, although some states and localities have a higher minimum wage. The federal minimum wage yields an annual income for a single person of $15,080, which is slightly higher than the Federal poverty line of $11,880. Congress periodically raises the federal minimum wage as the cost of living rises. As of March 2022, the most recent adjustment occurred in 2009, when the federal minimum wage was raised from $6.55 to $7.25.

Price floors are sometimes called "price supports," because they support a price by preventing it from falling below a certain level. Around the world, many countries have passed laws to create agricultural price supports. Farm prices and thus farm incomes fluctuate, sometimes widely. Even if, on average, farm incomes are adequate, some years they can be quite low. The purpose of price supports is to prevent these swings.

The most common way price supports work is that the government enters the market and buys up the product, adding to demand to keep prices higher than they otherwise would be. According to the Common Agricultural Policy reform effective in 2019, the European Union (EU) will spend about 58 billion euros per year, or 65.5 billion dollars per year (with the December 2021 exchange rate), or roughly 36% of the EU budget, on price supports for Europe's farmers.

Figure 3.22 illustrates the effects of a government program that assures a price above the equilibrium by focusing on the market for wheat in Europe. In the absence of government intervention, the price would adjust so that the quantity supplied would equal the quantity demanded at the equilibrium point $E_0$, with price $P_0$ and quantity $Q_0$. However, policies to keep prices high for farmers keep the price above what would have been the market equilibrium level—the price Pf shown by the dashed horizontal line in the diagram. The result is a quantity supplied in excess of the quantity demanded (Qd). When quantity supplied exceeds quantity demanded, a surplus exists.

Economists estimate that the high-income areas of the world, including the United States, Europe, and Japan, spend roughly $1 billion per day in supporting their farmers. If the government is willing to purchase the excess supply (or to provide payments for others to purchase it), then farmers will benefit from the price floor, but taxpayers and consumers of food will pay the costs. Agricultural economists and policy makers have offered numerous proposals for reducing farm subsidies. In many countries, however, political support for subsidies for farmers remains strong. This is either because the population views this as supporting the traditional rural way of life or because of industry's lobbying power of the agro-business.

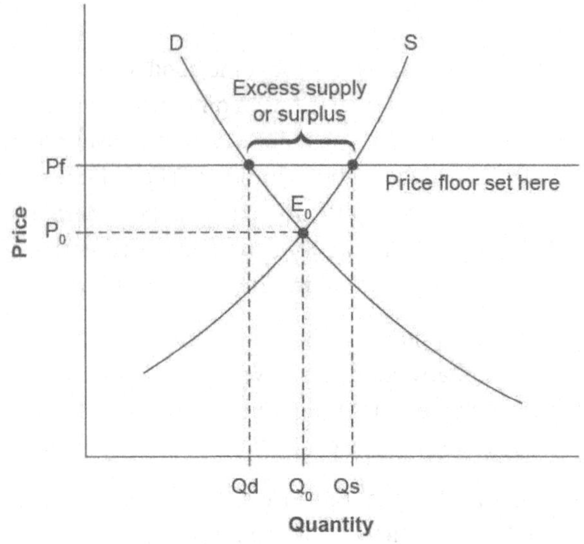

FIGURE 3.22 European Wheat Prices: A Price Floor Example The intersection of demand (D) and supply (S) would be at the equilibrium point $E_0$. However, a price floor set at Pf holds the price above $E_0$ and prevents it from falling. The result of the price floor is that the quantity supplied Qs exceeds the quantity demanded Qd. There is excess supply, also called a surplus.

## 3.5 Demand, Supply, and Efficiency

**LEARNING OBJECTIVES**

By the end of this section, you will be able to:
- Contrast consumer surplus, producer surplus, and social surplus
- Explain why price floors and price ceilings can be inefficient
- Analyze demand and supply as a social adjustment mechanism

The familiar demand and supply diagram holds within it the concept of economic efficiency. One typical way that economists define efficiency is when it is impossible to improve the situation of one party without imposing a cost on another. Conversely, if a situation is inefficient, it becomes possible to benefit at least one party without imposing costs on others.

Efficiency in the demand and supply model has the same basic meaning: The economy is getting as much benefit as possible from its scarce resources and all the possible gains from trade have been achieved. In other words, the optimal amount of each good and service is produced and consumed.

### Consumer Surplus, Producer Surplus, Social Surplus

Consider a market for tablet computers, as Figure 3.23 shows. The equilibrium price is $80 and the equilibrium quantity is 28 million. To see the benefits to consumers, look at the segment of the demand curve above the equilibrium point and to the left. This portion of the demand curve shows that at least some demanders would have been willing to pay more than $80 for a tablet.

For example, point J shows that if the price were $90, 20 million tablets would be sold. Those consumers who would have been willing to pay $90 for a tablet based on the utility they expect to receive from it, but who were able to pay the equilibrium price of $80, clearly received a benefit beyond what they had to pay. Remember, the demand curve traces consumers' willingness to pay for different quantities. The amount that individuals would have been willing to pay, minus the amount that they actually paid, is called **consumer surplus**. Consumer surplus is the area labeled F—that is, the area above the market price and below the demand curve.

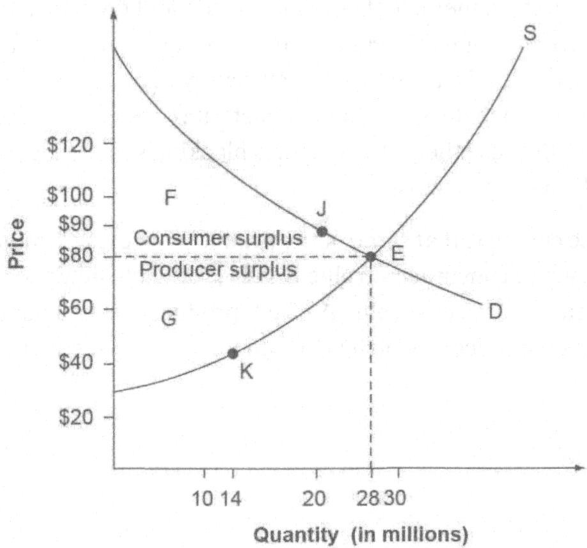

**FIGURE 3.23 Consumer and Producer Surplus** The somewhat triangular area labeled by F shows the area of consumer surplus, which shows that the equilibrium price in the market was less than what many of the consumers were willing to pay. Point J on the demand curve shows that, even at the price of $90, consumers would have been willing to purchase a quantity of 20 million. The somewhat triangular area labeled by G shows the area of producer surplus, which shows that the equilibrium price received in the market was more than what many of the producers were willing to accept for their products. For example, point K on the supply curve shows that at a price of $45, firms would have been willing to supply a quantity of 14 million.

The supply curve shows the quantity that firms are willing to supply at each price. For example, point K in Figure 3.23 illustrates that, at $45, firms would still have been willing to supply a quantity of 14 million. Those producers who would have been willing to supply the tablets at $45, but who were instead able to charge the equilibrium price of $80, clearly received an extra benefit beyond what they required to supply the product. The extra benefit producers receive from selling a good or service, measured by the price the producer actually received minus the price the producer would have been willing to accept is called **producer surplus**. In Figure 3.23, producer surplus is the area labeled G—that is, the area between the market price and the segment of the supply curve below the equilibrium.

The sum of consumer surplus and producer surplus is **social surplus**, also referred to as **economic surplus** or **total surplus**. In Figure 3.23 we show social surplus as the area F + G. Social surplus is larger at equilibrium quantity and price than it would be at any other quantity. This demonstrates the economic efficiency of the market equilibrium. In addition, at the efficient level of output, it is impossible to produce greater consumer surplus without reducing producer surplus, and it is impossible to produce greater producer surplus without reducing consumer surplus.

## Inefficiency of Price Floors and Price Ceilings

The imposition of a price floor or a price ceiling will prevent a market from adjusting to its equilibrium price and quantity, and thus will create an inefficient outcome. However, there is an additional twist here. Along with creating inefficiency, price floors and ceilings will also transfer some consumer surplus to producers, or some producer surplus to consumers.

Imagine that several firms develop a promising but expensive new drug for treating back pain. If this therapy is left to the market, the equilibrium price will be $600 per month and 20,000 people will use the drug, as shown in Figure 3.24 (a). The original level of consumer surplus is T + U and producer surplus is V + W + X. However, the government decides to impose a price ceiling of $400 to make the drug more affordable. At this price ceiling, firms in the market now produce only 15,000.

As a result, two changes occur. First, an inefficient outcome occurs and the total surplus of society is reduced. The loss in social surplus that occurs when the economy produces at an inefficient quantity is called **deadweight loss**. In a very real sense, it is like money thrown away that benefits no one. In Figure 3.24 (a), the deadweight loss is the area U + W. When deadweight loss exists, it is possible for both consumer and producer surplus to be higher, in this case because the price control is blocking some suppliers and demanders from transactions they would both be willing to make.

A second change from the price ceiling is that some of the producer surplus is transferred to consumers. After the price ceiling is imposed, the new consumer surplus is T + V, while the new producer surplus is X. In other words, the price ceiling transfers the area of surplus (V) from producers to consumers. Note that the gain to consumers is less than the loss to producers, which is just another way of seeing the deadweight loss.

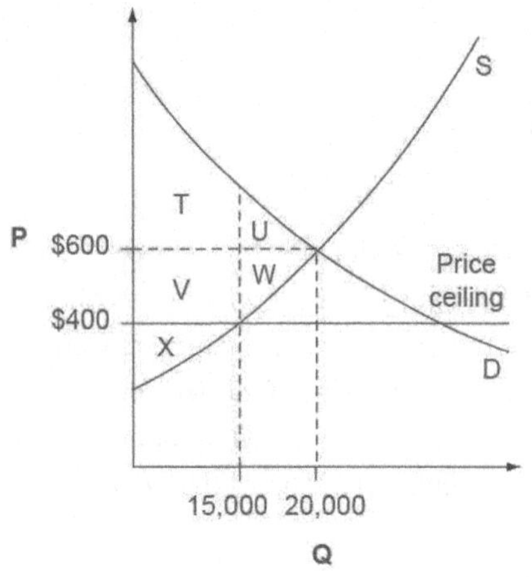


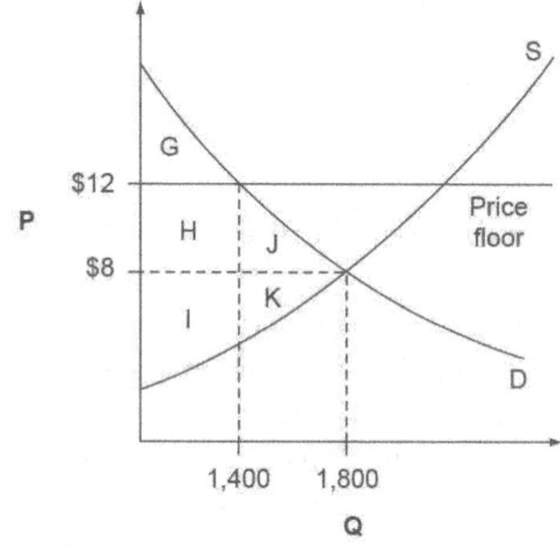


(a) Reduced social surplus from a price ceiling     (b) Reduced social surplus from a price floor

**FIGURE 3.24 Efficiency and Price Floors and Ceilings** (a) The original equilibrium price is $600 with a quantity of 20,000. Consumer surplus is T + U, and producer surplus is V + W + X. A price ceiling is imposed at $400, so firms in the market now produce only a quantity of 15,000. As a result, the new consumer surplus is T + V, while the new producer surplus is X. (b) The original equilibrium is $8 at a quantity of 1,800. Consumer surplus is G + H + J, and producer surplus is I + K. A price floor is imposed at $12, which means that quantity demanded falls to 1,400. As a result, the new consumer surplus is G, and the new producer surplus is H + I.

Figure 3.24 (b) shows a price floor example using a string of struggling movie theaters, all in the same city. The current equilibrium is $8 per movie ticket, with 1,800 people attending movies. The original consumer surplus is G + H + J, and producer surplus is I + K. The city government is worried that movie theaters will go out of business, reducing the entertainment options available to citizens, so it decides to impose a price floor of $12 per ticket. As a result, the quantity demanded of movie tickets falls to 1,400. The new consumer surplus is G, and the new producer surplus is H + I. In effect, the price floor causes the area H to be transferred from consumer to producer surplus, but also causes a deadweight loss of J + K.

This analysis shows that a price ceiling, like a law establishing rent controls, will transfer some producer surplus to consumers—which helps to explain why consumers often favor them. Conversely, a price floor like a guarantee that farmers will receive a certain price for their crops will transfer some consumer surplus to producers, which explains why producers often favor them. However, both price floors and price ceilings block some transactions that buyers and sellers would have been willing to make, and creates deadweight loss. Removing such barriers, so that prices and quantities can adjust to their equilibrium level, will increase the economy's social surplus.

## Demand and Supply as a Social Adjustment Mechanism

The demand and supply model emphasizes that prices are not set only by demand or only by supply, but by the interaction between the two. In 1890, the famous economist Alfred Marshall wrote that asking whether supply or demand determined a price was like arguing "whether it is the upper or the under blade of a pair of scissors that cuts a piece of paper." The answer is that both blades of the demand and supply scissors are always involved.

The adjustments of equilibrium price and quantity in a market-oriented economy often occur without much government direction or oversight. If the coffee crop in Brazil suffers a terrible frost, then the supply curve of coffee shifts to the left and the price of coffee rises. Some people continue to drink coffee and pay the higher price. Others switch to tea or soft drinks. No government commission is needed to figure out how to adjust coffee prices, which companies will be allowed to process the remaining supply, which supermarkets in which cities will get how much coffee to sell, or which consumers will ultimately be allowed to drink the brew. Such adjustments in response to price changes happen all the time in a market economy, often so smoothly and rapidly that we barely notice them.

Think for a moment of all the seasonal foods that are available and inexpensive at certain times of the year, like fresh corn in midsummer, but more expensive at other times of the year. People alter their diets and restaurants alter their menus in response to these fluctuations in prices without fuss or fanfare. For both the U.S. economy and the world economy as a whole, markets—that is, demand and supply—are the primary social mechanism for answering the basic questions about what is produced, how it is produced, and for whom it is produced.

 ## BRING IT HOME

### Why Can We Not Get Enough of Organic Food?

Organic food is grown without synthetic pesticides, chemical fertilizers or genetically modified seeds. In recent decades, the demand for organic products has increased dramatically. The Organic Trade Association reported sales increased from $1 billion in 1990 to nearly $62 billion in 2020, more than 90% of which were sales of food products.

Why, then, are organic foods more expensive than their conventional counterparts? The answer is a clear application of the theories of supply and demand. As people have learned more about the harmful effects of chemical fertilizers, growth hormones, pesticides and the like from large-scale factory farming, our tastes and preferences for safer, organic foods have increased. This change in tastes has been reinforced by increases in income, which allow people to purchase pricier products, and has made organic foods more mainstream. This shift, in addition to population growth, has led to an increased demand for organic foods. Graphically, the demand curve has shifted right, and we have moved up the supply curve as producers have responded to the higher prices by supplying a greater quantity.

In addition to the movement along the supply curve, we have also had an increase in the number of farmers converting to organic farming over time. This is represented by a shift to the right of the supply curve. Since both demand and supply have shifted to the right, the resulting equilibrium quantity of organic foods is definitely higher, but the price will only fall when the increase in supply is larger than the increase in demand. We may need more time before we see lower prices in organic foods. Since the production costs of these foods may remain higher than conventional farming, because organic fertilizers and pest management techniques are more expensive, they may never fully catch up with the lower prices of non-organic foods.

As a final, specific example: The Environmental Working Group's "Dirty Dozen" list of fruits and vegetables, which test high for pesticide residue even after washing, was released in April 2013. The inclusion of strawberries on the list led to an increase in demand for organic strawberries, resulting in both a higher equilibrium price and quantity of sales.

## Key Terms

**ceteris paribus** other things being equal

**complements** goods that are often used together so that consumption of one good tends to enhance consumption of the other

**consumer surplus** the extra benefit consumers receive from buying a good or service, measured by what the individuals would have been willing to pay minus the amount that they actually paid

**deadweight loss** the loss in social surplus that occurs when a market produces an inefficient quantity

**demand** the relationship between price and the quantity demanded of a certain good or service

**demand curve** a graphic representation of the relationship between price and quantity demanded of a certain good or service, with quantity on the horizontal axis and the price on the vertical axis

**demand schedule** a table that shows a range of prices for a certain good or service and the quantity demanded at each price

**economic surplus** see social surplus

**equilibrium** the situation where quantity demanded is equal to the quantity supplied; the combination of price and quantity where there is no economic pressure from surpluses or shortages that would cause price or quantity to change

**equilibrium price** the price where quantity demanded is equal to quantity supplied

**equilibrium quantity** the quantity at which quantity demanded and quantity supplied are equal for a certain price level

**excess demand** at the existing price, the quantity demanded exceeds the quantity supplied; also called a shortage

**excess supply** at the existing price, quantity supplied exceeds the quantity demanded; also called a surplus

**factors of production** the resources such as labor, materials, and machinery that are used to produce goods and services; also called inputs

**inferior good** a good in which the quantity demanded falls as income rises, and in which quantity demanded rises and income falls

**inputs** the resources such as labor, materials, and machinery that are used to produce goods and services; also called factors of production

**law of demand** the common relationship that a higher price leads to a lower quantity demanded of a certain good or service and a lower price leads to a higher quantity demanded, while all other variables are held constant

**law of supply** the common relationship that a higher price leads to a greater quantity supplied and a lower price leads to a lower quantity supplied, while all other variables are held constant

**normal good** a good in which the quantity demanded rises as income rises, and in which quantity demanded falls as income falls

**price** what a buyer pays for a unit of the specific good or service

**price ceiling** a legal maximum price

**price control** government laws to regulate prices instead of letting market forces determine prices

**price floor** a legal minimum price

**producer surplus** the extra benefit producers receive from selling a good or service, measured by the price the producer actually received minus the price the producer would have been willing to accept

**quantity demanded** the total number of units of a good or service consumers are willing to purchase at a given price

**quantity supplied** the total number of units of a good or service producers are willing to sell at a given price

**shift in demand** when a change in some economic factor (other than price) causes a different quantity to be demanded at every price

**shift in supply** when a change in some economic factor (other than price) causes a different quantity to be supplied at every price

**shortage** at the existing price, the quantity demanded exceeds the quantity supplied; also called excess demand

**social surplus** the sum of consumer surplus and producer surplus

**substitute** a good that can replace another to some extent, so that greater consumption of one good can mean less of the other

**supply** the relationship between price and the quantity supplied of a certain good or service

**supply curve** a line that shows the relationship between price and quantity supplied on a graph, with quantity supplied on the horizontal axis and price on the vertical axis

**supply schedule** a table that shows a range of prices for a good or service and the quantity supplied at each price

**surplus** at the existing price, quantity supplied exceeds the quantity demanded; also called excess supply

**total surplus** see social surplus

## Key Concepts and Summary

### 3.1 Demand, Supply, and Equilibrium in Markets for Goods and Services

A demand schedule is a table that shows the quantity demanded at different prices in the market. A demand curve shows the relationship between quantity demanded and price in a given market on a graph. The law of demand states that a higher price typically leads to a lower quantity demanded.

A supply schedule is a table that shows the quantity supplied at different prices in the market. A supply curve shows the relationship between quantity supplied and price on a graph. The law of supply says that a higher price typically leads to a higher quantity supplied.

The equilibrium price and equilibrium quantity occur where the supply and demand curves cross. The equilibrium occurs where the quantity demanded is equal to the quantity supplied. If the price is below the equilibrium level, then the quantity demanded will exceed the quantity supplied. Excess demand or a shortage will exist. If the price is above the equilibrium level, then the quantity supplied will exceed the quantity demanded. Excess supply or a surplus will exist. In either case, economic pressures will push the price toward the equilibrium level.

### 3.2 Shifts in Demand and Supply for Goods and Services

Economists often use the *ceteris paribus* or "other things being equal" assumption: while examining the economic impact of one event, all other factors remain unchanged for analysis purposes. Factors that can shift the demand curve for goods and services, causing a different quantity to be demanded at any given price, include changes in tastes, population, income, prices of substitute or complement goods, and expectations about future conditions and prices. Factors that can shift the supply curve for goods and services, causing a different quantity to be supplied at any given price, include input prices, natural conditions, changes in technology, and government taxes, regulations, or subsidies.

### 3.3 Changes in Equilibrium Price and Quantity: The Four-Step Process

When using the supply and demand framework to think about how an event will affect the equilibrium price and quantity, proceed through four steps: (1) sketch a supply and demand diagram to think about what the market looked like before the event; (2) decide whether the event will affect supply or demand; (3) decide whether the effect on supply or demand is negative or positive, and draw the appropriate shifted supply or demand curve; (4) compare the new equilibrium price and quantity to the original ones.

### 3.4 Price Ceilings and Price Floors

Price ceilings prevent a price from rising above a certain level. When a price ceiling is set below the equilibrium price, quantity demanded will exceed quantity supplied, and excess demand or shortages will result. Price floors prevent a price from falling below a certain level. When a price floor is set above the equilibrium price, quantity supplied will exceed quantity demanded, and excess supply or surpluses will result. Price floors and price ceilings often lead to unintended consequences.

### 3.5 Demand, Supply, and Efficiency

Consumer surplus is the gap between the price that consumers are willing to pay, based on their preferences, and the market equilibrium price. Producer surplus is the gap between the price for which producers are willing to sell a product, based on their costs, and the market equilibrium price. Social surplus is the sum of consumer surplus and producer surplus. Total surplus is larger at the equilibrium quantity and price than it will be at any other quantity and price. Deadweight loss is loss in total surplus that occurs when the economy produces at an inefficient quantity.

## Self-Check Questions

1. Review Figure 3.4. Suppose the price of gasoline is $1.60 per gallon. Is the quantity demanded higher or lower than at the equilibrium price of $1.40 per gallon? What about the quantity supplied? Is there a shortage or a surplus in the market? If so, how much?

2. Why do economists use the *ceteris paribus* assumption?

3. In an analysis of the market for paint, an economist discovers the facts listed below. State whether each of these changes will affect supply or demand, and in what direction.
    a. There have recently been some important cost-saving inventions in the technology for making paint.
    b. Paint is lasting longer, so that property owners need not repaint as often.
    c. Because of severe hailstorms, many people need to repaint now.
    d. The hailstorms damaged several factories that make paint, forcing them to close down for several months.

4. Many changes are affecting the market for oil. Predict how each of the following events will affect the equilibrium price and quantity in the market for oil. In each case, state how the event will affect the supply and demand diagram. Create a sketch of the diagram if necessary.
    a. Cars are becoming more fuel efficient, and therefore get more miles to the gallon.
    b. The winter is exceptionally cold.
    c. A major discovery of new oil is made off the coast of Norway.
    d. The economies of some major oil-using nations, like Japan, slow down.
    e. A war in the Middle East disrupts oil-pumping schedules.
    f. Landlords install additional insulation in buildings.
    g. The price of solar energy falls dramatically.
    h. Chemical companies invent a new, popular kind of plastic made from oil.

5. Let's think about the market for air travel. From August 2014 to January 2015, the price of jet fuel increased roughly 47%. Using the four-step analysis, how do you think this fuel price increase affected the equilibrium price and quantity of air travel?

6. A tariff is a tax on imported goods. Suppose the U.S. government cuts the tariff on imported flat screen televisions. Using the four-step analysis, how do you think the tariff reduction will affect the equilibrium price and quantity of flat screen TVs?

7. What is the effect of a price ceiling on the quantity demanded of the product? What is the effect of a price ceiling on the quantity supplied? Why exactly does a price ceiling cause a shortage?

8. Does a price ceiling change the equilibrium price?

9. What would be the impact of imposing a price floor below the equilibrium price?

10. Does a price ceiling increase or decrease the number of transactions in a market? Why? What about a price floor?

11. If a price floor benefits producers, why does a price floor reduce social surplus?

## Review Questions

**12.** What determines the level of prices in a market?

**13.** What does a downward-sloping demand curve mean about how buyers in a market will react to a higher price?

**14.** Will demand curves have the same exact shape in all markets? If not, how will they differ?

**15.** Will supply curves have the same shape in all markets? If not, how will they differ?

**16.** What is the relationship between quantity demanded and quantity supplied at equilibrium? What is the relationship when there is a shortage? What is the relationship when there is a surplus?

**17.** How can you locate the equilibrium point on a demand and supply graph?

**18.** If the price is above the equilibrium level, would you predict a surplus or a shortage? If the price is below the equilibrium level, would you predict a surplus or a shortage? Why?

**19.** When the price is above the equilibrium, explain how market forces move the market price to equilibrium. Do the same when the price is below the equilibrium.

**20.** What is the difference between the demand and the quantity demanded of a product, say milk? Explain in words and show the difference on a graph with a demand curve for milk.

**21.** What is the difference between the supply and the quantity supplied of a product, say milk? Explain in words and show the difference on a graph with the supply curve for milk.

**22.** When analyzing a market, how do economists deal with the problem that many factors that affect the market are changing at the same time?

**23.** Name some factors that can cause a shift in the demand curve in markets for goods and services.

**24.** Name some factors that can cause a shift in the supply curve in markets for goods and services.

**25.** How does one analyze a market where both demand and supply shift?

**26.** What causes a movement along the demand curve? What causes a movement along the supply curve?

**27.** Does a price ceiling attempt to make a price higher or lower?

**28.** How does a price ceiling set below the equilibrium level affect quantity demanded and quantity supplied?

**29.** Does a price floor attempt to make a price higher or lower?

**30.** How does a price floor set above the equilibrium level affect quantity demanded and quantity supplied?

**31.** What is consumer surplus? How is it illustrated on a demand and supply diagram?

**32.** What is producer surplus? How is it illustrated on a demand and supply diagram?

**33.** What is total surplus? How is it illustrated on a demand and supply diagram?

**34.** What is the relationship between total surplus and economic efficiency?

**35.** What is deadweight loss?

## Critical Thinking Questions

**36.** Review Figure 3.4. Suppose the government decided that, since gasoline is a necessity, its price should be legally capped at $1.30 per gallon. What do you anticipate would be the outcome in the gasoline market?

**37.** Explain why the following statement is false: "In the goods market, no buyer would be willing to pay more than the equilibrium price."

38. Explain why the following statement is false: "In the goods market, no seller would be willing to sell for less than the equilibrium price."

39. Consider the demand for hamburgers. If the price of a substitute good (for example, hot dogs) increases and the price of a complement good (for example, hamburger buns) increases, can you tell for sure what will happen to the demand for hamburgers? Why or why not? Illustrate your answer with a graph.

40. How do you suppose the demographics of an aging population of "Baby Boomers" in the United States will affect the demand for milk? Justify your answer.

41. We know that a change in the price of a product causes a movement along the demand curve. Suppose consumers believe that prices will be rising in the future. How will that affect demand for the product in the present? Can you show this graphically?

42. Suppose there is a soda tax to curb obesity. What should a reduction in the soda tax do to the supply of sodas and to the equilibrium price and quantity? Can you show this graphically? *Hint*: Assume that the soda tax is collected from the sellers.

43. Use the four-step process to analyze the impact of the advent of the iPod (or other portable digital music players) on the equilibrium price and quantity of the Sony Walkman (or other portable audio cassette players).

44. Use the four-step process to analyze the impact of a reduction in tariffs on imports of iPods on the equilibrium price and quantity of Sony Walkman-type products.

45. Suppose both of these events took place at the same time. Combine your analyses of the impacts of the iPod and the tariff reduction to determine the likely impact on the equilibrium price and quantity of Sony Walkman-type products. Show your answer graphically.

46. Most government policy decisions have winners and losers. What are the effects of raising the minimum wage? It is more complex than simply producers lose and workers gain. Who are the winners and who are the losers, and what exactly do they win and lose? To what extent does the policy change achieve its goals?

47. Agricultural price supports result in governments holding large inventories of agricultural products. Why do you think the government cannot simply give the products away to people experiencing poverty?

48. Can you propose a policy that would induce the market to supply more rental housing units?

49. What term would an economist use to describe what happens when a shopper gets a "good deal" on a product?

50. Explain why voluntary transactions improve social welfare.

51. Why would a free market never operate at a quantity greater than the equilibrium quantity? *Hint:* What would be required for a transaction to occur at that quantity?

## Problems

52. Review Figure 3.4 again. Suppose the price of gasoline is $1.00. Will the quantity demanded be lower or higher than at the equilibrium price of $1.40 per gallon? Will the quantity supplied be lower or higher? Is there a shortage or a surplus in the market? If so, of how much?

**53.** Table 3.8 shows information on the demand and supply for bicycles, where the quantities of bicycles are measured in thousands.

| Price | Qd | Qs |
|-------|----|----|
| $120  | 50 | 36 |
| $150  | 40 | 40 |
| $180  | 32 | 48 |
| $210  | 28 | 56 |
| $240  | 24 | 70 |

**TABLE 3.8**

a. What is the quantity demanded and the quantity supplied at a price of $210?
b. At what price is the quantity supplied equal to 48,000?
c. Graph the demand and supply curve for bicycles. How can you determine the equilibrium price and quantity from the graph? How can you determine the equilibrium price and quantity from the table? What are the equilibrium price and equilibrium quantity?
d. If the price was $120, what would the quantities demanded and supplied be? Would a shortage or surplus exist? If so, how large would the shortage or surplus be?

**54.** The computer market in recent years has seen many more computers sell at much lower prices. What shift in demand or supply is most likely to explain this outcome? Sketch a demand and supply diagram and explain your reasoning for each.
a. A rise in demand
b. A fall in demand
c. A rise in supply
d. A fall in supply

**55.** Table 3.9 illustrates the market's demand and supply for cheddar cheese. Graph the data and find the equilibrium. Next, create a table showing the change in quantity demanded or quantity supplied, and a graph of the new equilibrium, in each of the following situations:

   a.  The price of milk, a key input for cheese production, rises, so that the supply decreases by 80 pounds at every price.

   b.  A new study says that eating cheese is good for your health, so that demand increases by 20% at every price.

| Price per Pound | Qd | Qs |
| --- | --- | --- |
| $3.00 | 750 | 540 |
| $3.20 | 700 | 600 |
| **$3.40** | **650** | **650** |
| $3.60 | 620 | 700 |
| $3.80 | 600 | 720 |
| $4.00 | 590 | 730 |

**TABLE 3.9**

**56.** Table 3.10 shows the supply and demand for movie tickets in a city. Graph demand and supply and identify the equilibrium. Then calculate in a table and graph the effect of the following two changes.

   a.  Three new nightclubs open. They offer decent bands and have no cover charge, but make their money by selling food and drink. As a result, demand for movie tickets falls by six units at every price.

   b.  The city eliminates a tax that it placed on all local entertainment businesses. The result is that the quantity supplied of movies at any given price increases by 10%.

| Price per Ticket | Qd | Qs |
| --- | --- | --- |
| $5.00 | 26 | 16 |
| $6.00 | 24 | 18 |
| $7.00 | 22 | 20 |
| $8.00 | 21 | 21 |
| $9.00 | 20 | 22 |

**TABLE 3.10**

**57.** A low-income country decides to set a price ceiling on bread so it can make sure that bread is affordable to the poor. Table 3.11 provides the conditions of demand and supply. What are the equilibrium price and equilibrium quantity before the price ceiling? What will the excess demand or the shortage (that is, quantity demanded minus quantity supplied) be if the price ceiling is set at $2.40? At $2.00? At $3.60?

| Price | Qd | Qs |
|---|---|---|
| $1.60 | 9,000 | 5,000 |
| $2.00 | 8,500 | 5,500 |
| $2.40 | 8,000 | 6,400 |
| **$2.80** | **7,500** | **7,500** |
| $3.20 | 7,000 | 9,000 |
| $3.60 | 6,500 | 11,000 |
| $4.00 | 6,000 | 15,000 |

**TABLE 3.11**

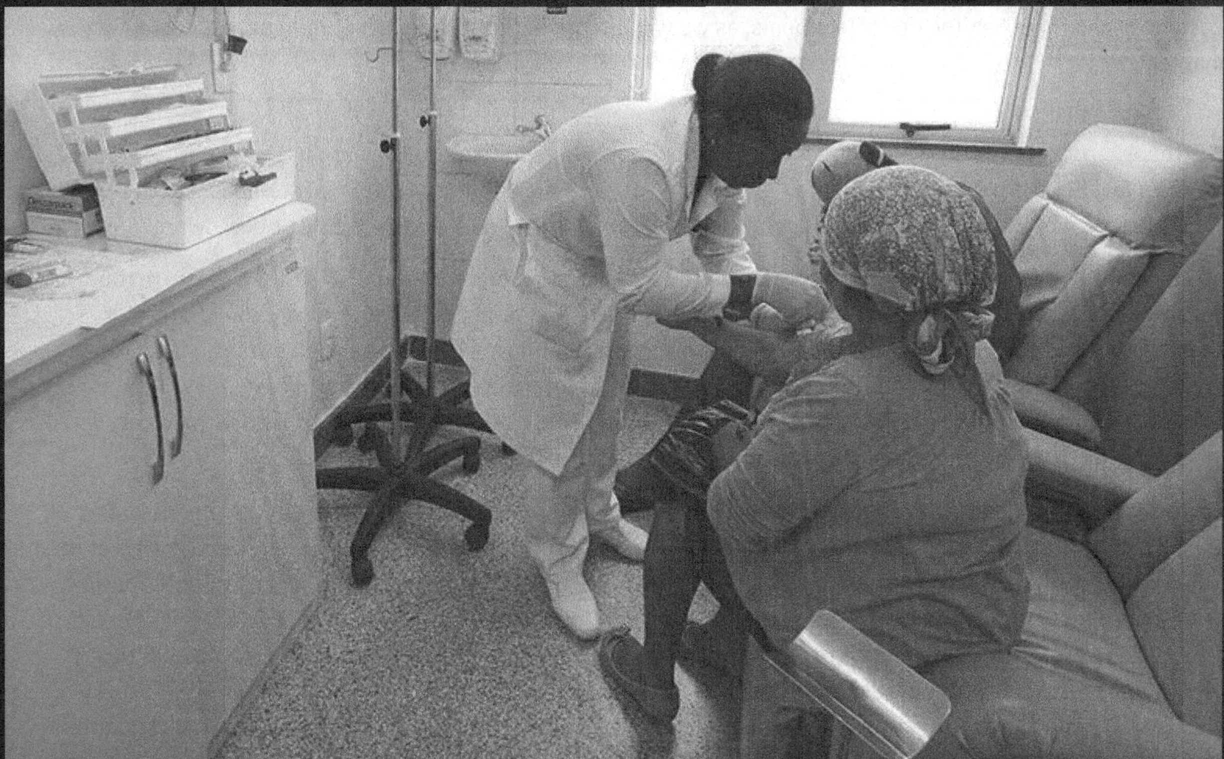

FIGURE 4.1 People often think of demand and supply in relation to goods, but labor markets, such as the nursing profession, can also apply to this analysis. (Credit: modification of "Hospital do Subúrbio" by Jaques Wagner Governador/Flickr Creative Commons, CC BY 2.0)

**CHAPTER OBJECTIVES**

In this chapter, you will learn about:

- Demand and Supply at Work in Labor Markets
- Demand and Supply in Financial Markets
- The Market System as an Efficient Mechanism for Information

## Introduction to Labor and Financial Markets

 **BRING IT HOME**

### Baby Boomers Come of Age

According to the 2020 Census, 22% of the U.S. population was 60 years old or older, which means that more than 74 million people have reached an age when they will need increased medical care.

The baby boomer population, the group born between 1946 and 1964, is comprised of more than 71 million people who have already reached retirement age or will soon reach retirement. As this population grows older, they will be faced with common healthcare issues such as heart conditions, arthritis, and Alzheimer's that may require hospitalization, long-term, or at-home nursing care. Aging baby boomers and advances in life-saving and life-extending technologies will increase the demand for healthcare and nursing. Additionally, the Affordable Care Act, which expands access to healthcare for millions of Americans, has further increased the demand.

These data tell us, as economists, that the market for healthcare professionals, and nurses in particular, will face several challenges. Our study of supply and demand will help us to analyze what might happen in the labor market for nursing and other healthcare professionals, as we will discuss in the second half of this case at the end of the chapter.

---

The theories of supply and demand do not apply just to markets for goods. They apply to any market, even markets for things we may not think of as goods and services like labor and financial services. Labor markets are markets for employees or jobs. Financial services markets are markets for saving or borrowing.

When we think about demand and supply curves in goods and services markets, it is easy to picture the demanders and suppliers: businesses produce the products and households buy them. Who are the demanders and suppliers in labor and financial service markets? In labor markets job seekers (individuals) are the suppliers of labor, while firms and other employers who hire labor are the demanders for labor. In financial markets, any individual or firm who saves contributes to the supply of money, and any entity that borrows (person, firm, or government) contributes to the demand for money.

As a college student, you most likely participate in both labor and financial markets. Employment is a fact of life for most college students: According to the National Center for Educational Statistics, in 2018 43% of full-time college students and 81% of part-time college students were employed. Most college students are also heavily involved in financial markets, primarily as borrowers. As of the 2018–19 school year, 43% of full-time undergraduate students were receiving loan aid to help finance their education, and those loans averaged $7,300 per year. Many students also borrow for other expenses, like purchasing a car. As this chapter will illustrate, we can analyze labor markets and financial markets with the same tools we use to analyze demand and supply in the goods markets.

## 4.1 Demand and Supply at Work in Labor Markets

**LEARNING OBJECTIVES**

By the end of this section, you will be able to:
- Predict shifts in the demand and supply curves of the labor market
- Explain the impact of new technology on the demand and supply curves of the labor market
- Explain price floors in the labor market such as minimum wage or a living wage

Markets for labor have demand and supply curves, just like markets for goods. The law of demand applies in labor markets this way: A higher **salary** or **wage**—that is, a higher price in the labor market—leads to a decrease in the quantity of labor demanded by employers, while a lower salary or wage leads to an increase in the quantity of labor demanded. The law of supply functions in labor markets, too: A higher price for labor leads to a higher quantity of labor supplied; a lower price leads to a lower quantity supplied.

### Equilibrium in the Labor Market

In 2020, nearly 41,000 registered nurses worked in the Minneapolis-St. Paul-Bloomington, Minnesota-Wisconsin metropolitan area, according to the BLS. They worked for a variety of employers: hospitals, doctors' offices, schools, health clinics, and nursing homes. Figure 4.2 illustrates how demand and supply determine equilibrium in this labor market. The demand and supply schedules in Table 4.1 list the quantity supplied and quantity demanded of nurses at different salaries.

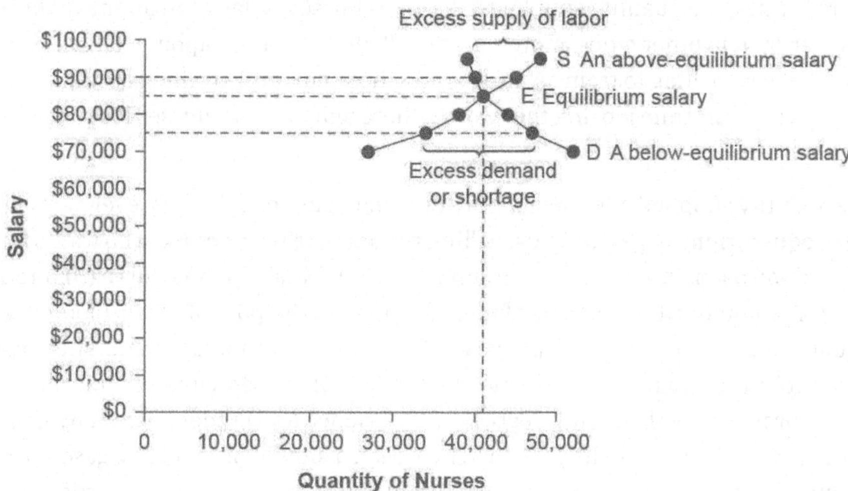


**FIGURE 4.2 Labor Market Example: Demand and Supply for Nurses in Minneapolis-St. Paul-Bloomington** The demand curve (D) of those employers who want to hire nurses intersects with the supply curve (S) of those who are qualified and willing to work as nurses at the equilibrium point (E). The equilibrium salary is $85,000 and the equilibrium quantity is 41,000 nurses. At an above-equilibrium salary of $90,000, quantity supplied increases to 45,000, but the quantity of nurses demanded at the higher pay declines to 40,000. At this above-equilibrium salary, an excess supply or surplus of nurses would exist. At a below-equilibrium salary of $75,000, quantity supplied declines to 34,000, while the quantity demanded at the lower wage increases to 47,000 nurses. At this below-equilibrium salary, excess demand or a shortage exists.

| Annual Salary | Quantity Demanded | Quantity Supplied |
| --- | --- | --- |
| $70,000 | 52,000 | 27,000 |
| $75,000 | 47,000 | 34,000 |
| $80,000 | 44,000 | 38,000 |
| $85,000 | 41,000 | 41,000 |
| $90,000 | 40,000 | 45,000 |
| $95,000 | 39,000 | 48,000 |

**TABLE 4.1 Demand and Supply of Nurses in Minneapolis-St. Paul-Bloomington**

The horizontal axis shows the quantity of nurses hired. In this example we measure labor by number of workers, but another common way to measure the quantity of labor is by the number of hours worked. The vertical axis shows the price for nurses' labor—that is, how much they are paid. In the real world, this "price" would be total labor compensation: salary plus benefits. It is not obvious, but benefits are a significant part (as high as 30 percent) of labor compensation. In this example we measure the price of labor by salary on an annual basis, although in other cases we could measure the price of labor by monthly or weekly pay, or even the wage paid per hour. As the salary for nurses rises, the quantity demanded will fall. Some hospitals and nursing homes may reduce the number of nurses they hire, or they may lay off some of their existing nurses, rather than pay them higher salaries. Employers who face higher nurses' salaries may also try to replace some nursing functions by investing in physical equipment, like computer monitoring and diagnostic systems to monitor patients, or by using lower-paid health care aides to reduce the number of nurses they need.

As the salary for nurses rises, the quantity supplied will rise. If nurses' salaries in Minneapolis-St. Paul-Bloomington are higher than in other cities, more nurses will move to Minneapolis-St. Paul-Bloomington to find jobs, more people will be willing to train as nurses, and those currently trained as nurses will be more likely to pursue nursing as a full-time job. In other words, there will be more nurses looking for jobs in the area.

At **equilibrium**, the quantity supplied and the quantity demanded are equal. Thus, every employer who wants to hire a nurse at this equilibrium wage can find a willing worker, and every nurse who wants to work at this equilibrium salary can find a job. In Figure 4.2, the supply curve (S) and demand curve (D) intersect at the equilibrium point (E). The equilibrium quantity of nurses in the Minneapolis-St. Paul-Bloomington area is 41,000, and the equilibrium salary is $86,000 per year. This example simplifies the nursing market by focusing on the "average" nurse. In reality, of course, the market for nurses actually comprises many smaller markets, like markets for nurses with varying degrees of experience and credentials. Many markets contain closely related products that differ in quality. For instance, even a simple product like gasoline comes in regular, premium, and super-premium, each with a different price. Even in such cases, discussing the average price of gasoline, like the average salary for nurses, can still be useful because it reflects what is happening in most of the submarkets.

When the price of labor is not at the equilibrium, economic incentives tend to move salaries toward the equilibrium. For example, if salaries for nurses in Minneapolis-St. Paul-Bloomington were above the equilibrium at $90,000 per year, then 43,000 people want to work as nurses, but employers want to hire only 39,000 nurses. At that above-equilibrium salary, excess supply or a surplus results. In a situation of excess supply in the **labor market**, with many applicants for every job opening, employers will have an incentive to offer lower wages than they otherwise would have. Nurses' salary will move down toward equilibrium.

In contrast, if the salary is below the equilibrium at, say, $60,000 per year, then a situation of excess demand or a shortage arises. In this case, employers encouraged by the relatively lower wage want to hire 40,000 nurses, but only 27,000 individuals want to work as nurses at that salary in Minneapolis-St. Paul-Bloomington. In response to the shortage, some employers will offer higher pay to attract the nurses. Other employers will have to match the higher pay to keep their own employees. The higher salaries will encourage more nurses to train or work in Minneapolis-St. Paul-Bloomington. Again, price and quantity in the labor market will move toward equilibrium.

## Shifts in Labor Demand

The demand curve for labor shows the quantity of labor employers wish to hire at any given salary or wage rate, under the *ceteris paribus* assumption. A change in the wage or salary will result in a change in the quantity demanded of labor. If the wage rate increases, employers will want to hire fewer employees. The quantity of labor demanded will decrease, and there will be a movement upward along the demand curve. If the wages and salaries decrease, employers are more likely to hire a greater number of workers. The quantity of labor demanded will increase, resulting in a downward movement along the demand curve.

Shifts in the demand curve for labor occur for many reasons. One key reason is that the demand for labor is based on the demand for the good or service that is produced. For example, the more new automobiles consumers demand, the greater the number of workers automakers will need to hire. Therefore the demand for labor is called a "derived demand." Here are some examples of derived demand for labor:

- The demand for chefs is dependent on the demand for restaurant meals.
- The demand for pharmacists is dependent on the demand for prescription drugs.
- The demand for attorneys is dependent on the demand for legal services.

As the demand for the goods and services increases, the demand for labor will increase, or shift to the right, to meet employers' production requirements. As the demand for the goods and services decreases, the demand for labor will decrease, or shift to the left. Table 4.2 shows that in addition to the derived demand for labor, demand can also increase or decrease (shift) in response to several factors.

| Factors | Results |
| --- | --- |
| Demand for Output | When the demand for the good produced (output) increases, both the output price and profitability increase. As a result, producers demand more labor to ramp up production. |
| Education and Training | A well-trained and educated workforce causes an increase in the demand for that labor by employers. Increased levels of productivity within the workforce will cause the demand for labor to shift to the right. If the workforce is not well-trained or educated, employers will not hire from within that labor pool, since they will need to spend a significant amount of time and money training that workforce. Demand for such will shift to the left. |
| Technology | Technology changes can act as either substitutes for or complements to labor. When technology acts as a substitute, it replaces the need for the number of workers an employer needs to hire. For example, word processing decreased the number of typists needed in the workplace. This shifted the demand curve for typists left. An increase in the availability of certain technologies may increase the demand for labor. Technology that acts as a complement to labor will increase the demand for certain types of labor, resulting in a rightward shift of the demand curve. For example, the increased use of word processing and other software has increased the demand for information technology professionals who can resolve software and hardware issues related to a firm's network. More and better technology will increase demand for skilled workers who know how to use technology to enhance workplace productivity. Those workers who do not adapt to changes in technology will experience a decrease in demand. |
| Number of Companies | An increase in the number of companies producing a given product will increase the demand for labor resulting in a shift to the right. A decrease in the number of companies producing a given product will decrease the demand for labor resulting in a shift to the left. |
| Government Regulations | Complying with government regulations can increase or decrease the demand for labor at any given wage. In the healthcare industry, government rules may require that nurses be hired to carry out certain medical procedures. This will increase the demand for nurses. Less-trained healthcare workers would be prohibited from carrying out these procedures, and the demand for these workers will shift to the left. |
| Price and Availability of Other Inputs | Labor is not the only input into the production process. For example, a salesperson at a call center needs a telephone and a computer terminal to enter data and record sales. If prices of other inputs fall, production will become more profitable and suppliers will demand more labor to increase production. This will cause a rightward shift in the demand curve for labor. The opposite is also true. Higher prices for other inputs lower demand for labor. |

**TABLE 4.2 Factors That Can Shift Demand**

## ⊘ LINK IT UP

Click here (http://openstax.org/l/Futurework) to read more about "Trends and Challenges for Work in the 21$^{st}$ Century."

## Shifts in Labor Supply

The supply of labor is upward-sloping and adheres to the law of supply: The higher the price, the greater the quantity supplied and the lower the price, the less quantity supplied. The supply curve models the tradeoff between supplying labor into the market or using time in leisure activities at every given price level. The higher the wage, the more labor is willing to work and forego leisure activities. Table 4.3 lists some of the factors that will cause the supply to increase or decrease.

| Factors | Results |
| --- | --- |
| Number of Workers | An increased number of workers will cause the supply curve to shift to the right. An increased number of workers can be due to several factors, such as immigration, increasing population, an aging population, and changing demographics. Policies that encourage immigration will increase the supply of labor, and vice versa. Population grows when birth rates exceed death rates. This eventually increases supply of labor when the former reach working age. Another example of changing demographics is more women working outside of the home, which increases the supply of labor. |
| Required Education | The more required education, the lower the supply. There is a lower supply of PhD mathematicians than of high school mathematics teachers; there is a lower supply of cardiologists than of primary care physicians; and there is a lower supply of physicians than of nurses. |
| Government Policies | Government policies can also affect the supply of labor for jobs. Alternatively, the government may support rules that set high qualifications for certain jobs: academic training, certificates or licenses, or experience. When these qualifications are made tougher, the number of qualified workers will decrease at any given wage. On the other hand, the government may also subsidize training or even reduce the required level of qualifications. For example, government might offer subsidies for nursing schools or nursing students. Such provisions would shift the supply curve of nurses to the right. In addition, government policies that change the relative desirability of working versus not working also affect the labor supply. These include unemployment benefits, maternity leave, child care benefits, and welfare policy. For example, child care benefits may increase the labor supply of working mothers. Long term unemployment benefits may discourage job searching for unemployed workers. All these policies must therefore be carefully designed to minimize any negative labor supply effects. |

**TABLE 4.3 Factors that Can Shift Supply**

A change in salary will lead to a movement along labor demand or labor supply curves, but it will not shift those curves. However, other events like those we have outlined here will cause either the demand or the supply of labor to shift, and thus will move the labor market to a new equilibrium salary and quantity.

## Technology and Wage Inequality: The Four-Step Process

Economic events can change the equilibrium salary (or wage) and quantity of labor. Consider how the wave of new information technologies, like computer and telecommunications networks, has affected low-skill and high-skill workers in the U.S. economy. From the perspective of employers who demand labor, these new technologies are often a substitute for low-skill laborers like file clerks who used to keep file cabinets full of paper records of transactions. However, the same new technologies are a complement to high-skill workers like managers, who benefit from the technological advances by having the ability to monitor more information, communicate more easily, and juggle a wider array of responsibilities. How will the new technologies affect the wages of high-skill and low-skill workers? For this question, the four-step process of analyzing how shifts in supply or demand affect a market (introduced in Demand and Supply) works in this way:

Step 1. What did the markets for low-skill labor and high-skill labor look like before the arrival of the new technologies? In Figure 4.3 (a) and Figure 4.3 (b), $S_0$ is the original supply curve for labor and $D_0$ is the original demand curve for labor in each market. In each graph, the original point of equilibrium, $E_0$, occurs at the price

$W_0$ and the quantity $Q_0$.

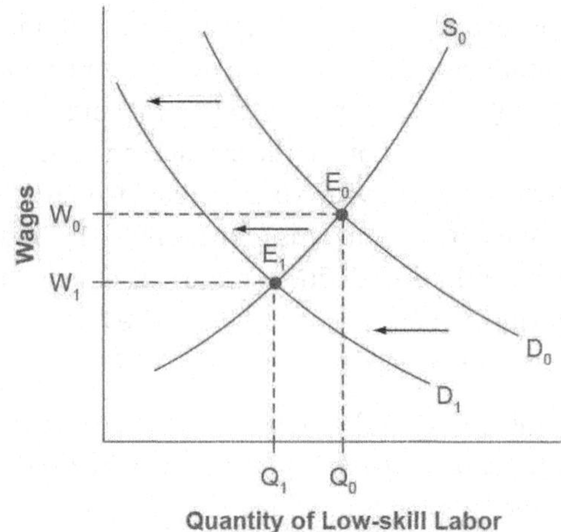


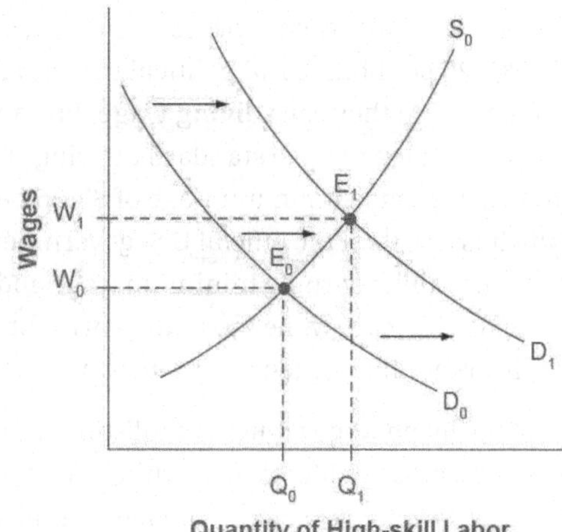


(a) Technological change and low-skill labor          (b) Technological change and high-skill labor

**FIGURE 4.3 Technology and Wages: Applying Demand and Supply** (a) The demand for low-skill labor shifts to the left when technology can do the job previously done by these workers. (b) New technologies can also increase the demand for high-skill labor in fields such as information technology and network administration.

Step 2. Does the new technology affect the supply of labor from households or the demand for labor from firms? The technology change described here affects demand for labor by firms that hire workers.

Step 3. Will the new technology increase or decrease demand? Based on the description earlier, as the substitute for low-skill labor becomes available, demand for low-skill labor will shift to the left, from $D_0$ to $D_1$. As the technology complement for high-skill labor becomes cheaper, demand for high-skill labor will shift to the right, from $D_0$ to $D_1$.

Step 4. The new equilibrium for low-skill labor, shown as point $E_1$ with price $W_1$ and quantity $Q_1$, has a lower wage and quantity hired than the original equilibrium, $E_0$. The new equilibrium for high-skill labor, shown as point $E_1$ with price $W_1$ and quantity $Q_1$, has a higher wage and quantity hired than the original equilibrium ($E_0$).

Thus, the demand and supply model predicts that the new computer and communications technologies will raise the pay of high-skill workers but reduce the pay of low-skill workers. From the 1970s to the mid-2000s, the wage gap widened between high-skill and low-skill labor. According to the National Center for Education Statistics, in 1980, for example, a college graduate earned about 30% more than a high school graduate with comparable job experience, but by 2019, a college graduate earned about 59% more than an otherwise comparable high school graduate. Many economists believe that the trend toward greater wage inequality across the U.S. economy is due to improvements in technology.

## ⊘ LINK IT UP

Visit this website (http://openstax.org/l/oldtechjobs) to read about ten tech skills that have lost relevance in today's workforce.

---

## Price Floors in the Labor Market: Living Wages and Minimum Wages

In contrast to goods and services markets, price ceilings are rare in labor markets, because rules that prevent people from earning income are not politically popular. There is one exception: boards of trustees or stockholders, as an example, propose limits on the high incomes of top business executives.

The labor market, however, presents some prominent examples of price floors, which are an attempt to increase the wages of low-paid workers. The U.S. government sets a **minimum wage**, a price floor that makes it illegal for an employer to pay employees less than a certain hourly rate. In mid-2009, the U.S. minimum wage was raised to $7.25 per hour. Local political movements in a number of U.S. cities have pushed for a higher minimum wage, which they call a **living wage**. Promoters of living wage laws maintain that the minimum wage is too low to ensure a reasonable standard of living. They base this conclusion on the calculation that, if you work 40 hours a week at a minimum wage of $7.25 per hour for 50 weeks a year, your annual income is $14,500, which is less than the official U.S. government definition of what it means for a family to be in poverty. (A family with two adults earning minimum wage and two young children will find it more cost efficient for one parent to provide childcare while the other works for income. Thus the family income would be $14,500, which is significantly lower than the federal poverty line for a family of four, which was $26,500 in 2021.)

Supporters of the living wage argue that full-time workers should be assured a high enough wage so that they can afford the essentials of life: food, clothing, shelter, and healthcare. Since Baltimore passed the first living wage law in 1994, several dozen cities enacted similar laws in the late 1990s and the 2000s. The living wage ordinances do not apply to all employers, but they have specified that all employees of the city or employees of firms that the city hires be paid at least a certain wage that is usually a few dollars per hour above the U.S. minimum wage.

Figure 4.4 illustrates the situation of a city considering a living wage law. For simplicity, we assume that there is no federal minimum wage. The wage appears on the vertical axis, because the wage is the price in the labor market. Before the passage of the living wage law, the equilibrium wage is $10 per hour and the city hires 1,200 workers at this wage. However, a group of concerned citizens persuades the city council to enact a living wage law requiring employers to pay no less than $12 per hour. In response to the higher wage, 1,600 workers look for jobs with the city. At this higher wage, the city, as an employer, is willing to hire only 700 workers. At the price floor, the quantity supplied exceeds the quantity demanded, and a surplus of labor exists in this market. For workers who continue to have a job at a higher salary, life has improved. For those who were willing to work at the old wage rate but lost their jobs with the wage increase, life has not improved. Table 4.4 shows the differences in supply and demand at different wages.

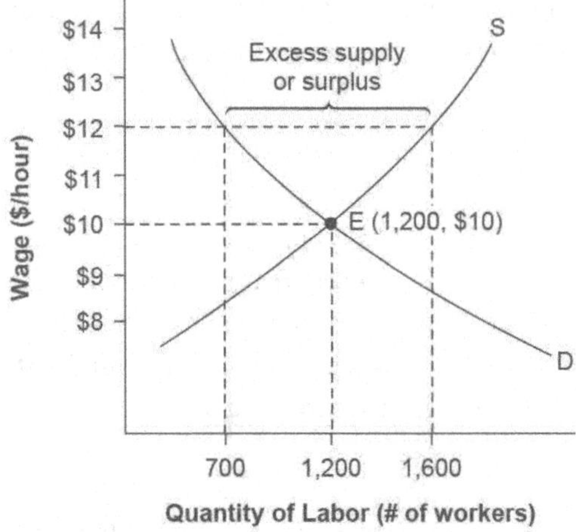


**FIGURE 4.4 A Living Wage: Example of a Price Floor** The original equilibrium in this labor market is a wage of $10/hour and a quantity of 1,200 workers, shown at point E. Imposing a wage floor at $12/hour leads to an excess supply of labor. At that wage, the quantity of labor supplied is 1,600 and the quantity of labor demanded is only 700.

| Wage | Quantity Labor Demanded | Quantity Labor Supplied |
|---|---|---|
| $8/hr | 1,900 | 500 |
| $9/hr | 1,500 | 900 |
| $10/hr | 1,200 | 1,200 |
| $11/hr | 900 | 1,400 |
| $12/hr | 700 | 1,600 |
| $13/hr | 500 | 1,800 |
| $14/hr | 400 | 1,900 |

**TABLE 4.4** Living Wage: Example of a Price Floor

## The Minimum Wage as an Example of a Price Floor

The U.S. minimum wage is a price floor that is set either very close to the equilibrium wage or even slightly below it. About 1.5% of hourly workers in the U.S. are paid the minimum wage. In other words, the vast majority of the U.S. labor force has its wages determined in the labor market, not as a result of the government price floor. However, for workers with low skills and little experience, like those without a high school diploma or teenagers, the minimum wage is quite important. In many cities, the federal minimum wage is apparently below the market price for unskilled labor, because employers offer more than the minimum wage to checkout clerks and other low-skill workers without any government prodding.

Economists have attempted to estimate how much the minimum wage reduces the quantity demanded of low-skill labor. A typical result of such studies is that a 10% increase in the minimum wage would decrease the hiring of unskilled workers by 1 to 2%, which seems a relatively small reduction. In fact, some studies have even found no effect of a higher minimum wage on employment at certain times and places—although these studies are controversial. Well-known economists Walter Williams and Thomas Sowell, who both focus on the intersections of race and economics, argue that minimum wages increase discrimination and limit economic mobility. Williams, for example, indicates that higher minimum wages would increase employment barriers for lower-skilled workers, reducing the opportunity for them to learn on the job and gain experience that would give them more choice in employment.

Let's suppose that the minimum wage lies just slightly *below* the equilibrium wage level. Wages could fluctuate according to market forces above this price floor, but they would not be allowed to move beneath the floor. In this situation, the price floor minimum wage is *nonbinding*—that is, the price floor is not determining the market outcome. Even if the minimum wage moves just a little higher, it will still have no effect on the quantity of employment in the economy, as long as it remains below the equilibrium wage. Even if the government increases the minimum wage by enough so that it rises slightly above the equilibrium wage and becomes binding, there will be only a small excess supply gap between the quantity demanded and quantity supplied.

These insights help to explain why U.S. minimum wage laws have historically had only a small impact on employment. Since the minimum wage has typically been set close to the equilibrium wage for low-skill labor and sometimes even below it, it has not had a large effect in creating an excess supply of labor. However, if the minimum wage increased dramatically—say, if it doubled to match the living wages that some U.S. cities have considered—then its impact on reducing the quantity demanded of employment would be far greater. The following Clear It Up feature describes in greater detail some of the arguments for and against changes to the minimum wage.

## CLEAR IT UP

### What's the harm in raising the minimum wage?

Because of the law of demand, a higher required wage will reduce the amount of low-skill employment either in terms of employees or in terms of work hours. Although there is controversy over the numbers, let's say for the sake of the argument that a 10% rise in the minimum wage will reduce the employment of low-skill workers by 2%. Does this outcome mean that raising the minimum wage by 10% is bad public policy? Not necessarily.

If 98% of those receiving the minimum wage have a pay increase of 10%, but 2% of those receiving the minimum wage lose their jobs, are the gains for society as a whole greater than the losses? The answer is not clear, because job losses, even for a small group, may cause more pain than modest income gains for others. For one thing, we need to consider which minimum wage workers are losing their jobs. If the 2% of minimum wage workers who lose their jobs are struggling to support families, that is one thing. If those who lose their job are high school students picking up spending money over summer vacation, that is something else.

Another complexity is that many minimum wage workers do not work full-time for an entire year. Imagine a minimum wage worker who holds different part-time jobs for a few months at a time, with bouts of unemployment in between. The worker in this situation receives the 10% raise in the minimum wage when working, but also ends up working 2% fewer hours during the year because the higher minimum wage reduces how much employers want people to work. Overall, this worker's income would rise because the 10% pay raise would more than offset the 2% fewer hours worked.

Of course, these arguments do not prove that raising the minimum wage is necessarily a good idea either. There may well be other, better public policy options for helping low-wage workers. (The Poverty and Economic Inequality chapter discusses some possibilities.) The lesson from this maze of minimum wage arguments is that complex social problems rarely have simple answers. Even those who agree on how a proposed economic policy affects quantity demanded and quantity supplied may still disagree on whether the policy is a good idea.

## 4.2 Demand and Supply in Financial Markets

**LEARNING OBJECTIVES**

By the end of this section, you will be able to:
- Identify the demanders and suppliers in a financial market
- Explain how interest rates can affect supply and demand
- Analyze the economic effects of U.S. debt in terms of domestic financial markets
- Explain the role of price ceilings and usury laws in the U.S.

United States' households, institutions, and domestic businesses saved almost $1.3 trillion in 2015. Where did that savings go and how was it used? Some of the savings ended up in banks, which in turn loaned the money to individuals or businesses that wanted to borrow money. Some was invested in private companies or loaned to government agencies that wanted to borrow money to raise funds for purposes like building roads or mass transit. Some firms reinvested their savings in their own businesses.

In this section, we will determine how the demand and supply model links those who wish to supply **financial capital** (i.e., savings) with those who demand financial capital (i.e., borrowing). Those who save money (or make financial investments, which is the same thing), whether individuals or businesses, are on the supply side of the financial market. Those who borrow money are on the demand side of the financial market. For a more detailed treatment of the different kinds of financial investments like bank accounts, stocks and bonds, see the Financial Markets chapter.

### Who Demands and Who Supplies in Financial Markets?

In any market, the price is what suppliers receive and what demanders pay. In financial markets, those who supply financial capital through saving expect to receive a rate of return, while those who demand financial capital by receiving funds expect to pay a rate of return. This rate of return can come in a variety of forms, depending on the type of investment.

The simplest example of a rate of return is the **interest rate**. For example, when you supply money into a savings account at a bank, you receive interest on your deposit. The interest the bank pays you as a percent of your deposits is the interest rate. Similarly, if you demand a loan to buy a car or a computer, you will need to pay interest on the money you borrow.

Let's consider the market for borrowing money with credit cards. In 2021, almost 200 million Americans were cardholders. Credit cards allow you to borrow money from the card's issuer, and pay back the borrowed amount plus interest, although most allow you a period of time in which you can repay the loan without paying interest. A typical credit card interest rate ranges from 12% to 18% per year. In May 2021, Americans had about $807 billion outstanding in credit card debts. As of 2021, just over 45% of American families carried some credit card debt. Let's say that, on average, the annual interest rate for credit card borrowing is 15% per year. Thus, Americans pay tens of billions of dollars every year in interest on their credit cards—plus basic fees for the credit card or fees for late payments.

Figure 4.5 illustrates demand and supply in the financial market for credit cards. The horizontal axis of the financial market shows the quantity of money loaned or borrowed in this market. The vertical or price axis shows the rate of return, which in the case of credit card borrowing we can measure with an interest rate. Table 4.5 shows the quantity of financial capital that consumers demand at various interest rates and the quantity that credit card firms (often banks) are willing to supply.

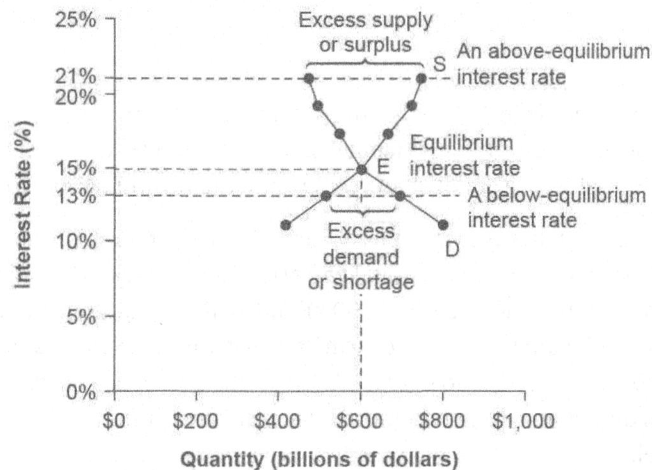


**FIGURE 4.5 Demand and Supply for Borrowing Money with Credit Cards** In this market for credit card borrowing, the demand curve (D) for borrowing financial capital intersects the supply curve (S) for lending financial capital at equilibrium E. At the equilibrium, the interest rate (the "price" in this market) is 15% and the quantity of financial capital loaned and borrowed is $600 billion. The equilibrium price is where the quantity demanded and the quantity supplied are equal. At an above-equilibrium interest rate like 21%, the quantity of financial capital supplied would increase to $750 billion, but the quantity demanded would decrease to $480 billion. At a below-equilibrium interest rate like 13%, the quantity of financial capital demanded would increase to $700 billion, but the quantity of financial capital supplied would decrease to $510 billion.

| Interest Rate (%) | Quantity of Financial Capital Demanded (Borrowing) ($ billions) | Quantity of Financial Capital Supplied (Lending) ($ billions) |
|---|---|---|
| 11 | $800 | $420 |
| 13 | $700 | $510 |
| 15 | $600 | $600 |
| 17 | $550 | $660 |
| 19 | $500 | $720 |
| 21 | $480 | $750 |

**TABLE 4.5** Demand and Supply for Borrowing Money with Credit Cards

The laws of demand and supply continue to apply in the financial markets. According to the **law of demand**, a higher rate of return (that is, a higher price) will decrease the quantity demanded. As the interest rate rises, consumers will reduce the quantity that they borrow. According to the law of supply, a higher price increases the quantity supplied. Consequently, as the interest rate paid on credit card borrowing rises, more firms will be eager to issue credit cards and to encourage customers to use them. Conversely, if the interest rate on credit cards falls, the quantity of financial capital supplied in the credit card market will decrease and the quantity demanded will increase.

### Equilibrium in Financial Markets

In the financial market for credit cards in Figure 4.5, the supply curve (S) and the demand curve (D) cross at the equilibrium point (E). The equilibrium occurs at an interest rate of 15%, where the quantity of funds demanded and the quantity supplied are equal at an equilibrium quantity of $600 billion.

If the interest rate (remember, this measures the "price" in the financial market) is above the equilibrium level, then an excess supply, or a surplus, of financial capital will arise in this market. For example, at an interest rate of 21%, the quantity of funds supplied increases to $750 billion, while the quantity demanded decreases to $480 billion. At this above-equilibrium interest rate, firms are eager to supply loans to credit card borrowers, but relatively few people or businesses wish to borrow. As a result, some credit card firms will lower the interest rates (or other fees) they charge to attract more business. This strategy will push the interest rate down toward the equilibrium level.

If the interest rate is below the equilibrium, then excess demand or a shortage of funds occurs in this market. At an interest rate of 13%, the quantity of funds credit card borrowers demand increases to $700 billion, but the quantity credit card firms are willing to supply is only $510 billion. In this situation, credit card firms will perceive that they are overloaded with eager borrowers and conclude that they have an opportunity to raise interest rates or fees. The interest rate will face economic pressures to creep up toward the equilibrium level.

The FRED database publishes some two dozen measures of interest rates, including interest rates on credit cards, automobile loans, personal loans, mortgage loans, and more. You can find these at the FRED website (https://openstax.org/l/FRED_stlouis).

### Shifts in Demand and Supply in Financial Markets

Those who supply financial capital face two broad decisions: how much to save, and how to divide up their savings among different forms of financial investments. We will discuss each of these in turn.

Participants in financial markets must decide when they prefer to consume goods: now or in the future.

Economists call this **intertemporal decision making** because it involves decisions across time. Unlike a decision about what to buy from the grocery store, people make investment or savings decisions across a period of time, sometimes a long period.

Most workers save for retirement because their income in the present is greater than their needs, while the opposite will be true once they retire. Thus, they save today and supply financial markets. If their income increases, they save more. If their perceived situation in the future changes, they change the amount of their saving. For example, there is some evidence that Social Security, the program that workers pay into in order to qualify for government checks after retirement, has tended to reduce the quantity of financial capital that workers save. If this is true, Social Security has shifted the supply of financial capital at any interest rate to the left.

By contrast, many college students need money today when their income is low (or nonexistent) to pay their college expenses. As a result, they borrow today and demand from financial markets. Once they graduate and become employed, they will pay back the loans. Individuals borrow money to purchase homes or cars. A business seeks financial investment so that it has the funds to build a factory or invest in a research and development project that will not pay off for five years, ten years, or even more. Thus, when consumers and businesses have greater confidence that they will be able to repay in the future, the quantity demanded of financial capital at any given interest rate will shift to the right.

For example, in the technology boom of the late 1990s, many businesses became extremely confident that investments in new technology would have a high rate of return, and their demand for financial capital shifted to the right. Conversely, during the 2008 and 2009 Great Recession, their demand for financial capital at any given interest rate shifted to the left.

To this point, we have been looking at saving in total. Now let us consider what affects saving in different types of financial investments. In deciding between different forms of financial investments, suppliers of financial capital will have to consider the rates of return and the risks involved. Rate of return is a positive attribute of investments, but risk is a negative. If Investment A becomes more risky, or the return diminishes, then savers will shift their funds to Investment B—and the supply curve of financial capital for Investment A will shift back to the left while the supply curve of capital for Investment B shifts to the right.

### The United States as a Global Borrower

In the global economy, trillions of dollars of financial investment cross national borders every year. In the early 2000s, financial investors from foreign countries were investing several hundred billion dollars per year more in the U.S. economy than U.S. financial investors were investing abroad. The following Work It Out deals with one of the macroeconomic concerns for the U.S. economy in recent years.

WORK IT OUT

#### The Effect of Growing U.S. Debt

Imagine that foreign investors viewed the U.S. economy as a less desirable place to put their money because of fears about the growth of the U.S. public debt. Using the four-step process for analyzing how changes in supply and demand affect equilibrium outcomes, how would increased U.S. public debt affect the equilibrium price and quantity for capital in U.S. financial markets?

Step 1. Draw a diagram showing demand and supply for financial capital that represents the original scenario in which foreign investors are pouring money into the U.S. economy. Figure 4.6 shows a demand curve, D, and a supply curve, S, where the supply of capital includes the funds arriving from foreign investors. The original equilibrium $E_0$ occurs at interest rate $R_0$ and quantity of financial investment $Q_0$.

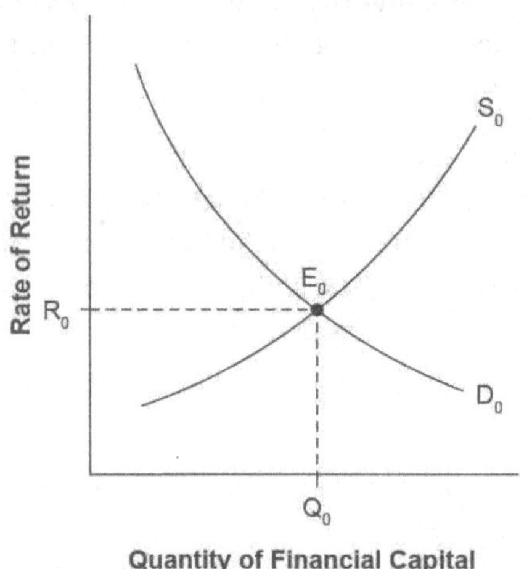



**FIGURE 4.6 The United States as a Global Borrower Before U.S. Debt Uncertainty** The graph shows the demand for financial capital from and supply of financial capital into the U.S. financial markets by the foreign sector before the increase in uncertainty regarding U.S. public debt. The original equilibrium ($E_0$) occurs at an equilibrium rate of return ($R_0$) and the equilibrium quantity is at $Q_0$.

Step 2. Will the diminished confidence in the U.S. economy as a place to invest affect demand or supply of financial capital? Yes, it will affect supply. Many foreign investors look to the U.S. financial markets to store their money in safe financial vehicles with low risk and stable returns. Diminished confidence means U.S. financial assets will be seen as more risky.

Step 3. Will supply increase or decrease? When the enthusiasm of foreign investors' for investing their money in the U.S. economy diminishes, the supply of financial capital shifts to the left. Figure 4.7 shows the supply curve shift from $S_0$ to $S_1$.

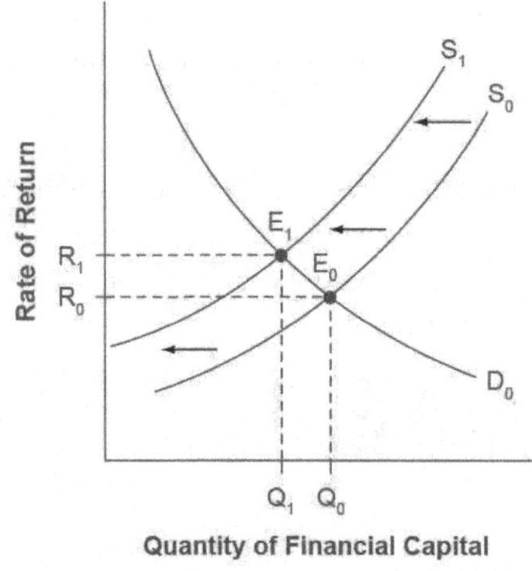



**FIGURE 4.7 The United States as a Global Borrower Before and After U.S. Debt Uncertainty** The graph shows the demand for financial capital and supply of financial capital into the U.S. financial markets by the foreign sector before and after the increase in uncertainty regarding U.S. public debt. The original equilibrium ($E_0$) occurs at an equilibrium rate of return ($R_0$) and the equilibrium quantity is at $Q_0$.

Step 4. Thus, foreign investors' diminished enthusiasm leads to a new equilibrium, $E_1$, which occurs at the higher interest rate, $R_1$, and the lower quantity of financial investment, $Q_1$. In short, U.S. borrowers will have to pay more interest on their borrowing.

The economy has experienced an enormous inflow of foreign capital. According to the U.S. Bureau of Economic Analysis, by the third quarter of 2021, U.S. investors had accumulated $34.45 trillion of foreign assets, but foreign investors owned a total of $50.53 trillion of U.S. assets. If foreign investors were to pull their money out of the U.S. economy and invest elsewhere in the world, the result could be a significantly lower quantity of financial investment in the United States, available only at a higher interest rate. This reduced inflow of foreign financial investment could impose hardship on U.S. consumers and firms interested in borrowing.

In a modern, developed economy, financial capital often moves invisibly through electronic transfers between one bank account and another. Yet we can analyze these flows of funds with the same tools of demand and supply as markets for goods or labor.

## Price Ceilings in Financial Markets: Usury Laws

As we noted earlier, about 200 million Americans own credit cards, and their interest payments and fees total tens of billions of dollars each year. It is little wonder that political pressures sometimes arise for setting limits on the interest rates or fees that credit card companies charge. The firms that issue credit cards, including banks, oil companies, phone companies, and retail stores, respond that the higher interest rates are necessary to cover the losses created by those who borrow on their credit cards and who do not repay on time or at all. These companies also point out that cardholders can avoid paying interest if they pay their bills on time.

Consider the credit card market as Figure 4.8 illustrates. In this financial market, the vertical axis shows the interest rate (which is the price in the financial market). Demanders in the credit card market are households and businesses. Suppliers are the companies that issue credit cards. This figure does not use specific numbers, which would be hypothetical in any case, but instead focuses on the underlying economic relationships. Imagine a law imposes a price ceiling that holds the interest rate charged on credit cards at the rate Rc, which lies below the interest rate $R_0$ that would otherwise have prevailed in the market. The horizontal dashed line at interest rate $R_c$ in Figure 4.8 shows the price ceiling. The demand and supply model predicts that at the lower price ceiling interest rate, the quantity demanded of credit card debt will increase from its original level of $Q_0$ to Qd; however, the quantity supplied of credit card debt will decrease from the original $Q_0$ to Qs. At the price ceiling (Rc), quantity demanded will exceed quantity supplied. Consequently, a number of people who want to have credit cards and are willing to pay the prevailing interest rate will find that companies are unwilling to issue cards to them. The result will be a credit shortage.

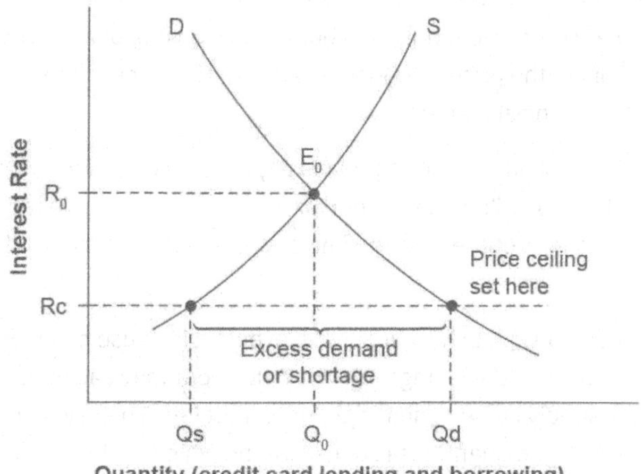


FIGURE 4.8 Credit Card Interest Rates: Another Price Ceiling Example The original intersection of demand D and supply S occurs at equilibrium $E_0$. However, a price ceiling is set at the interest rate Rc, below the equilibrium interest rate $R_0$, and so the interest rate cannot adjust upward to the equilibrium. At the price ceiling, the quantity demanded, Qd, exceeds the quantity supplied, Qs. There is excess demand, also called a shortage.

Many states do have **usury laws**, which impose an upper limit on the interest rate that lenders can charge. However, in many cases these upper limits are well above the market interest rate. For example, if the interest rate is not allowed to rise above 30% per year, it can still fluctuate below that level according to market forces. A price ceiling that is set at a relatively high level is nonbinding, and it will have no practical effect unless the equilibrium price soars high enough to exceed the price ceiling.

## 4.3 The Market System as an Efficient Mechanism for Information

### LEARNING OBJECTIVES

By the end of this section, you will be able to:
- Apply demand and supply models to analyze prices and quantities
- Explain the effects of price controls on the equilibrium of prices and quantities

Prices exist in markets for goods and services, for labor, and for financial capital. In all of these markets, prices serve as a remarkable social mechanism for collecting, combining, and transmitting information that is relevant to the market—namely, the relationship between demand and supply—and then serving as messengers to convey that information to buyers and sellers. In a market-oriented economy, no government agency or guiding intelligence oversees the set of responses and interconnections that result from a change in price. Instead, each consumer reacts according to that person's preferences and budget set, and each profit-seeking producer reacts to the impact on its expected profits. The following Clear It Up feature examines the **demand and supply models**.

 **CLEAR IT UP**

### Why are demand and supply curves important?

The demand and supply model is the second fundamental diagram for this course. (The opportunity set model that we introduced in the Choice in a World of Scarcity chapter was the first.) Just as it would be foolish to try to learn the arithmetic of long division by memorizing every possible combination of numbers that can be divided by each other, it would be foolish to try to memorize every specific example of demand and supply in this chapter, this textbook, or this course. Demand and supply is not primarily a list of examples. It is a model to analyze prices and quantities. Even though demand and supply diagrams have many labels, they are fundamentally the same in their logic. Your goal should be to understand the underlying model so you can use it to analyze *any* market.

Figure 4.9 displays a generic demand and supply curve. The horizontal axis shows the different measures of quantity: a quantity of a good or service, or a quantity of labor for a given job, or a quantity of financial capital. The vertical axis shows a measure of price: the price of a good or service, the wage in the labor market, or the rate of return (like the interest rate) in the financial market.

The demand and supply model can explain the existing levels of prices, wages, and rates of return. To carry out such an analysis, think about the quantity that will be demanded at each price and the quantity that will be supplied at each price—that is, think about the shape of the demand and supply curves—and how these forces will combine to produce equilibrium.

We can also use demand and supply to explain how economic events will cause changes in prices, wages, and rates of return. There are only four possibilities: the change in any single event may cause the demand curve to shift right or to shift left, or it may cause the supply curve to shift right or to shift left. The key to analyzing the effect of an economic event on equilibrium prices and quantities is to determine which of these four possibilities occurred. The way to do this correctly is to think back to the list of factors that shift the demand and supply curves. Note that if more than one variable is changing at the same time, the overall impact will depend on the degree of the shifts. When there are multiple variables, economists isolate each change and analyze it independently.

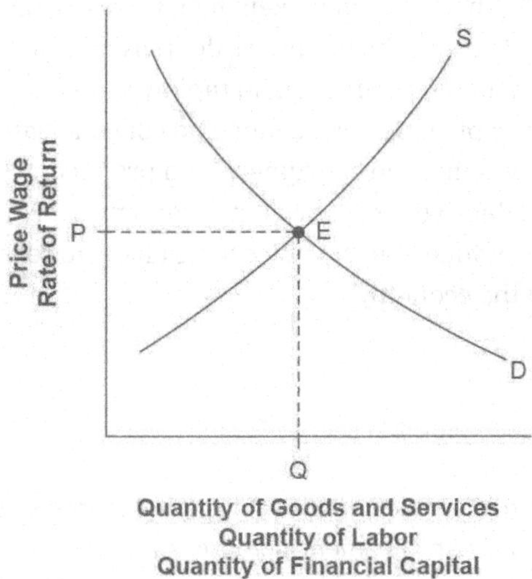


**FIGURE 4.9 Demand and Supply Curves** The figure displays a generic demand and supply curve. The horizontal axis shows the different measures of quantity: a quantity of a good or service, a quantity of labor for a given job, or a quantity of financial capital. The vertical axis shows a measure of price: the price of a good or service, the wage in the labor market, or the rate of return (like the interest rate) in the financial market. We can use the demand and supply curves explain how economic events will cause changes in prices, wages, and rates of return.

An increase in the price of some product signals consumers that there is a shortage; therefore, they may want to economize on buying this product. For example, if you are thinking about taking a plane trip to Hawaii, but the ticket turns out to be expensive during the week you intend to go, you might consider other weeks when the ticket might be cheaper. The price could be high because you were planning to travel during a holiday when demand for traveling is high. Maybe the cost of an input like jet fuel increased or the airline has raised the price temporarily to see how many people are willing to pay it. Perhaps all of these factors are present at the same time. You do not need to analyze the market and break down the price change into its underlying factors. You just have to look at the ticket price and decide whether and when to fly.

In the same way, price changes provide useful information to producers. Imagine the situation of a farmer who grows oats and learns that the price of oats has risen. The higher price could be due to an increase in demand caused by a new scientific study proclaiming that eating oats is especially healthful. Perhaps the price of a substitute grain, like corn, has risen, and people have responded by buying more oats. The oat farmer does not need to know the details. The farmer only needs to know that the price of oats has risen and that it will be profitable to expand production as a result.

The actions of individual consumers and producers as they react to prices overlap and interlock in markets for goods, labor, and financial capital. A change in any single market is transmitted through these multiple interconnections to other markets. The vision of the role of flexible prices helping markets to reach equilibrium and linking different markets together helps to explain why price controls can be so counterproductive. Price controls are government laws that serve to regulate prices rather than allow the various markets to determine prices. There is an old proverb: "Don't kill the messenger." In ancient times, messengers carried information between distant cities and kingdoms. When they brought bad news, there was an emotional impulse to kill the messenger. However, killing the messenger did not kill the bad news. Moreover, killing the messenger had an undesirable side effect: Other messengers would refuse to bring news to that city or kingdom, depriving its citizens of vital information.

Those who seek price controls are trying to kill the messenger—or at least to stifle an unwelcome message that prices are bringing about the equilibrium level of price and quantity. However, price controls do nothing to affect the underlying forces of demand and supply, and this can have serious repercussions. During China's

"Great Leap Forward" in the late 1950s, the government kept food prices artificially low, with the result that 30 to 40 million people died of starvation because the low prices depressed farm production. This was communist party leader Mao Zedong's social and economic campaign to rapidly transform the country from an agrarian economy to a socialist society through rapid industrialization and collectivization. Changes in demand and supply will continue to reveal themselves through consumers' and producers' behavior. Immobilizing the price messenger through price controls will deprive everyone in the economy of critical information. Without this information, it becomes difficult for everyone—buyers and sellers alike—to react in a flexible and appropriate manner as changes occur throughout the economy.

 **BRING IT HOME**

### Baby Boomers Come of Age

The theory of supply and demand can explain what happens in the labor markets and suggests that the demand for nurses will increase as healthcare needs of baby boomers increase, as Figure 4.10 shows. The impact of that increase will result in an average salary higher than the $75,330 earned in 2020 referenced in the first part of this case. The new equilibrium ($E_1$) will be at the new equilibrium price ($Pe_1$).Equilibrium quantity will also increase from $Qe_0$ to $Qe_1$.

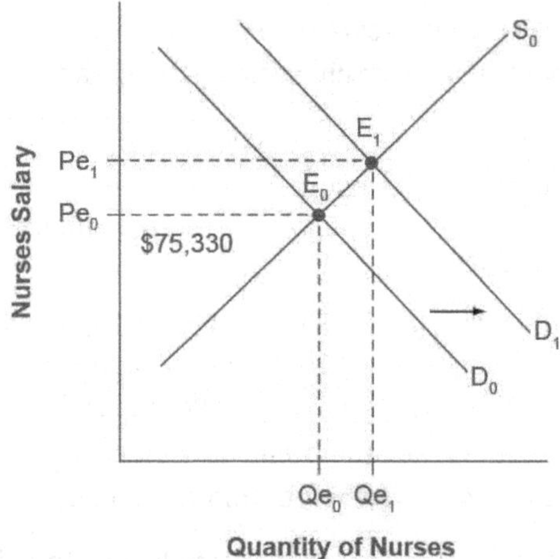


**FIGURE 4.10 Impact of Increasing Demand for Nurses 2020–2030** In 2020, the median salary for nurses was $75,330. As demand for services increases, the demand curve shifts to the right (from $D_0$ to $D_1$) and the equilibrium quantity of nurses increases from $Qe_0$ to $Qe_1$. The equilibrium salary increases from $Pe_0$ to $Pe_1$.

Suppose that as the demand for nurses increases, the supply shrinks due to an increasing number of nurses entering retirement and increases in the tuition of nursing degrees. The leftward shift of the supply curve in Figure 4.11 captures the impact of a decreasing supply of nurses. The shifts in the two curves result in higher salaries for nurses, but the overall impact on the quantity of nurses is uncertain, as it depends on the relative shifts of supply and demand.

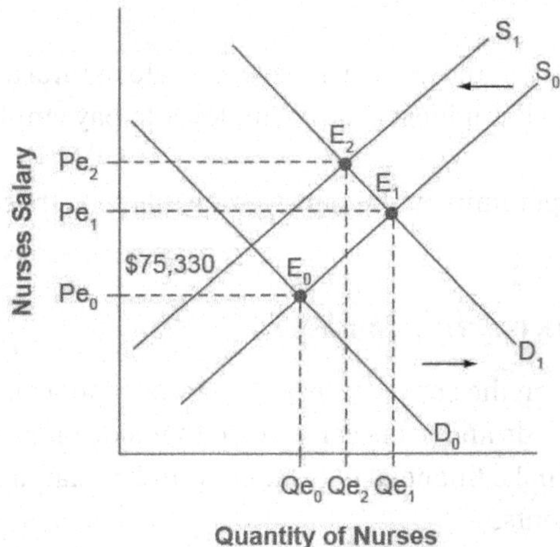



**FIGURE 4.11 Impact of Decreasing Supply of Nurses between 2020 and 2030** The increase in demand for nurses shown in Figure 4.10 leads to both higher prices and higher quantities demanded. As nurses retire from the work force, the supply of nurses decreases, causing a leftward shift in the supply curve and higher salaries for nurses at $Pe_2$. The net effect on the equilibrium quantity of nurses is uncertain, which in this representation is less than $Qe_1$, but more than the initial $Qe_0$.

While we do not know if the number of nurses will increase or decrease relative to their initial employment, we know they will have higher salaries.

## Key Terms

**interest rate** the "price" of borrowing in the financial market; a rate of return on an investment
**minimum wage** a price floor that makes it illegal for an employer to pay employees less than a certain hourly
rate
**usury laws** laws that impose an upper limit on the interest rate that lenders can charge

## Key Concepts and Summary

### 4.1 Demand and Supply at Work in Labor Markets

In the labor market, households are on the supply side of the market and firms are on the demand side. In the market for financial capital, households and firms can be on either side of the market: they are suppliers of financial capital when they save or make financial investments, and demanders of financial capital when they borrow or receive financial investments.

In the demand and supply analysis of labor markets, we can measure the price by the annual salary or hourly wage received. We can measure the quantity of labor various ways, like number of workers or the number of hours worked.

Factors that can shift the demand curve for labor include: a change in the quantity demanded of the product that the labor produces; a change in the production process that uses more or less labor; and a change in government policy that affects the quantity of labor that firms wish to hire at a given wage. Demand can also increase or decrease (shift) in response to: workers' level of education and training, technology, the number of companies, and availability and price of other inputs.

The main factors that can shift the supply curve for labor are: how desirable a job appears to workers relative to the alternatives, government policy that either restricts or encourages the quantity of workers trained for the job, the number of workers in the economy, and required education.

### 4.2 Demand and Supply in Financial Markets

In the demand and supply analysis of financial markets, the "price" is the rate of return or the interest rate received. We measure the quantity by the money that flows from those who supply financial capital to those who demand it.

Two factors can shift the supply of financial capital to a certain investment: if people want to alter their existing levels of consumption, and if the riskiness or return on one investment changes relative to other investments. Factors that can shift demand for capital include business confidence and consumer confidence in the future—since financial investments received in the present are typically repaid in the future.

### 4.3 The Market System as an Efficient Mechanism for Information

The market price system provides a highly efficient mechanism for disseminating information about relative scarcities of goods, services, labor, and financial capital. Market participants do not need to know why prices have changed, only that the changes require them to revisit previous decisions they made about supply and demand. Price controls hide information about the true scarcity of products and thereby cause misallocation of resources.

## Self-Check Questions

1. In the labor market, what causes a movement along the demand curve? What causes a shift in the demand curve?

2. In the labor market, what causes a movement along the supply curve? What causes a shift in the supply curve?

3. Why is a living wage considered a price floor? Does imposing a living wage have the same outcome as a minimum wage?

4. In the financial market, what causes a movement along the demand curve? What causes a shift in the demand curve?

5. In the financial market, what causes a movement along the supply curve? What causes a shift in the supply curve?

6. If a usury law limits interest rates to no more than 35%, what would the likely impact be on the amount of loans made and interest rates paid?

7. Which of the following changes in the financial market will lead to a decline in interest rates:
   a. a rise in demand
   b. a fall in demand
   c. a rise in supply
   d. a fall in supply

8. Which of the following changes in the financial market will lead to an increase in the quantity of loans made and received:
   a. a rise in demand
   b. a fall in demand
   c. a rise in supply
   d. a fall in supply

9. Identify the most accurate statement. A price floor will have the largest effect if it is set:
   a. substantially above the equilibrium price
   b. slightly above the equilibrium price
   c. slightly below the equilibrium price
   d. substantially below the equilibrium price

   Sketch all four of these possibilities on a demand and supply diagram to illustrate your answer.

10. A price ceiling will have the largest effect:
   a. substantially below the equilibrium price
   b. slightly below the equilibrium price
   c. substantially above the equilibrium price
   d. slightly above the equilibrium price

   Sketch all four of these possibilities on a demand and supply diagram to illustrate your answer.

11. Select the correct answer. A price floor will usually shift:
   a. demand
   b. supply
   c. both
   d. neither

   Illustrate your answer with a diagram.

12. Select the correct answer. A price ceiling will usually shift:
   a. demand
   b. supply
   c. both
   d. neither

## Review Questions

**13.** What is the "price" commonly called in the labor market?

**14.** Are households demanders or suppliers in the goods market? Are firms demanders or suppliers in the goods market? What about the labor market and the financial market?

**15.** Name some factors that can cause a shift in the demand curve in labor markets.

**16.** Name some factors that can cause a shift in the supply curve in labor markets.

**17.** How do economists define equilibrium in financial markets?

**18.** What would be a sign of a shortage in financial markets?

**19.** Would usury laws help or hinder resolution of a shortage in financial markets?

**20.** Whether the product market or the labor market, what happens to the equilibrium price and quantity for each of the four possibilities: increase in demand, decrease in demand, increase in supply, and decrease in supply.

## Critical Thinking Questions

**21.** Other than the demand for labor, what would be another example of a "derived demand?"

**22.** Suppose that a 5% increase in the minimum wage causes a 5% reduction in employment. How would this affect employers and how would it affect workers? In your opinion, would this be a good policy?

**23.** Under what circumstances would a minimum wage be a nonbinding price floor? Under what circumstances would a living wage be a binding price floor?

**24.** Suppose the U.S. economy began to grow more rapidly than other countries in the world. What would be the likely impact on U.S. financial markets as part of the global economy?

**25.** If the government imposed a federal interest rate ceiling of 20% on all loans, who would gain and who would lose?

**26.** Why are the factors that shift the demand for a product different from the factors that shift the demand for labor? Why are the factors that shift the supply of a product different from those that shift the supply of labor?

**27.** During a discussion several years ago on building a pipeline to Alaska to carry natural gas, the U.S. Senate passed a bill stipulating that there should be a guaranteed minimum price for the natural gas that would flow through the pipeline. The thinking behind the bill was that if private firms had a guaranteed price for their natural gas, they would be more willing to drill for gas and to pay to build the pipeline.
   a. Using the demand and supply framework, predict the effects of this price floor on the price, quantity demanded, and quantity supplied.
   b. With the enactment of this price floor for natural gas, what are some of the likely unintended consequences in the market?
   c. Suggest some policies other than the price floor that the government can pursue if it wishes to encourage drilling for natural gas and for a new pipeline in Alaska.

# Problems

**28.** Identify each of the following as involving either demand or supply. Draw a circular flow diagram and label the flows A through F. (Some choices can be on both sides of the goods market.)
   a.  Households in the labor market
   b.  Firms in the goods market
   c.  Firms in the financial market
   d.  Households in the goods market
   e.  Firms in the labor market
   f.  Households in the financial market

**29.** Predict how each of the following events will raise or lower the equilibrium wage and quantity of oil workers in Texas. In each case, sketch a demand and supply diagram to illustrate your answer.
   a.  The price of oil rises.
   b.  New oil-drilling equipment is invented that is cheap and requires few workers to run.
   c.  Several major companies that do not drill oil open factories in Texas, offering many well-paid jobs outside the oil industry.
   d.  Government imposes costly new regulations to make oil-drilling a safer job.

**30.** Predict how each of the following economic changes will affect the equilibrium price and quantity in the financial market for home loans. Sketch a demand and supply diagram to support your answers.
   a.  The number of people at the most common ages for home-buying increases.
   b.  People gain confidence that the economy is growing and that their jobs are secure.
   c.  Banks that have made home loans find that a larger number of people than they expected are not repaying those loans.
   d.  Because of a threat of a war, people become uncertain about their economic future.
   e.  The overall level of saving in the economy diminishes.
   f.  The federal government changes its bank regulations in a way that makes it cheaper and easier for banks to make home loans.

**31.** Table 4.6 shows the amount of savings and borrowing in a market for loans to purchase homes, measured in millions of dollars, at various interest rates. What is the equilibrium interest rate and quantity in the capital financial market? How can you tell? Now, imagine that because of a shift in the perceptions of foreign investors, the supply curve shifts so that there will be $10 million less supplied at every interest rate. Calculate the new equilibrium interest rate and quantity, and explain why the direction of the interest rate shift makes intuitive sense.

| Interest Rate | Qs | Qd |
|---|---|---|
| 5% | 130 | 170 |
| 6% | 135 | 150 |
| 7% | 140 | 140 |
| 8% | 145 | 135 |
| 9% | 150 | 125 |
| 10% | 155 | 110 |

**TABLE 4.6**

**32.** Imagine that to preserve the traditional way of life in small fishing villages, a government decides to impose a price floor that will guarantee all fishermen a certain price for their catch.
 a. Using the demand and supply framework, predict the effects on the price, quantity demanded, and quantity supplied.
 b. With the enactment of this price floor for fish, what are some of the likely unintended consequences in the market?
 c. Suggest some policies other than the price floor to make it possible for small fishing villages to continue.

**33.** What happens to the price and the quantity bought and sold in the cocoa market if countries producing cocoa experience a drought and a new study is released demonstrating the health benefits of cocoa? Illustrate your answer with a demand and supply graph.

FIGURE 5.1 **On-Demand Media Pricing** Many on-demand Internet streaming media providers, such as Netflix, have introduced tiered pricing for levels of access to services, begging the question, how will these prices affect buyer's purchasing choices? (Credit: modification of "160906_FF_CreditCardAgreements" by kdiwavvou/Flickr, Public Domain)

**CHAPTER OBJECTIVES**

In this chapter, you will learn about:

- Price Elasticity of Demand and Price Elasticity of Supply
- Polar Cases of Elasticity and Constant Elasticity
- Elasticity and Pricing
- Elasticity in Areas Other Than Price

## Introduction to Elasticity

 **BRING IT HOME**

### That Will Be How Much?

Imagine going to your favorite coffee shop and having the waiter inform you the pricing has changed. Instead of $3 for a cup of coffee, you will now be charged $2 for coffee, $1 for creamer, and $1 for your choice of sweetener. If you pay your usual $3 for a cup of coffee, you must choose between creamer and sweetener. If you want both, you now face an extra charge of $1. Sound absurd? Well, that is similar to the situation Netflix customers found themselves in—they faced a 60% price hike to retain the same service in 2011.

In early 2011, Netflix consumers paid about $10 a month for a package consisting of streaming video and DVD rentals. In July 2011, the company announced a packaging change. Customers wishing to retain both streaming video and DVD rental would be charged $15.98 per month, a price increase of about 60%. In 2014, Netflix also raised its streaming video subscription price from $7.99 to $8.99 per month for new U.S. customers. The company also changed its policy of 4K streaming content from $9.00 to $12.00 per month that year.

How would customers of the 18-year-old firm react? Would they abandon Netflix? Would the ease of access to other venues make a difference in how consumers responded to the Netflix price change? At the time, Netflix had few competitors; in the intervening years, the field has grown to ten major competitors and nearly 200 smaller ones. Is that likely to have a greater impact than the price changes? We will explore the answers to those questions in this chapter, which focuses on the change in quantity with respect to a change in price, a concept economists call elasticity.

Anyone who has studied economics knows the law of demand: a higher price will lead to a lower quantity demanded. What you may not know is how much lower the quantity demanded will be. Similarly, the law of supply states that a higher price will lead to a higher quantity supplied. The question is: How much higher? This chapter will explain how to answer these questions and why they are critically important in the real world.

To find answers to these questions, we need to understand the concept of elasticity. **Elasticity** is an economics concept that measures responsiveness of one variable to changes in another variable. Suppose you drop two items from a second-floor balcony. The first item is a tennis ball. The second item is a brick. Which will bounce higher? Obviously, the tennis ball. We would say that the tennis ball has greater elasticity.

Consider an economic example. Cigarette taxes are an example of a "sin tax," a tax on something that is bad for you, like alcohol. Governments tax cigarettes at the state and national levels. As of 2021, state taxes ranged from a low of 17 cents per pack in Missouri to $4.35 per pack in Connecticut and New York. The average state cigarette tax is $1.76 per pack. The 2021 federal tax rate on cigarettes was $1.01 per pack. In 2015, the Obama Administration proposed raising the federal tax nearly a dollar to $1.95 per pack. The key question is: How much would cigarette purchases decline?

Taxes on cigarettes serve two purposes: to raise tax revenue for government and to discourage cigarette consumption. However, if a higher cigarette tax discourages consumption considerably, meaning a greatly reduced quantity of cigarette sales, then the cigarette tax on each pack will not raise much revenue for the government. Alternatively, a higher cigarette tax that does not discourage consumption by much will actually raise more tax revenue for the government. Thus, when a government agency tries to calculate the effects of altering its cigarette tax, it must analyze how much the tax affects the quantity of cigarettes consumed. This issue reaches beyond governments and taxes. Every firm faces a similar issue. When a firm considers raising the sales price, it must consider how much a price increase will reduce the quantity demanded of what it sells. Conversely, when a firm puts its products on sale, it must expect (or hope) that the lower price will lead to a significantly higher quantity demanded.

## 5.1 Price Elasticity of Demand and Price Elasticity of Supply

**LEARNING OBJECTIVES**

By the end of this section, you will be able to:

- Calculate the price elasticity of demand
- Calculate the price elasticity of supply

Both the demand and supply curve show the relationship between price and the number of units demanded or supplied. **Price elasticity** is the ratio between the percentage change in the quantity demanded (Qd) or supplied (Qs) and the corresponding percent change in price. The **price elasticity of demand** is the percentage change in the quantity *demanded* of a good or service divided by the percentage change in the price. The **price elasticity of supply** is the percentage change in quantity *supplied* divided by the percentage change in price.

We can usefully divide elasticities into three broad categories: elastic, inelastic, and unitary. Because price and quantity demanded move in opposite directions, price elasticity of demand is always a negative number. Therefore, price elasticity of demand is usually reported as its absolute value, without a negative sign. The summary in Table 5.1 is assuming absolute values for price elasticity of demand. An **elastic demand** or **elastic supply** is one in which the elasticity is greater than one, indicating a high responsiveness to changes in price. Elasticities that are less than one indicate low responsiveness to price changes and correspond to **inelastic demand** or **inelastic supply**. **Unitary elasticities** indicate proportional responsiveness of either demand or supply, as Table 5.1 summarizes.

| If ... | Then ... | And It Is Called ... |
|---|---|---|
| % change in quantity > % change in price | $\dfrac{\%\ \text{change in quantity}}{\%\ \text{change in price}} > 1$ | Elastic |
| % change in quantity = % change in price | $\dfrac{\%\ \text{change in quantity}}{\%\ \text{change in price}} = 1$ | Unitary |
| % change in quantity < % change in price | $\dfrac{\%\ \text{change in quantity}}{\%\ \text{change in price}} < 1$ | Inelastic |

**TABLE 5.1** Elastic, Inelastic, and Unitary: Three Cases of Elasticity

## 🔗 LINK IT UP

Before we delve into the details of elasticity, enjoy this article (http://openstax.org/l/Super_Bowl) on elasticity and ticket prices at the Super Bowl.

To calculate elasticity along a demand or supply curve economists use the average percent change in both quantity and price. This is called the Midpoint Method for Elasticity, and is represented in the following equations:

$$\%\ \text{change in quantity} = \frac{Q_2 - Q_1}{(Q_2 + Q_1)/2} \times 100$$

$$\%\ \text{change in price} = \frac{P_2 - P_1}{(P_2 + P_1)/2} \times 100$$

The advantage of the Midpoint Method is that one obtains the same elasticity between two price points whether there is a price increase or decrease. This is because the formula uses the same base (average quantity and average price) for both cases.

## Calculating Price Elasticity of Demand

Let's calculate the elasticity between points A and B and between points G and H as Figure 5.2 shows.

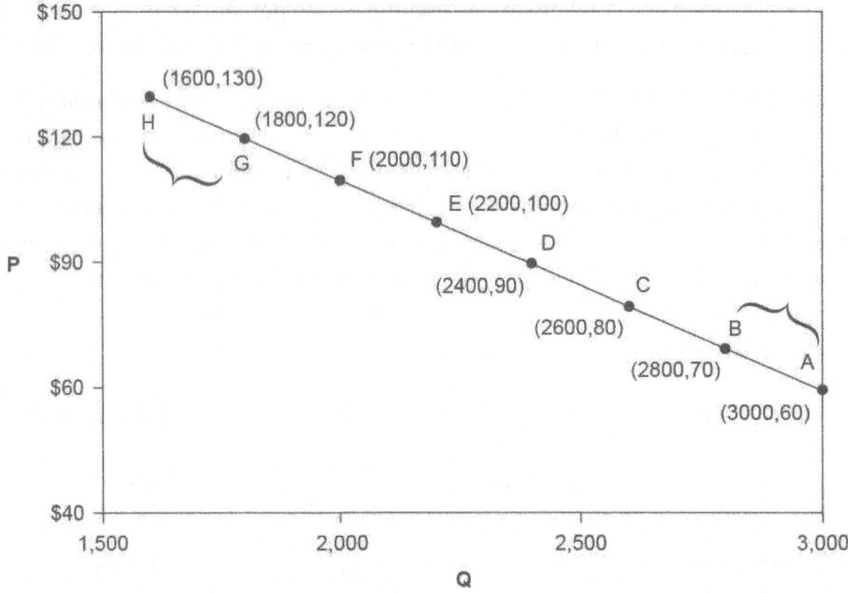


**FIGURE 5.2 Calculating the Price Elasticity of Demand** We calculate the price elasticity of demand as the percentage change in quantity divided by the percentage change in price.

First, apply the formula to calculate the elasticity as price decreases from $70 at point B to $60 at point A:

$$\% \text{ change in quantity} = \frac{3{,}000-2{,}800}{(3{,}000+2{,}800)/2} \times 100$$

$$= \frac{200}{2{,}900} \times 100$$

$$= 6.9$$

$$\% \text{ change in price} = \frac{60-70}{(60+70)/2} \times 100$$

$$= \frac{-10}{65} \times 100$$

$$= -15.4$$

$$\text{Price Elasticity of Demand} = \frac{6.9\%}{-15.4\%}$$

$$= 0.45$$

Therefore, the elasticity of demand between these two points is $\frac{6.9\%}{-15.4\%}$ which is 0.45, an amount smaller than one, showing that the demand is inelastic in this interval. Price elasticities of demand are *always* negative since price and quantity demanded always move in opposite directions (on the demand curve). By convention, we always talk about elasticities as positive numbers. Mathematically, we take the absolute value of the result. We will ignore this detail from now on, while remembering to interpret elasticities as positive numbers.

This means that, along the demand curve between point B and A, if the price changes by 1%, the quantity demanded will change by 0.45%. A change in the price will result in a smaller percentage change in the quantity demanded. For example, a 10% *increase* in the price will result in only a 4.5% *decrease* in quantity demanded. A 10% *decrease* in the price will result in only a 4.5% *increase* in the quantity demanded. Price elasticities of demand are negative numbers indicating that the demand curve is downward sloping, but we read them as absolute values. The following Work It Out feature will walk you through calculating the price elasticity of demand.

### Finding the Price Elasticity of Demand

Calculate the price elasticity of demand using the data in Figure 5.2 for an increase in price from G to H. Has the elasticity increased or decreased?

Step 1. We know that:

$$\text{Price Elasticity of Demand} = \frac{\%\text{ change in quantity}}{\%\text{ change in price}}$$

Step 2. From the Midpoint Formula we know that:

$$\%\text{ change in quantity} = \frac{Q_2 - Q_1}{(Q_2 + Q_1)/2} \times 100$$

$$\%\text{ change in price} = \frac{P_2 - P_1}{(P_2 + P_1)/2} \times 100$$

Step 3. So we can use the values provided in the figure in each equation:

$$\%\text{ change in quantity} = \frac{1{,}600 - 1{,}800}{(1{,}600 + 1{,}800)/2} \times 100$$

$$= \frac{-200}{1{,}700} \times 100$$

$$= -11.76$$

$$\%\text{ change in price} = \frac{130 - 120}{(130 + 120)/2} \times 100$$

$$= \frac{10}{125} \times 100$$

$$= 8.0$$

Step 4. Then, we can use those values to determine the price elasticity of demand:

$$\text{Price Elasticity of Demand} = \frac{\%\text{ change in quantity}}{\%\text{ change in price}}$$

$$= \frac{-11.76}{8}$$

$$= 1.47$$

Therefore, the elasticity of demand from G to is H 1.47. The magnitude of the elasticity has increased (in absolute value) as we moved up along the demand curve from points A to B. Recall that the elasticity between these two points was 0.45. Demand was inelastic between points A and B and elastic between points G and H. This shows us that price elasticity of demand changes at different points along a straight-line demand curve.

## Calculating the Price Elasticity of Supply

Assume that an apartment rents for $650 per month and at that price the landlord rents 10,000 units as Figure 5.3 shows. When the price increases to $700 per month, the landlord supplies 13,000 units into the market. By what percentage does apartment supply increase? What is the price sensitivity?

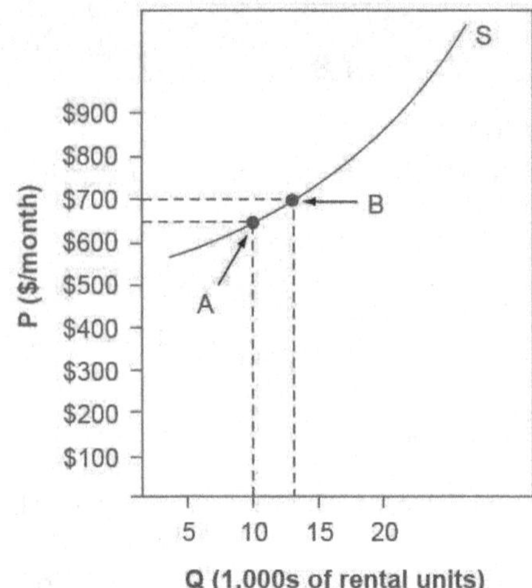


FIGURE 5.3 Price Elasticity of Supply We calculate the price elasticity of supply as the percentage change in quantity divided by the percentage change in price.

Using the Midpoint Method,

$$\text{\% change in quantity} = \frac{13{,}000-10{,}000}{(13{,}000+10{,}000)/2} \times 100$$

$$= \frac{3{,}000}{11{,}500} \times 100$$

$$= 26.1$$

$$\text{\% change in price} = \frac{\$700-\$650}{(\$700+\$650)/2} \times 100$$

$$= \frac{50}{675} \times 100$$

$$= 7.4$$

$$\text{Price Elasticity of Supply} = \frac{26.1\%}{7.4\%}$$

$$= 3.53$$

Again, as with the elasticity of demand, the elasticity of supply is not followed by any units. Elasticity is a ratio of one percentage change to another percentage change—nothing more—and we read it as an absolute value. In this case, a 1% rise in price causes an increase in quantity supplied of 3.5%. The greater than one elasticity of supply means that the percentage change in quantity supplied will be greater than a one percent price change. If you're starting to wonder if the concept of slope fits into this calculation, read the following Clear It Up box.

 **CLEAR IT UP**

### Is the elasticity the slope?

It is a common mistake to confuse the slope of either the supply or demand curve with its elasticity. The slope is the rate of change in units along the curve, or the rise/run (change in y over the change in x). For example, in Figure 5.2, at each point shown on the demand curve, price drops by $10 and the number of units demanded increases by 200 compared to the point to its left. The slope is −10/200 along the entire demand curve and does not change. The price elasticity, however, changes along the curve. Elasticity between points A and B was 0.45 and increased to 1.47 between points G and H. Elasticity is the *percentage* change, which is a different calculation from the slope and has a different meaning.

When we are at the upper end of a demand curve, where price is high and the quantity demanded is low, a small change in the quantity demanded, even in, say, one unit, is pretty big in percentage terms. A change in price of, say, a dollar, is going to be much less important in percentage terms than it would have been at the bottom of the demand curve. Likewise, at the bottom of the demand curve, that one unit change when the quantity demanded is high will be small as a percentage.

Thus, at one end of the demand curve, where we have a large percentage change in quantity demanded over a small percentage change in price, the elasticity value would be high, or demand would be relatively elastic. Even with the same change in the price and the same change in the quantity demanded, at the other end of the demand curve the quantity is much higher, and the price is much lower, so the percentage change in quantity demanded is smaller and the percentage change in price is much higher. That means at the bottom of the curve we'd have a small numerator over a large denominator, so the elasticity measure would be much lower, or inelastic.

As we move along the demand curve, the values for quantity and price go up or down, depending on which way we are moving, so the percentages for, say, a $1 difference in price or a one unit difference in quantity, will change as well, which means the ratios of those percentages and hence the elasticity will change.

## 5.2 Polar Cases of Elasticity and Constant Elasticity

**LEARNING OBJECTIVES**

By the end of this section, you will be able to:
- Differentiate between infinite and zero elasticity
- Analyze graphs in order to classify elasticity as constant unitary, infinite, or zero

There are two extreme cases of elasticity: when elasticity equals zero and when it is infinite. A third case of interest is that of constant unitary elasticity. We will describe each case. **Infinite elasticity** or **perfect elasticity** refers to the extreme case where either the quantity demanded (Qd) or supplied (Qs) changes by an infinite amount in response to any change in price at all. In both cases, the supply and the demand curve are horizontal as Figure 5.4 shows. While perfectly elastic supply curves are for the most part unrealistic, goods with readily available inputs and whose production can easily expand will feature highly elastic supply curves. Examples include pizza, bread, books, and pencils. Similarly, perfectly elastic demand is an extreme example. However, luxury goods, items that take a large share of individuals' income, and goods with many substitutes are likely to have highly elastic demand curves. Examples of such goods are Caribbean cruises and sports vehicles.

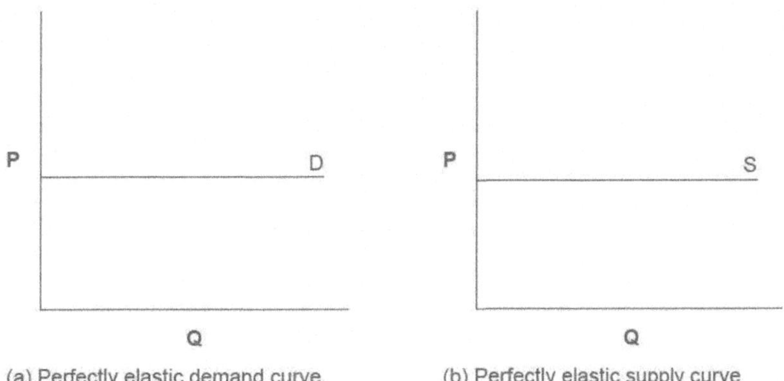


**FIGURE 5.4** Infinite Elasticity The horizontal lines show that an infinite quantity will be demanded or supplied at a specific price. This illustrates the cases of a perfectly (or infinitely) elastic demand curve and supply curve. The quantity supplied or demanded is extremely responsive to price changes, moving from zero for prices close to P to infinite when prices reach P.

**Zero elasticity** or **perfect inelasticity**, as Figure 5.5 depicts, refers to the extreme case in which a percentage change in price, no matter how large, results in zero change in quantity. While a perfectly inelastic supply is an extreme example, goods with limited supply of inputs are likely to feature highly inelastic supply curves. Examples include diamond rings or housing in prime locations such as apartments facing Central Park in New

York City. Similarly, while perfectly inelastic demand is an extreme case, necessities with no close substitutes are likely to have highly inelastic demand curves. This is the case of life-saving drugs and gasoline.

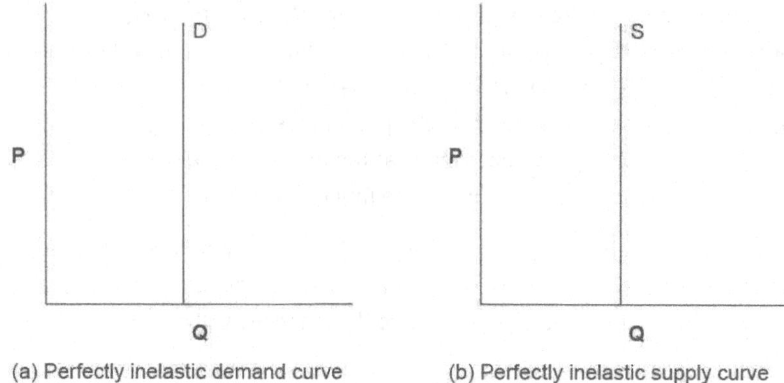


(a) Perfectly inelastic demand curve          (b) Perfectly inelastic supply curve

**FIGURE 5.5 Zero Elasticity** The vertical supply curve and vertical demand curve show that there will be zero percentage change in quantity (a) demanded or (b) supplied, regardless of the price.

Constant unitary elasticity, in either a supply or demand curve, occurs when a price change of one percent results in a quantity change of one percent. Figure 5.6 shows a demand curve with constant unit elasticity. Using the midpoint method, you can calculate that between points A and B on the demand curve, the price changes by 66.7% and quantity demanded also changes by 66.7%. Hence, the elasticity equals 1. Between points B and C, price again changes by 66.7% as does quantity, while between points C and D the corresponding percentage changes are again 66.7% for both price and quantity. In each case, then, the percentage change in price equals the percentage change in quantity, and consequently elasticity equals 1. Notice that in absolute value, the declines in price, as you step down the demand curve, are not identical. Instead, the price falls by $8.00 from A to B, by a smaller amount of $4.00 from B to C, and by a still smaller amount of $2.00 from C to D. As a result, a demand curve with constant unitary elasticity moves from a steeper slope on the left and a flatter slope on the right—and a curved shape overall.

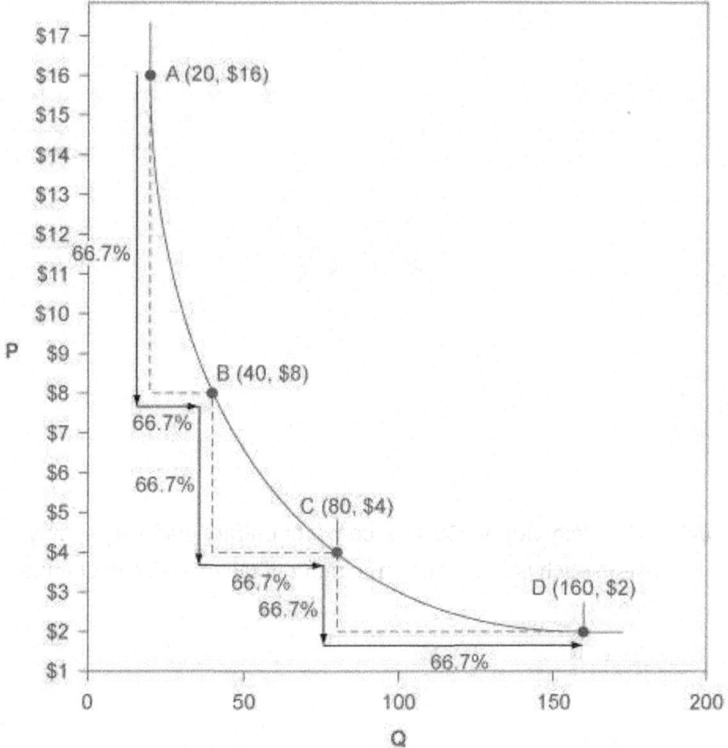


**FIGURE 5.6 A Constant Unitary Elasticity Demand Curve** A demand curve with constant unitary elasticity will be a curved line. Notice how price and quantity demanded change by an identical percentage amount between each pair of points on the demand curve.

Unlike the demand curve with unitary elasticity, the supply curve with unitary elasticity is represented by a straight line, and that line goes through the origin. In each pair of points on the supply curve there is an equal difference in quantity of 30. However, in percentage value, using the midpoint method, the steps are decreasing as one moves from left to right, from 28.6% to 22.2% to 18.2%, because the quantity points in each percentage calculation are getting increasingly larger, which expands the denominator in the elasticity calculation of the percentage change in quantity.

Consider the price changes moving up the supply curve in Figure 5.7. From points D to E to F and to G on the supply curve, each step of $1.50 is the same in absolute value. However, if we measure the price changes in percentage change terms, using the midpoint method, they are also decreasing, from 28.6% to 22.2% to 18.2%, because the original price points in each percentage calculation are getting increasingly larger in value, increasing the denominator in the calculation of the percentage change in price. Along the constant unitary elasticity supply curve, the percentage quantity increases on the horizontal axis exactly match the percentage price increases on the vertical axis—so this supply curve has a constant unitary elasticity at all points.

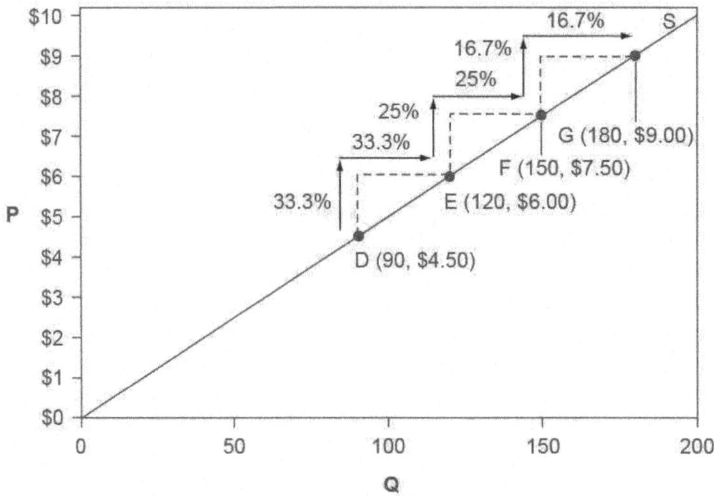


**FIGURE 5.7 A Constant Unitary Elasticity Supply Curve** A constant unitary elasticity supply curve is a straight line reaching up from the origin. Between each pair of points, the percentage increase in quantity supplied is the same as the percentage increase in price.

## 5.3 Elasticity and Pricing

**LEARNING OBJECTIVES**

By the end of this section, you will be able to:

- Analyze how price elasticities impact revenue
- Evaluate how elasticity can cause shifts in demand and supply
- Predict how the long-run and short-run impacts of elasticity affect equilibrium
- Explain how the elasticity of demand and supply determine the incidence of a tax on buyers and sellers

Studying elasticities is useful for a number of reasons, pricing being most important. Let's explore how elasticity relates to revenue and pricing, both in the long and short run. First, let's look at the elasticities of some common goods and services.

Table 5.2 shows a selection of demand elasticities for different goods and services drawn from a variety of different studies by economists, listed in order of increasing elasticity.

| Goods and Services | Elasticity of Price |
| --- | --- |
| Housing | 0.12 |
| Transatlantic air travel (economy class) | 0.12 |
| Rail transit (rush hour) | 0.15 |
| Electricity | 0.20 |
| Taxi cabs | 0.22 |
| Gasoline | 0.35 |
| Transatlantic air travel (first class) | 0.40 |
| Wine | 0.55 |

**TABLE 5.2** Some Selected Elasticities of Demand

| Goods and Services | Elasticity of Price |
| --- | --- |
| Beef | 0.59 |
| Transatlantic air travel (business class) | 0.62 |
| Kitchen and household appliances | 0.63 |
| Cable TV (basic rural) | 0.69 |
| Chicken | 0.64 |
| Soft drinks | 0.70 |
| Beer | 0.80 |
| New vehicle | 0.87 |
| Rail transit (off-peak) | 1.00 |
| Computer | 1.44 |
| Cable TV (basic urban) | 1.51 |
| Cable TV (premium) | 1.77 |
| Restaurant meals | 2.27 |

**TABLE 5.2** Some Selected Elasticities of Demand

Note that demand for necessities such as housing and electricity is inelastic, while items that are not necessities such as restaurant meals are more price-sensitive. If the price of a restaurant meal increases by 10%, the quantity demanded will decrease by 22.7%. A 10% increase in the price of housing will cause only a slight decrease of 1.2% in the quantity of housing demanded.

## ⊘ LINK IT UP

Read this article (http://openstax.org/l/Movietickets) for an example of price elasticity that may have affected you.

## Does Raising Price Bring in More Revenue?

Imagine that a band on tour is playing in an indoor arena with 15,000 seats. To keep this example simple, assume that the band keeps all the money from ticket sales. Assume further that the band pays the costs for its appearance, but that these costs, like travel, and setting up the stage, are the same regardless of how many people are in the audience. Finally, assume that all the tickets have the same price. (The same insights apply if ticket prices are more expensive for some seats than for others, but the calculations become more complicated.) The band knows that it faces a downward-sloping demand curve; that is, if the band raises the ticket price, it will sell fewer seats. How should the band set the ticket price to generate the most total revenue, which in this example, because costs are fixed, will also mean the highest profits for the band? Should the band sell more tickets at a lower price or fewer tickets at a higher price?

The key concept in thinking about collecting the most revenue is the price elasticity of demand. Total revenue is price times the quantity of tickets sold. Imagine that the band starts off thinking about a certain price, which will result in the sale of a certain quantity of tickets. The three possibilities are in Table 5.3. If demand is elastic at that price level, then the band should cut the price, because the percentage drop in price will result in an even larger percentage increase in the quantity sold—thus raising total revenue. However, if demand is inelastic at that original quantity level, then the band should raise the ticket price, because a certain percentage increase in price will result in a smaller percentage decrease in the quantity sold—and total revenue will rise. If demand has a unitary elasticity at that quantity, then an equal percentage change in quantity will offset a moderate percentage change in the price—so the band will earn the same revenue whether it (moderately) increases or decreases the ticket price.

| If Demand Is . . . | Then . . . | Therefore . . . |
|---|---|---|
| Elastic | % change in Qd >% change in P | A given % rise in P will be more than offset by a larger % fall in Q so that total revenue (P × Q) falls. |
| Unitary | % change in Qd =% change in P | A given % rise in P will be exactly offset by an equal % fall in Q so that total revenue (P × Q) is unchanged. |
| Inelastic | % change in Qd <% change in P | A given % rise in P will cause a smaller % fall in Q so that total revenue (P × Q) rises. |

**TABLE 5.3** Will the Band Earn More Revenue by Changing Ticket Prices?

What if the band keeps cutting price, because demand is elastic, until it reaches a level where it sells all 15,000 seats in the available arena? If demand remains elastic at that quantity, the band might try to move to a bigger arena, so that it could slash ticket prices further and see a larger percentage increase in the quantity of tickets sold. However, if the 15,000-seat arena is all that is available or if a larger arena would add substantially to costs, then this option may not work.

Conversely, a few bands are so famous, or have such fanatical followings, that demand for tickets may be inelastic right up to the point where the arena is full. These bands can, if they wish, keep raising the ticket price. Ironically, some of the most popular bands could make more revenue by setting prices so high that the arena is not full—but those who buy the tickets would have to pay very high prices. However, bands sometimes choose to sell tickets for less than the absolute maximum they might be able to charge, often in the hope that fans will feel happier and spend more on recordings, T-shirts, and other paraphernalia.

### Can Businesses Pass Costs on to Consumers?

Most businesses face a day-to-day struggle to figure out ways to produce at a lower cost, as one pathway to their goal of earning higher profits. However, in some cases, the price of a key input over which the firm has no control may rise. For example, many chemical companies use petroleum as a key input, but they have no control over the world market price for crude oil. Coffee shops use coffee as a key input, but they have no control over the world market price of coffee. If the cost of a key input rises, can the firm pass those higher costs along to consumers in the form of higher prices? Conversely, if new and less expensive ways of producing are invented, can the firm keep the benefits in the form of higher profits, or will the market pressure them to pass the gains along to consumers in the form of lower prices? The price elasticity of demand plays a key role in answering these questions.

Imagine that as a consumer of legal pharmaceutical products, you read a newspaper story that a technological breakthrough in the production of aspirin has occurred, so that every aspirin factory can now produce aspirin more cheaply. What does this discovery mean to you? Figure 5.8 illustrates two possibilities. In Figure 5.8 (a), the demand curve is highly inelastic. In this case, a technological breakthrough that shifts supply to the right, from $S_0$ to $S_1$, so that the equilibrium shifts from $E_0$ to $E_1$, creates a substantially lower price for the product with relatively little impact on the quantity sold. In Figure 5.8 (b), the demand curve is highly elastic. In this case, the technological breakthrough leads to a much greater quantity sold in the market at very close to the original price. Consumers benefit more, in general, when the demand curve is more inelastic because the shift in the supply results in a much lower price for consumers.

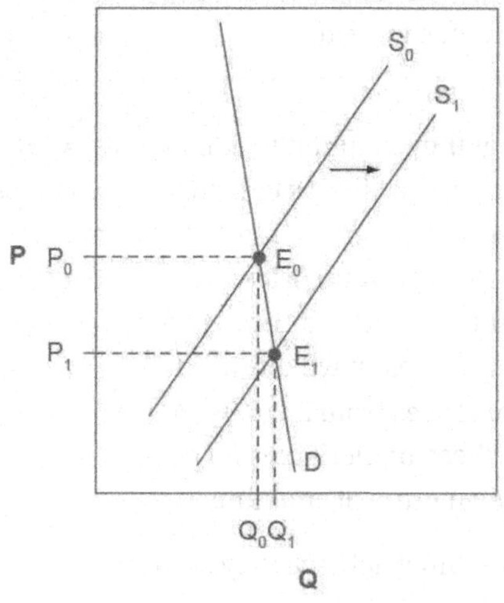

(a) Cost-saving with inelastic demand

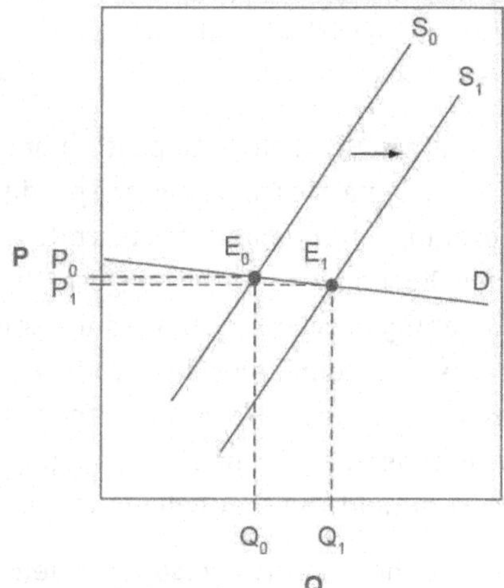

(b) Cost-saving with elastic demand

**FIGURE 5.8 Passing along Cost Savings to Consumers** Cost-saving gains cause supply to shift out to the right from $S_0$ to $S_1$; that is, at any given price, firms will be willing to supply a greater quantity. If demand is inelastic, as in (a), the result of this cost-saving technological improvement will be substantially lower prices. If demand is elastic, as in (b), the result will be only slightly lower prices. Consumers benefit in either case, from a greater quantity at a lower price, but the benefit is greater when demand is inelastic, as in (a).

Aspirin producers may find themselves in a nasty bind here. The situation in Figure 5.8, with extremely inelastic demand, means that a new invention may cause the price to drop dramatically while quantity changes little. As a result, the new production technology can lead to a drop in the revenue that firms earn from aspirin sales. However, if strong competition exists between aspirin producers, each producer may have little choice but to search for and implement any breakthrough that allows it to reduce production costs. After all, if one firm decides not to implement such a cost-saving technology, other firms that do can drive them out of business.

Since demand for food is generally inelastic, farmers may often face the situation in Figure 5.8 (a). That is, a surge in production leads to a severe drop in price that can actually decrease the total revenue that farmers receive. Conversely, poor weather or other conditions that cause a terrible year for farm production can sharply raise prices so that the total revenue that the farmer receives increases. The Clear It Up box discusses how these issues relate to coffee.

 **CLEAR IT UP**

### How do coffee prices fluctuate?

Coffee is an international crop. The top five coffee-exporting nations are Brazil, Vietnam, Colombia, Indonesia, and Ethiopia. In these nations and others, 20 million families depend on selling coffee beans as their main source of income. These families are exposed to enormous risk, because the world price of coffee bounces up and down. For example, in 1993, the world price of coffee was about 50 cents per pound. In 1995 it was four times as high, at $2 per pound. By 1997 it had fallen by half to $1.00 per pound. In 1998 it leaped back up to $2 per pound. By 2001 it had fallen back to 46 cents a pound. By early 2011 it rose to about $2.31 per pound. By the end of 2012, the price had fallen back to about $1.31 per pound. Since then, the price of coffee has continued to fluctuate.

The reason for these price fluctuations lies in a combination of inelastic demand and shifts in supply. The elasticity of coffee demand is only about 0.3; that is, a 10% rise in the price of coffee leads to a decline of about 3% in the quantity of coffee consumed. When a major frost hit the Brazilian coffee crop in 1994, coffee supply shifted to the left with an inelastic demand curve, leading to much higher prices. Conversely, when Vietnam entered the world coffee market as a major producer in the late 1990s, the supply curve shifted out to the right. With a highly inelastic demand curve, coffee prices fell dramatically. Figure 5.8 (a) illustrates this situation.

Elasticity also reveals whether firms can pass higher costs that they incur on to consumers. Addictive substances, for which demand is inelastic, are products for which producers can pass higher costs on to consumers. For example, the demand for cigarettes is relatively inelastic among regular smokers who are somewhat addicted. Economic research suggests that increasing cigarette prices by 10% leads to about a 3% reduction in the quantity of cigarettes that adults smoke, so the elasticity of demand for cigarettes is 0.3. If society increases taxes on companies that produce cigarettes, the result will be, as in Figure 5.9 (a), that the supply curve shifts from $S_0$ to $S_1$. However, as the equilibrium moves from $E_0$ to $E_1$, governments mainly pass along these taxes to consumers in the form of higher prices. These higher taxes on cigarettes will raise tax revenue for the government, but they will not much affect the quantity of smoking.

If the goal is to reduce the quantity of cigarettes demanded, we must achieve it by shifting this inelastic demand back to the left, perhaps with public programs to discourage cigarette use or to help people to quit. For example, anti-smoking advertising campaigns have shown some ability to reduce smoking. However, if cigarette demand were more elastic, as in Figure 5.9 (b), then an increase in taxes that shifts supply from $S_0$ to $S_1$ and equilibrium from $E_0$ to $E_1$ would reduce the quantity of cigarettes smoked substantially. Youth smoking seems to be more elastic than adult smoking—that is, the quantity of youth smoking will fall by a greater percentage than the quantity of adult smoking in response to a given percentage increase in price.

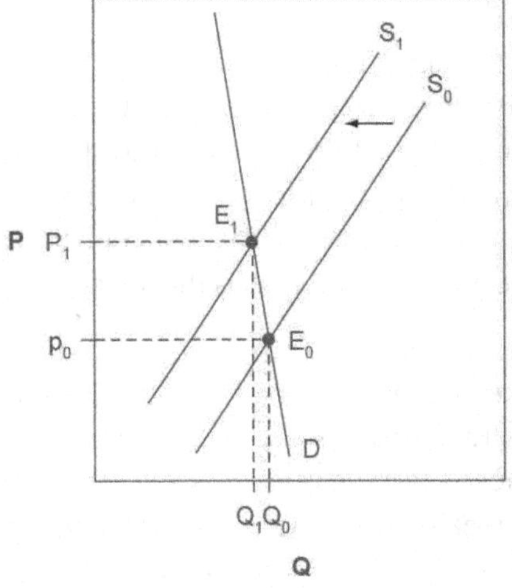


(a) Higher costs with inelastic demand

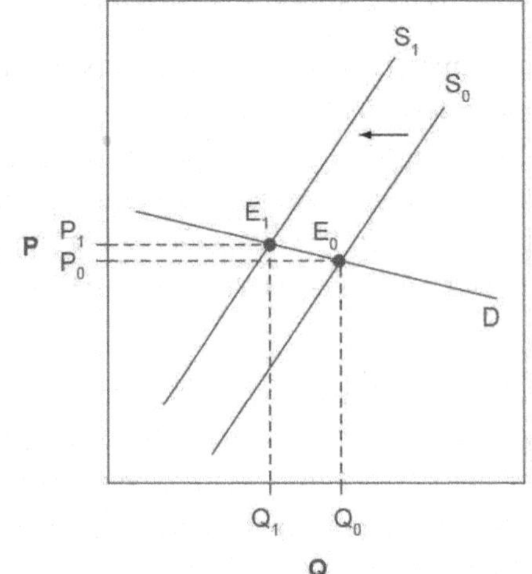


(b) Higher costs with elastic demand

**FIGURE 5.9 Passing along Higher Costs to Consumers** Higher costs, like a higher tax on cigarette companies for the example we gave in the text, lead supply to shift to the left. This shift is identical in (a) and (b). However, in (a), where demand is inelastic, companies largely can pass the cost increase along to consumers in the form of higher prices, without much of a decline in equilibrium quantity. In (b), demand is elastic, so the shift in supply results primarily in a lower equilibrium quantity. Consumers do not benefit in either case, but in (a), they pay a higher price for the same quantity, while in (b), they must buy a lower quantity (and presumably needing to shift their consumption elsewhere).

## Elasticity and Tax Incidence

The example of cigarette taxes demonstrated that because demand is inelastic, taxes are not effective at reducing the equilibrium quantity of smoking, and they are mainly passed along to consumers in the form of higher prices. The analysis, or manner, of how a tax burden is divided between consumers and producers is called **tax incidence**. Typically, the tax incidence, or burden, falls both on the consumers and producers of the taxed good. However, if one wants to predict which group will bear most of the burden, all one needs to do is examine the elasticity of demand and supply. In the tobacco example, the tax burden falls on the most inelastic side of the market.

If demand is more inelastic than supply, consumers bear most of the tax burden, and if supply is more inelastic than demand, sellers bear most of the tax burden.

The intuition for this is simple. When the demand is inelastic, consumers are not very responsive to price changes, and the quantity demanded reduces only modestly when the tax is introduced. In the case of smoking, the demand is inelastic because consumers are addicted to the product. The government can then pass the tax burden along to consumers in the form of higher prices, without much of a decline in the equilibrium quantity.

Similarly, when a government introduces a tax in a market with an inelastic supply, such as, for example, beachfront hotels, and sellers have no alternative than to accept lower prices for their business, taxes do not greatly affect the equilibrium quantity. The tax burden now passes on to the sellers. If the supply was elastic and sellers had the possibility of reorganizing their businesses to avoid supplying the taxed good, the tax burden on the sellers would be much smaller. The tax would result in a much lower quantity sold instead of lower prices received. Figure 5.10 illustrates this relationship between the tax incidence and elasticity of demand and supply.

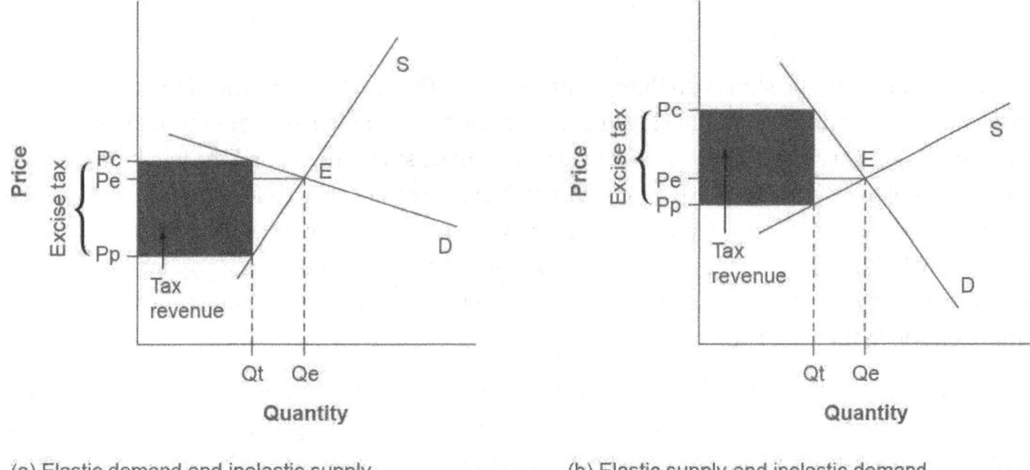


**FIGURE 5.10 Elasticity and Tax Incidence** An excise tax introduces a wedge between the price paid by consumers (Pc) and the price received by producers (Pp). The vertical distance between Pc and Pp is the amount of the tax per unit. Pe is the equilibrium price prior to introduction of the tax. (a) When the demand is more elastic than supply, the tax incidence on consumers Pc – Pe is lower than the tax incidence on producers Pe – Pp. (b) When the supply is more elastic than demand, the tax incidence on consumers Pc – Pe is larger than the tax incidence on producers Pe – Pp. The more elastic the demand and supply curves, the lower the tax revenue.

In Figure 5.10 (a), the supply is inelastic and the demand is elastic, such as in the example of beachfront hotels. While consumers may have other vacation choices, sellers can't easily move their businesses. By introducing a tax, the government essentially creates a wedge between the price paid by consumers Pc and the price received by producers Pp. In other words, of the total price paid by consumers, part is retained by the sellers and part is paid to the government in the form of a tax. The distance between Pc and Pp is the tax rate. The new market price is Pc, but sellers receive only Pp per unit sold, as they pay Pc-Pp to the government. Since we can view a tax as raising the costs of production, this could also be represented by a leftward shift of the supply curve, where the new supply curve would intercept the demand at the new quantity Qt. For simplicity, Figure 5.10 omits the shift in the supply curve.

The tax revenue is given by the shaded area, which we obtain by multiplying the tax per unit by the total quantity sold Qt. The tax incidence on the consumers is given by the difference between the price paid Pc and the initial equilibrium price Pe. The tax incidence on the sellers is given by the difference between the initial equilibrium price Pe and the price they receive after the tax is introduced Pp. In Figure 5.10 (a), the tax burden falls disproportionately on the sellers, and a larger proportion of the tax revenue (the shaded area) is due to the resulting lower price received by the sellers than by the resulting higher prices paid by the buyers. Figure 5.10 (b) describes the example of the tobacco excise tax where the supply is more elastic than demand. The tax incidence now falls disproportionately on consumers, as shown by the large difference between the price they pay, Pc, and the initial equilibrium price, Pe. Sellers receive a lower price than before the tax, but this difference is much smaller than the change in consumers' price. From this analysis one can also predict whether a tax is likely to create a large revenue or not. The more elastic the demand curve, the more likely that consumers will reduce quantity instead of paying higher prices. The more elastic the supply curve, the more likely that sellers will reduce the quantity sold, instead of taking lower prices. In a market where both the demand and supply are very elastic, the imposition of an excise tax generates low revenue.

Some believe that excise taxes hurt mainly the specific industries they target. For example, the medical device excise tax, which was implemented in 2013, has been controversial for it can delay industry profitability and therefore hamper start-ups and medical innovation. The tax was repealed in late 2019. However, whether the tax burden falls mostly on the medical device industry or on the patients depends simply on the elasticity of demand and supply.

## Long-Run vs. Short-Run Impact

Elasticities are often lower in the short run than in the long run. On the demand side of the market, it can sometimes be difficult to change Qd in the short run, but easier in the long run. Consumption of energy is a clear example. In the short run, it is not easy for a person to make substantial changes in energy consumption. Maybe you can carpool to work sometimes or adjust your home thermostat by a few degrees if the cost of energy rises, but that is about all. However, in the long run you can purchase a car that gets more miles to the gallon, choose a job that is closer to where you live, buy more energy-efficient home appliances, or install more insulation in your home. As a result, the elasticity of demand for energy is somewhat inelastic in the short run, but much more elastic in the long run.

Figure 5.11 is an example, based roughly on historical experience, for the responsiveness of Qd to price changes. In 1973, the price of crude oil was $12 per barrel and total consumption in the U.S. economy was 17 million barrels per day. That year, the nations who were members of the Organization of Petroleum Exporting Countries (OPEC) cut off oil exports to the United States for six months because the Arab members of OPEC disagreed with the U.S. support for Israel. OPEC did not bring exports back to their earlier levels until 1975—a policy that we can interpret as a shift of the supply curve to the left in the U.S. petroleum market. Figure 5.11 (a) and Figure 5.11 (b) show the same original equilibrium point and the same identical shift of a supply curve to the left from $S_0$ to $S_1$.

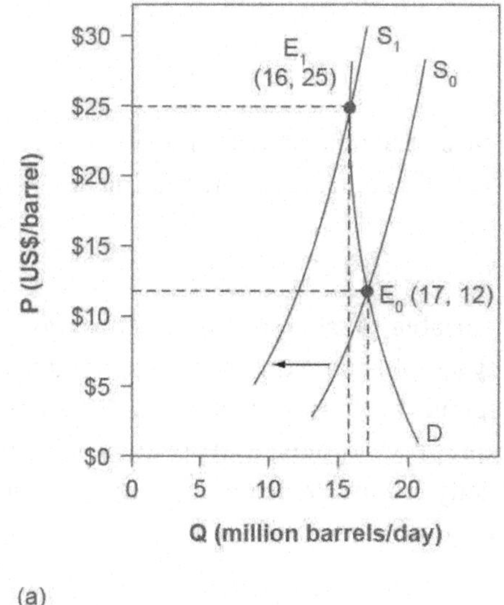


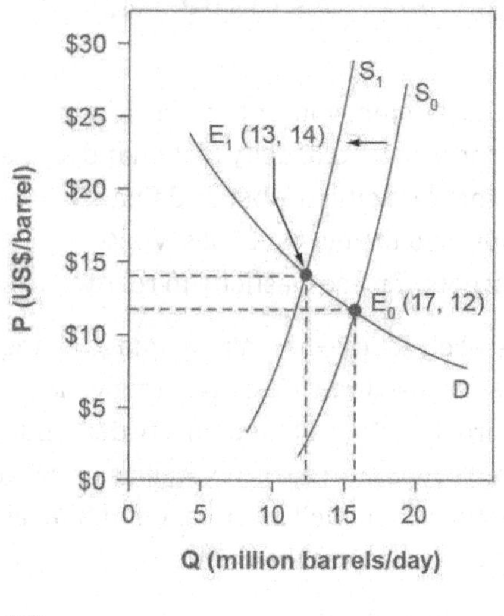


**FIGURE 5.11 How a Shift in Supply Can Affect Price or Quantity** The intersection ($E_0$) between demand curve D and supply curve $S_0$ is the same in both (a) and (b). The shift of supply to the left from $S_0$ to $S_1$ is identical in both (a) and (b). The new equilibrium ($E_1$) has a higher price and a lower quantity than the original equilibrium ($E_0$) in both (a) and (b). However, the shape of the demand curve D is different in (a) and (b), being more elastic in (b) than in (a). As a result, the shift in supply can result either in a new equilibrium with a much higher price and an only slightly smaller quantity, as in (a), with more inelastic demand, or in a new equilibrium with only a small increase in price and a relatively larger reduction in quantity, as in (b), with more elastic demand.

Figure 5.11 (a) shows inelastic demand for oil in the short run similar to that which existed for the United States in 1973. In Figure 5.11 (a), the new equilibrium ($E_1$) occurs at a price of $25 per barrel, roughly double the price before the OPEC shock, and an equilibrium quantity of 16 million barrels per day. Figure 5.11 (b) shows what the outcome would have been if the U.S. demand for oil had been more elastic, a result more likely over the long term. This alternative equilibrium ($E_1$) would have resulted in a smaller price increase to $14 per barrel and larger reduction in equilibrium quantity to 13 million barrels per day. In 1983, for example, U.S. petroleum consumption was 15.3 million barrels a day, which was lower than in 1973 or 1975. U.S. petroleum consumption was down even though the U.S. economy was about one-fourth larger in 1983 than it had been in 1973. The primary reason for the lower quantity was that higher energy prices spurred conservation efforts, and after a decade of home insulation, more fuel-efficient cars, more efficient appliances and machinery, and other fuel-conserving choices, the demand curve for energy had become more elastic.

On the supply side of markets, producers of goods and services typically find it easier to expand production in the long term of several years rather than in the short run of a few months. After all, in the short run it can be costly or difficult to build a new factory, hire many new workers, or open new stores. However, over a few years, all of these are possible.

In most markets for goods and services, prices bounce up and down more than quantities in the short run, but quantities often move more than prices in the long run. The underlying reason for this pattern is that supply and demand are often inelastic in the short run, so that shifts in either demand or supply can cause a relatively greater change in prices. However, since supply and demand are more elastic in the long run, the long-run movements in prices are more muted, while quantity adjusts more easily in the long run.

## 5.4 Elasticity in Areas Other Than Price

**LEARNING OBJECTIVES**

By the end of this section, you will be able to:
- Calculate the income elasticity of demand and the cross-price elasticity of demand
- Calculate the elasticity in labor and financial capital markets through an understanding of the elasticity of labor supply and the elasticity of savings
- Apply concepts of price elasticity to real-world situations

The basic idea of elasticity—how a percentage change in one variable causes a percentage change in another variable—does not just apply to the responsiveness of quantity supplied and quantity demanded to changes in the price of a product. Recall that quantity demanded (Qd) depends on income, tastes and preferences, the prices of related goods, and so on, as well as price. Similarly, quantity supplied (Qs) depends on factors such as the cost of production, as well as price. We can measure elasticity for any determinant of quantity supplied and quantity demanded, not just the price.

### Income Elasticity of Demand

The income elasticity of demand is the percentage change in quantity demanded divided by the percentage change in income.

$$\text{Income elasticity of demand} = \frac{\%\ \text{change in quantity demanded}}{\%\ \text{change in income}}$$

For most products, most of the time, the income elasticity of demand is positive: that is, a rise in income will cause an increase in the quantity demanded. This pattern is common enough that we refer to these goods as normal goods. However, for a few goods, an increase in income means that one might purchase less of the good. For example, those with a higher income might buy fewer hamburgers, because they are buying more steak instead, or those with a higher income might buy less cheap wine and more imported beer. When the income elasticity of demand is negative, we call the good an inferior good.

We introduced the concepts of normal and inferior goods in Demand and Supply. A higher level of income causes a demand curve to shift to the right for a normal good, which means that the income elasticity of demand is positive. How far the demand shifts depends on the income elasticity of demand. A higher income elasticity means a larger shift. However, for an inferior good, that is, when the income elasticity of demand is negative, a higher level of income would cause the demand curve for that good to shift to the left. Again, how much it shifts depends on how large the (negative) income elasticity is.

### Cross-Price Elasticity of Demand

A change in the price of one good can shift the quantity demanded for another good. If the two goods are complements, like bread and peanut butter, then a drop in the price of one good will lead to an increase in the quantity demanded of the other good. However, if the two goods are substitutes, like plane tickets and train tickets, then a drop in the price of one good will cause people to substitute toward that good, and to reduce consumption of the other good. Cheaper plane tickets lead to fewer train tickets, and vice versa.

The **cross-price elasticity of demand** puts some meat on the bones of these ideas. The term "cross-price" refers to the idea that the price of one good is affecting the quantity demanded of a different good. Specifically, the cross-price elasticity of demand is the percentage change in the quantity of good A that is demanded as a result of a percentage change in the price of good B.

$$\text{Cross-price elasticity of demand} = \frac{\%\ \text{change in Qd of good A}}{\%\ \text{change in price of good B}}$$

Substitute goods have positive cross-price elasticities of demand: if good A is a substitute for good B, like coffee and tea, then a higher price for B will mean a greater quantity consumed of A. Complement goods have negative cross-price elasticities: if good A is a complement for good B, like coffee and sugar, then a higher price for B will mean a lower quantity consumed of A.

## Elasticity in Labor and Financial Capital Markets

The concept of elasticity applies to any market, not just markets for goods and services. In the labor market, for example, the **wage elasticity of labor supply**—that is, the percentage change in hours worked divided by the percentage change in wages—will reflect the shape of the labor supply curve. Specifically:

$$\text{Elasticity of labor supply} = \frac{\%\text{ change in quantity of labor supplied}}{\%\text{ change in wage}}$$

The wage elasticity of labor supply for teenage workers is generally fairly elastic: that is, a certain percentage change in wages will lead to a larger percentage change in the quantity of hours worked. Conversely, the wage elasticity of labor supply for adult workers in their thirties and forties is fairly inelastic. When wages move up or down by a certain percentage amount, the quantity of hours that adults in their prime earning years are willing to supply changes but by a lesser percentage amount.

In markets for financial capital, the **elasticity of savings**—that is, the percentage change in the quantity of savings divided by the percentage change in interest rates—will describe the shape of the supply curve for financial capital. That is:

$$\text{Elasticity of savings} = \frac{\%\text{ change in quantity of financial savings}}{\%\text{ change in interest rate}}$$

Sometimes laws are proposed that seek to increase the quantity of savings by offering tax breaks so that the return on savings is higher. Such a policy will have a comparatively large impact on increasing the quantity saved if the supply curve for financial capital is elastic, because then a given percentage increase in the return to savings will cause a higher percentage increase in the quantity of savings. However, if the supply curve for financial capital is highly inelastic, then a percentage increase in the return to savings will cause only a small increase in the quantity of savings. The evidence on the supply curve of financial capital is controversial but, at least in the short run, the elasticity of savings with respect to the interest rate appears fairly inelastic.

## Expanding the Concept of Elasticity

The elasticity concept does not even need to relate to a typical supply or demand curve at all. For example, imagine that you are studying whether the Internal Revenue Service should spend more money on auditing tax returns. We can frame the question in terms of the elasticity of tax collections with respect to spending on tax enforcement; that is, what is the percentage change in tax collections derived from a given percentage change in spending on tax enforcement?

With all of the elasticity concepts that we have just described, some of which are in Table 5.4, the possibility of confusion arises. When you hear the phrases "elasticity of demand" or "elasticity of supply," they refer to the elasticity with respect to price. Sometimes, either to be extremely clear or because economists are discussing a wide variety of elasticities, we will call the elasticity of demand or the demand elasticity the price elasticity of demand or the "elasticity of demand with respect to price." Similarly, economists sometimes use the term elasticity of supply or the supply elasticity, to avoid any possibility of confusion, the price elasticity of supply or "the elasticity of supply with respect to price." However, in whatever context, the idea of elasticity always refers to percentage change in one variable, almost always a price or money variable, and how it causes a percentage change in another variable, typically a quantity variable of some kind.

$$\text{Income elasticity of demand} = \frac{\%\text{ change in Qd}}{\%\text{ change in income}}$$

$$\text{Cross-price elasticity of demand} = \frac{\%\text{ change in Qd of good A}}{\%\text{ change in price of good B}}$$

**TABLE 5.4** Formulas for Calculating Elasticity

$$\text{Wage elasticity of labor supply} = \frac{\%\ \text{change in quantity of labor supplied}}{\%\ \text{change in wage}}$$

$$\text{Wage elasticity of labor demand} = \frac{\%\ \text{change in quantity of labor demanded}}{\%\ \text{change in wage}}$$

$$\text{Interest rate elasticity of savings} = \frac{\%\ \text{change in quantity of savings}}{\%\ \text{change in interest rate}}$$

$$\text{Interest rate elasticity of borrowing} = \frac{\%\ \text{change in quantity of borrowing}}{\%\ \text{change in interest rate}}$$

**TABLE 5.4** Formulas for Calculating Elasticity

 **BRING IT HOME**

### That Will Be How Much?

How did the 60% price increase in 2011 end up for Netflix? It has been a very bumpy ride.

Before the price increase, there were about 24.6 million U.S. subscribers. After the price increase, 810,000 infuriated U.S. consumers canceled their Netflix subscriptions, dropping the total number of subscribers to 23.79 million. Fast forward to June 2013, when there were 36 million streaming Netflix subscribers in the United States. This was an increase of 11.4 million subscribers since the price increase—an average per quarter growth of about 1.6 million. This growth is less than the 2 million per quarter increases Netflix experienced in the fourth quarter of 2010 and the first quarter of 2011.

During the first year after the price increase, the firm's stock price (a measure of future expectations for the firm) fell from about $33.60 per share per share to just under $7.80. By the end of 2016, however, the stock price was at $123 per share. By the end of 2021, the stock price was just over $600 per share, and Netflix had more than 214 million subscribers in fifty countries.

What happened? Obviously, Netflix company officials understood the law of demand. Company officials reported, when announcing the price increase, this could result in the loss of about 600,000 existing subscribers. Using the elasticity of demand formula, it is easy to see company officials expected an inelastic response:

$$= \frac{-600{,}000/[(24\ \text{million} + 24.6\ \text{million})/2]}{\$6/[(\$10 + \$16)/2]}$$

$$= \frac{-600{,}000/24.3\ \text{million}}{\$6/\$13}$$

$$= \frac{-0.025}{0.46}$$

$$= -0.05$$

In addition, Netflix officials had anticipated the price increase would have little impact on attracting new customers. Netflix anticipated adding up to 1.29 million new subscribers in the third quarter of 2011. It is true this was slower growth than the firm had experienced—about 2 million per quarter.

Why was the estimate of customers leaving so far off? In the more than two decades since Netflix had been founded, there was an increase in the number of close, but not perfect, substitutes. Consumers now had choices ranging from Vudu, Amazon Prime, Hulu, and Redbox, to retail stores. Jaime Weinman reported in *Maclean's* that Redbox kiosks are "a five-minute drive for less from 68 percent of Americans, and it seems that many people still find a five-minute drive more convenient than loading up a movie online." It seems that in 2012, many consumers still preferred a physical DVD disk over streaming video.

What missteps did the Netflix management make? In addition to misjudging the elasticity of demand, by failing to account for close substitutes, it seems they may have also misjudged customers' preferences and tastes. However, the very substantial increase over time in the number of Netflix subscribers suggests that the preference for streaming video may well have overtaken the preference for physical DVD disks. Netflix, the source of numerous late night talk show laughs and jabs in 2011, may yet have the last laugh.

## Key Terms

**constant unitary elasticity** when a given percent price change in price leads to an equal percentage change in quantity demanded or supplied

**cross-price elasticity of demand** the percentage change in the quantity of good A that is demanded as a result of a percentage change in the price of good B

**elastic demand** when the elasticity of demand is greater than one, indicating a high responsiveness of quantity demanded or supplied to changes in price

**elastic supply** when the elasticity of either supply is greater than one, indicating a high responsiveness of quantity demanded or supplied to changes in price

**elasticity** an economics concept that measures responsiveness of one variable to changes in another variable

**elasticity of savings** the percentage change in the quantity of savings divided by the percentage change in interest rates

**inelastic demand** when the elasticity of demand is less than one, indicating that a 1 percent increase in price paid by the consumer leads to less than a 1 percent change in purchases (and vice versa); this indicates a low responsiveness by consumers to price changes

**inelastic supply** when the elasticity of supply is less than one, indicating that a 1 percent increase in price paid to the firm will result in a less than 1 percent increase in production by the firm; this indicates a low responsiveness of the firm to price increases (and vice versa if prices drop)

**infinite elasticity** the extremely elastic situation of demand or supply where quantity changes by an infinite amount in response to any change in price; horizontal in appearance

**perfect elasticity** see infinite elasticity

**perfect inelasticity** see zero elasticity

**price elasticity** the relationship between the percent change in price resulting in a corresponding percentage change in the quantity demanded or supplied

**price elasticity of demand** percentage change in the quantity *demanded* of a good or service divided the percentage change in price

**price elasticity of supply** percentage change in the quantity *supplied* divided by the percentage change in price

**tax incidence** manner in which the tax burden is divided between buyers and sellers

**unitary elasticity** when the calculated elasticity is equal to one indicating that a change in the price of the good or service results in a proportional change in the quantity demanded or supplied

**wage elasticity of labor supply** the percentage change in hours worked divided by the percentage change in wages

**zero inelasticity** the highly inelastic case of demand or supply in which a percentage change in price, no matter how large, results in zero change in the quantity; vertical in appearance

## Key Concepts and Summary

### 5.1 Price Elasticity of Demand and Price Elasticity of Supply

Price elasticity measures the responsiveness of the quantity demanded or supplied of a good to a change in its price. We compute it as the percentage change in quantity demanded (or supplied) divided by the percentage change in price. We can describe elasticity as elastic (or very responsive), unit elastic, or inelastic (not very responsive). Elastic demand or supply curves indicate that quantity demanded or supplied respond to price changes in a greater than proportional manner. An inelastic demand or supply curve is one where a given percentage change in price will cause a smaller percentage change in quantity demanded or supplied. A unitary elasticity means that a given percentage change in price leads to an equal percentage change in quantity demanded or supplied.

### 5.2 Polar Cases of Elasticity and Constant Elasticity

Infinite or perfect elasticity refers to the extreme case where either the quantity demanded or supplied changes by an infinite amount in response to any change in price at all. Zero elasticity refers to the extreme case in which a percentage change in price, no matter how large, results in zero change in quantity. Constant unitary elasticity in either a supply or demand curve refers to a situation where a price change of one percent results in a quantity change of one percent.

## 5.3 Elasticity and Pricing

In the market for goods and services, quantity supplied and quantity demanded are often relatively slow to react to changes in price in the short run, but react more substantially in the long run. As a result, demand and supply often (but not always) tend to be relatively inelastic in the short run and relatively elastic in the long run. A tax incidence depends on the relative price elasticity of supply and demand. When supply is more elastic than demand, buyers bear most of the tax burden, and when demand is more elastic than supply, producers bear most of the cost of the tax. Tax revenue is larger the more inelastic the demand and supply are.

## 5.4 Elasticity in Areas Other Than Price

Elasticity is a general term, that reflects responsiveness. It refers to the change of one variable divided by the percentage change of a related variable that we can apply to many economic connections. For instance, the income elasticity of demand is the percentage change in quantity demanded divided by the percentage change in income. The cross-price elasticity of demand is the percentage change in the quantity demanded of a good divided by the percentage change in the price of another good. Elasticity applies in labor markets and financial capital markets just as it does in markets for goods and services. The wage elasticity of labor supply is the percentage change in the quantity of hours supplied divided by the percentage change in the wage. The elasticity of savings with respect to interest rates is the percentage change in the quantity of savings divided by the percentage change in interest rates.

## Self-Check Questions

1. From the data in Table 5.5 about demand for smart phones, calculate the price elasticity of demand from: point B to point C, point D to point E, and point G to point H. Classify the elasticity at each point as elastic, inelastic, or unit elastic.

| Points | P | Q |
| --- | --- | --- |
| A | 60 | 3,000 |
| B | 70 | 2,800 |
| C | 80 | 2,600 |
| D | 90 | 2,400 |
| E | 100 | 2,200 |
| F | 110 | 2,000 |
| G | 120 | 1,800 |
| H | 130 | 1,600 |

**TABLE 5.5**

2. From the data in Table 5.6 about supply of alarm clocks, calculate the price elasticity of supply from: point J to point K, point L to point M, and point N to point P. Classify the elasticity at each point as elastic, inelastic, or unit elastic.

| Point | Price | Quantity Supplied |
|-------|-------|-------------------|
| J | $8 | 50 |
| K | $9 | 70 |
| L | $10 | 80 |
| M | $11 | 88 |
| N | $12 | 95 |
| P | $13 | 100 |

**TABLE 5.6**

3. Why is the demand curve with constant unitary elasticity concave?

4. Why is the supply curve with constant unitary elasticity a straight line?

5. The federal government decides to require that automobile manufacturers install new anti-pollution equipment that costs $2,000 per car. Under what conditions can carmakers pass almost all of this cost along to car buyers? Under what conditions can carmakers pass very little of this cost along to car buyers?

6. Suppose you are in charge of sales at a pharmaceutical company, and your firm has a new drug that causes bald men to grow hair. Assume that the company wants to earn as much revenue as possible from this drug. If the elasticity of demand for your company's product at the current price is 1.4, would you advise the company to raise the price, lower the price, or to keep the price the same? What if the elasticity were 0.6? What if it were 1? Explain your answer.

7. What would the gasoline price elasticity of supply mean to UPS or FedEx?

8. The average annual income rises from $25,000 to $38,000, and the quantity of bread consumed in a year by the average person falls from 30 loaves to 22 loaves. What is the income elasticity of bread consumption? Is bread a normal or an inferior good?

9. Suppose the cross-price elasticity of apples with respect to the price of oranges is 0.4, and the price of oranges falls by 3%. What will happen to the demand for apples?

## Review Questions

10. What is the formula for calculating elasticity?

11. What is the price elasticity of demand? Can you explain it in your own words?

12. What is the price elasticity of supply? Can you explain it in your own words?

13. Describe the general appearance of a demand or a supply curve with zero elasticity.

14. Describe the general appearance of a demand or a supply curve with infinite elasticity.

15. If demand is elastic, will shifts in supply have a larger effect on equilibrium quantity or on price?

16. If demand is inelastic, will shifts in supply have a larger effect on equilibrium price or on quantity?

17. If supply is elastic, will shifts in demand have a larger effect on equilibrium quantity or on price?

18. If supply is inelastic, will shifts in demand have a larger effect on equilibrium price or on quantity?

19. Would you usually expect elasticity of demand or supply to be higher in the short run or in the long run? Why?

20. Under which circumstances does the tax burden fall entirely on consumers?

21. What is the formula for the income elasticity of demand?

22. What is the formula for the cross-price elasticity of demand?

23. What is the formula for the wage elasticity of labor supply?

24. What is the formula for elasticity of savings with respect to interest rates?

## Critical Thinking Questions

25. Transatlantic air travel in business class has an estimated elasticity of demand of 0.62, while transatlantic air travel in economy class has an estimated price elasticity of 0.12. Why do you think this is the case?

26. What is the relationship between price elasticity and position on the demand curve? For example, as you move up the demand curve to higher prices and lower quantities, what happens to the measured elasticity? How would you explain that?

27. Can you think of an industry (or product) with near infinite elasticity of supply in the short term? That is, what is an industry that could increase Qs almost without limit in response to an increase in the price?

28. Would you expect supply to play a more significant role in determining the price of a basic necessity like food or a luxury like perfume? Explain. *Hint*: Think about how the price elasticity of demand will differ between necessities and luxuries.

29. A city has built a bridge over a river and it decides to charge a toll to everyone who crosses. For one year, the city charges a variety of different tolls and records information on how many drivers cross the bridge. The city thus gathers information about elasticity of demand. If the city wishes to raise as much revenue as possible from the tolls, where will the city decide to charge a toll: in the inelastic portion of the demand curve, the elastic portion of the demand curve, or the unit elastic portion? Explain.

30. In a market where the supply curve is perfectly inelastic, how does an excise tax affect the price paid by consumers and the quantity bought and sold?

31. Economists define normal goods as having a positive income elasticity. We can divide normal goods into two types: Those whose income elasticity is less than one and those whose income elasticity is greater than one. Think about products that would fall into each category. Can you come up with a name for each category?

32. Suppose you could buy shoes one at a time, rather than in pairs. What do you predict the cross-price elasticity for left shoes and right shoes would be?

## Problems

33. The equation for a demand curve is $P = 48 - 3Q$. What is the elasticity in moving from a quantity of 5 to a quantity of 6?

34. The equation for a demand curve is $P = 2/Q$. What is the elasticity of demand as price falls from 5 to 4? What is the elasticity of demand as the price falls from 9 to 8? Would you expect these answers to be the same?

35. The equation for a supply curve is 4P = Q. What is the elasticity of supply as price rises from 3 to 4? What is the elasticity of supply as the price rises from 7 to 8? Would you expect these answers to be the same?

36. The equation for a supply curve is P = 3Q − 8. What is the elasticity in moving from a price of 4 to a price of 7?

37. The supply of paintings by Leonardo Da Vinci, who painted the *Mona Lisa* and *The Last Supper* and died in 1519, is highly inelastic. Sketch a supply and demand diagram, paying attention to the appropriate elasticities, to illustrate that demand for these paintings will determine the price.

38. Say that a certain stadium for professional football has 70,000 seats. What is the shape of the supply curve for tickets to football games at that stadium? Explain.

39. When someone's kidneys fail, the person needs to have medical treatment with a dialysis machine (unless or until they receive a kidney transplant) or they will die. Sketch a supply and demand diagram, paying attention to the appropriate elasticities, to illustrate that the supply of such dialysis machines will primarily determine the price.

40. Assume that the supply of low-skilled workers is fairly elastic, but the employers' demand for such workers is fairly inelastic. If the policy goal is to expand employment for low-skilled workers, is it better to focus on policy tools to shift the supply of unskilled labor or on tools to shift the demand for unskilled labor? What if the policy goal is to raise wages for this group? Explain your answers with supply and demand diagrams.

# Consumer Choices

FIGURE 6.1 **Investment Choices** We generally view higher education as a good investment, if one can afford it, regardless of the state of the economy. (Credit: modification of "Commencement" by roanokecollege/Flickr, CC BY 2.0)

**CHAPTER OBJECTIVES**

In this chapter, you will learn about:

- Consumption Choices
- How Changes in Income and Prices Affect Consumption Choices
- How Consumer Choices Might Not Always be Rational

## Introduction to Consumer Choices

 **BRING IT HOME**

### Making Choices

The 2008–2009 Great Recession touched families around the globe. In too many countries, workers found themselves out of a job. In developed countries, unemployment compensation provided a safety net, but families still saw a marked decrease in disposable income and had to make tough spending decisions. Of course, non-essential, discretionary spending was the first to go.

Even so, there was one particular category that saw a universal increase in spending world-wide during that time—an 18% uptick in the United States, specifically. You might guess that consumers began eating more meals at home, increasing grocery store spending; however, the Bureau of Labor Statistics' Consumer Expenditure Survey, which tracks U.S. food spending over time, showed "real total food spending by U.S. households declined five percent between 2006 and 2009." So, it was not groceries. What product would people around the world demand more of during tough economic times, and more importantly, why? (Find out at chapter's end.)

That question leads us to this chapter's topic—analyzing how consumers make choices and how changes affect those choices. For instance, do changes in prices matter more or less than changes in a consumer's income? Can a small change in circumstances alter the consumers' perception of a product or even of their own resources? While many choices may seem straightforward, there is often much more to consider.

---

Microeconomics seeks to understand the behavior of individual economic agents such as individuals and businesses. Economists believe that we can analyze individuals' decisions, such as what goods and services to buy, as choices we make within certain budget constraints. Generally, consumers are trying to get the most for their limited budget. In economic terms they are trying to maximize total utility, or satisfaction, given their budget constraint.

Everyone has their own personal tastes and preferences. The French say: *Chacun à son goût*, or "Each to his own taste." An old Latin saying states, *De gustibus non est disputandum* or "There's no disputing about taste." If people base their decisions on their own tastes and personal preferences, however, then how can economists hope to analyze the choices consumers make?

An economic explanation for why people make different choices begins with accepting the proverbial wisdom that tastes are a matter of personal preference. However, economists also believe that the choices people make are influenced by their incomes, by the prices of goods and services they consume, and by factors like where they live. This chapter introduces the economic theory of how consumers make choices about what goods and services to buy with their limited income.

The analysis in this chapter will build on the budget constraint that we introduced in the Choice in a World of Scarcity chapter. This chapter will also illustrate how economic theory provides a tool to systematically look at the full range of possible consumption choices to predict how consumption responds to changes in prices or incomes. After reading this chapter, consult the appendix Indifference Curves to learn more about representing utility and choice through indifference curves.

## 6.1 Consumption Choices

### LEARNING OBJECTIVES

By the end of this section, you will be able to:

- Calculate total utility
- Propose decisions that maximize utility
- Explain marginal utility and the significance of diminishing marginal utility

Information on the consumption choices of Americans is available from the Consumer Expenditure Survey carried out by the U.S. Bureau of Labor Statistics. Table 6.1 shows spending patterns for the average U.S. household. The first row shows income and, after taxes and personal savings are subtracted, it shows that, in 2015, the average U.S. household spent $48,109 on consumption. The table then breaks down consumption into various categories. The average U.S. household spent roughly one-third of its consumption on shelter and other housing expenses, another one-third on food and vehicle expenses, and the rest on a variety of items, as shown. These patterns will vary for specific households by differing levels of family income, by geography, and by preferences.

| | |
|---|---|
| **Average Household Income before Taxes** | **$62,481** |
| **Average Annual Expenditures** | **$48.109** |
| Food at home | $3,264 |

**TABLE 6.1** U.S. Consumption Choices in 2015 (Source: http://www.bls.gov/cex/csxann13.pdf)

| | |
|---|---|
| Food away from home | $2,505 |
| Housing | $16,557 |
| Apparel and services | $1,700 |
| Transportation | $7,677 |
| Healthcare | $3,157 |
| Entertainment | $2,504 |
| Education | $1,074 |
| Personal insurance and pensions | $5,357 |
| All else: alcohol, tobacco, reading, personal care, cash contributions, miscellaneous | $3,356 |

**TABLE 6.1 U.S. Consumption Choices in 2015** (Source: http://www.bls.gov/cex/csxann13.pdf)

## Total Utility and Diminishing Marginal Utility

To understand how a household will make its choices, economists look at what consumers can afford, as shown in a **budget constraint (or budget line)**, and the **total utility** or satisfaction derived from those choices. In a budget constraint line, the quantity of one good is on the horizontal axis and the quantity of the other good on the vertical axis. The budget constraint line shows the various combinations of two goods that are affordable given consumer income. Consider José's situation, shown in Figure 6.2. José likes to collect T-shirts and watch movies.

In Figure 6.2 we show the quantity of T-shirts on the horizontal axis while we show the quantity of movies on the vertical axis. If José had unlimited income or goods were free, then he could consume without limit. However, José, like all of us, faces a budget constraint. José has a total of $56 to spend. The price of T-shirts is $14 and the price of movies is $7. Notice that the vertical intercept of the budget constraint line is at eight movies and zero T-shirts ($56/$7=8). The horizontal intercept of the budget constraint is four, where José spends of all of his money on T-shirts and no movies ($56/14=4). The slope of the budget constraint line is rise/run or −8/4=−2. The specific choices along the budget constraint line show the combinations of affordable T-shirts and movies.

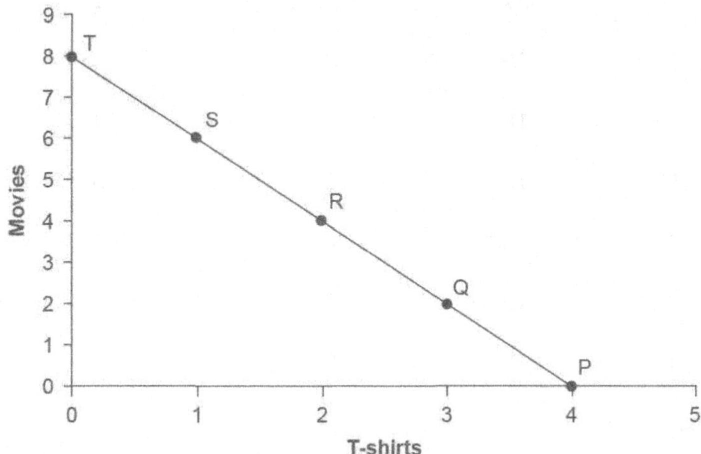


**FIGURE 6.2 A Choice between Consumption Goods** José has income of $56. Movies cost $7 and T-shirts cost $14. The points on the budget constraint line show the combinations of affordable movies and T-shirts.

José wishes to choose the combination that will provide him with the greatest utility, which is the term economists use to describe a person's level of satisfaction or happiness with their choices.

Let's begin with an assumption, which we will discuss in more detail later, that José can measure his own utility with something called *utils*. (It is important to note that you cannot make comparisons between the utils of individuals. If one person gets 20 utils from a cup of coffee and another gets 10 utils, this does not mean than the first person gets more enjoyment from the coffee than the other or that they enjoy the coffee twice as much. The reason why is that utils are subjective to an individual. The way one person measures utils is not the same as the way someone else does.) Table 6.2 shows how José's utility is connected with his T-shirt or movie consumption. The first column of the table shows the quantity of T-shirts consumed. The second column shows the total utility, or total amount of satisfaction, that José receives from consuming that number of T-shirts. The most common pattern of total utility, in this example, is that consuming additional goods leads to greater total utility, but at a decreasing rate. The third column shows **marginal utility**, which is the additional utility provided by one additional unit of consumption. This equation for marginal utility is:

$$MU = \frac{\text{change in total utility}}{\text{change in quantity}}$$

Notice that marginal utility diminishes as additional units are consumed, which means that each subsequent unit of a good consumed provides less *additional* utility. For example, the first T-shirt José picks is his favorite and it gives him an addition of 22 utils. The fourth T-shirt is just something to wear when all his other clothes are in the wash and yields only 18 additional utils. This is an example of the law of **diminishing marginal utility**, which holds that the additional utility decreases with each unit added. Diminishing marginal utility is another example of the more general law of diminishing returns we learned earlier in the chapter on Choice in a World of Scarcity.

The rest of Table 6.2 shows the quantity of movies that José attends, and his total and marginal utility from seeing each movie. Total utility follows the expected pattern: it increases as the number of movies that José watches rises. Marginal utility also follows the expected pattern: each additional movie brings a smaller gain in utility than the previous one. The first movie José attends is the one he wanted to see the most, and thus provides him with the highest level of utility or satisfaction. The fifth movie he attends is just to kill time. Notice that total utility is also the sum of the marginal utilities. Read the next Work It Out feature for instructions on how to calculate total utility.

| T-Shirts (Quantity) | Total Utility | Marginal Utility | Movies (Quantity) | Total Utility | Marginal Utility |
|---|---|---|---|---|---|
| 1 | 22 | 22 | 1 | 16 | 16 |
| 2 | 43 | 21 | 2 | 31 | 15 |
| 3 | 63 | 20 | 3 | 45 | 14 |
| 4 | 81 | 18 | 4 | 58 | 13 |
| 5 | 97 | 16 | 5 | 70 | 12 |
| 6 | 111 | 14 | 6 | 81 | 11 |
| 7 | 123 | 12 | 7 | 91 | 10 |
| 8 | 133 | 10 | 8 | 100 | 9 |

**TABLE 6.2** Total and Marginal Utility

Table 6.3 looks at each point on the budget constraint in Figure 6.2, and adds up José's total utility for five possible combinations of T-shirts and movies.

| Point | T-Shirts | Movies | Total Utility |
|---|---|---|---|
| P | 4 | 0 | 81 + 0 = 81 |
| Q | 3 | 2 | 63 + 31 = 94 |
| R | 2 | 4 | 43 + 58 = 101 |
| S | 1 | 6 | 22 + 81 = 103 |
| T | 0 | 8 | 0 + 100 = 100 |

**TABLE 6.3** Finding the Choice with the Highest Utility

**WORK IT OUT**

## Calculating Total Utility

Let's look at how José makes his decision in more detail.

Step 1. Observe that, at point Q (for example), José consumes three T-shirts and two movies.

Step 2. Look at Table 6.2. You can see from the fourth row/second column that three T-shirts are worth 63 utils. Similarly, the second row/fifth column shows that two movies are worth 31 utils.

Step 3. From this information, you can calculate that point Q has a total utility of 94 (63 + 31).

Step 4. You can repeat the same calculations for each point on Table 6.3, in which the total utility numbers are shown in the last column.

For José, the highest total utility for all possible combinations of goods occurs at point S, with a total utility of 103 from consuming one T-shirt and six movies.

## Choosing with Marginal Utility

Most people approach their utility-maximizing combination of choices in a step-by-step way. This approach is based on looking at the tradeoffs, measured in terms of marginal utility, of consuming less of one good and more of another.

For example, say that José starts off thinking about spending all his money on T-shirts and choosing point P, which corresponds to four T-shirts and no movies, as Figure 6.2 illustrates. José chooses this starting point randomly as he has to start somewhere. Then he considers giving up the last T-shirt, the one that provides him the least marginal utility, and using the money he saves to buy two movies instead. Table 6.4 tracks the step-by-step series of decisions José needs to make (*Key:* T-shirts are $14, movies are $7, and income is $56). The following Work It Out feature explains how marginal utility can affect decision making.

| Try | Which Has | Total Utility | Marginal Gain and Loss of Utility, Compared with Previous Choice | Conclusion |
|---|---|---|---|---|
| Choice 1: P | 4 T-shirts and 0 movies | 81 from 4 T-shirts + 0 from 0 movies = 81 | – | – |
| Choice 2: Q | 3 T-shirts and 2 movies | 63 from 3 T-shirts + 31 from 0 movies = 94 | Loss of 18 from 1 less T-shirt, but gain of 31 from 2 more movies, for a net utility gain of 13 | Q is preferred over P |
| Choice 3: R | 2 T-shirts and 4 movies | 43 from 2 T-shirts + 58 from 4 movies = 101 | Loss of 20 from 1 less T-shirt, but gain of 27 from two more movies for a net utility gain of 7 | R is preferred over Q |
| Choice 4: S | 1 T-shirt and 6 movies | 22 from 1 T-shirt + 81 from 6 movies = 103 | Loss of 21 from 1 less T-shirt, but gain of 23 from two more movies, for a net utility gain of 2 | S is preferred over R |
| Choice 5: T | 0 T-shirts and 8 movies | 0 from 0 T-shirts + 100 from 8 movies = 100 | Loss of 22 from 1 less T-shirt, but gain of 19 from two more movies, for a net utility loss of 3 | S is preferred over T |

**TABLE 6.4** A Step-by-Step Approach to Maximizing Utility

WORK IT OUT

### Decision Making by Comparing Marginal Utility

José could use the following thought process (if he thought in utils) to make his decision regarding how many T-shirts and movies to purchase:

Step 1. From Table 6.2, José can see that the marginal utility of the fourth T-shirt is 18. If José gives up the fourth T-shirt, then he loses 18 utils.

Step 2. Giving up the fourth T-shirt, however, frees up $14 (the price of a T-shirt), allowing José to buy the first two movies (at $7 each).

Step 3. José knows that the marginal utility of the first movie is 16 and the marginal utility of the second movie is 15. Thus, if José moves from point P to point Q, he gives up 18 utils (from the T-shirt), but gains 31 utils (from the movies).

Step 4. Gaining 31 utils and losing 18 utils is a net gain of 13. This is just another way of saying that the total utility at Q (94 according to the last column in Table 6.3) is 13 more than the total utility at P (81).

Step 5. Thus, for José, it makes sense to give up the fourth T-shirt in order to buy two movies.

José clearly prefers point Q to point P. Now repeat this step-by-step process of decision making with marginal utilities. José thinks about giving up the third T-shirt and surrendering a marginal utility of 20, in exchange for purchasing two more movies that promise a combined marginal utility of 27. José prefers point R to point Q. What if José thinks about going beyond R to point S? Giving up the second T-shirt means a marginal utility loss of 21, and the marginal utility gain from the fifth and sixth movies would combine to make a marginal utility gain of 23, so José prefers point S to R.

However, if José seeks to go beyond point S to point T, he finds that the loss of marginal utility from giving up the first T-shirt is 22, while the marginal utility gain from the last two movies is only a total of 19. If José were to choose point T, his utility would fall to 100. Through these stages of thinking about marginal tradeoffs, José again concludes that S, with one T-shirt and six movies, is the choice that will provide him with the highest level of total utility. This step-by-step approach will reach the same conclusion regardless of José's starting point.

We can develop a more systematic way of using this approach by focusing on satisfaction per dollar. If an item costing $5 yields 10 utils, then it's worth 2 utils per dollar spent. **Marginal utility per dollar** is the amount of additional utility José receives divided by the product's price. Table 6.5 shows the marginal utility per dollar for José's T shirts and movies.

$$\text{marginal utility per dollar} = \frac{\text{marginal utility}}{\text{price}}$$

If José wants to maximize the utility he gets from his limited budget, he will always purchase the item with the greatest marginal utility per dollar of expenditure (assuming he can afford it with his remaining budget). José starts with no purchases. If he purchases a T-shirt, the marginal utility per dollar spent will be 1.6. If he purchases a movie, the marginal utility per dollar spent will be 2.3. Therefore, José's first purchase will be the movie. Why? Because it gives him the highest marginal utility per dollar and is affordable. Next, José will purchase another movie. Why? Because the marginal utility of the next movie (2.14) is greater than the marginal utility of the next T-shirt (1.6). Note that when José has no T- shirts, the next one is the first one. José will continue to purchase the next good with the highest marginal utility per dollar until he exhausts his budget. He will continue purchasing movies because they give him a greater "bang for the buck" until the sixth movie which gives the same marginal utility per dollar as the first T-shirt purchase. José has just enough budget to purchase both. So in total, José will purchase six movies and one T-shirt.

| Quantity of T-Shirts | Total Utility | Marginal Utility | Marginal Utility per Dollar | Quantity of Movies | Total Utility | Marginal Utility | Marginal Utility per Dollar |
|---|---|---|---|---|---|---|---|
| **1** | **22** | **22** | **22/$14=1.6** | 1 | 16 | 16 | 16/$7=2.3 |
| 2 | 43 | 21 | 21/$14=1.5 | 2 | 31 | 15 | 15/$7=2.14 |
| 3 | 63 | 20 | 20/$14=1.4 | 3 | 45 | 14 | 14/$7=2 |
| 4 | 81 | 18 | 18/$14=1.3 | 4 | 58 | 13 | 13/$7=1.9 |
| 5 | 97 | 16 | 16/$14=1.1 | 5 | 70 | 12 | 12/$7=1.7 |
| 6 | 111 | 14 | 14/$14=1 | **6** | **81** | **11** | **11/$7=1.6** |
| 7 | 123 | 12 | 12/$14=1.2 | 7 | 91 | 10 | 10/$7=1.4 |

**TABLE 6.5** Marginal Utility per Dollar

## A Rule for Maximizing Utility

This process of decision making suggests a rule to follow when maximizing utility. Since the price of T-shirts is twice as high as the price of movies, to maximize utility the last T-shirt that José chose needs to provide exactly twice the marginal utility (MU) of the last movie. If the last T-shirt provides less than twice the marginal utility of the last movie, then the T-shirt is providing less "bang for the buck" (i.e., marginal utility per dollar spent) than José would receive from spending the same money on movies. If this is so, José should trade the T-shirt for more movies to increase his total utility.

If the last T-shirt provides more than twice the marginal utility of the last movie, then the T-shirt is providing more "bang for the buck" or marginal utility per dollar, than if the money were spent on movies. As a result, José should buy more T-shirts. Notice that at José's optimal choice of point S, the marginal utility from the first T-shirt, of 22 is exactly twice the marginal utility of the sixth movie, which is 11. At this choice, the marginal utility per dollar is the same for both goods. This is a tell-tale signal that José has found the point with highest total utility.

We can write this argument as a general rule: If you always choose the item with the greatest marginal utility per dollar spent, when your budget is exhausted, the utility maximizing choice should occur where the marginal utility per dollar spent is the same for both goods.

$$\frac{MU_1}{P_1} = \frac{MU_2}{P_2}$$

A sensible economizer will pay twice as much for something only if, in the marginal comparison, the item confers twice as much utility. Notice that the formula for the table above is:

$$\frac{22}{\$14} = \frac{11}{\$7}$$
$$1.6 = 1.6$$

The following Work It Out feature provides step by step guidance for this concept of utility-maximizing choices.

## WORK IT OUT

### Maximizing Utility

The general rule, $\frac{MU_1}{P_1} = \frac{MU_2}{P_2}$ , means that the last dollar spent on each good provides exactly the same marginal utility. This is the case at point S. So:

Step 1. If we traded a dollar more of movies for a dollar more of T-shirts, the marginal utility gained from T-shirts would exactly offset the marginal utility lost from fewer movies. In other words, the net gain would be zero.

Step 2. Products, however, usually cost more than a dollar, so we cannot trade a dollar's worth of movies. The best we can do is trade two movies for another T-shirt, since in this example T-shirts cost twice what a movie does.

Step 3. If we trade two movies for one T-shirt, we would end up at point R (two T-shirts and four movies).

Step 4. Choice 4 in Table 6.4 shows that if we move to point R, we would gain 21 utils from one more T-shirt, but lose 23 utils from two fewer movies, so we would end up with less total utility at point R.

In short, the general rule shows us the utility-maximizing choice, which is called the **consumer equilibrium**.

There is another equivalent way to think about this. We can also express the general rule as *the ratio of the prices of the two goods should be equal to the ratio of the marginal utilities.* When we divide the price of good 1 by the price of good 2, at the utility-maximizing point this will equal the marginal utility of good 1 divided by the marginal utility of good 2.

$$\frac{P_1}{P_2} = \frac{MU_1}{MU_2}$$

Along the budget constraint, the total price of the two goods remains the same, so the ratio of the prices does not change. However, the marginal utility of the two goods changes with the quantities consumed. At the optimal choice of one T-shirt and six movies, point S, the ratio of marginal utility to price for T-shirts (22:14) matches the ratio of marginal utility to price for movies (of 11:7).

## Measuring Utility with Numbers

This discussion of utility began with an assumption that it is possible to place numerical values on utility, an assumption that may seem questionable. You can buy a thermometer for measuring temperature at the hardware store, but what store sells a "utilimometer" for measuring utility? While measuring utility with numbers is a convenient assumption to clarify the explanation, the key assumption is not that an outside party can measure utility but only that individuals can decide which of two alternatives they prefer.

To understand this point, think back to the step-by-step process of finding the choice with highest total utility by comparing the marginal utility you gain and lose from different choices along the budget constraint. As José compares each choice along his budget constraint to the previous choice, what matters is not the specific numbers that he places on his utility—or whether he uses any numbers at all—but only that he personally can identify which choices he prefers.

In this way, the step-by-step process of choosing the highest level of utility resembles rather closely how many people make consumption decisions. We think about what will make us the happiest. We think about what things cost. We think about buying a little more of one item and giving up a little of something else. We choose what provides us with the greatest level of satisfaction. The vocabulary of comparing the points along a budget constraint and total and marginal utility is just a set of tools for discussing this everyday process in a clear and specific manner. It is welcome news that specific utility numbers are not central to the argument, since a good utilimometer is hard to find. Do not worry—while we cannot measure utils, by the end of the next module, we will have transformed our analysis into something we can measure—demand.

# 6.2 How Changes in Income and Prices Affect Consumption Choices

**LEARNING OBJECTIVES**

By the end of this section, you will be able to:

- Explain how income, prices, and preferences affect consumer choices
- Contrast the substitution effect and the income effect
- Utilize concepts of demand to analyze consumer choices
- Apply utility-maximizing choices to governments and businesses

Just as we can use utility and marginal utility to discuss making consumer choices along a budget constraint, we can also use these ideas to think about how consumer choices change when the budget constraint shifts in response to changes in income or price. Because we can use the budget constraint framework to analyze how quantities demanded change because of price movements, the budget constraint model can illustrate the underlying logic behind demand curves.

## How Changes in Income Affect Consumer Choices

Let's begin with a concrete example illustrating how changes in income level affect consumer choices. Figure 6.3 shows a budget constraint that represents Kimberly's choice between concert tickets at $50 each and getting away overnight to a bed-and-breakfast for $200 per night. Kimberly has $1,000 per year to spend between these two choices. After thinking about her total utility and marginal utility and applying the decision rule that the ratio of the marginal utilities to the prices should be equal between the two products, Kimberly chooses point M, with eight concerts and three overnight getaways as her utility-maximizing choice.

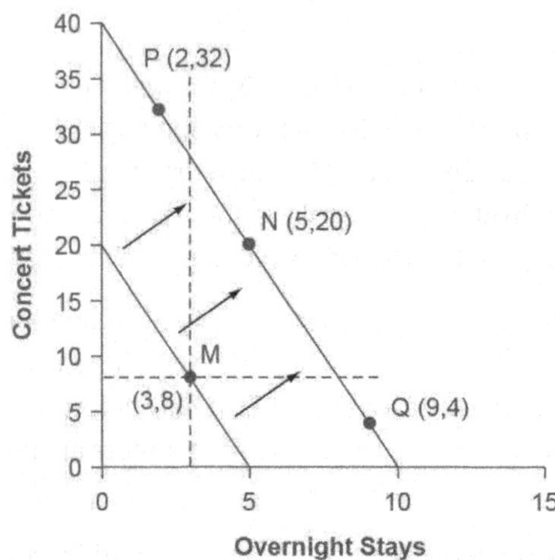


**FIGURE 6.3 How a Change in Income Affects Consumption Choices** The utility-maximizing choice on the original budget constraint is M. The dashed horizontal and vertical lines extending through point M allow you to see at a glance whether the quantity consumed of goods on the new budget constraint is higher or lower than on the original budget constraint. On the new budget constraint, Kimberly will make a choice like N if both goods are normal goods. If overnight stays is an inferior good, Kimberly will make a choice like P. If concert tickets are an inferior good, Kimberly will make a choice like Q.

Now, assume that the income Kimberly has to spend on these two items rises to $2,000 per year, causing her budget constraint to shift out to the right. How does this rise in income alter her utility-maximizing choice? Kimberly will again consider the utility and marginal utility that she receives from concert tickets and overnight getaways and seek her utility-maximizing choice on the new budget line, but how will her new choice relate to her original choice?

We can replace the possible choices along the new budget constraint into three groups, which the dashed horizontal and vertical lines that pass through the original choice M in the figure divide. All choices on the upper left of the new budget constraint that are to the left of the vertical dashed line, like choice P with two overnight stays and 32 concert tickets, involve less of the good on the horizontal axis but much more of the good on the vertical axis. All choices to the right of the vertical dashed line and above the horizontal dashed line—like choice N with five overnight getaways and 20 concert tickets—have more consumption of both goods. Finally, all choices that are to the right of the vertical dashed line but below the horizontal dashed line, like choice Q with four concerts and nine overnight getaways, involve less of the good on the vertical axis but much more of the good on the horizontal axis.

All of these choices are theoretically possible, depending on Kimberly's personal preferences as expressed through the total and marginal utility she would receive from consuming these two goods. When income rises, the most common reaction is to purchase more of both goods, like choice N, which is to the upper right relative to Kimberly's original choice M, although exactly how much more of each good will vary according to personal taste. Conversely, when income falls, the most typical reaction is to purchase less of both goods. As we defined in the chapter on Demand and Supply and again in the chapter on Elasticity, we call goods and services normal goods when a rise in income leads to a rise in the quantity consumed of that good and a fall in income leads to a fall in quantity consumed.

However, depending on Kimberly's preferences, a rise in income could cause consumption of one good to increase while consumption of the other good declines. A choice like P means that a rise in income caused her quantity consumed of overnight stays to decline, while a choice like Q would mean that a rise in income caused her quantity of concerts to decline. Goods where demand declines as income rises (or conversely, where the demand rises as income falls) are called "inferior goods." An inferior good occurs when people trim back on a good as income rises, because they can now afford the more expensive choices that they prefer. For example, a higher-income household might eat fewer hamburgers or be less likely to buy a used car, and instead eat more steak and buy a new car.

## How Price Changes Affect Consumer Choices

For analyzing the possible effect of a change in price on consumption, let's again use a concrete example. Figure 6.4 represents Sergei's consumer choice, who chooses between purchasing baseball bats and cameras. A price increase for baseball bats would have no effect on the ability to purchase cameras, but it would reduce the number of bats Sergei could afford to buy. Thus a price increase for baseball bats, the good on the horizontal axis, causes the budget constraint to rotate inward, as if on a hinge, from the vertical axis. As in the previous section, the point labeled M represents the originally preferred point on the original budget constraint, which Sergei has chosen after contemplating his total utility and marginal utility and the tradeoffs involved along the budget constraint. In this example, the units along the horizontal and vertical axes are not numbered, so the discussion must focus on whether Sergei will consume more or less of certain goods, not on numerical amounts.

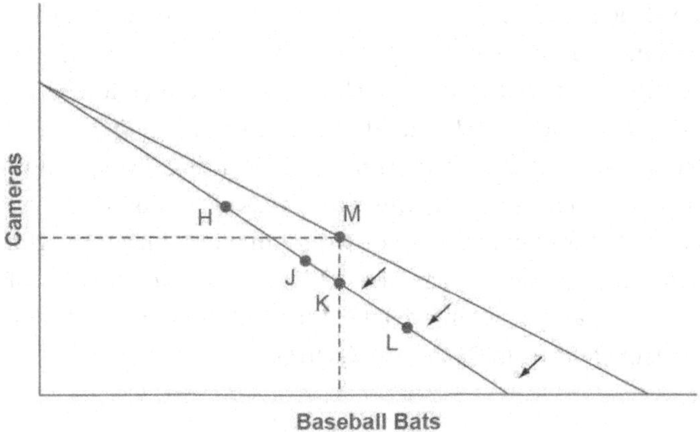


**FIGURE 6.4 How a Change in Price Affects Consumption Choices** The original utility-maximizing choice is M. When the price rises, the budget constraint rotates clockwise. The dashed lines make it possible to see at a glance whether the new consumption choice involves less of both goods, or less of one good and more of the other. The new possible choices would be fewer baseball bats and more cameras, like point H, or less of both goods, as at point J. Choice K would mean that the higher price of bats led to exactly the same quantity of bat consumption, but fewer cameras. Theoretically possible, but unlikely in the real world, we rule out choices like L because they would mean that a higher price for baseball bats means a greater consumption of baseball bats.

After the price increase, Sergei will make a choice along the new budget constraint. Again, we can divide his choices into three segments by the dashed vertical and horizontal lines. In the upper left portion of the new budget constraint, at a choice like H, Sergei consumes more cameras and fewer bats. In the central portion of the new budget constraint, at a choice like J, he consumes less of both goods. At the right-hand end, at a choice like L, he consumes more bats but fewer cameras.

The typical response to higher prices is that a person chooses to consume less of the product with the higher price. This occurs for two reasons, and both effects can occur simultaneously. The **substitution effect** occurs when a price changes and consumers have an incentive to consume less of the good with a relatively higher price and more of the good with a relatively lower price. The **income effect** is that a higher price means, in effect, the buying power of income has been reduced (even though actual income has not changed), which leads to buying less of the good (when the good is normal). In this example, the higher price for baseball bats would cause Sergei to buy fewer bats for both reasons. Exactly how much will a higher price for bats cause Sergei's bat consumption to fall? Figure 6.4 suggests a range of possibilities. Sergei might react to a higher price for baseball bats by purchasing the same quantity of bats, but cutting his camera consumption. This choice is the point K on the new budget constraint, straight below the original choice M. Alternatively, Sergei might react by dramatically reducing his bat purchases and instead buy more cameras.

The key is that it would be imprudent to assume that a change in the price of one good will only affect consumption of that good. In our example, since Sergei purchases all his products out of the same budget, a change in the price of baseball bats can also have a range of effects, either positive or negative, on his purchases of cameras. Since Sergei purchases all his products out of the same budget, a change in the price of one good can also have a range of effects, either positive or negative, on the quantity consumed of other goods.

In short, a higher price typically causes reduced consumption of the good in question, but it can affect the consumption of other goods as well.

 **LINK IT UP**

Read this article (http://openstax.org/l/vending) about the potential of variable prices in vending machines.

## The Foundations of Demand Curves

Changes in the price of a good lead the budget constraint to rotate. A rotation in the budget constraint means that when individuals are seeking their highest utility, the quantity that is demanded of that good will change. In this way, the logical foundations of demand curves—which show a connection between prices and quantity demanded—are based on the underlying idea of individuals seeking utility. Figure 6.5 (a) shows a budget constraint with a choice between housing and "everything else." (Putting "everything else" on the vertical axis can be a useful approach in some cases, especially when the focus of the analysis is on one particular good.) We label the preferred choice on the original budget constraint that provides the highest possible utility $M_0$. The other three budget constraints represent successively higher prices for housing of $P_1$, $P_2$, and $P_3$. As the budget constraint rotates in, and in, and in again, we label the utility-maximizing choices $M_1$, $M_2$, and $M_3$, and the quantity demanded of housing falls from $Q_0$ to $Q_1$ to $Q_2$ to $Q_3$.

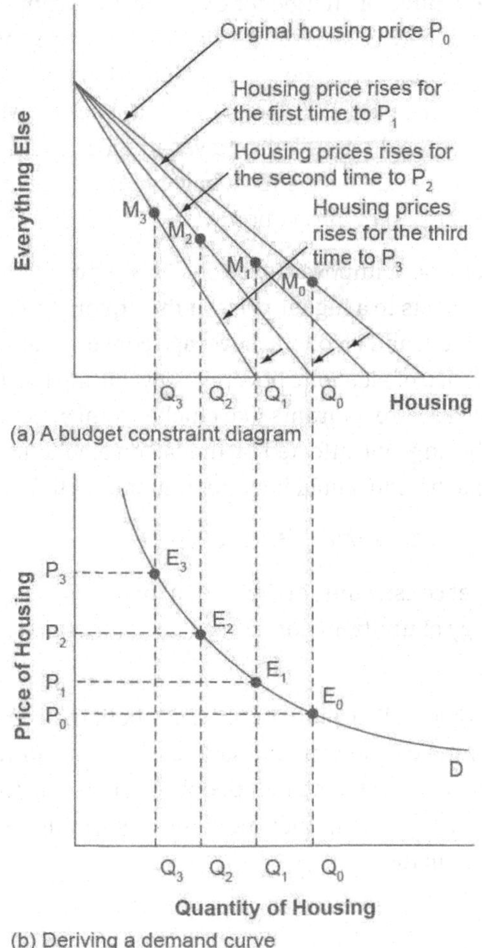


**FIGURE 6.5 The Foundations of a Demand Curve: An Example of Housing** (a) As the price increases from $P_0$ to $P_1$ to $P_2$ to $P_3$, the budget constraint on the upper part of the diagram rotates clockwise. The utility-maximizing choice changes from $M_0$ to $M_1$ to $M_2$ to $M_3$. As a result, the quantity demanded of housing shifts from $Q_0$ to $Q_1$ to $Q_2$ to $Q_3$, *ceteris paribus*. (b) The demand curve graphs each combination of the price of housing and the quantity of housing demanded, *ceteris paribus*. The quantities of housing are the same at the points on both (a) and (b). Thus, the original price of housing ($P_0$) and the original quantity of housing ($Q_0$) appear on the demand curve as point $E_0$. The higher price of housing ($P_1$) and the corresponding lower quantity demanded of housing ($Q_1$) appear on the demand curve as point $E_1$.

Thus, as the price of housing rises, the budget constraint rotates clockwise and the quantity consumed of housing falls, *ceteris paribus* (meaning, with all other things being the same). We graph this relationship—the price of housing rising from $P_0$ to $P_1$ to $P_2$ to $P_3$, while the quantity of housing demanded falls from $Q_0$ to $Q_1$ to $Q_2$ to $Q_3$—on the demand curve in Figure 6.5 (b). The vertical dashed lines stretching between the top and bottom of Figure 6.5 show that the quantity of housing demanded at each point is the same in both (a) and (b). We ultimately determine the shape of a demand curve by the underlying choices about maximizing utility subject to a budget constraint. While economists may not be able to measure "utils," they can certainly measure price and quantity demanded.

## Applications in Government and Business

The budget constraint framework for making utility-maximizing choices offers a reminder that people can react to a change in price or income in a range of different ways. For example, in the winter months of 2005, costs for heating homes increased significantly in many parts of the country as prices for natural gas and electricity soared, due in large part to the disruption caused by Hurricanes Katrina and Rita. Some people reacted by reducing the quantity demanded of energy; for example, by turning down the thermostats in their homes by a few degrees and wearing a heavier sweater inside. Even so, many home heating bills rose, so people adjusted their consumption in other ways, too. As you learned in the chapter on Elasticity, the short run demand for home heating is generally inelastic. Each household cut back on what it valued least on the margin. For some it might have been some dinners out, or a vacation, or postponing buying a new refrigerator or a new car. Sharply higher energy prices can have effects beyond the energy market, leading to a widespread reduction in purchasing throughout the rest of the economy.

A similar issue arises when the government imposes taxes on certain products, such as on gasoline, cigarettes, and alcohol. Say that a tax on alcohol leads to a higher price at the liquor store. The higher price of alcohol causes the budget constraint to pivot left, and alcoholic beverage consumption is likely to decrease. However, people may also react to the higher price of alcoholic beverages by cutting back on other purchases. For example, they might cut back on snacks at restaurants like chicken wings and nachos. It would be unwise to assume that the liquor industry is the only one affected by the tax on alcoholic beverages. Read the next Clear It Up to learn about how who controls the household income influences buying decisions.

### The Unifying Power of the Utility-Maximizing Budget Set Framework

An interaction between prices, budget constraints, and personal preferences determine household choices. The flexible and powerful terminology of utility-maximizing gives economists a vocabulary for bringing these elements together.

Not even economists believe that people walk around mumbling about their marginal utilities before they walk into a shopping mall, accept a job, or make a deposit in a savings account. However, economists do believe that individuals seek their own satisfaction or utility and that people often decide to try a little less of one thing and a little more of another. If we accept these assumptions, then the idea of utility-maximizing households facing budget constraints becomes highly plausible.

 **CLEAR IT UP**

### Does who controls household income make a difference?

In the mid-1970s, the United Kingdom made an interesting policy change in its "child allowance" policy. This program provides a fixed amount of money per child to every family, regardless of family income. Traditionally, the child allowance had been distributed to families by withholding less in taxes from the paycheck of the family wage earner—typically the father in this time period. The new policy instead provided the child allowance as a cash payment to the mother. As a result of this change, households have the same level of income and face the same prices in the market, but the money is more likely to be in the mother's purse than in the father's wallet.

Should this change in policy alter household consumption patterns? Basic models of consumption decisions, of the sort that we examined in this chapter, assume that it does not matter which parent or guardian receives the money, because both seek to maximize the family's utility as a whole. In effect, this model assumes that everyone in the family has the same makeup or has the same preferences.

There has not been extensive research on diverse family structures and guardian/parent sex and gender related to spending. However, the older research on families with one man and one woman parent indicates that gender does affect spending decisions. When the mother controls a larger share of family income a number of studies, in the United Kingdom and in a wide variety of other countries, have found that the family tends to spend more on restaurant meals, child care, and women's clothing, and less on alcohol and tobacco. As the mother controls a larger share of household resources, children's health improves, too. These findings suggest that when providing assistance to families, in high-income countries and low-income countries alike, the monetary amount of assistance is not all that matters: it also matters which family member actually receives the money.

The budget constraint framework serves as a constant reminder to think about the full range of effects that can arise from changes in income or price, not just effects on the one product that might seem most immediately affected.

## 6.3 Behavioral Economics: An Alternative Framework for Consumer Choice

**LEARNING OBJECTIVES**

By the end of this section, you will be able to:

- Evaluate the reasons for making intertemporal choices
- Interpret an intertemporal budget constraint
- Analyze why people in America tend to save such a small percentage of their income

As we know, people sometimes make decisions that seem "irrational" and not in their own best interest. People's decisions can seem inconsistent from one day to the next and they even deliberately ignore ways to save money or time. The traditional economic models assume rationality, which means that people take all available information and make consistent and informed decisions that are in their best interest. (In fact, economics professors often delight in pointing out so-called "irrational behavior" each semester to their new students, and present economics as a way to become more rational.)

However, a new group of economists, known as behavioral economists, argue that the traditional method omits something important: people's state of mind. For example, one can think differently about money if one is feeling revenge, optimism, or loss. These are not necessarily irrational states of mind, but part of a range of emotions that can affect anyone on a given day. In addition, actions under these conditions are predictable, if one better understands the underlying environment. **Behavioral economics** seeks to enrich our understanding of decision-making by integrating the insights of psychology into economics. It does this by investigating how given dollar amounts can mean different things to individuals depending on the situation. This can lead to decisions that appear outwardly inconsistent, or irrational, to the outside observer.

The way the mind works, according to this view, may seem inconsistent to traditional economists but is actually far more complex than an unemotional cost-benefit adding machine. For example, a traditional economist would say that if you lost a $10 bill today, and also received an extra $10 in your paycheck, you should feel perfectly neutral. After all, −$10 + $10 = $0. You are the same financially as you were before. However, behavioral economists have conducted research that shows many people will feel some negative emotion, such as anger or frustration, after those two things happen. We tend to focus more on the loss than the gain. We call this loss aversion, where a $1 loss pains us 2.25 times more than a $1 gain helps us, according to the economists Daniel Kahneman and Amos Tversky in a famous 1979 article in the journal *Econometrica*. This insight has implications for investing, as people tend to "overplay" the stock market by reacting more to losses than to gains. This behavior looks irrational to traditional economists, but is consistent once we understand better how the mind works, these economists argue.

Traditional economists also assume human beings have complete self control, but, for instance, people will buy cigarettes by the pack instead of the carton even though the carton saves them money, to keep usage down. They purchase locks for their refrigerators and overpay on taxes to force themselves to save. In other words, we protect ourselves from our worst temptations but pay a price to do so. One way behavioral economists are responding to this is by establishing ways for people to keep themselves free of these temptations. This includes what we call "nudges" toward more rational behavior rather than mandatory regulations from government. For example, up to 20 percent of new employees do not enroll in retirement savings plans immediately, because of procrastination or feeling overwhelmed by the different choices. Some companies are now moving to a new system, where employees are automatically enrolled unless they "opt out." Almost no-one opts out in this program and employees begin saving at the early years, which are most critical for retirement.

Another area that seems illogical is the idea of mental accounting, or putting dollars in different mental categories where they take different values. Economists typically consider dollars to be **fungible**, or having equal value to the individual, regardless of the situation.

You might, for instance, think of the $25 you found in the street differently from the $25 you earned from three hours working in a fast food restaurant. You might treat the street money as "mad money" with little rational regard to getting the best value. This is in one sense strange, since it is still equivalent to three hours of hard work in the restaurant. Yet the "easy come-easy go" mentality replaces the rational economizer because of the situation, or context, in which you attained the money.

In another example of mental accounting that seems inconsistent to a traditional economist, a person could carry a credit card debt of $1,000 that has a 15% yearly interest cost, and simultaneously have a $2,000 savings account that pays only 2% per year. That means she pays $150 a year to the credit card company, while collecting only $40 annually in bank interest, so she loses $110 a year. That doesn't seem wise.

The "rational" decision would be to pay off the debt, since a $1,000 savings account with $0 in debt is the equivalent net worth, and she would now net $20 per year. Curiously, it is not uncommon for people to ignore this advice, since they will treat a loss to their savings account as higher than the benefit of paying off their credit card. They do not treat the dollars as fungible so it looks irrational to traditional economists.

Which view is right, the behavioral economists' or the traditional view? Both have their advantages, but behavioral economists have at least identified trying to describe and explain behavior that economists have historically dismissed as irrational. If most of us are engaged in some "irrational behavior," perhaps there are deeper underlying reasons for this behavior in the first place.

 **BRING IT HOME**

## Making Choices

In what category did consumers worldwide increase their spending during the Great Recession? Higher education. According to the United Nations Educational, Scientific, and Cultural Organization (UNESCO), enrollment in colleges and universities rose one-third in China and almost two-thirds in Saudi Arabia, nearly doubled in Pakistan, tripled in Uganda, and surged by three million—18 percent—in the United States. Why were consumers willing to spend on education during lean times? Both individuals and countries view higher education as the way to prosperity. Many feel that increased earnings are a significant benefit of attending college.

U.S. Bureau of Labor Statistics data from May 2012 supports this view, as Figure 6.6 shows. They show a positive correlation between earnings and education. The data also indicate that unemployment rates fall with higher levels of education and training.

Why spend the money to go to college during recession? Because if you are unemployed (or underemployed, working fewer hours than you would like), the opportunity cost of your time is low. If you're unemployed, you don't have to give up work hours and income by going to college.

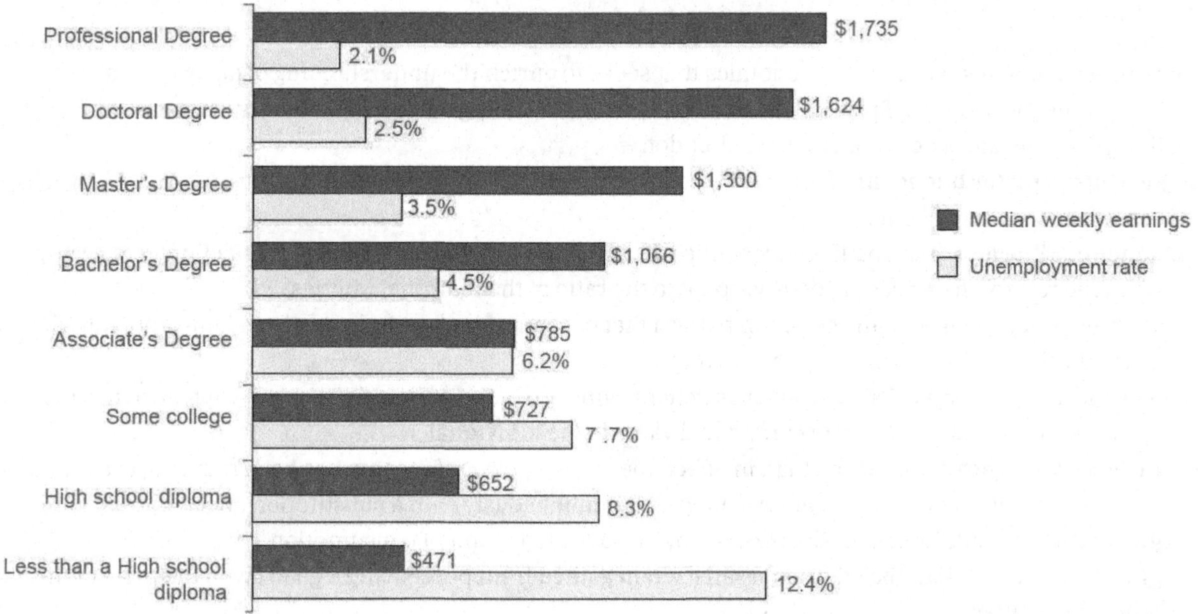


**FIGURE 6.6 The Impact of Education on Earnings and Unemployment Rates, 2012** Those with the highest degrees in 2012 had substantially lower unemployment rates; whereas, those with the least formal education suffered from the highest unemployment rates. The national median average weekly income was $815, and the nation unemployment average in 2012 was 6.8%. (Source: U.S. Bureau of Labor Statistics, May 22, 2013)

## Key Terms

**behavioral economics** a branch of economics that seeks to enrich the understanding of decision-making by integrating the insights of psychology and by investigating how given dollar amounts can mean different things to individuals depending on the situation

**budget constraint (or budget line)** shows the possible combinations of two goods that are affordable given a consumer's limited income

**consumer equilibrium** point on the budget line where the consumer gets the most satisfaction; this occurs when the ratio of the prices of goods is equal to the ratio of the marginal utilities.

**diminishing marginal utility** the common pattern that each marginal unit of a good consumed provides less of an addition to utility than the previous unit

**fungible** the idea that units of a good, such as dollars, ounces of gold, or barrels of oil are capable of mutual substitution with each other and carry equal value to the individual

**income effect** a higher price means that, in effect, the buying power of income has been reduced, even though actual income has not changed; always happens simultaneously with a substitution effect

**marginal utility** the additional utility provided by one additional unit of consumption

**marginal utility per dollar** the additional satisfaction gained from purchasing a good given the price of the product; MU/Price

**substitution effect** when a price changes, consumers have an incentive to consume less of the good with a relatively higher price and more of the good with a relatively lower price; always happens simultaneously with an income effect

**total utility** satisfaction derived from consumer choices

## Key Concepts and Summary

### 6.1 Consumption Choices

Economic analysis of household behavior is based on the assumption that people seek the highest level of utility or satisfaction. Individuals are the only judge of their own utility. In general, greater consumption of a good brings higher total utility. However, the additional utility people receive from each unit of greater consumption tends to decline in a pattern of diminishing marginal utility.

We can find the utility-maximizing choice on a consumption budget constraint in several ways. You can add up total utility of each choice on the budget line and choose the highest total. You can select a starting point at random and compare the marginal utility gains and losses of moving to neighboring points—and thus eventually seek out the preferred choice. Alternatively, you can compare the ratio of the marginal utility to price of good 1 with the marginal utility to price of good 2 and apply the rule that at the optimal choice, the two ratios should be equal:

$$\frac{MU_1}{P_1} = \frac{MU_2}{P_2}$$

### 6.2 How Changes in Income and Prices Affect Consumption Choices

The budget constraint framework suggest that when income or price changes, a range of responses are possible. When income rises, households will demand a higher quantity of normal goods, but a lower quantity of inferior goods. When the price of a good rises, households will typically demand less of that good—but whether they will demand a much lower quantity or only a slightly lower quantity will depend on personal preferences. Also, a higher price for one good can lead to more or less demand of the other good.

### 6.3 Behavioral Economics: An Alternative Framework for Consumer Choice

People regularly make decisions that seem less than rational, decisions that contradict traditional consumer theory. This is because traditional theory ignores people's state of mind or feelings, which can influence behavior. For example, people tend to value a dollar lost more than a dollar gained, even though the amounts are the same. Similarly, many people over withhold on their taxes, essentially giving the government a free loan until they file their tax returns, so that they are more likely to get money back than have to pay money on their taxes.

## Self-Check Questions

1. Jeremy is deeply in love with Jasmine. Jasmine lives where cell phone coverage is poor, so he can either call her on the land-line phone for five cents per minute or he can drive to see her, at a round-trip cost of $2 in gasoline money. He has a total of $10 per week to spend on staying in touch. To make his preferred choice, Jeremy uses a handy utilimometer that measures his total utility from personal visits and from phone minutes. Using the values in Table 6.6, figure out the points on Jeremy's consumption choice budget constraint (it may be helpful to do a sketch) and identify his utility-maximizing point.

| Round Trips | Total Utility | Phone Minutes | Total Utility |
|---|---|---|---|
| 0 | 0 | 0 | 0 |
| 1 | 80 | 20 | 200 |
| 2 | 150 | 40 | 380 |
| 3 | 210 | 60 | 540 |
| 4 | 260 | 80 | 680 |
| 5 | 300 | 100 | 800 |
| 6 | 330 | 120 | 900 |
| 7 | 200 | 140 | 980 |
| 8 | 180 | 160 | 1040 |
| 9 | 160 | 180 | 1080 |
| 10 | 140 | 200 | 1100 |

**TABLE 6.6**

2. Take Jeremy's total utility information in Exercise 6.1, and use the marginal utility approach to confirm the choice of phone minutes and round trips that maximize Jeremy's utility.

3. Explain all the reasons why a decrease in a product's price would lead to an increase in purchases.

4. As a college student you work at a part-time job, but your parents also send you a monthly "allowance." Suppose one month your parents forgot to send the check. Show graphically how your budget constraint is affected. Assuming you only buy normal goods, what would happen to your purchases of goods?

## Review Questions

5. Who determines how much utility an individual will receive from consuming a good?

6. Would you expect total utility to rise or fall with additional consumption of a good? Why?

7. Would you expect marginal utility to rise or fall with additional consumption of a good? Why?

8. Is it possible for total utility to increase while marginal utility diminishes? Explain.

9. If people do not have a complete mental picture of total utility for every level of consumption, how can they find their utility-maximizing consumption choice?

10. What is the rule relating the ratio of marginal utility to prices of two goods at the optimal choice? Explain why, if this rule does not hold, the choice cannot be utility-maximizing.

11. As a general rule, is it safe to assume that a change in the price of a good will always have its most significant impact on the quantity demanded of that good, rather than on the quantity demanded of other goods? Explain.

12. Why does a change in income cause a parallel shift in the budget constraint?

## Critical Thinking Questions

13. Think back to a purchase that you made recently. How would you describe your thinking before you made that purchase?

14. The rules of politics are not always the same as the rules of economics. In discussions of setting budgets for government agencies, there is a strategy called "closing the Washington Monument." When an agency faces the unwelcome prospect of a budget cut, it may decide to close a high-visibility attraction enjoyed by many people (like the Washington Monument). Explain in terms of diminishing marginal utility why the Washington Monument strategy is so misleading. *Hint*: If you are really trying to make the best of a budget cut, should you cut the items in your budget with the highest marginal utility or the lowest marginal utility? Does the Washington Monument strategy cut the items with the highest marginal utility or the lowest marginal utility?

15. Income effects depend on the income elasticity of demand for each good that you buy. If one of the goods you buy has a negative income elasticity, that is, it is an inferior good, what must be true of the income elasticity of the other good you buy?

## Problems

16. Praxilla, who lived in ancient Greece, derives utility from reading poems and from eating cucumbers. Praxilla gets 30 units of marginal utility from her first poem, 27 units of marginal utility from her second poem, 24 units of marginal utility from her third poem, and so on, with marginal utility declining by three units for each additional poem. Praxilla gets six units of marginal utility for each of her first three cucumbers consumed, five units of marginal utility for each of her next three cucumbers consumed, four units of marginal utility for each of the following three cucumbers consumed, and so on, with marginal utility declining by one for every three cucumbers consumed. A poem costs three bronze coins but a cucumber costs only one bronze coin. Praxilla has 18 bronze coins. Sketch Praxilla's budget set between poems and cucumbers, placing poems on the vertical axis and cucumbers on the horizontal axis. Start off with the choice of zero poems and 18 cucumbers, and calculate the changes in marginal utility of moving along the budget line to the next choice of one poem and 15 cucumbers. Using this step-by-step process based on marginal utility, create a table and identify Praxilla's utility-maximizing choice. Compare the marginal utility of the two goods and the relative prices at the optimal choice to see if the expected relationship holds. *Hint*: Label the table columns: 1) Choice, 2) Marginal Gain from More Poems, 3) Marginal Loss from Fewer Cucumbers, 4) Overall Gain or Loss, 5) Is the previous choice optimal? Label the table rows: 1) 0 Poems and 18 Cucumbers, 2) 1 Poem and 15 Cucumbers, 3) 2 Poems and 12 Cucumbers, 4) 3 Poems and 9 Cucumbers, 5) 4 Poems and 6 Cucumbers, 6) 5 Poems and 3 Cucumbers, 7) 6 Poems and 0 Cucumbers.

17. If a 10% decrease in the price of one product that you buy causes an 8% increase in quantity demanded of that product, will another 10% decrease in the price cause another 8% increase (no more and no less) in quantity demanded?

# Production, Costs, and Industry Structure

**FIGURE 7.1** Amazon is an American international electronic commerce company that sells books, among many other things, shipping them directly to the consumer. Until recently there were no brick and mortar Amazon stores. (Credit: modification of "Amazon Prime Delivery Van (50072389511)" by Tony Webster/Wikimedia Commons, CC BY 2.0)

**CHAPTER OBJECTIVES**

In this chapter, you will learn about:

- Explicit and Implicit Costs, and Accounting and Economic Profit
- Production in the Short Run
- Costs in the Short Run
- Production in the Long Run
- Costs in the Long Run

## Introduction to Production, Costs, and Industry Structure

 **BRING IT HOME**

### Amazon

In less than two decades, Amazon.com has transformed the way consumers sell, buy, and even read. Prior to Amazon, independent bookstores with limited inventories in small retail locations primarily sold books. There were exceptions, of course. Borders and Barnes & Noble offered larger stores in urban areas. In the last decade, however, independent bookstores have mostly disappeared, Borders has gone out of business, and Barnes & Noble is struggling. Online delivery and purchase of books has overtaken the more traditional business models. How has

Amazon changed the book selling industry? How has it managed to crush its competition?

A major reason for the giant retailer's success is its production model and cost structure, which has enabled Amazon to undercut the competitors' prices even when factoring in the cost of shipping. Read on to see how firms great (like Amazon) and small (like your corner deli) determine what to sell, at what output, and price.

This chapter is the first of four chapters that explores the *theory of the firm*. This theory explains how firms behave. What does that mean? Let's define what we mean by the firm. A **firm** (or producer or business) combines inputs of labor, capital, land, and raw or finished component materials to produce outputs. If the firm is successful, the outputs are more valuable than the inputs. This activity of **production** goes beyond manufacturing (i.e., making things). It includes any process or service that creates value, including transportation, distribution, wholesale and retail sales.

Production involves a number of important decisions that define a firm's behavior. These decisions include, but are not limited to:

- What product or products should the firm produce?
- How should the firm produce the products (i.e., what production process should the firm use)?
- How much output should the firm produce?
- What price should the firm charge for its products?
- How much labor should the firm employ?

The answers to these questions depend on the production and cost conditions facing each firm. That is the subject of this chapter. The answers also depend on the market structure for the product(s) in question. Market structure is a multidimensional concept that involves how competitive the industry is. We define it by questions such as these:

- How much market power does each firm in the industry possess?
- How similar is each firm's product to the products of other firms in the industry?
- How difficult is it for new firms to enter the industry?
- Do firms compete on the basis of price, advertising, or other product differences?

Figure 7.2 illustrates the range of different market structures, which we will explore in Perfect Competition, Monopoly, and Monopolistic Competition and Oligopoly.

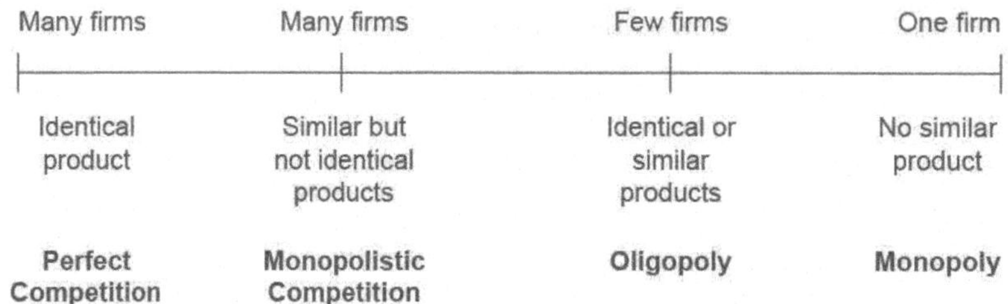


**FIGURE 7.2 The Spectrum of Competition** Firms face different competitive situations. At one extreme—perfect competition—many firms are all trying to sell identical products. At the other extreme—monopoly—only one firm is selling the product, and this firm faces no competition. Monopolistic competition and oligopoly fall between the extremes of perfect competition and monopoly. Monopolistic competition is a situation with many firms selling similar, but not identical products. Oligopoly is a situation with few firms that sell identical or similar products.

Let's examine how firms determine their costs and desired profit levels. Then we will discuss the origins of cost, both in the short and long run. Private enterprise, which can be private individual or group business ownership, characterizes the U.S. economy. In the U.S. system, we have the option to organize private businesses as sole proprietorships (one owner), partners (more than one owner), and corporations (legal entitles separate from the owners.

When people think of businesses, often corporate giants like Wal-Mart, Microsoft, or General Motors come to mind. However, firms come in all sizes, as Table 7.1 shows. The vast majority of American firms have fewer than 20 employees. As of 2010, the U.S. Census Bureau counted 5.7 million firms with employees in the U.S. economy. Slightly less than half of all the workers in private firms are at the 17,000 large firms, meaning they employ more than 500 workers. Another 35% of workers in the U.S. economy are at firms with fewer than 100 workers. These small-scale businesses include everything from dentists and lawyers to businesses that mow lawns or clean houses. Table 7.1 does not include a separate category for the millions of small "non-employer" businesses where a single owner or a few partners are not officially paid wages or a salary, but simply receive whatever they can earn.

| Number of Employees | Firms (% of total firms) | Number of Paid Employees (% of total employment) |
| --- | --- | --- |
| Total | 5,734,538 | 112.0 million |
| 0–9 | 4,543,315 (79.2%) | 12.3 million (11.0%) |
| 10–19 | 617,089 (10.8%) | 8.3 million (7.4%) |
| 20–99 | 475,125 (8.3%) | 18.6 million (16.6%) |
| 100–499 | 81,773 (1.4%) | 15.9 million (14.2%) |
| 500 or more | 17,236 (0.30%) | 50.9 million (49.8%) |

**TABLE 7.1 Range in Size of U.S. Firms** (Source: U.S. Census, 2010 www.census.gov)

## 7.1 Explicit and Implicit Costs, and Accounting and Economic Profit

**LEARNING OBJECTIVES**

By the end of this section, you will be able to:
- Explain the difference between explicit costs and implicit costs
- Understand the relationship between cost and revenue

Each business, regardless of size or complexity, tries to earn a profit:

$$\text{Profit} = \text{Total Revenue} - \text{Total Cost}$$

Total **revenue** is the income the firm generates from selling its products. We calculate it by multiplying the price of the product times the quantity of output sold:

$$\text{Total Revenue} = \text{Price} \times \text{Quantity}$$

We will see in the following chapters that revenue is a function of the demand for the firm's products.

Total cost is what the firm pays for producing and selling its products. Recall that production involves the firm converting inputs to outputs. Each of those inputs has a cost to the firm. The sum of all those costs is total cost. We will learn in this chapter that short run costs are different from long run costs.

We can distinguish between two types of cost: explicit and implicit. **Explicit costs** are out-of-pocket costs, that is, actual payments. Wages that a firm pays its employees or rent that a firm pays for its office are explicit costs. **Implicit costs** are more subtle, but just as important. They represent the opportunity cost of using resources that the firm already owns. Often for small businesses, they are resources that the owners contribute. For example, working in the business while not earning a formal salary, or using the ground floor of a home as a retail store are both implicit costs. Implicit costs also include the depreciation of goods, materials, and equipment that are necessary for a company to operate. (See the Work It Out feature for an extended example.)

These two definitions of cost are important for distinguishing between two conceptions of profit, accounting profit, and economic profit. **Accounting profit** is a cash concept. It means total revenue minus explicit costs—the difference between dollars brought in and dollars paid out. **Economic profit** is total revenue minus total cost, including both explicit and implicit costs. The difference is important because even though a business pays income taxes based on its accounting profit, whether or not it is economically successful depends on its economic profit.

**WORK IT OUT**

## Calculating Implicit Costs

Consider the following example. Eryn currently works for a corporate law firm. She is considering opening her own legal practice, where she expects to earn $200,000 per year once she establishes herself. To run her own firm, she would need an office and a law clerk. She has found the perfect office, which rents for $50,000 per year. She could hire a law clerk for $35,000 per year. If these figures are accurate, would Eryn's legal practice be profitable?

Step 1. First you have to calculate the costs. You can take what you know about explicit costs and total them:

| | |
|---|---|
| Office rental: | $50,000 |
| Law clerk's salary: | +$35,000 |
| Total explicit costs: | $85,000 |

Step 2. Subtracting the explicit costs from the revenue gives you the accounting profit.

| | |
|---|---|
| Revenues: | $200,000 |
| Explicit costs: | –$85,000 |
| Accounting profit: | $115,000 |

However, these calculations consider only the explicit costs. To open her own practice, Eryn would have to quit her current job, where she is earning an annual salary of $125,000. This would be an implicit cost of opening her own firm.

Step 3. You need to subtract both the explicit and implicit costs to determine the true economic profit:

$$\text{Economic profit} = \text{total revenues} - \text{explicit costs} - \text{implicit costs}$$
$$= \$200,000 - \$85,000 - \$125,000$$
$$= -\$10,000 \text{ per year}$$

Eryn would be losing $10,000 per year. That does not mean she would not want to open her own business, but it does mean she would be earning $10,000 less than if she worked for the corporate firm.

Implicit costs can include other things as well. Maybe Eryn values her leisure time, and starting her own firm would require her to put in more hours than at the corporate firm. In this case, the lost leisure would also be an implicit cost that would subtract from economic profits.

Now that we have an idea about the different types of costs, let's look at cost structures. A firm's cost structure in the long run may be different from that in the short run. We turn to that distinction in the next few sections.

## 7.2 Production in the Short Run

**LEARNING OBJECTIVES**

By the end of this section, you will be able to:
- Understand the concept of a production function
- Differentiate between the different types of inputs or factors in a production function
- Differentiate between fixed and variable inputs
- Differentiate between production in the short run and in the long run
- Differentiate between total and marginal product
- Understand the concept of diminishing marginal productivity

In this chapter, we want to explore the relationship between the quantity of output a firm produces, and the cost of producing that output. We mentioned that the cost of the product depends on how many inputs are required to produce the product and what those inputs cost. We can answer the former question by looking at the firm's production function.

**FIGURE 7.3** The production process for pizza includes inputs such as ingredients, the efforts of the pizza maker, and tools and materials for cooking and serving. (Credit: "Grilled gluten-free BBQ chicken pizza" by Keith McDuffee/ Flickr, CC BY 2.0)

Production is the process (or processes) a firm uses to transform inputs (e.g., labor, capital, raw materials) into outputs, i.e. the goods or services the firm wishes to sell. Consider pizza making. The pizzaiolo (pizza maker) takes flour, water, and yeast to make dough. Similarly, the pizzaiolo may take tomatoes, spices, and water to make pizza sauce. The cook rolls out the dough, brushes on the pizza sauce, and adds cheese and other toppings. The pizzaiolo uses a peel—the shovel-like wooden tool—to put the pizza into the oven to cook. Once baked, the pizza goes into a box (if it's for takeout) and the customer pays for the good. What are the inputs (or factors of production) in the production process for this pizza?

Economists divide factors of production into several categories:

- **Natural Resources (Land and Raw Materials)** - The ingredients for the pizza are raw materials. These include the flour, yeast, and water for the dough, the tomatoes, herbs, and water for the sauce, the cheese, and the toppings. If the pizza place uses a wood-burning oven, we would include the wood as a raw material. If the establishment heats the oven with natural gas, we would count this as a raw material. Don't forget electricity for lights. If, instead of pizza, we were looking at an agricultural product, like wheat, we would include the land the farmer used for crops here.
- **Labor** – When we talk about production, labor means human effort, both physical and mental. The pizzaiolo was the primary example of labor here. They need to be strong enough to roll out the dough and to insert and retrieve the pizza from the oven, but they also must know **how** to make the pizza, how long it cooks in the oven and a myriad of other aspects of pizza-making. The business may also have one or more people to work the counter, take orders, and receive payment.
- **Capital** – When economists uses the term capital, they do not mean financial capital (money); rather, they mean physical capital, the machines, equipment, and buildings that one uses to produce the product. In the case of pizza, the capital includes the peel, the oven, the building, and any other necessary equipment (for example, tables and chairs).
- **Technology** – Technology refers to the process or processes for producing the product. How does the pizzaiolo combine ingredients to make pizza? How hot should the oven be? How long should the pizza cook? What is the best oven to use? Gas or wood burning? Should the restaurant make its own dough, sauce, cheese, toppings, or should it buy them?
- **Entrepreneurship** – Production involves many decisions and much knowledge, even for something as simple as pizza. Who makes those decisions? Ultimately, it is the entrepreneur, the person who creates the business, whose idea it is to combine the inputs to produce the outputs.

The cost of producing pizza (or any output) depends on the amount of labor capital, raw materials, and other inputs required and the price of each input to the entrepreneur. Let's explore these ideas in more detail.

We can summarize the ideas so far in terms of a **production function**, a mathematical expression or equation that explains the engineering relationship between inputs and outputs:

$$Q = f[NR, L, K, t, E]$$

The production function gives the answer to the question, how much output can the firm produce given different amounts of inputs? Production functions are specific to the product. Different products have different production functions. The amount of labor a farmer uses to produce a bushel of wheat is likely different than that required to produce an automobile. Firms in the same industry may have somewhat different production functions, since each firm may produce a little differently. One pizza restaurant may make its own dough and sauce, while another may buy those pre-made. A sit-down pizza restaurant probably uses more labor (to handle table service) than a purely take-out restaurant.

We can describe inputs as either **fixed** or **variable**.

**Fixed inputs** are those that can't easily be increased or decreased in a short period of time. In the pizza example, the building is a fixed input. The restaurant owner signs a lease and is stuck in the building until the lease expires. Fixed inputs define the firm's maximum output capacity. This is analogous to the potential real GDP shown by society's production possibilities curve, i.e., the maximum quantities of outputs a society can produce at a given time with its available resources.

**Variable inputs** are those that can easily be increased or decreased in a short period of time. The pizzaiolo can order more ingredients with a phone call, so ingredients would be variable inputs. The owner could hire a new person to work the counter pretty quickly as well.

Economists often use a short-hand form for the production function:

$$Q = f[L, K],$$

where L represents all the variable inputs, and K represents all the fixed inputs.

Economists differentiate between short and long run production.

The **short run** is the period of time during which at least some factors of production are fixed. During the period of the pizza restaurant lease, the pizza restaurant is operating in the short run, because it is limited to using the current building—the owner can't choose a larger or smaller building.

The **long run** is the period of time during which all factors are variable. Once the lease expires for the pizza restaurant, the shop owner can move to a larger or smaller place.

Let's explore production in the short run using a specific example: tree cutting (for lumber) with a two-person crosscut saw.

**FIGURE 7.4** Production in the short run may be explored through the example of lumberjacks using a two-person saw. (Credit: "DO - Apple Day Civilian Conservation Corps Demonstration Crosscut Saw (Gladden)" by Virginia State Parks/Flickr, CC BY 2.0)

Since by definition capital is fixed in the short run, our production function becomes

$$Q = f[L, \bar{K}] \text{ or } Q = f[L]$$

This equation simply indicates that since capital is fixed, the amount of output (e.g., trees cut down per day) depends only on the amount of labor employed (e.g., number of lumberjacks working). We can express this production function numerically as Table 7.2 below shows.

| # Lumberjacks | 1 | 2 | 3 | 4 | 5 |
|---|---|---|---|---|---|
| # Trees (TP) | 4 | 10 | 12 | 13 | 13 |
| MP | 4 | 6 | 2 | 1 | 0 |

**TABLE 7.2 Short Run Production Function for Trees**

Note that we have introduced some new language. We also call Output (Q) Total Product (TP), which means the amount of output produced with a given amount of labor and a fixed amount of capital. In this example, one lumberjack using a two-person saw can cut down four trees in an hour. Two lumberjacks using a two-person saw can cut down ten trees in an hour.

We should also introduce a critical concept: **marginal product**. Marginal product is the additional output of one more worker. Mathematically, Marginal Product is the change in total product divided by the change in labor: $MP = \Delta TP/\Delta L$. In the table above, since 0 workers produce 0 trees, the marginal product of the first worker is four trees per day, but the marginal product of the second worker is six trees per day. Why might that be the case? It's because of the nature of the capital the workers are using. A two-person saw works much better with two persons than with one. Suppose we add a third lumberjack to the story. What will that person's marginal product be? What will that person contribute to the team? Perhaps they can oil the saw's teeth to keep it sawing smoothly or they could bring water to the two people sawing. What you see in the table is a critically important conclusion about production in the short run: It may be that as we add workers, the marginal product increases at first, but sooner or later additional workers will have decreasing marginal product. In fact, there may eventually be no effect or a negative effect on output. This is called the **Law of Diminishing Marginal Product** and it's a characteristic of production in the short run. Diminishing marginal productivity is very similar to the concept of diminishing marginal utility that we learned about in the chapter on consumer choice. Both concepts are examples of the more general concept of diminishing marginal returns. Why does diminishing marginal productivity occur? It's because of fixed capital. We will see this more clearly when we discuss production in the long run.

We can show these concepts graphically as Figure 7.5 and Figure 7.6 illustrate. Figure 7.5 graphically shows the data from Table 7.2. Figure 7.6 shows the more general cases of total product and marginal product curves.

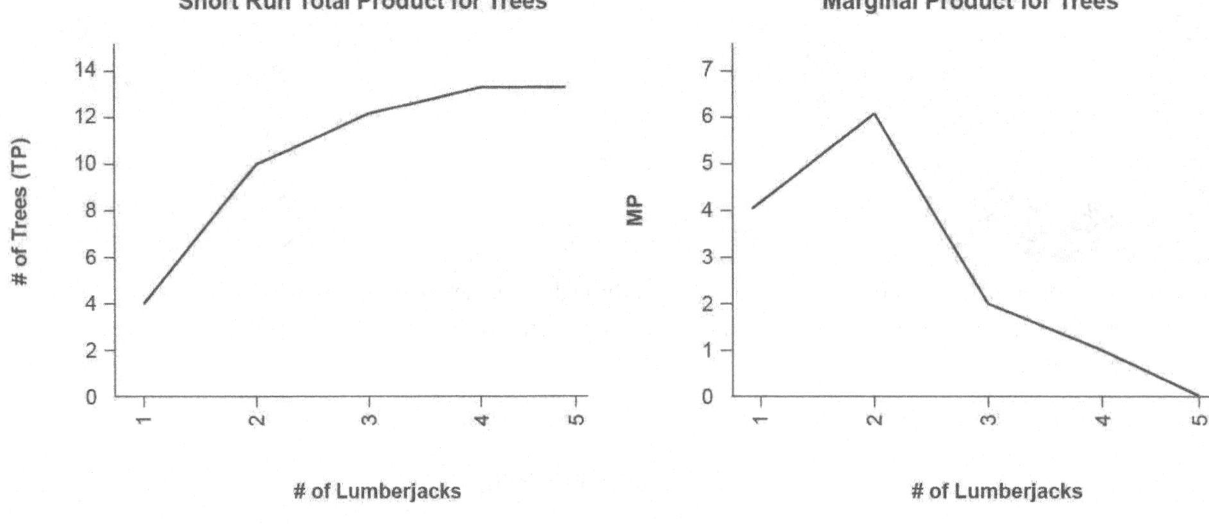


**FIGURE 7.5**

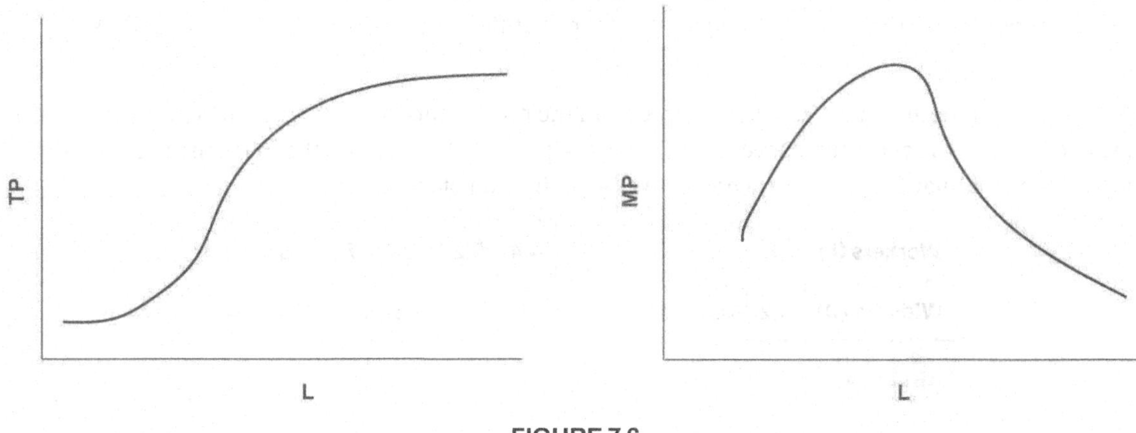

**FIGURE 7.6**

## 7.3 Costs in the Short Run

**LEARNING OBJECTIVES**

By the end of this section, you will be able to:
- Understand the relationship between production and costs
- Understand that every factor of production has a corresponding factor price
- Analyze short-run costs in terms of total cost, fixed cost, variable cost, marginal cost, and average cost
- Calculate average profit
- Evaluate patterns of costs to determine potential profit

We've explained that a firm's total costs depend on the quantities of inputs the firm uses to produce its output and the cost of those inputs to the firm. The firm's production function tells us how much output the firm will produce with given amounts of inputs. However, if we think about that backwards, it tells us how many inputs the firm needs to produce a given quantity of output, which is the first thing we need to determine total cost. Let's move to the second factor we need to determine.

For every factor of production (or input), there is an associated factor payment. **Factor payments** are what the firm pays for the use of the factors of production. From the firm's perspective, factor payments are costs. From the owner of each factor's perspective, factor payments are income. Factor payments include:

- **Raw materials prices** for raw materials
- **Rent** for land or buildings
- **Wages and salaries** for labor
- **Interest and dividends** for the use of financial capital (loans and equity investments)
- **Profit** for entrepreneurship. Profit is the residual, what's left over from revenues after the firm pays all the other costs. While it may seem odd to treat profit as a "cost", it is what entrepreneurs earn for taking the risk of starting a business. You can see this correspondence between factors of production and factor payments in the inside loop of the circular flow diagram in Figure 1.7.

We now have all the information necessary to determine a firm's costs.

A cost function is a mathematical expression or equation that shows the cost of producing different levels of output.

| Q | 1 | 2 | 3 | 4 |
|---|---|---|---|---|
| Cost | $32.50 | $44 | $52 | $90 |

**TABLE 7.3** Cost Function for Producing Widgets

What we observe is that the cost increases as the firm produces higher quantities of output. This is pretty intuitive, since producing more output requires greater quantities of inputs, which cost more dollars to acquire.

What is the origin of these cost figures? They come from the production function and the factor payments. The discussion of costs in the short run above, Costs in the Short Run, was based on the following production function, which is similar to Table 7.3 except for "widgets" instead of trees.

| Workers (L) | 1 | 2 | 3 | 3.25 | 4.4 | 5.2 | 6 | 7 | 8 | 9 |
|---|---|---|---|---|---|---|---|---|---|---|
| Widgets (Q) | 0.2 | 0.4 | 0.8 | 1 | 2 | 3 | 3.5 | 3.8 | 3.95 | 4 |

**TABLE 7.4**

We can use the information from the production function to determine production costs. What we need to know is how many workers are required to produce any quantity of output. If we flip the order of the rows, we "invert" the production function so it shows $L = f(Q)$.

| Widgets (Q) | 0.2 | 0.4 | 0.8 | 1 | 2 | 3 | 3.5 | 3.8 | 3.95 | 4 |
|---|---|---|---|---|---|---|---|---|---|---|
| Workers (L) | 1 | 2 | 3 | 3.25 | 4.4 | 5.2 | 6 | 7 | 8 | 9 |

**TABLE 7.5**

Now focus on the whole number quantities of output. We'll eliminate the fractions from the table:

| Widgets (Q) |  |  | 1 | 2 | 3 |  | 4 |
|---|---|---|---|---|---|---|---|
| Workers (L) |  |  | 3.25 | 4.4 | 5.2 |  | 9 |

**TABLE 7.6**

Suppose widget workers receive $10 per hour. Multiplying the Workers row by $10 (and eliminating the blanks) gives us the cost of producing different levels of output.

| Widgets (Q) | 1.00 | 2.00 | 3.00 | 4.00 |
|---|---|---|---|---|
| Workers (L) | 3.25 | 4.4 | 5.2 | 9 |
| × Wage Rate per hour | $10 | $10 | $10 | $10 |
| = Cost | $32.50 | $44.00 | $52.00 | $90.00 |

**TABLE 7.7**

This is same cost function with which we began! (shown in Table 7.3)

Now that we have the basic idea of the cost origins and how they are related to production, let's drill down into the details.

## Average and Marginal Costs

The cost of producing a firm's output depends on how much labor and physical capital the firm uses. A list of the costs involved in producing cars will look very different from the costs involved in producing computer software or haircuts or fast-food meals.

We can measure costs in a variety of ways. Each way provides its own insight into costs. Sometimes firms need to look at their cost per unit of output, not just their total cost. There are two ways to measure per unit costs. The most intuitive way is average cost. Average cost is the cost on average of producing a given quantity. We define **average cost** as total cost divided by the quantity of output produced. $AC = TC/Q$ If producing two widgets costs a total of \$44, the average cost per widget is \$44/2 = \$22 per widget. The other way of measuring cost per unit is marginal cost. If average cost is the cost of the average unit of output produced, marginal cost is the cost of each individual unit produced. More formally, marginal cost is the cost of producing one more unit of output. Mathematically, **marginal cost** is the change in total cost divided by the change in output: $MC = \Delta TC/\Delta Q$. If the cost of the first widget is \$32.50 and the cost of two widgets is \$44, the marginal cost of the second widget is \$44 − \$32.50 = \$11.50. We can see the Widget Cost table redrawn below with average and marginal cost added.

| Q | 1 | 2 | 3 | 4 |
|---|---|---|---|---|
| Total Cost | \$32.50 | \$44.00 | \$52.00 | \$90.00 |
| Average Cost | \$32.50 | \$22.00 | \$17.33 | \$22.50 |
| Marginal Cost | \$32.50 | \$11.50 | \$8.00 | \$38.00 |

**TABLE 7.8 Extended Cost Function for Producing Widgets**

Note that the marginal cost of the first unit of output is always the same as total cost.

### Fixed and Variable Costs

We can decompose costs into fixed and variable costs. Fixed costs are the costs of the fixed inputs (e.g., capital). Because fixed inputs do not change in the short run, fixed costs are expenditures that do not change regardless of the level of production. Whether you produce a great deal or a little, the fixed costs are the same. One example is the rent on a factory or a retail space. Once you sign the lease, the rent is the same regardless of how much you produce, at least until the lease expires. Fixed costs can take many other forms: for example, the cost of machinery or equipment to produce the product, research and development costs to develop new products, even an expense like advertising to popularize a brand name. The amount of fixed costs varies according to the specific line of business: for instance, manufacturing computer chips requires an expensive factory, but a local moving and hauling business can get by with almost no fixed costs at all if it rents trucks by the day when needed.

**Variable costs** are the costs of the variable inputs (e.g., labor). The only way to increase or decrease output is by increasing or decreasing the variable inputs. Therefore, variable costs increase or decrease with output. We treat labor as a variable cost, since producing a greater quantity of a good or service typically requires more workers or more work hours. Variable costs would also include raw materials.

Total costs are the sum of fixed plus variable costs. Let's look at another example. Consider the barber shop called "The Clip Joint" in Figure 7.7. The data for output and costs are in Table 7.9. The fixed costs of operating the barber shop, including the space and equipment, are \$160 per day. The variable costs are the costs of hiring barbers, which in our example is \$80 per barber each day. The first two columns of the table show the quantity of haircuts the barbershop can produce as it hires additional barbers. The third column shows the fixed costs, which do not change regardless of the level of production. The fourth column shows the variable costs at each level of output. We calculate these by taking the amount of labor hired and multiplying by the wage. For example, two barbers cost: 2 × $80 = $160. Adding together the fixed costs in the third column and the variable costs in the fourth column produces the total costs in the fifth column. For example, with two barbers the total cost is: $160 + $160 = $320.

| Labor | Quantity | Fixed Cost | Variable Cost | Total Cost |
|-------|----------|------------|---------------|------------|
| 1 | 16 | $160 | $80 | $240 |
| 2 | 40 | $160 | $160 | $320 |
| 3 | 60 | $160 | $240 | $400 |
| 4 | 72 | $160 | $320 | $480 |
| 5 | 80 | $160 | $400 | $560 |
| 6 | 84 | $160 | $480 | $640 |
| 7 | 82 | $160 | $560 | $720 |

**TABLE 7.9** Output and Total Costs

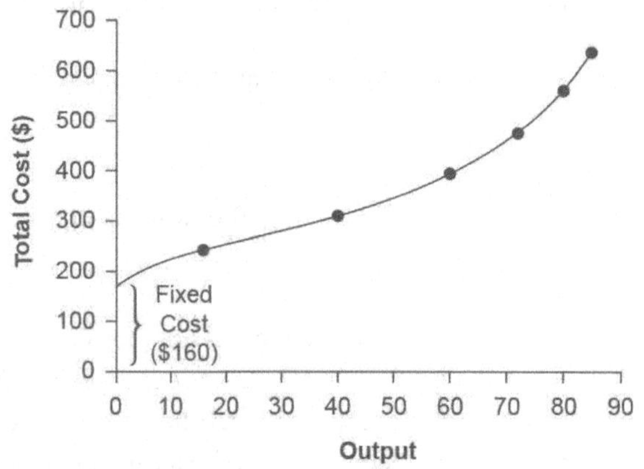


**FIGURE 7.7** How Output Affects Total Costs At zero production, the fixed costs of $160 are still present. As production increases, variable costs are added to fixed costs, and the total cost is the sum of the two.

At zero production, the fixed costs of $160 are still present. As production increases, we add variable costs to fixed costs, and the total cost is the sum of the two. Figure 7.7 graphically shows the relationship between the quantity of output produced and the cost of producing that output. We always show the fixed costs as the vertical intercept of the total cost curve; that is, they are the costs incurred when output is zero so there are no variable costs.

You can see from the graph that once production starts, total costs and variable costs rise. While variable costs may initially increase at a decreasing rate, at some point they begin increasing at an increasing rate. This is caused by diminishing marginal productivity which we discussed earlier in the Production in the Short Run section of this chapter, which is easiest to see with an example. As the number of barbers increases from zero to one in the table, output increases from 0 to 16 for a marginal gain (or marginal product) of 16. As the number rises from one to two barbers, output increases from 16 to 40, a marginal gain of 24. From that point on, though, the marginal product diminishes as we add each additional barber. For example, as the number of barbers rises from two to three, the marginal product is only 20; and as the number rises from three to four, the marginal product is only 12.

To understand the reason behind this pattern, consider that a one-man barber shop is a very busy operation. The single barber needs to do everything: say hello to people entering, answer the phone, cut hair, sweep, and run the cash register. A second barber reduces the level of disruption from jumping back and forth between these tasks, and allows a greater division of labor and specialization. The result can be increasing marginal productivity. However, as the shop adds other barbers, the advantage of each additional barber is less, since the specialization of labor can only go so far. The addition of a sixth or seventh or eighth barber just to greet people at the door will have less impact than the second one did. This is the pattern of diminishing marginal productivity. As a result, the total costs of production will begin to rise more rapidly as output increases. At some point, you may even see negative returns as the additional barbers begin bumping elbows and getting in each other's way. In this case, the addition of still more barbers would actually cause output to decrease, as the last row of Table 7.9 shows.

This pattern of diminishing marginal productivity is common in production. As another example, consider the problem of irrigating a crop on a farmer's field. The plot of land is the fixed factor of production, while the water that the farmer can add to the land is the key variable cost. As the farmer adds water to the land, output increases. However, adding increasingly more water brings smaller increases in output, until at some point the water floods the field and actually reduces output. Diminishing marginal productivity occurs because, with fixed inputs (land in this example), each additional unit of input (e.g., water) contributes less to overall production.

## Average Total Cost, Average Variable Cost, Marginal Cost

The breakdown of total costs into fixed and variable costs can provide a basis for other insights as well. The first five columns of Table 7.10 duplicate the previous table, but the last three columns show average total costs, average variable costs, and marginal costs. These new measures analyze costs on a per-unit (rather than a total) basis and are reflected in the curves in Figure 7.8.

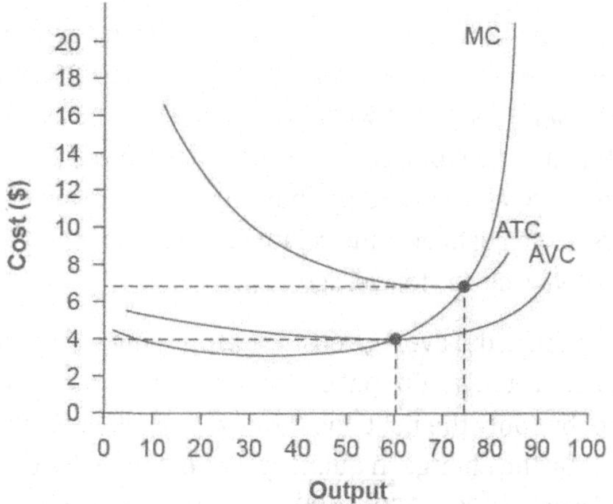


FIGURE 7.8 Cost Curves at the Clip Joint We can also present the information on total costs, fixed cost, and variable cost on a per-unit basis. We calculate average total cost (ATC) by dividing total cost by the total quantity produced. The average total cost curve is typically U-shaped. We calculate average variable cost (AVC) by dividing variable cost by the quantity produced. The average variable cost curve lies below the average total cost curve and is also typically U-shaped. We calculate marginal cost (MC) by taking the change in total cost between two levels of output and dividing by the change in output. The marginal cost curve is upward-sloping.

| Labor | Quantity | Fixed Cost | Variable Cost | Total Cost | Marginal Cost | Average Total Cost | Average Variable Cost |
|---|---|---|---|---|---|---|---|
| 1 | 16 | $160 | $80 | $240 | $15.00 | $15.00 | $5.00 |
| 2 | 40 | $160 | $160 | $320 | $3.33 | $8.00 | $4.00 |
| 3 | 60 | $160 | $240 | $400 | $4.00 | $6.67 | $4.00 |
| 4 | 72 | $160 | $320 | $480 | $6.67 | $6.67 | $4.44 |
| 5 | 80 | $160 | $400 | $560 | $10.00 | $7.00 | $5.00 |
| 6 | 84 | $160 | $480 | $640 | $20.00 | $7.62 | $5.71 |

**TABLE 7.10** Different Types of Costs

**Average total cost** (sometimes referred to simply as average cost) is total cost divided by the quantity of output. Since the total cost of producing 40 haircuts is $320, the average total cost for producing each of 40 haircuts is $320/40, or $8 per haircut. Average cost curves are typically U-shaped, as Figure 7.8 shows. Average total cost starts off relatively high, because at low levels of output total costs are dominated by the fixed cost. Mathematically, the denominator is so small that average total cost is large. Average total cost then declines, as the fixed costs are spread over an increasing quantity of output. In the average cost calculation, the rise in the numerator of total costs is relatively small compared to the rise in the denominator of quantity produced. However, as output expands still further, the average cost begins to rise. At the right side of the average cost curve, total costs begin rising more rapidly as diminishing returns come into effect.

We obtain **average variable cost** when we divide variable cost by quantity of output. For example, the variable cost of producing 80 haircuts is $400, so the average variable cost is $400/80, or $5 per haircut. Note that at any level of output, the average variable cost curve will always lie below the curve for average total cost, as Figure 7.8 shows. The reason is that average total cost includes average variable cost and average fixed cost. Thus, for Q = 80 haircuts, the average total cost is $8 per haircut, while the average variable cost is $5 per haircut. However, as output grows, fixed costs become relatively less important (since they do not rise with output), so average variable cost sneaks closer to average cost.

Average total and variable costs measure the average costs of producing some quantity of output. Marginal cost is somewhat different. **Marginal cost** is the additional cost of producing one more unit of output. It is not the cost per unit of *all* units produced, but only the next one (or next few). We calculate marginal cost by taking the change in total cost and dividing it by the change in quantity. For example, as quantity produced increases from 40 to 60 haircuts, total costs rise by 400 − 320, or 80. Thus, the marginal cost for each of those marginal 20 units will be 80/20, or $4 per haircut. The marginal cost curve is generally upward-sloping, because diminishing marginal returns implies that additional units are more costly to produce. We can see small range of increasing marginal returns in the figure as a dip in the marginal cost curve before it starts rising. There is a point at which marginal and average costs meet, as the following Clear it Up feature discusses.

## CLEAR IT UP

### Where do marginal and average costs meet?

The marginal cost line intersects the average cost line exactly at the bottom of the average cost curve—which occurs at a quantity of 72 and cost of $6.60 in Figure 7.8. The reason why the intersection occurs at this point is built into the economic meaning of marginal and average costs. If the marginal cost of production is below the average cost for producing previous units, as it is for the points to the left of where MC crosses ATC, then producing one more additional unit will reduce average costs overall—and the ATC curve will be downward-sloping in this zone. Conversely, if the marginal cost of production for producing an additional unit is above the average cost for producing the earlier units, as it is for points to the right of where MC crosses ATC, then producing a marginal unit will increase average costs overall—and the ATC curve must be upward-sloping in this zone. The point of transition, between where MC is pulling ATC down and where it is pulling it up, must occur at the minimum point of the ATC curve.

This idea of the marginal cost "pulling down" the average cost or "pulling up" the average cost may sound abstract, but think about it in terms of your own grades. If the score on the most recent quiz you take is lower than your average score on previous quizzes, then the marginal quiz pulls down your average. If your score on the most recent quiz is higher than the average on previous quizzes, the marginal quiz pulls up your average. In this same way, low marginal costs of production first pull down average costs and then higher marginal costs pull them up.

The numerical calculations behind average cost, average variable cost, and marginal cost will change from firm to firm. However, the general patterns of these curves, and the relationships and economic intuition behind them, will not change.

### Lessons from Alternative Measures of Costs

Breaking down total costs into fixed cost, marginal cost, average total cost, and average variable cost is useful because each statistic offers its own insights for the firm.

Whatever the firm's quantity of production, total revenue must exceed total costs if it is to earn a profit. As explored in the chapter Choice in a World of Scarcity, fixed costs are often sunk costs that a firm cannot recoup. In thinking about what to do next, typically you should ignore sunk costs, since you have already spent this money and cannot make any changes. However, you can change variable costs, so they convey information about the firm's ability to cut costs in the present and the extent to which costs will increase if production rises.

 **CLEAR IT UP**

### Why are total cost and average cost not on the same graph?
Total cost, fixed cost, and variable cost each reflect different aspects of the cost of production over the entire quantity of output produced. We measure these costs in dollars. In contrast, marginal cost, average cost, and average variable cost are costs per unit. In the previous example, we measured them as dollars per haircut. Thus, it would not make sense to put all of these numbers on the same graph, since we measure them in different units ($ versus $ per unit of output).

It would be as if the vertical axis measured two different things. In addition, as a practical matter, if they were on the same graph, the lines for marginal cost, average cost, and average variable cost would appear almost flat against the horizontal axis, compared to the values for total cost, fixed cost, and variable cost. Using the figures from the previous example, the total cost of producing 40 haircuts is $320. However, the average cost is $320/40, or $8. If you graphed both total and average cost on the same axes, the average cost would hardly show.

Average cost tells a firm whether it can earn profits given the current price in the market. If we divide profit by the quantity of output produced we get **average profit**, also known as the firm's *profit margin*. Expanding the equation for profit gives:

$$\begin{aligned}
\text{average profit} &= \frac{\text{profit}}{\text{quantity produced}} \\
&= \frac{\text{total revenue} - \text{total cost}}{\text{quantity produced}} \\
&= \frac{\text{total revenue}}{\text{quantity produced}} - \frac{\text{total cost}}{\text{quantity produced}} \\
&= \text{average revenue} - \text{average cost}
\end{aligned}$$

However, note that:

$$\begin{aligned}
\text{average revenue} &= \frac{\text{price} \times \text{quantity produced}}{\text{quantity produced}} \\
&= \text{price}
\end{aligned}$$

Thus:

$$\text{average profit} = \text{price} - \text{average cost}$$

This is the firm's **profit margin**. This definition implies that if the market price is above average cost, average profit, and thus total profit, will be positive. If price is below average cost, then profits will be negative.

We can compare this marginal cost of producing an additional unit with the marginal revenue gained by selling that additional unit to reveal whether the additional unit is adding to total profit—or not. Thus, marginal cost helps producers understand how increasing or decreasing production affects profits.

### A Variety of Cost Patterns

The pattern of costs varies among industries and even among firms in the same industry. Some businesses have high fixed costs, but low marginal costs. Consider, for example, an internet company that provides medical advice to customers. Consumers might pay such a company directly, or perhaps hospitals or healthcare practices might subscribe on behalf of their patients. Setting up the website, collecting the information, writing the content, and buying or leasing the computer space to handle the web traffic are all fixed costs that the company must undertake before the site can work. However, when the website is up and running, it can provide a high quantity of service with relatively low variable costs, like the cost of monitoring the system and updating the information. In this case, the total cost curve might start at a high level, because of the high fixed costs, but then might appear close to flat, up to a large quantity of output, reflecting the low variable costs of operation. If the website is popular, however, a large rise in the number of visitors will overwhelm the website, and increasing output further could require a purchase of additional computer space.

For other firms, fixed costs may be relatively low. For example, consider firms that rake leaves in the fall or shovel snow off sidewalks and driveways in the winter. For fixed costs, such firms may need little more than a car to transport workers to homes of customers and some rakes and shovels. Still other firms may find that diminishing marginal returns set in quite sharply. If a manufacturing plant tried to run 24 hours a day, seven days a week, little time remains for routine equipment maintenance, and marginal costs can increase dramatically as the firm struggles to repair and replace overworked equipment.

Every firm can gain insight into its task of earning profits by dividing its total costs into fixed and variable costs, and then using these calculations as a basis for average total cost, average variable cost, and marginal cost. However, making a final decision about the profit-maximizing quantity to produce and the price to charge will require combining these perspectives on cost with an analysis of sales and revenue, which in turn requires looking at the market structure in which the firm finds itself. Before we turn to the analysis of market structure in other chapters, we will analyze the firm's cost structure from a long-run perspective.

## 7.4 Production in the Long Run

### LEARNING OBJECTIVES

By the end of this section, you will be able to:
- Understand how long run production differs from short run production.

In the long run, all factors (including capital) are variable, so our production function is $Q = f[L, K]$.

Consider a secretarial firm that does typing for hire using typists for labor and personal computers for capital. To start, the firm has just enough business for one typist and one PC to keep busy for a day. Say that's five documents. Now suppose the firm receives a rush order from a good customer for 10 documents tomorrow. Ideally, the firm would like to use two typists and two PCs to produce twice their normal output of five documents. However, in the short turn, the firm has fixed capital, i.e. only one PC. The table below shows the situation:

| # Typists (L) | 1 | 2 | 3 | 4 | 5 | 6 | |
|---|---|---|---|---|---|---|---|
| Letters/hr (TP) | 5 | 7 | 8 | 8 | 8 | 8 | For K = 1PC |
| MP | | 5 | 2 | 1 | 0 | 0 | 0 |

**TABLE 7.11** Short Run Production Function for Typing

In the short run, the only variable factor is labor so the only way the firm can produce more output is by hiring additional workers. What could the second worker do? What can they contribute to the firm? Perhaps they can answer the phone, which is a major impediment to completing the typing assignment. What about a third worker? Perhaps the third worker could bring coffee to the first two workers. You can see both total product and marginal product for the firm above. Now here's something to think about: At what point (e.g., after how many workers) does diminishing marginal productivity kick in, and more importantly, why?

In this example, marginal productivity starts to decline after the second worker. This is because capital is fixed. The production process for typing works best with one worker and one PC. If you add more than one typist, you get seriously diminishing marginal productivity.

Consider the long run. Suppose the firm's demand increases to 15 documents per day. What might the firm do to operate more efficiently? If demand has tripled, the firm could acquire two more PCs, which would give us a new short run production function as Table 7.12 below shows.

| # Typists (L) | 1 | 2 | 3 | 4 | 5 | 5 | |
|---|---|---|---|---|---|---|---|
| Letters/hr (TP) | 5 | 6 | 8 | 8 | 8 | 8 | For K = 1PC |
| MP | | 5 | 2 | 1 | 0 | 0 | 0 |
| Letters/hr (TP) | 5 | 10 | 15 | 17 | 18 | 18 | For K = 3PC |
| MP | | 5 | 5 | 5 | 2 | 1 | 0 |

**TABLE 7.12** Long Run Production Function for Typing

With more capital, the firm can hire three workers before diminishing productivity comes into effect. More generally, because all factors are variable, the long run production function shows the most efficient way of producing any level of output.

## 7.5 Costs in the Long Run

**LEARNING OBJECTIVES**

By the end of this section, you will be able to:

- Calculate long run total cost
- Identify economies of scale, diseconomies of scale, and constant returns to scale
- Interpret graphs of long-run average cost curves and short-run average cost curves
- Analyze cost and production in the long run and short run

The long run is the period of time when all costs are variable. The long run depends on the specifics of the firm in question—it is not a precise period of time. If you have a one-year lease on your factory, then the long run is any period longer than a year, since after a year you are no longer bound by the lease. No costs are fixed in the long run. A firm can build new factories and purchase new machinery, or it can close existing facilities. In planning for the long run, the firm will compare alternative **production technologies** (or processes).

In this context, technology refers to all alternative methods of combining inputs to produce outputs. It does not refer to a specific new invention like the tablet computer. The firm will search for the production technology that allows it to produce the desired level of output at the lowest cost. After all, lower costs lead to higher profits—at least if total revenues remain unchanged. Moreover, each firm must fear that if it does not seek out the lowest-cost methods of production, then it may lose sales to competitor firms that find a way to produce and sell for less.

### Choice of Production Technology

A firm can perform many tasks with a range of combinations of labor and physical capital. For example, a firm can have human beings answering phones and taking messages, or it can invest in an automated voicemail system. A firm can hire file clerks and secretaries to manage a system of paper folders and file cabinets, or it can invest in a computerized recordkeeping system that will require fewer employees. A firm can hire workers to push supplies around a factory on rolling carts, it can invest in motorized vehicles, or it can invest in robots that carry materials without a driver. Firms often face a choice between buying a many small machines, which need a worker to run each one, or buying one larger and more expensive machine, which requires only one or two workers to operate it. In short, physical capital and labor can often substitute for each other.

Consider the example of local governments hiring a private firm to clean up public parks. Three different combinations of labor and physical capital for cleaning up a single average-sized park appear in Table 7.13. The first production technology is heavy on workers and light on machines, while the next two technologies substitute machines for workers. Since all three of these production methods produce the same thing—one cleaned-up park—a profit-seeking firm will choose the production technology that is least expensive, given the prices of labor and machines.

| | | |
|---|---|---|
| Production technology 1 | 10 workers | 2 machines |
| Production technology 2 | 7 workers | 4 machines |
| Production technology 3 | 3 workers | 7 machines |

**TABLE 7.13 Three Ways to Clean a Park**

Production technology 1 uses the most labor and least machinery, while production technology 3 uses the least labor and the most machinery. Table 7.14 outlines three examples of how the total cost will change with each production technology as the cost of labor changes. As the cost of labor rises from example A to B to C, the firm will choose to substitute away from labor and use more machinery.

**Example A: Workers cost $40, machines cost $80**

|  | Labor Cost | Machine Cost | Total Cost |
|---|---|---|---|
| Cost of technology 1 | 10 × $40 = $400 | 2 × $80 = $160 | $560 |
| Cost of technology 2 | 7 × $40 = $280 | 4 × $80 = $320 | $600 |
| Cost of technology 3 | 3 × $40 = $120 | 7 × $80 = $560 | $680 |

**Example B: Workers cost $55, machines cost $80**

|  | Labor Cost | Machine Cost | Total Cost |
|---|---|---|---|
| Cost of technology 1 | 10 × $55 = $550 | 2 × $80 = $160 | $710 |
| Cost of technology 2 | 7 × $55 = $385 | 4 × $80 = $320 | $705 |
| Cost of technology 3 | 3 × $55 = $165 | 7 × $80 = $560 | $725 |

**Example C: Workers cost $90, machines cost $80**

|  | Labor Cost | Machine Cost | Total Cost |
|---|---|---|---|
| Cost of technology 1 | 10 × $90 = $900 | 2 × $80 = $160 | $1,060 |
| Cost of technology 2 | 7 × $90 = $630 | 4 × $80 = $320 | $950 |
| Cost of technology 3 | 3 × $90 = $270 | 7 × $80 = $560 | $830 |

**TABLE 7.14 Total Cost with Rising Labor Costs**

Example A shows the firm's cost calculation when wages are $40 and machines costs are $80. In this case, technology 1 is the low-cost production technology. In example B, wages rise to $55, while the cost of machines does not change, in which case technology 2 is the low-cost production technology. If wages keep rising up to $90, while the cost of machines remains unchanged, then technology 3 clearly becomes the low-cost form of production, as example C shows.

This example shows that as an input becomes more expensive (in this case, the labor input), firms will attempt to conserve on using that input and will instead shift to other inputs that are relatively less expensive. This pattern helps to explain why the demand curve for labor (or any input) slopes down; that is, as labor becomes relatively more expensive, profit-seeking firms will seek to substitute the use of other inputs. When a multinational employer like Coca-Cola or McDonald's sets up a bottling plant or a restaurant in a high-wage economy like the United States, Canada, Japan, or Western Europe, it is likely to use production technologies that conserve on the number of workers and focuses more on machines. However, that same employer is likely to use production technologies with more workers and less machinery when producing in a lower-wage country like Mexico, China, or South Africa.

## Economies of Scale

Once a firm has determined the least costly production technology, it can consider the optimal scale of production, or quantity of output to produce. Many industries experience economies of scale. Economies of scale refers to the situation where, as the quantity of output goes up, the cost per unit goes down. This is the idea behind "warehouse stores" like Costco or Walmart. In everyday language: a larger factory can produce at a lower average cost than a smaller factory.

Figure 7.9 illustrates the idea of economies of scale, showing the average cost of producing an alarm clock falling as the quantity of output rises. For a small-sized factory like S, with an output level of 1,000, the average cost of production is $12 per alarm clock. For a medium-sized factory like M, with an output level of 2,000, the average cost of production falls to $8 per alarm clock. For a large factory like L, with an output of 5,000, the average cost of production declines still further to $4 per alarm clock.

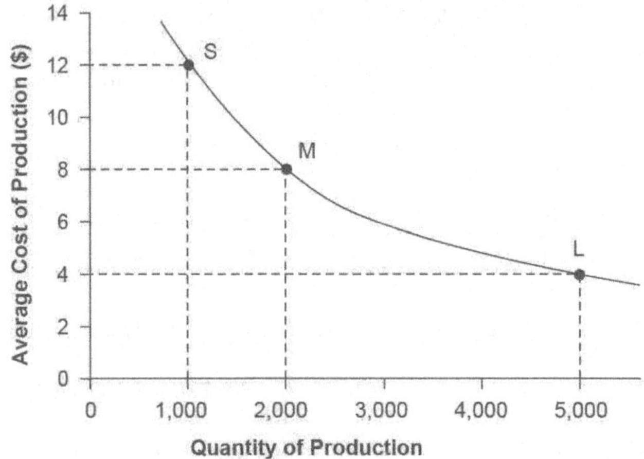


**FIGURE 7.9 Economies of Scale** A small factory like S produces 1,000 alarm clocks at an average cost of $12 per clock. A medium factory like M produces 2,000 alarm clocks at a cost of $8 per clock. A large factory like L produces 5,000 alarm clocks at a cost of $4 per clock. Economies of scale exist when the larger scale of production leads to lower average costs.

The average cost curve in Figure 7.9 may appear similar to the average cost curves we presented earlier in this chapter, although it is downward-sloping rather than U-shaped. However, there is one major difference. The economies of scale curve is a long-run average cost curve, because it allows all factors of production to change. The short-run average cost curves we presented earlier in this chapter assumed the existence of fixed costs, and only variable costs were allowed to change.

One prominent example of economies of scale occurs in the chemical industry. Chemical plants have many pipes. The cost of the materials for producing a pipe is related to the circumference of the pipe and its length. However, the cross-section area of the pipe determines the volume of chemicals that can flow through it. The calculations in Table 7.15 show that a pipe which uses twice as much material to make (as shown by the circumference) can actually carry four times the volume of chemicals because the pipe's cross-section area rises by a factor of four (as the Area column below shows).

|  | **Circumference ($2\pi r$)** | **Area ($\pi r^2$)** |
|---|---|---|
| 4-inch pipe | 12.5 inches | 12.5 square inches |
| 8-inch pipe | 25.1 inches | 50.2 square inches |
| 16-inch pipe | 50.2 inches | 201.1 square inches |

**TABLE 7.15 Comparing Pipes: Economies of Scale in the Chemical Industry**

A doubling of the cost of producing the pipe allows the chemical firm to process four times as much material. This pattern is a major reason for economies of scale in chemical production, which uses a large quantity of pipes. Of course, economies of scale in a chemical plant are more complex than this simple calculation suggests. However, the chemical engineers who design these plants have long used what they call the "six-tenths rule," a rule of thumb which holds that increasing the quantity produced in a chemical plant by a certain percentage will increase total cost by only six-tenths as much.

## Shapes of Long-Run Average Cost Curves

While in the short run firms are limited to operating on a single average cost curve (corresponding to the level of fixed costs they have chosen), in the long run when all costs are variable, they can choose to operate on any average cost curve. Thus, the **long-run average cost (LRAC) curve** is actually based on a group of **short-run average cost (SRAC) curves**, each of which represents one specific level of fixed costs. More precisely, the long-run average cost curve will be the least expensive average cost curve for any level of output. Figure 7.10 shows how we build the long-run average cost curve from a group of short-run average cost curves. Five short-run-average cost curves appear on the diagram. Each SRAC curve represents a different level of fixed costs. For example, you can imagine $SRAC_1$ as a small factory, $SRAC_2$ as a medium factory, $SRAC_3$ as a large factory, and $SRAC_4$ and $SRAC_5$ as very large and ultra-large. Although this diagram shows only five SRAC curves, presumably there are an infinite number of other SRAC curves between the ones that we show. Think of this family of short-run average cost curves as representing different choices for a firm that is planning its level of investment in fixed cost physical capital—knowing that different choices about capital investment in the present will cause it to end up with different short-run average cost curves in the future.

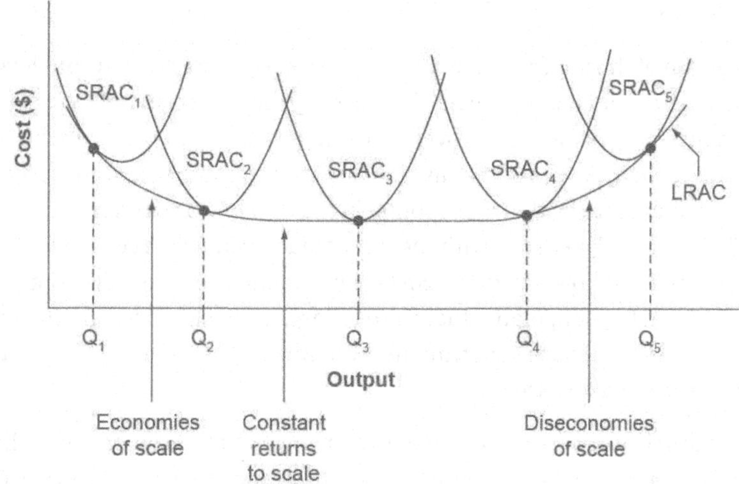


FIGURE 7.10 From Short-Run Average Cost Curves to Long-Run Average Cost Curves The five different short-run average cost (SRAC) curves each represents a different level of fixed costs, from the low level of fixed costs at $SRAC_1$ to the high level of fixed costs at $SRAC_5$. Other SRAC curves, not in the diagram, lie between the ones that are here. The long-run average cost (LRAC) curve shows the lowest cost for producing each quantity of output when fixed costs can vary, and so it is formed by the bottom edge of the family of SRAC curves. If a firm wished to produce quantity $Q_3$, it would choose the fixed costs associated with $SRAC_3$.

The long-run average cost curve shows the cost of producing each quantity in the long run, when the firm can choose its level of fixed costs and thus choose which short-run average costs it desires. If the firm plans to produce in the long run at an output of $Q_3$, it should make the set of investments that will lead it to locate on $SRAC_3$, which allows producing $q_3$ at the lowest cost. A firm that intends to produce $Q_3$ would be foolish to choose the level of fixed costs at $SRAC_2$ or $SRAC_4$. At $SRAC_2$ the level of fixed costs is too low for producing $Q_3$ at lowest possible cost, and producing $q_3$ would require adding a very high level of variable costs and make the average cost very high. At $SRAC_4$, the level of fixed costs is too high for producing $q_3$ at lowest possible cost, and again average costs would be very high as a result.

The shape of the long-run cost curve, in Figure 7.10, is fairly common for many industries. The left-hand portion of the long-run average cost curve, where it is downward- sloping from output levels $Q_1$ to $Q_2$ to $Q_3$, illustrates the case of economies of scale. In this portion of the long-run average cost curve, larger scale leads to lower average costs. We illustrated this pattern earlier in Figure 7.9.

In the middle portion of the long-run average cost curve, the flat portion of the curve around $Q_3$, economies of scale have been exhausted. In this situation, allowing all inputs to expand does not much change the average cost of production. We call this **constant returns to scale**. In this LRAC curve range, the average cost of production does not change much as scale rises or falls. The following Clear It Up feature explains where diminishing marginal returns fit into this analysis.

## CLEAR IT UP

### How do economies of scale compare to diminishing marginal returns?

The concept of economies of scale, where average costs decline as production expands, might seem to conflict with the idea of diminishing marginal returns, where marginal costs rise as production expands. However, diminishing marginal returns refers only to the short-run average cost curve, where one variable input (like labor) is increasing, but other inputs (like capital) are fixed. Economies of scale refers to the long-run average cost curve where all inputs are allowed to increase together. Thus, it is quite possible and common to have an industry that has both diminishing marginal returns when only one input is allowed to change, and at the same time has economies of scale when all inputs change together to produce a larger-scale operation.

---

Finally, the right-hand portion of the long-run average cost curve, running from output level $Q_4$ to $Q_5$, shows a situation where, as the level of output and the scale rises, average costs rise as well. We call this situation **diseconomies of scale**. A firm or a factory can grow so large that it becomes very difficult to manage, resulting in unnecessarily high costs as many layers of management try to communicate with workers and with each other, and as failures to communicate lead to disruptions in the flow of work and materials. Not many overly large factories exist in the real world, because with their very high production costs, they are unable to compete for long against plants with lower average costs of production. However, in some planned economies, like the economy of the old Soviet Union, plants that were so large as to be grossly inefficient were able to continue operating for a long time because government economic planners protected them from competition and ensured that they would not make losses.

Diseconomies of scale can also be present across an entire firm, not just a large factory. The leviathan effect can hit firms that become too large to run efficiently, across the entirety of the enterprise. Firms that shrink their operations are often responding to finding itself in the diseconomies region, thus moving back to a lower average cost at a lower output level.

## LINK IT UP

Visit this website (http://openstax.org/l/Toobig) to read an article about the complexity of the belief that banks can be "too-big-to-fail."

### The Size and Number of Firms in an Industry

The shape of the long-run average cost curve has implications for how many firms will compete in an industry, and whether the firms in an industry have many different sizes, or tend to be the same size. For example, say that the appliance industry sells one million dishwashers every year at a price of $500 each and the long-run average cost curve for dishwashers is in Figure 7.11 (a). In Figure 7.11 (a), the lowest point of the LRAC curve occurs at a quantity of 10,000 produced. Thus, the market for dishwashers will consist of 100 different manufacturing plants of this same size. If some firms built a plant that produced 5,000 dishwashers per year or 25,000 dishwashers per year, the average costs of production at such plants would be well above $500, and the firms would not be able to compete.

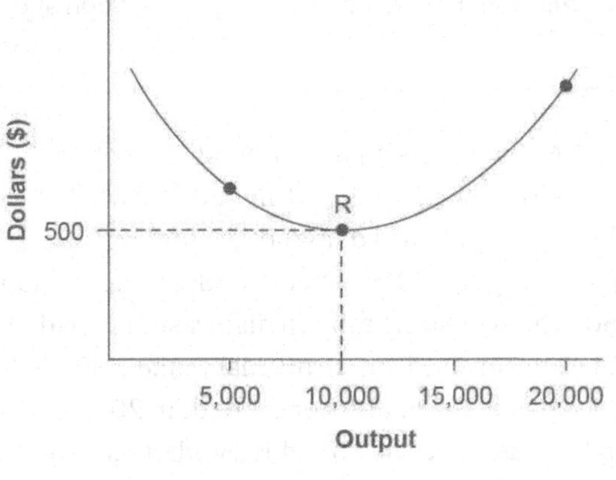

(a) LRAC curve with a clear minimum point

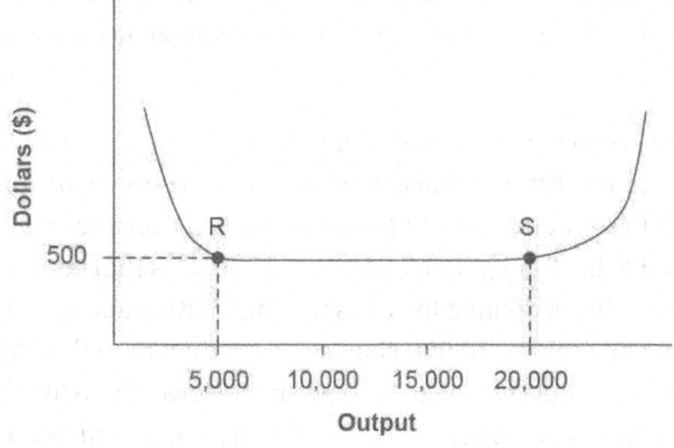

(b) A flat-bottomed LRAC curve

**FIGURE 7.11 The LRAC Curve and the Size and Number of Firms** (a) Low-cost firms will produce at output level R. When the LRAC curve has a clear minimum point, then any firm producing a different quantity will have higher costs. In this case, a firm producing at a quantity of 10,000 will produce at a lower average cost than a firm producing, say, 5,000 or 20,000 units. (b) Low-cost firms will produce between output levels R and S. When the LRAC curve has a flat bottom, then firms producing at any quantity along this flat bottom can compete. In this case, any firm producing a quantity between 5,000 and 20,000 can compete effectively, although firms producing less than 5,000 or more than 20,000 would face higher average costs and be unable to compete.

 ## CLEAR IT UP

### How can we view cities as examples of economies of scale?

Why are people and economic activity concentrated in cities, rather than distributed evenly across a country? The fundamental reason must be related to the idea of economies of scale—that grouping economic activity is more productive in many cases than spreading it out. For example, cities provide a large group of nearby customers, so that businesses can produce at an efficient economy of scale. They also provide a large group of workers and suppliers, so that business can hire easily and purchase whatever specialized inputs they need. Many of the attractions of cities, like sports stadiums and museums, can operate only if they can draw on a large nearby population base. Cities are big enough to offer a wide variety of products, which is what appeals to many shoppers.

These factors are not exactly economies of scale in the narrow sense of the production function of a single firm, but they are related to growth in the overall size of population and market in an area. Cities are sometimes called "agglomeration economies."

These agglomeration factors help to explain why every economy, as it develops, has an increasing proportion of its population living in urban areas. In the United States, about 80% of the population now lives in metropolitan areas (which include the suburbs around cities), compared to just 40% in 1900. However, in poorer nations of the world, including much of Africa, the proportion of the population in urban areas is only about 30%. One of the great challenges for these countries as their economies grow will be to manage the growth of the great cities that will arise.

If cities offer economic advantages that are a form of economies of scale, then why don't all or most people live in one giant city? At some point, agglomeration economies must turn into diseconomies. For example, traffic congestion may reach a point where the gains from being geographically nearby are counterbalanced by how long it takes to travel. High densities of people, cars, and factories can mean more garbage and air and water pollution. Facilities like parks or museums may become overcrowded. There may be economies of scale for negative activities like crime, because high densities of people and businesses, combined with the greater impersonality of cities, make it easier for illegal activities as well as legal ones. The future of cities, both in the United States and in other countries around the world, will be determined by their ability to benefit from the economies of agglomeration and to minimize or counterbalance the corresponding diseconomies.

We illustrate a more common case in Figure 7.11 (b), where the LRAC curve has a flat-bottomed area of constant returns to scale. In this situation, any firm with a level of output between 5,000 and 20,000 will be able to produce at about the same level of average cost. Given that the market will demand one million dishwashers per year at a price of $500, this market might have as many as 200 producers (that is, one million dishwashers divided by firms making 5,000 each) or as few as 50 producers (one million dishwashers divided by firms making 20,000 each). The producers in this market will range in size from firms that make 5,000 units to firms that make 20,000 units. However, firms that produce below 5,000 units or more than 20,000 will be unable to compete, because their average costs will be too high. Thus, if we see an industry where almost all plants are the same size, it is likely that the long-run average cost curve has a unique bottom point as in Figure 7.11 (a). However, if the long-run average cost curve has a wide flat bottom like Figure 7.11 (b), then firms of a variety of different sizes will be able to compete with each other.

We can interpret the flat section of the long-run average cost curve in Figure 7.11 (b) in two different ways. One interpretation is that a single manufacturing plant producing a quantity of 5,000 has the same average costs as a single manufacturing plant with four times as much capacity that produces a quantity of 20,000. The other interpretation is that one firm owns a single manufacturing plant that produces a quantity of 5,000, while another firm owns four separate manufacturing plants, which each produce a quantity of 5,000. This second explanation, based on the insight that a single firm may own a number of different manufacturing plants, is especially useful in explaining why the long-run average cost curve often has a large flat segment—and thus why a seemingly smaller firm may be able to compete quite well with a larger firm. At some point, however, the task of coordinating and managing many different plants raises the cost of production sharply, and the long-run average cost curve slopes up as a result.

In the examples to this point, the quantity demanded in the market is quite large (one million) compared with the quantity produced at the bottom of the long-run average cost curve (5,000, 10,000 or 20,000). In such a situation, the market is set for competition between many firms. However, what if the bottom of the long-run average cost curve is at a quantity of 10,000 and the total market demand at that price is only slightly higher than that quantity—or even somewhat lower?

Return to Figure 7.11 (a), where the bottom of the long-run average cost curve is at 10,000, but now imagine that the total quantity of dishwashers demanded in the market at that price of $500 is only 30,000. In this situation, the total number of firms in the market would be three. We call a handful of firms in a market an "oligopoly," and the chapter on Monopolistic Competition and Oligopoly will discuss the range of competitive strategies that can occur when oligopolies compete.

Alternatively, consider a situation, again in the setting of Figure 7.11 (a), where the bottom of the long-run average cost curve is 10,000, but total demand for the product is only 5,000. (For simplicity, imagine that this demand is highly inelastic, so that it does not vary according to price.) In this situation, the market may well end up with a single firm—a monopoly—producing all 5,000 units. If any firm tried to challenge this monopoly while producing a quantity lower than 5,000 units, the prospective competitor firm would have a higher average cost, and so it would not be able to compete in the longer term without losing money. The chapter on Monopoly discusses the situation of a monopoly firm.

Thus, the shape of the long-run average cost curve reveals whether competitors in the market will be different sizes. If the LRAC curve has a single point at the bottom, then the firms in the market will be about the same size, but if the LRAC curve has a flat-bottomed segment of constant returns to scale, then firms in the market may be a variety of different sizes.

The relationship between the quantity at the minimum of the long-run average cost curve and the quantity demanded in the market at that price will predict how much competition is likely to exist in the market. If the quantity demanded in the market far exceeds the quantity at the minimum of the LRAC, then many firms will compete. If the quantity demanded in the market is only slightly higher than the quantity at the minimum of the LRAC, a few firms will compete. If the quantity demanded in the market is less than the quantity at the minimum of the LRAC, a single-producer monopoly is a likely outcome.

## Shifting Patterns of Long-Run Average Cost

New developments in production technology can shift the long-run average cost curve in ways that can alter the size distribution of firms in an industry.

For much of the twentieth century, the most common change had been to see alterations in technology, like the assembly line or the large department store, where large-scale producers seemed to gain an advantage over smaller ones. In the long-run average cost curve, the downward-sloping economies of scale portion of the curve stretched over a larger quantity of output.

However, new production technologies do not inevitably lead to a greater average size for firms. For example, in recent years some new technologies for generating electricity on a smaller scale have appeared. The traditional coal-burning electricity plants needed to produce 300 to 600 megawatts of power to exploit economies of scale fully. However, high-efficiency turbines to produce electricity from burning natural gas can produce electricity at a competitive price while producing a smaller quantity of 100 megawatts or less. These new technologies create the possibility for smaller companies or plants to generate electricity as efficiently as large ones. Another example of a technology-driven shift to smaller plants may be taking place in the tire industry. A traditional mid-size tire plant produces about six million tires per year. However, in 2000, the Italian company Pirelli introduced a new tire factory that uses many robots. The Pirelli tire plant produced only about one million tires per year, but did so at a lower average cost than a traditional mid-sized tire plant.

Controversy has simmered in recent years over whether the new information and communications technologies will lead to a larger or smaller size for firms. On one side, the new technology may make it easier for small firms to reach out beyond their local geographic area and find customers across a state, or the nation, or even across international boundaries. This factor might seem to predict a future with a larger number of small competitors. On the other side, perhaps the new information and communications technology will create "winner-take-all" markets where one large company will tend to command a large share of total sales, as Microsoft has done producing of software for personal computers or Amazon has done in online bookselling. Moreover, improved information and communication technologies might make it easier to manage many different plants and operations across the country or around the world, and thus encourage larger firms. This ongoing battle between the forces of smallness and largeness will be of great interest to economists, businesspeople, and policymakers.

 **BRING IT HOME**

### Amazon

Traditionally, bookstores have operated in retail locations with inventories held either on the shelves or in the back of the store. These retail locations were very pricey in terms of rent. Until recently, Amazon had no retail locations. It only sold online and delivered by mail. Amazon now has retail stores in California, Oregon and Washington State and retail stores are coming to Illinois, Massachusetts, New Jersey, and New York. Amazon offers almost any book in print, convenient purchasing, and prompt delivery by mail. Amazon holds its inventories in huge warehouses in low-rent locations around the world. The warehouses are highly computerized using robots and relatively low-skilled workers, making for low average costs per sale. Amazon demonstrates the significant advantages economies of scale can offer to a firm that exploits those economies.

## Key Terms

**accounting profit**  total revenues minus explicit costs, including depreciation

**average profit**  profit divided by the quantity of output produced; also known as profit margin

**average total cost**  total cost divided by the quantity of output

**average variable cost**  variable cost divided by the quantity of output

**constant returns to scale**  expanding all inputs proportionately does not change the average cost of production

**diminishing marginal productivity**  general rule that as a firm employs more labor, eventually the amount of additional output produced declines

**diseconomies of scale**  the long-run average cost of producing output increases as total output increases

**economic profit**  total revenues minus total costs (explicit plus implicit costs)

**economies of scale**  the long-run average cost of producing output decreases as total output increases

**economies of scale**  the long-run average cost of producing output decreases as total output increases

**explicit costs**  out-of-pocket costs for a firm, for example, payments for wages and salaries, rent, or materials

**factors of production (or inputs)**  resources that firms use to produce their products, for example, labor and capital

**firm**  an organization that combines inputs of labor, capital, land, and raw or finished component materials to produce outputs.

**fixed cost**  cost of the fixed inputs; expenditure that a firm must make before production starts and that does not change regardless of the production level

**fixed inputs**  factors of production that can't be easily increased or decreased in a short period of time

**implicit costs**  opportunity cost of resources already owned by the firm and used in business, for example, expanding a factory onto land already owned

**long run**  period of time during which all of a firm's inputs are variable

**long-run average cost (LRAC) curve**  shows the lowest possible average cost of production, allowing all the inputs to production to vary so that the firm is choosing its production technology

**marginal cost**  the additional cost of producing one more unit; mathematically, $MC = \Delta TC/\Delta L$

**marginal product**  change in a firm's output when it employees more labor; mathematically, $MP = \Delta TP/\Delta L$

**private enterprise**  the ownership of businesses by private individuals

**production**  the process of combining inputs to produce outputs, ideally of a value greater than the value of the inputs

**production function**  mathematical equation that tells how much output a firm can produce with given amounts of the inputs

**production technologies**  alternative methods of combining inputs to produce output

**revenue**  income from selling a firm's product; defined as price times quantity sold

**short run**  period of time during which at least one or more of the firm's inputs is fixed

**short-run average cost (SRAC) curve**  the average total cost curve in the short term; shows the total of the average fixed costs and the average variable costs

**total cost**  the sum of fixed and variable costs of production

**total product**  synonym for a firm's output

**variable cost**  cost of production that increases with the quantity produced; the cost of the variable inputs

**variable inputs**  factors of production that a firm can easily increase or decrease in a short period of time

## Key Concepts and Summary

### 7.1 Explicit and Implicit Costs, and Accounting and Economic Profit

Privately owned firms are motivated to earn profits. Profit is the difference between revenues and costs. While accounting profit considers only explicit costs, economic profit considers both explicit and implicit costs.

## 7.2 Production in the Short Run

Production is the process a firm uses to transform inputs (e.g., labor, capital, raw materials, etc.) into outputs. It is not possible to vary fixed inputs (e.g., capital) in a short period of time. Thus, in the short run the only way to change output is to change the variable inputs (e.g., labor). Marginal product is the additional output a firm obtains by employing more labor in production. At some point, employing additional labor leads to diminishing marginal productivity, meaning the additional output obtained is less than for the previous increment to labor. Mathematically, marginal product is the slope of the total product curve.

## 7.3 Costs in the Short Run

For every input (e.g., labor), there is an associated factor payment (e.g., wages and salaries). The cost of production for a given quantity of output is the sum of the amount of each input required to produce that quantity of output times the associated factor payment.

In a short-run perspective, we can divide a firm's total costs into fixed costs, which a firm must incur before producing any output, and variable costs, which the firm incurs in the act of producing. Fixed costs are sunk costs; that is, because they are in the past and the firm cannot alter them, they should play no role in economic decisions about future production or pricing. Variable costs typically show diminishing marginal returns, so that the marginal cost of producing higher levels of output rises.

We calculate marginal cost by taking the change in total cost (or the change in variable cost, which will be the same thing) and dividing it by the change in output, for each possible change in output. Marginal costs are typically rising. A firm can compare marginal cost to the additional revenue it gains from selling another unit to find out whether its marginal unit is adding to profit.

We calculate average total cost by taking total cost and dividing by total output at each different level of output. Average costs are typically U-shaped on a graph. If a firm's average cost of production is lower than the market price, a firm will be earning profits.

We calculate average variable cost by taking variable cost and dividing by the total output at each level of output. Average variable costs are typically U-shaped. If a firm's average variable cost of production is lower than the market price, then the firm would be earning profits if fixed costs are left out of the picture.

## 7.4 Production in the Long Run

In the long run, all inputs are variable. Since diminishing marginal productivity is caused by fixed capital, there are no diminishing returns in the long run. Firms can choose the optimal capital stock to produce their desired level of output.

## 7.5 Costs in the Long Run

A production technology refers to a specific combination of labor, physical capital, and technology that makes up a particular method of production.

In the long run, firms can choose their production technology, and so all costs become variable costs. In making this choice, firms will try to substitute relatively inexpensive inputs for relatively expensive inputs where possible, so as to produce at the lowest possible long-run average cost.

Economies of scale refers to a situation where as the level of output increases, the average cost decreases. Constant returns to scale refers to a situation where average cost does not change as output increases. Diseconomies of scale refers to a situation where as output increases, average costs also increase.

The long-run average cost curve shows the lowest possible average cost of production, allowing all the inputs to production to vary so that the firm is choosing its production technology. A downward-sloping LRAC shows economies of scale; a flat LRAC shows constant returns to scale; an upward-sloping LRAC shows diseconomies of scale. If the long-run average cost curve has only one quantity produced that results in the lowest possible average cost, then all of the firms competing in an industry should be the same size. However, if the LRAC has a flat segment at the bottom, so that a firm can produce a range of different quantities at the lowest average cost, the firms competing in the industry will display a range of sizes. The market demand in conjunction with the long-run average cost curve determines how many firms will exist in a given industry.

If the quantity demanded in the market of a certain product is much greater than the quantity found at the bottom of the long-run average cost curve, where the cost of production is lowest, the market will have many firms competing. If the quantity demanded in the market is less than the quantity at the bottom of the LRAC, there will likely be only one firm.

## Self-Check Questions

1. A firm had sales revenue of $1 million last year. It spent $600,000 on labor, $150,000 on capital and $200,000 on materials. What was the firm's accounting profit?

2. Continuing from Exercise 7.1, the firm's factory sits on land owned by the firm that it could rent for $30,000 per year. What was the firm's economic profit last year?

3. The WipeOut Ski Company manufactures skis for beginners. Fixed costs are $30. Fill in Table 7.16 for total cost, average variable cost, average total cost, and marginal cost.

| Quantity | Variable Cost | Fixed Cost | Total Cost | Average Variable Cost | Average Total Cost | Marginal Cost |
|---|---|---|---|---|---|---|
| 0 | 0 | $30 | | | | |
| 1 | $10 | $30 | | | | |
| 2 | $25 | $30 | | | | |
| 3 | $45 | $30 | | | | |
| 4 | $70 | $30 | | | | |
| 5 | $100 | $30 | | | | |
| 6 | $135 | $30 | | | | |

**TABLE 7.16**

4. Based on your answers to the WipeOut Ski Company in Exercise 7.3, now imagine a situation where the firm produces a quantity of 5 units that it sells for a price of $25 each.
   a. What will be the company's profits or losses?
   b. How can you tell at a glance whether the company is making or losing money at this price by looking at average cost?
   c. At the given quantity and price, is the marginal unit produced adding to profits?

5. If two painters can paint 200 square feet of wall in an hour, and three painters can paint 275 square feet, what is the marginal product of the third painter?

6. Return to the problem explained in Table 7.13 and Table 7.14. If the cost of labor remains at $40, but the cost of a machine decreases to $50, what would be the total cost of each method of production? Which method should the firm use, and why?

7. Suppose the cost of machines increases to $55, while the cost of labor stays at $40. How would that affect the total cost of the three methods? Which method should the firm choose now?

8. Automobile manufacturing is an industry subject to significant economies of scale. Suppose there are four domestic auto manufacturers, but the demand for domestic autos is no more than 2.5 times the quantity produced at the bottom of the long-run average cost curve. What do you expect will happen to the domestic auto industry in the long run?

## Review Questions

9. What are explicit and implicit costs?

10. Would you consider an interest payment on a loan to a firm an explicit or implicit cost?

11. What is the difference between accounting and economic profit?

12. What is a production function?

13. What is the difference between a fixed input and a variable input?

14. How do we calculate marginal product?

15. What shapes would you generally expect a total product curve and a marginal product curve to have?

16. What are the factor payments for land, labor, and capital?

17. What is the difference between fixed costs and variable costs?

18. How do we calculate each of the following: marginal cost, average total cost, and average variable cost?

19. What shapes would you generally expect each of the following cost curves to have: fixed costs, variable costs, marginal costs, average total costs, and average variable costs?

20. Are there fixed costs in the long-run? Explain briefly.

21. Are fixed costs also sunk costs? Explain.

22. What are diminishing marginal returns as they relate to costs?

23. Which costs are measured on per-unit basis: fixed costs, average cost, average variable cost, variable costs, and marginal cost?

24. What is a production technology?

25. In choosing a production technology, how will firms react if one input becomes relatively more expensive?

26. What is a long-run average cost curve?

27. What is the difference between economies of scale, constant returns to scale, and diseconomies of scale?

28. What shape of a long-run average cost curve illustrates economies of scale, constant returns to scale, and diseconomies of scale?

29. Why will firms in most markets be located at or close to the bottom of the long-run average cost curve?

## Critical Thinking Questions

30. Small "Mom and Pop firms," like inner city grocery stores, sometimes exist even though they do not earn economic profits. How can you explain this?

31. A common name for fixed cost is "overhead." If you divide fixed cost by the quantity of output produced, you get average fixed cost. Suppose fixed cost is $1,000. What does the average fixed cost curve look like? Use your response to explain what "spreading the overhead" means.

**32.** How does fixed cost affect marginal cost? Why is this relationship important?

**33.** Average cost curves (except for average fixed cost) tend to be U-shaped, decreasing and then increasing. Marginal cost curves have the same shape, though this may be harder to see since most of the marginal cost curve is increasing. Why do you think that average and marginal cost curves have the same general shape?

**34.** What is the relationship between marginal product and marginal cost? (Hint: Look at the curves.) Why do you suppose that is? Is this relationship the same in the long run as in the short run?

**35.** It is clear that businesses operate in the short run, but do they ever operate in the long run? Discuss.

**36.** Return to Table 7.12. In the top half of the table, at what point does diminishing marginal productivity kick in? What about in the bottom half of the table? How do you explain this?

**37.** How would an improvement in technology, like the high-efficiency gas turbines or Pirelli tire plant, affect the long-run average cost curve of a firm? Can you draw the old curve and the new one on the same axes? How might such an improvement affect other firms in the industry?

**38.** Do you think that the taxicab industry in large cities would be subject to significant economies of scale? Why or why not?

## Problems

**39.** A firm is considering an investment that will earn a 6% rate of return. If it were to borrow the money, it would have to pay 8% interest on the loan, but it currently has the cash, so it will not need to borrow. Should the firm make the investment? Show your work.

**40.** Return to Figure 7.7. What is the marginal gain in output from increasing the number of barbers from 4 to 5 and from 5 to 6? Does it continue the pattern of diminishing marginal returns?

**41.** Compute the average total cost, average variable cost, and marginal cost of producing 60 and 72 haircuts. Draw the graph of the three curves between 60 and 72 haircuts.

**42.** A small company that shovels sidewalks and driveways has 100 homes signed up for its services this winter. It can use various combinations of capital and labor: intensive labor with hand shovels, less labor with snow blowers, and still less labor with a pickup truck that has a snowplow on front. To summarize, the method choices are:
Method 1: 50 units of labor, 10 units of capital
Method 2: 20 units of labor, 40 units of capital
Method 3: 10 units of labor, 70 units of capital
If hiring labor for the winter costs $100/unit and a unit of capital costs $400, what is the best production method? What method should the company use if the cost of labor rises to $200/unit?

# Perfect Competition 8

FIGURE 8.1 Depending on the competition and prices offered, a soybean farmer may choose to grow a different crop. (Credit: modification "Agronomist & Farmer Inspecting Weeds" by United Soybean Board/Flickr, CC BY 2.0)

**CHAPTER OBJECTIVES**

In this chapter, you will learn about:

- Perfect Competition and Why It Matters
- How Perfectly Competitive Firms Make Output Decisions
- Entry and Exit Decisions in the Long Run
- Efficiency in Perfectly Competitive Markets

## Introduction to Perfect Competition

 **BRING IT HOME**

### A Dime a Dozen

When you were younger did you babysit, deliver papers, or mow the lawn for money? If so, you faced stiff competition from many other competitors who offered identical services. There was nothing to stop others from also offering their services.

All of you charged the "going rate." If you tried to charge more, your customers would simply buy from someone else. These conditions are very similar to the conditions agricultural growers face.

Growing a crop may be more difficult to start than a babysitting or lawn mowing service, but growers face the same fierce competition. In the grand scale of world agriculture, farmers face competition from thousands of others because they sell an identical product. After all, winter wheat is winter wheat, but if they find it hard to make money with that crop, it is relatively easy for farmers to leave the marketplace for another crop. In this case, they do not sell the family farm, they switch crops.

Take the case of the upper Midwest region of the United States—for many generations the area was called "King Wheat." According to the United States Department of Agriculture National Agricultural Statistics Service, statistics by state, in 1997, 11.6 million acres of wheat and 780,000 acres of corn were planted in North Dakota. In the intervening 25 or so years has the mix of crops changed? Since it is relatively easy to switch crops, did farmers change what they planted in response to changes in relative crop prices? We will find out at chapter's end.

In the meantime, let's consider the topic of this chapter—the perfectly competitive market. This is a market in which entry and exit are relatively easy and competitors are "a dime a dozen."

---

Most businesses face two realities: no one is required to buy their products, and even customers who might want those products may buy from other businesses instead. Firms that operate in perfectly competitive markets face this reality. In this chapter, you will learn how such firms make decisions about how much to produce, how much profit they make, whether to stay in business or not, and many others. Industries differ from one another in terms of how many sellers there are in a specific market, how easy or difficult it is for a new firm to enter, and the type of products that they sell. Economists refer to this as an industry's **market structure**. In this chapter, we focus on perfect competition. However, in other chapters we will examine other industry types: Monopoly and Monopolistic Competition and Oligopoly.

## 8.1 Perfect Competition and Why It Matters

**LEARNING OBJECTIVES**

By the end of this section, you will be able to:
- Explain the characteristics of a perfectly competitive market
- Discuss how perfectly competitive firms react in the short run and in the long run

Firms are in **perfect competition** when the following conditions occur: (1) many firms produce identical products; (2) many buyers are available to buy the product, and many sellers are available to sell the product; (3) sellers and buyers have all relevant information to make rational decisions about the product that they are buying and selling; and (4) firms can enter and leave the market without any restrictions—in other words, there is free entry and exit into and out of the market.

A perfectly competitive firm is known as a **price taker**, because the pressure of competing firms forces it to accept the prevailing equilibrium price in the market. If a firm in a perfectly competitive market raises the price of its product by so much as a penny, it will lose all of its sales to competitors. When a wheat grower, as we discussed in the Bring It Home feature, wants to know the going price of wheat, they have to check on the computer or listen to the radio. Supply and demand in the entire market solely determine the market price, not the individual farmer. A perfectly competitive firm must be a very small player in the overall market, so that it can increase or decrease output without noticeably affecting the overall quantity supplied and price in the market.

A perfectly competitive market is a hypothetical extreme; however, producers in a number of industries do face many competitor firms selling highly similar goods, in which case they must often act as price takers. Economists often use agricultural markets as an example. The same crops that different farmers grow are largely interchangeable. According to the United States Department of Agriculture monthly reports, in December 2021, U.S. corn farmers received an average of $5.47 per bushel. A corn farmer who attempted to sell at $6.00 per bushel would not have found any buyers. A perfectly competitive firm will not sell below the equilibrium price either. Why should they when they can sell all they want at the higher price? Other examples of agricultural markets that operate in close to perfectly competitive markets are small roadside produce markets and small organic farmers.

 **LINK IT UP**

Visit this website (http://openstax.org/l/commodities) that reveals the current value of various commodities.

---

This chapter examines how profit-seeking firms decide how much to produce in perfectly competitive markets. Such firms will analyze their costs as we discussed in the chapter on Production, Costs and Industry Structure. In the short run, the perfectly competitive firm will seek the quantity of output where profits are highest or, if profits are not possible, where losses are lowest.

In the long run, positive economic profits will attract competition as other firms enter the market. Economic losses will cause firms to exit the market. Ultimately, perfectly competitive markets will attain long-run *equilibrium* when no new firms want to enter the market and existing firms do not want to leave the market, as economic profits have been driven down to zero.

## 8.2 How Perfectly Competitive Firms Make Output Decisions

**LEARNING OBJECTIVES**
By the end of this section, you will be able to:
- Calculate profits by comparing total revenue and total cost
- Identify profits and losses with the average cost curve
- Explain the shutdown point
- Determine the price at which a firm should continue producing in the short run

A perfectly competitive firm has only one major decision to make—namely, what quantity to produce. To understand this, consider a different way of writing out the basic definition of profit:

$$\text{Profit} = \text{Total revenue} - \text{Total cost}$$
$$= (\text{Price})(\text{Quantity produced}) - (\text{Average cost})(\text{Quantity produced})$$

Since a perfectly competitive firm must accept the price for its output as determined by the product's market demand and supply, it cannot choose the price it charges. This is already determined in the profit equation, and so the perfectly competitive firm can sell any number of units at exactly the same price. It implies that the firm faces a perfectly elastic demand curve for its product: buyers are willing to buy any number of units of output from the firm at the market price. When the perfectly competitive firm chooses what quantity to produce, then this quantity—along with the prices prevailing in the market for output and inputs—will determine the firm's total revenue, total costs, and ultimately, level of profits.

### Determining the Highest Profit by Comparing Total Revenue and Total Cost

A perfectly competitive firm can sell as large a quantity as it wishes, as long as it accepts the prevailing market price. The formula above shows that total revenue depends on the quantity sold and the price charged. If the firm sells a higher quantity of output, then total revenue will increase. If the market price of the product increases, then total revenue also increases whatever the quantity of output sold. As an example of how a perfectly competitive firm decides what quantity to produce, consider the case of a small farmer who produces raspberries and sells them frozen for $4 per pack. Sales of one pack of raspberries will bring in $4, two packs will be $8, three packs will be $12, and so on. If, for example, the price of frozen raspberries doubles to $8 per pack, then sales of one pack of raspberries will be $8, two packs will be $16, three packs will be $24, and so on.

Table 8.1 shows total revenue and total costs for the raspberry farm; these data also appear in Figure 8.2. The horizontal axis shows the quantity of frozen raspberries produced in packs. The vertical axis shows both total revenue and total costs, measured in dollars. The total cost curve intersects with the vertical axis at a value that shows the level of fixed costs, and then slopes upward. All these cost curves follow the same characteristics as the curves that we covered in the Production, Costs and Industry Structure chapter.

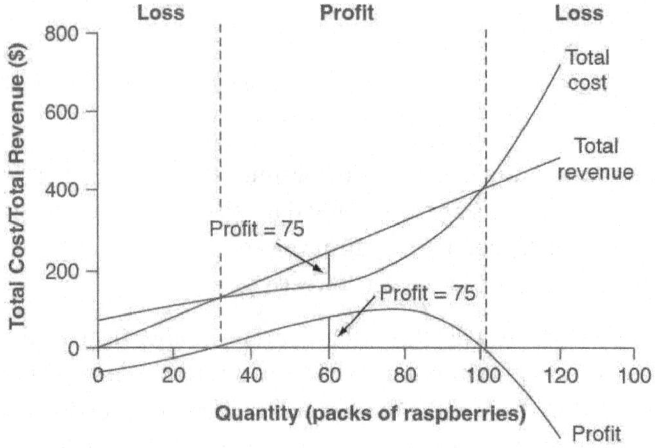


FIGURE 8.2 Total Cost and Total Revenue at the Raspberry Farm Total revenue for a perfectly competitive firm is a straight line sloping up. The slope is equal to the price of the good. Total cost also slopes up, but with some curvature. At higher levels of output, total cost begins to slope upward more steeply because of diminishing marginal returns. The maximum profit will occur at the quantity where the difference between total revenue and total cost is largest.

| Quantity (Q) | Total Cost (TC) | Total Revenue (TR) | Profit |
| --- | --- | --- | --- |
| 0 | $62 | $0 | –$62 |
| 10 | $90 | $40 | –$50 |
| 20 | $110 | $80 | –$30 |
| 30 | $126 | $120 | –$6 |
| 40 | $138 | $160 | $22 |
| 50 | $150 | $200 | $50 |
| 60 | $165 | $240 | $75 |
| 70 | $190 | $280 | $90 |
| 80 | $230 | $320 | $90 |
| 90 | $296 | $360 | $64 |
| 100 | $400 | $400 | $0 |
| 110 | $550 | $440 | $–110 |
| 120 | $715 | $480 | $–235 |

TABLE 8.1 Total Cost and Total Revenue at the Raspberry Farm

Based on its total revenue and total cost curves, a perfectly competitive firm like the raspberry farm can calculate the quantity of output that will provide the highest level of profit. At any given quantity, total revenue minus total cost will equal profit. One way to determine the most profitable quantity to produce is to see at what quantity total revenue exceeds total cost by the largest amount. Figure 8.2 shows total revenue, total cost and profit using the data from Table 8.1. The vertical gap between total revenue and total cost is profit, for example, at Q = 60, TR = 240 and TC = 165. The difference is 75, which is the height of the profit curve at that output level. The firm doesn't make a profit at every level of output. In this example, total costs will exceed total revenues at output levels from 0 to approximately 30, and so over this range of output, the firm will be making losses. At output levels from 40 to 100, total revenues exceed total costs, so the firm is earning profits. However, at any output greater than 100, total costs again exceed total revenues and the firm is making increasing losses. Total profits appear in the final column of Table 8.1. Maximum profit occurs at an output between 70 and 80, when profit equals $90.

A higher price would mean that total revenue would be higher for every quantity sold. A lower price would mean that total revenue would be lower for every quantity sold. What happens if the price drops low enough so that the total revenue line is completely below the total cost curve; that is, at every level of output, total costs are higher than total revenues? In this instance, the best the firm can do is to suffer losses. However, a profit-maximizing firm will prefer the quantity of output where total revenues come closest to total costs and thus where the losses are smallest.

(Later we will see that sometimes it will make sense for the firm to close, rather than stay in operation producing output.)

## Comparing Marginal Revenue and Marginal Costs

The approach that we described in the previous section, using total revenue and total cost, is not the only approach to determining the profit maximizing level of output. In this section, we provide an alternative approach which uses marginal revenue and marginal cost.

Firms often do not have the necessary data they need to draw a complete total cost curve for all levels of production. They cannot be sure of what total costs would look like if they, say, doubled production or cut production in half, because they have not tried it. Instead, firms experiment. They produce a slightly greater or lower quantity and observe how it affects profits. In economic terms, this practical approach to maximizing profits means examining how changes in production affect marginal revenue and marginal cost.

Figure 8.3 presents the marginal revenue and marginal cost curves based on the total revenue and total cost in Table 8.1. The **marginal revenue** curve shows the additional revenue gained from selling one more unit. As mentioned before, a firm in perfect competition faces a perfectly elastic demand curve for its product—that is, the firm's demand curve is a horizontal line drawn at the market price level. This also means that the firm's marginal revenue curve is the same as the firm's demand curve: Every time a consumer demands one more unit, the firm sells one more unit and revenue increases by exactly the same amount equal to the market price. In this example, every time the firm sells a pack of frozen raspberries, the firm's revenue increases by $4. Table 8.2 shows an example of this. This condition only holds for price taking firms in perfect competition where:

$$\text{marginal revenue} = \text{price}$$

The formula for marginal revenue is:

$$\text{marginal revenue} = \frac{\text{change in total revenue}}{\text{change in quantity}}$$

| Price | Quantity | Total Revenue | Marginal Revenue |
|-------|----------|---------------|------------------|
| $4 | 1 | $4 | - |
| $4 | 2 | $8 | $4 |
| $4 | 3 | $12 | $4 |
| $4 | 4 | $16 | $4 |

**TABLE 8.2**

Notice that marginal revenue does not change as the firm produces more output. That is because under perfect competition, the price is determined through the interaction of supply and demand in the market and does not change as the farmer produces more (keeping in mind that, due to the relative small size of each firm, increasing their supply has no impact on the total market supply where price is determined).

Since a perfectly competitive firm is a price taker, it can sell whatever quantity it wishes at the market-determined price. We calculate marginal cost, the cost per additional unit sold, by dividing the change in total cost by the change in quantity. The formula for marginal cost is:

$$\text{marginal cost} = \frac{\text{change in total cost}}{\text{change in quantity}}$$

Ordinarily, marginal cost changes as the firm produces a greater quantity.

In the raspberry farm example, in Figure 8.3 and Table 8.3, marginal cost at first declines as production increases from 10 to 20 to 30 to 40 packs of raspberries—which represents the area of increasing marginal returns that is not uncommon at low levels of production. At some point, though, marginal costs start to increase, displaying the typical pattern of diminishing marginal returns. If the firm is producing at a quantity where MR > MC, like 40 or 50 packs of raspberries, then it can increase profit by increasing output because the marginal revenue is exceeding the marginal cost. If the firm is producing at a quantity where MC > MR, like 90 or 100 packs, then it can increase profit by reducing output because the reductions in marginal cost will exceed the reductions in marginal revenue. The firm's profit-maximizing choice of output will occur where MR = MC (or at a choice close to that point).

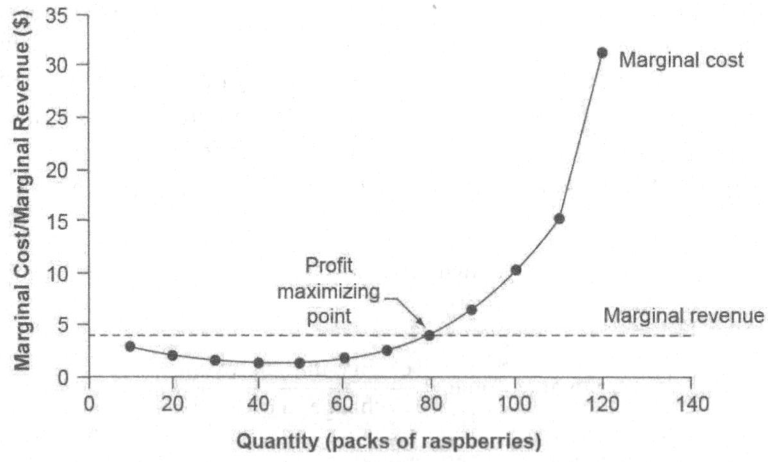


**FIGURE 8.3 Marginal Revenues and Marginal Costs at the Raspberry Farm: Individual Farmer** For a perfectly competitive firm, the marginal revenue (MR) curve is a horizontal line because it is equal to the price of the good, which is determined by the market, as Figure 8.4 illustrates. The marginal cost (MC) curve is sometimes initially

downward-sloping, if there is a region of increasing marginal returns at low levels of output, but is eventually upward-sloping at higher levels of output as diminishing marginal returns kick in.

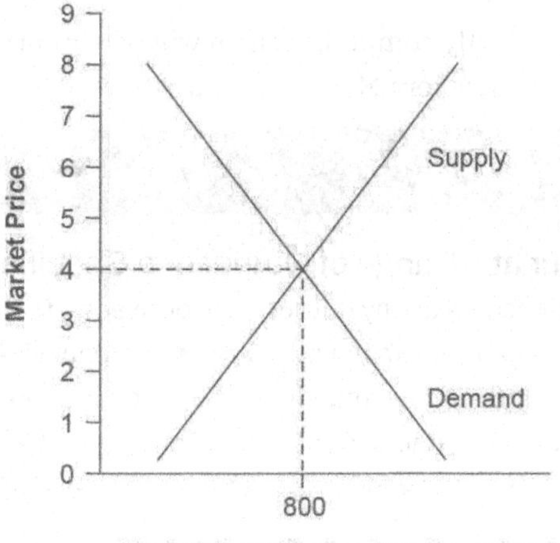


**FIGURE 8.4 Supply, Demand, and Equilibrium Price in the Market for Raspberries** The equilibrium price of raspberries is determined through the interaction of market supply and market demand at $4.00.

| Quantity | Total Cost | Marginal Cost | Total Revenue | Marginal Revenue | Profit |
|---|---|---|---|---|---|
| 0 | $62 | - | $0 | $4 | -$62 |
| 10 | $90 | $2.80 | $40 | $4 | -$50 |
| 20 | $110 | $2.00 | $80 | $4 | -$30 |
| 30 | $126 | $1.60 | $120 | $4 | -$6 |
| 40 | $138 | $1.20 | $160 | $4 | $22 |
| 50 | $150 | $1.20 | $200 | $4 | $50 |
| 60 | $165 | $1.50 | $240 | $4 | $75 |
| 70 | $190 | $2.50 | $280 | $4 | $90 |
| 80 | $230 | $4.00 | $320 | $4 | $90 |
| 90 | $296 | $6.60 | $360 | $4 | $64 |
| 100 | $400 | $10.40 | $400 | $4 | $0 |
| 110 | $550 | $15.00 | $440 | $4 | -$110 |
| 120 | $715 | $16.50 | $480 | $4 | -$235 |

**TABLE 8.3 Marginal Revenues and Marginal Costs at the Raspberry Farm**

In this example, the marginal revenue and marginal cost curves cross at a price of $4 and a quantity of 80 produced. If the farmer started out producing at a level of 60, and then experimented with increasing production to 70, marginal revenues from the increase in production would exceed marginal costs—and so profits would rise. The farmer has an incentive to keep producing. At a level of output of 80, marginal cost and marginal revenue are equal so profit doesn't change. If the farmer then experimented further with increasing production from 80 to 90, he would find that marginal costs from the increase in production are greater than marginal revenues, and so profits would decline.

The profit-maximizing choice for a perfectly competitive firm will occur at the level of output where marginal revenue is equal to marginal cost—that is, where MR = MC. This occurs at Q = 80 in the figure.

## WORK IT OUT

### Does Profit Maximization Occur at a Range of Output or a Specific Level of Output?

Table 8.1 shows that maximum profit occurs at any output level between 70 and 80 units of output. But MR = MC occurs only at 80 units of output. How can we explain this slight discrepancy? As long as MR > MC, a profit-seeking firm should keep expanding production. Expanding production into the zone where MR < MC reduces economic profits. It's true that profit is the same at Q = 70 and Q = 80, but it's only when the firm goes beyond that Q that it will see that profits fall. Thus, MR = MC is the signal to stop expanding, so that is the level of output they should target.

Because the marginal revenue received by a perfectly competitive firm is equal to the price P, we can also write the profit-maximizing rule for a perfectly competitive firm as a recommendation to produce at the quantity of output where P = MC.

### Profits and Losses with the Average Cost Curve

Does maximizing profit (producing where MR = MC) imply an actual economic profit? The answer depends on the relationship between price and average total cost, which is the average profit or **profit margin**. If the market price is higher than the firm's average cost of production for that quantity produced, then the profit margin is positive and the firm will earn profits. Conversely, if the market price is lower than the average cost of production, the profit margin is negative and the firm will suffer losses. You might think that, in this situation, the firm may want to shut down immediately. Remember, however, that the firm has already paid for fixed costs, such as equipment, so it may continue to produce for a while and incur a loss. Table 8.3 continues the raspberry farm example. Figure 8.5 illustrates the three possible scenarios: (a) where price intersects marginal cost at a level above the average cost curve, (b) where price intersects marginal cost at a level equal to the average cost curve, and (c) where price intersects marginal cost at a level below the average cost curve.

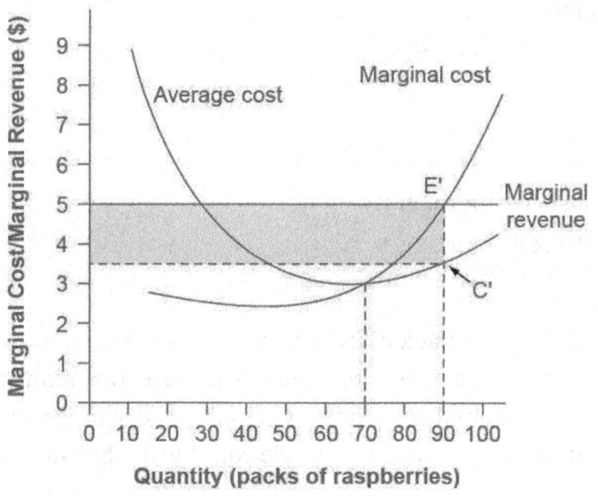



(a) Price is above average cost

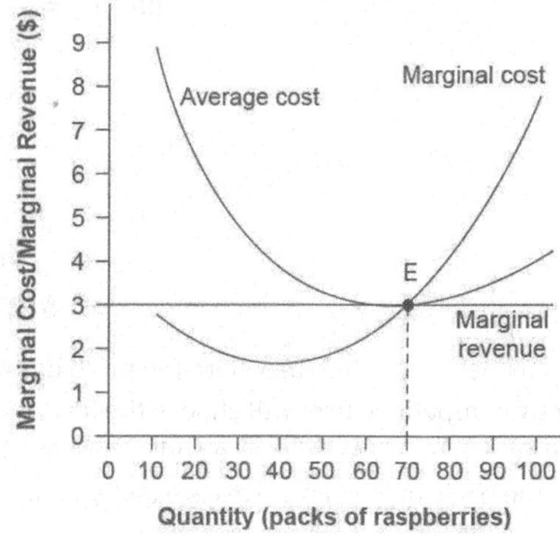



(b) Price equals average cost

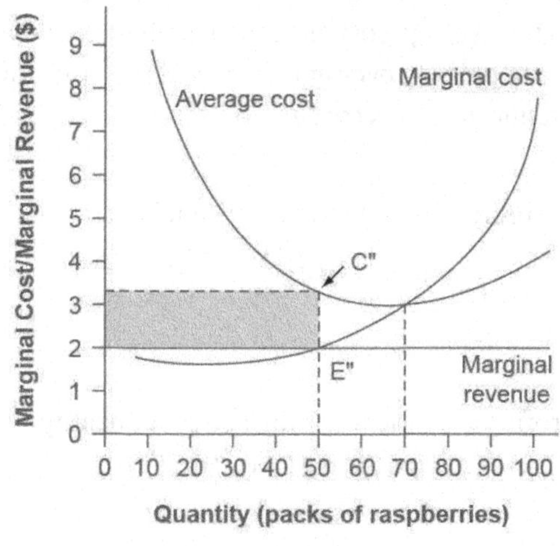



(c) Price is below average cost

**FIGURE 8.5 Price and Average Cost at the Raspberry Farm** In (a), price intersects marginal cost above the average cost curve. Since price is greater than average cost, the firm is making a profit. In (b), price intersects marginal cost at the minimum point of the average cost curve. Since price is equal to average cost, the firm is breaking even. In (c), price intersects marginal cost below the average cost curve. Since price is less than average cost, the firm is making a loss.

First consider a situation where the price is equal to $5 for a pack of frozen raspberries. The rule for a profit-maximizing perfectly competitive firm is to produce the level of output where Price= MR = MC, so the raspberry farmer will produce a quantity of approximately 85, which is labeled as E' in Figure 8.5 (a). Remember that the area of a rectangle is equal to its base multiplied by its height. The farm's total revenue at this price will be shown by the rectangle from the origin over to a quantity of 85 packs (the base) up to point E' (the height), over to the price of $5, and back to the origin. The average cost of producing 80 packs is shown by point C or about $3.50. Total costs will be the quantity of 85 times the average cost of $3.50, which is shown by the area of the rectangle from the origin to a quantity of 90, up to point C, over to the vertical axis and down to the origin. The difference between total revenues and total costs is profits. Thus, profits will be the blue shaded rectangle on top.

We calculate this as:

$$
\begin{aligned}
\text{profit} \quad &= \quad \text{total revenue} - \text{total cost} \\
&= \quad (85)(\$5.00) - (85)(\$3.50) \\
&= \quad \$127.50
\end{aligned}
$$

Or, we can calculate it as:

$$
\begin{aligned}
\text{profit} \quad &= \quad (\text{price} - \text{average cost}) \times \text{quantity} \\
&= \quad (\$5.00 - \$3.50) \times 85 \\
&= \quad \$127.50
\end{aligned}
$$

Now consider Figure 8.5 (b), where the price has fallen to $2.75 for a pack of frozen raspberries. Again, the perfectly competitive firm will choose the level of output where Price = MR = MC, but in this case, the quantity produced will be 75. At this price and output level, where the marginal cost curve is crossing the average cost curve, the price the firm receives is exactly equal to its average cost of production. We call this the **break even point**.

The farm's total revenue at this price will be shown by the large shaded rectangle from the origin over to a quantity of 75 packs (the base) up to point E (the height), over to the price of $2.75, and back to the origin. The height of the average cost curve at Q = 75, i.e. point E, shows the average cost of producing this quantity. Total costs will be the quantity of 75 times the average cost of $2.75, which is shown by the area of the rectangle from the origin to a quantity of 75, up to point E, over to the vertical axis and down to the origin. It should be clear that the rectangles for total revenue and total cost are the same. Thus, the firm is making zero profit. The calculations are as follows:

$$
\begin{aligned}
\text{profit} \quad &= \quad \text{total revenue} - \text{total cost} \\
&= \quad (75)(\$2.75) - (75)(\$2.75) \\
&= \quad \$0
\end{aligned}
$$

Or, we can calculate it as:

$$
\begin{aligned}
\text{profit} \quad &= \quad (\text{price} - \text{average cost}) \times \text{quantity} \\
&= \quad (\$2.75 - \$2.75) \times 75 \\
&= \quad \$0
\end{aligned}
$$

In Figure 8.5 (c), the market price has fallen still further to $2.00 for a pack of frozen raspberries. At this price, marginal revenue intersects marginal cost at a quantity of 65. The farm's total revenue at this price will be shown by the large shaded rectangle from the origin over to a quantity of 65 packs (the base) up to point E" (the height), over to the price of $2, and back to the origin. The average cost of producing 65 packs is shown by Point C" or shows the average cost of producing 50 packs is about $2.73. Total costs will be the quantity of 65 times the average cost of $2.73, which the area of the rectangle from the origin to a quantity of 50, up to point C", over to the vertical axis and down to the origin shows. It should be clear from examining the two rectangles that total revenue is less than total cost. Thus, the firm is losing money and the loss (or negative profit) will be the rose-shaded rectangle.

The calculations are:

$$
\begin{aligned}
\text{profit} \quad &= \quad (\text{total revenue} - \text{total cost}) \\
&= \quad (65)(\$2.00) - (65)(\$2.73) \\
&= \quad -\$47.45
\end{aligned}
$$

Or:

$$
\begin{aligned}
\text{profit} \quad &= \quad (\text{price} - \text{average cost}) \times \text{quantity} \\
&= \quad (\$2.00 - \$2.73) \times 65 \\
&= \quad -\$47.45
\end{aligned}
$$

If the market price that perfectly competitive firm receives leads it to produce at a quantity where the price is greater than average cost, the firm will earn profits. If the price the firm receives causes it to produce at a quantity where price equals average cost, which occurs at the minimum point of the AC curve, then the firm earns zero profits. Finally, if the price the firm receives leads it to produce at a quantity where the price is less than average cost, the firm will earn losses. Table 8.4 summarizes this.

| If... | Then... |
| --- | --- |
| Price > ATC | Firm earns an economic profit |
| Price = ATC | Firm earns zero economic profit |
| Price < ATC | Firm earns a loss |

**TABLE 8.4**

 **CLEAR IT UP**

## Which intersection should a firm choose?

At a price of $2, MR intersects MC at two points: Q = 20 and Q = 65. It never makes sense for a firm to choose a level of output on the downward sloping part of the MC curve, because the profit is lower (the loss is bigger). Thus, the correct choice of output is Q = 65.

## The Shutdown Point

The possibility that a firm may earn losses raises a question: Why can the firm not avoid losses by shutting down and not producing at all? The answer is that shutting down can reduce variable costs to zero, but in the short run, the firm has already paid for fixed costs. As a result, if the firm produces a quantity of zero, it would still make losses because it would still need to pay for its fixed costs. Therefore when a firm is experiencing losses, it must face a question: should it continue producing or should it shut down?

As an example, consider the situation of the Yoga Center, which has signed a contract to rent space that costs $10,000 per month. If the firm decides to operate, its marginal costs for hiring yoga teachers is $15,000 for the month. If the firm shuts down, it must still pay the rent, but it would not need to hire labor. Table 8.5 shows three possible scenarios. In the first scenario, the Yoga Center does not have any clients, and therefore does not make any revenues, in which case it faces losses of $10,000 equal to the fixed costs. In the second scenario, the Yoga Center has clients that earn the center revenues of $10,000 for the month, but ultimately experiences losses of $15,000 due to having to hire yoga instructors to cover the classes. In the third scenario, the Yoga Center earns revenues of $20,000 for the month, but experiences losses of $5,000.

In all three cases, the Yoga Center loses money. In all three cases, when the rental contract expires in the long run, assuming revenues do not improve, the firm should exit this business. In the short run, though, the decision varies depending on the level of losses and whether the firm can cover its variable costs. In scenario 1, the center does not have any revenues, so hiring yoga teachers would increase variable costs and losses, so it should shut down and only incur its fixed costs. In scenario 2, the center's losses are greater because it does not make enough revenue to offset the increased variable costs, so it should shut down immediately and only incur its fixed costs. If price is below the minimum average variable cost, the firm must shut down. In contrast, in scenario 3 the revenue that the center can earn is high enough that the losses diminish when it remains open, so the center should remain open in the short run.

**Scenario 1**

If the center shuts down now, revenues are zero but it will not incur any variable costs and would only need to pay fixed costs of $10,000.

$$\text{profit} = \text{total revenue--(fixed costs + variable cost)}$$
$$= 0 - \$10{,}000$$
$$= -\$10{,}000$$

**Scenario 2**

The center earns revenues of $10,000, and variable costs are $15,000. The center should shut down now.

$$\text{profit} = \text{total revenue} - \text{(fixed costs + variable cost)}$$
$$= \$10{,}000 - (\$10{,}000 + \$15{,}000)$$
$$= -\$15{,}000$$

**Scenario 3**

The center earns revenues of $20,000, and variable costs are $15,000. The center should continue in business.

$$\text{profit} = \text{total revenue} - \text{(fixed costs + variable cost)}$$
$$= \$20{,}000 - (\$10{,}000 + \$15{,}000)$$
$$= -\$5{,}000$$

**TABLE 8.5 Should the Yoga Center Shut Down Now or Later?**

Figure 8.6 illustrates the lesson that remaining open requires the price to exceed the firm's average variable cost. When the firm is operating below the break-even point, where price equals average cost, it is operating at a loss so it faces two options: continue to produce and lose money or shutdown. Which option is preferable? The one that loses the least money is the best choice.

At a price of $2.00 per pack, as Figure 8.6 (a) illustrates, if the farm stays in operation it will produce at a level of 65 packs of raspberries, and it will make losses of $47.45 (as explained earlier). The alternative would be to shut down and lose all the fixed costs of $62.00. Since losing $47.45 is preferable to losing $62.00, the profit maximizing (or in this case the loss minimizing) choice is to stay in operation. The key reason is because price is above average variable cost. This means that at the current price the farm can pay all its variable costs, and have some revenue left over to pay some of the fixed costs. So the loss represents the part of the fixed costs the farm can't pay, which is less than the entire fixed costs. However, if the price declined to $1.50 per pack, as Figure 8.6 (b) shows, and if the firm applied its rule of producing where P = MR = MC, it would produce a quantity of 60. This price is below average variable cost for this level of output. If the farmer cannot pay workers (the variable costs), then it has to shut down. At this price and output, total revenues would be $90 (quantity of 60 times price of $1.50) and total cost would be $165, for overall losses of $75. If the farm shuts down, it must pay only its fixed costs of $62, so shutting down is preferable to selling at a price of $1.50 per pack.

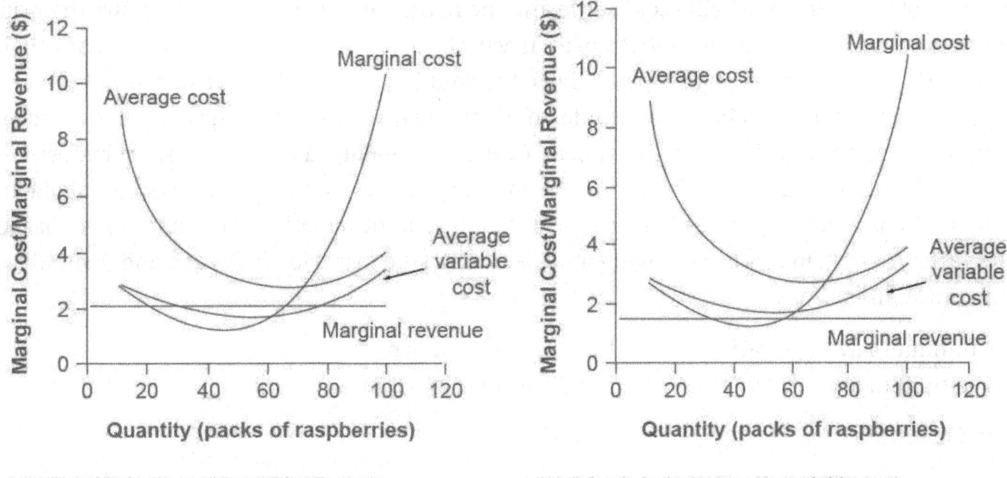


(a) Price is above average variable cost        (b) Price is below average variable cost

**FIGURE 8.6 The Shutdown Point for the Raspberry Farm** In (a), the farm produces at a level of 65. It is making losses of $47.50, but price is above average variable cost, so it continues to operate. In (b), total revenues are $90 and total cost is $165, for overall losses of $75. If the farm shuts down, it must pay only its fixed costs of $62. Shutting down is preferable to selling at a price of $1.50 per pack.

Looking at Table 8.6, if the price falls below about $1.72, the minimum average variable cost, the firm must shut down.

| Quantity Q | Average Variable Cost AVC | Average Cost AC | Marginal Cost MC |
|---|---|---|---|
| 0 | - | - | - |
| 10 | $2.80 | $9.00 | $2.80 |
| 20 | $2.40 | $5.50 | $2.00 |
| 30 | $2.13 | $4.20 | $1.60 |
| 40 | $1.90 | $3.45 | $1.20 |
| 50 | $1.76 | $3.00 | $1.20 |
| 60 | $1.72 | $2.75 | $1.50 |
| 70 | $1.83 | $2.71 | $2.50 |
| 80 | $2.10 | $2.88 | $4.00 |
| 90 | $2.60 | $3.29 | $6.60 |
| 100 | $3.38 | $4.00 | $10.40 |
| 110 | $4.44 | $5.00 | $15.00 |
| 120 | $5.44 | $5.96 | $31.50 |

**TABLE 8.6 Cost of Production for the Raspberry Farm**

The intersection of the average variable cost curve and the marginal cost curve, which shows the price below which the firm would lack enough revenue to cover its variable costs, is called the **shutdown point**. If the perfectly competitive firm faces a market price above the shutdown point, then the firm is at least covering its average variable costs. At a price above the shutdown point, the firm is also making enough revenue to cover at least a portion of fixed costs, so it should limp ahead even if it is making losses in the short run, since at least those losses will be smaller than if the firm shuts down immediately and incurs a loss equal to total fixed costs. However, if the firm is receiving a price below the price at the shutdown point, then the firm is not even covering its variable costs. In this case, staying open is making the firm's losses larger, and it should shut down immediately. To summarize, if:

- price < minimum average variable cost, then firm shuts down
- price > minimum average variable cost, then firm stays in business

## Short-Run Outcomes for Perfectly Competitive Firms

The average cost and average variable cost curves divide the marginal cost curve into three segments, as Figure 8.7 shows. At the market price, which the perfectly competitive firm accepts as given, the profit-maximizing firm chooses the output level where price or marginal revenue, which are the same thing for a perfectly competitive firm, is equal to marginal cost: P = MR = MC.

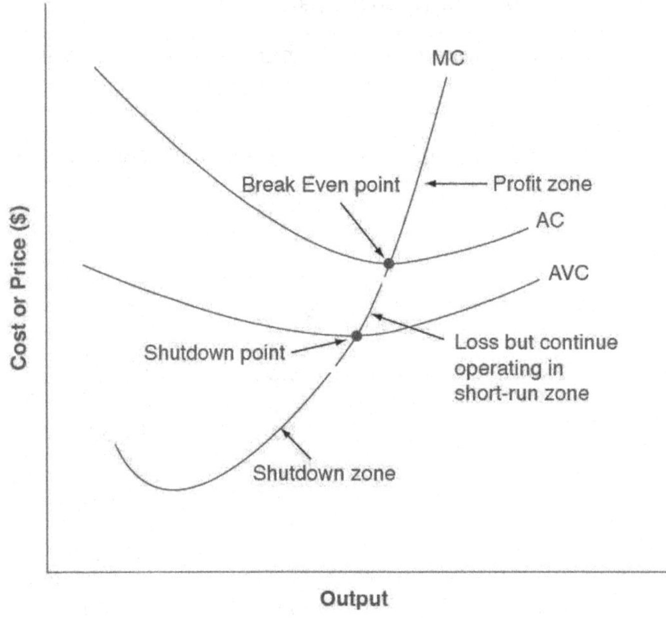


**FIGURE 8.7 Profit, Loss, Shutdown** We can divide the marginal cost curve into three zones, based on where it is crossed by the average cost and average variable cost curves. We call the point where MC crosses AC the break even point. If the firm is operating where the market price is at a level higher than the break even point, then price will be greater than average cost and the firm is earning profits. If the price is exactly at the break even point, then the firm is making zero profits. If price falls in the zone between the shutdown point and the break even point, then the firm is making losses but will continue to operate in the short run, since it is covering its variable costs, and more if price is above the shutdown-point price. However, if price falls below the price at the shutdown point, then the firm will shut down immediately, since it is not even covering its variable costs.

First consider the upper zone, where prices are above the level where marginal cost (MC) crosses average cost (AC) at the zero profit point. At any price above that level, the firm will earn profits in the short run. If the price falls exactly on the break even point where the MC and AC curves cross, then the firm earns zero profits. If a price falls into the zone between the break even point, where MC crosses AC, and the shutdown point, where MC crosses AVC, the firm will be making losses in the short run—but since the firm is more than covering its variable costs, the losses are smaller than if the firm shut down immediately. Finally, consider a price at or below the shutdown point where MC crosses AVC. At any price like this one, the firm will shut down immediately, because it cannot even cover its variable costs.

## Marginal Cost and the Firm's Supply Curve

For a perfectly competitive firm, the marginal cost curve is identical to the firm's supply curve starting from the minimum point on the average variable cost curve. To understand why this perhaps surprising insight holds true, first think about what the supply curve means. A firm checks the market price and then looks at its supply curve to decide what quantity to produce. Now, think about what it means to say that a firm will maximize its profits by producing at the quantity where P = MC. This rule means that the firm checks the market price, and then looks at its marginal cost to determine the quantity to produce—and makes sure that the price is greater than the minimum average variable cost. In other words, the marginal cost curve above the minimum point on the average variable cost curve becomes the firm's supply curve.

## LINK IT UP

Watch this video (http://openstax.org/l/foodprice) that addresses how drought in the United States can impact food prices across the world.

---

As we discussed in the chapter on Demand and Supply, many of the reasons that supply curves shift relate to underlying changes in costs. For example, a lower price of key inputs or new technologies that reduce production costs cause supply to shift to the right. In contrast, bad weather or added government regulations can add to costs of certain goods in a way that causes supply to shift to the left. We can also interpret these shifts in the firm's supply curve as shifts of the marginal cost curve. A shift in costs of production that increases marginal costs at all levels of output—and shifts MC upward and to the left—will cause a perfectly competitive firm to produce less at any given market price. Conversely, a shift in costs of production that decreases marginal costs at all levels of output will shift MC downward and to the right and as a result, a competitive firm will choose to expand its level of output at any given price. The following Work It Out feature will walk you through an example.

### WORK IT OUT

**At What Price Should the Firm Continue Producing in the Short Run?**

To determine the short-run economic condition of a firm in perfect competition, follow the steps outlined below. Use the data in Table 8.7.

| Q | P | TFC | TVC | TC | AVC | ATC | MC | TR | Profits |
|---|---|---|---|---|---|---|---|---|---|
| 0 | $28 | $20 | $0 | - | - | - | - | - | - |
| 1 | $28 | $20 | $20 | - | - | - | - | - | - |
| 2 | $28 | $20 | $25 | - | - | - | - | - | - |
| 3 | $28 | $20 | $35 | - | - | - | - | - | - |
| 4 | $28 | $20 | $52 | - | - | - | - | - | - |
| 5 | $28 | $20 | $80 | - | - | - | - | - | - |

**TABLE 8.7**

Step 1. Determine the cost structure for the firm. For a given total fixed costs and variable costs, calculate total cost, average variable cost, average total cost, and marginal cost. Follow the formulas given in the Production, Costs, and Industry Structure chapter. These calculations are in Table 8.8.

| Q | P | TFC | TVC | TC (TFC+TVC) | AVC (TVC/Q) | ATC (TC/Q) | MC $(TC_2-TC_1)/(Q_2-Q_1)$ |
|---|---|---|---|---|---|---|---|
| 0 | $28 | $20 | $0 | $20+$0=$20 | - | - | - |
| 1 | $28 | $20 | $20 | $20+$20=$40 | $20/1=$20.00 | $40/1=$40.00 | ($40–$20)/(1–0)= $20 |
| 2 | $28 | $20 | $25 | $20+$25=$45 | $25/2=$12.50 | $45/2=$22.50 | ($45–$40)/(2–1)= $5 |
| 3 | $28 | $20 | $35 | $20+$35=$55 | $35/3=$11.67 | $55/3=$18.33 | ($55–$45)/(3–2)= $10 |
| 4 | $28 | $20 | $52 | $20+$52=$72 | $52/4=$13.00 | $72/4=$18.00 | ($72–$55)/(4–3)= $17 |
| 5 | $28 | $20 | $80 | $20+$80=$100 | $80/5=$16.00 | $100/5=$20.00 | ($100–$72)/(5–4)= $28 |

**TABLE 8.8**

Step 2. Determine the market price that the firm receives for its product. Since the firm in perfect competition is a price taker, the market price is constant. With the given price, calculate total revenue as equal to price multiplied by quantity for all output levels produced. In this example, the given price is $28. You can see that in the second column of Table 8.9.

| Quantity | Price | Total Revenue (P × Q) |
|---|---|---|
| 0 | $28 | $28×0=$0 |
| 1 | $28 | $28×1=$28 |
| 2 | $28 | $28×2=$56 |
| 3 | $28 | $28×3=$84 |
| 4 | $28 | $28×4=$112 |
| 5 | $28 | $28×5=$140 |

**TABLE 8.9**

Step 3. Calculate profits as total cost subtracted from total revenue, as Table 8.10 shows.

| Quantity | Total Revenue | Total Cost | Profits (TR–TC) |
|---|---|---|---|
| 0 | $0 | $20 | $0–$20=–$20 |
| 1 | $28 | $40 | $28–$40=–$12 |
| 2 | $56 | $45 | $56–$45=$11 |
| 3 | $84 | $55 | $84–$55=$29 |
| 4 | $112 | $72 | $112–$72=$40 |
| 5 | $140 | $100 | $140–$100=$40 |

**TABLE 8.10**

Step 4. To find the profit-maximizing output level, look at the Marginal Cost column (at every output level produced), as Table 8.11 shows, and determine where it is equal to the market price. The output level where price equals the marginal cost is the output level that maximizes profits.

| Q | P | TFC | TVC | TC | AVC | ATC | MC | TR | Profits |
|---|---|---|---|---|---|---|---|---|---|
| 0 | $28 | $20 | $0 | $20 | - | - | - | $0 | –$20 |
| 1 | $28 | $20 | $20 | $40 | $20.00 | $40.00 | $20 | $28 | –$12 |
| 2 | $28 | $20 | $25 | $45 | $12.50 | $22.50 | $5 | $56 | $11 |
| 3 | $28 | $20 | $35 | $55 | $11.67 | $18.33 | $10 | $84 | $29 |
| 4 | $28 | $20 | $52 | $72 | $13.00 | $18.00 | $17 | $112 | $40 |
| **5** | **$28** | $20 | $80 | $100 | $16.40 | $20.40 | **$28** | $140 | **$40** |

**TABLE 8.11**

Step 5. Once you have determined the profit-maximizing output level (in this case, output quantity 5), you can look at the amount of profits made (in this case, $40).

Step 6. If the firm is making economic losses, the firm needs to determine whether it produces the output level where price equals marginal revenue and equals marginal cost or it shuts down and only incurs its fixed costs.

Step 7. For the output level where marginal revenue is equal to marginal cost, check if the market price is greater than the average variable cost of producing that output level.

- If P > AVC but P < ATC, then the firm continues to produce in the short-run, making economic losses.
- If P < AVC, then the firm stops producing and only incurs its fixed costs.

In this example, the price of $28 is greater than the AVC ($16.40) of producing 5 units of output, so the firm continues producing.

# 8.3 Entry and Exit Decisions in the Long Run

**LEARNING OBJECTIVES**

By the end of this section, you will be able to:

- Explain how entry and exit lead to zero profits in the long run
- Discuss the long-run adjustment process

It is impossible to precisely define the line between the short run and the long run with a stopwatch, or even with a calendar. It varies according to the specific business. Therefore, the distinction between the short run and the long run is more technical: in the short run, firms cannot change the usage of fixed inputs, while in the long run, the firm can adjust all factors of production.

In a competitive market, profits are a red cape that incites businesses to charge. If a business is making a profit in the short run, it has an incentive to expand existing factories or to build new ones. New firms may start production, as well. When new firms enter the industry in response to increased industry profits it is called **entry**.

Losses are the black thundercloud that causes businesses to flee. If a business is making losses in the short run, it will either keep limping along or just shut down, depending on whether its revenues are covering its variable costs. But in the long run, firms that are facing losses will cease production altogether. The long-run process of reducing production in response to a sustained pattern of losses is called **exit**. The following Clear It Up feature discusses where some of these losses might come from, and the reasons why some firms go out of business.

 **CLEAR IT UP**

### Why do firms cease to exist?

Can we say anything about what causes a firm to exit an industry? Profits are the measurement that determines whether a business stays operating or not. Individuals start businesses with the purpose of making profits. They invest their money, time, effort, and many other resources to produce and sell something that they hope will give them something in return. Unfortunately, not all businesses are successful, and many new startups soon realize that their "business venture" must eventually end.

In the model of perfectly competitive firms, those that consistently cannot make money will "exit," which is a nice, bloodless word for a more painful process. When a business fails, after all, workers lose their jobs, investors lose their money, and owners and managers can lose their dreams. Many businesses fail. The U.S. Small Business Administration indicates that in 2011, 534,907 new firms "entered," and 575,691 firms failed.

Sometimes a business fails because of poor management or workers who are not very productive, or because of tough domestic or foreign competition. Businesses also fail from a variety of causes. For example, conditions of demand and supply in the market may shift in an unexpected way, so that the prices that a business charges for outputs fall or the prices for inputs rise. With millions of businesses in the U.S. economy, even a small fraction of them failing will affect many people—and business failures can be very hard on the workers and managers directly involved. However, from the standpoint of the overall economic system, business exits are sometimes a necessary evil if a market-oriented system is going to offer a flexible mechanism for satisfying customers, keeping costs low, and inventing new products.

### How Entry and Exit Lead to Zero Profits in the Long Run

No perfectly competitive firm acting alone can affect the market price. However, the combination of many firms entering or exiting the market will affect overall supply in the market. In turn, a shift in supply for the market as a whole will affect the market price. Entry and exit to and from the market are the driving forces behind a process that, in the long run, pushes the price down to minimum average total costs so that all firms are earning a zero profit.

To understand how short-run profits for a perfectly competitive firm will evaporate in the long run, imagine the following situation. The market is in **long-run equilibrium**, where all firms earn zero economic profits producing the output level where $P = MR = MC$ and $P = AC$. No firm has the incentive to enter or leave the market. Let's say that the product's demand increases, and with that, the market price goes up. The existing firms in the industry are now facing a higher price than before, so they will increase production to the new output level where $P = MR = MC$.

This will temporarily make the market price rise above the minimum point on the average cost curve, and therefore, the existing firms in the market will now be earning economic profits. However, these economic profits attract other firms to enter the market. Entry of many new firms causes the market supply curve to shift to the right. As the supply curve shifts to the right, the market price starts decreasing, and with that, economic profits fall for new and existing firms. As long as there are still profits in the market, entry will continue to shift supply to the right. This will stop whenever the market price is driven down to the zero-profit level, where no firm is earning economic profits.

Short-run losses will fade away by reversing this process. Say that the market is in long-run equilibrium. This time, instead, demand decreases, and with that, the market price starts falling. The existing firms in the industry are now facing a lower price than before, and as it will be below the average cost curve, they will now be making economic losses. Some firms will continue producing where the new $P = MR = MC$, as long as they are able to cover their average variable costs. Some firms will have to shut down immediately as they will not be able to cover their average variable costs, and will then only incur their fixed costs, minimizing their losses. Exit of many firms causes the market supply curve to shift to the left. As the supply curve shifts to the left, the market price starts rising, and economic losses start to be lower. This process ends whenever the market price rises to the zero-profit level, where the existing firms are no longer losing money and are at zero profits again. Thus, while a perfectly competitive firm can earn profits in the short run, in the long run the process of entry will push down prices until they reach the zero-profit level. Conversely, while a perfectly competitive firm may earn losses in the short run, firms will not continually lose money. In the long run, firms making losses are able to escape from their fixed costs, and their exit from the market will push the price back up to the zero-profit level. In the long run, this process of entry and exit will drive the price in perfectly competitive markets to the zero-profit point at the bottom of the AC curve, where marginal cost crosses average cost.

## The Long-Run Adjustment and Industry Types

Whenever there are expansions in an industry, costs of production for the existing and new firms could either stay the same, increase, or even decrease. Therefore, we can categorize an industry as being (1) a constant-cost industry (as demand increases, the cost of production for firms stays the same), (2) an increasing cost industry (as demand increases, the cost of production for firms increases), or (3) a decreasing cost industry (as demand increases the costs of production for the firms decreases).

For a constant-cost industry, whenever there is an increase in market demand and price, then the supply curve shifts to the right with new firms' entry and stops at the point where the new long-run equilibrium intersects at the same market price as before. This is the case of constant returns to scale, which we discussed earlier in the chapter on Production, Costs, and Industry Structure. However, why will costs remain the same? In this type of industry, the supply curve is very elastic. Firms can easily supply any quantity that consumers demand. In addition, there is a perfectly elastic supply of inputs—firms can easily increase their demand for employees, for example, with no increase to wages. Tying in to our Bring it Home discussion, an increased demand for ethanol in recent years has caused the demand for corn to increase. Consequently, many farmers switched from growing wheat to growing corn. Agricultural markets are generally good examples of constant-cost industries.

For an increasing cost industry, as the market expands, the old and new firms experience increases in their costs of production, which makes the new zero-profit level intersect at a higher price than before. Here companies may have to deal with limited inputs, such as skilled labor. As the demand for these workers rises, wages rise and this increases the cost of production for all firms. The industry supply curve in this type of industry is more inelastic.

For a decreasing cost industry, as the market expands, the old and new firms experience lower costs of production, which makes the new zero-profit level intersect at a lower price than before. In this case, the industry and all the firms in it are experiencing falling average total costs. This can be due to an improvement in technology in the entire industry or an increase in the education of employees. High-tech industries may be a good example of a decreasing cost market.

Figure 8.8 (a) presents the case of an adjustment process in a constant-cost industry. Whenever there are output expansions in this type of industry, the long-run outcome implies more output produced at exactly the same original price. Note that supply was able to increase to meet the increased demand. When we join the before and after long-run equilibriums, the resulting line is the long run supply (LRS) curve in perfectly competitive markets. In this case, it is a flat curve. Figure 8.8 (b) and Figure 8.8 (c) present the cases for an increasing cost and decreasing cost industry, respectively. For an increasing cost industry, the LRS is upward sloping, while for a decreasing cost industry, the LRS is downward sloping.

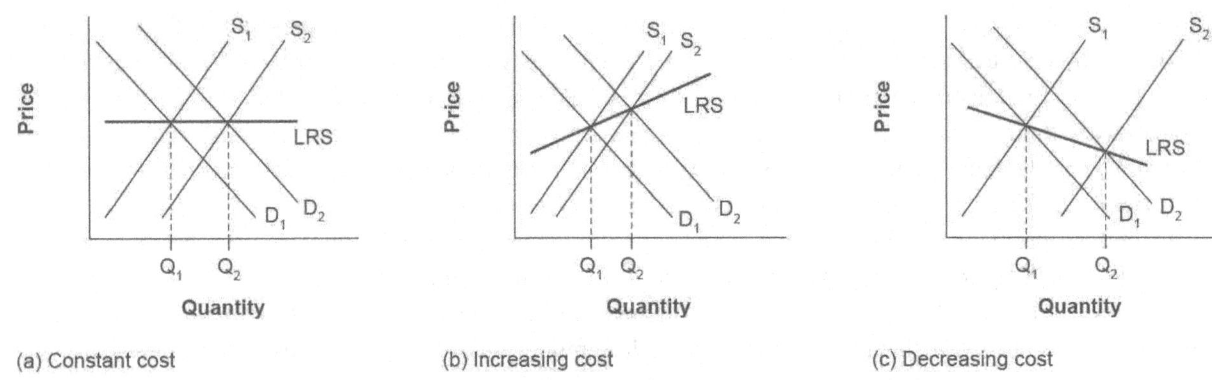


(a) Constant cost          (b) Increasing cost          (c) Decreasing cost

**FIGURE 8.8 Adjustment Process in a Constant-Cost Industry** In (a), demand increased and supply met it. Notice that the supply increase is equal to the demand increase. The result is that the equilibrium price stays the same as quantity sold increases. In (b), notice that sellers were not able to increase supply as much as demand. Some inputs were scarce, or wages were rising. The equilibrium price rises. In (c), sellers easily increased supply in response to the demand increase. Here, new technology or economies of scale caused the large increase in supply, resulting in declining equilibrium price.

## 8.4 Efficiency in Perfectly Competitive Markets

**LEARNING OBJECTIVES**

By the end of this section, you will be able to:

- Apply concepts of productive efficiency and allocative efficiency to perfectly competitive markets
- Compare the model of perfect competition to real-world markets

When profit-maximizing firms in perfectly competitive markets combine with utility-maximizing consumers, something remarkable happens: the resulting quantities of outputs of goods and services demonstrate both productive and allocative efficiency (terms that we first introduced in (Choice in a World of Scarcity) .

Productive efficiency means producing without waste, so that the choice is on the production possibility frontier. In the long run in a perfectly competitive market, because of the process of entry and exit, the price in the market is equal to the minimum of the long-run average cost curve. In other words, firms produce and sell goods at the lowest possible average cost.

Allocative efficiency means that among the points on the production possibility frontier, the chosen point is socially preferred—at least in a particular and specific sense. In a perfectly competitive market, price will be equal to the marginal cost of production. Think about the price that one pays for a good as a measure of the social benefit one receives for that good; after all, willingness to pay conveys what the good is worth to a buyer. Then think about the marginal cost of producing the good as representing not just the cost for the firm, but more broadly as the social cost of producing that good. When perfectly competitive firms follow the rule that profits are maximized by producing at the quantity where price is equal to marginal cost, they are thus ensuring that the social benefits they receive from producing a good are in line with the social costs of production.

To explore what economists mean by allocative efficiency, it is useful to walk through an example. Begin by assuming that the market for wholesale flowers is perfectly competitive, and so P = MC. Now, consider what it would mean if firms in that market produced a lesser quantity of flowers. At a lesser quantity, marginal costs will not yet have increased as much, so that price will exceed marginal cost; that is, P > MC. In that situation, the benefit to society as a whole of producing additional goods, as measured by the willingness of consumers to pay for marginal units of a good, would be higher than the cost of the inputs of labor and physical capital needed to produce the marginal good. In other words, the gains to society as a whole from producing additional marginal units will be greater than the costs.

Conversely, consider what it would mean if, compared to the level of output at the allocatively efficient choice when P = MC, firms produced a greater quantity of flowers. At a greater quantity, marginal costs of production will have increased so that P < MC. In that case, the marginal costs of producing additional flowers is greater than the benefit to society as measured by what people are willing to pay. For society as a whole, since the costs are outstripping the benefits, it will make sense to produce a lower quantity of such goods.

When perfectly competitive firms maximize their profits by producing the quantity where P = MC, they also assure that the benefits to consumers of what they are buying, as measured by the price they are willing to pay, is equal to the costs to society of producing the marginal units, as measured by the marginal costs the firm must pay—and thus that allocative efficiency holds.

We should view the statements that a perfectly competitive market in the long run will feature both productive and allocative efficiency with a degree of skepticism about its truth. Remember, economists are using the concept of "efficiency" in a particular and specific sense, not as a synonym for "desirable in every way." For one thing, consumers' ability to pay reflects the income distribution in a particular society. For example, a person with a low income may not be able to purchase their own car because they have insufficient income.

Perfect competition, in the long run, is a hypothetical benchmark. For market structures such as monopoly, monopolistic competition, and oligopoly, which are more frequently observed in the real world than perfect competition, firms will not always produce at the minimum of average cost, nor will they always set price equal to marginal cost. Thus, these other competitive situations will not produce productive and allocative efficiency.

Moreover, real-world markets include many issues that are assumed away in the model of perfect competition, including pollution, inventions of new technology, poverty which may make some people unable to pay for basic necessities of life, government programs like national defense or education, discrimination in labor markets, and buyers and sellers who must deal with imperfect and unclear information. We explore these issues in other chapters. However, the theoretical efficiency of perfect competition does provide a useful benchmark for comparing the issues that arise from these real-world problems.

 **BRING IT HOME**

### A Dime a Dozen

A quick glance at Table 8.12 reveals the dramatic increase in North Dakota corn production—almost a tenfold increase since 1972. Recent allocation of land to corn (as of mid-2019) is estimated to have increased to more than

4 million acres. Taking into consideration that corn typically yields two to three times as many bushels per acre as wheat, it is obvious there has been a significant increase in bushels of corn. Why the increase in corn acreage? Converging prices.

| Year | Corn (millions of acres) |
| --- | --- |
| 1972 | 495,000 |
| 2013 | 3,850,000 |

**TABLE 8.12** (Source: USDA National Agricultural Statistics Service)

Historically, wheat prices have been higher than corn prices, offsetting wheat's lower yield per acre. However, in recent years wheat and corn prices have been converging. In April 2013, *Agweek* reported the gap was just 71 cents per bushel. As the difference in price narrowed, switching to the production of higher yield per acre of corn simply made good business sense. Erik Younggren, president of the National Association of Wheat Growers said in the *Agweek* article, "I don't think we're going to see mile after mile of waving amber fields [of wheat] anymore." (Until wheat prices rise, we will probably be seeing field after field of tasseled corn.)

# Key Terms

**break even point** level of output where the marginal cost curve intersects the average cost curve at the
minimum point of AC; if the price is at this point, the firm is earning zero economic profits
**entry** the long-run process of firms entering an industry in response to industry profits
**exit** the long-run process of firms reducing production and shutting down in response to industry losses
**long-run equilibrium** where all firms earn zero economic profits producing the output level where P = MR =
MC and P = AC
**marginal revenue** the additional revenue gained from selling one more unit
**market structure** the conditions in an industry, such as number of sellers, how easy or difficult it is for a new
firm to enter, and the type of products that are sold
**perfect competition** each firm faces many competitors that sell identical products
**price taker** a firm in a perfectly competitive market that must take the prevailing market price as given
**shutdown point** level of output where the marginal cost curve intersects the average variable cost curve at the
minimum point of AVC; if the price is below this point, the firm should shut down immediately

## Key Concepts and Summary

### 8.1 Perfect Competition and Why It Matters

A perfectly competitive firm is a price taker, which means that it must accept the equilibrium price at which it
sells goods. If a perfectly competitive firm attempts to charge even a tiny amount more than the market price,
it will be unable to make any sales. In a perfectly competitive market there are thousands of sellers, easy entry,
and identical products. A short-run production period is when firms are producing with some fixed inputs.
Long-run equilibrium in a perfectly competitive industry occurs after all firms have entered and exited the
industry and seller profits are driven to zero.

Perfect competition means that there are many sellers, there is easy entry and exiting of firms, products are
identical from one seller to another, and sellers are price takers.

### 8.2 How Perfectly Competitive Firms Make Output Decisions

As a perfectly competitive firm produces a greater quantity of output, its total revenue steadily increases at a
constant rate determined by the given market price. Profits will be highest (or losses will be smallest) at the
quantity of output where total revenues exceed total costs by the greatest amount (or where total revenues fall
short of total costs by the smallest amount). Alternatively, profits will be highest where marginal revenue,
which is price for a perfectly competitive firm, is equal to marginal cost. If the market price faced by a perfectly
competitive firm is above average cost at the profit-maximizing quantity of output, then the firm is making
profits. If the market price is below average cost at the profit-maximizing quantity of output, then the firm is
making losses.

If the market price is equal to average cost at the profit-maximizing level of output, then the firm is making
zero profits. We call the point where the marginal cost curve crosses the average cost curve, at the minimum of
the average cost curve, the "zero profit point." If the market price that a perfectly competitive firm faces is
below average variable cost at the profit-maximizing quantity of output, then the firm should shut down
operations immediately. If the market price that a perfectly competitive firm faces is above average variable
cost, but below average cost, then the firm should continue producing in the short run, but exit in the long run.
We call the point where the marginal cost curve crosses the average variable cost curve the shutdown point.

### 8.3 Entry and Exit Decisions in the Long Run

In the long run, firms will respond to profits through a process of entry, where existing firms expand output
and new firms enter the market. Conversely, firms will react to losses in the long run through a process of exit,
in which existing firms cease production altogether. Through the process of entry in response to profits and
exit in response to losses, the price level in a perfectly competitive market will move toward the zero-profit

point, where the marginal cost curve crosses the AC curve at the minimum of the average cost curve.

The long-run supply curve shows the long-run output supplied by firms in three different types of industries: constant cost, increasing cost, and decreasing cost.

## 8.4 Efficiency in Perfectly Competitive Markets

Long-run equilibrium in perfectly competitive markets meets two important conditions: allocative efficiency and productive efficiency. These two conditions have important implications. First, resources are allocated to their best alternative use. Second, they provide the maximum satisfaction attainable by society.

## Self-Check Questions

1. Firms in a perfectly competitive market are said to be "price takers"—that is, once the market determines an equilibrium price for the product, firms must accept this price. If you sell a product in a perfectly competitive market, but you are not happy with its price, would you raise the price, even by a cent?

2. Would independent trucking fit the characteristics of a perfectly competitive industry?

3. Look at Table 8.13. What would happen to the firm's profits if the market price increases to $6 per pack of raspberries?

| Quantity | Total Cost | Fixed Cost | Variable Cost | Total Revenue | Profit |
|---|---|---|---|---|---|
| 0 | $62 | $62 | - | $0 | −$62 |
| 10 | $90 | $62 | $28 | $60 | −$30 |
| 20 | $110 | $62 | $48 | $120 | $10 |
| 30 | $126 | $62 | $64 | $180 | $54 |
| 40 | $144 | $62 | $82 | $240 | $96 |
| 50 | $166 | $62 | $104 | $300 | $134 |
| 60 | $192 | $62 | $130 | $360 | $168 |
| 70 | $224 | $62 | $162 | $420 | $196 |
| 80 | $264 | $62 | $202 | $480 | $216 |
| 90 | $324 | $62 | $262 | $540 | $216 |
| 100 | $404 | $62 | $342 | $600 | $196 |

**TABLE 8.13**

4. Suppose that the market price increases to $6, as Table 8.14 shows. What would happen to the profit-maximizing output level?

| Quantity | Total Cost | Fixed Cost | Variable Cost | Marginal Cost | Total Revenue | Marginal Revenue |
|---|---|---|---|---|---|---|
| 0 | $62 | $62 | - | - | $0 | - |
| 10 | $90 | $62 | $28 | $2.80 | $60 | $6.00 |
| 20 | $110 | $62 | $48 | $2.00 | $120 | $6.00 |
| 30 | $126 | $62 | $64 | $1.60 | $180 | $6.00 |
| 40 | $144 | $62 | $82 | $1.80 | $240 | $6.00 |
| 50 | $166 | $62 | $104 | $2.20 | $300 | $6.00 |
| 60 | $192 | $62 | $130 | $2.60 | $360 | $6.00 |
| 70 | $224 | $62 | $162 | $3.20 | $420 | $6.00 |
| 80 | $264 | $62 | $202 | $4.00 | $480 | $6.00 |
| **90** | $324 | $62 | $262 | **$6.00** | $540 | **$6.00** |
| 100 | $404 | $62 | $342 | $8.00 | $600 | $6.00 |

**TABLE 8.14**

5. Explain in words why a profit-maximizing firm will not choose to produce at a quantity where marginal cost exceeds marginal revenue.

6. A firm's marginal cost curve above the average variable cost curve is equal to the firm's individual supply curve. This means that every time a firm receives a price from the market it will be willing to supply the amount of output where the price equals marginal cost. What happens to the firm's individual supply curve if marginal costs increase?

7. If new technology in a perfectly competitive market brings about a substantial reduction in costs of production, how will this affect the market?

8. A market in perfect competition is in long-run equilibrium. What happens to the market if labor unions are able to increase wages for workers?

9. Productive efficiency and allocative efficiency are two concepts achieved in the long run in a perfectly competitive market. These are the two reasons why we call them "perfect." How would you use these two concepts to analyze other market structures and label them "imperfect?"

10. Explain how the profit-maximizing rule of setting P = MC leads a perfectly competitive market to be allocatively efficient.

## Review Questions

11. A single firm in a perfectly competitive market is relatively small compared to the rest of the market. What does this mean? How "small" is "small"?

12. What are the four basic assumptions of perfect competition? Explain in words what they imply for a perfectly competitive firm.

13. What is a "price taker" firm?

14. How does a perfectly competitive firm decide what price to charge?

15. What prevents a perfectly competitive firm from seeking higher profits by increasing the price that it charges?

16. How does a perfectly competitive firm calculate total revenue?

17. Briefly explain the reason for the shape of a marginal revenue curve for a perfectly competitive firm.

18. What two rules does a perfectly competitive firm apply to determine its profit-maximizing quantity of output?

19. How does the average cost curve help to show whether a firm is making profits or losses?

20. What two lines on a cost curve diagram intersect at the zero-profit point?

21. Should a firm shut down immediately if it is making losses?

22. How does the average variable cost curve help a firm know whether it should shut down immediately?

23. What two lines on a cost curve diagram intersect at the shutdown point?

24. Why does entry occur?

25. Why does exit occur?

26. Do entry and exit occur in the short run, the long run, both, or neither?

27. What price will a perfectly competitive firm end up charging in the long run? Why?

28. Will a perfectly competitive market display productive efficiency? Why or why not?

29. Will a perfectly competitive market display allocative efficiency? Why or why not?

## Critical Thinking Questions

30. Finding a life partner is a complicated process that may take many years. It is hard to think of this process as being part of a very complex market, with a demand and a supply for partners. Think about how this market works and some of its characteristics, such as search costs. Would you consider it a perfectly competitive market?

31. Can you name five examples of perfectly competitive markets? Why or why not?

32. Your company operates in a perfectly competitive market. You have been told that advertising can help you increase your sales in the short run. Would you create an aggressive advertising campaign for your product?

33. Since a perfectly competitive firm can sell as much as it wishes at the market price, why can the firm not simply increase its profits by selling an extremely high quantity?

34. Many firms in the United States file for bankruptcy every year, yet they still continue operating. Why would they do this instead of completely shutting down?

35. Why will profits for firms in a perfectly competitive industry tend to vanish in the long run?

36. Why will losses for firms in a perfectly competitive industry tend to vanish in the long run?

37. Assuming that the market for cigarettes is in perfect competition, what does allocative and productive efficiency imply in this case? What does it not imply?

**38.** In the argument for why perfect competition is allocatively efficient, the price that people are willing to pay represents the gains to society and the marginal cost to the firm represents the costs to society. Can you think of some social costs or issues that are not included in the marginal cost to the firm? Or some social gains that are not included in what people pay for a good?

## Problems

**39.** The AAA Aquarium Co. sells aquariums for $20 each. Fixed costs of production are $20. The total variable costs are $20 for one aquarium, $25 for two units, $35 for the three units, $50 for four units, and $80 for five units. In the form of a table, calculate total revenue, marginal revenue, total cost, and marginal cost for each output level (one to five units). What is the profit-maximizing quantity of output? On one diagram, sketch the total revenue and total cost curves. On another diagram, sketch the marginal revenue and marginal cost curves.

**40.** Perfectly competitive firm Doggies Paradise Inc. sells winter coats for dogs. Dog coats sell for $72 each. The fixed costs of production are $100. The total variable costs are $64 for one unit, $84 for two units, $114 for three units, $184 for four units, and $270 for five units. In the form of a table, calculate total revenue, marginal revenue, total cost and marginal cost for each output level (one to five units). On one diagram, sketch the total revenue and total cost curves. On another diagram, sketch the marginal revenue and marginal cost curves. What is the profit maximizing quantity?

**41.** A computer company produces affordable, easy-to-use home computer systems and has fixed costs of $250. The marginal cost of producing computers is $700 for the first computer, $250 for the second, $300 for the third, $350 for the fourth, $400 for the fifth, $450 for the sixth, and $500 for the seventh.
   a. Create a table that shows the company's output, total cost, marginal cost, average cost, variable cost, and average variable cost.
   b. At what price is the zero-profit point? At what price is the shutdown point?
   c. If the company sells the computers for $500, is it making a profit or a loss? How big is the profit or loss? Sketch a graph with AC, MC, and AVC curves to illustrate your answer and show the profit or loss.
   d. If the firm sells the computers for $300, is it making a profit or a loss? How big is the profit or loss? Sketch a graph with AC, MC, and AVC curves to illustrate your answer and show the profit or loss.

**FIGURE 9.1 Political Power from a Cotton Monopoly** In the mid-nineteenth century, the United States, specifically the Southern states, had a near monopoly in the cotton that they supplied to Great Britain. These states attempted to leverage this economic power into political power—trying to sway Great Britain to formally recognize the Confederate States of America. (Credit: modification of "cotton!" by ashley/Flickr, CC BY 2.0)

**CHAPTER OBJECTIVES**

In this chapter, you will learn about:
- How Monopolies form: Barriers to Entry
- How a Profit-Maximizing Monopoly Chooses Output and Price

## Introduction to a Monopoly

 **BRING IT HOME**

### The Rest is History

Many of the opening case studies have focused on current events. This one steps into the past to observe how monopoly, or near monopolies, have helped shape history. In spring 1773, the East India Company, a firm that, in its time, was designated "too big to fail," was experiencing financial difficulties. To help shore up the failing firm, the British Parliament authorized the Tea Act. The act continued the tax on teas and made the East India Company the sole legal supplier of tea to the American colonies. By November, the citizens of Boston had had enough. They refused to permit the unloading of tea, citing their main complaint: "No taxation without representation." Several newspapers, including *The Massachusetts Gazette*, warned arriving tea-bearing ships, "We are prepared, and shall not fail to pay them an unwelcome visit by The Mohawks."

Step forward in time to 1860—the eve of the American Civil War—to another near monopoly supplier of historical significance: the U.S. cotton industry. At that time, the Southern states provided the majority of the cotton Britain imported. The South, wanting to secede from the Union, hoped to leverage Britain's high dependency on its cotton into formal diplomatic recognition of the Confederate States of America.

This leads us to this chapter's topic: a firm that controls all (or nearly all) of the supply of a good or service—a monopoly. How do monopoly firms behave in the marketplace? Do they have "power?" Does this power potentially have unintended consequences? We'll return to this case at the end of the chapter to see how the tea and cotton monopolies influenced U.S. history.

---

Many believe that top executives at firms are the strongest supporters of market competition, but this belief is far from the truth. Think about it this way: If you very much wanted to win an Olympic gold medal, would you rather be far better than everyone else, or locked in competition with many athletes just as good as you? Similarly, if you would like to attain a very high level of profits, would you rather manage a business with little or no competition, or struggle against many tough competitors who are trying to sell to your customers? By now, you might have read the chapter on Perfect Competition. In this chapter, we explore the opposite extreme: monopoly.

If perfect competition is a market where firms have no market power and they simply respond to the market price, monopoly is a market with no competition at all, and firms have a great deal of market power. In the case of **monopoly**, one firm produces all of the output in a market. Since a monopoly faces no significant competition, it can charge any price it wishes, subject to the demand curve. While a monopoly, by definition, refers to a single firm, in practice people often use the term to describe a market in which one firm merely has a very high market share. This tends to be the definition that the U.S. Department of Justice uses.

Even though there are very few true monopolies in existence, we do deal with some of those few every day, often without realizing it: The U.S. Postal Service, your electric, and garbage collection companies are a few examples. Some new drugs are produced by only one pharmaceutical firm—and no close substitutes for that drug may exist.

From the mid-1990s until 2004, the U.S. Department of Justice prosecuted the Microsoft Corporation for including Internet Explorer as the default web browser with its operating system. The Justice Department's argument was that, since Microsoft possessed an extremely high market share in the industry for operating systems, the inclusion of a free web browser constituted unfair competition to other browsers, such as Netscape Navigator. Since nearly everyone was using Windows, including Internet Explorer eliminated the incentive for consumers to explore other browsers and made it impossible for competitors to gain a foothold in the market. In 2013, the Windows system ran on more than 90% of the most commonly sold personal computers. In 2015, a U.S. federal court tossed out antitrust charges that Google had an agreement with mobile device makers to set Google as the default search engine.

This chapter begins by describing how monopolies are protected from competition, including laws that prohibit competition, technological advantages, and certain configurations of demand and supply. It then discusses how a monopoly will choose its profit-maximizing quantity to produce and what price to charge. While a monopoly must be concerned about whether consumers will purchase its products or spend their money on something altogether different, the monopolist need not worry about the actions of other competing firms producing its products. As a result, a monopoly is not a price taker like a perfectly competitive firm, but instead exercises some power to choose its market price.

# 9.1 How Monopolies Form: Barriers to Entry

**LEARNING OBJECTIVES**

By the end of this section, you will be able to:
- Distinguish between a natural monopoly and a legal monopoly.
- Explain how economies of scale and the control of natural resources led to the necessary formation of legal monopolies
- Analyze the importance of trademarks and patents in promoting innovation
- Identify examples of predatory pricing

Because of the lack of competition, monopolies tend to earn significant economic profits. These profits should attract vigorous competition as we described in Perfect Competition, and yet, because of one particular characteristic of monopoly, they do not. **Barriers to entry** are the legal, technological, or market forces that discourage or prevent potential competitors from entering a market. Barriers to entry can range from the simple and easily surmountable, such as the cost of renting retail space, to the extremely restrictive. For example, there are a finite number of radio frequencies available for broadcasting. Once an entrepreneur or firm has purchased the rights to all of them, no new competitors can enter the market.

In some cases, barriers to entry may lead to monopoly. In other cases, they may limit competition to a few firms. Barriers may block entry even if the firm or firms currently in the market are earning profits. Thus, in markets with significant barriers to entry, it is *not* necessarily true that abnormally high profits will attract new firms, and that this entry of new firms will eventually cause the price to decline so that surviving firms earn only a normal level of profit in the long run.

There are five types of monopoly, based on the types of barriers to entry they exploit.

## Natural Monopoly

Economies of scale can combine with the size of the market to limit competition. (We introduced this theme in Production, Cost and Industry Structure). Figure 9.2 presents a long-run average cost curve for the airplane manufacturing industry. It shows economies of scale up to an output of 8,000 planes per year and a price of $P_0$, then constant returns to scale from 8,000 to 20,000 planes per year, and diseconomies of scale at a quantity of production greater than 20,000 planes per year.

Now consider the market demand curve in the diagram, which intersects the long-run average cost (LRAC) curve at an output level of 5,000 planes per year and at a price $P_1$, which is higher than $P_0$. In this situation, the market has room for only one producer. If a second firm attempts to enter the market at a smaller size, say by producing a quantity of 4,000 planes, then its average costs will be higher than those of the existing firm, and it will be unable to compete. If the second firm attempts to enter the market at a larger size, like 8,000 planes per year, then it could produce at a lower average cost—but it could not sell all 8,000 planes that it produced because of insufficient demand in the market.

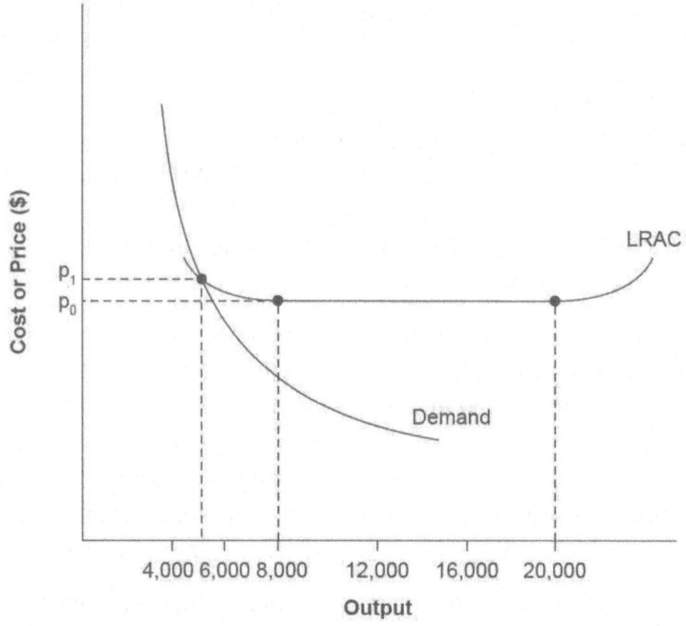


**FIGURE 9.2 Economies of Scale and Natural Monopoly** In this market, the demand curve intersects the long-run average cost (LRAC) curve at its downward-sloping part. A natural monopoly occurs when the quantity demanded is less than the minimum quantity it takes to be at the bottom of the long-run average cost curve.

Economists call this situation, when economies of scale are large relative to the quantity demanded in the market, a natural monopoly. Natural monopolies often arise in industries where the marginal cost of adding an additional customer is very low, once the fixed costs of the overall system are in place. This results in situations where there are substantial economies of scale. For example, once a water company lays the main water pipes through a neighborhood, the marginal cost of providing water service to another home is fairly low. Once the electric company installs lines in a new subdivision, the marginal cost of providing additional electrical service to one more home is minimal. It would be costly and duplicative for a second water company to enter the market and invest in a whole second set of main water pipes, or for a second electricity company to enter the market and invest in a whole new set of electrical wires. These industries offer an example where, because of economies of scale, one producer can serve the entire market more efficiently than a number of smaller producers that would need to make duplicate physical capital investments.

A natural monopoly can also arise in smaller local markets for products that are difficult to transport. For example, cement production exhibits economies of scale, and the quantity of cement demanded in a local area may not be much larger than what a single plant can produce. Moreover, the costs of transporting cement over land are high, and so a cement plant in an area without access to water transportation may be a natural monopoly.

## Control of a Physical Resource

Another type of monopoly occurs when a company has control of a scarce physical resource. In the U.S. economy, one historical example of this pattern occurred when ALCOA—the Aluminum Company of America—controlled most of the supply of bauxite, a key mineral used in making aluminum. Back in the 1930s, when ALCOA controlled most of the bauxite, other firms were simply unable to produce enough aluminum to compete.

As another example, the majority of global diamond production is controlled by DeBeers, a multi-national company that has mining and production operations in South Africa, Botswana, Namibia, and Canada. It also has exploration activities on four continents, while directing a worldwide distribution network of rough cut diamonds. Although in recent years they have experienced growing competition, their impact on the rough diamond market is still considerable.

## Legal Monopoly

For some products, the government erects barriers to entry by prohibiting or limiting competition. Under U.S. law, no organization but the U.S. Postal Service is legally allowed to deliver first-class mail. Many states or cities have laws or regulations that allow households a choice of only one electric company, one water company, and one company to pick up the garbage. Most legal monopolies are utilities—products necessary for everyday life—that are socially beneficial. As a consequence, the government allows producers to become regulated monopolies, to ensure that customers have access to an appropriate amount of these products or services. Additionally, legal monopolies are often subject to economies of scale, so it makes sense to allow only one provider.

## Promoting Innovation

Innovation takes time and resources to achieve. Suppose a company invests in research and development and finds the cure for the common cold. In this world of near ubiquitous information, other companies could take the formula, produce the drug, and because they did not incur the costs of research and development (R&D), undercut the price of the company that discovered the drug. Given this possibility, many firms would choose not to invest in research and development, and as a result, the world would have less innovation. To prevent this from happening, the Constitution of the United States specifies in Article I, Section 8: "The Congress shall have Power . . . to Promote the Progress of Science and Useful Arts, by securing for limited Times to Authors and Inventors the Exclusive Right to their Writings and Discoveries." Congress used this power to create the U.S. Patent and Trademark Office, as well as the U.S. Copyright Office. A **patent** gives the inventor the exclusive legal right to make, use, or sell the invention for a limited time. In the United States, exclusive patent rights last for 20 years. The idea is to provide limited monopoly power so that innovative firms can recoup their investment in R&D, but then to allow other firms to produce the product more cheaply once the patent expires.

A **trademark** is an identifying symbol or name for a particular good, like Chiquita bananas, Chevrolet cars, or the Nike "swoosh" that appears on shoes and athletic gear. Between 2003 and 2019, roughly 6.8 million trademarks were registered with the U.S. government. A firm can renew a trademark repeatedly, as long as it remains in active use.

A **copyright**, according to the U.S. Copyright Office, "is a form of protection provided by the laws of the United States for 'original works of authorship' including literary, dramatic, musical, architectural, cartographic, choreographic, pantomimic, pictorial, graphic, sculptural, and audiovisual creations." No one can reproduce, display, or perform a copyrighted work without the author's permission. Copyright protection ordinarily lasts for the life of the author plus 70 years.

Roughly speaking, patent law covers inventions and copyright protects books, songs, and art. However, in certain areas, like the invention of new software, it has been unclear whether patent or copyright protection should apply. There is also a body of law known as **trade secrets**. Even if a company does not have a patent on an invention, competing firms are not allowed to steal their secrets. One famous trade secret is the formula for Coca-Cola, which is not protected under copyright or patent law, but is simply kept secret by the company.

Taken together, we call this combination of patents, trademarks, copyrights, and trade secret law **intellectual property**, because it implies ownership over an idea, concept, or image, not a physical piece of property like a house or a car. Countries around the world have enacted laws to protect intellectual property, although the time periods and exact provisions of such laws vary across countries. There are ongoing negotiations, both through the World Intellectual Property Organization (WIPO) and through international treaties, to bring greater harmony to the intellectual property laws of different countries to determine the extent to which those in other countries will respect patents and copyrights of those in other countries.

Government limitations on competition used to be more common in the United States. For most of the twentieth century, only one phone company—AT&T—was legally allowed to provide local and long distance service. From the 1930s to the 1970s, one set of federal regulations limited which destinations airlines could choose to fly to and what fares they could charge. Another set of regulations limited the interest rates that banks could pay to depositors; yet another specified how much trucking firms could charge customers.

What products we consider utilities depends, in part, on the available technology. Fifty years ago, telephone companies provided local and long distance service over wires. It did not make much sense to have many companies building multiple wiring systems across towns and the entire country. AT&T lost its monopoly on long distance service when the technology for providing phone service changed from wires to microwave and satellite transmission, so that multiple firms could use the same transmission mechanism. The same thing happened to local service, especially in recent years, with the growth in cellular phone systems.

The combination of improvements in production technologies and a general sense that the markets could provide services adequately led to a wave of **deregulation**, starting in the late 1970s and continuing into the 1990s. This wave eliminated or reduced government restrictions on the firms that could enter, the prices that they could charge, and the quantities that many industries could produce, including telecommunications, airlines, trucking, banking, and electricity.

Around the world, from Europe to Latin America to Africa and Asia, many governments continue to control and limit competition in what those governments perceive to be key industries, including airlines, banks, steel companies, oil companies, and telephone companies.

##  LINK IT UP

Vist this website (http://openstax.org/l/patents) for examples of some pretty bizarre patents.

---

### Intimidating Potential Competition

Businesses have developed a number of schemes for creating barriers to entry by deterring potential competitors from entering the market. One method is known as **predatory pricing**, in which a firm uses the threat of sharp price cuts to discourage competition. Predatory pricing is a violation of U.S. antitrust law, but it is difficult to prove.

Consider a large airline that provides most of the flights between two particular cities. A new, small start-up airline decides to offer service between these two cities. The large airline immediately slashes prices on this route to the bone, so that the new entrant cannot make any money. After the new entrant has gone out of business, the incumbent firm can raise prices again.

After the company repeats this pattern once or twice, potential new entrants may decide that it is not wise to try to compete. Small airlines often accuse larger airlines of predatory pricing: in the early 2000s, for example, ValuJet accused Delta of predatory pricing, Frontier accused United, and Reno Air accused Northwest. In 2015, the Justice Department ruled against American Express and Mastercard for imposing restrictions on retailers that encouraged customers to use lower swipe fees on credit transactions.

In some cases, large advertising budgets can also act as a way of discouraging the competition. If the only way to launch a successful new national cola drink is to spend more than the promotional budgets of Coca-Cola and Pepsi Cola, not too many companies will try. A firmly established brand name can be difficult to dislodge.

### Summing Up Barriers to Entry

Table 9.1 lists the barriers to entry that we have discussed. This list is not exhaustive, since firms have proved to be highly creative in inventing business practices that discourage competition. When barriers to entry exist, perfect competition is no longer a reasonable description of how an industry works. When barriers to entry are high enough, monopoly can result.

| Barrier to Entry | Government Role? | Example |
|---|---|---|
| Natural monopoly | Government often responds with regulation (or ownership) | Water and electric companies |
| Control of a physical resource | No | DeBeers for diamonds |
| Legal monopoly | Yes | Post office, past regulation of airlines and trucking |
| Patent, trademark, and copyright | Yes, through protection of intellectual property | New drugs or software |
| Intimidating potential competitors | Somewhat | Predatory pricing; well-known brand names |

**TABLE 9.1 Barriers to Entry**

## 9.2 How a Profit-Maximizing Monopoly Chooses Output and Price

**LEARNING OBJECTIVES**

By the end of this section, you will be able to:
- Explain the perceived demand curve for a perfect competitor and a monopoly
- Analyze a demand curve for a monopoly and determine the output that maximizes profit and revenue
- Calculate marginal revenue and marginal cost
- Explain allocative efficiency as it pertains to the efficiency of a monopoly

Consider a monopoly firm, comfortably surrounded by barriers to entry so that it need not fear competition from other producers. How will this monopoly choose its profit-maximizing quantity of output, and what price will it charge? Profits for the monopolist, like any firm, will be equal to total revenues minus total costs. We can analyze the pattern of costs for the monopoly within the same framework as the costs of a perfectly competitive firm—that is, by using total cost, fixed cost, variable cost, marginal cost, average cost, and average variable cost. However, because a monopoly faces no competition, its situation and its decision process will differ from that of a perfectly competitive firm. (The Clear It Up feature discusses how hard it is sometimes to define "market" in a monopoly situation.)

### Demand Curves Perceived by a Perfectly Competitive Firm and by a Monopoly

A perfectly competitive firm acts as a price taker, so we calculate total revenue taking the given market price and multiplying it by the quantity of output that the firm chooses. The demand curve *as it is perceived by a perfectly competitive firm* appears in Figure 9.3 (a). The flat perceived demand curve means that, from the viewpoint of the perfectly competitive firm, it could sell either a relatively low quantity like Ql or a relatively high quantity like Qh at the market price P.

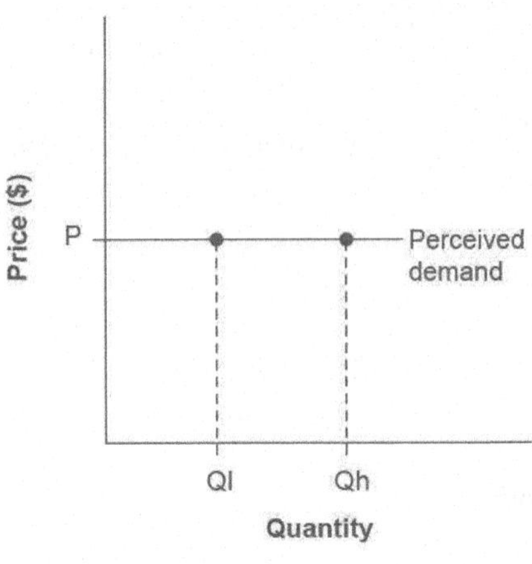

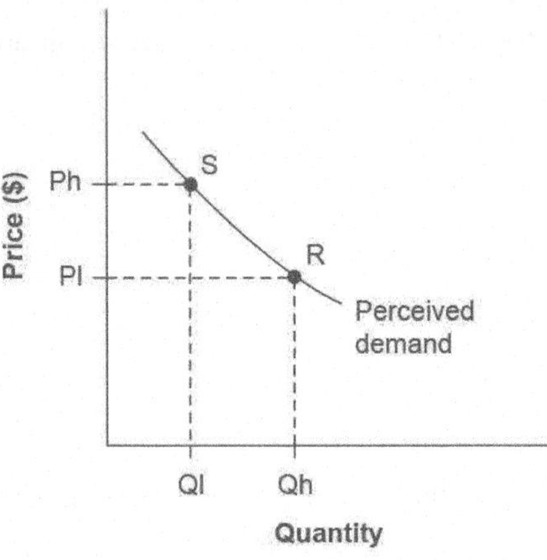

(a) Perceived demand for a perfect competitor          (b) Perceived demand for a monopolist

**FIGURE 9.3 The Perceived Demand Curve for a Perfect Competitor and a Monopolist** (a) A perfectly competitive firm perceives the demand curve that it faces to be flat. The flat shape means that the firm can sell either a low quantity (Ql) or a high quantity (Qh) at exactly the same price (P). (b) A monopolist perceives the demand curve that it faces to be the same as the market demand curve, which for most goods is downward-sloping. Thus, if the monopolist chooses a high level of output (Qh), it can charge only a relatively low price (Pl). Conversely, if the monopolist chooses a low level of output (Ql), it can then charge a higher price (Ph). The challenge for the monopolist is to choose the combination of price and quantity that maximizes profits.

 **CLEAR IT UP**

### What defines the market?

A monopoly is a firm that sells all or nearly all of the goods and services in a given market. However, what defines the "market"?

In a famous 1947 case, the federal government accused the DuPont company of having a monopoly in the cellophane market, pointing out that DuPont produced 75% of the cellophane in the United States. DuPont countered that even though it had a 75% market share in cellophane, it had less than a 20% share of the "flexible packaging materials," which includes all other moisture-proof papers, films, and foils. In 1956, after years of legal appeals, the U.S. Supreme Court held that the broader market definition was more appropriate, and it dismissed the case against DuPont.

Questions over how to define the market continue today. True, Microsoft in the 1990s had a dominant share of the software for computer operating systems, but in the total market for all computer software and services, including everything from games to scientific programs, the Microsoft share was only about 14% in 2014. The Greyhound bus company may have a near-monopoly on the market for intercity bus transportation, but it is only a small share of the market for intercity transportation if that market includes private cars, airplanes, and railroad service. DeBeers has a monopoly in diamonds, but it is a much smaller share of the total market for precious gemstones and an even smaller share of the total market for jewelry. A small town in the country may have only one gas station: is this gas station a "monopoly," or does it compete with gas stations that might be five, 10, or 50 miles away?

In general, if a firm produces a product without close substitutes, then we can consider the firm a monopoly producer in a single market. However, if buyers have a range of similar—even if not identical—options available from other firms, then the firm is not a monopoly. Still, arguments over whether substitutes are close or not close can be controversial.

While a monopolist can charge *any* price for its product, nonetheless the demand for the firm's product constrains the price. No monopolist, even one that is thoroughly protected by high barriers to entry, can require consumers to purchase its product. Because the monopolist is the only firm in the market, its demand curve is the same as the market demand curve, which is, unlike that for a perfectly competitive firm, downward-sloping.

Figure 9.3 illustrates this situation. The monopolist can either choose a point like R with a low price (Pl) and high quantity (Qh), or a point like S with a high price (Ph) and a low quantity (Ql), or some intermediate point. Setting the price too high will result in a low quantity sold, and will not bring in much revenue. Conversely, setting the price too low may result in a high quantity sold, but because of the low price, it will not bring in much revenue either. The challenge for the monopolist is to strike a profit-maximizing balance between the price it charges and the quantity that it sells. However, why isn't the perfectly competitive firm's demand curve also the market demand curve? See the following Clear It Up feature for the answer to this question.

## CLEAR IT UP

### What is the difference between perceived demand and market demand?

The demand curve as perceived by a perfectly competitive firm is not the overall market demand curve for that product. However, the firm's demand curve as perceived by a monopoly is the same as the market demand curve. The reason for the difference is that each perfectly competitive firm perceives the demand for its products in a market that includes many other firms. In effect, the demand curve perceived by a perfectly competitive firm is a tiny slice of the entire market demand curve. In contrast, a monopoly perceives demand for its product in a market where the monopoly is the only producer.

## Total Cost and Total Revenue for a Monopolist

We can illustrate profits for a monopolist with a graph of total revenues and total costs, with the example of the hypothetical HealthPill firm in Figure 9.4. The total cost curve has its typical shape that we learned about in Production, Costs and Industry Structure, and that we used in Perfect Competition; that is, total costs rise and the curve grows steeper as output increases, as the final column of Table 9.2 shows.

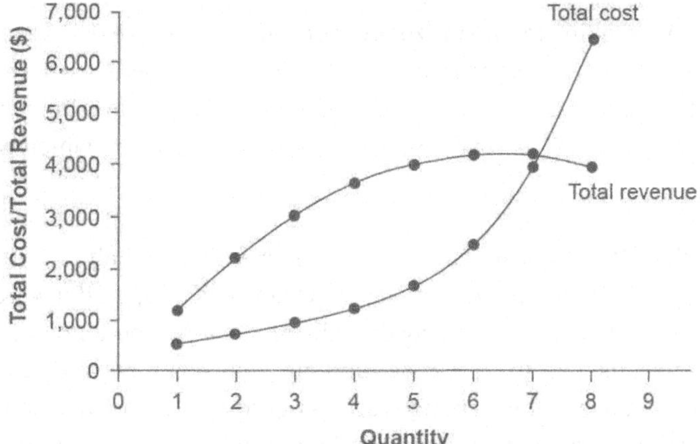


**FIGURE 9.4 Total Revenue and Total Cost for the HealthPill Monopoly** Total revenue for the monopoly firm called HealthPill first rises, then falls. Low levels of output bring in relatively little total revenue, because the quantity is low. High levels of output bring in relatively less revenue, because the high quantity pushes down the market price. The total cost curve is upward-sloping. Profits will be highest at the quantity of output where total revenue is most above total cost. The profit-maximizing level of output is not the same as the revenue-maximizing level of output, which should make sense, because profits take costs into account and revenues do not.

| Quantity<br>Q | Price<br>P | Total Revenue<br>TR | Total Cost<br>TC |
|---|---|---|---|
| 1 | 1,200 | 1,200 | 500 |
| 2 | 1,100 | 2,200 | 750 |
| 3 | 1,000 | 3,000 | 1,000 |
| 4 | 900 | 3,600 | 1,250 |
| 5 | 800 | 4,000 | 1,650 |
| 6 | 700 | 4,200 | 2,500 |
| 7 | 600 | 4,200 | 4,000 |
| 8 | 500 | 4,000 | 6,400 |

**TABLE 9.2** Total Costs and Total Revenues of HealthPill

Total revenue, though, is different. Since a monopolist faces a downward sloping demand curve, the only way it can sell more output is by reducing its price. Selling more output raises revenue, but lowering price reduces it. Thus, the shape of total revenue isn't clear. Let's explore this using the data in Table 9.2, which shows quantities along the demand curve and the price at each quantity demanded, and then calculates total revenue by multiplying price times quantity at each level of output. (In this example, we give the output as 1, 2, 3, 4, and so on, for the sake of simplicity. If you prefer a dash of greater realism, you can imagine that the pharmaceutical company measures these output levels and the corresponding prices per 1,000 or 10,000 pills.) As the figure illustrates, total revenue for a monopolist has the shape of a hill, first rising, next flattening out, and then falling. In this example, total revenue is highest at a quantity of 6 or 7.

However, the monopolist is not seeking to maximize revenue, but instead to earn the highest possible profit. In the HealthPill example in Figure 9.4, the highest profit will occur at the quantity where total revenue is the farthest above total cost. This looks to be somewhere in the middle of the graph, but where exactly? It is easier to see the profit maximizing level of output by using the marginal approach, to which we turn next.

## Marginal Revenue and Marginal Cost for a Monopolist

In the real world, a monopolist often does not have enough information to analyze its entire total revenues or total costs curves. After all, the firm does not know exactly what would happen if it were to alter production dramatically. However, a monopolist often has fairly reliable information about how changing output by small or moderate amounts will affect its marginal revenues and marginal costs, because it has had experience with such changes over time and because modest changes are easier to extrapolate from current experience. A monopolist can use information on marginal revenue and marginal cost to seek out the profit-maximizing combination of quantity and price.

Table 9.3 expands Table 9.2 using the figures on total costs and total revenues from the HealthPill example to calculate marginal revenue and marginal cost. This monopoly faces typical upward-sloping marginal cost and downward-sloping marginal revenue curves, as Figure 9.5 shows.

Notice that marginal revenue is zero at a quantity of 7, and turns negative at quantities higher than 7. It may seem counterintuitive that marginal revenue could ever be zero or negative: after all, doesn't an increase in quantity sold not always mean more revenue? For a perfect competitor, each additional unit sold brought a positive marginal revenue, because marginal revenue was equal to the given market price. However, a monopolist can sell a larger quantity and see a decline in total revenue. When a monopolist increases sales by one unit, it gains some marginal revenue from selling that extra unit, but also loses some marginal revenue because it must now sell every other unit at a lower price. As the quantity sold becomes higher, at some point the drop in price is proportionally more than the increase in greater quantity of sales, causing a situation where more sales bring in less revenue. In other words, marginal revenue is negative.

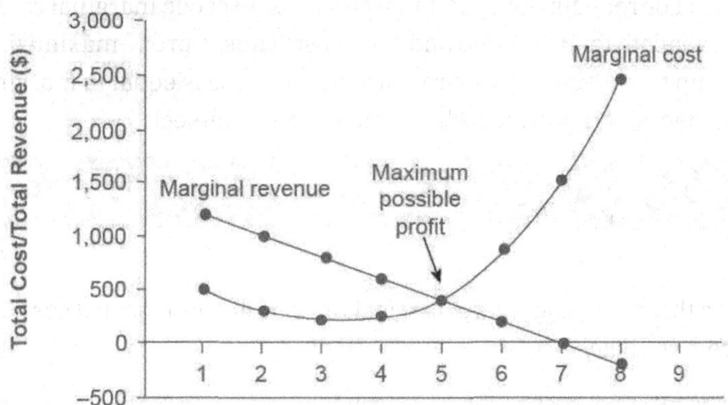


**FIGURE 9.5 Marginal Revenue and Marginal Cost for the HealthPill Monopoly** For a monopoly like HealthPill, marginal revenue decreases as it sells additional units of output. The marginal cost curve is upward-sloping. The profit-maximizing choice for the monopoly will be to produce at the quantity where marginal revenue is equal to marginal cost: that is, MR = MC. If the monopoly produces a lower quantity, then MR > MC at those levels of output, and the firm can make higher profits by expanding output. If the firm produces at a greater quantity, then MC > MR, and the firm can make higher profits by reducing its quantity of output.

| Quantity Q | Total Revenue TR | Marginal Revenue MR | Total Cost TC | Marginal Cost MC |
|---|---|---|---|---|
| 1 | 1,200 | 1,200 | 500 | 500 |
| 2 | 2,200 | 1,000 | 775 | 275 |
| 3 | 3,000 | 800 | 1,000 | 225 |
| 4 | 3,600 | 600 | 1,250 | 250 |
| 5 | 4,000 | 400 | 1,650 | 400 |
| 6 | 4,200 | 200 | 2,500 | 850 |
| 7 | 4,200 | 0 | 4,000 | 1,500 |
| 8 | 4,000 | −200 | 6,400 | 2,400 |

**TABLE 9.3 Costs and Revenues of HealthPill**

A monopolist can determine its profit-maximizing price and quantity by analyzing the marginal revenue and marginal costs of producing an extra unit. If the marginal revenue exceeds the marginal cost, then the firm should produce the extra unit.

For example, at an output of 4 in Figure 9.5, marginal revenue is 600 and marginal cost is 250, so producing this unit will clearly add to overall profits. At an output of 5, marginal revenue is 400 and marginal cost is 400, so producing this unit still means overall profits are unchanged. However, expanding output from 5 to 6 would involve a marginal revenue of 200 and a marginal cost of 850, so that sixth unit would actually reduce profits. Thus, the monopoly can tell from the marginal revenue and marginal cost that of the choices in the table, the profit-maximizing level of output is 5.

The monopoly could seek out the profit-maximizing level of output by increasing quantity by a small amount, calculating marginal revenue and marginal cost, and then either increasing output as long as marginal revenue exceeds marginal cost or reducing output if marginal cost exceeds marginal revenue. This process works without any need to calculate total revenue and total cost. Thus, a profit-maximizing monopoly should follow the rule of producing up to the quantity where marginal revenue is equal to marginal cost—that is, MR = MC. This quantity is easy to identify graphically, where MR and MC intersect.

## WORK IT OUT

### Maximizing Profits

If you find it counterintuitive that producing where marginal revenue equals marginal cost will maximize profits, working through the numbers will help.

Step 1. Remember, we define marginal cost as the change in total cost from producing a small amount of additional output.

$$MC = \frac{\text{change in total cost}}{\text{change in quantity produced}}$$

Step 2. Note that in Table 9.3, as output increases from 1 to 2 units, total cost increases from $500 to $775. As a result, the marginal cost of the second unit will be:

$$MC = \frac{\$775 - \$500}{1}$$
$$= \$275$$

Step 3. Remember that, similarly, marginal revenue is the change in total revenue from selling a small amount of additional output.

$$MR = \frac{\text{change in total revenue}}{\text{change in quantity sold}}$$

Step 4. Note that in Table 9.3, as output increases from 1 to 2 units, total revenue increases from $1200 to $2200. As a result, the marginal revenue of the second unit will be:

$$MR = \frac{\$2200 - \$1200}{1}$$
$$= \$1000$$

| Quantity Q | Marginal Revenue MR | Marginal Cost MC | Marginal Profit MP | Total Profit P |
|---|---|---|---|---|
| 1 | 1,200 | 500 | 700 | 700 |
| 2 | 1,000 | 275 | 725 | 1,425 |
| 3 | 800 | 225 | 575 | 2,000 |
| 4 | 600 | 250 | 350 | 2,350 |

**TABLE 9.4** Marginal Revenue, Marginal Cost, Marginal and Total Profit

| Quantity Q | Marginal Revenue MR | Marginal Cost MC | Marginal Profit MP | Total Profit P |
|---|---|---|---|---|
| 5 | 400 | 400 | 0 | 2,350 |
| 6 | 200 | 850 | −650 | 1,700 |
| 7 | 0 | 1,500 | −1,500 | 200 |
| 8 | −200 | 2,400 | −2,600 | −2,400 |

**TABLE 9.4** Marginal Revenue, Marginal Cost, Marginal and Total Profit

Table 9.4 repeats the marginal cost and marginal revenue data from Table 9.3, and adds two more columns: **Marginal profit** is the profitability of each additional unit sold. We define it as marginal revenue minus marginal cost. Finally, **total profit** is the sum of marginal profits. As long as marginal profit is positive, producing more output will increase total profits. When marginal profit turns negative, producing more output will decrease total profits. Total profit is maximized where marginal revenue equals marginal cost. In this example, maximum profit occurs at 5 units of output.

A perfectly competitive firm will also find its profit-maximizing level of output where MR = MC. The key difference with a perfectly competitive firm is that in the case of perfect competition, marginal revenue is equal to price (MR = P), while for a monopolist, marginal revenue is not equal to the price, because changes in quantity of output affect the price.

## Illustrating Monopoly Profits

It is straightforward to calculate profits of given numbers for total revenue and total cost. However, the size of monopoly profits can also be illustrated graphically with Figure 9.6, which takes the marginal cost and marginal revenue curves from the previous exhibit and adds an average cost curve and the monopolist's perceived demand curve. Table 9.5 shows the data for these curves.

| Quantity Q | Demand P | Marginal Revenue MR | Marginal Cost MC | Average Cost AC |
|---|---|---|---|---|
| 1 | 1,200 | 1,200 | 500 | 500 |
| 2 | 1,100 | 1,000 | 275 | 388 |
| 3 | 1,000 | 800 | 225 | 333 |
| 4 | 900 | 600 | 250 | 313 |
| 5 | 800 | 400 | 400 | 330 |
| 6 | 700 | 200 | 850 | 417 |
| 7 | 600 | 0 | 1,500 | 571 |
| 8 | 500 | −200 | 2,400 | 800 |

**TABLE 9.5**

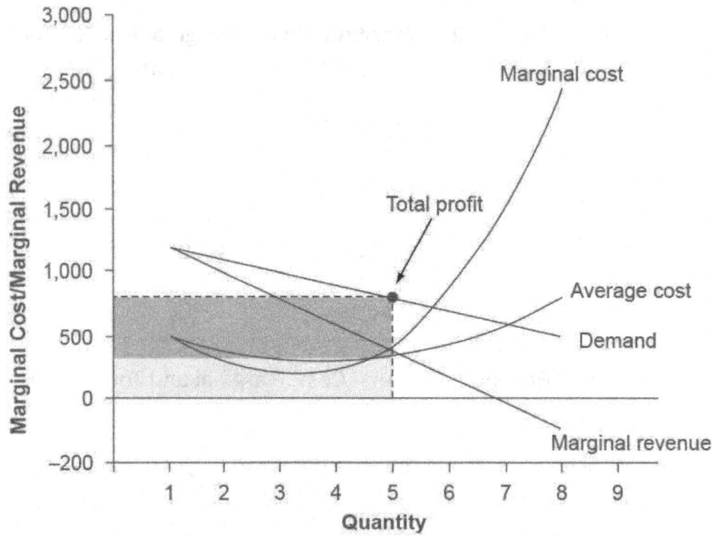


**FIGURE 9.6 Illustrating Profits at the HealthPill Monopoly** This figure begins with the same marginal revenue and marginal cost curves from the HealthPill monopoly from Figure 9.5. It then adds an average cost curve and the demand curve that the monopolist faces. The HealthPill firm first chooses the quantity where MR = MC. In this example, the quantity is 5. The monopolist then decides what price to charge by looking at the demand curve it faces. The large box, with quantity on the horizontal axis and demand (which shows the price) on the vertical axis, shows total revenue for the firm. The lighter-shaded box, which is quantity on the horizontal axis and average cost of production on the vertical axis shows the firm's total costs. The large total revenue box minus the smaller total cost box leaves the darkly shaded box that shows total profits. Since the price charged is above average cost, the firm is earning positive profits.

Figure 9.7 illustrates the three-step process where a monopolist: selects the profit-maximizing quantity to produce; decides what price to charge; determines total revenue, total cost, and profit.

### Step 1: The Monopolist Determines Its Profit-Maximizing Level of Output

The firm can use the points on the demand curve D to calculate total revenue, and then, based on total revenue, calculate its marginal revenue curve. The profit-maximizing quantity will occur where MR = MC—or at the last possible point before marginal costs start exceeding marginal revenue. On Figure 9.6, MR = MC occurs at an output of 5.

### Step 2: The Monopolist Decides What Price to Charge

The monopolist will charge what the market is willing to pay. A dotted line drawn straight up from the profit-maximizing quantity to the demand curve shows the profit-maximizing price which, in Figure 9.6, is $800. This price is above the average cost curve, which shows that the firm is earning profits.

### Step 3: Calculate Total Revenue, Total Cost, and Profit

Total revenue is the overall shaded box, where the width of the box is the quantity sold and the height is the price. In Figure 9.6, this is 5 x $800 = $4000. In Figure 9.6, the bottom part of the shaded box, which is shaded more lightly, shows total costs; that is, quantity on the horizontal axis multiplied by average cost on the vertical axis or 5 x $330 = $1650. The larger box of total revenues minus the smaller box of total costs will equal profits, which the darkly shaded box shows. Using the numbers gives $4000 - $1650 = $2350. In a perfectly competitive market, the forces of entry would erode this profit in the long run. However, a monopolist is protected by barriers to entry. In fact, one obvious sign of a possible monopoly is when a firm earns profits year after year, while doing more or less the same thing, without ever seeing increased competition eroding those profits.

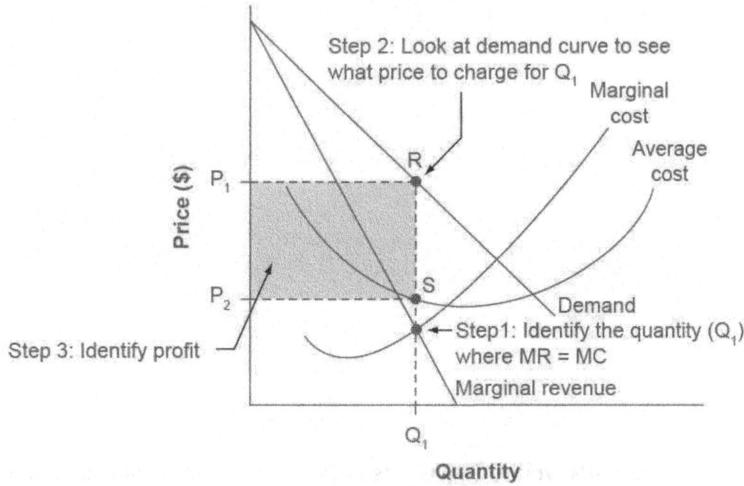


**FIGURE 9.7 How a Profit-Maximizing Monopoly Decides Price** In Step 1, the monopoly chooses the profit-maximizing level of output $Q_1$, by choosing the quantity where MR = MC. In Step 2, the monopoly decides how much to charge for output level $Q_1$ by drawing a line straight up from $Q_1$ to point R on its perceived demand curve. Thus, the monopoly will charge a price ($P_1$). In Step 3, the monopoly identifies its profit. Total revenue will be $Q_1$ multiplied by $P_1$. Total cost will be $Q_1$ multiplied by the average cost of producing $Q_1$, which point S shows on the average cost curve to be $P_2$. Profits will be the total revenue rectangle minus the total cost rectangle, which the shaded zone in the figure shows.

##  CLEAR IT UP

### Why is a monopolist's marginal revenue always less than the price?

The marginal revenue curve for a monopolist always lies beneath the market demand curve. To understand why, think about increasing the quantity along the demand curve by one unit, so that you take one step down the demand curve to a slightly higher quantity but a slightly lower price. A demand curve is not sequential: It is not that first we sell $Q_1$ at a higher price, and then we sell $Q_2$ at a lower price. Rather, a demand curve is conditional: If we charge the higher price, we would sell $Q_1$. If, instead, we charge a lower price (on all the units that we sell), we would sell $Q_2$.

When we think about increasing the quantity sold by one unit, marginal revenue is affected in two ways. First, we sell one additional unit at the new market price. Second, all the previous units, which we sold at the higher price, now sell for less. Because of the lower price on all units sold, the marginal revenue of selling a unit is less than the price of that unit—and the marginal revenue curve is below the demand curve. *Tip*: For a straight-line demand curve, MR and demand have the same vertical intercept. As output increases, marginal revenue decreases twice as fast as demand, so that the horizontal intercept of MR is halfway to the horizontal intercept of demand. You can see this in the Figure 9.8.

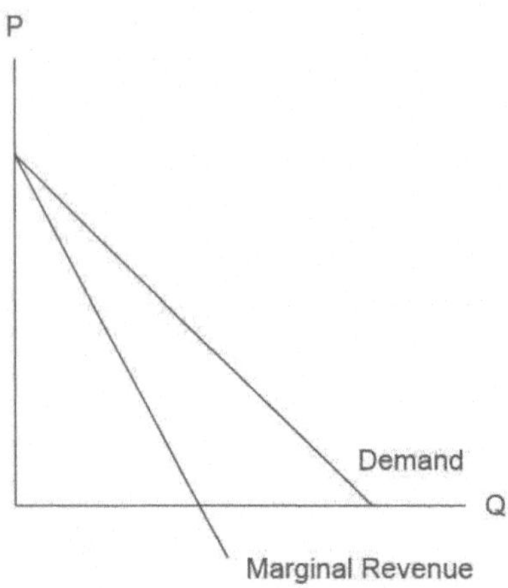



**FIGURE 9.8 The Monopolist's Marginal Revenue Curve versus Demand Curve** Because the market demand curve is conditional, the marginal revenue curve for a monopolist lies beneath the demand curve.

## The Inefficiency of Monopoly

Most people criticize monopolies because they charge too high a price, but what economists object to is that monopolies do not supply enough output to be allocatively efficient. To understand why a monopoly is inefficient, it is useful to compare it with the benchmark model of perfect competition.

**Allocative efficiency** is an economic concept regarding efficiency at the social or societal level. It refers to producing the optimal quantity of some output, the quantity where the marginal benefit to society of one more unit just equals the marginal cost. The rule of profit maximization in a world of perfect competition was for each firm to produce the quantity of output where P = MC, where the price (P) is a measure of how much buyers value the good and the marginal cost (MC) is a measure of what marginal units cost society to produce. Following this rule assures allocative efficiency. If P > MC, then the marginal benefit to society (as measured by P) is greater than the marginal cost to society of producing additional units, and a greater quantity should be produced. However, in the case of monopoly, price is always greater than marginal cost at the profit-maximizing level of output, as you can see by looking back at Figure 9.6. Thus, consumers do not benefit from a monopoly because it will sell a lower quantity in the market, at a higher price, than would have been the case in a perfectly competitive market.

The problem of inefficiency for monopolies often runs even deeper than these issues, and also involves incentives for efficiency over longer periods of time. There are counterbalancing incentives here. On one side, firms may strive for new inventions and new intellectual property because they want to become monopolies and earn high profits—at least for a few years until the competition catches up. In this way, monopolies may come to exist because of competitive pressures on firms. However, once a barrier to entry is in place, a monopoly that does not need to fear competition can just produce the same old products in the same old way—while still ringing up a healthy rate of profit. John Hicks, who won the Nobel Prize for economics in 1972, wrote in 1935: "The best of all monopoly profits is a quiet life." He did not mean the comment in a complimentary way. He meant that monopolies may bank their profits and slack off on trying to please their customers.

When AT&T provided all of the local and long-distance phone service in the United States, along with manufacturing most of the phone equipment, the payment plans and types of phones did not change much. The old joke was that you could have any color phone you wanted, as long as it was black. However, in 1982, government litigation split up AT&T into a number of local phone companies, a long-distance phone company, and a phone equipment manufacturer. An explosion of innovation followed. Services like call waiting, caller ID, three-way calling, voice mail through the phone company, mobile phones, and wireless connections to the internet all became available. Companies offered a wide range of payment plans, as well. It was no longer true that all phones were black. Instead, phones came in a wide variety of shapes and colors. The end of the telephone monopoly brought lower prices, a greater quantity of services, and also a wave of innovation aimed at attracting and pleasing customers.

 **BRING IT HOME**

## The Rest is History

In the opening case, we presented the East India Company and the Confederate States as a monopoly or near monopoly provider of a good. Nearly every American schoolchild knows the result of the "unwelcome visit" the "Mohawks" bestowed upon Boston Harbor's tea-bearing ships—the Boston Tea Party. Regarding the cotton industry, we also know Great Britain remained neutral during the Civil War, taking neither side during the conflict.

Did the monopoly nature of these business have unintended and historical consequences? Might the American Revolution have been deterred, if the East India Company had sailed the tea-bearing ships back to England? Might the southern states have made different decisions had they not been so confident "King Cotton" would force diplomatic recognition of the Confederate States of America? Of course, it is not possible to definitively answer these questions. We cannot roll back the clock and try a different scenario. We can, however, consider the monopoly nature of these businesses and the roles they played and hypothesize about what might have occurred under different circumstances.

Perhaps if there had been legal free tea trade, the colonists would have seen things differently. There was smuggled Dutch tea in the colonial market. If the colonists had been able to freely purchase Dutch tea, they would have paid lower prices and avoided the tax.

What about the cotton monopoly? With one in five jobs in Great Britain depending on Southern cotton and the Confederate States as nearly the sole provider of that cotton, why did Great Britain remain neutral during the Civil War? At the beginning of the war, Britain simply drew down massive stores of cotton. These stockpiles lasted until near the end of 1862. Why did Britain not recognize the Confederacy at that point? Two reasons: The Emancipation Proclamation and new sources of cotton. Having outlawed slavery throughout the United Kingdom in 1833, it was politically impossible for Great Britain, empty cotton warehouses or not, to recognize, diplomatically, the Confederate States. In addition, during the two years it took to draw down the stockpiles, Britain expanded cotton imports from India, Egypt, and Brazil.

Monopoly sellers often see no threats to their superior marketplace position. In these examples did the power of the monopoly hide other possibilities from the decision makers? Perhaps. As a result of their actions, this is how history unfolded.

# Key Terms

**allocative efficiency** producing the optimal quantity of some output; the quantity where the marginal benefit to society of one more unit just equals the marginal cost

**barriers to entry** the legal, technological, or market forces that may discourage or prevent potential competitors from entering a market

**copyright** a form of legal protection to prevent copying, for commercial purposes, original works of authorship, including books and music

**deregulation** removing government controls over setting prices and quantities in certain industries

**intellectual property** the body of law including patents, trademarks, copyrights, and trade secret law that protect the right of inventors to produce and sell their inventions

**legal monopoly** legal prohibitions against competition, such as regulated monopolies and intellectual property protection

**marginal profit** profit of one more unit of output, computed as marginal revenue minus marginal cost

**monopoly** a situation in which one firm produces all of the output in a market

**natural monopoly** economic conditions in the industry, for example, economies of scale or control of a critical resource, that limit effective competition

**patent** a government rule that gives the inventor the exclusive legal right to make, use, or sell the invention for a limited time

**predatory pricing** when an existing firm uses sharp but temporary price cuts to discourage new competition

**trade secrets** methods of production kept secret by the producing firm

**trademark** an identifying symbol or name for a particular good and can only be used by the firm that registered that trademark

# Key Concepts and Summary

## 9.1 How Monopolies Form: Barriers to Entry

Barriers to entry prevent or discourage competitors from entering the market. These barriers include: economies of scale that lead to natural monopoly; control of a physical resource; legal restrictions on competition; patent, trademark and copyright protection; and practices to intimidate the competition like predatory pricing. Intellectual property refers to legally guaranteed ownership of an idea, rather than a physical item. The laws that protect intellectual property include patents, copyrights, trademarks, and trade secrets. A natural monopoly arises when economies of scale persist over a large enough range of output that if one firm supplies the entire market, no other firm can enter without facing a cost disadvantage.

## 9.2 How a Profit-Maximizing Monopoly Chooses Output and Price

A monopolist is not a price taker, because when it decides what quantity to produce, it also determines the market price. For a monopolist, total revenue is relatively low at low quantities of output, because it is not selling much. Total revenue is also relatively low at very high quantities of output, because a very high quantity will sell only at a low price. Thus, total revenue for a monopolist will start low, rise, and then decline. The marginal revenue for a monopolist from selling additional units will decline. Each additional unit a monopolist sells will push down the overall market price, and as it sells more units, this lower price applies to increasingly more units.

The monopolist will select the profit-maximizing level of output where MR = MC, and then charge the price for that quantity of output as determined by the market demand curve. If that price is above average cost, the monopolist earns positive profits.

Monopolists are not productively efficient, because they do not produce at the minimum of the average cost curve. Monopolists are not allocatively efficient, because they do not produce at the quantity where P = MC. As a result, monopolists produce less, at a higher average cost, and charge a higher price than would a combination of firms in a perfectly competitive industry. Monopolists also may lack incentives for innovation, because they need not fear entry.

## Self-Check Questions

1. Classify the following as a government-enforced barrier to entry, a barrier to entry that is not government-enforced, or a situation that does not involve a barrier to entry.
   a. A patented invention
   b. A popular but easily copied restaurant recipe
   c. An industry where economies of scale are very small compared to the size of demand in the market
   d. A well-established reputation for slashing prices in response to new entry
   e. A well-respected brand name that has been carefully built up over many years

2. Classify the following as a government-enforced barrier to entry, a barrier to entry that is not government-enforced, or a situation that does not involve a barrier to entry.
   a. A city passes a law on how many licenses it will issue for taxicabs
   b. A city passes a law that all taxicab drivers must pass a driving safety test and have insurance
   c. A well-known trademark
   d. Owning a spring that offers very pure water
   e. An industry where economies of scale are very large compared to the size of demand in the market

3. Suppose the local electrical utility, a legal monopoly based on economies of scale, was split into four firms of equal size, with the idea that eliminating the monopoly would promote competitive pricing of electricity. What do you anticipate would happen to prices?

4. If Congress reduced the period of patent protection from 20 years to 10 years, what would likely happen to the amount of private research and development?

5. Suppose demand for a monopoly's product falls so that its profit-maximizing price is below average variable cost. How much output should the firm supply? *Hint*: Draw the graph.

6. Imagine a monopolist could charge a different price to every customer based on how much the customer is willing to pay. How would this affect monopoly profits?

## Review Questions

7. How is monopoly different from perfect competition?

8. What is a barrier to entry? Give some examples.

9. What is a natural monopoly?

10. What is a legal monopoly?

11. What is predatory pricing?

12. How is intellectual property different from other property?

13. What legal mechanisms protect intellectual property?

14. In what sense is a natural monopoly "natural"?

15. How is the demand curve perceived by a perfectly competitive firm different from the demand curve perceived by a monopolist?

16. How does the demand curve perceived by a monopolist compare with the market demand curve?

17. Is a monopolist a price taker? Explain briefly.

18. What is the usual shape of a total revenue curve for a monopolist? Why?

19. What is the usual shape of a marginal revenue curve for a monopolist? Why?

20. How can a monopolist identify the profit-maximizing level of output if it knows its total revenue and total cost curves?

21. How can a monopolist identify the profit-maximizing level of output if it knows its marginal revenue and marginal costs?

22. When a monopolist identifies its profit-maximizing quantity of output, how does it decide what price to charge?

23. Is a monopolist allocatively efficient? Why or why not?

24. How does the quantity produced and price charged by a monopolist compare to that of a perfectly competitive firm?

## Critical Thinking Questions

25. ALCOA does not have the monopoly power it once had. How do you suppose their barriers to entry were weakened?

26. Why are generic pharmaceuticals significantly cheaper than name brand ones?

27. For many years, the Justice Department has tried to break up large firms like IBM, Microsoft, and most recently Google, on the grounds that their large market share made them essentially monopolies. In a global market, where U.S. firms compete with firms from other countries, would this policy make the same sense as it might in a purely domestic context?

28. Intellectual property laws are intended to promote innovation, but some economists, such as Milton Friedman, have argued that such laws are not desirable. In the United States, there is no intellectual property protection for food recipes or for fashion designs. Considering the state of these two industries, and bearing in mind the discussion of the inefficiency of monopolies, can you think of any reasons why intellectual property laws might hinder innovation in some cases?

29. Imagine that you are managing a small firm and thinking about entering the market of a monopolist. The monopolist is currently charging a high price, and you have calculated that you can make a nice profit charging 10% less than the monopolist. Before you go ahead and challenge the monopolist, what possibility should you consider for how the monopolist might react?

30. If a monopoly firm is earning profits, how much would you expect these profits to be diminished by entry in the long run?

## Problems

31. Return to Figure 9.2. Suppose $P_0$ is $10 and $P_1$ is $11. Suppose a new firm with the same LRAC curve as the incumbent tries to break into the market by selling 4,000 units of output. Estimate from the graph what the new firm's average cost of producing output would be. If the incumbent continues to produce 6,000 units, how much output would the two firms supply to the market? Estimate what would happen to the market price as a result of the supply of both the incumbent firm and the new entrant. Approximately how much profit would each firm earn?

32. Draw the demand curve, marginal revenue, and marginal cost curves from Figure 9.6, and identify the quantity of output the monopoly wishes to supply and the price it will charge. Suppose demand for the monopoly's product increases dramatically. Draw the new demand curve. What happens to the marginal revenue as a result of the increase in demand? What happens to the marginal cost curve? Identify the new profit-maximizing quantity and price. Does the answer make sense to you?

33. Draw a monopolist's demand curve, marginal revenue, and marginal cost curves. Identify the monopolist's profit-maximizing output level. Now, think about a slightly higher level of output (say $Q_0 + 1$). According to the graph, is there any consumer willing to pay more than the marginal cost of that new level of output? If so, what does this mean?

# Monopolistic Competition and Oligopoly

FIGURE 10.1 **Competing Brands?** The laundry detergent market is one that is characterized neither as perfect competition nor monopoly. (Credit: modification of "DSC_7174" by Pixel Drip/Flickr Creative Commons, CC BY 2.0)

**CHAPTER OBJECTIVES**

In this chapter, you will learn about:

- Monopolistic Competition
- Oligopoly

## Introduction to Monopolistic Competition and Oligopoly

 **BRING IT HOME**

### The Temptation to Defy the Law

Laundry detergent and bags of ice—products of industries that seem pretty mundane, maybe even boring. Hardly! Both have been the center of clandestine meetings and secret deals worthy of a spy novel. In France, between 1997 and 2004, the top four laundry detergent producers (Proctor & Gamble, Henkel, Unilever, and Colgate-Palmolive) controlled about 90 percent of the French soap market. Officials from the soap firms were meeting secretly, in out-of-the-way, small cafés around Paris. Their goals: Stamp out competition and set prices.

Around the same time, the top five Midwest ice makers (Home City Ice, Lang Ice, Tinley Ice, Sisler's Dairy, and Products of Ohio) had similar goals in mind when they secretly agreed to divide up the bagged ice market.

If both groups could meet their goals, it would enable each to act as though they were a single firm—in essence, a monopoly—and enjoy monopoly-size profits. The problem? In many parts of the world, including the European Union and the United States, it is illegal for firms to divide markets and set prices collaboratively.

These two cases provide examples of markets that are characterized neither as perfect competition nor monopoly. Instead, these firms are competing in market structures that lie between the extremes of monopoly and perfect competition. How do they behave? Why do they exist? We will revisit this case later, to find out what happened.

---

Perfect competition and monopoly are at opposite ends of the competition spectrum. A perfectly competitive market has many firms selling identical products, who all act as price takers in the face of the competition. If you recall, price takers are firms that have no market power. They simply have to take the market price as given.

Monopoly arises when a single firm sells a product for which there are no close substitutes. We consider Microsoft, for instance, as a monopoly because it dominates the operating systems market.

What about the vast majority of real world firms and organizations that fall between these extremes, firms that we could describe as **imperfectly competitive**? What determines their behavior? They have more influence over the price they charge than perfectly competitive firms, but not as much as a monopoly. What will they do?

One type of imperfectly competitive market is **monopolistic competition**. Monopolistically competitive markets feature a large number of competing firms, but the products that they sell are not identical. Consider, as an example, the Mall of America in Minnesota, the largest shopping mall in the United States. In 2010, the Mall of America had 24 stores that sold women's "ready-to-wear" clothing (like Ann Taylor and Urban Outfitters), another 50 stores that sold clothing for both men and women (like Banana Republic, J. Crew, and Nordstrom's), plus 14 more stores that sold women's specialty clothing (like Motherhood Maternity and Victoria's Secret). Most of the markets that consumers encounter at the retail level are monopolistically competitive.

The other type of imperfectly competitive market is **oligopoly**. Oligopolistic markets are those which a small number of firms dominate. Commercial aircraft provides a good example: Boeing and Airbus each produce slightly less than 50% of the large commercial aircraft in the world. Another example is the U.S. soft drink industry, which Coca-Cola and Pepsi dominate. We characterize oligopolies by high barriers to entry with firms choosing output, pricing, and other decisions strategically based on the decisions of the other firms in the market. In this chapter, we first explore how monopolistically competitive firms will choose their profit-maximizing level of output. We will then discuss oligopolistic firms, which face two conflicting temptations: to collaborate as if they were a single monopoly, or to individually compete to gain profits by expanding output levels and cutting prices. Oligopolistic markets and firms can also take on elements of monopoly and of perfect competition.

## 10.1 Monopolistic Competition

### LEARNING OBJECTIVES

By the end of this section, you will be able to:
- Explain the significance of differentiated products
- Describe how a monopolistic competitor chooses price and quantity
- Discuss entry, exit, and efficiency as they pertain to monopolistic competition
- Analyze how advertising can impact monopolistic competition

Monopolistic competition involves many firms competing against each other, but selling products that are distinctive in some way. Examples include stores that sell different styles of clothing; restaurants or grocery stores that sell a variety of food; and even products like golf balls or beer that may be at least somewhat similar but differ in public perception because of advertising and brand names. There are over 600,000 restaurants in the United States. When products are distinctive, each firm has a mini-monopoly on its particular style or flavor or brand name. However, firms producing such products must also compete with other styles and flavors and brand names. The term "monopolistic competition" captures this mixture of mini-monopoly and tough competition, and the following Clear It Up feature introduces its derivation.

 ## CLEAR IT UP

### Who invented the theory of imperfect competition?

Two economists independently but simultaneously developed the theory of imperfect competition in 1933. The first was Edward Chamberlin of Harvard University who published *The Economics of Monopolistic Competition*. The second was Joan Robinson of Cambridge University who published *The Economics of Imperfect Competition*. Robinson subsequently became interested in macroeconomics and she became a prominent Keynesian, and later a post-Keynesian economist. (See the Welcome to Economics! and The Keynesian Perspective (http://openstax.org/books/principles-economics-3e/pages/25-introduction-to-the-keynesian-perspective) chapters for more on Keynes.)

## Differentiated Products

A firm can try to make its products different from those of its competitors in several ways: physical aspects of the product, location from which it sells the product, intangible aspects of the product, and perceptions of the product. We call products that are distinctive in one of these ways **differentiated products**.

Physical aspects of a product include all the phrases you hear in advertisements: unbreakable bottle, nonstick surface, freezer-to-microwave, non-shrink, extra spicy, newly redesigned for your comfort. A firm's location can also create a difference between producers. For example, a gas station located at a heavily traveled intersection can probably sell more gas, because more cars drive by that corner. A supplier to an automobile manufacturer may find that it is an advantage to locate close to the car factory.

Intangible aspects can differentiate a product, too. Some intangible aspects may be promises like a guarantee of satisfaction or money back, a reputation for high quality, services like free delivery, or offering a loan to purchase the product. Finally, product differentiation may occur in the minds of buyers. For example, many people could not tell the difference in taste between common varieties of ketchup or mayonnaise if they were blindfolded but, because of past habits and advertising, they have strong preferences for certain brands. Advertising can play a role in shaping these intangible preferences.

The concept of differentiated products is closely related to the degree of variety that is available. If everyone in the economy wore only blue jeans, ate only white bread, and drank only tap water, then the markets for clothing, food, and drink would be much closer to perfectly competitive. The variety of styles, flavors, locations, and characteristics creates product differentiation and monopolistic competition.

### Perceived Demand for a Monopolistic Competitor

A monopolistically competitive firm perceives a demand for its goods that is an intermediate case between monopoly and competition. Figure 10.2 offers a reminder that the demand curve that a perfectly competitive firm faces is perfectly elastic or flat, because the perfectly competitive firm can sell any quantity it wishes at the prevailing market price. In contrast, the demand curve, as faced by a monopolist, is the market demand curve, since a monopolist is the only firm in the market, and hence is downward sloping.

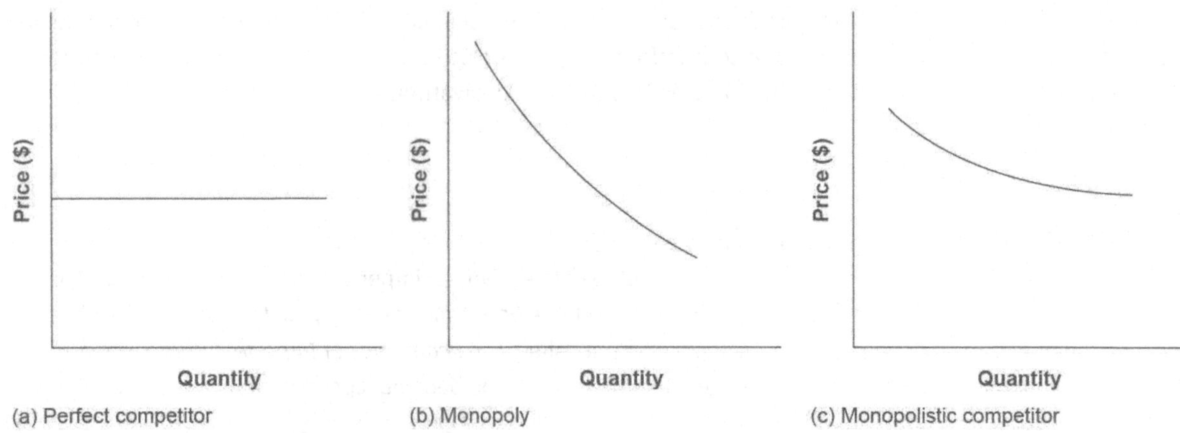


**FIGURE 10.2 Perceived Demand for Firms in Different Competitive Settings** The demand curve that a perfectly competitive firm faces is perfectly elastic, meaning it can sell all the output it wishes at the prevailing market price. The demand curve that a monopoly faces is the market demand. It can sell more output only by decreasing the price it charges. The demand curve that a monopolistically competitive firm faces falls in between.

The demand curve as a monopolistic competitor faces is not flat, but rather downward-sloping, which means that the monopolistic competitor can raise its price without losing all of its customers or lower the price and gain more customers. Since there are substitutes, the demand curve facing a monopolistically competitive firm is more elastic than that of a monopoly where there are no close substitutes. If a monopolist raises its price, some consumers will choose not to purchase its product—but they will then need to buy a completely different product. However, when a monopolistic competitor raises its price, some consumers will choose not to purchase the product at all, but others will choose to buy a similar product from another firm. If a monopolistic competitor raises its price, it will not lose as many customers as would a perfectly competitive firm, but it will lose more customers than would a monopoly that raised its prices.

At a glance, the demand curves that a monopoly and a monopolistic competitor face look similar—that is, they both slope down. However, the underlying economic meaning of these perceived demand curves is different, because a monopolist faces the market demand curve and a monopolistic competitor does not. Rather, a monopolistically competitive firm's demand curve is but one of many firms that make up the "before" market demand curve. Are you following? If so, how would you categorize the market for golf balls? Take a swing, then see the following Clear It Up feature.

 **CLEAR IT UP**

### Are golf balls really differentiated products?

Monopolistic competition refers to an industry that has more than a few firms, each offering a product which, from the consumer's perspective, is different from its competitors. The U.S. Golf Association runs a laboratory that tests 20,000 golf balls a year. There are strict rules for what makes a golf ball legal. A ball's weight cannot exceed 1.620 ounces and its diameter cannot be less than 1.680 inches (which is a weight of 45.93 grams and a diameter of 42.67 millimeters, in case you were wondering). The Association also tests the balls by hitting them at different speeds. For example, the distance test involves having a mechanical golfer hit the ball with a titanium driver and a swing speed of 120 miles per hour. As the testing center explains: "The USGA system then uses an array of sensors that accurately measure the flight of a golf ball during a short, indoor trajectory from a ball launcher. From this flight data, a computer calculates the lift and drag forces that are generated by the speed, spin, and dimple pattern of the ball. ... The distance limit is 317 yards."

Over 1800 golf balls made by more than 100 companies meet the USGA standards. The balls do differ in various ways, such as the pattern of dimples on the ball, the types of plastic on the cover and in the cores, and other factors.

Since all balls need to conform to the USGA tests, they are much more alike than different. In other words, golf ball manufacturers are monopolistically competitive.

However, retail sales of golf balls are about $500 million per year, which means that many large companies have a powerful incentive to persuade players that golf balls are highly differentiated and that it makes a huge difference which one you choose. Sure, Tiger Woods can tell the difference. For the average amateur golfer who plays a few times a summer—and who loses many golf balls to the woods and lake and needs to buy new ones—most golf balls are pretty much indistinguishable.

## How a Monopolistic Competitor Chooses Price and Quantity

The monopolistically competitive firm decides on its profit-maximizing quantity and price in much the same way as a monopolist. A monopolistic competitor, like a monopolist, faces a downward-sloping demand curve, and so it will choose some combination of price and quantity along its perceived demand curve.

As an example of a profit-maximizing monopolistic competitor, consider the Authentic Chinese Pizza store, which serves pizza with cheese, sweet and sour sauce, and your choice of vegetables and meats. Although Authentic Chinese Pizza must compete against other pizza businesses and restaurants, it has a differentiated product. The firm's perceived demand curve is downward sloping, as Figure 10.3 shows and the first two columns of Table 10.1.

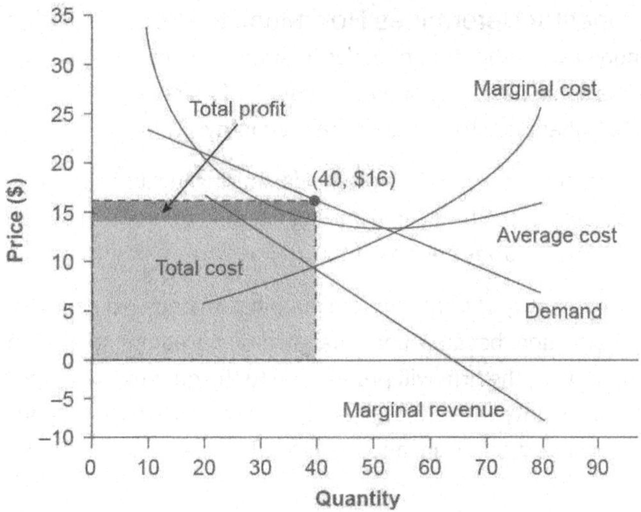


**FIGURE 10.3 How a Monopolistic Competitor Chooses its Profit Maximizing Output and Price** To maximize profits, the Authentic Chinese Pizza shop would choose a quantity where marginal revenue equals marginal cost, or Q where MR = MC. Here it would choose a quantity of 40 and a price of $16.

| Quantity | Price | Total Revenue | Marginal Revenue | Total Cost | Marginal Cost | Average Cost |
|---|---|---|---|---|---|---|
| 10 | $23 | $230 | $23 | $340 | $34 | $34 |
| 20 | $20 | $400 | $17 | $400 | $6 | $20 |
| 30 | $18 | $540 | $14 | $480 | $8 | $16 |
| 40 | $16 | $640 | $10 | $580 | $10 | $14.50 |
| 50 | $14 | $700 | $6 | $700 | $12 | $14 |

**TABLE 10.1 Revenue and Cost Schedule**

| Quantity | Price | Total Revenue | Marginal Revenue | Total Cost | Marginal Cost | Average Cost |
|---|---|---|---|---|---|---|
| 60 | $12 | $720 | $2 | $840 | $14 | $14 |
| 70 | $10 | $700 | −$2 | $1,020 | $18 | $14.57 |
| 80 | $8 | $640 | −$6 | $1,280 | $26 | $16 |

**TABLE 10.1** Revenue and Cost Schedule

We can multiply the combinations of price and quantity at each point on the demand curve to calculate the total revenue that the firm would receive, which is in the third column of Table 10.1. We calculate marginal revenue, in the fourth column, as the change in total revenue divided by the change in quantity. The final columns of Table 10.1 show total cost, marginal cost, and average cost. As always, we calculate marginal cost by dividing the change in total cost by the change in quantity, while we calculate average cost by dividing total cost by quantity. The following Work It Out feature shows how these firms calculate how much of their products to supply at what price.

## WORK IT OUT

### How a Monopolistic Competitor Determines How Much to Produce and at What Price

The process by which a monopolistic competitor chooses its profit-maximizing quantity and price resembles closely how a monopoly makes these decisions process. First, the firm selects the profit-maximizing quantity to produce. Then the firm decides what price to charge for that quantity.

Step 1. The monopolistic competitor determines its profit-maximizing level of output. In this case, the Authentic Chinese Pizza company will determine the profit-maximizing quantity to produce by considering its marginal revenues and marginal costs. Two scenarios are possible:

- If the firm is producing at a quantity of output where marginal revenue exceeds marginal cost, then the firm should keep expanding production, because each marginal unit is adding to profit by bringing in more revenue than its cost. In this way, the firm will produce up to the quantity where MR = MC.
- If the firm is producing at a quantity where marginal costs exceed marginal revenue, then each marginal unit is costing more than the revenue it brings in, and the firm will increase its profits by reducing the quantity of output until MR = MC.

In this example, MR and MC intersect at a quantity of 40, which is the profit-maximizing level of output for the firm.

Step 2. The monopolistic competitor decides what price to charge. When the firm has determined its profit-maximizing quantity of output, it can then look to its perceived demand curve to find out what it can charge for that quantity of output. On the graph, we show this process as a vertical line reaching up through the profit-maximizing quantity until it hits the firm's perceived demand curve. For Authentic Chinese Pizza, it should charge a price of $16 per pizza for a quantity of 40.

Once the firm has chosen price and quantity, it's in a position to calculate total revenue, total cost, and profit. At a quantity of 40, the price of $16 lies above the average cost curve, so the firm is making economic profits. From Table 10.1 we can see that, at an output of 40, the firm's total revenue is $640 and its total cost is $580, so profits are $60. In Figure 10.3, the firm's total revenues are the rectangle with the quantity of 40 on the horizontal axis and the price of $16 on the vertical axis. The firm's total costs are the light shaded rectangle with the same quantity of 40 on the horizontal axis but the average cost of $14.50 on the vertical axis. Profits are total revenues minus total costs, which is the shaded area above the average cost curve.

Although the process by which a monopolistic competitor makes decisions about quantity and price is similar to the way in which a monopolist makes such decisions, two differences are worth remembering. First, although both a monopolist and a monopolistic competitor face downward-sloping demand curves, the monopolist's perceived demand curve is the market demand curve, while the perceived demand curve for a monopolistic competitor is based on the extent of its product differentiation and how many competitors it faces. Second, a monopolist is surrounded by barriers to entry and need not fear entry, but a monopolistic competitor who earns profits must expect the entry of firms with similar, but differentiated, products.

## Monopolistic Competitors and Entry

If one monopolistic competitor earns positive economic profits, other firms will be tempted to enter the market. A gas station with a great location must worry that other gas stations might open across the street or down the road—and perhaps the new gas stations will sell coffee or have a carwash or some other attraction to lure customers. A successful restaurant with a unique barbecue sauce must be concerned that other restaurants will try to copy the sauce or offer their own unique recipes. A laundry detergent with a great reputation for quality must take note that other competitors may seek to build their own reputations.

The entry of other firms into the same general market (like gas, restaurants, or detergent) shifts the demand curve that a monopolistically competitive firm faces. As more firms enter the market, the quantity demanded at a given price for any particular firm will decline, and the firm's perceived demand curve will shift to the left. As a firm's perceived demand curve shifts to the left, its marginal revenue curve will shift to the left, too. The shift in marginal revenue will change the profit-maximizing quantity that the firm chooses to produce, since marginal revenue will then equal marginal cost at a lower quantity.

Figure 10.4 (a) shows a situation in which a monopolistic competitor was earning a profit with its original perceived demand curve ($D_0$). The intersection of the marginal revenue curve ($MR_0$) and marginal cost curve (MC) occurs at point S, corresponding to quantity $Q_0$, which is associated on the demand curve at point T with price $P_0$. The combination of price $P_0$ and quantity $Q_0$ lies above the average cost curve, which shows that the firm is earning positive economic profits.

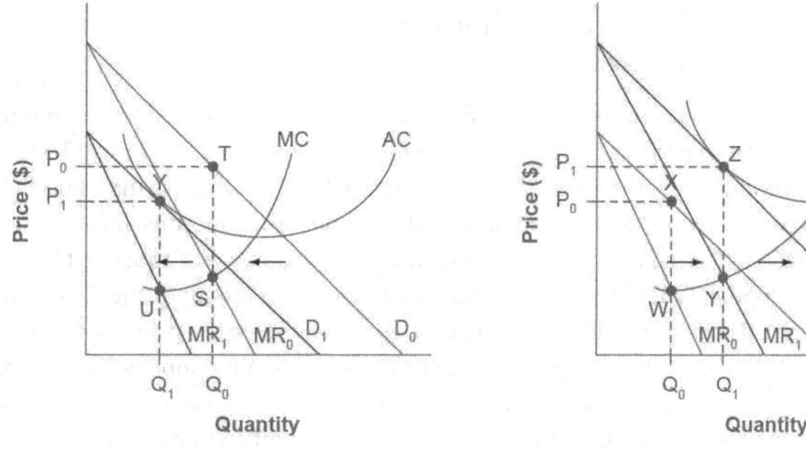


(a) Profit induces entry; shift to zero profit          (b) Loss induces exit; shift to zero profit

**FIGURE 10.4 Monopolistic Competition, Entry, and Exit** (a) At $P_0$ and $Q_0$, the monopolistically competitive firm in this figure is making a positive economic profit. This is clear because if you follow the dotted line above $Q_0$, you can see that price is above average cost. Positive economic profits attract competing firms to the industry, driving the original firm's demand down to $D_1$. At the new equilibrium quantity ($P_1$, $Q_1$), the original firm is earning zero economic profits, and entry into the industry ceases. In (b) the opposite occurs. At $P_0$ and $Q_0$, the firm is losing money. If you follow the dotted line above $Q_0$, you can see that average cost is above price. Losses induce firms to leave the industry. When they do, demand for the original firm rises to $D_1$, where once again the firm is earning zero economic profit.

Unlike a monopoly, with its high barriers to entry, a monopolistically competitive firm with positive economic profits will attract competition. When another competitor enters the market, the original firm's perceived demand curve shifts to the left, from $D_0$ to $D_1$, and the associated marginal revenue curve shifts from $MR_0$ to $MR_1$. The new profit-maximizing output is $Q_1$, because the intersection of the $MR_1$ and MC now occurs at point U. Moving vertically up from that quantity on the new demand curve, the optimal price is at $P_1$.

As long as the firm is earning positive economic profits, new competitors will continue to enter the market, reducing the original firm's demand and marginal revenue curves. The long-run equilibrium is in the figure at point Y, where the firm's perceived demand curve touches the average cost curve. When price is equal to average cost, economic profits are zero. Thus, although a monopolistically competitive firm may earn positive economic profits in the short term, the process of new entry will drive down economic profits to zero in the long run. Remember that zero economic profit is not equivalent to zero accounting profit. A zero economic profit means the firm's accounting profit is equal to what its resources could earn in their next best use. Figure 10.4 (b) shows the reverse situation, where a monopolistically competitive firm is originally losing money. The adjustment to long-run equilibrium is analogous to the previous example. The economic losses lead to firms exiting, which will result in increased demand for this particular firm, and consequently lower losses. Firms exit up to the point where there are no more losses in this market, for example when the demand curve touches the average cost curve, as in point Z.

Monopolistic competitors can make an economic profit or loss in the short run, but in the long run, entry and exit will drive these firms toward a zero economic profit outcome. However, the zero economic profit outcome in monopolistic competition looks different from the zero economic profit outcome in perfect competition in several ways relating both to efficiency and to variety in the market.

## Monopolistic Competition and Efficiency

The long-term result of entry and exit in a perfectly competitive market is that all firms end up selling at the price level determined by the lowest point on the average cost curve. This outcome is why perfect competition displays productive efficiency: goods are produced at the lowest possible average cost. However, in monopolistic competition, the end result of entry and exit is that firms end up with a price that lies on the downward-sloping portion of the average cost curve, not at the very bottom of the AC curve. Thus, monopolistic competition will not be productively efficient.

In a perfectly competitive market, each firm produces at a quantity where price is set equal to marginal cost, both in the short and long run. This outcome is why perfect competition displays allocative efficiency: the social benefits of additional production, as measured by the marginal benefit, which is the same as the price, equal the marginal costs to society of that production. In a monopolistically competitive market, the rule for maximizing profit is to set MR = MC—and price is higher than marginal revenue, not equal to it because the demand curve is downward sloping. When P > MC, which is the outcome in a monopolistically competitive market, the benefits to society of providing additional quantity, as measured by the price that people are willing to pay, exceed the marginal costs to society of producing those units. A monopolistically competitive firm does not produce more, which means that society loses the net benefit of those extra units. This is the same argument we made about monopoly, but in this case the allocative inefficiency will be smaller. Thus, a monopolistically competitive industry will produce a lower quantity of a good and charge a higher price for it than would a perfectly competitive industry. See the following Clear It Up feature for more detail on the impact of demand shifts.

## CLEAR IT UP

### Why does a shift in perceived demand cause a shift in marginal revenue?

We use the combinations of price and quantity at each point on a firm's perceived demand curve to calculate total revenue for each combination of price and quantity. We then use this information on total revenue to calculate marginal revenue, which is the change in total revenue divided by the change in quantity. A change in perceived demand will change total revenue at every quantity of output and in turn, the change in total revenue will shift marginal revenue at each quantity of output. Thus, when entry occurs in a monopolistically competitive industry, the perceived demand curve for each firm will shift to the left, because a smaller quantity will be demanded at any given price. Another way of interpreting this shift in demand is to notice that, for each quantity sold, the firm will charge a lower price. Consequently, the marginal revenue will be lower for each quantity sold—and the marginal revenue curve will shift to the left as well. Conversely, exit causes the perceived demand curve for a monopolistically competitive firm to shift to the right and the corresponding marginal revenue curve to shift right, too.

A monopolistically competitive industry does not display productive or allocative efficiency in either the short run, when firms are making economic profits and losses, nor in the long run, when firms are earning zero profits.

## The Benefits of Variety and Product Differentiation

Even though monopolistic competition does not provide productive efficiency or allocative efficiency, it does have benefits of its own. Product differentiation is based on variety and innovation. Most people would prefer to live in an economy with many kinds of clothes, foods, and car styles; not in a world of perfect competition where everyone will always wear blue jeans and white shirts, eat only spaghetti with plain red sauce, and drive an identical model of car. Most people would prefer to live in an economy where firms are struggling to figure out ways of attracting customers by methods like friendlier service, free delivery, guarantees of quality, variations on existing products, and a better shopping experience.

Economists have struggled, with only partial success, to address the question of whether a market-oriented economy produces the optimal amount of variety. Critics of market-oriented economies argue that society does not really need dozens of different athletic shoes or breakfast cereals or automobiles. They argue that much of the cost of creating such a high degree of product differentiation, and then of advertising and marketing this differentiation, is socially wasteful—that is, most people would be just as happy with a smaller range of differentiated products produced and sold at a lower price. Defenders of a market-oriented economy respond that if people do not want to buy differentiated products or highly advertised brand names, no one is forcing them to do so. Moreover, they argue that consumers benefit substantially when firms seek short-term profits by providing differentiated products. This controversy may never be fully resolved, in part because deciding on the optimal amount of variety is very difficult, and in part because the two sides often place different values on what variety means for consumers. Read the following Clear It Up feature for a discussion on the role that advertising plays in monopolistic competition.

## CLEAR IT UP

### How does advertising impact monopolistic competition?

The U.S. economy spent about $180.12 billion on advertising in 2014, according to eMarketer.com. Roughly one third of this was television advertising, and another third was divided roughly equally between internet, newspapers, and radio. The remaining third was divided between direct mail, magazines, telephone directory yellow pages, and billboards. Mobile devices are increasing the opportunities for advertisers.

Advertising is all about explaining to people, or making people believe, that the products of one firm are differentiated from another firm's products. In the framework of monopolistic competition, there are two ways to conceive of how advertising works: either advertising causes a firm's perceived demand curve to become more inelastic (that is, it causes the perceived demand curve to become steeper); or advertising causes demand for the firm's product to increase (that is, it causes the firm's perceived demand curve to shift to the right). In either case, a successful advertising campaign may allow a firm to sell either a greater quantity or to charge a higher price, or both, and thus increase its profits.

However, economists and business owners have also long suspected that much of the advertising may only offset other advertising. Economist A. C. Pigou wrote the following back in 1920 in his book, *The Economics of Welfare*:

> It may happen that expenditures on advertisement made by competing monopolists [that is, what we now call monopolistic competitors] will simply neutralise one another, and leave the industrial position exactly as it would have been if neither had expended anything. For, clearly, if each of two rivals makes equal efforts to attract the favour of the public away from the other, the total result is the same as it would have been if neither had made any effort at all.

## 10.2 Oligopoly

**LEARNING OBJECTIVES**

By the end of this section, you will be able to:

- Explain why and how oligopolies exist
- Contrast collusion and competition
- Interpret and analyze the prisoner's dilemma diagram
- Evaluate the tradeoffs of imperfect competition

Many purchases that individuals make at the retail level are produced in markets that are neither perfectly competitive, monopolies, nor monopolistically competitive. Rather, they are oligopolies. Oligopoly arises when a small number of large firms have all or most of the sales in an industry. Examples of oligopoly abound and include the auto industry, cable television, and commercial air travel. Oligopolistic firms are like cats in a bag. They can either scratch each other to pieces or cuddle up and get comfortable with one another. If oligopolists compete hard, they may end up acting very much like perfect competitors, driving down costs and leading to zero profits for all. If oligopolists collude with each other, they may effectively act like a monopoly and succeed in pushing up prices and earning consistently high levels of profit. We typically characterize oligopolies by mutual interdependence where various decisions such as output, price, and advertising depend on other firm(s)' decisions. Analyzing the choices of oligopolistic firms about pricing and quantity produced involves considering the pros and cons of competition versus collusion at a given point in time.

### Why Do Oligopolies Exist?

A combination of the barriers to entry that create monopolies and the product differentiation that characterizes monopolistic competition can create the setting for an oligopoly. For example, when a government grants a patent for an invention to one firm, it may create a monopoly. When the government grants patents to, for example, three different pharmaceutical companies that each has its own drug for reducing high blood pressure, those three firms may become an oligopoly.

Similarly, a natural monopoly will arise when the quantity demanded in a market is only large enough for a single firm to operate at the minimum of the long-run average cost curve. In such a setting, the market has room for only one firm, because no smaller firm can operate at a low enough average cost to compete, and no larger firm could sell what it produced given the quantity demanded in the market.

Quantity demanded in the market may also be two or three times the quantity needed to produce at the minimum of the average cost curve—which means that the market would have room for only two or three oligopoly firms (and they need not produce differentiated products). Again, smaller firms would have higher average costs and be unable to compete, while additional large firms would produce such a high quantity that they would not be able to sell it at a profitable price. This combination of economies of scale and market demand creates the barrier to entry, which led to the Boeing-Airbus oligopoly (also called a duopoly) for large passenger aircraft.

The product differentiation at the heart of monopolistic competition can also play a role in creating oligopoly.

For example, firms may need to reach a certain minimum size before they are able to spend enough on advertising and marketing to create a recognizable brand name. The problem in competing with, say, Coca-Cola or Pepsi is not that producing fizzy drinks is technologically difficult, but rather that creating a brand name and marketing effort to equal Coke or Pepsi is an enormous task.

## Collusion or Competition?

When oligopoly firms in a certain market decide what quantity to produce and what price to charge, they face a temptation to act as if they were a monopoly. By acting together, oligopolistic firms can hold down industry output, charge a higher price, and divide the profit among themselves. When firms act together in this way to reduce output and keep prices high, it is called **collusion**. A group of firms that have a formal agreement to collude to produce the monopoly output and sell at the monopoly price is called a **cartel**. See the following Clear It Up feature for a more in-depth analysis of the difference between the two.

## CLEAR IT UP

### Collusion versus cartels: How to differentiate

In the United States, as well as many other countries, it is illegal for firms to collude since collusion is anti-competitive behavior, which is a violation of antitrust law. Both the Antitrust Division of the Justice Department and the Federal Trade Commission have responsibilities for preventing collusion in the United States.

The problem of enforcement is finding hard evidence of collusion. Cartels are formal agreements to collude. Because cartel agreements provide evidence of collusion, they are rare in the United States. Instead, most collusion is tacit, where firms implicitly reach an understanding that competition is bad for profits.

---

Economists have understood for a long time the desire of businesses to avoid competing so that they can instead raise the prices that they charge and earn higher profits. Adam Smith wrote in *Wealth of Nations* in 1776: "People of the same trade seldom meet together, even for merriment and diversion, but the conversation ends in a conspiracy against the public, or in some contrivance to raise prices."

Even when oligopolists recognize that they would benefit as a group by acting like a monopoly, each individual oligopoly faces a private temptation to produce just a slightly higher quantity and earn slightly higher profit—while still counting on the other oligopolists to hold down their production and keep prices high. If at least some oligopolists give in to this temptation and start producing more, then the market price will fall. A small handful of oligopoly firms may end up competing so fiercely that they all find themselves earning zero economic profits—as if they were perfect competitors.

## The Prisoner's Dilemma

Because of the complexity of oligopoly, which is the result of mutual interdependence among firms, there is no single, generally-accepted theory of how oligopolies behave, in the same way that we have theories for all the other market structures. Instead, economists use **game theory**, a branch of mathematics that analyzes situations in which players must make decisions and then receive payoffs based on what other players decide to do. Game theory has found widespread applications in the social sciences, as well as in business, law, and military strategy.

The **prisoner's dilemma** is a scenario in which the gains from cooperation are larger than the rewards from pursuing self-interest. It applies well to oligopoly. (Note that the term "prisoner" is not typically an accurate term for someone who has recently been arrested, but we will use the term here, since this scenario is widely used and referenced in economic, business, and social contexts.) The story behind the prisoner's dilemma goes like this:

Two co-conspirators are arrested. When they are taken to the police station, they refuse to say anything and are put in separate interrogation rooms. Eventually, a police officer enters the room where Prisoner A is being held and says: "You know what? Your partner in the other room is confessing. Your partner is going to get a light prison sentence of just one year, and because you're remaining silent, the judge is going to stick you with eight years in prison. Why don't you get smart? If you confess, too, we'll cut your jail time down to five years, and your partner will get five years, also." Over in the next room, another police officer is giving exactly the same speech to Prisoner B. What the police officers do not say is that if both prisoners remain silent, the evidence against them is not especially strong, and the prisoners will end up with only two years in jail each.

The game theory situation facing the two prisoners is in Table 10.2. To understand the dilemma, first consider the choices from Prisoner A's point of view. If A believes that B will confess, then A should confess, too, so as to not get stuck with the eight years in prison. However, if A believes that B will not confess, then A will be tempted to act selfishly and confess, so as to serve only one year. The key point is that A has an incentive to confess regardless of what choice B makes! B faces the same set of choices, and thus will have an incentive to confess regardless of what choice A makes. To confess is called the dominant strategy. It is the strategy an individual (or firm) will pursue regardless of the other individual's (or firm's) decision. The result is that if prisoners pursue their own self-interest, both are likely to confess, and end up being sentenced to a total of 10 years of jail time between them.

|  |  | Prisoner B | |
| --- | --- | --- | --- |
|  |  | Remain Silent (cooperate with other prisoner) | Confess (do not cooperate with other prisoner) |
| Prisoner A | Remain Silent (cooperate with other prisoner) | A gets 2 years, B gets 2 years | A gets 8 years, B gets 1 year |
|  | Confess (do not cooperate with other prisoner) | A gets 1 year, B gets 8 years | A gets 5 years B gets 5 years |

**TABLE 10.2 The Prisoner's Dilemma Problem**

The game is called a dilemma because if the two prisoners had cooperated by both remaining silent, they would only have been incarcerated for two years each, for a total of four years between them. If the two prisoners can work out some way of cooperating so that neither one will confess, they will both be better off than if they each follow their own individual self-interest, which in this case leads straight into longer terms.

## The Oligopoly Version of the Prisoner's Dilemma

The members of an oligopoly can face a prisoner's dilemma, also. If each of the oligopolists cooperates in holding down output, then high monopoly profits are possible. Each oligopolist, however, must worry that while it is holding down output, other firms are taking advantage of the high price by raising output and earning higher profits. Table 10.3 shows the prisoner's dilemma for a two-firm oligopoly—known as a **duopoly**. If Firms A and B both agree to hold down output, they are acting together as a monopoly and will each earn $1,000 in profits. However, both firms' dominant strategy is to increase output, in which case each will earn $400 in profits.

|  | Firm B | |
| --- | --- | --- |
|  | Hold Down Output (cooperate with other firm) | Increase Output (do not cooperate with other firm) |

**TABLE 10.3 A Prisoner's Dilemma for Oligopolists**

| Firm A | Hold Down Output (cooperate with other firm) | A gets $1,000, B gets $1,000 | A gets $200, B gets $1,500 |
|---|---|---|---|
| | Increase Output (do not cooperate with other firm) | A gets $1,500, B gets $200 | A gets $400, B gets $400 |

**TABLE 10.3** A Prisoner's Dilemma for Oligopolists

Can the two firms trust each other? Consider the situation of Firm A:

- If A thinks that B will cheat on their agreement and increase output, then A will increase output, too, because for A the profit of $400 when both firms increase output (the bottom right-hand choice in Table 10.3) is better than a profit of only $200 if A keeps output low and B raises output (the upper right-hand choice in the table).
- If A thinks that B will cooperate by holding down output, then A may seize the opportunity to earn higher profits by raising output. After all, if B is going to hold down output, then A can earn $1,500 in profits by expanding output (the bottom left-hand choice in the table) compared with only $1,000 by holding down output as well (the upper left-hand choice in the table).

Thus, firm A will reason that it makes sense to expand output if B holds down output and that it also makes sense to expand output if B raises output. Again, B faces a parallel set of decisions that will lead B also to expand output.

The result of this prisoner's dilemma is often that even though A and B could make the highest combined profits by cooperating in producing a lower level of output and acting like a monopolist, the two firms may well end up in a situation where they each increase output and earn only $400 each in profits. The following Clear It Up feature discusses one cartel scandal in particular.

## CLEAR IT UP

### What is the Lysine cartel?

Lysine, a $600 million-a-year industry, is an amino acid that farmers use as a feed additive to ensure the proper growth of swine and poultry. The primary U.S. producer of lysine is Archer Daniels Midland (ADM), but several other large European and Japanese firms are also in this market. For a time in the first half of the 1990s, the world's major lysine producers met together in hotel conference rooms and decided exactly how much each firm would sell and what it would charge. The U.S. Federal Bureau of Investigation (FBI), however, had learned of the cartel and placed wire taps on a number of their phone calls and meetings.

From FBI surveillance tapes, following is a comment that Terry Wilson, president of the corn processing division at ADM, made to the other lysine producers at a 1994 meeting in Mona, Hawaii:

> I wanna go back and I wanna say something very simple. If we're going to trust each other, okay, and if I'm assured that I'm gonna get 67,000 tons by the year's end, we're gonna sell it at the prices we agreed to . . . The only thing we need to talk about there because we are gonna get manipulated by these [expletive] buyers—they can be smarter than us if we let them be smarter. . . . They [the customers] are not your friend. They are not my friend. And we gotta have 'em, but they are not my friends. You are my friend. I wanna be closer to you than I am to any customer. Cause you can make us ... money. ... And all I wanna tell you again is let's—let's put the prices on the board. Let's all agree that's what we're gonna do and then walk out of here and do it.

The price of lysine doubled while the cartel was in effect. Confronted by the FBI tapes, Archer Daniels Midland pled guilty in 1996 and paid a fine of $100 million. A number of top executives, both at ADM and other firms, later paid fines of up to $350,000 and were sentenced to 24–30 months in prison.

In another one of the FBI recordings, the president of Archer Daniels Midland told an executive from another competing firm that ADM had a slogan that, in his words, had "penetrated the whole company." The company president stated the slogan this way: "Our competitors are our friends. Our customers are the enemy." That slogan could stand as the motto of cartels everywhere.

## How to Enforce Cooperation

How can parties who find themselves in a prisoner's dilemma situation avoid the undesired outcome and cooperate with each other? The way out of a prisoner's dilemma is to find a way to penalize those who do not cooperate.

Perhaps the easiest approach for colluding oligopolists, as you might imagine, would be to sign a contract with each other that they will hold output low and keep prices high. If a group of U.S. companies signed such a contract, however, it would be illegal. Certain international organizations, like the nations that are members of the Organization of Petroleum Exporting Countries (OPEC), have signed international agreements to act like a monopoly, hold down output, and keep prices high so that all of the countries can make high profits from oil exports. Such agreements, however, because they fall in a gray area of international law, are not legally enforceable. If Nigeria, for example, decides to start cutting prices and selling more oil, Saudi Arabia cannot sue Nigeria in court and force it to stop.

## ⊘ LINK IT UP

Visit the Organization of the Petroleum Exporting Countries website (http://openstax.org/l/OPEC) and learn more about its history and how it defines itself.

Because oligopolists cannot sign a legally enforceable contract to act like a monopoly, the firms may instead keep close tabs on what other firms are producing and charging. Alternatively, oligopolists may choose to act in a way that generates pressure on each firm to stick to its agreed quantity of output.

One example of the pressure these firms can exert on one another is the **kinked demand curve**, in which competing oligopoly firms commit to match price cuts, but not price increases. Figure 10.5 shows this situation. Say that an oligopoly airline has agreed with the rest of a cartel to provide a quantity of 10,000 seats on the New York to Los Angeles route, at a price of $500. This choice defines the kink in the firm's perceived demand curve. The reason that the firm faces a kink in its demand curve is because of how the other oligopolists react to changes in the firm's price. If the oligopoly decides to produce more and cut its price, the other members of the cartel will immediately match any price cuts—and therefore, a lower price brings very little increase in quantity sold.

If one firm cuts its price to $300, it will be able to sell only 11,000 seats. However, if the airline seeks to raise prices, the other oligopolists will not raise their prices, and so the firm that raised prices will lose a considerable share of sales. For example, if the firm raises its price to $550, its sales drop to 5,000 seats sold. Thus, if oligopolists always match price cuts by other firms in the cartel, but do not match price increases, then none of the oligopolists will have a strong incentive to change prices, since the potential gains are minimal. This strategy can work like a silent form of cooperation, in which the cartel successfully manages to hold down output, increase price, and share a monopoly level of profits even without any legally enforceable agreement.

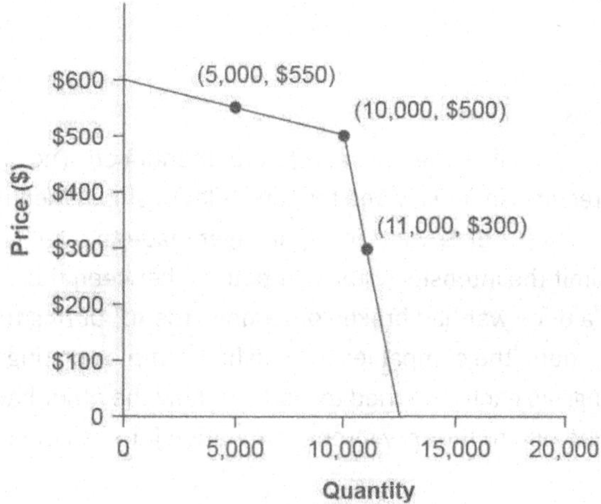


**FIGURE 10.5 A Kinked Demand Curve** Consider a member firm in an oligopoly cartel that is supposed to produce a quantity of 10,000 and sell at a price of $500. The other members of the cartel can encourage this firm to honor its commitments by acting so that the firm faces a kinked demand curve. If the oligopolist attempts to expand output and reduce price slightly, other firms also cut prices immediately—so if the firm expands output to 11,000, the price per unit falls dramatically, to $300. On the other side, if the oligopoly attempts to raise its price, other firms will not do so, so if the firm raises its price to $550, its sales decline sharply to 5,000. Thus, the members of a cartel can discipline each other to stick to the pre-agreed levels of quantity and price through a strategy of matching all price cuts but not matching any price increases.

Many real-world oligopolies, prodded by economic changes, legal and political pressures, and the egos of their top executives, go through episodes of cooperation and competition. If oligopolies could sustain cooperation with each other on output and pricing, they could earn profits as if they were a single monopoly. However, each firm in an oligopoly has an incentive to produce more and grab a bigger share of the overall market; when firms start behaving in this way, the market outcome in terms of prices and quantity can be similar to that of a highly competitive market.

## Tradeoffs of Imperfect Competition

Monopolistic competition is probably the single most common market structure in the U.S. economy. It provides powerful incentives for innovation, as firms seek to earn profits in the short run, while entry assures that firms do not earn economic profits in the long run. However, monopolistically competitive firms do not produce at the lowest point on their average cost curves. In addition, the endless search to impress consumers through product differentiation may lead to excessive social expenses on advertising and marketing.

Oligopoly is probably the second most common market structure. When oligopolies result from patented innovations or from taking advantage of economies of scale to produce at low average cost, they may provide considerable benefit to consumers. Oligopolies are often buffered by significant barriers to entry, which enable the oligopolists to earn sustained profits over long periods of time. Oligopolists also do not typically produce at the minimum of their average cost curves. When they lack vibrant competition, they may lack incentives to provide innovative products and high-quality service.

The task of public policy with regard to competition is to sort through these multiple realities, attempting to encourage behavior that is beneficial to the broader society and to discourage behavior that only adds to the profits of a few large companies, with no corresponding benefit to consumers. Monopoly and Antitrust Policy discusses the delicate judgments that go into this task.

 **BRING IT HOME**

## The Temptation to Defy the Law

Oligopolistic firms have been called "cats in a bag," as this chapter mentioned. The French detergent makers chose to "cozy up" with each other. The result? An uneasy and tenuous relationship. When the *Wall Street Journal* reported on the matter, it wrote: "According to a statement a Henkel manager made to the [French anti-trust] commission, the detergent makers wanted 'to limit the intensity of the competition between them and clean up the market.' Nevertheless, by the early 1990s, a price war had broken out among them." During the soap executives' meetings, sometimes lasting more than four hours, the companies established complex pricing structures. "One [soap] executive recalled 'chaotic' meetings as each side tried to work out how the other had bent the rules." Like many cartels, the soap cartel disintegrated due to the very strong temptation for each member to maximize its own individual profits.

How did this soap opera end? After an investigation, French antitrust authorities fined Colgate-Palmolive, Henkel, and Proctor & Gamble a total of €361 million ($484 million). A similar fate befell the icemakers. Bagged ice is a commodity, a perfect substitute, generally sold in 7- or 22-pound bags. No one cares what label is on the bag. By agreeing to carve up the ice market, control broad geographic swaths of territory, and set prices, the icemakers moved from perfect competition to a monopoly model. After the agreements, each firm was the sole supplier of bagged ice to a region. There were profits in both the long run and the short run. According to the courts: "These companies illegally conspired to manipulate the marketplace." Fines totaled about $600,000—a steep fine considering a bag of ice sells for under $3 in most parts of the United States.

Even though it is illegal in many parts of the world for firms to set prices and carve up a market, the temptation to earn higher profits makes it extremely tempting to defy the law.

## Key Terms

**cartel** a group of firms that collude to produce the monopoly output and sell at the monopoly price
**collusion** when firms act together to reduce output and keep prices high
**differentiated product** a product that consumers perceive as distinctive in some way
**duopoly** an oligopoly with only two firms
**game theory** a branch of mathematics that economists use to analyze situations in which players must make decisions and then receive payoffs based on what decisions the other players make
**imperfectly competitive** firms and organizations that fall between the extremes of monopoly and perfect competition
**kinked demand curve** a perceived demand curve that arises when competing oligopoly firms commit to match price cuts, but not price increases
**monopolistic competition** many firms competing to sell similar but differentiated products
**oligopoly** when a few large firms have all or most of the sales in an industry
**prisoner's dilemma** a game in which the gains from cooperation are larger than the rewards from pursuing self-interest
**product differentiation** any action that firms do to make consumers think their products are different from their competitors'

## Key Concepts and Summary

### 10.1 Monopolistic Competition

Monopolistic competition refers to a market where many firms sell differentiated products. Differentiated products can arise from characteristics of the good or service, location from which the firm sells the product, intangible aspects of the product, and perceptions of the product.

The perceived demand curve for a monopolistically competitive firm is downward-sloping, which shows that it is a price maker and chooses a combination of price and quantity. However, the perceived demand curve for a monopolistic competitor is more elastic than the perceived demand curve for a monopolist, because the monopolistic competitor has direct competition, unlike the pure monopolist. A profit-maximizing monopolistic competitor will seek out the quantity where marginal revenue is equal to marginal cost. The monopolistic competitor will produce that level of output and charge the price that the firm's demand curve indicates.

If the firms in a monopolistically competitive industry are earning economic profits, the industry will attract entry until profits are driven down to zero in the long run. If the firms in a monopolistically competitive industry are suffering economic losses, then the industry will experience exit of firms until economic losses are driven up to zero in the long run.

A monopolistically competitive firm is not productively efficient because it does not produce at the minimum of its average cost curve. A monopolistically competitive firm is not allocatively efficient because it does not produce where P = MC, but instead produces where P > MC. Thus, a monopolistically competitive firm will tend to produce a lower quantity at a higher cost and to charge a higher price than a perfectly competitive firm.

Monopolistically competitive industries do offer benefits to consumers in the form of greater variety and incentives for improved products and services. There is some controversy over whether a market-oriented economy generates too much variety.

### 10.2 Oligopoly

An oligopoly is a situation where a few firms sell most or all of the goods in a market. Oligopolists earn their highest profits if they can band together as a cartel and act like a monopolist by reducing output and raising price. Since each member of the oligopoly can benefit individually from expanding output, such collusion often breaks down—especially since explicit collusion is illegal.

The prisoner's dilemma is an example of the application of game theory to analysis of oligopoly. It shows how, in certain situations, all sides can benefit from cooperative behavior rather than self-interested behavior. However, the challenge for the parties is to find ways to encourage cooperative behavior.

## Self-Check Questions

1. Suppose that, due to a successful advertising campaign, a monopolistic competitor experiences an increase in demand for its product. How will that affect the price it charges and the quantity it supplies?

2. Continuing with the scenario in question 1, in the long run, the positive economic profits that the monopolistic competitor earns will attract a response either from existing firms in the industry or firms outside. As those firms capture the original firm's profit, what will happen to the original firm's profit-maximizing price and output levels?

3. Consider the curve in the figure below, which shows the market demand, marginal cost, and marginal revenue curve for firms in an oligopolistic industry. In this example, we assume firms have zero fixed costs.

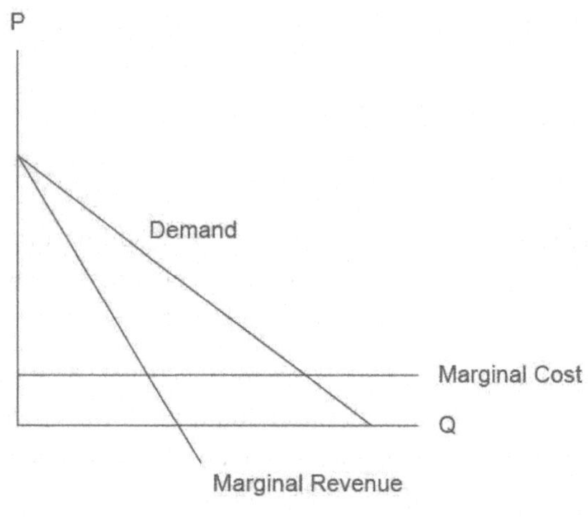


**FIGURE 10.6**

   a. Suppose the firms collude to form a cartel. What price will the cartel charge? What quantity will the cartel supply? How much profit will the cartel earn?
   b. Suppose now that the cartel breaks up and the oligopolistic firms compete as vigorously as possible by cutting the price and increasing sales. What will be the industry quantity and price? What will be the collective profits of all firms in the industry?
   c. Compare the equilibrium price, quantity, and profit for the cartel and cutthroat competition outcomes.

4. Sometimes oligopolies in the same industry are very different in size. Suppose we have a duopoly where one firm (Firm A) is large and the other firm (Firm B) is small, as the prisoner's dilemma box in Table 10.4 shows.

|  | Firm B colludes with Firm A | Firm B cheats by selling more output |
|---|---|---|
| Firm A colludes with Firm B | A gets $1,000, B gets $100 | A gets $800, B gets $200 |
| Firm A cheats by selling more output | A gets $1,050, B gets $50 | A gets $500, B gets $20 |

**TABLE 10.4**

Assuming that both firms know the payoffs, what is the likely outcome in this case?

## Review Questions

5. What is the relationship between product differentiation and monopolistic competition?

6. How is the perceived demand curve for a monopolistically competitive firm different from the perceived demand curve for a monopoly or a perfectly competitive firm?

7. How does a monopolistic competitor choose its profit-maximizing quantity of output and price?

8. How can a monopolistic competitor tell whether the price it is charging will cause the firm to earn profits or experience losses?

9. If the firms in a monopolistically competitive market are earning economic profits or losses in the short run, would you expect them to continue doing so in the long run? Why?

10. Is a monopolistically competitive firm productively efficient? Is it allocatively efficient? Why or why not?

11. Will the firms in an oligopoly act more like a monopoly or more like competitors? Briefly explain.

12. Does each individual in a prisoner's dilemma benefit more from cooperation or from pursuing self-interest? Explain briefly.

13. What stops oligopolists from acting together as a monopolist and earning the highest possible level of profits?

## Critical Thinking Questions

14. Aside from advertising, how can monopolistically competitive firms increase demand for their products?

15. Make a case for why monopolistically competitive industries never reach long-run equilibrium.

16. Would you rather have efficiency or variety? That is, one opportunity cost of the variety of products we have is that each product costs more per unit than if there were only one kind of product of a given type, like shoes. Perhaps a better question is, "What is the right amount of variety? Can there be too many varieties of shoes, for example?"

17. Would you expect the kinked demand curve to be more extreme (like a right angle) or less extreme (like a normal demand curve) if each firm in the cartel produces a near-identical product like OPEC and petroleum? What if each firm produces a somewhat different product? Explain your reasoning.

18. When OPEC raised the price of oil dramatically in the mid-1970s, experts said it was unlikely that the cartel could stay together over the long term—that the incentives for individual members to cheat would become too strong. More than forty years later, OPEC still exists. Why do you think OPEC has been able to beat the odds and continue to collude? *Hint:* You may wish to consider non-economic reasons.

## Problems

**19.** Andrea's Day Spa began to offer a relaxing aromatherapy treatment. The firm asks you how much to charge to maximize profits. The first two columns in Table 10.5 provide the price and quantity for the demand curve for treatments. The third column shows its total costs. For each level of output, calculate total revenue, marginal revenue, average cost, and marginal cost. What is the profit-maximizing level of output for the treatments and how much will the firm earn in profits?

| Price | Quantity | TC |
|---|---|---|
| $25.00 | 0 | $130 |
| $24.00 | 10 | $275 |
| $23.00 | 20 | $435 |
| $22.50 | 30 | $610 |
| $22.00 | 40 | $800 |
| $21.60 | 50 | $1,005 |
| $21.20 | 60 | $1,225 |

**TABLE 10.5**

**20.** Mary and Raj are the only two growers who provide organically grown corn to a local grocery store. They know that if they cooperated and produced less corn, they could raise the price of the corn. If they work independently, they will each earn $100. If they decide to work together and both lower their output, they can each earn $150. If one person lowers output and the other does not, the person who lowers output will earn $0 and the other person will capture the entire market and will earn $200. Table 10.6 represents the choices available to Mary and Raj. What is the best choice for Raj if he is sure that Mary will cooperate? If Mary thinks Raj will cheat, what should Mary do and why? What is the prisoner's dilemma result? What is the preferred choice if they could ensure cooperation? A = Work independently; B = Cooperate and Lower Output. (Each results entry lists Raj's earnings first, and Mary's earnings second.)

| | | Mary | |
|---|---|---|---|
| | | A | B |
| Raj | A | ($100, $100) | ($200, $0) |
| | B | ($0, $200) | ($150, $150) |

**TABLE 10.6**

**21.** Jane and Bill are apprehended for a bank robbery. They are taken into separate rooms and questioned by the police about their involvement in the crime. The police tell them each that if they confess and turn the other person in, they will receive a lighter sentence. If they both confess, they will be each be sentenced to 30 years. If neither confesses, they will each receive a 20-year sentence. If only one confesses, the confessor will receive 15 years and the one who stayed silent will receive 35 years. Table 10.7 below represents the choices available to Jane and Bill. If Jane trusts Bill to stay silent, what should she do? If Jane thinks that Bill will confess, what should she do? Does Jane have a dominant strategy? Does Bill have a dominant strategy? A = Confess; B = Stay Silent. (Each results entry lists Jane's sentence first (in years), and Bill's sentence second.)

|  |  | Jane | |
|---|---|---|---|
|  |  | A | B |
| **Bill** | A | (30, 30) | (15, 35) |
|  | B | (35, 15) | (20, 20) |

**TABLE 10.7**

**FIGURE 11.1 Oligopoly versus Competitors in the Marketplace** Large corporations, such as the natural gas producer Kinder Morgan, can bring economies of scale to the marketplace. Will that benefit consumers, or is more competition better? (Credit: modification of "Aerial view of Kinder Morgan Brisbane Terminal" by Chiara Coetzee/ Flickr Creative Commons, Public Domain)

## CHAPTER OBJECTIVES

In this chapter, you will learn about:

- Corporate Mergers
- Regulating Anticompetitive Behavior
- Regulating Natural Monopolies
- The Great Deregulation Experiment

## Introduction to Monopoly and Antitrust Policy

 **BRING IT HOME**

### More than Cooking, Heating, and Cooling

If you live in the United States, there is a slightly better than 50–50 chance your home is heated and cooled using natural gas. You may even use natural gas for cooking. However, those uses are not the primary uses of natural gas in the U.S. In late 2021, according to the U.S. Energy Information Administration, home heating, cooling, and cooking accounted for nearly 20% of natural gas usage. What accounts for the rest? The greatest uses for natural gas are the generation of electric power (almost 37%) and in industry (30%). Together these three uses for natural gas touch many areas of our lives, so why would there be any opposition to a merger of two natural gas firms? After all, a merger could mean increased efficiencies and reduced costs to people like you and me.

In October 2011, Kinder Morgan and El Paso Corporation, two natural gas firms, announced they were merging. The announcement stated the combined firm would link "nearly every major production region with markets," cut costs by "eliminating duplication in pipelines and other assets," and that "the savings could be passed on to consumers."

The objection? The $21.1 billion deal would give Kinder Morgan control of more than 80,000 miles of pipeline, making the new firm the third largest energy producer in North America. Policymakers and the public wondered whether the new conglomerate really would pass on cost savings to consumers, or would the merger give Kinder Morgan a strong oligopoly position in the natural gas marketplace?

That brings us to the central questions this chapter poses: What should the balance be between corporate size and a larger number of competitors in a marketplace, and what role should the government play in this balancing act?

---

The previous chapters on the theory of the firm identified three important lessons: First, that competition, by providing consumers with lower prices and a variety of innovative products, is a good thing; second, that large-scale production can dramatically lower average costs; and third, that markets in the real world are rarely perfectly competitive. As a consequence, government policymakers must determine how much to intervene to balance the potential benefits of large-scale production against the potential loss of competition that can occur when businesses grow in size, especially through mergers.

For example, in 2006, AT&T and BellSouth proposed a merger. At the time, there were very few mobile phone service providers. Both the Justice Department and the FCC blocked the proposal.

The two companies argued that the merger would benefit consumers, who would be able to purchase better telecommunications services at a cheaper price because the newly created firm would take advantage of economies of scale and eliminate duplicate investments. However, a number of activist groups like the Consumer Federation of America and Public Knowledge expressed fears that the merger would reduce competition and lead to higher prices for consumers for decades to come. In December 2006, the federal government allowed the merger to proceed. By 2009, the new post-merger AT&T was the eighth largest company by revenues in the United States, and by that measure the largest telecommunications company in the world. Economists have spent – and will still spend – years trying to determine whether the merger of AT&T and BellSouth, as well as other smaller mergers of telecommunications companies at about this same time, helped consumers, hurt them, or did not make much difference.

This chapter discusses public policy issues about competition. How can economists and governments determine when mergers of large companies like AT&T and BellSouth should be allowed and when they should be blocked? The government also plays a role in policing anticompetitive behavior other than mergers, like prohibiting certain kinds of contracts that might restrict competition. In the case of natural monopoly, however, trying to preserve competition probably will not work very well, and so government will often resort to regulation of price and/or quantity of output. In recent decades, there has been a global trend toward less government intervention in the price and output decisions of businesses.

## 11.1 Corporate Mergers

**LEARNING OBJECTIVES**

By the end of this section, you will be able to:

- Explain antitrust law and its significance
- Calculate concentration ratios
- Calculate the Herfindahl-Hirschman Index (HHI)
- Evaluate methods of antitrust regulation

A corporate **merger** occurs when two formerly separate firms combine to become a single firm. When one firm purchases another, it is called an **acquisition**. An acquisition may not look just like a merger, since the newly purchased firm may continue to operate under its former company name. Mergers can also be lateral, where two firms of similar sizes combine to become one. However, both mergers and acquisitions lead to two formerly separate firms operating under common ownership, and so they are commonly grouped together.

### Regulations for Approving Mergers

Since a merger combines two firms into one, it can reduce the extent of competition between firms. Therefore, when two U.S. firms announce a merger or acquisition where at least one of the firms is above a minimum size of sales (a threshold that moves up gradually over time, and was at $101 million in 2022), or certain other conditions are met, they are required under law to notify the U.S. Federal Trade Commission (FTC). The left-hand panel of Figure 11.2 (a) shows the number of mergers submitted for review to the FTC each year from 1999 to 2012. Mergers follow the business cycle, falling after the 2001 recession, peaking in 2007 as the Great Recession struck, and then rising since 2009. The right-hand panel of Figure 11.2 (b) shows the distribution of those mergers submitted for review in 2015 as measured by the size of the transaction. It is important to remember that this total leaves out many small mergers under $50 million, which companies only need to report in certain limited circumstances. In 2012, 26 percent of all reported merger and acquisition transactions exceeded $500 million, while 11 percent exceeded $1 billion.

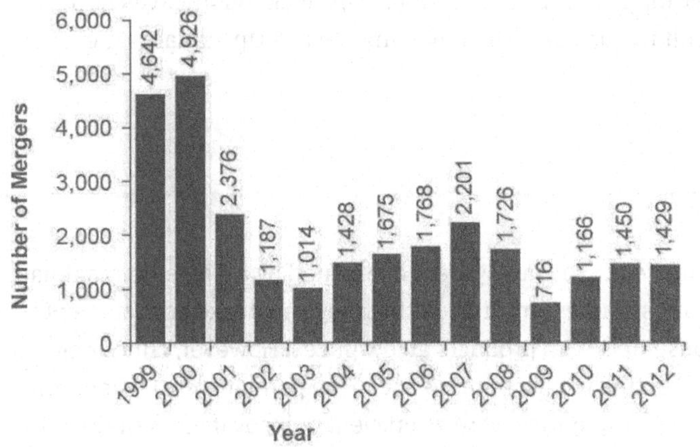

(a) Number of mergers submitted for review by the Federal Trade Commission, 1999-2012

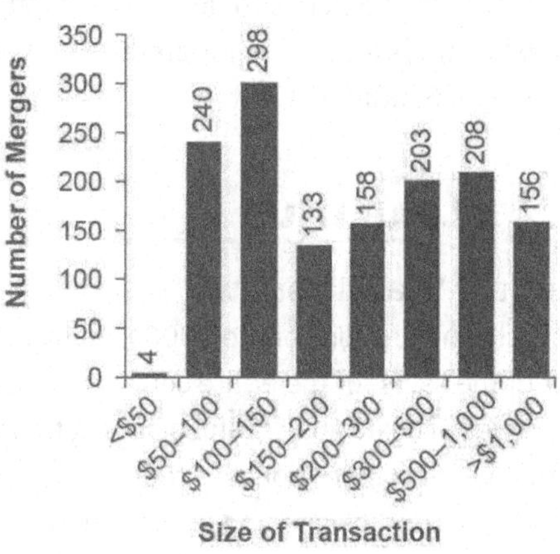

(b) Size of transaction for mergers submitted for review in 2012 (in millions of dollars)

**FIGURE 11.2 Number and Size of Mergers** (a) The number of mergers grew from 2003 to 2007, then fell dramatically during the 2008-2009 Great Recession, before recovering since. (b) In 2012, the greatest number of mergers submitted for review by the Federal Trade Commission was for transactions between $100–$150 million.

The laws that give government the power to block certain mergers, and even in some cases to break up large firms into smaller ones, are called **antitrust laws**. Before a large merger happens, the antitrust regulators at the FTC and the U.S. Department of Justice can allow the merger, prohibit it, or allow it if certain conditions are met. One common condition is that the merger will be allowed if the firm agrees to sell off certain parts. For example, in 2006, Johnson & Johnson bought the Pfizer's "consumer health" division, which included well-known brands like Listerine mouthwash and Sudafed cold medicine. As a condition of allowing the merger, Johnson & Johnson was required to sell off six brands to other firms, including Zantac® heartburn relief medication, Cortizone anti-itch cream, and Balmex diaper rash medication, to preserve a greater degree of competition in these markets.

The U.S. government approves most proposed mergers. In a market-oriented economy, firms have the freedom to make their own choices. Private firms generally have the freedom to:

- expand or reduce production
- set the price they choose
- open new factories or sales facilities or close them
- hire workers or to lay them off
- start selling new products or stop selling existing ones

If the owners want to acquire a firm or be acquired, or to merge with another firm, this decision is just one of many that firms are free to make. In these conditions, the managers of private firms will sometimes make mistakes. They may close down a factory which, it later turns out, would have been profitable. They may start selling a product that ends up losing money. A merger between two companies can sometimes lead to a clash of corporate personalities that makes both firms worse off. However, the fundamental belief behind a market-oriented economy is that firms, not governments, are in the best position to know if their actions will lead to attracting more customers or producing more efficiently.

Government regulators agree that most mergers are beneficial to consumers. As the Federal Trade Commission has noted on its website (as of November, 2013): "Most mergers actually benefit competition and consumers by allowing firms to operate more efficiently." At the same time, the FTC recognizes, "Some [mergers] are likely to lessen competition. That, in turn, can lead to higher prices, reduced availability of goods or services, lower quality of products, and less innovation. Some mergers create a concentrated market, while others enable a single firm to raise prices." The challenge for the antitrust regulators at the FTC and the U.S. Department of Justice is to figure out when a merger may hinder competition. This decision involves both numerical tools and some judgments that are difficult to quantify. The following Clear It Up explains the origins of U.S. antitrust law.

## CLEAR IT UP

### What is U.S. antitrust law?

In the closing decades of the 1800s, many industries in the U.S. economy were dominated by a single firm that had most of the sales for the entire country. Supporters of these large firms argued that they could take advantage of economies of scale and careful planning to provide consumers with products at low prices. However, critics pointed out that when competition was reduced, these firms were free to charge more and make permanently higher profits, and that without the goading of competition, it was not clear that they were as efficient or innovative as they could be.

In many cases, these large firms were organized in the legal form of a "trust," in which a group of formerly independent firms were consolidated by mergers and purchases, and a group of "trustees" then ran the companies as if they were a single firm. Thus, when the U.S. government sought to limit the power of these trusts, it passed the **Sherman Antitrust Act** in 1890 - the nation's first antitrust law. In an early demonstration of the law's power, the U.S. Supreme Court in 1911 upheld the government's right to break up Standard Oil, which had controlled about 90% of the country's oil refining, into 34 independent firms, including Exxon, Mobil, Amoco, and Chevron. In 1914, the **Clayton Antitrust Act** outlawed mergers and acquisitions (where the outcome would be to "substantially lessen competition" in an industry), price discrimination (where different customers are charged different prices for the same product), and tied sales (where purchase of one product commits the buyer to purchase some other product). Also in 1914, the Federal Trade Commission (FTC) was created to define more specifically what competition was unfair. In 1950, the **Celler-Kefauver Act** extended the Clayton Act by restricting vertical and conglomerate mergers. A vertical merger occurs when two or more firms, operating at different levels within an industry's supply chain, merge operations. A conglomerate merger is a merger between firms that are involved in totally unrelated business activities. In the twenty-first century, the FTC and the U.S. Department of Justice continue to enforce antitrust laws.

### The Four-Firm Concentration Ratio

Regulators have struggled for decades to measure the degree of monopoly power in an industry. An early tool was the **concentration ratio**, which measures the combined market share (or percent of total industry sales) which is accounted for by the largest firms (typically the top four to eight). For an explanation of how high market concentrations can create inefficiencies in an economy, refer to Monopoly.

Say that the market for replacing broken automobile windshields in a certain city has 18 firms with the market shares in Table 11.1, where the **market share** is each firm's proportion of total sales in that market. We calculate the four-firm concentration ratio by adding the market shares of the four largest firms: in this case, 16 + 10 + 8 + 6 = 40. We do not consider this concentration ratio especially high, because the largest four firms have less than half the market.

<table>
<tr><td colspan="2">If the market shares for replacing automobile windshields are:</td></tr>
<tr><td>Smooth as Glass Repair Company</td><td>16% of the market</td></tr>
<tr><td>The Auto Glass Doctor Company</td><td>10% of the market</td></tr>
<tr><td>Your Car Shield Company</td><td>8% of the market</td></tr>
<tr><td>Seven firms that each have 6% of the market</td><td>42% of the market, combined</td></tr>
<tr><td>Eight firms that each have 3% of the market</td><td>24% of the market, combined</td></tr>
<tr><td colspan="2">Then the four-firm concentration ratio is 16 + 10 + 8 + 6 = 40.</td></tr>
</table>

**TABLE 11.1 Calculating Concentration Ratios from Market Shares**

The concentration ratio approach can help to clarify some of the fuzziness over deciding when a merger might affect competition. For instance, if two of the smallest firms in the hypothetical market for repairing automobile windshields merged, the four-firm concentration ratio would not change—which implies that there is not much worry that the degree of competition in the market has notably diminished. However, if the top two firms merged, then the four-firm concentration ratio would become 46 (that is, 26 + 8 + 6 + 6). While this concentration ratio is modestly higher, the four-firm concentration ratio would still be less than half, so such a proposed merger might barely raise an eyebrow among antitrust regulators.

## LINK IT UP

Visit this website (http://openstax.org/l/Google_FTC) to read an article about Google's run-in with the FTC.

### The Herfindahl-Hirschman Index

A four-firm concentration ratio is a simple tool, which may reveal only part of the story. For example, consider two industries that both have a four-firm concentration ratio of 80. However, in one industry five firms each control 20% of the market, while in the other industry, the top firm holds 77% of the market and all the other firms have 1% each. Although the four-firm concentration ratios are identical, it would be reasonable to worry more about the extent of competition in the second case—where the largest firm is nearly a monopoly—than in the first.

Another approach to measuring industry concentration that can distinguish between these two cases is called the **Herfindahl-Hirschman Index (HHI)**. We calculate HHI by summing the squares of the market share of each firm in the industry, as the following Work It Out shows.

### WORK IT OUT

**Calculating HHI**

Step 1. Calculate the HHI for a monopoly with a market share of 100%. Because there is only one firm, it has 100% market share. The HHI is $100^2 = 10,000$.

Step 2. For an extremely competitive industry, with dozens or hundreds of extremely small competitors, the HHI value might drop as low as 100 or even less. Calculate the HHI for an industry with 100 firms that each have 1% of the market. In this case, the HHI is $100(1^2) = 100$.

Step 3. Calculate the HHI for the industry in Table 11.1. In this case, the HHI is $16^2 + 10^2 + 8^2 + 7(6^2) + 8(3^2) = 744$.

Step 4. Note that the HHI gives greater weight to large firms.

Step 5. Consider the earlier example, comparing one industry where five firms each have 20% of the market with an industry where one firm has 77% and the other 23 firms have 1% each. The two industries have the same four-firm concentration ratio of 80. However, the HHI for the first industry is $5(20^2) = 2,000$, while the HHI for the second industry is much higher at $77^2 + 23(1^2) = 5,952$.

Step 6. Note that the near-monopolist in the second industry drives up the HHI measure of industrial concentration.

Step 7. Review Table 11.2 which gives some examples of the four-firm concentration ratio and the HHI in various U.S. industries in 2016. (You can find market share data from multiple industry sources. Data in the table are from: Statista.com (for wireless), *The Wall Street Journal* (for automobiles), Gartner.com (for computers) and the U.S. Bureau of Transportation Statistics (for airlines).)

| U.S. Industry | Four-Firm Ratio | HHI |
|---|---|---|
| *Wireless* | 98 | 2,736 |
| Largest five: Verizon, AT&T, Sprint, T-Mobile, US Cellular | | |
| *Personal Computers* | 76 | 1,234 |
| Largest five: HP, Lenovo, Dell, Asus, Apple, Acer | | |
| *Airlines* | 69 | 1,382 |
| Largest five: American, Southwest, Delta, United, JetBlue | | |
| *Automobiles* | 58 | 1,099 |
| Largest five: Ford, GM, Toyota, Chrysler, Nissan | | |

**TABLE 11.2 Examples of Concentration Ratios and HHIs in the U.S. Economy, 2016**

In the 1980s, the FTC followed these guidelines: If a merger would result in an HHI of less than 1,000, the FTC would probably approve it. If a merger would result in an HHI of more than 1,800, the FTC would probably challenge it. If a merger would result in an HHI between 1,000 and 1,800, then the FTC would scrutinize the plan and make a case-by-case decision. However, in the last several decades, the antitrust enforcement authorities have moved away from relying as heavily on measures of concentration ratios and HHIs to determine whether they will allow a merger, and instead they carry out more case-by-case analysis on the extent of competition in different industries.

## New Directions for Antitrust

Both the four-firm concentration ratio and the Herfindahl-Hirschman index share some weaknesses. First, they begin from the assumption that the "market" under discussion is well-defined, and the only question is measuring how sales are divided in that market. Second, they are based on an implicit assumption that competitive conditions across industries are similar enough that a broad measure of concentration in the market is enough to make a decision about the effects of a merger. These assumptions, however, are not always correct. In response to these two problems, the antitrust regulators have been changing their approach in the last decade or two.

Defining a **market** is often controversial. For example, Microsoft in the early 2000s had a dominant share of the software for computer operating systems. However, in the total market for all computer software and services, including everything from games to scientific programs, the Microsoft share was only about 14% in 2014. A narrowly defined market will tend to make concentration appear higher, while a broadly defined market will tend to make it appear smaller.

In recent decades, there have been two especially important shifts affecting how we define markets: one centers on technology and the other centers on globalization. In addition, these two shifts are interconnected. With the vast improvement in communications technologies, including the development of the internet, a consumer can order books or pet supplies from all over the country or the world. As a result, the degree of competition many local retail businesses face has increased. The same effect may operate even more strongly in markets for business supplies, where so-called "business-to-business" websites can allow buyers and suppliers from anywhere in the world to find each other.

Globalization has changed the market boundaries. As recently as the 1970s, it was common for measurements of concentration ratios and HHIs to stop at national borders. Now, many industries find that their competition comes from the global market. A few decades ago, three companies, General Motors, Ford, and Chrysler, dominated the U.S. auto market. By 2014, however, production of these three firms accounted for less than half of U.S. auto sales, although by 2021, with the emergence of COVID-19, the three firms accounted for essentially half of U.S. auto sales. The three firms face competition from well-known car manufacturers such as Toyota, Honda, Nissan, Volkswagen, Mitsubishi, and Mazda. When analysts calculate HHIs with a global perspective, concentration in most major industries—including cars—is lower than in a purely domestic context.

Because attempting to define a particular market can be difficult and controversial, the Federal Trade Commission has begun to look less at market share and more at the data on actual competition between businesses. For example, in February 2007, Whole Foods Market and Wild Oats Market announced that they wished to merge. These were the two largest companies in the market that the government defined as "premium natural and organic supermarket chains." However, one could also argue that they were two relatively small companies in the broader market for all stores that sell groceries or specialty food products.

Rather than relying on a market definition, the government antitrust regulators looked at detailed evidence on profits and prices for specific stores in different cities, both before and after other competitive stores entered or exited. Based on that evidence, the Federal Trade Commission decided to block the merger. After two years of legal battles, the FTC eventually allowed the merger in 2009 under the conditions that Whole Foods sell off the Wild Oats brand name and a number of individual stores, to preserve competition in certain local markets. For more on the difficulties of defining markets, refer to Monopoly.

This new approach to antitrust regulation involves detailed analysis of specific markets and companies, instead of defining a market and counting up total sales. A common starting point is for antitrust regulators to use statistical tools and real-world evidence to estimate the **demand curves** and **supply curves** the firms proposing a merger face. A second step is to specify how competition occurs in this specific industry. Some possibilities include competing to cut prices, to raise output, to build a brand name through advertising, and to build a reputation for good service or high quality. With these pieces of the puzzle in place, it is then possible to build a statistical model that estimates the likely outcome for consumers if the two firms are allowed to merge. These models do require some degree of subjective judgment, and so they can become the subject of legal disputes between the antitrust authorities and the companies that wish to merge.

## 11.2 Regulating Anticompetitive Behavior

**LEARNING OBJECTIVES**

By the end of this section, you will be able to:

- Analyze restrictive practices
- Explain tying sales, bundling, and predatory pricing
- Evaluate a real-world situation of possible anticompetitive and restrictive practices

The U.S. antitrust laws reach beyond blocking mergers that would reduce competition to include a wide array of anticompetitive practices. For example, it is illegal for competitors to form a cartel to collude to make pricing and output decisions, as if they were a monopoly firm. The Federal Trade Commission and the U.S. Department of Justice prohibit firms from agreeing to fix prices or output, rigging bids, or sharing or dividing markets by allocating customers, suppliers, territories, or lines of commerce.

In the late 1990s, for example, the antitrust regulators prosecuted an international cartel of vitamin manufacturers, including the Swiss firm Hoffman-La Roche, the German firm BASF, and the French firm Rhone-Poulenc. These firms reached agreements on how much to produce, how much to charge, and which firm would sell to which customers. Firms like General Mills, Kellogg, Purina Mills, and Proctor and Gamble bought the high-priced vitamins, which pushed up the prices more. Hoffman-La Roche pleaded guilty in May 1999 and agreed both to pay a fine of $500 million and to have at least one top executive be incarcerated for four months.

Under U.S. antitrust laws, monopoly itself is not illegal. If a firm has a monopoly because of a newly patented invention, for example, the law explicitly allows a firm to earn higher-than-normal profits for a time as a reward for innovation. If a firm achieves a large share of the market by producing a better product at a lower price, such behavior is not prohibited by antitrust law.

### Restrictive Practices

Antitrust law includes rules against **restrictive practices**—practices that do not involve outright agreements to raise price or to reduce the quantity produced, but that might have the effect of reducing competition. Antitrust cases involving restrictive practices are often controversial, because they delve into specific contracts or agreements between firms that are allowed in some cases but not in others.

For example, an **exclusive dealing** agreement between a manufacturer and a dealer can be legal or illegal. It is legal if the purpose of the contract is to encourage competition between dealers. For example, it is legal for the Ford Motor Company to sell its cars to only Ford dealers, and for General Motors to sell to only GM dealers, and so on. However, exclusive deals may also limit competition. If one large retailer obtained the exclusive rights to be the sole distributor of televisions, computers, and audio equipment made by a number of companies, then this exclusive contract would have an anticompetitive effect on other retailers.

**Tying sales** happen when a customer is allowed to buy one product only if the customer also buys a second product. Tying sales are controversial because they force consumers to purchase a product that they may not actually want or need. Further, the additional, required products are not necessarily advantageous to the customer. Suppose that to purchase a popular DVD, the store required that you also purchase a certain portable TV model. These products are only loosely related, thus there is no reason to make the purchase of one contingent on the other. Even if a customer were interested in a portable TV, the tying to a particular model prevents the customer from having the option of selecting one from the numerous types available in the market.

A related, but not identical, concept is **bundling**, where a firm sells two or more products as one. Bundling typically offers an advantage for consumers by allowing them to acquire multiple products or services for a better price. For example, several cable companies allow customers to buy products like cable, internet, and a phone line through a special price available through bundling. Customers are also welcome to purchase these products separately, but the price of bundling is usually more appealing.

In some cases, we can view tying sales and bundling as anticompetitive. However, in other cases they may be legal and even common. It is common for people to purchase season tickets to a sports team or a set of concerts so as to guarantee tickets to the few contests or shows that are most popular and likely to sell out. Computer software manufacturers may often bundle a number of different programs, even when the buyer wants only a few. Think about the software that is included in a new computer purchase, for example.

Recall from the chapter on Monopoly that predatory pricing occurs when the existing firm (or firms) reacts to a new firm by dropping prices very low, until the new firm is driven out of the market, at which point the existing firm raises prices again. This pattern of pricing is aimed at deterring new firms from entering the market. However, in practice, it can be hard to figure out when pricing is predatory. Say that American Airlines is flying between two cities, and a new airline starts flying between the same two cities, at a lower price. If American Airlines cuts its price to match the new entrant, is this predatory pricing or is it just market competition at work? A commonly proposed rule is that if a firm is selling for less than its average variable cost—that is, at a price where it should be shutting down—then there is evidence for predatory pricing. However, calculating in the real world what costs are variable and what costs are fixed is often not obvious, either.

The Microsoft antitrust case embodies many of these gray areas in restrictive practices, as the next Clear It Up shows.

## CLEAR IT UP

### Did Microsoft® engage in anticompetitive and restrictive practices?

The most famous restrictive practices case of recent years was a series of lawsuits by the U.S. government against Microsoft—lawsuits that some of Microsoft's competitors encouraged. All sides admitted that Microsoft's Windows program had a near-monopoly position in the market for the software used in general computer operating systems. All sides agreed that the software had many satisfied customers and that the computer software capabilities were compatible with Windows. Software that Microsoft and other companies produced had expanded dramatically in the 1990s. Having a **monopoly** or a near-monopoly is not necessarily illegal in and of itself, but in cases where one company controls a great deal of the market, antitrust regulators look at any allegations of restrictive practices with special care.

The antitrust regulators argued that Microsoft had gone beyond profiting from its software innovations and its dominant position in the software market for operating systems, and had tried to use its market power in operating systems software to take over other parts of the software industry. For example, the government argued that Microsoft had engaged in an anticompetitive form of exclusive dealing by threatening computer makers that, if they did not leave another firm's software off their machines (specifically, Netscape's Internet browser), then Microsoft would not sell them its operating system software. Government antitrust regulators accused Microsoft of tying together its Windows operating system software, where it had a monopoly, with its Internet Explorer browser software, where it did not have a monopoly, and thus using this bundling as an anticompetitive tool. The government also accused Microsoft of a form of predatory pricing; namely, giving away certain additional software products for free as part of Windows, as a way of driving out the competition from other software makers.

In April 2000, a federal court held that Microsoft's behavior had crossed the line into unfair competition, and recommended that the company be split into two competing firms. However, the court overturned that penalty on appeal, and in November 2002 Microsoft reached a settlement with the government that it would end its restrictive practices.

---

The concept of restrictive practices is continually evolving, as firms seek new ways to earn profits and government regulators define what is permissible. A situation where the law is evolving and changing is always somewhat troublesome, since laws are most useful and fair when firms know what they are in advance. In addition, since the law is open to interpretation, competitors who are losing out in the market can accuse successful firms of anticompetitive restrictive practices, and try to win through government regulation what they have failed to accomplish in the market. Officials at the Federal Trade Commission and the Department of Justice are, of course, aware of these issues, but there is no easy way to resolve them.

# 11.3 Regulating Natural Monopolies

**LEARNING OBJECTIVES**

By the end of this section, you will be able to:

- Evaluate the appropriate competition policy for a natural monopoly
- Interpret a graph of regulatory choices
- Contrast cost-plus and price cap regulation

Most true monopolies today in the U.S. are regulated, natural monopolies. A natural monopoly poses a difficult challenge for competition policy, because the structure of costs and demand makes competition unlikely or costly. A **natural monopoly** arises when average costs are declining over the range of production that satisfies market demand. This typically happens when fixed costs are large relative to variable costs. As a result, one firm is able to supply the total quantity demanded in the market at lower cost than two or more firms—so splitting up the natural monopoly would raise the average cost of production and force customers to pay more.

Public utilities, the companies that have traditionally provided water and electrical service across much of the United States, are leading examples of natural monopoly. It would make little sense to argue that a local water company should be divided into several competing companies, each with its own separate set of pipes and water supplies. Installing four or five identical sets of pipes under a city, one for each water company, so that each household could choose its own water provider, would be terribly costly. The same argument applies to the idea of having many competing companies for delivering electricity to homes, each with its own set of wires. Before the advent of wireless phones, the argument also applied to the idea of many different phone companies, each with its own set of phone wires running through the neighborhood.

## The Choices in Regulating a Natural Monopoly

What then is the appropriate competition policy for a natural monopoly? Figure 11.3 illustrates the case of natural monopoly, with a market demand curve that cuts through the downward-sloping portion of the **average cost curve**. Points A, B, C, and F illustrate four of the main choices for regulation. Table 11.3 outlines the regulatory choices for dealing with a natural monopoly.

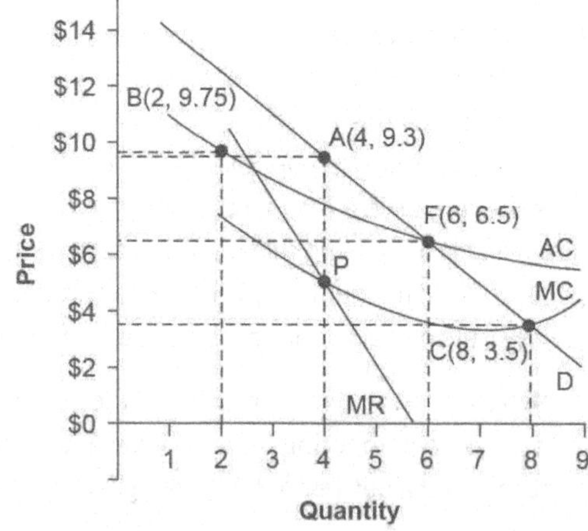


**FIGURE 11.3 Regulatory Choices in Dealing with Natural Monopoly** A natural monopoly will maximize profits by producing at the quantity where marginal revenue (MR) equals marginal costs (MC) and by then looking to the market demand curve to see what price to charge for this quantity. This monopoly will produce at point A, with a quantity of 4 and a price of 9.3. If antitrust regulators split this company exactly in half, then each half would

produce at point B, with average costs of 9.75 and output of 2. The regulators might require the firm to produce where marginal cost crosses the market demand curve at point C. However, if the firm is required to produce at a quantity of 8 and sell at a price of 3.5, the firm will incur losses. The most likely choice is point F, where the firm is required to produce a quantity of 6 and charge a price of 6.5.

| Quantity | Price | Total Revenue[*] | Marginal Revenue | Total Cost | Marginal Cost | Average Cost |
|---|---|---|---|---|---|---|
| 1 | 14.7 | 14.7 | 14.7 | 11.0 | - | 11.00 |
| 2 | 12.4 | 24.7 | 10.0 | 19.5 | 8.5 | 9.75 |
| 3 | 10.6 | 31.7 | 7.0 | 25.5 | 6.0 | 8.50 |
| 4 | 9.3 | 37.2 | 5.5 | 31.0 | 5.5 | 7.75 |
| 5 | 8.0 | 40.0 | 2.8 | 35.0 | 4.0 | 7.00 |
| 6 | 6.5 | 39.0 | −1.0 | 39.0 | 4.0 | 6.50 |
| 7 | 5.0 | 35.0 | −4.0 | 42.0 | 3.0 | 6.00 |
| 8 | 3.5 | 28.0 | −7.0 | 45.5 | 3.5 | 5.70 |
| 9 | 2.0 | 18.0 | −10.0 | 49.5 | 4.0 | 5.5 |

**TABLE 11.3 Regulatory Choices in Dealing with Natural Monopoly** (*We obtain total revenue by multiplying price and quantity. However, we have rounded some of the price values in this table for ease of presentation.)

The first possibility is to leave the natural monopoly alone. In this case, the monopoly will follow its normal approach to maximizing profits. It determines the quantity where MR = MC, which happens at point P at a quantity of 4. The firm then looks to point A on the demand curve to find that it can charge a price of 9.3 for that profit-maximizing quantity. Since the price is above the average cost curve, the natural monopoly would earn economic profits.

A second outcome arises if antitrust authorities decide to divide the company, so that the new firms can compete. As a simple example, imagine that the company is cut in half. Thus, instead of one large firm producing a quantity of 4, two half-size firms each produce a quantity of 2. Because of the declining average cost curve (AC), the average cost of production for each of the half-size companies producing 2, as point B shows, would be 9.75, while the average cost of production for a larger firm producing 4 would only be 7.75. Thus, the economy would become less productively efficient, since the good is produced at a higher average cost. In a situation with a downward-sloping average cost curve, two smaller firms will always have higher average costs of production than one larger firm for any quantity of total output. In addition, the antitrust authorities must worry that splitting the natural monopoly into pieces may be only the start of their problems. If one of the two firms grows larger than the other, it will have lower average costs and may be able to drive its competitor out of the market. Alternatively, two firms in a market may discover subtle ways of coordinating their behavior and keeping prices high. Either way, the result will not be the greater competition that was desired.

A third alternative is that regulators may decide to set prices and quantities produced for this industry. The regulators will try to choose a point along the market demand curve that benefits both consumers and the broader social interest. Point C illustrates one tempting choice: the regulator requires that the firm produce the quantity of output where marginal cost crosses the demand curve at an output of 8, and charge the price of

3.5, which is equal to **marginal cost** at that point. This rule is appealing because it requires price to be set equal to marginal cost, which is what would occur in a perfectly competitive market, and it would assure consumers a higher quantity and lower price than at the monopoly choice A. In fact, efficient allocation of resources would occur at point C, since the value to the consumers of the last unit bought and sold in this market is equal to the marginal cost of producing it.

Attempting to bring about point C through force of regulation, however, runs into a severe difficulty. At point C, with an output of 8, a price of 3.5 is below the average cost of production, which is 5.7, so if the firm charges a price of 3.5, it will be suffering losses. Unless the regulators or the government offer the firm an ongoing public subsidy (and there are numerous political problems with that option), the firm will lose money and go out of business.

Perhaps the most plausible option for the regulator is point F; that is, to set the price where AC crosses the demand curve at an output of 6 and a price of 6.5. This plan makes some sense at an intuitive level: let the natural monopoly charge enough to cover its average costs and earn a normal rate of profit, so that it can continue operating, but prevent the firm from raising prices and earning abnormally high monopoly profits, as it would at the monopoly choice A. Determining this level of output and price with the political pressures, time constraints, and limited information of the real world is much harder than identifying the point on a graph. For more on the problems that can arise from a centrally determined price, see the discussion of price floors and price ceilings in Demand and Supply.

### Cost-Plus versus Price Cap Regulation

Regulators of public utilities for many decades followed the general approach of attempting to choose a point like F in Figure 11.3. They calculated the average cost of production for the water or electricity companies, added in an amount for the normal rate of profit the firm should expect to earn, and set the price for consumers accordingly. This method was known as **cost-plus regulation**.

Cost-plus regulation raises difficulties of its own. If producers receive reimbursement for their costs, plus a bit more, then at a minimum, producers have less reason to be concerned with high costs—because they can just pass them along in higher prices. Worse, firms under cost-plus regulation even have an incentive to generate high costs by building huge factories or employing many staff, because what they can charge is linked to the costs they incur.

Thus, in the 1980s and 1990s, some public utility regulators began to use **price cap regulation**, where the regulator sets a price that the firm can charge over the next few years. A common pattern was to require a price that declined slightly over time. If the firm can find ways of reducing its costs more quickly than the price caps, it can make a high level of profits. However, if the firm cannot keep up with the price caps or suffers bad luck in the market, it may suffer losses. A few years down the road, the regulators will then set a new series of price caps based on the firm's performance.

Price cap regulation requires delicacy. It will not work if the price regulators set the price cap unrealistically low. It may not work if the market changes dramatically so that the firm is doomed to incurring losses no matter what it does—say, if energy prices rise dramatically on world markets, then the company selling natural gas or heating oil to homes may not be able to meet price caps that seemed reasonable a year or two ago. However, if the regulators compare the prices with producers of the same good in other areas, they can, in effect, pressure a natural monopoly in one area to compete with the prices charged in other areas. Moreover, the possibility of earning greater profits or experiencing losses—instead of having an average rate of profit locked in every year by cost-plus regulation—can provide the natural monopoly with incentives for efficiency and innovation.

With natural monopoly, market competition is unlikely to take root, so if consumers are not to suffer the high prices and restricted output of an unrestricted monopoly, government regulation will need to play a role. In attempting to design a system of price cap regulation with flexibility and incentive, government regulators do not have an easy task.

# 11.4 The Great Deregulation Experiment

**LEARNING OBJECTIVES**

By the end of this section, you will be able to:
- Evaluate the effectiveness of price regulation and antitrust policy
- Explain regulatory capture and its significance

Governments at all levels across the United States have regulated prices in a wide range of industries. In some cases, like water and electricity that have natural monopoly characteristics, there is some room in economic theory for such regulation. However, once politicians are given a basis to intervene in markets and to choose prices and quantities, it is hard to know where to stop.

## Doubts about Regulation of Prices and Quantities

Beginning in the 1970s, it became clear to policymakers of all political leanings that the existing price regulation was not working well. The United States carried out a great policy experiment—the **deregulation** that we discussed in Monopoly—removing government controls over prices and quantities produced in airlines, railroads, trucking, intercity bus travel, natural gas, and bank interest rates. The Clear It Up discusses the outcome of deregulation in one industry in particular—airlines.

## CLEAR IT UP

### What are the results of airline deregulation?

Why did the pendulum swing in favor of deregulation? Consider the airline industry. In the early days of air travel, no airline could make a profit just by flying passengers. Airlines needed something else to carry and the Postal Service provided that something with airmail. Thus, the first U.S. government regulation of the airline industry happened through the Postal Service, when in 1926 the Postmaster General began giving airlines permission to fly certain routes based on mail delivery needs—and the airlines took some passengers along for the ride. In 1934, the antitrust authorities charged the Postmaster General with colluding with the major airlines of that day to monopolize the nation's airways. In 1938, the U.S. government created the Civil Aeronautics Board (CAB) to regulate airfares and routes instead. For 40 years, from 1938 to 1978, the CAB approved all fares, controlled all entry and exit, and specified which airlines could fly which routes. There was zero entry of new airlines on the main routes across the country for 40 years, because the CAB did not think it was necessary.

In 1978, the Airline Deregulation Act took the government out of the business of determining airfares and schedules. The new law shook up the industry. Famous old airlines like Pan American, Eastern, and Braniff went bankrupt and disappeared. Some new airlines like People Express were created—and then vanished.

The greater competition from deregulation reduced airfares by about one-third over the next two decades, saving consumers billions of dollars a year. The average flight used to take off with just half its seats full; now it is two-thirds full, which is far more efficient. Airlines have also developed hub-and-spoke systems, where planes all fly into a central hub city at a certain time and then depart. As a result, one can fly between any of the spoke cities with just one connection—and there is greater service to more cities than before deregulation. With lower fares and more service, the number of air passengers doubled from the late 1970s to the start of the 2000s—an increase that, in turn, doubled the number of jobs in the airline industry. Meanwhile, with the watchful oversight of government safety inspectors, commercial air travel has continued to get safer over time.

The U.S. airline industry is far from perfect. For example, a string of mergers in recent years has raised concerns over how competition might be compromised.

One difficulty with government price regulation is what economists call **regulatory capture**, in which the firms that are supposedly regulated end up playing a large role in setting the regulations that they will follow. When the airline industry was regulated, for example, it suggested appointees to the regulatory board, sent lobbyists to argue with the board, provided most of the information on which the board made decisions, and offered well-paid jobs to at least some of the people leaving the board. In this situation, it is easy for regulators to poorly represent consumers. The result of regulatory capture is that government price regulation can often become a way for existing competitors to work together to reduce output, keep prices high, and limit competition.

### The Effects of Deregulation

Deregulation, both of airlines and of other industries, has its negatives. The greater pressure of competition led to entry and exit. When firms went bankrupt or contracted substantially in size, they laid off workers who had to find other jobs. Market competition is, after all, a full-contact sport.

A number of major accounting scandals involving prominent corporations such as Enron, Tyco International, and WorldCom led to the **Sarbanes-Oxley Act** in 2002. The government designed Sarbanes-Oxley to increase confidence in financial information provided by public corporations to protect investors from accounting fraud.

The Great Recession, which began in late 2007, was caused at least in part by a global financial crisis, which began in the United States. The key component of the crisis was the creation and subsequent failure of several types of unregulated financial assets, such as collateralized mortgage obligations (CMOs, a type of mortgage-backed security), and credit default swaps (CDSs, insurance contracts on assets like CMOs that provided a payoff even if the holder of the CDS did not own the CMO). Private credit rating agencies such as Standard & Poors, Moody's, and Fitch rated many of these assets very safe.

The collapse of the markets for these assets precipitated the financial crisis and led to the failure of Lehman Brothers, a major investment bank, numerous large commercial banks, such as Wachovia, and even the Federal National Mortgage Corporation (Fannie Mae), which had to be nationalized—that is, taken over by the federal government. One response to the financial crisis was the **Dodd-Frank Act**, which majorly attempted to reform the financial system. The legislation's purpose, as noted on dodd-frank.com is:

> To promote the financial stability of the United States by improving accountability and transparency in the financial system, to end "too big to fail," to protect the American taxpayer by ending bailouts, [and] to protect consumers from abusive financial services practices. . .

All market-based economies operate against a background of laws and regulations, including laws about enforcing contracts, collecting taxes, and protecting health and the environment. The government policies that we discussed in this chapter—like blocking certain anticompetitive mergers, ending restrictive practices, imposing price cap regulation on natural monopolies, and deregulation—demonstrate the role of government to strengthen the incentives that come with a greater degree of competition.

 **BRING IT HOME**

### More than Cooking, Heating, and Cooling

What did the Federal Trade Commission (FTC) decide on the Kinder Morgan / El Paso Corporation merger? After careful examination, federal officials decided there was only one area of significant overlap that might provide the merged firm with strong market power. The FTC approved the merger, provided Kinder Morgan divest itself of the overlap area. Tallgrass purchased Kinder Morgan Interstate Gas Transmission, Trailblazer Pipeline Co. LLC, two processing facilities in Wyoming, and Kinder Morgan's 50 percent interest in the Rockies Express Pipeline to meet the FTC requirements. The FTC was attempting to strike a balance between potential cost reductions resulting from economies of scale and concentration of market power.

Did the price of natural gas decrease? Yes, rather significantly. In 2010, the wellhead price of natural gas was $4.48 per thousand cubic foot. In 2012 the price had fallen to just $2.66. Was the merger responsible for the large drop in price? The answer is uncertain. The larger contributor to the sharp drop in price was the overall increase in the supply of natural gas. Increasingly, more natural gas was able to be recovered by fracturing shale deposits, a process called fracking. Fracking, which is controversial for environmental reasons, enabled the recovery of known reserves of natural gas that previously were not economically feasible to tap. Kinder Morgan's control of 80,000-plus miles of pipeline likely made moving the gas from wellheads to end users smoother and allowed for an even greater benefit from the increased supply.

## Key Terms

**acquisition** when one firm purchases another

**antitrust laws** laws that give government the power to block certain mergers, and even in some cases to break up large firms into smaller ones

**bundling** a situation in which multiple products are sold as one

**concentration ratio** an early tool to measure the degree of monopoly power in an industry; measures what share of the total sales in the industry are accounted for by the largest firms, typically the top four to eight firms

**cost-plus regulation** when regulators permit a regulated firm to cover its costs and to make a normal level of profit

**exclusive dealing** an agreement that a dealer will sell only products from one manufacturer

**four-firm concentration ratio** the percentage of the total sales in the industry that are accounted for by the largest four firms

**Herfindahl-Hirschman Index (HHI)** approach to measuring market concentration by adding the square of the market share of each firm in the industry

**market share** the percentage of total sales in the market

**merger** when two formerly separate firms combine to become a single firm

**minimum resale price maintenance agreement** an agreement that requires a dealer who buys from a manufacturer to sell for at least a certain minimum price

**price cap regulation** when the regulator sets a price that a firm cannot exceed over the next few years

**regulatory capture** when the supposedly regulated firms end up playing a large role in setting the regulations that they will follow and as a result, they "capture" the people usually through the promise of a job in that "regulated" industry once their term in government has ended

**restrictive practices** practices that reduce competition but that do not involve outright agreements between firms to raise prices or to reduce the quantity produced

**tying sales** a situation where a customer is allowed to buy one product only if the customer also buys another product

## Key Concepts and Summary

### 11.1 Corporate Mergers

A corporate merger involves two private firms joining together. An acquisition refers to one firm buying another firm. In either case, two formerly independent firms become one firm. Antitrust laws seek to ensure active competition in markets, sometimes by preventing large firms from forming through mergers and acquisitions, sometimes by regulating business practices that might restrict competition, and sometimes by breaking up large firms into smaller competitors.

A four-firm concentration ratio is one way of measuring the extent of competition in a market. We calculate it by adding the market shares—that is, the percentage of total sales—of the four largest firms in the market. A Herfindahl-Hirschman Index (HHI) is another way of measuring the extent of competition in a market. We calculate it by taking the market shares of all firms in the market, squaring them, and then summing the total.

The forces of globalization and new communications and information technology have increased the level of competition that many firms face by increasing the amount of competition from other regions and countries.

### 11.2 Regulating Anticompetitive Behavior

Antitrust firms block authorities from openly colluding to form a cartel that will reduce output and raise prices. Companies sometimes attempt to find other ways around these restrictions and, consequently, many antitrust cases involve restrictive practices that can reduce competition in certain circumstances, like tie-in sales, bundling, and predatory pricing.

## 11.3 Regulating Natural Monopolies

In the case of a natural monopoly, market competition will not work well and so, rather than allowing an unregulated monopoly to raise price and reduce output, the government may wish to regulate price and/or output. Common examples of regulation are public utilities, the regulated firms that often provide electricity and water service.

Cost-plus regulation refers to government regulating a firm which sets the price that a firm can charge over a period of time by looking at the firm's accounting costs and then adding a normal rate of profit. Price cap regulation refers to government regulation of a firm where the government sets a price level several years in advance. In this case, the firm can either earn high profits if it manages to produce at lower costs or sell a higher quantity than expected or suffer low profits or losses if costs are high or it sells less than expected.

## 11.4 The Great Deregulation Experiment

The U.S. economy experienced a wave of deregulation in the late 1970s and early 1980s, when the government eliminated a number of regulations that had set prices and quantities produced in a number of industries. Major accounting scandals in the early 2000s and, more recently, the Great Recession have spurred new regulation to prevent similar occurrences in the future. Regulatory capture occurs when the regulated industries end up having a strong influence over what regulations exist.

## Self-Check Questions

1. Is it true that a merger between two firms that are not already in the top four by size can affect both the four-firm concentration ratio and the Herfindahl-Hirschman Index? Explain briefly.

2. Is it true that the four-firm concentration ratio puts more emphasis on one or two very large firms, while the Herfindahl-Hirschman Index puts more emphasis on all the firms in the entire market? Explain briefly.

3. Some years ago, two intercity bus companies, Greyhound Lines, Inc. and Trailways Transportation System, wanted to merge. One possible definition of the market in this case was "the market for intercity bus service." Another possible definition was "the market for intercity transportation, including personal cars, car rentals, passenger trains, and commuter air flights." Which definition do you think the bus companies preferred, and why?

4. As a result of globalization and new information and communications technology, would you expect that the definitions of markets that antitrust authorities use will become broader or narrower?

5. Why would a firm choose to use one or more of the anticompetitive practices described in Regulating Anticompetitive Behavior?

6. Urban transit systems, especially those with rail systems, typically experience significant economies of scale in operation. Consider the transit system data in Table 11.4. Note that the quantity is in millions of riders.

| Demand: | Quantity | 1 | 2 | 3 | 4 | 5 | 6 | 7 | 8 | 9 | 10 |
|---|---|---|---|---|---|---|---|---|---|---|---|
| | Price | 10 | 9 | 8 | 7 | 6 | 5 | 4 | 3 | 2 | 1 |
| | Marginal Revenue | 10 | 8 | 6 | 4 | 2 | 0 | −2 | −4 | −6 | −8 |
| Costs: | Marginal Cost | 9 | 6 | 5 | 3 | 2 | 3 | 4 | 5 | 7 | 10 |
| | Average Cost | 9 | 7.5 | 6.7 | 5.8 | 5 | 4.7 | 4.6 | 4.6 | 4.9 | 5.4 |

**TABLE 11.4**

Draw the demand, marginal revenue, marginal cost, and average cost curves. Do they have the normal shapes?

7. From the graph you drew to answer Exercise 11.6, would you say this transit system is a natural monopoly? Justify.

Use the following information to answer the next three questions. In the years before wireless phones, when telephone technology required having a wire running to every home, it seemed plausible that telephone service had diminishing average costs and might require regulation like a natural monopoly. For most of the twentieth century, the national U.S. phone company was AT&T, and the company functioned as a regulated monopoly. Think about the deregulation of the U.S. telecommunications industry that has occurred over the last few decades. (This is not a research assignment, but a thought assignment based on what you have learned in this chapter.)

8. What real-world changes made the deregulation possible?

9. What are some of the benefits of the deregulation?

10. What might some of the negatives of deregulation be?

## Review Questions

11. What is a corporate merger? What is an acquisition?

12. What is the goal of antitrust policies?

13. How do we measure a four-firm concentration ratio? What does a high measure mean about the extent of competition?

14. How do we measure a Herfindahl-Hirschman Index? What does a low measure mean about the extent of competition?

15. Why can it be difficult to decide what a "market" is for purposes of measuring competition?

16. What is a minimum resale price maintenance agreement? How might it reduce competition and when might it be acceptable?

17. What is exclusive dealing? How might it reduce competition and when might it be acceptable?

18. What is a tie-in sale? How might it reduce competition and when might it be acceptable?

19. What is predatory pricing? How might it reduce competition, and why might it be difficult to tell when it should be illegal?

20. If public utilities are a natural monopoly, what would be the danger in deregulating them?

21. If public utilities are a natural monopoly, what would be the danger in splitting them into a number of separate competing firms?

22. What is cost-plus regulation?

23. What is price cap regulation?

24. What is deregulation? Name some industries that have been deregulated in the United States.

25. What is regulatory capture?

26. Why does regulatory capture reduce the persuasiveness of the case for regulating industries for the benefit of consumers?

## Critical Thinking Questions

27. Does either the four-firm concentration ratio or the HHI directly measure the amount of competition in an industry? Why or why not?

28. What would be evidence of serious competition between firms in an industry? Can you identify two highly competitive industries?

29. Can you think of any examples of successful predatory pricing in the real world?

30. If you were developing a product (like a web browser) for a market with significant barriers to entry, how would you try to get your product into the market successfully?

31. In the middle of the twentieth century, major U.S. cities had multiple competing city bus companies. Today, there is usually only one and it runs as a subsidized, regulated monopoly. What do you suppose caused the change?

32. Why are urban areas willing to subsidize urban transit systems? Does the argument for subsidies make sense to you?

33. Deregulation, like all changes in government policy, always has pluses and minuses. What do you think some of the minuses might be for airline deregulation?

34. Do you think it is possible for government to outlaw everything that businesses could do wrong? If so, why does government not do that? If not, how can regulation stay ahead of rogue businesses that push the limits of the system until it breaks?

# Problems

**35**.  Use Table 11.5 to calculate the four-firm concentration ratio for the U.S. auto market. Does this indicate a concentrated market or not?

| GM | 19% |
|---|---|
| Ford | 17% |
| Toyota | 14% |
| Chrysler | 11% |

**TABLE 11.5 Global Auto Manufacturers with Top Four U.S. Market Share, June 2013** (Source: http://www.zacks.com/commentary/27690/auto-industry-stock-outlook-june-2013)

**36**.  Use Table 11.5 and Table 11.6 to calculate the Herfindahl-Hirschman Index for the U.S. auto market. Would the FTC approve a merger between GM and Ford?

| Honda | 10% |
|---|---|
| Nissan | 7% |
| Hyundai | 5% |
| Kia | 4% |
| Subaru | 3% |
| Volkswagen | 3% |

**TABLE 11.6 Global Auto Manufacturers with additional U.S. Market Share, June 2013** (Source: http://www.zacks.com/commentary/27690/auto-industry-stock-outlook-june-2013)

Use Table 11.4 to answer the following questions.

**37.** If the transit system were allowed to operate as an unregulated monopoly, what output would it supply and what price would it charge?

**38.** If the transit system were regulated to operate with no subsidy (i.e., at zero economic profit), what approximate output would it supply and what approximate price would it charge?

**39.** If the transit system were regulated to provide the most allocatively efficient quantity of output, what output would it supply and what price would it charge? What subsidy would be necessary to ensure this efficient provision of transit services?

# Environmental Protection and Negative Externalities

FIGURE 12.1 **Environmental Debate** Across the country, countless people have protested, even risking arrest, against the Keystone XL Pipeline. (Credit: modification of "People Risk Arrest at State Department Office in Boston Protesting Keystone XL Pipeline" by NoKXL/Flickr, CC BY 2.0)

## CHAPTER OBJECTIVES

In this chapter, you will learn about:

- The Economics of Pollution
- Command-and-Control Regulation
- Market-Oriented Environmental Tools
- The Benefits and Costs of U.S. Environmental Laws
- International Environmental Issues
- The Tradeoff between Economic Output and Environmental Protection

# Introduction to Environmental Protection and Negative Externalities

 **BRING IT HOME**

### Keystone XL

You might have heard about Keystone XL in the news. It was a pipeline system designed to bring oil from Canada to the refineries near the Gulf of Mexico, as well as to boost crude oil production in the United States. While a private company, TransCanada, planned to build and own the pipeline, U.S. government approval was required because of its size and location. There were four phases in plans to build the pipeline, and the first two of these had been in operation.

Sounds like a great idea, right? A pipeline that would move much needed crude oil to the Gulf refineries would increase oil production for manufacturing needs, reduce price pressure at the gas pump, and increase overall economic growth. Supporters argued that the pipeline would be one of the safest pipelines built yet, and would reduce America's dependence on politically vulnerable Middle Eastern oil imports.

Not so fast, said its critics. The Keystone XL would be constructed over an enormous aquifer (one of the largest in the world) in the Midwest, and through an environmentally fragile area in Nebraska, causing great concern among environmentalists about possible destruction to the natural surroundings. They argued that leaks could taint valuable water sources and pipeline construction could disrupt and even harm indigenous species. Environmentalist groups fought government approval of the proposed pipeline construction, and in November 2015, the Obama administration refused to grant the cross-border permit necessary to build the Keystone XL pipeline. In 2017, the Trump administration sought to grant the necessary cross-border permit, and legal challenges emerged. In 2021, President Biden, on his first day in office, canceled the cross-border permit, effectively ending (for now) the Keystone XL pipeline.

Environmental concerns matter when discussing issues related to economic growth. However, how much should economists factor in these issues when deciding policy? In the case of the pipeline, how do we know how much damage it would cause when we do not know how to put a value on the environment? Would the pipeline's benefits outweigh the opportunity cost? The issue of how to balance economic progress with unintended effects on our planet is the subject of this chapter.

---

In 1969, the Cuyahoga River in Ohio was so polluted that it spontaneously burst into flame. Air pollution was so bad at that time that Chattanooga, Tennessee was a city where, as an article from *Sports Illustrated* put it: "the death rate from tuberculosis was double that of the rest of Tennessee and triple that of the rest of the United States, a city in which the filth in the air was so bad it melted nylon stockings off women's legs, in which executives kept supplies of clean white shirts in their offices so they could change when a shirt became too gray to be presentable, in which headlights were turned on at high noon because the sun was eclipsed by the gunk in the sky."

The problem of pollution arises for every economy in the world, whether high-income or low-income, and whether market-oriented or command-oriented. Every country needs to strike some balance between production and environmental quality. This chapter begins by discussing how firms may fail to take certain social costs, like pollution, into their planning if they do not need to pay these costs. Traditionally, policies for environmental protection have focused on governmental limits on how much of each pollutant could be emitted. While this approach has had some success, economists have suggested a range of more flexible, market-oriented policies that reduce pollution at a lower cost. We will consider both approaches, but first let's see how economists frame and analyze these issues.

## 12.1 The Economics of Pollution

**LEARNING OBJECTIVES**

By the end of this section, you will be able to:
- Explain and give examples of positive and negative externalities
- Identify equilibrium price and quantity
- Evaluate how firms can contribute to market failure

From 1970 to 2020, the U.S. population increased by 63 percent, and the size of the U.S. economy increased by more than 3.8-fold. Since the 1970s, however, the United States, using a variety of anti-pollution policies, has made genuine progress against a number of pollutants. Table 12.1 lists the change in carbon dioxide emissions by energy users (from residential to industrial) according to the U.S. Energy Information Administration (EIA). The table shows that emissions of certain key air pollutants declined substantially from 2007 to 2012. They dropped 740 million metric tons (MMT) a year—a 12% reduction. This seems to indicate that there has been progress made in the United States in reducing overall carbon dioxide emissions, which contribute to the greenhouse effect.

| Year | Coal | Natural Gas | Petroleum | Total |
|---|---|---|---|---|
| 1973 | 1,221 | 1,175 | 2,325 | 4,721 |
| 2007 | 2,171 | 1,245 | 2,587 | 6,016 |
| 2020 | 875 | 1,648 | 2,042 | 4,576 |

**TABLE 12.1** Carbon Dioxide Emissions from Energy Consumption, by Source (Source: EIA Monthly Energy Review)

Despite the gradual reduction in emissions from fossil fuels, many important environmental issues remain. Along with the still high levels of air and water pollution, other issues include hazardous waste disposal, destruction of wetlands and other wildlife habitats, and the impact on human health from pollution.

## Externalities

Private markets, such as the cell phone industry, offer an efficient way to put buyers and sellers together and determine what goods they produce, how they produce them and who gets them. The principle that voluntary exchange benefits both buyers and sellers is a fundamental building block of the economic way of thinking. However, what happens when a voluntary exchange affects a third party who is neither the buyer nor the seller?

As an example, consider a concert producer who wants to build an outdoor arena that will host country music concerts a half-mile from your neighborhood. You will be able to hear these outdoor concerts while sitting on your back porch—or perhaps even in your dining room. In this case, the sellers and buyers of concert tickets may both be quite satisfied with their voluntary exchange, but you have no voice in their market transaction. The effect of a market exchange on a third party who is outside or "external" to the exchange is called an **externality**. Because externalities that occur in market transactions affect other parties beyond those involved, they are sometimes called **spillovers**.

Externalities can be negative or positive. If you hate country music, then having it waft into your house every night would be a **negative externality**. If you love country music, then what amounts to a series of free concerts would be a **positive externality**.

## Pollution as a Negative Externality

Pollution is a negative externality. Economists illustrate the **social costs** of production with a demand and supply diagram. The social costs include the private costs of production that a company incurs and the external costs of pollution that pass on to society. Figure 12.2 shows the demand and supply for manufacturing refrigerators. The demand curve (D) shows the quantity demanded at each price. The supply curve ($S_{private}$) shows the quantity of refrigerators that all firms in the industry supply at each price assuming they are taking only their private costs into account and they are allowed to emit pollution at zero cost. The market equilibrium ($E_0$), where quantity supplied equals quantity demanded, is at a price of $650 per refrigerator and a quantity of 45,000 refrigerators. Table 12.2 reflects this information in the first three columns.

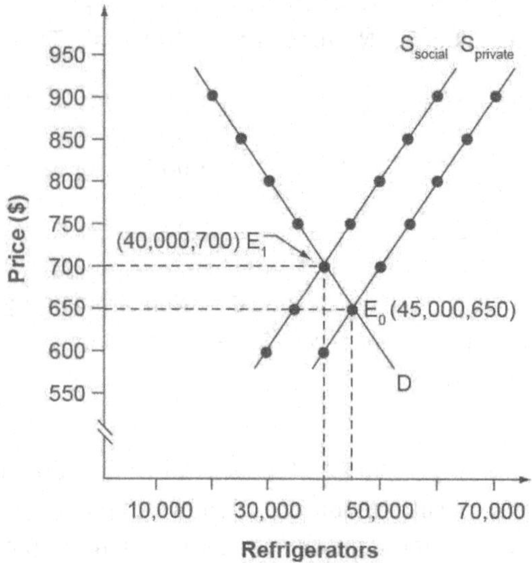


**FIGURE 12.2 Taking Social Costs into Account: A Supply Shift** If the firm takes only its own costs of production into account, then its supply curve will be $S_{private}$, and the market equilibrium will occur at $E_0$. Accounting for additional external costs of $100 for every unit produced, the firm's supply curve will be $S_{social}$. The new equilibrium will occur at $E_1$.

| Price | Quantity Demanded | Quantity Supplied before Considering Pollution Cost | Quantity Supplied after Considering Pollution Cost |
|---|---|---|---|
| $600 | 50,000 | 40,000 | 30,000 |
| $650 | 45,000 | 45,000 | 35,000 |
| $700 | 40,000 | 50,000 | 40,000 |
| $750 | 35,000 | 55,000 | 45,000 |
| $800 | 30,000 | 60,000 | 50,000 |
| $850 | 25,000 | 65,000 | 55,000 |
| $900 | 20,000 | 70,000 | 60,000 |

**TABLE 12.2 A Supply Shift Caused by Pollution Costs**

However, as a by-product of the metals, plastics, chemicals and energy that refrigerator manufacturers use, some pollution is created. Let's say that, if these pollutants were emitted into the air and water, they would create costs of $100 per refrigerator produced. These costs might occur because of adverse effects on human health, property values, or wildlife habitat, reduction of recreation possibilities, or because of other negative impacts. In a market with no anti-pollution restrictions, firms can dispose of certain wastes absolutely free. Now imagine that firms which produce refrigerators must factor in these external costs of pollution—that is, the firms have to consider not only labor and material costs, but also the broader costs to society of harm to health and other costs caused by pollution. If the firm is required to pay $100 for the **additional external costs** of pollution each time it produces a refrigerator, production becomes more costly and the entire supply curve shifts up by $100.

As Table 12.2 and Figure 12.2 illustrate, the firm will need to receive a price of $700 per refrigerator and produce a quantity of 40,000—and the firm's new supply curve will be $S_{social}$. The new equilibrium will occur at

$E_1$. In short, taking the additional external costs of pollution into account results in a higher price, a lower quantity of production, and a lower quantity of pollution. The following Work It Out feature will walk you through an example, this time with musical accompaniment.

## WORK IT OUT

### Identifying the Equilibrium Price and Quantity

Table 12.3 shows the supply and demand conditions for a firm that will play trumpets on the streets when requested. We measure output as the number of songs played.

| Price | Quantity Demanded | Quantity Supplied without paying the costs of the externality | Quantity Supplied after paying the costs of the externality |
|---|---|---|---|
| $20 | 0 | 10 | 8 |
| $18 | 1 | 9 | 7 |
| $15 | 2.5 | 7.5 | 5.5 |
| $12 | 4 | 6 | 4 |
| $10 | 5 | 5 | 3 |
| $5 | 7.5 | 2.5 | 0.5 |

**TABLE 12.3 Supply and Demand Conditions for a Trumpet-Playing Firm**

Step 1. Determine the negative externality in this situation. To do this, you must think about the situation and consider all parties that might be impacted. A negative externality might be the increase in noise pollution in the area where the firm is playing.

Step 2. Identify the initial equilibrium price and quantity only taking private costs into account. Next, identify the new equilibrium taking into account social costs as well as private costs. Remember that equilibrium is where the quantity demanded is equal to the quantity supplied.

Step 3. Look down the columns to where the quantity demanded (the second column) is equal to the "quantity supplied without paying the costs of the externality" (the third column). Then refer to the first column of that row to determine the equilibrium price. In this case, the equilibrium price and quantity would be at a price of $10 and a quantity of five when we only take into account private costs.

Step 4. Identify the equilibrium price and quantity when we take into account the additional external costs. Look down the columns of quantity demanded (the second column) and the "quantity supplied after paying the costs of the externality" (the fourth column) then refer to the first column of that row to determine the equilibrium price. In this case, the equilibrium will be at a price of $12 and a quantity of four.

Step 5. Consider how taking into account the externality affects the equilibrium price and quantity. Do this by comparing the two equilibrium situations. If the firm is forced to pay its additional external costs, then production of trumpet songs becomes more costly, and the supply curve will shift up.

Remember that the supply curve is based on choices about production that firms make while looking at their marginal costs, while the demand curve is based on the benefits that individuals perceive while maximizing utility. If no externalities existed, private costs would be the same as the costs to society as a whole, and private benefits would be the same as the benefits to society as a whole. Thus, if no externalities existed, the interaction of demand and supply will coordinate social costs and benefits.

However, when the externality of pollution exists, the supply curve no longer represents all social costs. Because externalities represent a case where markets no longer consider all social costs, but only some of them, economists commonly refer to externalities as an example of **market failure**. When there is market failure, the private market fails to achieve efficient output, because either firms do not account for all costs incurred in the production of output and/or consumers do not account for all benefits obtained (a positive externality). In the case of pollution, at the market output, social costs of production exceed social benefits to consumers, and the market produces too much of the product.

We can see a general lesson here. If firms were required to pay the social costs of pollution, they would create less pollution but produce less of the product and charge a higher price. In the next module, we will explore how governments require firms to account for the social costs of pollution.

## 12.2 Command-and-Control Regulation

**LEARNING OBJECTIVES**

By the end of this section, you will be able to:

- Explain command-and-control regulation
- Evaluate the effectiveness of command-and-control regulation

When the United States started passing comprehensive environmental laws in the late 1960s and early 1970s, a typical law specified to companies how much pollution their smokestacks or drainpipes could emit and imposed penalties if companies exceeded the limit. Other laws required that companies install certain equipment—for example, on automobile tailpipes or on smokestacks—to reduce pollution. These types of laws, which specify allowable quantities of pollution and which also may detail which pollution-control technologies companies must use, fall under the category of **command-and-control regulation**. In effect, command-and-control regulation requires that firms increase their costs by installing anti-pollution equipment. Thus, firms are required to account for the social costs of pollution in deciding how much output to produce.

Command-and-control regulation has been highly successful in protecting and cleaning up the U.S. environment. In 1970, the Federal government created the Environmental Protection Agency (EPA) to oversee all environmental laws. In the same year, Congress enacted the Clean Air Act to address air pollution. Just two years later, in 1972, Congress passed and the president signed the far-reaching Clean Water Act. These command-and-control environmental laws, and their amendments and updates, have been largely responsible for America's cleaner air and water in recent decades. However, economists have pointed out three difficulties with command-and-control environmental regulation.

First, command-and-control regulation offers no incentive to improve the quality of the environment beyond the standard set by a particular law. Once firms meet the standard, polluters have zero incentive to do better.

Second, command-and-control regulation is inflexible. It usually requires the same standard for all polluters, and often the same pollution-control technology as well. This means that command-and-control regulation draws no distinctions between firms that would find it easy and inexpensive to meet the pollution standard—or to reduce pollution even further—and firms that might find it difficult and costly to meet the standard. Firms have no reason to rethink their production methods in fundamental ways that might reduce pollution even more and at lower cost.

Third, legislators and EPA analysts write the command-and-control regulations, and so they are subject to compromises in the political process. Existing firms often argue (and lobby) that stricter environmental standards should not apply to them, only to new firms that wish to start production. Consequently, real-world environmental laws are full of fine print, loopholes, and exceptions.

Although critics accept the goal of reducing pollution, they question whether command-and-control regulation is the best way to design policy tools for accomplishing that goal. A different approach is the use of market-oriented tools, which we discussed in the next section.

## 12.3 Market-Oriented Environmental Tools

**LEARNING OBJECTIVES**

By the end of this section, you will be able to:
- Show how pollution charges impact firm decisions
- Suggest other laws and regulations that could fall under pollution charges
- Explain the significance of marketable permits and property rights
- Evaluate which policies are most appropriate for various situations

Market-oriented environmental policies create incentives to allow firms some flexibility in reducing pollution. The three main categories of market-oriented approaches to pollution control are pollution charges, marketable permits, and better-defined property rights. All of these policy tools which we discuss, below, address the shortcomings of command-and-control regulation—albeit in different ways.

### Pollution Charges

A **pollution charge** is a tax imposed on the quantity of pollution that a firm emits. A pollution charge gives a profit-maximizing firm an incentive to determine ways to reduce its emissions—as long as the marginal cost of reducing the emissions is less than the tax.

For example, consider a small firm that emits 50 pounds per year of small particles, such as soot, into the air. This particulate matter causes respiratory illnesses and also imposes costs on firms and individuals.

Figure 12.3 illustrates the marginal costs that a firm faces in reducing pollution. The marginal cost of pollution reduction, like most marginal cost curves, increases with output, at least in the short run. Reducing the first 10 pounds of particulate emissions costs the firm $300. Reducing the second 10 pounds would cost $500; reducing the third ten pounds would cost $900; reducing the fourth 10 pounds would cost $1,500; and the fifth 10 pounds would cost $2,500. This pattern for the costs of reducing pollution is common, because the firm can use the cheapest and easiest method to make initial reductions in pollution, but additional reductions in pollution become more expensive.

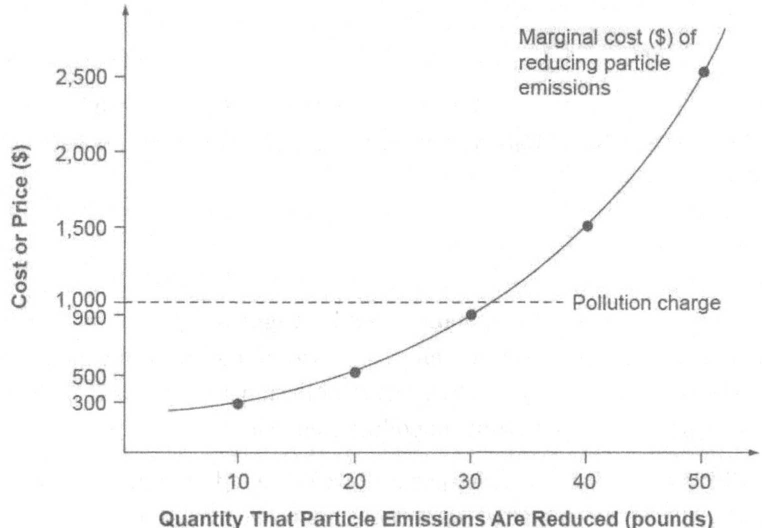


**FIGURE 12.3 A Pollution Charge** If a pollution charge is set equal to $1,000, then the firm will have an incentive to reduce pollution by 30 pounds because the $900 cost of these reductions would be less than the cost of paying the pollution charge.

Imagine the firm now faces a pollution tax of $1,000 for every 10 pounds of particulates it emits. The firm has the choice of either polluting and paying the tax, or reducing the amount of particulates it emits and paying the cost of abatement as the figure shows. How much will the firm pollute and how much will the firm abate? The first 10 pounds would cost the firm $300 to abate. This is substantially less than the $1,000 tax, so the firm will choose to abate. The second 10 pounds would cost $500 to abate, which is still less than the tax, so it will choose to abate. The third 10 pounds would cost $900 to abate, which is slightly less than the $1,000 tax. The fourth 10 pounds would cost $1,500, which is much more costly than paying the tax. As a result, the firm will decide to reduce pollutants by 30 pounds, because the marginal cost of reducing pollution by this amount is less than the pollution tax. With a tax of $1,000, the firm has no incentive to reduce pollution more than 30 pounds.

A firm that has to pay a pollution tax will have an incentive to figure out the least expensive technologies for reducing pollution. Firms that can reduce pollution cheaply and easily will do so to minimize their pollution taxes; whereas firms that will incur high costs for reducing pollution will end up paying the pollution tax instead. If the pollution tax applies to every source of pollution, then there are no special favoritism or loopholes for politically well-connected producers.

For an example of a pollution charge at the household level, consider two ways of charging for garbage collection. One method is to have a flat fee per household, no matter how much garbage a household produces. An alternative approach is to have several levels of fees, depending on how much garbage the household produces—and to offer lower or free charges for recyclable materials. As of 2006 (latest statistics available), the EPA had recorded over 7,000 communities that have implemented "pay as you throw" programs. When people have a financial incentive to put out less garbage and to increase recycling, they find ways to make it happen.

A number of environmental policies are really pollution charges, although they often do not travel under that name. For example, the federal government and many state governments impose taxes on gasoline. We can view this tax as a charge on the air pollution that cars generate as well as a source of funding for maintaining roads. Gasoline taxes are far higher in most other countries than in the United States.

Similarly, the refundable charge of five or 10 cents that only 10 states have for returning recyclable cans and bottles works like a pollution tax that provides an incentive to avoid littering or throwing bottles in the trash. Compared with command-and-control regulation, a pollution tax reduces pollution in a more flexible and cost-effective way.

### 🔗 LINK IT UP

Visit this website (http://openstax.org/l/bottlebill) to see the current U.S. states with bottle bills and the states that have active campaigns for new bottle bills. You can also view current and proposed bills in Canada and other countries around the world.

---

## Marketable Permits

When a city or state government sets up a **marketable permit program** (e.g., cap-and-trade), it must start by determining the overall quantity of pollution it will allow as it tries to meet national pollution standards. Then, it divides a number of permits allowing only this quantity of pollution among the firms that emit that pollutant. The government can sell or provide these permits to pollute free to firms.

Now, add two more conditions. Imagine that these permits are designed to reduce total emissions over time. For example, a permit may allow emission of 10 units of pollution one year, but only nine units the next year, then eight units the year after that, and so on down to some lower level. In addition, imagine that these are marketable permits, meaning that firms can buy and sell them.

To see how marketable permits can work to reduce pollution, consider the four firms in Table 12.4. The table shows current emissions of lead from each firm. At the start of the marketable permit program, each firm receives permits to allow this level of pollution. However, these permits are shrinkable, and next year the permits allow the firms to emit only half as much pollution. Let's say that in a year, Firm Gamma finds it easy and cheap to reduce emissions from 600 tons of lead to 200 tons, which means that it has permits that it is not using that allow emitting 100 tons of lead. Firm Beta reduces its lead pollution from 400 tons to 200 tons, so it does not need to buy any permits, and it does not have any extra permits to sell. However, although Firm Alpha can easily reduce pollution from 200 tons to 150 tons, it finds that it is cheaper to purchase permits from Gamma rather than to reduce its own emissions to 100. Meanwhile, Firm Delta did not even exist in the first period, so the only way it can start production is to purchase permits to emit 50 tons of lead.

The total quantity of pollution will decline. However, buying and selling the marketable permits will determine exactly which firms reduce pollution and by how much. With a system of marketable permits, the firms that find it least expensive to do so will reduce pollution the most.

|  | Firm Alpha | Firm Beta | Firm Gamma | Firm Delta |
|---|---|---|---|---|
| Current emissions—permits distributed free for this amount | 200 tons | 400 tons | 600 tons | 0 tons |
| How much pollution will these permits allow in one year? | 100 tons | 200 tons | 300 tons | 0 tons |
| Actual emissions one year in the future | 150 tons | 200 tons | 200 tons | 50 tons |
| Buyer or seller of marketable permit? | Buys permits for 50 tons | Doesn't buy or sell permits | Sells permits for 100 tons | Buys permits for 50 tons |

**TABLE 12.4 How Marketable Permits Work**

Another application of marketable permits occurred when the U.S. government amended the Clean Air Act in 1990. The revised law sought to reduce sulfur dioxide emissions from electric power plants to half of the 1980 levels out of concern that sulfur dioxide was causing acid rain, which harms forests as well as buildings. In this case, the marketable permits the federal government issued were free of charge (no pun intended) to electricity-generating plants across the country, especially those that were burning coal (which produces sulfur dioxide). These permits were of the "shrinkable" type; that is, the amount of pollution allowed by a given permit declined with time.

## Better-Defined Property Rights

A clarified and strengthened idea of property rights can also strike a balance between economic activity and pollution. Ronald Coase (1910–2013), who won the 1991 Nobel Prize in economics, offered a vivid illustration of an externality: a railroad track running beside a farmer's field where the railroad locomotive sometimes emits sparks and sets the field ablaze. Coase asked whose responsibility it was to address this spillover. Should the farmer be required to build a tall fence alongside the field to block the sparks, or should the railroad be required to place a gadget on the locomotive's smokestack to reduce the number of sparks?

Coase pointed out that one cannot resolve this issue until one clearly defines **property rights**—that is, the legal rights of ownership on which others are not allowed to infringe without paying compensation. Does the farmer have a property right not to have a field burned? Does the railroad have a property right to run its own trains on its own tracks? If neither party has a property right, then the two sides may squabble endlessly, doing nothing, and sparks will continue to set the field aflame. However, if either the farmer or the railroad has a well-defined legal responsibility, then that party will seek out and pay for the least costly method of reducing the risk that sparks will hit the field. The property right determines whether the farmer or the railroad pays the bills.

The property rights approach is highly relevant in cases involving endangered species. The U.S. government's endangered species list includes about 1,000 plants and animals, and about 90% of these species live on privately owned land. The protection of these endangered species requires careful thinking about incentives and property rights. The discovery of an endangered species on private land has often triggered an automatic reaction from the government to prohibit the landowner from using that land for any purpose that might disturb the imperiled creatures. Consider the incentives of that policy: If you admit to the government that you have an endangered species, the government effectively prohibits you from using your land. As a result, rumors abounded of landowners who followed a policy of "shoot, shovel, and shut up" when they found an endangered animal on their land. Other landowners have deliberately cut trees or managed land in a way that they knew would discourage endangered animals from locating there.

 **CLEAR IT UP**

### How effective are market-oriented environmental policy tools?

Environmentalists sometimes fear that market-oriented environmental tools are an excuse to weaken or eliminate strict limits on pollution emissions and instead to allow more pollution. It is true that if pollution charges are set very low or if marketable permits do not reduce pollution by very much then market-oriented tools will not work well. However, command-and-control environmental laws can also be full of loopholes or have exemptions that do not reduce pollution by much, either. The advantage of market-oriented environmental tools is not that they reduce pollution by more or less, but because of their incentives and flexibility, they can achieve any desired reduction in pollution at a lower cost to society.

A more productive policy would consider how to provide private landowners with an incentive to protect the endangered species that they find and to provide a habitat for additional endangered species. For example, the government might pay landowners who provide and maintain suitable habitats for endangered species or who restrict the use of their land to protect an endangered species. Again, an environmental law built on incentives and flexibility offers greater promise than a command-and-control approach when trying to oversee millions of acres of privately owned land.

### Applying Market-Oriented Environmental Tools

Market-oriented environmental policies are a tool kit. Specific policy tools will work better in some situations than in others. For example, marketable permits work best when a few dozen or a few hundred parties are highly interested in trading, as in the cases of oil refineries that trade lead permits or electrical utilities that trade sulfur dioxide permits. However, for cases in which millions of users emit small amounts of pollution—such as emissions from car engines or unrecycled soda cans—and have no strong interest in trading, pollution charges will typically offer a better choice. We can also combine market-oriented environmental tools. We can view marketable permits as a form of improved property rights. Alternatively, the government could combine marketable permits with a pollution tax on any emissions not covered by a permit.

## 12.4 The Benefits and Costs of U.S. Environmental Laws

**LEARNING OBJECTIVES**

By the end of this section, you will be able to:
- Evaluate the benefits and costs of environmental protection
- Explain the effects of ecotourism
- Apply marginal analysis to illustrate the marginal costs and marginal benefits of reducing pollution

Government economists have estimated that U.S. firms may pay more than $200 billion per year to comply with federal environmental laws. That is a sizable amount of money. Is the money well spent?

## Benefits and Costs of Clean Air and Clean Water

We can divide the benefits of a cleaner environment into four areas: (1) people may stay healthier and live longer; (2) certain industries that rely on clean air and water, such as farming, fishing, and tourism, may benefit; (3) property values may be higher; and (4) people may simply enjoy a cleaner environment in a way that does not need to involve a market transaction. Some of these benefits, such as gains to tourism or farming, are relatively easy to value in economic terms. It is harder to assign a monetary value to others, such as the value of clean air for someone with asthma. It seems difficult to put a clear-cut monetary value on still others, such as the satisfaction you might feel from knowing that the air is clear over the Grand Canyon, even if you have never visited the Grand Canyon, but advanced techniques in economics allow one to generate estimates.

Although estimates of environmental benefits are not precise, they can still be revealing. For example, a study by the Environmental Protection Agency looked at the costs and benefits of the Clean Air Act from 1970 to 1990. It found that total costs over that time period were roughly $500 billion—a huge amount. However, it also found that a middle-range estimate of the health and other benefits from cleaner air was $22 trillion—about 44 times higher than the costs. A more recent EPA study estimated that the environmental benefits to Americans from the Clean Air Act will exceed their costs by a margin of four to one. The EPA estimated that "in 2010 the benefits of Clean Air Act programs will total about $110 billion. This estimate represents the value of avoiding increases in illness and premature death which would have prevailed." Saying that overall benefits of environmental regulation have exceeded costs in the past, however, is very different from saying that every environmental regulation makes sense. For example, studies suggest that when breaking down emission reductions by type of contaminants, the benefits of air pollution control outweigh the costs primarily for particulates and lead, but when looking at other air pollutants, the costs of reducing them may be comparable to or greater than the benefits. Just because some environmental regulations have had benefits much higher than costs does not prove that every individual regulation is a sensible idea.

## Ecotourism: Making Environmentalism Pay

The definition of ecotourism is a little vague. Does it mean sleeping on the ground, eating roots, and getting close to wild animals? Does it mean flying in a helicopter to shoot anesthetic darts at African wildlife, or a little of both? The definition may be fuzzy, but tourists who hope to appreciate the ecology of their destination—"eco tourists"—are the impetus to a big and growing business. The International Ecotourism Society estimates that international tourists interested in seeing nature or wildlife would take 1.56 billion trips by 2020. While COVID-19 prevented this from happening in 2020, it is clear that there is a strong demand for ecotourism.

## 🔗 LINK IT UP

Visit The International Ecotourism Society's website (http://openstax.org/l/ecotourism) to learn more about The International Ecotourism Society, its programs, and tourism's role in sustainable community development.

---

Realizing the attraction of ecotourism, the residents of low-income countries may come to see that preserving wildlife habitats is more lucrative than, say, cutting down forests or grazing livestock. In South Africa, Namibia, and Zimbabwe, for example, ecotourism has given local communities an economic interest in protecting elephant and rhinoceros populations. Some of the leading ecotourism destinations include Costa Rica and Panama in Central America; the Caribbean; Malaysia, and other South Pacific destinations; New Zealand; the Serengeti in Tanzania; the Amazon rain forests; and the Galapagos Islands. In many of these countries and regions, governments have enacted policies whereby they share revenues from ecotourism with local communities, to give people in those local communities a kind of property right that encourages them to conserve their local environment.

Ecotourism needs careful management, so that the combination of eager tourists and local entrepreneurs does not destroy what the visitors are coming to see. And recent research indicates that wild animals that are continually exposed to tourists and vehicles exhibit stress and atypical behaviors. In general, however, well-managed ecotourism is viewed as a net positive, which provides an alternative to damaging the local environment.

## Marginal Benefits and Marginal Costs

We can use the tools of marginal analysis to illustrate the marginal costs and the marginal benefits of reducing pollution. Figure 12.4 illustrates a theoretical model of this situation. When the quantity of environmental protection is low so that pollution is extensive—for example, at quantity Qa—there are usually numerous relatively cheap and easy ways to reduce pollution, and the marginal benefits of doing so are quite high. At Qa, it makes sense to allocate more resources to fight pollution. However, as the extent of environmental protection increases, the cheap and easy ways of reducing pollution begin to decrease, and one must use more costly methods. The marginal cost curve rises. Also, as environmental protection increases, one achieves the largest marginal benefits first, followed by reduced marginal benefits. As the quantity of environmental protection increases to, say, Qb, the gap between marginal benefits and marginal costs narrows. At point Qc the marginal costs will exceed the marginal benefits. At this level of environmental protection, society is not allocating resources efficiently, because it is forfeiting too many resources to reduce pollution.

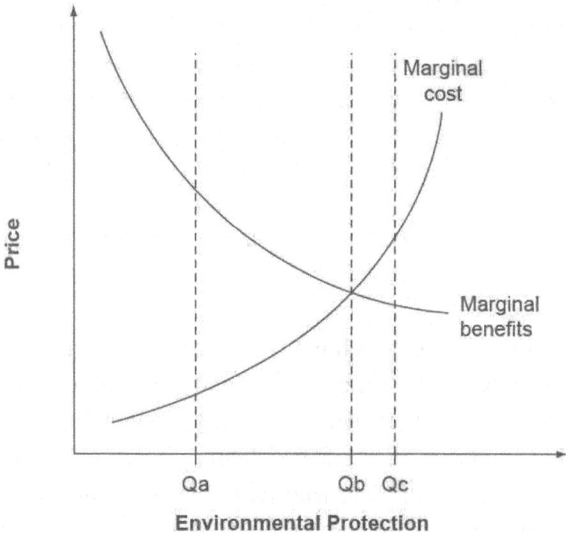


**FIGURE 12.4 Marginal Costs and Marginal Benefits of Environmental Protection** Reducing pollution is costly—one must sacrifice resources. The marginal costs of reducing pollution are generally increasing, because one can first make the least expensive and easiest reductions, leaving the more expensive methods for later. The marginal benefits of reducing pollution are generally declining, because one can take the steps that provide the greatest benefit first, and steps that provide less benefit can wait until later.

As society draws closer to Qb, some might argue that it becomes more important to use market-oriented environmental tools to hold down the costs of reducing pollution. Their objective would be to avoid environmental rules that would provide the quantity of environmental protection at Qc, where marginal costs exceed marginal benefits. The following Clear It Up feature delves into how the EPA measures its policies – and the monetary value of our lives.

 **CLEAR IT UP**

### What's a life worth?

The U.S. Environmental Protection Agency (EPA) must estimate the value of saving lives by reducing pollution against the additional costs. In measuring the benefits of government environmental policies, the EPA's National

Center for Environmental Economics (NCEE) values a statistical human life at $7.4 million (in 2006 U.S. dollars, which corresponds to a little more than $10.5 million in February 2022.)

Economists value a human life on the basis of studies of the value that people actually place on human lives in their own decisions. For example, some jobs have a higher probability of death than others, and these jobs typically pay more to compensate for the risk. Examples are ocean fishery as opposed to fish farming, and ice trucking in Alaska as opposed to truck driving in the "lower forty-eight" states.

Government regulators use estimates such as these when deciding what proposed regulations are "reasonable," which means deciding which proposals have high enough benefits to justify their cost. For example, when the U.S. Department of Transportation makes decisions about what safety systems should be required in cars or airplanes, it will approve rules only where the estimated cost per life saved is $3 million or less.

Resources that we spend on life-saving regulations create a tradeoff. A study by W. Kip Viscusi of Vanderbilt University estimated that when a regulation costs $50 million, it diverts enough spending in the rest of the economy from health care and safety expenditures that it costs a life. This finding suggests that any regulation that costs more than $50 million per life saved actually costs lives, rather than saving them.

---

### References

Ryan, Dave. "New Report Shows Benefits of 1990 Clean Air Amendments Outweigh Costs by Four-to-One Margin," press release, November 16, 1999. *United States Environmental Protection Agency.* Accessed December 19, 2013. http://www.epa.gov/oar/sect812/r-140.html.

National Center for Environmental Economics (NCEE). "Frequently Asked Questions on Mortality Risk Valuation." *United States Environmental Protection Agency.* Accessed December 19, 2013. http://yosemite.epa.gov/ee/epa/eed.nsf/pages/MortalityRiskValuation.html#whatvalue World Tourism Organization, "Tourism 2020 Vision." Accessed December 19, 2013. http://www.world-tourism.org/market_research/facts/market_trends.htm.

Viscusi, Kip W. *Fatal Tradeoffs: Public and Private Responsibilities for Risk.* New York: Oxford University Press, 1995.

## 12.5 International Environmental Issues

**LEARNING OBJECTIVES**

By the end of this section, you will be able to:

- Explain biodiversity
- Analyze the partnership of high-income and low-income countries in efforts to address international externalities

Many countries around the world have become more aware of the benefits of environmental protection. Yet even if most nations individually took steps to address their environmental issues, no nation acting alone can solve certain environmental problems which spill over national borders. No nation by itself can reduce emissions of carbon dioxide and other gases by enough to solve the problem of global warming—not without the cooperation of other nations. Another issue is the challenge of preserving **biodiversity**, which includes the full spectrum of animal and plant genetic material. Although a nation can protect biodiversity within its own borders, no nation acting alone can protect biodiversity around the world. Global warming and biodiversity are examples of **international externalities**.

Bringing the nations of the world together to address environmental issues requires a difficult set of negotiations between countries with different income levels and different sets of priorities. If nations such as China, India, Brazil, Mexico, and others are developing their economies by burning vast amounts of fossil fuels or by stripping their forest and wildlife habitats, then the world's high-income countries acting alone will not be able to reduce greenhouse gases. However, low-income countries, with some understandable exasperation, point out that high-income countries do not have much moral standing to lecture them on the necessities of putting environmental protection ahead of economic growth. After all, high-income countries have historically been the primary contributors to greenhouse warming by burning **fossil fuels**—and still are today. It is hard to tell people who are living in a low-income country, where adequate diet, health care, and education are lacking, that they should sacrifice an improved quality of life for a cleaner environment.

Can rich and poor countries come together to address global environmental spillovers? At the initiative of the European Union and the most vulnerable developing nations, the Durban climate conference in December 2011 launched negotiations to develop a new international climate change agreement that covers all countries. The outcome of these negotiations was the Paris Climate Agreement, passed in 2015. The Paris Agreement committed participating countries to significant limits on $CO_2$ emissions. To date, 196 entities have signed on, including the two biggest emitters of greenhouse gases—China and the United States. The U.S. contribution to the agreement was the Clean Power Plan, which planned to reduce power plant $CO_2$ emissions across the U.S. by 17% to pre-2005 levels by 2020, and to further reduce emissions by a cumulative 32% by 2030. In early 2017, the Trump Administration announced plans to back out of the Paris Climate Agreement. Trump opposed the Clean Power plan, opting instead to shift focus to the use of natural gas. This represented a significant blow to the success of the Paris Agreement. However, on his first day in office, President Biden, on behalf of the United States, rejoined the Paris Climate Agreement.

## 🔗 LINK IT UP

Visit this website (http://openstax.org/l/EC) to learn more about the European Commission.

---

If high-income countries want low-income countries to reduce their emission of greenhouse gases, then the high-income countries may need to pay some of the costs. Perhaps some of these payments will happen through private markets. For example, some tourists from rich countries will pay handsomely to vacation near the natural treasures of low-income countries. Perhaps some of the transfer of resources can happen through making modern pollution-control technology available to poorer countries.

The practical details of what such an international system might look like and how it would operate across international borders are forbiddingly complex. However, it seems highly unlikely that some form of world government will impose a detailed system of environmental command-and-control regulation around the world. As a result, a decentralized and market-oriented approach may be the only practical way to address international issues such as global warming and biodiversity.

## 12.6 The Tradeoff between Economic Output and Environmental Protection

### LEARNING OBJECTIVES

By the end of this section, you will be able to:
- Apply the production possibility frontier to evaluate the tradeoff between economic output and the environment
- Interpret a graphic representation of the tradeoff between economic output and environmental protection

We can analyze the tradeoff between economic output and the environment with a production possibility frontier (PPF) such as the one in Figure 12.5. At one extreme, at a choice like P, a country would be selecting a high level of economic output but very little environmental protection. At the other extreme, at a choice like T, a country would be selecting a high level of environmental protection but little economic output. According to the graph, an increase in environmental protection involves an opportunity cost of less economic output. No matter what their preferences, all societies should wish to avoid choices like M, which are productively inefficient. Efficiency requires that the choice should be on the production possibility frontier.

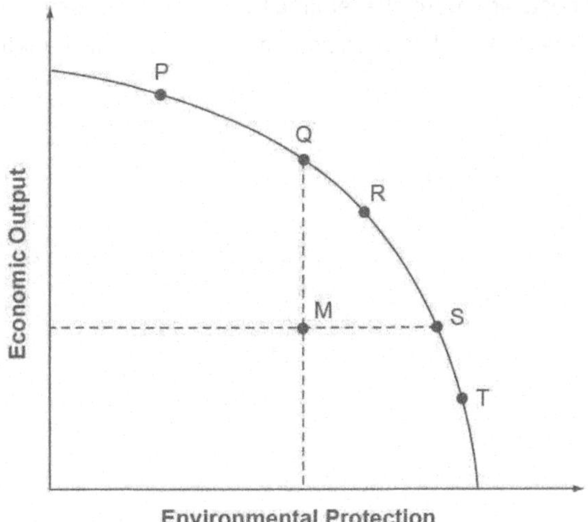


**FIGURE 12.5 The Tradeoff between Economic Output and Environmental Protection** Each society will have to weigh its own values and decide whether it prefers a choice like P with more economic output and less environmental protection, or a choice like T with more environmental protection and less economic output.

Economists do not have a great deal to say about the choice between P, Q, R, S and T in Figure 12.5, all of which lie along the production possibility frontier. Countries with low per capita gross domestic product (GDP), such as India, place a greater emphasis on economic output—which in turn helps to produce nutrition, shelter, health, education, and desirable consumer goods. Countries with higher income levels, where a greater share of people have access to the basic necessities of life, may be willing to place a relatively greater emphasis on environmental protection.

However, economists are united in their belief that an inefficient choice such as M is undesirable. Rather than choosing M, a nation could achieve either greater economic output with the same environmental protection, as at point Q, or greater environmental protection with the same level of output, as at point S. The problem with command-and-control environmental laws is that they sometimes involve a choice like M. Market-oriented environmental tools offer a mechanism for providing either the same environmental protection at lower cost, or providing a greater degree of environmental protection for the same cost.

 **BRING IT HOME**

### Keystone XL

How would an economist respond to claims of environmental damage caused by the Keystone XL project? Clearly, we can consider the environmental cost of oil spills a negative externality, but how large would these external costs be? Furthermore, are these costs "too high" when we measure them against any potential for economic benefit?

As this chapter indicates, in deciding whether pipeline construction is a good idea, an economist would want to know not only about the marginal benefits resulting from the additional pipeline construction, but also the potential marginal costs—and especially the pipeline's marginal external costs. Typically these come in the form of environmental impact statements, which are usually required for such projects. For example, an impact statement, released in March 2013 by the Nebraska Department of State, considered the possibility of fewer pipeline miles going over the aquifer system and avoiding completely environmentally fragile areas. It indicated that pipeline construction would not harm "most resources".

As noted at the outset of this chapter, the Obama Administration declined to approve construction of the Keystone XL project. However, the Trump administration announced its willingness to do so, but as noted earlier, the Biden administration effectively ended the project. While we may fairly easily quantify the economic benefits of additional oil in the United States, the social costs are more challenging to measure. Consequently, different observers may reach different conclusions about the balance between estimates of economic benefits and estimates of the social costs of the pipeline project.

---

## Key Terms

**additional external cost** additional costs incurred by third parties outside the production process when a unit of output is produced

**biodiversity** the full spectrum of animal and plant genetic material

**command-and-control regulation** laws that specify allowable quantities of pollution and that also may detail which pollution-control technologies one must use

**externality** a market exchange that affects a third party who is outside or "external" to the exchange; sometimes called a "spillover"

**international externalities** externalities that cross national borders and that a single nation acting alone cannot resolve

**market failure** When the market on its own does not allocate resources efficiently in a way that balances social costs and benefits; externalities are one example of a market failure

**marketable permit program** a permit that allows a firm to emit a certain amount of pollution; firms with more permits than pollution can sell the remaining permits to other firms

**negative externality** a situation where a third party, outside the transaction, suffers from a market transaction by others

**pollution charge** a tax imposed on the quantity of pollution that a firm emits; also called a pollution tax

**positive externality** a situation where a third party, outside the transaction, benefits from a market transaction by others

**property rights** the legal rights of ownership on which others are not allowed to infringe without paying compensation

**social costs** costs that include both the private costs incurred by firms and also additional costs incurred by third parties outside the production process, like costs of pollution

**spillover** see externality

## Key Concepts and Summary

### 12.1 The Economics of Pollution

Economic production can cause environmental damage. This tradeoff arises for all countries, whether high-income or low-income, and whether their economies are market-oriented or command-oriented.

An externality occurs when an exchange between a buyer and seller has an impact on a third party who is not part of the exchange. An externality, which is sometimes also called a spillover, can have a negative or a positive impact on the third party. If those parties imposing a negative externality on others had to account for the broader social cost of their behavior, they would have an incentive to reduce the production of whatever is causing the negative externality. In the case of a positive externality, the third party obtains benefits from the exchange between a buyer and a seller, but they are not paying for these benefits. If this is the case, then markets would tend to under produce output because suppliers are not aware of the additional demand from others. If the parties generating benefits to others would somehow receive compensation for these external benefits, they would have an incentive to increase production of whatever is causing the positive externality.

### 12.2 Command-and-Control Regulation

Command-and-control regulation sets specific limits for pollution emissions and/or specific pollution-control technologies that firms must use. Although such regulations have helped to protect the environment, they have three shortcomings: they provide no incentive for going beyond the limits they set; they offer limited flexibility on where and how to reduce pollution; and they often have politically-motivated loopholes.

### 12.3 Market-Oriented Environmental Tools

Examples of market-oriented environmental policies, also called cap and trade programs, include pollution charges, marketable permits, and better-defined property rights. Market-oriented environmental policies include taxes, markets, and property rights so that those who impose negative externalities must face the social cost.

## 12.4 The Benefits and Costs of U.S. Environmental Laws

We can make a strong case, taken as a whole, that the benefits of U.S. environmental regulation have outweighed the costs. As the extent of environment regulation increases, additional expenditures on environmental protection will probably have increasing marginal costs and decreasing marginal benefits. This pattern suggests that the flexibility and cost savings of market-oriented environmental policies will become more important.

## 12.5 International Environmental Issues

Certain global environmental issues, such as global warming and biodiversity, spill over national borders and require addressing with some form of international agreement.

## 12.6 The Tradeoff between Economic Output and Environmental Protection

Depending on their different income levels and political preferences, countries are likely to make different choices about allocative efficiency—that is, the choice between economic output and environmental protection along the production possibility frontier. However, all countries should prefer to make a choice that shows productive efficiency—that is, the choice is somewhere on the production possibility frontier rather than inside it. Revisit Choice in a World of Scarcity for more on these terms.

# Self-Check Questions

1. Identify the following situations as an example of a negative or a positive externality:
   a. You are a birder (bird watcher), and your neighbor has put up several birdhouses in the yard as well as planting trees and flowers that attract birds.
   b. Your neighbor paints his house a hideous color.
   c. Investments in private education raise your country's standard of living.
   d. Trash dumped upstream flows downstream right past your home.
   e. Your roommate is a smoker, but you are a nonsmoker.

2. Identify whether the market supply curve will shift right or left or will stay the same for the following:
   a. Firms in an industry are required to pay a fine for their carbon dioxide emissions.
   b. Companies are sued for polluting the water in a river.
   c. Power plants in a specific city are not required to address the impact of their air quality emissions.
   d. Companies that use fracking to remove oil and gas from rock are required to clean up the damage.

3. For each of your answers to Exercise 12.2, will equilibrium price rise or fall or stay the same?

4. Table 12.5 provides the supply and demand conditions for a manufacturing firm. The third column represents a supply curve without accounting for the social cost of pollution. The fourth column represents the supply curve when the firm is required to account for the social cost of pollution. Identify the equilibrium before the social cost of production is included and after the social cost of production is included.

| Price | Quantity Demanded | Quantity Supplied without paying the cost of the pollution | Quantity Supplied after paying the cost of the pollution |
|---|---|---|---|
| $10 | 450 | 400 | 250 |
| $15 | 440 | 440 | 290 |
| $20 | 430 | 480 | 330 |
| $25 | 420 | 520 | 370 |
| $30 | 410 | 560 | 410 |

**TABLE 12.5**

5. Consider two approaches to reducing emissions of $CO_2$ into the environment from manufacturing industries in the United States. In the first approach, the U.S. government makes it a policy to use only predetermined technologies. In the second approach, the U.S. government determines which technologies are cleaner and subsidizes their use. Of the two approaches, which is the command-and-control policy?

6. Classify the following pollution-control policies as command-and-control or market incentive based.
   a.  A state emissions tax on the quantity of carbon emitted by each firm.
   b.  The federal government requires domestic auto companies to improve car emissions by 2020.
   c.  The EPA sets national standards for water quality.
   d.  A city sells permits to firms that allow them to emit a specified quantity of pollution.
   e.  The federal government pays fishermen to preserve salmon.

7. An emissions tax on a quantity of emissions from a firm is not a command-and-control approach to reducing pollution. Why?

8. Four firms called Elm, Maple, Oak, and Cherry, produce wooden chairs. However, they also produce a great deal of garbage (a mixture of glue, varnish, sandpaper, and wood scraps). The first row of Table 12.6 shows the total amount of garbage (in tons) that each firm currently produces. The other rows of the table show the cost of reducing garbage produced by the first five tons, the second five tons, and so on. First, calculate the cost of requiring each firm to reduce the weight of its garbage by one-fourth. Now, imagine that the government issues marketable permits for the current level of garbage, but the permits will shrink the weight of allowable garbage for each firm by one-fourth. What will be the result of this alternative approach to reducing pollution?

| | Elm | Maple | Oak | Cherry |
|---|---|---|---|---|
| Current production of garbage (in tons) | 20 | 40 | 60 | 80 |
| Cost of reducing garbage by first five tons | $5,500 | $6,300 | $7,200 | $3,000 |
| Cost of reducing garbage by second five tons | $6,000 | $7,200 | $7,500 | $4,000 |
| Cost of reducing garbage by third five tons | $6,500 | $8,100 | $7,800 | $5,000 |
| Cost of reducing garbage by fourth five tons | $7,000 | $9,000 | $8,100 | $6,000 |
| Cost of reducing garbage by fifth five tons | $0 | $9,900 | $8,400 | $7,000 |

**TABLE 12.6**

9. The rows in Table 12.7 show three market-oriented tools for reducing pollution. The columns of the table show three complaints about command-and-control regulation. Fill in the table by stating briefly how each market-oriented tool addresses each of the three concerns.

| | Incentives to Go Beyond | Flexibility about Where and How Pollution Will Be Reduced | Political Process Creates Loopholes and Exceptions |
|---|---|---|---|
| Pollution Charges | | | |
| Marketable Permits | | | |
| Property Rights | | | |

**TABLE 12.7**

10. Suppose a city releases 16 million gallons of raw sewage into a nearby lake. Table 12.8 shows the total costs of cleaning up the sewage to different levels, together with the total benefits of doing so. (Benefits include environmental, recreational, health, and industrial benefits.)

|  | Total Cost (in thousands of dollars) | Total Benefits (in thousands of dollars) |
|---|---|---|
| 16 million gallons | Current situation | Current situation |
| 12 million gallons | 50 | 800 |
| 8 million gallons | 150 | 1300 |
| 4 million gallons | 500 | 1650 |
| 0 gallons | 1200 | 1900 |

**TABLE 12.8**

a. Using the information in Table 12.8, calculate the marginal costs and marginal benefits of reducing sewage emissions for this city. See Production, Costs and Industry Structure if you need a refresher on how to calculate marginal costs.
b. What is the optimal level of sewage for this city?
c. Why not just pass a law that firms can emit zero sewage? After all, the total benefits of zero emissions exceed the total costs.

11. The state of Colorado requires oil and gas companies who use fracking techniques to return the land to its original condition after the oil and gas extractions. Table 12.9 shows the total cost and total benefits (in dollars) of this policy.

| Land Restored (in acres) | Total Cost | Total Benefit |
|---|---|---|
| 0 | $0 | $0 |
| 100 | $20 | $140 |
| 200 | $80 | $240 |
| 300 | $160 | $320 |
| 400 | $280 | $380 |

**TABLE 12.9**

a. Calculate the marginal cost and the marginal benefit at each quantity (acre) of land restored. See Production, Costs and Industry Structure if you need a refresher on how to calculate marginal costs and benefits.
b. If we apply marginal analysis, what is the optimal amount of land to be restored?

12. Consider the case of global environmental problems that spill across international borders as a prisoner's dilemma of the sort studied in Monopolistic Competition and Oligopoly. Say that there are two countries, A and B. Each country can choose whether to protect the environment, at a cost of 10, or not to protect it, at a cost of zero. If one country decides to protect the environment, there is a benefit of 16, but the benefit is divided equally between the two countries. If both countries decide to protect the environment, there is a benefit of 32, which is divided equally between the two countries.

    a.   In Table 12.10, fill in the costs, benefits, and total payoffs to the countries of the following decisions. Explain why, without some international agreement, they are likely to end up with neither country acting to protect the environment.

|  |  | Country B | |
| --- | --- | --- | --- |
|  |  | Protect | Not Protect |
| **Country A** | Protect |  |  |
|  | Not Protect |  |  |

**TABLE 12.10**

13. A country called Sherwood is very heavily covered with a forest of 50,000 trees. There are proposals to clear some of Sherwood's forest and grow corn, but obtaining this additional economic output will have an environmental cost from reducing the number of trees. Table 12.11 shows possible combinations of economic output and environmental protection.

| *Combos* | **Corn Bushels (thousands)** | **Number of Trees (thousands)** |
| --- | --- | --- |
| **P** | 9 | 5 |
| **Q** | 2 | 30 |
| **R** | 7 | 20 |
| **S** | 2 | 40 |
| **T** | 6 | 10 |

**TABLE 12.11**

    a.   Sketch a graph of a production possibility frontier with environmental quality on the horizontal axis, measured by the number of trees, and the quantity of economic output, measured in corn, on the vertical axis.
    b.   Which choices display productive efficiency? How can you tell?
    c.   Which choices show allocative efficiency? How can you tell?
    d.   In the choice between T and R, decide which one is better. Why?
    e.   In the choice between T and S, can you say which one is better, and why?
    f.   If you had to guess, which choice would you think is more likely to represent a command-and-control environmental policy and which choice is more likely to represent a market-oriented environmental policy, choice Q or S? Why?

## Review Questions

**14.** What is an externality?

**15.** Give an example of a positive externality and an example of a negative externality.

**16.** What is the difference between private costs and social costs?

**17.** In a market without environmental regulations, will the supply curve for a firm account for private costs, external costs, both, or neither? Explain.

**18.** What is command-and-control environmental regulation?

**19.** What are the three problems that economists have noted with regard to command-and-control regulation?

**20.** What is a pollution charge and what incentive does it provide for a firm to take external costs into account?

**21.** What is a marketable permit and what incentive does it provide for a firm to account for external costs?

**22.** What are better-defined property rights and what incentive do they provide to account for external costs?

**23.** As the extent of environmental protection expands, would you expect marginal costs of environmental protection to rise or fall? Why or why not?

**24.** As the extent of environmental protection expands, would you expect the marginal benefits of environmental protection to rise or fall? Why or why not?

**25.** What are the economic tradeoffs between low-income and high-income countries in international conferences on global environmental damage?

**26.** What arguments do low-income countries make in international discussions of global environmental clean-up?

**27.** In the tradeoff between economic output and environmental protection, what do the combinations on the protection possibility curve represent?

**28.** What does a point inside the production possibility frontier represent?

## Critical Thinking Questions

**29.** Suppose you want to put a dollar value on the external costs of carbon emissions from a power plant. What information or data would you obtain to measure the external [not social] cost?

**30.** Would environmentalists favor command-and-control policies as a way to reduce pollution? Why or why not?

**31.** Consider two ways of protecting elephants from poachers in African countries. In one approach, the government sets up enormous national parks that have sufficient habitat for elephants to thrive and forbids all local people to enter the parks or to injure either the elephants or their habitat in any way. In a second approach, the government sets up national parks and designates 10 villages around the edges of the park as official tourist centers that become places where tourists can stay and bases for guided tours inside the national park. Consider the different incentives of local villagers—who often are living in poverty—in each of these plans. Which plan seems more likely to help the elephant population?

**32.** Will a system of marketable permits work with thousands of firms? Why or why not?

**33.** Is zero pollution possible under a marketable permits system? Why or why not?

**34.** Is zero pollution an optimal goal? Why or why not?

**35.** From an economic perspective, is it sound policy to pursue a goal of zero pollution? Why or why not?

**36.** Recycling is a relatively inexpensive solution to much of the environmental contamination from plastics, glass, and other waste materials. Is it a sound policy to make it mandatory for everybody to recycle?

**37.** Can extreme levels of pollution hurt the economic development of a high-income country? Why or why not?

**38.** How can high-income countries benefit from covering much of the cost of reducing pollution created by low-income countries?

**39.** Technological innovations shift the production possibility curve. Look at graph you sketched for Exercise 12.13. Which types of technologies should a country promote? Should "clean" technologies be promoted over other technologies? Why or why not?

## Problems

**40.** Show the market for cigarettes in equilibrium, assuming that there are no laws banning smoking in public. Label the equilibrium private market price and quantity as Pm and Qm. Add whatever is needed to the model to show the impact of the negative externality from second-hand smoking. (Hint: In this case it is the consumers, not the sellers, who are creating the negative externality.) Label the socially optimal output and price as Pe and Qe. On the graph, shade in the deadweight loss at the market output.

**41.** Refer to Table 12.2. The externality created by the refrigerator production was $100. However, once we accounted for both the private and additional external costs, the market price increased by only $50. If the external costs were $100 why did the price only increase by $50 when we accounted for all costs?

**42.** Table 12.12 shows the supply and demand conditions for a firm that will play trumpets on the streets when requested. $Qs_1$ is the quantity supplied without social costs. $Qs_2$ is the quantity supplied with social costs. What is the negative externality in this situation? Identify the equilibrium price and quantity when we account only for private costs, and then when we account for social costs. How does accounting for the externality affect the equilibrium price and quantity?

| P | Qd | $Qs_1$ | $Qs_2$ |
|---|---|---|---|
| $20 | 0 | 10 | 8 |
| $18 | 1 | 9 | 7 |
| $15 | 2.5 | 7.5 | 5.5 |
| $12 | 4 | 6 | 4 |
| $10 | 5 | 5 | 3 |
| $5 | 7.5 | 2.5 | 0.5 |

**TABLE 12.12**

**43.** A city currently emits 16 million gallons (MG) of raw sewage into a lake that is beside the city. Table 12.13 shows the total costs (TC) in thousands of dollars of cleaning up the sewage to different levels, together with the total benefits (TB) of doing so. Benefits include environmental, recreational, health, and industrial benefits.

|        | TC      | TB      |
|--------|---------|---------|
| 16 MG  | Current | Current |
| 12 MG  | 50      | 800     |
| 8 MG   | 150     | 1300    |
| 4 MG   | 500     | 1850    |
| 0 MG   | 1200    | 2000    |

**TABLE 12.13**

a. Using the information in Table 12.13, calculate the marginal costs and marginal benefits of reducing sewage emissions for this city.
b. What is the optimal level of sewage for this city? How can you tell?

**44.** In the Land of Purity, there is only one form of pollution, called "gunk." Table 12.14 shows possible combinations of economic output and reduction of gunk, depending on what kinds of environmental regulations you choose.

| *Combos* | Eco Output | Gunk Cleaned Up |
|----------|------------|-----------------|
| **J**    | 800        | 10%             |
| **K**    | 500        | 30%             |
| **L**    | 600        | 40%             |
| **M**    | 400        | 40%             |
| **N**    | 100        | 90%             |

**TABLE 12.14**

a. Sketch a graph of a production possibility frontier with environmental quality on the horizontal axis, measured by the percentage reduction of gunk, and with the quantity of economic output on the vertical axis.
b. Which choices display productive efficiency? How can you tell?
c. Which choices show allocative efficiency? How can you tell?
d. In the choice between K and L, can you say which one is better and why?
e. In the choice between K and N, can you say which one is better, and why?
f. If you had to guess, which choice would you think is more likely to represent a command-and-control environmental policy and which choice is more likely to represent a market-oriented environmental policy, choice L or M? Why?

# Positive Externalities and Public Goods

**FIGURE 13.1 View from Voyager I (http://openstax.org/l/voyager1)** Launched by NASA on September 5, 1977, Voyager I's primary mission was to provide detailed images of Jupiter, Saturn, and their moons. It took this photograph of Jupiter on its journey. In August of 2012, Voyager I entered interstellar space—the first human-made object to do so—and it is expected to send data and images back to earth until 2025. Such a technological feat entails many economic principles. (Credit: modification of "Voyager's View of Jupiter's Great Red Spot" by NASA/ JPL, Public Domain)

**CHAPTER OBJECTIVES**

In this chapter, you will learn about:

- Why the Private Sector Underinvests in Technologies
- How Governments Can Encourage Innovation
- Public Goods

## Introduction to Positive Externalities and Public Goods

 **BRING IT HOME**

### The Benefits of Voyager I Endure

The rapid growth of technology has increased our ability to access and process data, to navigate through a busy city, and to communicate with friends on the other side of the globe. The research and development efforts of citizens, scientists, firms, universities, and governments have truly revolutionized the modern economy. To get a sense of how far we have come in a short period of time, let's compare one of humankind's greatest achievements to the smartphone.

In 1977 the United States launched Voyager I, a spacecraft originally intended to reach Jupiter and Saturn, to send back photographs and other cosmic measurements. Voyager I, however, kept going, and going—past Jupiter and Saturn—right out of our solar system. At the time of its launch, Voyager had some of the most sophisticated computing processing power NASA could engineer (8,000 instructions per second), but today, we Earthlings use handheld devices that can process 14 billion instructions per second.

Still, the technology of today is a spillover product of the incredible feats NASA accomplished over forty years ago. NASA research, for instance, is responsible for the kidney dialysis and mammogram machines that we use today. Research in new technologies not only produces private benefits to the investing firm, or in this case to NASA, but it also creates benefits for the broader society. In this way, new knowledge often becomes what economists refer to as a public good. This leads us to the topic of this chapter—technology, positive externalities, public goods, and the role of government in encouraging innovation and the social benefits that it provides.

As economist Mariana Mazzucato explores in her well-known work *The Entrepreneurial State*, what makes a smartphone smart? What allows its apps to help you navigate new towns while getting updates about your home, all while your hands are on the steering wheel and your children are in the back seat watching their shows? For starters, the internet, cell tower networks, GPS, and voice activation. Each of these, and many other technologies we rely on, were developed with intensive government support. For example, GPS, which enables many cell phone functions beyond the frequently used mapping and ride-sharing applications, was developed by the U.S. Department of Defense over several generations of satellite tracking and complex computer algorithm development. The U.S. government still provides GPS for many of the world's users.

We do not often think of the government when we consider our leading products and entrepreneurs. We think of Apple, Google, Lyft, Tesla, Fitbit, and so on—creative innovators who built on the tools provided by these government efforts, using them in transformative ways. We may not think of the estimated $19 billion per year that the U.S. spends to maintain the GPS system, but we would certainly think of it if it suddenly went away. (Beyond the impact on our daily lives, economists estimate U.S. businesses alone would lose about $1 billion per day without GPS.)

Mazzucato is one of several prominent economists advocating for an embrace of continued government-sponsored innovations in order to build economic prosperity, reduce inequality, and manage ongoing challenges such as drought, coastal changes, and extreme weather. She argues that competitive, private sector markets are often resistant to the risks involved with large-scale innovation, because failed experiments and lack of uptake lead to massive corporate and personal losses. Governments can take on riskier research and development projects. Because government spending is fueled by taxpayers, and all innovation leads to some level of employment change, these proposals are certainly complex and challenging to implement.

This chapter deals with some of these issues: Will private companies be willing to invest in new technology? In what ways does new technology have positive externalities? What motivates inventors? What role should government play in encouraging research and technology? Are there certain types of goods that markets fail to provide efficiently, and that only government can produce? What happens when consumption or production of a product creates positive externalities? Why is it unsurprising when we overuse a common resource, like marine fisheries?

## 13.1 Investments in Innovation

**LEARNING OBJECTIVES**

By the end of this section, you will be able to:

- Identify the positive externalities of new technology.
- Explain the difference between private benefits and social benefits and give examples of each.
- Calculate and analyze rates of return

Market competition can provide an incentive for discovering new technology because a firm can earn higher profits by finding a way to produce products more cheaply or to create products with characteristics consumers want. As Gregory Lee, CEO of Samsung said, "Relentless pursuit of new innovation is the key principle of our business and enables consumers to discover a world of possibilities with technology." An innovative firm knows that it will usually have a temporary edge over its competitors and thus an ability to earn above-normal profits before competitors can catch up.

In certain cases, however, competition can discourage new technology, especially when other firms can quickly copy a new idea. Consider a pharmaceutical firm deciding to develop a new drug. On average, it can cost $800 million and take more than a decade to discover a new drug, perform the necessary safety tests, and bring the drug to market. If the research and development (R&D) effort fails—and every R&D project has some chance of failure—then the firm will suffer losses and could even be driven out of business. If the project succeeds, then the firm's competitors may figure out ways of adapting and copying the underlying idea, but without having to pay the costs themselves. As a result, the innovative company will bear the much higher costs of the R&D and will enjoy at best only a small, temporary advantage over the competition.

Many inventors over the years have discovered that their inventions brought them less profit than they might have reasonably expected.

- Eli Whitney (1765–1825) invented the cotton gin, but then southern cotton planters built their own seed-separating devices with a few minor changes in Whitney's design. When Whitney sued, he found that the courts in southern states would not uphold his patent rights.
- Thomas Edison (1847–1931) still holds the record for most patents granted to an individual. His first invention was an automatic vote counter, and despite the social benefits, he could not find a government that wanted to buy it.
- Gordon Gould came up with the idea behind the laser in 1957. He put off applying for a patent and, by the time he did apply, other scientists had laser inventions of their own. A lengthy legal battle resulted, in which Gould spent $100,000 on lawyers, before he eventually received a patent for the laser in 1977. Compared to the enormous social benefits of the laser, Gould received relatively little financial reward.
- In 1936, Alan Turing delivered a paper titled, "On Computable Numbers, with an Application to the Entscheidungsproblem," in which he presented the notion of a universal machine (later called the "Universal Turing Machine," and then the "Turing machine") capable of computing anything that is computable. The central concept of the modern computer was based on Turing's paper. Today scholars widely consider Turing as the father of theoretical computer science and artificial intelligence; however, the UK government prosecuted Turing in 1952 for engaging in same-sex sexual acts and gave him the choice of chemical castration or prison. Turing chose castration and died in 1954 from cyanide poisoning.

A variety of studies by economists have found that the original inventor receives one-third to one-half of the total economic benefits from innovations, while other businesses and new product users receive the rest.

## The Positive Externalities of New Technology

Will private firms in a market economy underinvest in research and technology? If a firm builds a factory or buys a piece of equipment, the firm receives all the economic benefits that result from the investments. However, when a firm invests in new technology, the **private benefits**, or profits, that the firm receives are only a portion of the overall social benefits. The **social benefits** of an innovation account for the value of all the positive externalities of the new idea or product, whether enjoyed by other companies or society as a whole, as well as the private benefits the firm that developed the new technology receives. As you learned in Environmental Protection and Negative Externalities, **positive externalities** are beneficial spillovers to a third party, or parties.

Consider the example of the Big Drug Company, which is planning its R&D budget for the next year. Economists and scientists working for Big Drug have compiled a list of potential research and development projects and estimated rates of return. (The rate of return is the estimated payoff from the project.) Figure 13.2 shows how the calculations work. The downward-sloping $D_{Private}$ curve represents the firm's demand for financial capital and reflects the company's willingness to borrow to finance research and development projects at various interest rates. Suppose that this firm's investment in research and development creates a spillover benefit to other firms and households. After all, new innovations often spark other creative endeavors that society also values. If we add the spillover benefits society enjoys to the firm's private demand for financial capital, we can draw $D_{Social}$ that lies above $D_{Private}$.

If there were a way for the firm to fully monopolize those social benefits by somehow making them unavailable to the rest of us, the firm's private demand curve would be the same as society's demand curve. According to Figure 13.2 and Table 13.1, if the going rate of interest on borrowing is 8%, and the company can receive the private benefits of innovation only, then the company would finance $30 million. Society, at the same rate of 8%, would find it optimal to have $52 million of borrowing. Unless there is a way for the company to fully enjoy the total benefits, then it will borrow less than the socially optimal level of $52 million.

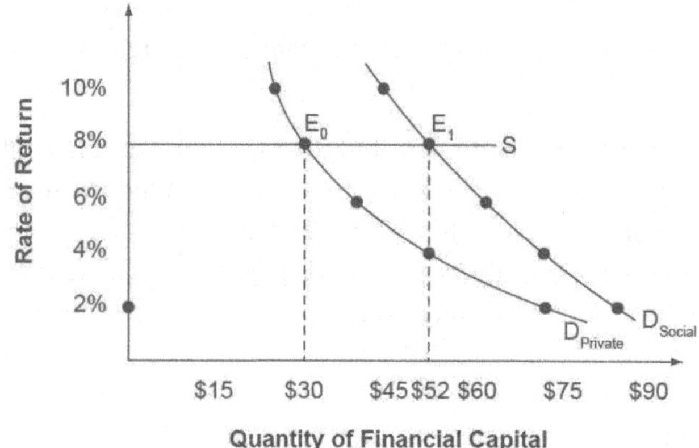


**FIGURE 13.2 Positive Externalities and Technology** Big Drug faces a cost of borrowing of 8%. If the firm receives only the private benefits of investing in R&D, then we show its demand curve for financial capital by $D_{Private}$, and the equilibrium will occur at $30 million. Because there are spillover benefits, society would find it optimal to have $52 million of investment. If the firm could keep the social benefits of its investment for itself, its demand curve for financial capital would be $D_{Social}$ and it would be willing to borrow $52 million.

| Rate of Return | $D_{Private}$ (in millions) | $D_{Social}$ (in millions) |
| --- | --- | --- |
| 2% | $72 | $84 |
| 4% | $52 | $72 |
| 6% | $38 | $62 |
| 8% | $30 | $52 |
| 10% | $26 | $44 |

**TABLE 13.1 Return and Demand for Capital**

Big Drug's original demand for financial capital ($D_{Private}$) is based on the profits the firm receives. However, other pharmaceutical firms and health care companies may learn new lessons about how to treat certain medical conditions and are then able to create their own competing products. The social benefit of the drug takes into account the value of all the drug's positive externalities. If Big Drug were able to gain this social return instead of other companies, its demand for financial capital would shift to the demand curve $D_{Social}$, and it would be willing to borrow and invest $52 million. However, if Big Drug is receiving only 50 cents of each dollar of social benefits, the firm will not spend as much on creating new products. The amount it would be willing to spend would fall somewhere in between $D_{Private}$ and $D_{Social}$.

## Why Invest in Human Capital?

The investment in anything, whether it is the construction of a new power plant or research in a new cancer treatment, usually requires a certain upfront cost with an uncertain future benefit. The investment in education, or human capital, is no different. Over the span of many years, a student and her family invest significant amounts of time and money into that student's education. The idea is that higher levels of educational attainment will eventually serve to increase the student's future productivity and subsequent ability to earn. Once the student crunches the numbers, does this investment pay off for her?

Almost universally, economists have found that the answer to this question is a clear "Yes." For example, several studies of the return to education in the United States estimate that the rate of return to a college education is approximately 10-15%. Data in Table 13.2, from the U.S. Bureau of Labor Statistics' *Usual Weekly Earnings of Wage and Salary Workers, Fourth Quarter 2021,* demonstrate that median weekly earnings are higher for workers who have completed more education. While these rates of return will beat equivalent investments in Treasury bonds or savings accounts, the estimated returns to education go primarily to the individual worker, so these returns are **private rates of return** to education.

|  | Less than a High School Degree | High School Degree, No College | Bachelor's Degree or Higher |
|---|---|---|---|
| Median Weekly Earnings (full-time workers over the age of 25) | $651 | $831 | $1,467 |

**TABLE 13.2 Usual Weekly Earnings of Wage and Salary Workers, Fourth Quarter 2021** (Source: https://www.bls.gov/news.release/pdf/wkyeng.pdf)

What does society gain from investing in the education of another student? After all, if the government is spending taxpayer dollars to subsidize public education, society should expect some kind of return on that spending. Economists like George Psacharopoulos have found that, across a variety of nations, the **social rate of return** on schooling is also positive. After all, positive externalities exist from investment in education. While not always easy to measure, according to Walter McMahon, the positive externalities to education typically include better health outcomes for the population, lower levels of crime, a cleaner environment and a more stable, democratic government. For these reasons, many nations have chosen to use taxpayer dollars to subsidize primary, secondary, and higher education. Education clearly benefits the person who receives it, but a society where most people have a good level of education provides positive externalities for all.

## Other Examples of Positive Externalities

Although technology may be the most prominent example of a positive externality, it is not the only one. For example, vaccinations against disease are not only a protection for the individual, but they have the positive spillover of protecting others who may become infected. When a number of homes in a neighborhood are modernized, updated, and restored, not only does it increase the homes' value, but other property values in the neighborhood may increase as well.

The appropriate public policy response to a positive externality, like a new technology, is to help the party creating the positive externality receive a greater share of the social benefits. In the case of vaccines, like flu shots, an effective policy might be to provide a subsidy to those who choose to get vaccinated.

Figure 13.3 shows the market for flu shots. The market demand curve $D_{Market}$ for flu shots reflects only the marginal private benefits (MPB) that the vaccinated individuals receive from the shots. Assuming that there are no spillover costs in the production of flu shots, the market supply curve is given by the marginal private cost (MPC) of producing the vaccinations.

The equilibrium quantity of flu shots produced in the market, where MPB is equal to MPC, is $Q_{Market}$ and the price of flu shots is $P_{Market}$. However, spillover benefits exist in this market because others, those who chose not to purchase a flu shot, receive a positive externality in the form of a reduced chance of contracting the flu. When we add the spillover benefits to the marginal private benefit of flu shots, the marginal social benefit (MSB) of flu shots is given by $D_{Social}$. Because the MSB is greater than MPB, we see that the socially optimal level of flu shots is greater than the market quantity ($Q_{Social}$ exceeds $Q_{Market}$) and the corresponding price of flu shots, if the market were to produce $Q_{Social}$, would be at $P_{Social}$. Unfortunately, the marketplace does not recognize the positive externality and flu shots will go under-produced and under-consumed.

How can government try to move the market level of output closer to the socially desirable level of output? One policy would be to provide a subsidy, like a voucher, to any citizen who wishes to get vaccinated. This voucher would act as "income" that one could use to purchase only a flu shot and, if the voucher were exactly equal to the per-unit spillover benefits, would increase market equilibrium to a quantity of $Q_{Social}$ and a price of $P_{Social}$ where MSB equals MSC (which equals MPC given the assumption that there are no spillover costs in producing the vaccine). Suppliers of the flu shots would receive payment of $P_{Social}$ per vaccination, while consumers of flu shots would redeem the voucher and only pay a price of $P_{Subsidy}$. When the government uses a subsidy in this way, it produces the socially optimal quantity of vaccinations.

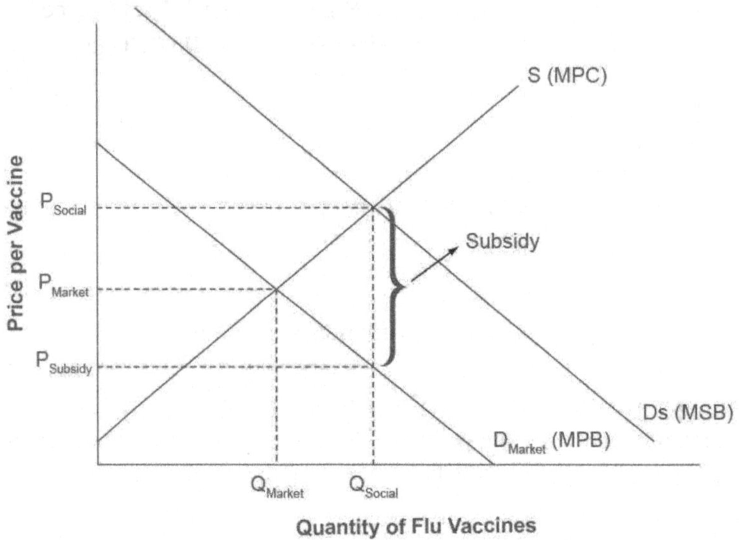


**FIGURE 13.3 The Market for Flu Shots with Spillover Benefits (A Positive Externality)** The market demand curve does not reflect the positive externality of flu vaccinations, so only $Q_{Market}$ will be exchanged. This outcome is inefficient because the marginal social benefit exceeds the marginal social cost. If the government provides a subsidy to consumers of flu shots, equal to the marginal social benefit minus the marginal private benefit, the level of vaccinations can increase to the socially optimal quantity of $Q_{Social}$.

### Societal Change as an Innovation Outcome

Economist Carlota Perez draws on the lessons of past innovations to understand the current state of our economy. She demonstrates that prior technological turning points, such as the proliferation of railroads and the emergence of mass production, created initial periods of employment and wealth shifting but eventually led to greater well-being and economic growth. After difficult transition periods and sometimes economic meltdowns during the "installment" phase of widespread new technologies, many economies and the people within them have benefited from prolonged periods of economic and lifestyle improvement, including lower unemployment and better quality of life.

Most prior innovation periods, such as the Industrial Revolution, had one significant downside: negative impacts on the environment, such as pollution and habitat destruction. Perez notes that our current revolution—in information and communications technology (ICT)—has the potential for significant positive externalities related to the environment. ICT is shifting many areas of society (and therefore industry) to digital experiences and services that do not require fossil fuels or similar natural resources. Vehicle sharing, product rental-reuse networks, and new manufacturing methods offer the promise of far less consumable consumption. And even though the appearance of delivery trucks and shipping boxes gives the impression of environmental damage, most studies indicate that online shopping is better for the environment than individuals shopping in person. (This is partly attributed to greater efficiency in a few trucks driving to a neighborhood rather than everyone in the neighborhood driving to several stores.) Consumers and governments can spur on those environmental benefits by choosing or partnering with companies that focus on furthering their environmental impact, such as by using solar power to fuel their computer servers or by using electrically powered delivery trucks.

Like other innovations, ICT has created some employment and economic opportunities while it has reduced others. Increased globalization and efficiencies have shuttered businesses and reduced wages in some areas. Perez's research indicates that those types of employment shifts can be managed through proper regulation and investment (especially in human capital), particularly as firms in the relevant industries become mature and profitable. The prospects aren't simple: ICT has created megafirms like Amazon and Apple, which despite pleasing their consumers can wield significant power over governments and employees. But on the environmental and societal front at least, ICT has offered a wealth of opportunities and externalities.

## 13.2 How Governments Can Encourage Innovation

### LEARNING OBJECTIVES

By the end of this section, you will be able to:
- Explain the effects of intellectual property rights on social and private rates of return.
- Identify three U.S. Government policies and explain how they encourage innovation

A number of different government policies can increase the incentives to innovate, including: guaranteeing intellectual property rights, government assistance with the costs of research and development, and cooperative research ventures between universities and companies.

### Intellectual Property Rights

One way to increase new technology is to guarantee the innovator an exclusive right to that new product or process. **Intellectual property** rights include patents, which give the inventor the exclusive legal right to make, use, or sell the invention for a limited time, and copyright laws, which give the author an exclusive legal right over works of literature, music, film/video, and pictures. For example, if a pharmaceutical firm has a patent on a new drug, then no other firm can manufacture or sell that drug for 20 years, unless the firm with the patent grants permission. Without a patent, the pharmaceutical firm would have to face competition for any successful products, and could earn no more than a normal rate of profit. With a patent, a firm is able to earn monopoly profits on its product for a period of time—which offers an incentive for research and development. In general, how long can "a period of time" be? The Clear It Up discusses patent and copyright protection timeframes for some works you might know.

## CLEAR IT UP

### How long is Mickey Mouse protected from being copied?

All patents and copyrights are scheduled to end someday. In 2003, copyright protection for Mickey Mouse was scheduled to run out. Once the copyright had expired, anyone would be able to copy Mickey Mouse cartoons or draw and sell new ones. In 1998, however, Congress passed the Sonny Bono Copyright Term Extension Act. For copyrights owned by companies or other entities, it increased or extended the copyright from 75 years to 95 years after publication. For copyrights owned by individuals, it increased or extended the copyright coverage from 50 years to 70 years after death. Along with protecting Mickey for another 20 years, the copyright extension affected about 400,000 books, movies, and songs.

---

Figure 13.4 illustrates how the total number of patent applications filed with the U.S. Patent and Trademark Office, as well as the total number of patents granted, surged in the mid-1990s with the invention of the internet, and is still going strong today.

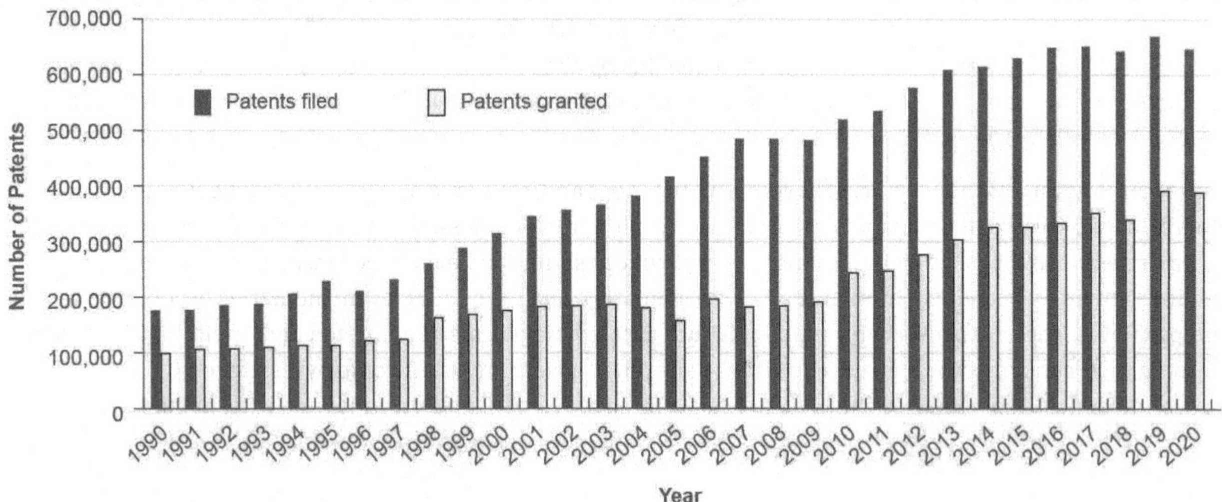


**FIGURE 13.4 Patents Filed and Granted, 1981–2012** The number of applications filed for patents increased substantially beginning in the 1990s, due in part to the invention of the internet, which has led to many other inventions and to the 1998 Copyright Term Extension Act. (Source: http://www.uspto.gov/web/offices/ac/ido/oeip/taf/us_stat.htm)

While patents provide an incentive to innovate by protecting the innovator, they are not perfect. For example:

- In countries that already have patents, economic studies show that inventors receive only one-third to one-half of the total economic value of their inventions.
- In a fast-moving high-technology industry like biotechnology or semiconductor design, patents may be almost irrelevant because technology is advancing so quickly.
- Not every new idea can be protected with a patent or a copyright—for example, a new way of organizing a factory or a new way of training employees.
- Patents may sometimes cover too much or be granted too easily. In the early 1970s, Xerox had received over 1,700 patents on various elements of the photocopy machine. Every time Xerox improved the photocopier, it received a patent on the improvement.
- The 20-year time period for a patent is somewhat arbitrary. Ideally, a patent should cover a long enough period of time for the inventor to earn a good return, but not so long that it allows the inventor to charge a monopoly price permanently.

Because patents are imperfect and do not apply well to all situations, alternative methods of improving the rate of return for inventors of new technology are desirable. The following sections describe some of these possible alternative policies.

## Policy #1: Government Spending on Research and Development

If the private sector does not have sufficient incentive to carry out research and development, one possibility is for the government to fund such work directly. Government spending can provide direct financial support for research and development (R&D) conducted at colleges and universities, nonprofit research entities, and sometimes by private firms, as well as at government-run laboratories. While government spending on research and development produces technology that is broadly available for firms to use, it costs taxpayers money and can sometimes be directed more for political than for scientific or economic reasons.

## LINK IT UP

Visit the NASA website (http://openstax.org/l/NASA) and the USDA website (http://openstax.org/l/USDA) to read about government research that would not take place were it left to firms, due to the externalities.

The first column of Table 13.3 shows the sources of total U.S. spending on research and development. The second column shows the total dollars of R&D funding by each source. The third column shows that, relative to the total amount of funding, 22.7% comes from the federal government, about 69% of R&D is done by industry, and less than 4% is done by universities and colleges. (The percentages below do not add up to exactly 100% due to rounding.)

| Sources of R&D Funding | Amount ($ billions) | Percent of the Total |
|---|---|---|
| **Federal government** | **$129.6** | **21.4%** |
| Industry | $426.0 | 70.3% |
| Universities and colleges | $20.7 | 3.4% |
| Nonprofits | $25.0 | 4.1% |
| Nonfederal government | $4.8 | 0.8% |
| Total | $606.1 | |

TABLE 13.3 U.S. Research and Development Expenditures, 2018
(Source: https://ncses.nsf.gov/pubs/nsf21324)

In the 1960s the federal government paid for about two-thirds of the nation's R&D. Over time, the U.S. economy has come to rely much more heavily on industry-funded R&D. The federal government has tried to focus its direct R&D spending on areas where private firms are not as active. One difficulty with direct government support of R&D is that it inevitably involves political decisions about which projects are worthy. The scientific question of whether research is worthwhile can easily become entangled with considerations like the location of the congressional district in which the research funding is spent.

## Policy #2: Tax Breaks for Research and Development

A complementary approach to supporting R&D that does not involve the government's close scrutiny of specific projects is to give firms a reduction in taxes depending on how much research and development they do. The federal government refers to this policy as the research and experimentation (R&E) tax credit. According to the Treasury Department: "... the R&E Credit is also a cost-effective policy for stimulating additional private sector investment. Most recent studies find that each dollar of foregone tax revenue through the R&E Tax Credit causes firms to invest at least a dollar in R&D, with some studies finding a benefit to cost ratio of 2 or 2.96."

## LINK IT UP

Visit this website (http://openstax.org/l/REtaxcredit) for more information on how the R&E Tax Credit encourages investment.

### Policy #3 Cooperative Research

State and federal governments support research in a variety of ways. For example, United for Medical Research, a coalition of groups that seek funding for the National Institutes of Health, (which is supported by federal grants), states: "NIH-supported research added $69 billion to our GDP and supported seven million jobs in 2011 alone." The United States remains the leading sponsor of medical-related research, spending $117 billion in 2011. Other institutions, such as the National Academy of Sciences and the National Academy of Engineering, receive federal grants for innovative projects. The Agriculture and Food Research Initiative (AFRI) at the United States Department of Agriculture awards federal grants to projects that apply the best science to the most important agricultural problems, from food safety to childhood obesity. Cooperation between government-funded universities, academies, and the private sector can spur product innovation and create whole new industries.

## 13.3 Public Goods

**LEARNING OBJECTIVES**

By the end of this section, you will be able to:
- Identify a public good using nonexcludable and non-rival as criteria
- Explain the free rider problem
- Identify several sources of public goods

Even though new technology creates positive externalities so that perhaps one-half or two-thirds of the social benefit of new inventions spills over to others, the inventor still receives some private return. What about a situation where the positive externalities are so extensive that private firms could not expect to receive any of the social benefit? We call this kind of good a **public good**. Spending on national defense is a good example of a public good. Let's begin by defining the characteristics of a public good and discussing why these characteristics make it difficult for private firms to supply public goods. Then we will see how government may step in to address the issue.

### The Definition of a Public Good

Economists have a strict definition of a public good, and it does not necessarily include all goods financed through taxes. To understand the defining characteristics of a public good, first consider an ordinary private good, like a piece of pizza. We can buy and sell a piece of pizza fairly easily because it is a separate and identifiable item. However, public goods are not separate and identifiable in this way.

Instead, public goods have two defining characteristics: they are nonexcludable and non-rival. The first characteristic, that a public good is **nonexcludable**, means that it is costly or impossible to exclude someone from using the good. If Larry buys a private good like a piece of pizza, then he can exclude others, like Lorna, from eating that pizza. However, if national defense is provided, then it includes everyone. Even if you strongly disagree with America's defense policies or with the level of defense spending, the national defense still protects you. You cannot choose to be unprotected, and national defense cannot protect everyone else and exclude you.

The second main characteristic of a public good, that it is **non-rival**, means that when one person uses the public good, another can also use it. With a private good like pizza, if Max is eating the pizza then Michelle cannot also eat it; that is, the two people are rivals in consumption. With a public good like national defense, Max's consumption of national defense does not reduce the amount left for Michelle, so they are non-rival in this area.

A number of government services are examples of public goods. For instance, it would not be easy to provide fire and police service so that some people in a neighborhood would be protected from the burning and burglary of their property, while others would not be protected at all. Protecting some necessarily means protecting others, too.

Positive externalities and public goods are closely related concepts. Public goods have positive externalities, like police protection or public health funding. Not all goods and services with positive externalities, however, are public goods. Investments in education have huge positive spillovers but can be provided by a private company. Private companies can invest in new inventions such as the Apple iPad and reap profits that may not capture all of the social benefits. We can also describe patents as an attempt to make new inventions into private goods, which are excludable and rivalrous, so that no one but the inventor can use them during the length of the patent.

## The Free Rider Problem of Public Goods

Private companies find it difficult to produce public goods. If a good or service is nonexcludable, like national defense, so that it is impossible or very costly to exclude people from using this good or service, then how can a firm charge people for it?

## LINK IT UP

Visit this website (http://openstax.org/l/freerider) to read about a connection between free riders and "bad music."

When individuals make decisions about buying a public good, a **free rider** problem can arise, in which people have an incentive to let others pay for the public good and then to "free ride" on the purchases of others. We can express the free rider problem in terms of the prisoner's dilemma game, which we discussed as a representation of oligopoly in Monopolistic Competition and Oligopoly.

There is a dilemma with the Prisoner's Dilemma, though. See the Work It Out feature.

## WORK IT OUT

### The Problem with the Prisoner's Dilemma

Suppose two people, Rachel and Samuel, are considering purchasing a public good. The difficulty with the prisoner's dilemma arises as each person thinks through their strategic choices.

Step 1. Rachel reasons in this way: If Samuel does not contribute, then I would be a fool to contribute. However, if Samuel does contribute, then I can come out ahead by not contributing.

Step 2. Either way, I should choose not to contribute, and instead hope that I can be a free rider who uses the public good paid for by Samuel.

Step 3. Samuel reasons the same way about Rachel.

Step 4. When both people reason in that way, the public good never gets built, and there is no movement to the option where everyone cooperates—which is actually best for all parties.

## The Role of Government in Paying for Public Goods

The key insight in paying for public goods is to find a way of assuring that everyone will make a contribution and to prevent free riders. For example, if people come together through the political process and agree to pay taxes and make group decisions about the quantity of public goods, they can defeat the free rider problem by requiring, through the law, that everyone contributes.

However, government spending and taxes are not the only way to provide public goods. In some cases, markets can produce public goods. For example, think about radio. It is nonexcludable, since once the radio signal is broadcast, it would be very difficult to stop someone from receiving it. It is non-rival, since one person listening to the signal does not prevent others from listening as well. Because of these features, it is practically impossible to charge listeners directly for listening to conventional radio broadcasts.

Radio has found a way to collect revenue by selling advertising, which is an indirect way of "charging" listeners by taking up some of their time. Ultimately, consumers who purchase the goods advertised are also paying for the radio service, since the station builds in the cost of advertising into the product cost. In a more recent development, satellite radio companies, such as SiriusXM, charge a regular subscription fee for streaming music without commercials. In this case, however, the product is excludable—only those who pay for the subscription will receive the broadcast.

Some public goods will also have a mixture of public provision at no charge along with fees for some purposes, like a public city park that is free to use, but the government charges a fee for parking your car, for reserving certain picnic grounds, and for food sold at a refreshment stand.

## 🔗 LINK IT UP

Read this article (http://openstax.org/l/governmentpay) to find out what economists say the government should pay for.

---

In other cases, we can use social pressures and personal appeals, rather than the force of law, to reduce the number of free riders and to collect resources for the public good. For example, neighbors sometimes form an association to carry out beautification projects or to patrol their area after dark to discourage crime. In low-income countries, where social pressure strongly encourages all farmers to participate, farmers in a region may come together to work on a large irrigation project that will benefit all. We can view many fundraising efforts, including raising money for local charities and for the endowments of colleges and universities, as an attempt to use social pressure to discourage free riding and to generate the outcome that will produce a public benefit.

### Common Resources and the "Tragedy of the Commons"

There are some goods that do not fall neatly into the categories of private good or public good. While it is easy to classify a pizza as a private good and a city park as a public good, what about an item that is nonexcludable and rivalrous, such as the queen conch?

In the Caribbean, the queen conch is a large marine mollusk that lives in shallow waters of sea grass. These waters are so shallow, and so clear, that a single diver may harvest many conch in a single day. Not only is conch meat a local delicacy and an important part of the local diet, but artists use the large ornate shells and craftsmen transform them. Because almost anyone with a small boat, snorkel, and mask, can participate in the conch harvest, it is essentially nonexcludable. At the same time, fishing for conch is rivalrous. Once a diver catches one conch another diver cannot catch it.

We call goods that are nonexcludable and rivalrous common resources. Because the waters of the Caribbean are open to all conch fishermen, and because any conch that *you* catch is a conch that *I* cannot catch, fishermen tend to overharvest common resources like the conch.

The problem of overharvesting common resources is not a new one, but ecologist Garret Hardin put the tag "tragedy of the commons" to the problem in a 1968 article in the magazine *Science*. Economists view this as a problem of property rights. Since nobody owns the ocean, or the conch that crawl on the sand beneath it, no one individual has an incentive to protect that resource and responsibly harvest it. To address the issue of overharvesting conch and other marine fisheries, economists have advocated simple devices like fishing licenses, harvest limits, and shorter fishing seasons. One approach that has been turned to more recently is the implementation of catch shares, whereby regulators establish a total allowable catch, and then fishermen are allocated a portion of that total allowable catch. Catch shares appear to slow the race to fish. When the population of a species drops to critically low numbers, governments have even banned the harvest until biologists determine that the population has returned to sustainable levels. In fact, such is the case with the conch, the harvesting of which the government has effectively banned in the United States since 1986.

The tragedy of the commons is a frequent economic and social framework for discussions about a range of common resources, even extending into digital resources such as open media repositories and online libraries. Prominent economist Elinor Ostrom, the first woman to receive the Nobel Prize in Economics, proposed an alternate version, sometimes referred to as the "non-tragedy of the commons." After extensive fieldwork in areas as diverse as Indonesia, Kenya, Maine (U.S.), and Nepal, she challenged the notion that people would only avoid depletion of common resources if they were forced to by regulatory laws and property rights. She noted that farmers working shared land could communicate and cooperate in order to maximize and preserve the fields over time. She argued that when those who benefit most from a resource are in close proximity to it (like a farm field that directly serves a town), the resource is better managed without external influence.

 ## LINK IT UP

Visit this website (http://openstax.org/l/queenconch) for more on the queen conch industry.

---

## Positive Externalities in Public Health Programs

One of the most remarkable changes in the standard of living in the last several centuries is that people are living longer. Scientists believe that, thousands of years ago, human life expectancy ranged between 20 to 30 years. By 1900, average life expectancy in the United States was 47 years. By 2015, life expectancy was 79 years; due to COVID-19, life expectancy declined slightly to 77 years in 2020. Most of the gains in life expectancy in the history of the human race happened in the twentieth century.

The rise in life expectancy seems to stem from three primary factors. First, systems for providing clean water and disposing of human waste helped to prevent the transmission of many diseases. Second, changes in public behavior have advanced health. Early in the twentieth century, for example, people learned the importance of boiling bottles before using them for food storage and baby's milk, washing their hands, and protecting food from flies. More recent behavioral changes include reducing the number of people who smoke tobacco and precautions to limit sexually transmitted diseases. Third, medicine has played a large role. Scientists developed immunizations for diphtheria, cholera, pertussis, tuberculosis, tetanus, and yellow fever between 1890 and 1930. Penicillin, discovered in 1941, led to a series of other antibiotic drugs for bringing infectious diseases under control. In recent decades, drugs that reduce the risks of high blood pressure have had a dramatic effect in extending lives.

These advances in public health have all been closely linked to positive externalities and public goods. Public health officials taught hygienic practices to mothers in the early 1900s and encouraged less smoking in the late 1900s. Government funded many public sanitation systems and storm sewers because they have the key traits of public goods. In the twentieth century, many medical discoveries emerged from government or university-funded research. Patents and intellectual property rights provided an additional incentive for private inventors. The reason for requiring immunizations, phrased in economic terms, is that it prevents spillovers of illness to others—as well as helping the person immunized.

 ## BRING IT HOME

### The Benefits of Voyager I Endure

While we applaud the technology spillovers of NASA's space projects, we should also acknowledge that those benefits are not shared equally. Economists like Tyler Cowen, a professor at George Mason University, are seeing increasing evidence of a widening gap between those who have access to rapidly improving technology, and those who do not. According to Cowen, author of the 2013 book, *Average Is Over: Powering America Beyond the Age of the Great Stagnation*, this inequality in access to technology and information is going to deepen the inequality in skills, and ultimately, in wages and global standards of living.

## Key Terms

**external benefits (or positive externalities)** beneficial spillovers to a third party of parties, who did not purchase the good or service that provided the externalities

**free rider** those who want others to pay for the public good and then plan to use the good themselves; if many people act as free riders, the public good may never be provided

**intellectual property** the body of law including patents, trademarks, copyrights, and trade secret law that protect the right of inventors to produce and sell their inventions

**nonexcludable** when it is costly or impossible to exclude someone from using the good, and thus hard to charge for it

**nonrivalrous** even when one person uses the good, others can also use it

**positive externalities** beneficial spillovers to a third party or parties

**private benefits** the benefits a person who consumes a good or service receives, or a new product's benefits or process that a company invents that the company captures

**private rates of return** when the estimated rates of return go primarily to an individual; for example, earning interest on a savings account

**public good** good that is nonexcludable and non-rival, and thus is difficult for market producers to sell to individual consumers

**social benefits** the sum of private benefits and external benefits

**social rate of return** when the estimated rates of return go primarily to society; for example, providing free education

## Key Concepts and Summary

### 13.1 Investments in Innovation

Competition creates pressure to innovate. However, if one can easily copy new inventions, then the original inventor loses the incentive to invest further in research and development. New technology often has positive externalities; that is, there are often spillovers from the invention of new technology that benefit firms other than the innovator. The social benefit of an invention, once the firm accounts for these spillovers, typically exceeds the private benefit to the inventor. If inventors could receive a greater share of the broader social benefits for their work, they would have a greater incentive to seek out new inventions.

### 13.2 How Governments Can Encourage Innovation

Public policy with regard to technology must often strike a balance. For example, patents provide an incentive for inventors, but they should be limited to genuinely new inventions and not extend forever.

Government has a variety of policy tools for increasing the rate of return for new technology and encouraging its development, including: direct government funding of R&D, tax incentives for R&D, protection of intellectual property, and forming cooperative relationships between universities and the private sector.

### 13.3 Public Goods

A public good has two key characteristics: it is nonexcludable and non-rival. Nonexcludable means that it is costly or impossible for one user to exclude others from using the good. Non-rival means that when one person uses the good, it does not prevent others from using it. Markets often have a difficult time producing public goods because free riders will attempt to use the public good without paying for it. One can overcome the free rider problem through measures to assure that users of the public good pay for it. Such measures include government actions, social pressures, and specific situations where markets have discovered a way to collect payments.

## Self-Check Questions

1. Do market demand curves reflect positive externalities? Why or why not?

2. Suppose that Sony's R&D investment in digital devices has increased profits by 20%. Is this a private or social benefit?

3. The Gizmo Company is planning to develop new household gadgets. Table 13.4 shows the company's demand for financial capital for research and development of these gadgets, based on expected rates of return from sales. Now, say that every investment would have an additional 5% social benefit—that is, an investment that pays at least a 6% return to the Gizmo Company will pay at least an 11% return for society as a whole; an investment that pays at least 7% for the Gizmo Company will pay at least 12% for society as a whole, and so on. Answer the questions that follow based on this information.

| Estimated Rate of Return | Private profits of the firm from an R&D project (in $ millions) |
| --- | --- |
| 10% | $100 |
| 9% | $102 |
| 8% | $108 |
| 7% | $118 |
| 6% | $133 |
| 5% | $153 |
| 4% | $183 |
| 3% | $223 |

**TABLE 13.4**

   a. If the going interest rate is 9%, how much will Gizmo invest in R&D if it receives only the private benefits of this investment?

   b. Assume that the interest rate is still 9%. How much will the firm invest if it also receives the social benefits of its investment? (Add an additional 5% return on all levels of investment.)

4. The Junkbuyers Company travels from home to home, looking for opportunities to buy items that would otherwise end up with the garbage, but which the company can resell or recycle. Which will be larger, the private or the social benefits?

5. When residents in a neighborhood tidy it and keep it neat, there are a number of positive spillovers: higher property values, less crime, happier residents. What types of government policies can encourage neighborhoods to clean up?

6. Education provides both private benefits to those who receive it and broader social benefits for the economy as a whole. Think about the types of policies a government can follow to address the issue of positive spillovers in technology and then suggest a parallel set of policies that governments could follow for addressing positive externalities in education.

7. Which of the following goods or services are nonexcludable?
   a. police protection
   b. streaming music from satellite transmission programs
   c. roads
   d. primary education
   e. cell phone service

8. Are the following goods non-rival in consumption?
   a. slice of pizza
   b. laptop computer
   c. public radio
   d. ice cream cone

## Review Questions

9. In what ways do company investments in research and development create positive externalities?

10. Will the demand for borrowing and investing in R&D be higher or lower if there are no external benefits?

11. Why might private markets tend to provide too few incentives for the development of new technology?

12. What can government do to encourage the development of new technology?

13. What are the two key characteristics of public goods?

14. Name two public goods and explain why they are public goods.

15. What is the free rider problem?

16. Explain why the federal government funds national defense.

## Critical Thinking Questions

17. Can a company be guaranteed all of the social benefits of a new invention? Why or why not?

18. Is it inevitable that government must become involved in supporting investments in new technology?

19. How do public television stations, like PBS, try to overcome the free rider problem?

20. Why is a football game on ESPN a quasi-public good but a game on the NBC, CBS, or ABC is a public good?

21. Provide two examples of goods/services that are classified as private goods/services even though they are provided by a federal government.

22. Radio stations, tornado sirens, light houses, and street lights are all public goods in that all are nonrivalrous and nonexclusionary. Therefore why does the government provide tornado sirens, street lights and light houses but not radio stations (other than PBS stations)?

## Problems

**23.** HighFlyer Airlines wants to build new airplanes with greatly increased cabin space. This will allow HighFlyer Airlines to give passengers more comfort and sell more tickets at a higher price. However, redesigning the cabin means rethinking many other elements of the airplane as well, like engine and luggage placement and the most efficient shape of the plane for moving through the air. HighFlyer Airlines has developed a list of possible methods to increase cabin space, along with estimates of how these approaches would affect the plane's operating costs and ticket sales. Based on these estimates, Table 13.5 shows the value of R&D projects that provide at least a certain private rate of return. Column 1 = Private Rate of Return. Column 2 = Value of R&D Projects that Return at Least the Private Rate of Return to HighFlyer Airlines. Use the data to answer the following questions.

| Private Rate of Return | Value of R&D |
| --- | --- |
| 12% | $100 |
| 10% | $200 |
| 8% | $300 |
| 6% | $400 |
| 4% | $500 |

**TABLE 13.5**

   a. If the opportunity cost of financial capital for HighFlyer Airlines is 6%, how much should the firm invest in R&D?

   b. Assume that the social rate of return for R&D is an additional 2% on top of the private return; that is, an R&D investment that had a 7% private return to HighFlyer Airlines would have a 9% social return. How much investment is socially optimal at the 6% interest rate?

**24.** Assume that the marginal private costs of a firm producing fuel-efficient cars is greater than the marginal social costs. Assume that the marginal private benefits of a firm producing fuel-efficient cars is the same as the marginal social benefits. Discuss one way that the government can try to increase production and sales of fuel efficient cars to the socially desirable amount. *Hint*: the government is trying to affect production through costs, not benefits.

**25.** Becky and Sarah are sisters who share a room. Their room can easily get messy, and their parents are always telling them to tidy it. Here are the costs and benefits to both Becky and Sarah, of taking the time to clean their room: If both Becky and Sarah clean, they each spends two hours and get a clean room. If Becky decides not to clean and Sarah does all the cleaning, then Sarah spends 10 hours cleaning (Becky spends 0) but Sarah is exhausted. The same would occur for Becky if Sarah decided not to clean—Becky spends 10 hours and becomes exhausted. If both girls decide not to clean, they both have a dirty room.

   a. What is the best outcome for Becky and Sarah? What is the worst outcome? (It would help you to construct a prisoner's dilemma table.)

   b. Unfortunately, we know that the optimal outcome will most likely not happen, and that the sisters probably will choose the worst one instead. Explain what it is about Becky's and Sarah's reasoning that will lead them both to choose the worst outcome.

# Labor Markets and Income

**FIGURE 14.1 What determines incomes?** In the U.S., income is primarily based on one's value to an employer, which depends in part on education. (Credit: modification of work by AFL-CIO America's Unions/Flickr Creative Commons and COD Newsroom/Flickr Creative Commons)

**CHAPTER OBJECTIVES**

In this chapter, you will learn about:

- The theory of labor markets
- How wages are determined in an imperfectly competitive labor market
- How unions affect wages and employment
- How labor market outcomes are determined under Bilateral Monopoly
- Theories of Employment Discrimination, and
- How Immigration affects labor market outcomes

## Introduction to Labor Markets and Income

 **BRING IT HOME**

### The Increasing Value of a College Degree

Working your way through college used to be fairly common in the United States. According to a 2015 study by the Georgetown Center on Education and the Workforce, 40% of college students work 30 hours or more per week.

At the same time, the cost of college seems to rise every year. The data show that between the 2000–2001 academic year and the 2019–2020 academic year, the cost of tuition, fees, and room and board has slightly more than doubled for private four-year colleges, and has increased by a factor of almost 2.5 for public four-year colleges. Thus, even full time employment may not be enough to cover college expenses anymore. Working full time at minimum wage—40 hours per week, 52 weeks per year—earns $15,080 before taxes, which is substantially less than the more than \$25,000 estimated as the average cost in 2022 for a year of college at a public university. The result of these costs is that student loan debt topped \$1.3 trillion this year.

Despite these disheartening figures, the value of a bachelor's degree has never been higher. How do we explain this? This chapter will tell us.

In a market economy like the United States, income comes from ownership of the means of production: resources or assets. More precisely, one's income is a function of two things: the quantity of each resource one owns, and the value society places on those resources. Recall from the chapter on Production, Costs, and Industry Structure, each factor of production has an associated factor payment. For the majority of us, the most important resource we own is our labor. Thus, most of our income is wages, salaries, commissions, tips and other types of labor income. Your labor income depends on how many hours you work and the wage rate an employer will pay you for those hours. At the same time, some people own real estate, which they can either use themselves or rent out to other users. Some people have financial assets like bank accounts, stocks and bonds, for which they earn interest, dividends or some other form of income.

Each of these factor payments, like wages for labor and interest for financial capital, is determined in their respective factor markets. For the rest of this chapter, we will focus on labor markets, but other factor markets operate similarly. Later in Chapter 17 we will describe how this works for financial capital.

## 14.1 The Theory of Labor Markets

**LEARNING OBJECTIVES**

By the end of this section, you will be able to:
- Describe the demand for labor in perfectly competitive output markets
- Describe the demand for labor in imperfectly competitive output markets
- Identify what determines the going market rate for labor

   **CLEAR IT UP**

### What is the labor market?

The labor market is the term that economists use for all the different markets for labor. There is no single labor market. Rather, there is a different market for every different type of labor. Labor differs by type of work (e.g. retail sales vs. scientist), skill level (entry level or more experienced), and location (the market for administrative assistants is probably more local or regional than the market for university presidents). While each labor market is different, they all tend to operate in similar ways. For example, when wages go up in one labor market, they tend to go up in others too. When economists talk about the labor market, they are describing these similarities.

The labor market, like all markets, has a demand and a supply. Why do firms demand labor? Why is an employer willing to pay you for your labor? It's not because the employer likes you or is socially conscious. Rather, it's because your labor is worth something to the employer--your work brings in revenues to the firm. How much is an employer willing to pay? That depends on the skills and experience you bring to the firm.

If a firm wants to maximize profits, it will never pay more (in terms of wages and benefits) for a worker than the value of their marginal productivity to the firm. We call this the **first rule of labor markets**.

Suppose a worker can produce two widgets per hour and the firm can sell each widget for \$4 each. Then the worker is generating \$8 per hour in revenues to the firm, and a profit-maximizing employer will pay the worker up to, but no more than, \$8 per hour, because that is what the worker is worth to the firm.

Recall the definition of marginal product. Marginal product is the additional output a firm can produce by adding one more worker to the production process. Since employers often hire labor by the hour, we'll define marginal product as the additional output the firm produces by adding one more worker hour to the production process. In this chapter, we assume that workers in a particular labor market are homogeneous—they have the same background, experience and skills and they put in the same amount of effort. Thus, marginal product depends on the capital and technology with which workers have to work.

A typist can type more pages per hour with an electric typewriter than a manual typewriter, and the typist can type even more pages per hour with a personal computer and word processing software. A ditch digger can dig more cubic feet of dirt in an hour with a backhoe than with a shovel.

Thus, we can define the demand for labor as the marginal product of labor times the value of that output to the firm.

| # Workers (L) | 1 | 2 | 3 | 4 |
|---|---|---|---|---|
| $MP_L$ | 4 | 3 | 2 | 1 |

**TABLE 14.1 Marginal Product of Labor**

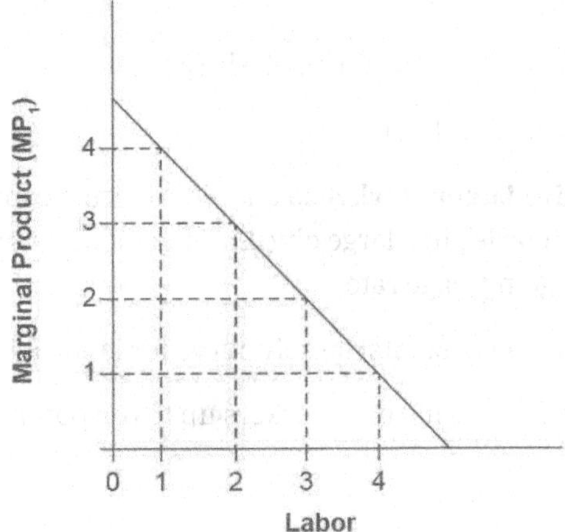


**FIGURE 14.2 Marginal Product of Labor** Because of fixed capital, the marginal product of labor declines as the employer hires additional workers.

On what does the value of each worker's marginal product depend? If we assume that the employer sells its output in a perfectly competitive market, the value of each worker's output will be the market price of the product. Thus,

Demand for Labor = $MP_L$ x P = Value of the Marginal Product of Labor

We show this in Table 14.2, which is an expanded version of Table 14.1

| # Workers (L) | 1 | 2 | 3 | 4 |
|---|---|---|---|---|
| $MP_L$ | 4 | 3 | 2 | 1 |
| Price of Output | $4 | $4 | $4 | $4 |
| $VMP_L$ | $16 | $12 | $8 | $4 |

**TABLE 14.2 Value of the Marginal Product of Labor**

Note that the value of each additional worker is less than the value of the ones who came before.

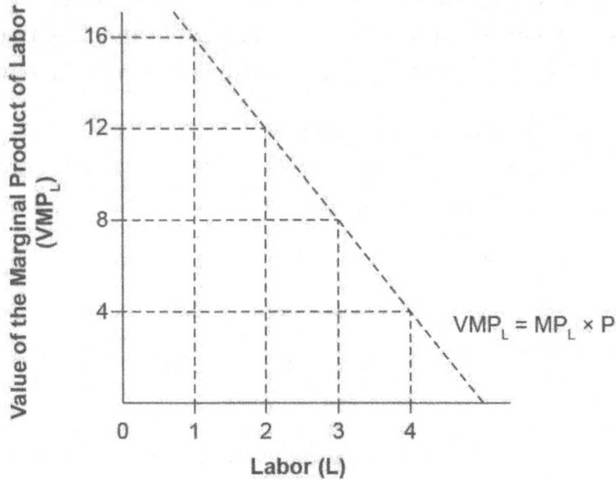


**FIGURE 14.3 Value of the Marginal Product of Labor** For firms operating in a competitive output market, the value of additional output sold is the price the firms receive for the output. Since $MP_L$ declines with additional labor employed, while that marginal product is worth the market price, the value of the marginal product declines as employment increases.

## Demand for Labor in Perfectly Competitive Output Markets

The question for any firm is how much labor to hire.

We can define a **Perfectly Competitive Labor Market** as one where firms can hire all the labor they want at the going market wage. Think about secretaries in a large city. Employers who need secretaries can probably hire as many as they need if they pay the going wage rate.

Graphically, this means that firms face a horizontal supply curve for labor, as Figure 14.3 shows.

Given the market wage, profit maximizing firms hire workers up to the point where: $W_{mkt} = VMP_L$

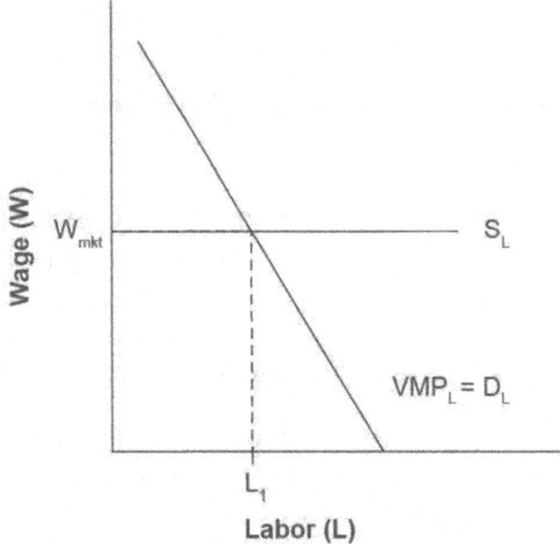


**FIGURE 14.4 Equilibrium Employment for Firms in a Competitive Labor Market** In a perfectly competitive labor market, firms can hire all the labor they want at the going market wage. Therefore, they hire workers up to the point $L_1$ where the going market wage equals the value of the marginal product of labor.

## CLEAR IT UP

### Derived Demand

Economists describe the demand for inputs like labor as a **derived demand**. Since the demand for labor is MPL*P, it is dependent on the demand for the product the firm is producing. We show this by the P term in the demand for labor. An increase in demand for the firm's product drives up the product's price, which increases the firm's demand for labor. Thus, we derive the demand for labor from the demand for the firm's output.

## Demand for Labor in Imperfectly Competitive Output Markets

If the employer does not sell its output in a perfectly competitive industry, they face a downward sloping demand curve for output, which means that in order to sell additional output the firm must lower its price. This is true if the firm is a monopoly, but it's also true if the firm is an oligopoly or monopolistically competitive. In this situation, the value of a worker's marginal product is the marginal revenue, not the price. Thus, the demand for labor is the marginal product times the marginal revenue.

The Demand for Labor = $MP_L$ x MR = Marginal Revenue Product

| # Workers (L) | 1 | 2 | 3 | 4 |
|---|---|---|---|---|
| $MP_L$ | 4 | 3 | 2 | 1 |
| Marginal Revenue | $4 | $3 | $2 | $1 |
| $MRP_L$ | $16 | $9 | $4 | $1 |

**TABLE 14.3 Marginal Revenue Product**

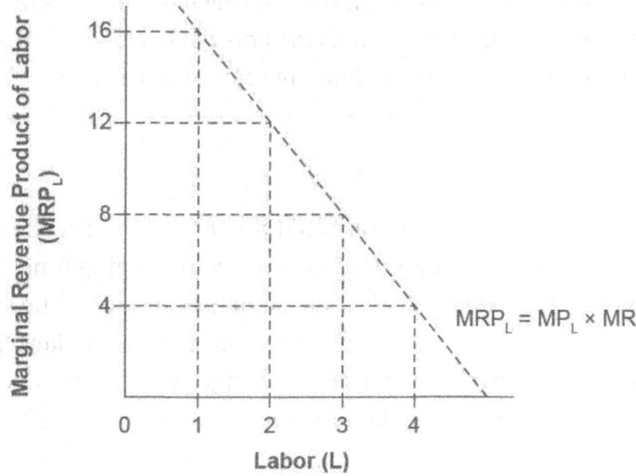


**FIGURE 14.5 Marginal Revenue Product** For firms with some market power in their output market, the value of additional output sold is the firm's marginal revenue. Since $MP_L$ declines with additional labor employed and since MR declines with additional output sold, the firm's marginal revenue declines as employment increases.

Everything else remains the same as we described above in the discussion of the labor demand in perfectly competitive labor markets. Given the market wage, profit-maximizing firms will hire workers up to the point where the market wage equals the marginal revenue product, as Figure 14.6 shows.

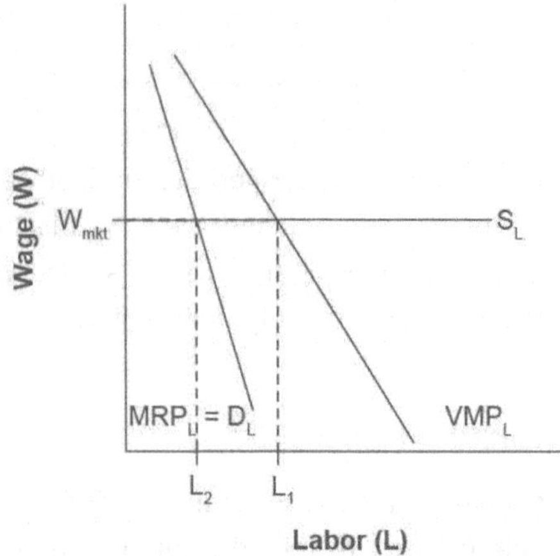


**FIGURE 14.6 Equilibrium Level of Employment for Firms with Market Power** For firms with market power in their output market, they choose the number of workers, $L_2$, where the going market wage equals the firm's marginal revenue product. Note that since marginal revenue is less than price, the demand for labor for a firm which has market power in its output market is less than the demand for labor ($L_1$) for a perfectly competitive firm. As a result, employment will be lower in an imperfectly competitive industry than in a perfectly competitive industry.

 **CLEAR IT UP**

### Do Profit Maximizing Employers Exploit Labor?

If you look back at Figure 14.4, you will see that the firm pays only the last worker it hires what they're worth to the firm. Every other worker brings in more revenue than the firm pays them. This has sometimes led to the claim that employers exploit workers because they do not pay workers what they are worth. Let's think about this claim. The first worker is worth $x to the firm, and the second worker is worth $y, but why are they worth that much? It is because of the capital and technology with which they work. The difference between workers' worth and their compensation goes to pay for the capital and technology, without which the workers wouldn't have a job. The difference also goes to the employer's profit, without which the firm would close and workers wouldn't have a job. The firm may be earning excessive profits, but that is a different topic of discussion.

## What Determines the Going Market Wage Rate?

In the chapter on Labor and Financial Markets, we learned that the labor market has demand and supply curves like other markets. The demand for labor curve is a downward sloping function of the wage rate. The market demand for labor is the horizontal sum of all firms' demands for labor. The supply of labor curve is an upward sloping function of the wage rate. This is because if wages for a particular type of labor increase in a particular labor market, people with appropriate skills may change jobs, and vacancies will attract people from outside the geographic area. The market supply of labor is the horizontal summation of all individuals' supplies of labor.

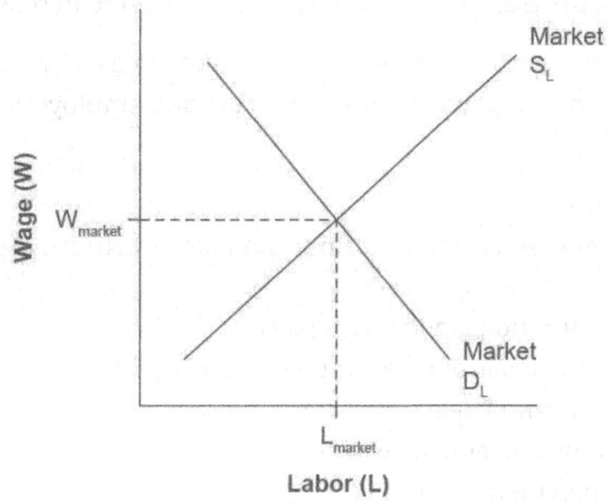


**FIGURE 14.7 The Market Wage Rate** In a competitive labor market, the equilibrium wage and employment level are determined where the market demand for labor equals the market supply of labor.

Like all equilibrium prices, the market wage rate is determined through the interaction of supply and demand in the labor market. Thus, we can see in Figure 14.7 for competitive markets the wage rate and number of workers hired.

The FRED database has a great deal of data on labor markets, starting at the wage rate and number of workers hired (https://openstax.org/l/cat10).

The United States Census Bureau for the Bureau of Labor Statistics publishes *The Current Population Survey*, which is a monthly survey of households (you can find a link to it by going to the FRED database found in the previous link), which provides data on labor supply, including numerous measures of the labor force size (disaggregated by age, gender and educational attainment), labor force participation rates for different demographic groups, and employment. It also includes more than 3,500 measures of earnings by different demographic groups.

*The Current Employment Statistics*, which is a survey of businesses, offers alternative estimates of employment across all sectors of the economy.

The FRED database, found in the previous link, also has a link labeled "Productivity and Costs" has a wide range of data on productivity, labor costs, and profits across the business sector.

## 14.2 Wages and Employment in an Imperfectly Competitive Labor Market

### LEARNING OBJECTIVES

By the end of this section, you will be able to:
- Define monopsony power
- Explain how imperfectly competitive labor markets determine wages and employment, where employers have market power

In the chapters on market structure, we observed that while economists use the theory of perfect competition as an ideal case of market structure, there are very few examples of perfectly competitive industries in the real world. What about labor markets? How many labor markets are perfectly competitive? There are probably more examples of perfectly competitive labor markets than perfectly competitive product markets, but that doesn't mean that all labor markets are competitive.

When a job applicant is bargaining with an employer for a position, the applicant is often at a disadvantage—needing the job more than the employer needs that particular applicant. John Bates Clark (1847–1938), often named as the first great American economist, wrote in 1907: "In the making of the wages contract the individual laborer is always at a disadvantage. He has something which he is obliged to sell and which his employer is not obliged to take, since he [that is, the employer] can reject single men with impunity."

To give workers more power, the U.S. government has passed, in response to years of labor protests, a number of laws to create a more equal balance of power between workers and employers. These laws include some of the following:

- Setting minimum hourly wages
- Setting maximum hours of work (at least before employers pay overtime rates)
- Prohibiting child labor
- Regulating health and safety conditions in the workplace
- Preventing discrimination on the basis of race, ethnicity, gender, sexual orientation, and age
- Requiring employers to provide family leave
- Requiring employers to give advance notice of layoffs
- Covering workers with unemployment insurance
- Setting a limit on the number of immigrant workers from other countries

Table 14.4 lists some prominent U.S. workplace protection laws. Many of the laws listed in the table were only the start of labor market regulations in these areas and have been followed, over time, by other related laws, regulations, and court rulings.

| Law | Protection |
| --- | --- |
| National Labor-Management Relations Act of 1935 (the "Wagner Act") | Establishes procedures for establishing a union that firms are obligated to follow; sets up the National Labor Relations Board for deciding disputes |
| Social Security Act of 1935 | Under Title III, establishes a state-run system of unemployment insurance, in which workers pay into a state fund when they are employed and received benefits for a time when they are unemployed |
| Fair Labor Standards Act of 1938 | Establishes the minimum wage, limits on child labor, and rules requiring payment of overtime pay for those in jobs that are paid by the hour and exceed 40 hours per week |
| Taft-Hartley Act of 1947 | Allows states to decide whether all workers at a firm can be required to join a union as a condition of employment; in the case of a disruptive union strike, permits the president to declare a "cooling-off period" during which workers have to return to work |
| Civil Rights Act of 1964 | Title VII of the Act prohibits discrimination in employment on the basis of race, gender, national origin, religion, or sexual orientation |
| Occupational Health and Safety Act of 1970 | Creates the Occupational Safety and Health Administration (OSHA), which protects workers from physical harm in the workplace |
| Employee Retirement and Income Security Act of 1974 | Regulates employee pension rules and benefits |
| Pregnancy Discrimination Act of 1978 | Prohibits discrimination against women in the workplace who are planning to get pregnant or who are returning to work after pregnancy |

**TABLE 14.4 Prominent U.S. Workplace Protection Laws**

| Law | Protection |
|---|---|
| Immigration Reform and Control Act of 1986 | Prohibits hiring of illegal immigrants; requires employers to ask for proof of citizenship; protects rights of legal immigrants |
| Worker Adjustment and Retraining Notification Act of 1988 | Requires employers with more than 100 employees to provide written notice 60 days before plant closings or large layoffs |
| Americans with Disabilities Act of 1990 | Prohibits discrimination against those with disabilities and requires reasonable accommodations for them on the job |
| Family and Medical Leave Act of 1993 | Allows employees to take up to 12 weeks of unpaid leave per year for family reasons, including birth or family illness |
| Pension Protection Act of 2006 | Penalizes firms for underfunding their pension plans and gives employees more information about their pension accounts |
| Lilly Ledbetter Fair Pay Act of 2009 | Restores protection for pay discrimination claims on the basis of sex, race, national origin, age, religion, or disability |

**TABLE 14.4 Prominent U.S. Workplace Protection Laws**

There are two sources of imperfect competition in labor markets. These are demand side sources, that is, labor market power by employers, and supply side sources: labor market power by employees. In this section we will discuss the former. In the next section we will discuss the latter.

A competitive labor market is one where there are many potential employers for a given type of worker, say a secretary or an accountant. Suppose there is only one employer in a labor market. Because that employer has no direct competition in hiring, if they offer lower wages than would exist in a competitive market, employees will have few options. If they want a job, they must accept the offered wage rate. Since the employer is exploiting its market power, we call the firm a **monopsony**, a term introduced and widely discussed by Joan Robinson (though she credited scholar Bertrand Hallward with invention of the word). The classical example of monopsony is the sole coal company in a West Virginia town. If coal miners want to work, they must accept what the coal company is paying. This is not the only example of monopsony. Think about surgical nurses in a town with only one hospital. A situation in which employers have at least some market power over potential employees is not that unusual. After all, most firms have many employees while there is only one employer. Thus, even if there is some competition for workers, it may not feel that way to potential employees unless they do their research and find the opposite.

How does market power by an employer affect labor market outcomes? Intuitively, one might think that wages will be lower than in a competitive labor market. Let's prove it. We will tell the story for a monopsonist, but the results will be qualitatively similar, although less extreme, for any firm with labor market power.

Think back to monopoly. The good news for the firm is that because the monopolist is the sole supplier in the market, it can charge any price it wishes. The bad news is that if it wants to sell a greater quantity of output, it must lower the price it charges. Monopsony is analogous. Because the monopsonist is the sole employer in a labor market, it can offer any wage that it wishes. However, because they face the market supply curve for labor, if they want to hire more workers, they must raise the wage they pay. This creates a quandary, which we can understand by introducing a new concept: the marginal cost of labor. The **marginal cost of labor** is the cost to the firm of hiring one more worker. However, here is the thing: we assume that the firm is determining how many workers to hire in total. They are not hiring sequentially. Let's look how this plays out with the example in Table 14.5.

| Supply of Labor | 1 | 2 | 3 | 4 | 5 |
|---|---|---|---|---|---|
| Wage Rate | $1 per hour | $2 per hour | $3 per hour | $4 per hour | $5 per hour |
| Total Cost of Labor | $1 | $4 | $9 | $16 | $25 |
| Marginal Cost of Labor | $1 | $3 | $5 | $7 | $9 |

**TABLE 14.5 The Marginal Cost of Labor**

There are a couple of things to notice from the table. First, the marginal cost increases faster than the wage rate. In fact, for any number of workers more than one, the marginal cost of labor is greater than the wage. This is because to hire one more worker requires paying a higher wage rate, not just for the new worker but for all the previous hires also. We can see this graphically in Figure 14.7.

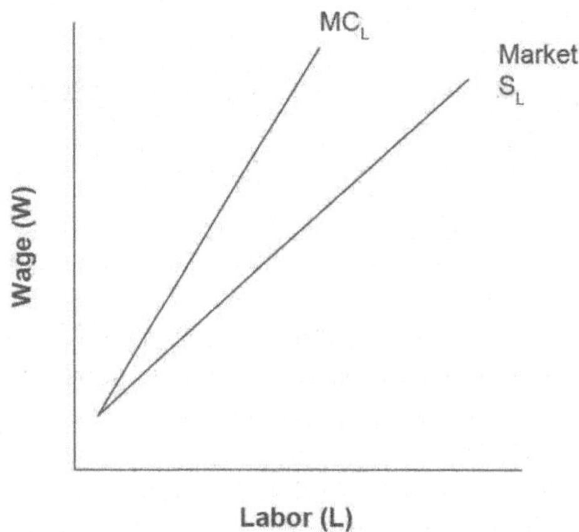


**FIGURE 14.8 The Marginal Cost of Labor** Since monopsonies are the sole demander for labor, they face the market supply curve for labor. In order to increase employment they must raise the wage they pay not just for new workers, but for all the existing workers they could have hired at the previous lower wage. As a result, the marginal cost of hiring additional labor is greater than the wage, and thus for any level of employment (above the first worker), $MC_L$ is above the Market Supply of Labor.

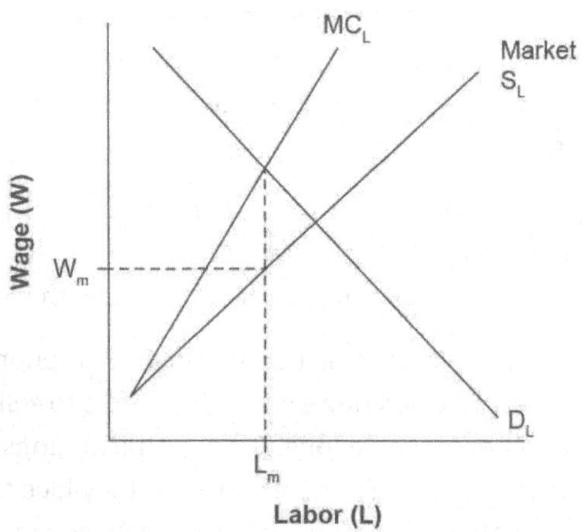


**FIGURE 14.9 Labor Market Outcomes Under Monopsony** A monopsony will hire workers up to the point Lm where its demand for labor equals the marginal cost of additional labor, paying the wage Wm given by the supply curve of

labor necessary to obtain Lm workers.

If the firm wants to maximize profits, it will hire labor up to the point Lm where $D_L$ = VMP (or MRP) = $MC_L$, as Figure 14.9 shows. Then, the supply curve for labor shows the wage the firm will have to pay to attract Lm workers. Graphically, we can draw a vertical line up from Lm to the Supply Curve for the label and then read the wage Wm off the vertical axis to the left.

How does this outcome compare to what would occur in a perfectly competitive market? A competitive market would operate where $D_L$ = $S_L$, hiring Lc workers and paying Wc wage. In other words, under monopsony employers hire fewer workers and pay a lower wage. While pure monopsony may be rare, many employers have some degree of market power in labor markets. The outcomes for those employers will be qualitatively similar though not as extreme as monopsony.

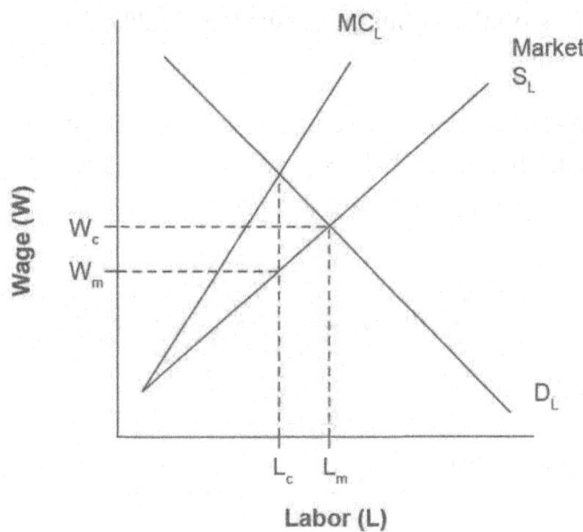


FIGURE 14.10 Comparison of labor market outcomes: Monopsony vs. Perfect Competition A monopsony hires fewer workers (Lm) than would be hired in a competitive labor market (Lc). In exploiting its market power, the monopsony can also pay a lower wage (Wm) than workers would earn in a competitive labor market (Wc).

## 14.3 Market Power on the Supply Side of Labor Markets: Unions

### LEARNING OBJECTIVES

By the end of this section, you will be able to:
- Explain the concept of labor unions, including membership levels and wages
- Evaluate arguments for and against labor unions
- Analyze reasons for the decline in U.S. union membership

A labor union is an organization of workers that negotiates with employers over wages and working conditions. A labor union seeks to change the balance of power between employers and workers by requiring employers to deal with workers collectively, rather than as individuals. As such, a labor union operates like a monopoly in a labor market. We sometimes call negotiations between unions and firms **collective bargaining**.

The subject of labor unions can be controversial. Supporters of labor unions view them as the workers' primary line of defense against efforts by profit-seeking firms to hold down wages and benefits. Critics of labor unions view them as having a tendency to grab as much as they can in the short term, even if it means injuring workers in the long run by driving firms into bankruptcy or by blocking the new technologies and production methods that lead to economic growth. We will start with some facts about union membership in the United States.

### Facts about Union Membership and Pay

According to the U.S. Bureau of Labor and Statistics, about 10.3% of all U.S. workers belong to unions. This represents nearly a 50% reduction since 1983 (the earliest year for which comparable data are available), when union members were 20.1% of all workers. Following are some facts about unions for 2021 (note that we are using the population categories and group names utilized in the data collection and publication):

- 10.6% of U.S. male workers belong to unions; 9.9% of female workers do
- 10.7% of White workers, 12.3% of Black workers, and 9.8 % of Hispanic workers belong to unions
- 11.8% of full-time workers and 5.7% of part-time workers are union members
- 4.4% of workers ages 16–24 belong to unions, as do 13.2% of workers ages 45-54
- Occupations in which relatively high percentages of workers belong to unions are the federal government (26.0% belong to a union), state government (29.9%), local government (41.7%); transportation and utilities (17.6%); natural resources, construction, and maintenance (15.9%); and production, transportation, and material moving (13.3%)
- Occupations that have relatively low percentages of unionized workers are agricultural workers (1.7%), financial services (1.9%), professional and business services (2.2%), leisure and hospitality (2.2%), and wholesale and retail trade (4.5%)

In summary, the percentage of workers belonging to a union is higher for men than women; higher for Black than for White or Hispanic people; higher for the 45–64 age range; and higher among workers in government and manufacturing than workers in agriculture or service-oriented jobs. Table 14.6 lists the largest U.S. labor unions and their membership.

| Union | Membership |
|---|---|
| National Education Association (NEA) | 3.0 million |
| Service Employees International Union (SEIU) | 2.0 million |
| American Federation of Teachers (AFT) | 1.7 million |
| International Brotherhood of Teamsters (IBT) | 1.4 million |
| The American Federation of State, County, and Municipal Workers (AFSCME) | 1.6 million |
| United Food and Commercial Workers International Union | 1.3 million |
| International Brotherhood of Electrical Workers (IBEW) | 775,000 |
| United Steelworkers | 625,000 |
| International Association of Machinists and Aerospace Workers | 569,000 |
| International Union, United Automobile, Aerospace and Agricultural Implement Workers of America (UAW) | 408,000 |

**TABLE 14.6 The Largest American Unions in 2021** (Source: U.S. Department of Labor and individual union websites)

In terms of pay, benefits, and hiring, U.S. unions offer a good news/bad news story. The good news for unions and their members is that their members earn about 20% more than nonunion workers, even after adjusting for factors such as years of work experience and education level. The bad news for unions is that the share of U.S. workers who belong to a labor union has been steadily declining for 50 years, as Figure 14.11 shows. About one-quarter of all U.S. workers belonged to a union in the mid-1950s, but only 10.3% of U.S. workers are union members today. If you leave out government workers (which includes teachers in public schools), only 6.1% of the workers employed by private firms now work for a union.

**FIGURE 14.11 Percentage of Wage and Salary Workers Who Are Union Members** The share of wage and salary workers who belong to unions rose sharply in the 1930s and 1940s, but has tailed off since then to 10.3% of all workers in 2021.

The following section analyzes the higher pay union workers receive compared the pay rates for nonunion workers. The section after that analyzes declining union membership levels. An overview of these two issues will allow us to discuss many aspects of how unions work.

### Higher Wages for Union Workers

How does a union affect wages and employment? Because a union is the sole supplier of labor, it can act like a monopoly and ask for whatever wage rate it can obtain for its workers. If employers need workers, they have to meet the union's wage demand.

What are the limits on how much higher pay union workers can receive? To analyze these questions, let's consider a situation where all firms in an industry must negotiate with a single union, and no firm is allowed to hire nonunion labor. If no labor union existed in this market, then equilibrium (E) in the labor market would occur at the intersection of the demand for labor (D) and the supply of labor (S) as we see in Figure 14.12. This is the same result as we showed in Figure 14.6 above. The union can, however, threaten that, unless firms agree to the wages they demand, the workers will strike. As a result, the labor union manages to achieve, through negotiations with the firms, a union wage of Wu for its members, above what the equilibrium wage would otherwise have been.

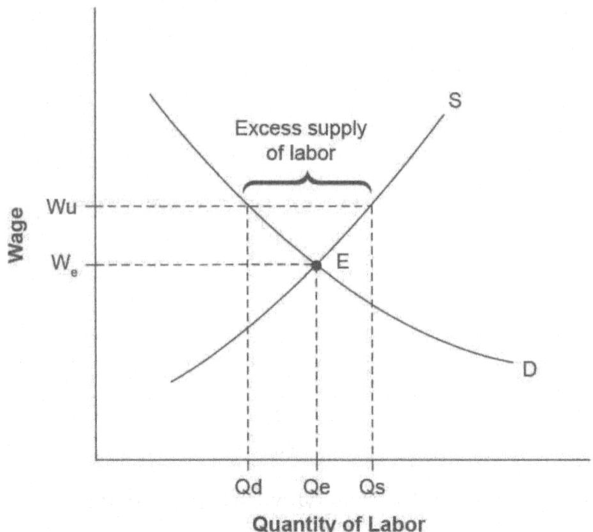


**FIGURE 14.12 Union Wage Negotiations** Without a union, the equilibrium at E would have involved the wage We and the quantity of labor Qe. However, the union is able to use its bargaining power to raise the wage to Wu. The result is an excess supply of labor for union jobs. That is, a quantity of labor supplied, Qs is greater than firms' quantity demanded for labor, Qd.

This labor market situation resembles what a monopoly firm does in selling a product, but in this case a union is a monopoly selling labor to firms. At the higher union wage Wu, the firms in this industry will hire less labor than they would have hired in equilibrium. Moreover, an excess supply of workers want union jobs, but firms will not be hiring for such jobs.

From the union point of view, workers who receive higher wages are better off. However, notice that the quantity of workers (Qd) hired at the union wage Wu is smaller than the quantity Qe that the firm would have hired at the original equilibrium wage. A sensible union must recognize that when it pushes up the wage, it also reduces the firms' incentive to hire. This situation does not necessarily mean that union workers are fired. Instead, it may be that when union workers move on to other jobs or retire, they are not always replaced, or perhaps when a firm expands production, it expands employment somewhat less with a higher union wage than it would have done with the lower equilibrium wage. Other situations could be that a firm decides to purchase inputs from nonunion producers, rather than producing them with its own highly paid unionized workers, or perhaps the firm moves or opens a new facility in a state or country where unions are less powerful.

From the firm's point of view, the key question is whether union workers' higher wages are matched by higher productivity. If so, then the firm can afford to pay the higher union wages and, the demand curve for "unionized" labor could actually shift to the right. This could reduce the job losses as the equilibrium employment level shifts to the right and the difference between the equilibrium and the union wages will have been reduced. If worker unionization does not increase productivity, then the higher union wage will cause lower profits or losses for the firm.

Union workers might have higher productivity than nonunion workers for a number of reasons. First, higher wages may elicit higher productivity. Second, union workers tend to stay longer at a given job, a trend that reduces the employer's costs for training and hiring and results in workers with more years of experience. Many unions also offer job training and apprenticeship programs.

In addition, firms that are confronted with union demands for higher wages may choose production methods that involve more physical capital and less labor, resulting in increased labor productivity. Table 14.7 provides an example. Assume that a firm can produce a home exercise cycle with three different combinations of labor and manufacturing equipment. Say that the firm pays labor $16 an hour (including benefits) and the machines for manufacturing cost $200 each. Under these circumstances, the total cost of producing a home exercise cycle will be lowest if the firm adopts the plan of 50 hours of labor and one machine, as the table shows. Now, suppose that a union negotiates a wage of $20 an hour including benefits. In this case, it makes no difference to the firm whether it uses more hours of labor and fewer machines or less labor and more machines, although it might prefer to use more machines and to hire fewer union workers. (After all, machines never threaten to strike—but they do not buy the final product or service either.)

In the final column of the table, the wage has risen to $24 an hour. In this case, the firm clearly has an incentive for using the plan that involves paying for fewer hours of labor and using three machines. If management responds to union demands for higher wages by investing more in machinery, then union workers can be more productive because they are working with more or better physical capital equipment than the typical nonunion worker. However, the firm will need to hire fewer workers.

| Hours of Labor | Number of Machines | Cost of Labor + Cost of Machine $16/hour | Cost of Labor + Cost of Machine $20/hour | Cost of Labor + Cost of Machine $24/hour |
|---|---|---|---|---|
| 30 | 3 | $480 + $600 = $1,080 | $600 + $600 = $1,200 | $720 + $600 = $1,320 |
| 40 | 2 | $640 + $400 = $1,040 | $800 + $400 = $1,200 | $960 + $400 = $1,360 |
| 50 | 1 | $800 + $200 = $1,000 | $1,000 + $200 = $1,200 | $1,200 + $200 = $1,400 |

**TABLE 14.7** Three Production Choices to Manufacture a Home Exercise Cycle

In some cases, unions have discouraged the use of labor-saving physical capital equipment—out of the reasonable fear that new machinery will reduce the number of union jobs. For example, in 2015, the union representing longshoremen who unload ships and the firms that operate shipping companies and port facilities staged a work stoppage that shut down the ports on the western coast of the United States. Two key issues in the dispute were the desire of the shipping companies and port operators to use handheld scanners for record-keeping and computer-operated cabs for loading and unloading ships—changes which the union opposed, along with overtime pay. President Obama threatened to use the Labor Management Relations Act of 1947—commonly known as the Taft-Hartley Act—where a court can impose an 80-day "cooling-off period" in order to allow time for negotiations to proceed without the threat of a work stoppage. Federal mediators were called in, and the two sides agreed to a deal in February 2015. The ultimate agreement allowed the new technologies, but also kept wages, health, and pension benefits high for workers. In the past, presidential use of the Taft-Hartley Act sometimes has made labor negotiations more bitter and argumentative but, in this case, it seems to have smoothed the road to an agreement.

In other instances, unions have proved quite willing to adopt new technologies. In one prominent example, during the 1950s and 1960s, the United Mineworkers union demanded that mining companies install labor-saving machinery in the mines. The mineworkers' union realized that over time, the new machines would reduce the number of jobs in the mines, but the union leaders also knew that the mine owners would have to pay higher wages if the workers became more productive, and mechanization was a necessary step toward greater productivity.

In fact, in some cases union workers may be more willing to accept new technology than nonunion workers, because the union workers believe that the union will negotiate to protect their jobs and wages, whereas nonunion workers may be more concerned that the new technology will replace their jobs. In addition, union workers, who typically have higher job market experience and training, are likely to suffer less and benefit more than non-union workers from the introduction of new technology. Overall, it is hard to make a definitive case that union workers as a group are always either more or less welcoming to new technology than are nonunion workers

### The Decline in U.S. Union Membership

The proportion of U.S. workers belonging to unions has declined dramatically since the early 1950s. Economists have offered a number of possible explanations:

- The shift from manufacturing to service industries
- The force of globalization and increased competition from foreign producers
- A reduced desire for unions because of the workplace protection laws now in place
- U.S. legal environment that makes it relatively more difficult for unions to organize workers and expand their membership

Let's discuss each of these four explanations in more detail.

A first possible explanation for the decline in the share of U.S. workers belonging to unions involves the patterns of job growth in the manufacturing and service sectors of the economy as Figure 14.13 shows. The U.S. economy had about 15 million manufacturing jobs in 1960. This total rose to 19 million by the late 1970s and then declined to 17 million in 2013. Meanwhile, the number of jobs in service industries (including government employment) rose from 35 million in 1960 to over 118 million by 2013, according to the Bureau of Labor Statistics. Because over time unions were stronger in manufacturing than in service industries, the growth in jobs was not happening where the unions were. It is interesting to note that government workers comprise several of the biggest unions in the country, including the **American Federation of State, County and Municipal Employees (AFSCME)**; the **Service Employees International Union**; and the **National Education Association**. Table 14.8 lists the membership of each of these unions. Outside of government employees, however, unions have not had great success in organizing the service sector.

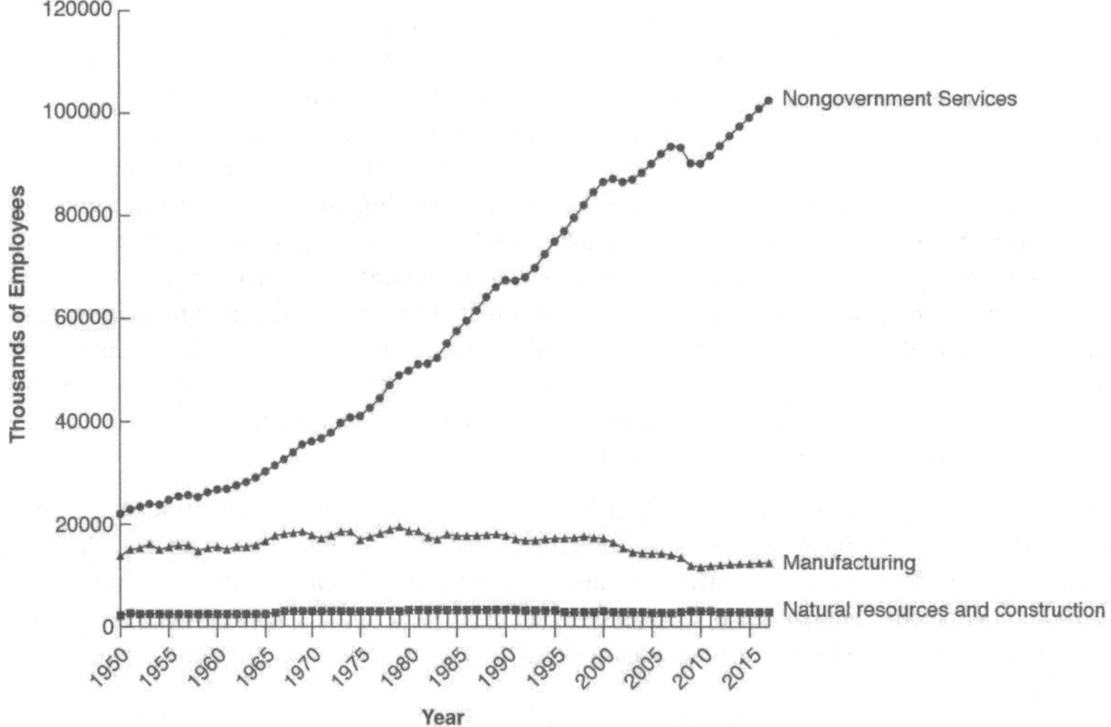


**FIGURE 14.13 The Growth of Service Jobs** Jobs in services have increased dramatically for more than the past 50 years. Jobs in government have increased modestly until 1990 and then declined slightly since then. Jobs in manufacturing peaked in the late 1970s and have declined more than a third since then.

A second explanation for the decline in the share of unionized workers looks at import competition. Starting in the 1960s, U.S. carmakers and steelmakers faced increasing competition from Japanese and European manufacturers. As sales of imported cars and steel rose, the number of jobs in U.S. auto manufacturing fell.

This industry is heavily unionized. Not surprisingly, membership in the United Auto Workers, which was 975,000 in 1985, had fallen to roughly 390,000 by 2015. Import competition not only decreases the employment in sectors where unions were once strong, but also decreases the bargaining power of unions in those sectors. However, as we have seen, unions that organize public-sector workers, who are not threatened by import competition, have continued to see growth.

A third possible reason for the decline in the number of union workers is that citizens often call on their elected representatives to pass laws concerning work conditions, overtime, parental leave, regulation of pensions, and other issues. Unions offered strong political support for these laws aimed at protecting workers but, in an ironic twist, the passage of those laws then made many workers feel less need for unions.

These first three possible reasons for the decline of unions are all somewhat plausible, but they have a common problem. Most other developed economies have experienced similar economic and political trends, such as the shift from manufacturing to services, globalization, and increasing government social benefits and regulation of the workplace. Clearly there are cultural differences between countries as to their acceptance of unions in the workplace. The share of the population belonging to unions in other countries is very high compared with the share in the United States. Table 14.8 shows the proportion of workers in a number of the world's high-income economies who belong to unions. The United States is near the bottom, along with France and Spain. The last column shows union coverage, defined as including those workers whose wages are determined by a union negotiation even if the workers do not officially belong to the union. In the United States, union membership is almost identical to union coverage. However, in many countries, the wages of many workers who do not officially belong to a union are still determined by collective bargaining between unions and firms.

| Country | Union Density: Percentage of Workers Belonging to a Union | Union Coverage: Percentage of Workers Whose Wages Are Determined by Union Bargaining |
|---|---|---|
| Austria | 37% | 99% |
| France | 9% | 95% |
| Germany | 26% | 63% |
| Japan | 22% | 23% |
| Netherlands | 25% | 82% |
| Spain | 11.3% | 81% |
| Sweden | 82% | 92% |
| United Kingdom | 29% | 35% |
| United States | 11.1% | 12.5% |

**TABLE 14.8** International Comparisons of Union Membership and Coverage in 2012 (Source, CIA World Factbook, retrieved from www.cia.gov)

These international differences in union membership suggest a fourth reason for the decline of union membership in the United States: perhaps U.S. laws are less friendly to the formation of unions than such laws in other countries. The close connection between union membership and a friendly legal environment is apparent in the history of U.S. unions. The great rise in union membership in the 1930s followed the passage of the **National Labor Relations Act** of 1935, which specified that workers had a right to organize unions and that management had to give them a fair chance to do so. The U.S. government strongly encouraged forming unions during the early 1940s in the belief that unions would help to coordinate the all-out production efforts needed during World War II. However, after World War II came the passage of the Taft-Hartley Act of 1947, which gave states the power to allow workers to opt out of the union in their workplace if they so desired. This law made the legal climate less encouraging to those seeking to form unions, and union membership levels soon started declining.

The procedures for forming a union differ substantially from country to country. For example, the procedures in the United States and those in Canada are strikingly different. When a group of workers wishes to form a union in the United States, they announce this fact and set an election date when the firm's employees will vote in a secret ballot on whether to form a union. Supporters of the union lobby for a "yes" vote, and the firm's management lobbies for a "no" vote—often even hiring outside consultants for assistance in swaying workers to vote "no." In Canada, by contrast, a union is formed when a sufficient proportion of workers (usually about 60%) signs an official card saying that they want a union. There is no separate "election date." The management of Canadian firms is limited by law in its ability to lobby against the union. In addition, although it is illegal to discriminate and fire workers based on their union activity in the United States, the penalties are slight, making this a not so costly way of deterring union activity. In short, forming unions is easier in Canada—and in many other countries—than in the United States.

In summary, union membership in the United States is lower than in many other high-income countries, a difference that may be due to different legal environments and cultural attitudes toward unions.

## ⊘ LINK IT UP

Visit this website (http://openstax.org/l/fastfoodwages) to read more about recent protests regarding minimum wage for fast food employees.

---

## 14.4 Bilateral Monopoly

**LEARNING OBJECTIVES**

By the end of this section, you will be able to explain:

- How firms determine wages and employment when a specific labor market combines a union and a monopsony

What happens when there is market power on both sides of the labor market, in other words, when a union meets a monopsony? Economists call such a situation a **bilateral monopoly**.

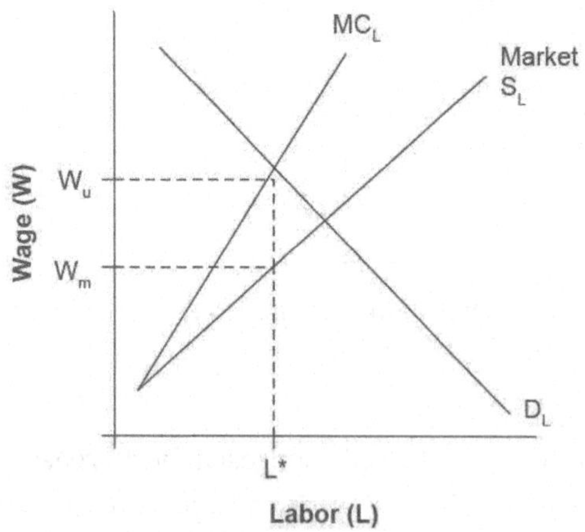


**FIGURE 14.14 Bilateral Monopoly** Employment, L*, will be lower in a bilateral monopoly than in a competitive labor

market, but the equilibrium wage is indeterminate, somewhere in the range between Wu, what the union would choose, and Wm, what the monopsony would choose.

Figure 14.14 is a combination of Figure 14.6 and Figure 14.11. A monopsony wants to reduce wages as well as employment, Wm and L* in the figure. A union wants to increase wages, but at the cost of lower employment, Wu and L* in the figure. Since both sides want to reduce employment, we can be sure that the outcome will be lower employment compared to a competitive labor market. What happens to the wage, though, is based on the monopsonist's relative bargaining power compared to the bargaining power of the union. The actual outcome is indeterminate in the graph, but it will be closer to Wu if the union has more power and closer to Wm if the monopsonist has more power.

## 14.5 Employment Discrimination

**LEARNING OBJECTIVES**

By the end of this section, you will be able to:
- Analyze earnings gaps based on race and gender
- Explain the impact of discrimination in a competitive market
- Identify U.S. public policies designed to reduce discrimination

Barriers to equitable participation in the labor market drive down economic growth. When certain populations are underrepresented, underpaid, or mistreated in a labor market or industry, the negative outcomes can effect the larger economy. For example, many science and technology fields were either unwelcoming or overtly unaccepting of women and people of color. Some major contributors to these fields overcame these challenges. Mexican-American scientist Lydia Villa-Komaroff, for example, faced overt discrimination when her college advisor told her not to pursue chemistry because women didn't "belong" in chemistry. She pursued biology instead; she developed the first instance of synthetic insulin (the chemical that people with diabetes need in order to survive) through a process that has saved million of lives and is credited with launching the entire industry of biotechnology—one of the most important in the U.S. economy. But for every Villa-Komaroff, there have been thousands of women who were prevented from making those contributions. Beyond the personal impact on those people, consider the impact on those scientific fields, our overall quality of life, and the economy itself. Economist Lisa D. Cook has quantified the costs of these innovation losses. She estimates that GDP could be as much as 4.4% higher if women and people from minority populations were fully able to participate in the science and technology innovation process.

**Discrimination** involves acting on the belief that members of a certain group are inferior or deserve less solely because of a factor such as race, gender, or religion. There are many types of discrimination but the focus here will be on discrimination in labor markets, which arises if workers with the same skill levels—as measured by education, experience, and expertise—receive different pay or have different job opportunities because of their race or gender. Much of the data collected and published on these topics are limited in terms of the diversity of people represented, and focus particularly on binary gender, single-race, and single-ethnicity identities. While these characterizations do not capture the diversity of Americans, the findings are important in order to understand discrimination and other practices, and to consider the impacts of policies and changes. Also, while sex and gender are different, many data sets, laws, court decisions, and media accounts use the terms interchangeably. For consistency, we will use the terminology found in the source material and government data.

### Earnings Gaps by Race and Gender

A possible signal of labor market discrimination is when an employer pays one group less than another. Figure 14.15 shows the average wage of Black workers as a ratio of the average wage of White workers and the average wage of female workers as a ratio of the average wage of male workers. Research by the economists Francine Blau and Laurence Kahn shows that the gap between the earnings of women and men did not move much in the 1970s, but has declined since the 1980s. Detailed analysis by economists Kerwin Kofi Charles and Patrick

Bayer show that the gap between the earnings of Black and White people diminished in the 1970s, but grew again so that current differences are as wide as they were nearly 70 years ago. In both gender and race, an earnings gap remains.

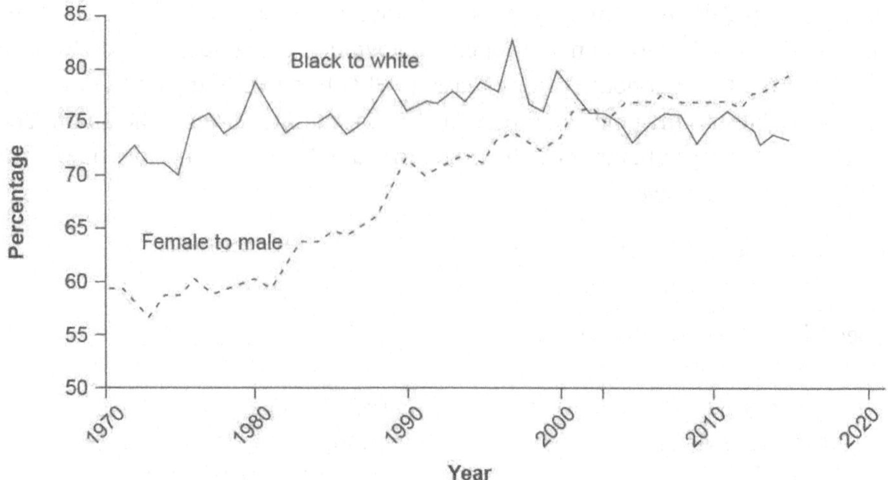


**FIGURE 14.15 Wage Ratios by Sex and Race** The ratio of wages for Black workers to White workers rose substantially in the late 1960s and through the 1970s. The 1990s saw a peak above 80% followed by a bumpy decline to the low 70s. The ratio of wages for female to male workers changed little through the 1970s. In both cases, a gap remains between the average wages of Black and White workers and between the average wages of female and male workers. Source: U.S. Department of Labor, Bureau of Labor Statistics.

An earnings gap between average wages, in and of itself, does not prove that discrimination is occurring in the labor market. We need to apply the same productivity characteristics to all parties (employees) involved. Gender discrimination in the labor market occurs when employers pay people of a specific gender less despite those people having comparable levels of education, experience, and expertise. (Read the Clear It Up about the sex-discrimination suit brought against Walmart.) Similarly, racial discrimination in the labor market exists when employers pay racially diverse employees less than their coworkers of the majority race despite having comparable levels of education, experience, and expertise. To bring a successful gender discrimination lawsuit, an employee must prove the employer is paying them less than an employee of a different gender who holds a similar job, with similar educational attainment, and with similar expertise. Likewise, someone who wants to sue on the grounds of racial discrimination must prove that the employer pays them less than an employee of another race who holds a similar job, with similar educational attainment, and with similar expertise.

The FRED database includes earnings data at earnings by age, gender and race/ethnicity (https://openstax.org/l/33501).

As stated previously and as we will see below, not every instance of a wage gap or employment inequity is a product of overt discrimination on the part of individual employers. Significant overall issues in societies, such as inequitable education or housing segregation, can lead to earning gaps and limitations on economic mobility. However, these wider issues usually affect people from minority populations and/or those who have been historically underrepresented in positions of power. Economist William A. Darity Jr., whose work is discussed in more detail below, indicates that individualized employer racism still exists, but it is largely practiced in "covert and subtle forms."

## CLEAR IT UP

### What was the sex-discrimination case against Walmart?

In one of the largest class-action sex-discrimination cases in U.S. history, 1.2 million female employees of Walmart claimed that the company engaged in wage and promotion discrimination. In 2011, the Supreme Court threw out the case on the grounds that the group was too large and too diverse to consider the case a class action suit. Lawyers for the women regrouped and were subsequently suing in smaller groups. Part of the difficulty for the female employees is that the court said that local managers made pay and promotion decisions that were not necessarily the company's policies as a whole. Consequently, female Walmart employees in Texas argued that their new suit would challenge the management of a "discrete group of regional district and store managers." They claimed that these managers made biased pay and promotion decisions. However, in 2013, a federal district court rejected a smaller California class action suit against the company.

On other issues, Walmart made the news again in 2013 when the National Labor Relations Board found Walmart guilty of illegally penalizing and firing workers who took part in labor protests and strikes. Walmart paid $11.7 million in back wages and compensation damages to women in Kentucky who were denied jobs due to their sex. And in 2020, a sex-based hiring discrimination lawsuit was filed by the U.S. Equal Employment Opportunity Commission (EEOC), in which the EEOC alleged that Walmart conducted a physical ability test (known as the PAT) as a requirement for applicants to be hired as order fillers at Walmart's grocery distribution centers nationwide, and that the PAT disproportionately excluded female applicants from jobs as grocery order fillers. In September 2020, Walmart and the EEOC agreed to a consent decree, which requires Walmart to cease all physical ability testing that had been used for purposes of hiring grocery distribution center order fillers. The decree also required Walmart to pay $20 million into a settlement fund to pay lost wages to women across the country who were denied grocery order filler positions because of the testing.

## Investigating the Female/Male Earnings Gap

As a result of changes in law and culture, women began to enter the paid workforce in substantial numbers in the mid- to late-twentieth century. As of February 2022, 56.0% of women aged 20 and over held jobs, while 67.6% of men aged 20 and over did. Moreover, along with entering the workforce, women began to ratchet up their education levels. In 1971, 44% of undergraduate college degrees went to women. As of the 2018–19 academic year, women earned 57% of bachelor's degrees. In 1970, women received 5.4% of the degrees from law schools and 8.4% of the degrees from medical schools. By 2017, women were receiving just over 50% of the law degrees, and by 2019, 48% of the medical degrees. There are now slightly more women than men in both law schools and medical schools. These gains in education and experience have reduced the female/male wage gap over time. However, concerns remain about the extent to which women have not yet assumed a substantial share of the positions at the top of the largest companies or in the U.S. Congress.

There are factors that can lower women's average wages. Women are likely to bear a disproportionately large share of household responsibilities. A mother of young children is more likely to drop out of the labor force for several years or work on a reduced schedule than is the father. As a result, women in their 30s and 40s are likely, on average, to have less job experience than men. In the United States, childless women with the same education and experience levels as men are typically paid comparably. However, women with families and children are typically paid about 7% to 14% less than other women of similar education and work experience. Meanwhile, married men earn about 10% to 15% more than single men with comparable education and work experience. This circumstance or practice is often referred to as the "motherhood penalty" and the "fatherhood bonus."

Another aspect of the gender pay gap relates to work that isn't actually paid, such as household chores, caring for children and other family members, and cooking. Studies have found that globally and within the United States, women undertake far more of this work than do men; even women who work full time and/or bring in the majority of family income take on more of this unpaid work than the men in their households.

Economists study many aspects of sex- and gender-based earnings gaps, often revealing unexpected causes and impacts. For example, economists Jessica Pan, Jonathan Guryan, and Kerwin Kofi Charles analyzed decades of sociological and employment data and uncovered that the amount of sexism in the U.S. state where a woman was born is an indicator of the woman's earnings throughout her life, even if she moves away from her home state. In other words, women born in states with more pronounced sexist attitudes earn less, no matter where they live later on. Other economists showed that from 1950–2000, as women's representation increased in the workforce, jobs that became occupied by women experienced wage reductions relative to jobs being done by men—an outcome often referred to as "devaluation." The value of this research and similar investigations comes from the deeper understanding of the origins of the earnings gap, so that workers, employers, and governments can take steps to address them.

## ⊘ LINK IT UP

Visit this website (https://openstax.org/l/numberswomen) to read more about the persistently low numbers of women in executive roles in business and in the U.S. Congress.

---

### Investigating the Earnings Gap Related to Race and Ethnicity

Black people experienced blatant labor market discrimination during much of the twentieth century. Until the passage of the Civil Rights Act of 1964, it was legal in many states to refuse to hire a Black worker, regardless of the credentials or experience of that worker. Moreover, Black people were often denied access to educational opportunities, which in turn meant that they had lower levels of qualifications for many jobs. At least one economic study has shown that the 1964 law is partially responsible for the narrowing of the gap in Black–White earnings in the late 1960s and into the 1970s. For example, the ratio of total earnings of Black male workers to White male workers rose from 62% in 1964 to 75.3% in 2013, according to the Bureau of Labor Statistics.

However, the earnings gap between Black and White workers has not changed as much as the earnings gap between men and women has in the last half century. The remaining racial gap seems related both to continuing differences in education levels and to the presence of discrimination. Table 14.9 shows that the percentage of Black people who complete a four-year college degree remains substantially lower than the percentage of White people who complete college. According to the U.S. Census, both White and Black people have higher levels of educational attainment than Hispanic people and lower levels than Asian people. The lower average levels of education for Black workers surely explain part of the earnings gap. In fact, Black women who have the same levels of education and experience as White women receive, on average, about the same level of pay. One study shows that White and Black college graduates have identical salaries immediately after college; however, the racial wage gap widens over time, an outcome that suggests the possibility of continuing discrimination. Other researchers conducted a field experiment by responding to job advertisements with fictitious resumes using names that were either commonly associated with Black/African American people or names commonly associated with White people; they found that the White-associated names received 50 percent more callbacks for interviews. This is suggestive of discrimination in job opportunities. Further, as the following Clear It Up feature explains, there is evidence to support that discrimination in the housing market is connected to employment discrimination.

|                                              | White | Hispanic | Black | Asian |
|----------------------------------------------|-------|----------|-------|-------|
| Completed four years of high school or more  | 93.8% | 73.0%    | 87.2% | 91.0% |
| Completed four years of college or more      | 37.6% | 16.8%    | 23.7% | 54.7% |

**TABLE 14.9 Educational Attainment by Race and Ethnicity for Individuals Aged 18 and Above in 2019** (Source: https://www.census.gov/content/census/en/data/tables/2019/demo/educational-attainment/cps-detailed-tables.html)

 **CLEAR IT UP**

## How is discrimination in the housing market connected to employment discrimination?

A recent study by the Housing and Urban Development (HUD) department found that realtors showed Black homebuyers 18 percent fewer homes compared to White homebuyers. Realtors showed Asian homebuyers 19 percent fewer properties. Additionally, Hispanic people experience more discrimination in renting apartments and undergo stiffer credit checks than White renters. In a 2012 study by the U.S. Department of Housing and Urban Development and the nonprofit Urban Institute, Hispanic testers who contacted agents about advertised rental units received information about 12 percent fewer units available and were shown seven percent fewer units than White renters. The $9 million study, based on research in 28 metropolitan areas, concluded that blatant "door slamming" forms of discrimination are on the decline but that the discrimination that does exist is harder to detect, and as a result, more difficult to remedy. According to the *Chicago Tribune*, HUD Secretary Shaun Donovan, who served in his role from 2009-2014, told reporters, "Just because it's taken on a hidden form doesn't make it any less harmful. You might not be able to move into that community with the good schools."

These practices are viewed as a continuation of **redlining**, which is the intentional and discriminatory withholding of services or products based on race or other factors. Redlining was practiced extensively by banks and other lenders who refused to issue mortgages or other loans to people from racial or ethnic minorities living in neighborhoods that were deemed "hazardous" to investment, even though the same lenders would issue loans to White people with similar economic status. Redlining has lasting effects today, demonstrated by significant divides in educational and financial opportunity in certain neighborhoods or cities.

The lower levels of education for Black workers can also be a result of discrimination—although it may be pre-labor market discrimination, rather than direct discrimination by employers in the labor market. For example, if redlining and other discrimination in housing markets causes Black families to live clustered together in certain neighborhoods and those areas have under-resourced schools, then those children will continue to have lower educational attainment then their White counterparts and, consequently, not be able to obtain the higher paying jobs that require higher levels of education. Another element to consider is that in the past, when Black people were effectively barred from many high-paying jobs, obtaining additional education could have seemed not to be worth the investment, because the educational degrees would not pay off. While the government has legally abolished discriminatory labor practices, structures and systems take a very long time to eradicate.

## Competitive Markets and Discrimination

Gary Becker (1930–2014), who won the Nobel Prize in economics in 1992, was one of the first to analyze discrimination in economic terms. Becker pointed out that while competitive markets can allow some employers to practice discrimination, it can also provide profit-seeking firms with incentives not to discriminate. Given these incentives, Becker explored the question of why discrimination persists.

If a business is located in an area with a large minority population and refuses to sell to minorities, it will cut into its own profits. If some businesses run by bigoted employers refuse to pay women and/or minorities a wage based on their productivity, then other profit-seeking employers can hire these workers. In a competitive market, if the business owners care more about the color of money than about the color of skin, they will have an incentive to make buying, selling, hiring, and promotion decisions strictly based on economic factors.

Do not underestimate the power of markets to offer at least a degree of freedom to oppressed groups. In many countries, cohesive minority population groups like Jewish people and emigrant Chinese people have managed to carve out a space for themselves through their economic activities, despite legal and social discrimination against them. Many immigrants, including those who come to the United States, have taken advantage of economic freedom to make new lives for themselves. However, history teaches that market forces alone are unlikely to eliminate discrimination. After all, discrimination against African Americans persisted in the market-oriented U.S. economy during the century between the ratification of the 13th Amendment, which abolished slavery in 1865, and the passage of the Civil Rights Act of 1964—and has continued since then, too.

Why does discrimination persist in competitive markets? Gary Becker sought to explain this persistence. Discriminatory impulses can emerge at a number of levels: among managers, among workers, and among customers. Consider the situation of a store owner or manager who is not personally prejudiced, but who has many customers who are prejudiced. If that manager treats all groups fairly, the manager may find it drives away prejudiced customers. In such a situation, a policy of nondiscrimination could reduce the firm's profits. After all, a business firm is part of society, and a firm that does not follow the societal norms is likely to suffer.

As economist William A. Darity Jr. points out, however, the "prejudiced customer" rationale falls apart when considering the many jobs that have no customer contact. Darity examined several theories regarding the persistence of employment discrimination, including rationales regarding group membership and employers' lack of information about candidates of other genders or races. Darity also directly studies and interprets others' work on discrimination in other countries, such as wage disparities between Sikh and Hindu men in India. Darity concludes that the competitive forces of the market have not been enough to overcome employment and wage discrimination, and, on their own, are unlikely to end such discrimination in the future.

## ⊘ LINK IT UP

Read this article (http://openstax.org/l/censusincome) to learn more about wage discrimination.

---

## Public Policies to Reduce Discrimination

A first public policy step against discrimination in the labor market is to make it illegal. For example, the Equal Pay Act of 1963 said that employers must pay men and women who do equal work the same. The Civil Rights Act of 1964 prohibits employment discrimination based on race, color, religion, sex, or national origin. The Age Discrimination in Employment Act of 1967 prohibited discrimination on the basis of age against individuals who are 40 years of age or older. The Civil Rights Act of 1991 provides monetary damages in cases of intentional employment discrimination. The Pregnancy Discrimination Act of 1978 was aimed at prohibiting discrimination against people in the workplace who are planning pregnancy, are pregnant, or are returning after pregnancy. Passing a law, however, is only part of the answer, since discrimination by prejudiced employers may be less important than broader social patterns and systems.

The 1964 Civil Rights Act created an important government organization, the Equal Employment Opportunity Commission, to investigate employment discrimination and protect workers who filed complaints against employers. Economist Phyllis Ann Wallace, who had previously worked for U.S. intelligence services, was appointed as the commission's chief of technical studies. In this role she collected and organized a massive amount of public and private sector data, as well as mentored and directed economists and other analysts in their investigations.

These laws against discrimination have reduced the gender wage gap. A 2007 Department of Labor study compared salaries of men and women who have similar educational achievement, work experience, and occupation and found that the gender wage gap is only 5%.

In the case of the earnings gap between Black people and White people (and also between Hispanic people and White people), probably the single largest step that could be taken at this point in U.S. history to close the earnings gap would be to reduce the gap in educational attainment. Part of the answer to this issue involves finding ways to improve the performance of schools, which is a highly controversial topic in itself. In addition, the education gap is unlikely to close unless Black and Hispanic families and peer groups strengthen their culture of support for educational attainment.

**Affirmative action** is the name given to active efforts by government or businesses that give special rights to minorities in hiring and promotion to make up for past discrimination. Affirmative action, in its limited and not especially controversial form, means making an effort to reach out to a broader range of minority candidates for jobs. In its more aggressive and controversial form, affirmative action required government and companies to hire a specific number or percentage of minority employees. However, the U.S. Supreme Court has ruled against state affirmative action laws. Today, the government applies affirmative action policies only to federal contractors who have lost a discrimination lawsuit. The federal Equal Employment Opportunity Commission (EEOC) enforces this type of redress.

## An Increasingly Diverse Workforce

Racial and ethnic diversity is on the rise in the U.S. population and workforce. As Figure 14.16 shows, while the White Americans comprised 78% of the population in 2012, the U.S. Bureau of the Census projects that Whites will comprise 69% of the U.S. population by 2060. Forecasters predict that the proportion of U.S. citizens who are of Hispanic background to rise substantially. Moreover, in addition to expected changes in the population, workforce diversity is increasing as the women who entered the workforce in the 1970s and 1980s are now moving up the promotion ladders within their organizations.

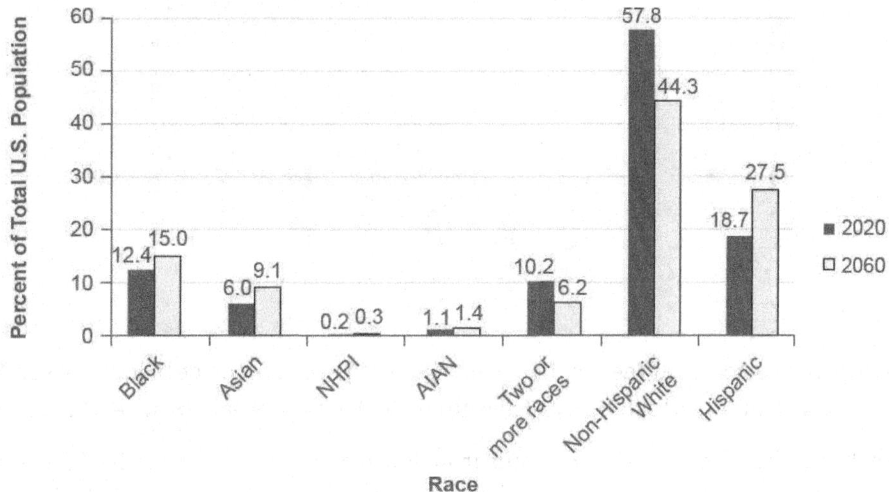


**FIGURE 14.16 Projected Changes in America's Racial and Ethnic Diversity** This figure shows projected changes in the ethnic makeup of the U.S. population by 2060. Note that "NHPI" stands for Native Hawaiian and Other Pacific Islander. "AIAN" stands for American Indian and Alaska Native. Source: US Department of Commerce

Regarding the future, optimists argue that the growing proportions of minority workers will break down remaining discriminatory barriers. The economy will benefit as an increasing proportion of workers from traditionally disadvantaged groups have a greater opportunity to fulfill their potential. Pessimists worry that the social tensions between different genders and between ethnic groups will rise and that workers will be less productive as a result. Anti-discrimination policy, at its best, seeks to help society move toward the more optimistic outcome.

The FRED database includes data on foreign and native born civilian population (https://openstax.org/l/104)

and labor force (https://openstax.org/l/32442).

## 14.6 Immigration

Most Americans would be outraged if a law prevented them from moving to another city or another state. However, when the conversation turns to crossing national borders and is about other people arriving in the United States, laws preventing such movement often seem more reasonable. Some of the tensions over immigration stem from worries over how it might affect a country's culture, including differences in language, and patterns of family, authority, or gender relationships. Economics does not have much to say about such cultural issues. Some of the worries about immigration do, however, have to do with its effects on wages and income levels, and how it affects government taxes and spending. On those topics, economists have insights and research to offer.

### Historical Patterns of Immigration

Supporters and opponents of immigration look at the same data and see different patterns. Those who express concern about immigration levels to the United States point to graphics like Figure 14.17 which shows total inflows of immigrants decade by decade through the twentieth and into the twenty-first century. Clearly, the level of immigration has been high and rising in recent years, reaching and exceeding the towering levels of the early twentieth century. However, those who are less worried about immigration point out that the high immigration levels of the early twentieth century happened when total population was much lower. Since the U.S. population roughly tripled during the twentieth century, the seemingly high levels in immigration in the 1990s and 2000s look relatively smaller when they are divided by the population.

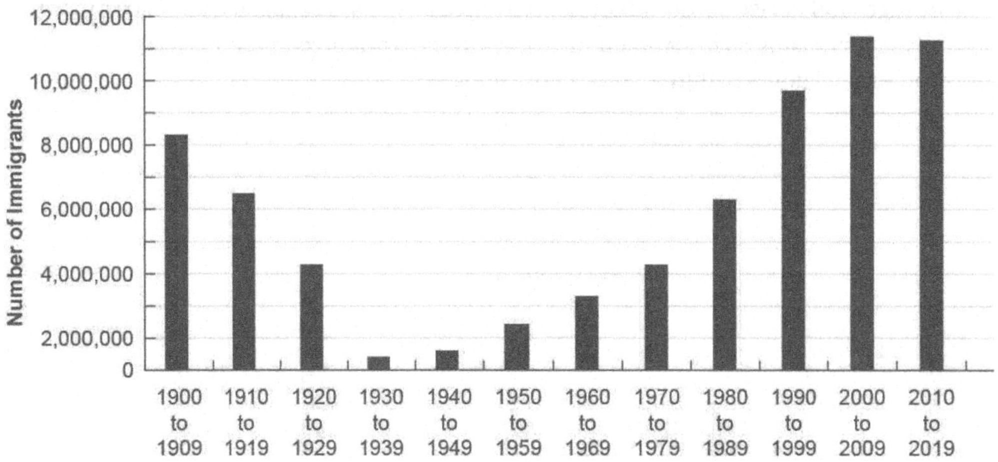

FIGURE 14.17 Immigration Since 1900 The number of immigrants in each decade declined between 1900 and the 1940s, rose sharply through 2009 and started to decline from 2010 to the present. (Source: U.S. Census)

From where have the immigrants come? Immigrants from Europe were more than 90% of the total in the first decade of the twentieth century, but less than 20% of the total by the end of the century. By the 2000s, about half of U.S. immigration came from the rest of the Americas, especially Mexico, and about a quarter came from various countries in Asia.

### Economic Effects of Immigration

A surge of immigration can affect the economy in a number of different ways. In this section, we will consider how immigrants might benefit the rest of the economy, how they might affect wage levels, and how they might affect government spending at the federal and local level.

To understand the economic consequences of immigration, consider the following scenario. Imagine that the immigrants entering the United States matched the existing U.S. population in age range, education, skill levels, family size, and occupations. How would immigration of this type affect the rest of the U.S. economy?

Immigrants themselves would be much better off, because their standard of living would be higher in the United States. Immigrants would contribute to both increased production and increased consumption. Given enough time for adjustment, the range of jobs performed, income earned, taxes paid, and public services needed would not be much affected by this kind of immigration. It would be as if the population simply increased a little.

Now, consider the reality of recent immigration to the United States. Immigrants are not identical to the rest of the U.S. population. About one-third of immigrants over the age of 25 lack a high school diploma. As a result, many of the recent immigrants end up in jobs like restaurant and hotel work, lawn care, and janitorial work. This kind of immigration represents a shift to the right in the supply of unskilled labor for a number of jobs, which will lead to lower wages for these jobs. The middle- and upper-income households that purchase the services of these unskilled workers will benefit from these lower wages. However, low-skilled U.S. workers who must compete with low-skilled immigrants for jobs will tend to be negatively impacted by immigration.

The difficult policy questions about immigration are not so much about the overall gains to the rest of the economy, which seem to be real but small in the context of the U.S. economy, as they are about the disruptive effects of immigration in specific labor markets. One disruptive effect, as we noted, is that immigration weighted toward low-skill workers tends to reduce wages for domestic low-skill workers. A study by Michael S. Clune found that for each 10% rise in the number of employed immigrants with no more than a high school diploma in the labor market, high school students reduced their annual number of hours worked by 3%. The effects on wages of low-skill workers are not large—perhaps in the range of decline of about 1%. These effects are likely kept low, in part, because of the legal floor of federal and state minimum wage laws. In addition, immigrants are also thought to contribute to increased demand for local goods and services which can stimulate the local low skilled labor market. It is also possible that employers, in the face of abundant low-skill workers, may choose production processes which are more labor intensive than otherwise would have been. These various factors would explain the small negative wage effect that the native low-skill workers observed as a result of immigration.

Another potential disruptive effect is the impact on state and local government budgets. Many of the costs imposed by immigrants are costs that arise in state-run programs, like the cost of public schooling and of welfare benefits. However, many of the taxes that immigrants pay are federal taxes like income taxes and Social Security taxes. Many immigrants do not own property (such as homes and cars), so they do not pay property taxes, which are one of the main sources of state and local tax revenue. However, they do pay sales taxes, which are state and local, and the landlords of property they rent pay property taxes. According to the nonprofit Rand Corporation, the effects of immigration on taxes are generally positive at the federal level, but they are negative at the state and local levels in places where there are many low-skilled immigrants.

 **LINK IT UP**

Visit this website (http://openstax.org/l/nber) to obtain more context regarding immigration.

## Proposals for Immigration Reform

The Congressional Jordan Commission of the 1990s proposed reducing overall levels of immigration and refocusing U.S. immigration policy to give priority to immigrants with higher skill levels. In the labor market, focusing on high-skilled immigrants would help prevent any negative effects on low-skilled workers' wages. For government budgets, higher-skilled workers find jobs more quickly, earn higher wages, and pay more in taxes. Several other immigration-friendly countries, notably Canada and Australia, have immigration systems where those with high levels of education or job skills have a much better chance of obtaining permission to immigrate. For the United States, high tech companies regularly ask for a more lenient immigration policy to admit a greater quantity of highly skilled workers under the H1B visa program.

The Obama Administration proposed the so-called "DREAM Act" legislation, which would have offered a path to citizenship for those classified as illegal immigrants who were brought to the United States before the age of 16. Despite bipartisan support, the legislation failed to pass at the federal level. However, some state legislatures, such as California, have passed their own Dream Acts.

Between its plans for a border wall, increased deportation of undocumented immigrants, and even reductions in the number of highly skilled legal H1B immigrants, the Trump Administration had a much less positive approach to immigration. Most economists, whether conservative or liberal, believe that while immigration harms some domestic workers, the benefits to the nation exceed the costs. President Biden has been considerably more positive about immigration than his predecessor. However, given the presence of considerable disagreement within the overall population about the desirability of immigration, it is unlikely that any significant immigration reform will take place in the near future.

The FRED database includes data on the national origin of the civilian population (https://fred.stlouisfed.org/categories/104) (https://fred.stlouisfed.org/categories/104) and labor force (https://fred.stlouisfed.org/categories/32442) (https://fred.stlouisfed.org/categories/32442).

 **BRING IT HOME**

### The Increasing Value of a College Degree

The cost of college has increased dramatically in recent decades, causing many college students to take student loans to afford it. Despite this, the value of a college degree has never been higher. How can we explain this?

We can estimate the value of a bachelor's degree as the difference in lifetime earnings between the average holder of a bachelor's degree and the average high school graduate. According to a 2021 report from the Georgetown University Center on Education and the Workforce, adults with a bachelor's degree earn an average of $2.8 million during their careers, $1.2 million more than the median for workers with a high school diploma. College graduates also have a significantly lower unemployment rate than those with lower educational attainments.

While a college degree holder's wages have increased somewhat, the major reason for the increase in value of a bachelor's degree has been the plummeting value of a high school diploma. In the twenty-first century, the majority of jobs require at least some post-secondary education. This includes manufacturing jobs that in the past would have afforded workers a middle class income with only a high school diploma. Those jobs are increasingly scarce. This phenomenon has also no doubt contributed to the increasing inequality of income that we observe in the U.S. today. We will discuss that topic next, in Chapter 15.

## Key Terms

**affirmative action** active efforts by government or businesses that give special rights to minorities in hiring, promotion, or access to education to make up for past discrimination

**bilateral monopoly** a labor market with a monopsony on the demand side and a union on the supply side

**collective bargaining** negotiations between unions and a firm or firms

**discrimination** actions based on the belief that members of a certain group or groups are in some way inferior solely because of a factor such as race, gender, or religion

**first rule of labor markets** an employer will never pay a worker more than the value of the worker's marginal productivity to the firm

**monopsony** a labor market where there is only one employer

**perfectly competitive labor market** a labor market where neither suppliers of labor nor demanders of labor have any market power; thus, an employer can hire all the workers they would like at the going market wage

## Key Concepts and Summary

### 14.1 The Theory of Labor Markets

A firm demands labor because of the value of the labor's marginal productivity. For a firm operating in a perfectly competitive output market, this will be the value of the marginal product, which we define as the marginal product of labor multiplied by the firm's output price. For a firm which is not perfectly competitive, the appropriate concept is the marginal revenue product, which we define as the marginal product of labor multiplied by the firm's marginal revenue. Profit maximizing firms employ labor up to the point where the market wage is equal to the firm's demand for labor. In a competitive labor market, we determine market wage through the interaction between the market supply and market demand for labor.

### 14.2 Wages and Employment in an Imperfectly Competitive Labor Market

A monopsony is the sole employer in a labor market. The monopsony can pay any wage it chooses, subject to the market supply of labor. This means that if the monopsony offers too low a wage, they may not find enough workers willing to work for them. Since to obtain more workers, they must offer a higher wage, the marginal cost of additional labor is greater than the wage. To maximize profits, a monopsonist will hire workers up to the point where the marginal cost of labor equals their labor demand. This results in a lower level of employment than a competitive labor market would provide, but also a lower equilibrium wage.

### 14.3 Market Power on the Supply Side of Labor Markets: Unions

A labor union is an organization of workers that negotiates as a group with employers over compensation and work conditions. Union workers in the United States are paid more on average than other workers with comparable education and experience. Thus, either union workers must be more productive to match this higher pay or the higher pay will lead employers to find ways of hiring fewer union workers than they otherwise would. American union membership has been falling for decades. Some possible reasons include the shift of jobs to service industries; greater competition from globalization; the passage of worker-friendly legislation; and U.S. laws that are less favorable to organizing unions.

### 14.4 Bilateral Monopoly

A bilateral monopoly is a labor market with a union on the supply side and a monopsony on the demand side. Since both sides have monopoly power, the equilibrium level of employment will be lower than that for a competitive labor market, but the equilibrium wage could be higher or lower depending on which side negotiates better. The union favors a higher wage, while the monopsony favors a lower wage, but the outcome is indeterminate in the model.

## 14.5 Employment Discrimination

Discrimination occurs in a labor market when employers pay workers with the same economic characteristics, such as education,experience, and skill, are paid different amounts because of race, gender, religion, age, or disability status. In the United States, female workers on average earn less than male workers, and Black workers on average earn less than White workers. There is controversy over to which discrimination differences in factors like education and job experience can explain these earnings gaps. Free markets can allow discrimination to occur, but the threat of a loss of sales or a loss of productive workers can also create incentives for a firm not to discriminate. A range of public policies can be used to reduce earnings gaps between men and women or between White and other racial/ethnic groups: requiring equal pay for equal work, and attaining more equal educational outcomes.

## 14.6 Immigration

The recent level of U.S. immigration is at a historically high level if we measure it in absolute numbers, but not if we measure it as a share of population. The overall gains to the U.S. economy from immigration are real but relatively small. However, immigration also causes effects like slightly lower wages for low-skill workers and budget problems for certain state and local governments.

## Self-Check Questions

1. Table 14.10 shows levels of employment (Labor), the marginal product at each of those levels, and the price at which the firm can sell output in the perfectly competitive market where it operates.

| Labor | Marginal Product of Labor | Price of the Product |
|---|---|---|
| 1 | 10 | $4 |
| 2 | 8 | $4 |
| 3 | 7 | $4 |
| 4 | 5 | $4 |
| 5 | 3 | $4 |
| 6 | 1 | $4 |

**TABLE 14.10**

   a. What is the value of the marginal product at each level of labor?
   b. If the firm operates in a perfectly competitive labor market where the going market wage is $12, what is the firm's profit maximizing level of employment?

2. Table 14.11 shows levels of employment (Labor), the marginal product at each of those levels, and a monopoly's marginal revenue.

| Labor | Marginal Product of Labor | Price of the Product |
|---|---|---|
| 1 | 10 | $10 |
| 2 | 8 | $7 |
| 3 | 7 | $5 |
| 4 | 5 | $4 |
| 5 | 3 | $2 |
| 6 | 1 | $1 |

**TABLE 14.11**

   a.  What is the monopoly's marginal revenue product at each level of employment?
   b.  If the monopoly operates in a perfectly competitive labor market where the going market wage is $20, what is the firm's profit maximizing level of employment?

3. Table 14.12 shows the quantity demanded and supplied in the labor market for driving city buses in the town of Unionville, where all the bus drivers belong to a union.

| Wage Per Hour | Quantity of Workers Demanded | Quantity of Workers Supplied |
|---|---|---|
| $14 | 12,000 | 6,000 |
| $16 | 10,000 | 7,000 |
| $18 | 8,000 | 8,000 |
| $20 | 6,000 | 9,000 |
| $22 | 4,000 | 10,000 |
| $24 | 2,000 | 11,000 |

**TABLE 14.12**

   a.  What would the equilibrium wage and quantity be in this market if no union existed?
   b.  Assume that the union has enough negotiating power to raise the wage to $4 per hour higher than it would otherwise be. Is there now excess demand or excess supply of labor?

4. Do unions typically oppose new technology out of a fear that it will reduce the number of union jobs? Why or why not?

5. Compared with the share of workers in most other high-income countries, is the share of U.S. workers whose wages are determined by union bargaining higher or lower? Why or why not?

6. Are firms with a high percentage of union employees more likely to go bankrupt because of the higher wages that they pay? Why or why not?

7. Do countries with a higher percentage of unionized workers usually have less growth in productivity because of strikes and other disruptions caused by the unions? Why or why not?

8. Table 14.13 shows information from the supply curve for labor for a monopsonist, that is, the wage rate required at each level of employment.

| Labor | Wage |
|---|---|
| 1 | 1 |
| 2 | 3 |
| 3 | 5 |
| 4 | 7 |
| 5 | 8 |
| 6 | 10 |

**TABLE 14.13**

   a. What is the monopsonist's marginal cost of labor at each level of employment?
   b. If each unit of labor's marginal revenue product is $13, what is the firm's profit maximizing level of employment and wage?

9. Explain in each of the following situations how market forces might give a business an incentive to act in a less discriminatory fashion.
   a. A local flower delivery business that had intentionally served only White customers notices that many of the local residents are Black.
   b. An assembly line has traditionally only hired men, but it is having a hard time hiring sufficiently qualified workers.
   c. A relationship counselor who had a strict policy of only serving straight couples notes the significant increase of LGBTQ people moving into the town.

10. Does the earnings gap between the average wages of females and the average wages of males prove labor market discrimination? Why or why not?

11. If immigration is reduced, what is the impact on the wage for low-skilled labor? Explain.

## Review Questions

12. What determines the demand for labor for a firm operating in a perfectly competitive output market?

13. What determines the demand for labor for a firm with market power in the output market?

14. What is a perfectly competitive labor market?

15. What is a labor union?

16. Why do employers have a natural advantage in bargaining with employees?

17. What are some of the most important laws that protect employee rights?

18. How does the presence of a labor union change negotiations between employers and workers?

19. What is the long-term trend in American union membership?

20. Would you expect the presence of labor unions to lead to higher or lower pay for worker-members? Would you expect a higher or lower quantity of workers hired by those employers? Explain briefly.

21. What are the main causes for the recent trends in union membership rates in the United States? Why are union rates lower in the United States than in many other developed countries?

22. What is a monopsony?

23. What is the marginal cost of labor?

24. How does monopsony affect the equilibrium wage and employment levels?

25. What is a bilateral monopoly?

26. How does a bilateral monopoly affect the equilibrium wage and employment levels compared to a perfectly competitive labor market?

27. Describe how the earnings gap between men and women has evolved in recent decades.

28. Describe how the earnings gap between Black and White people has evolved in recent decades.

29. Does a gap between the average earnings of men and women, or between White and Black people, prove that employers are discriminating in the labor market? Explain briefly.

30. Will a free market tend to encourage or discourage discrimination? Explain briefly.

31. What policies, when used together with antidiscrimination laws, might help to reduce the earnings gap between men and women or between White and Black workers?

32. Describe how affirmative action is applied in the labor market.

33. What factors can explain the relatively small effect of low-skilled immigration on the wages of low-skilled workers?

34. Have levels of immigration to the United States been relatively high or low in recent years? Explain.

35. How would you expect immigration by primarily low-skill workers to affect American low-skilled workers?

## Critical Thinking Questions

36. What is the marginal cost of labor for a firm that operates in a competitive labor market? How does this compare with the MCL for a monopsony?

37. Given the decline in union membership over the past 50 years, what does the theory of bilateral monopoly suggest will have happened to the equilibrium level of wages over time? Why?

38. Are unions and technological improvements complementary? Why or why not?

39. Will union membership continue to decline? Why or why not?

40. If it is not profitable to discriminate, why does discrimination persist?

41. If a company has discriminated against minorities in the past, should it be required to give priority to minority applicants today? Why or why not?

42. If the United States allows a greater quantity of highly skilled workers, what will be the impact on the average wages of highly skilled employees?

43. If all countries eliminated all barriers to immigration, would global economic growth increase? Why or why not?

# Poverty and Economic Inequality

**FIGURE 15.1 Occupying Wall Street** On September 17, 2011, Occupy Wall Street began in New York City's Wall Street financial district. (Credit: modification of "Occupy Wall Street Day 2 2011 Shankbone" by David Shankbone/ Flickr Creative Commons, CC BY 2.0)

**CHAPTER OBJECTIVES**

In this chapter, you will learn about:

- Drawing the Poverty Line
- The Poverty Trap
- The Safety Net
- Income Inequality: Measurement and Causes
- Government Policies to Reduce Income Inequality

## Introduction to Poverty and Economic Inequality

 **BRING IT HOME**

### Occupy Wall Street

In September 2011, a group of protesters gathered in Zuccotti Park in New York City to decry what they perceived as increasing social and economic inequality in the United States. Calling their protest "Occupy Wall Street," they argued that the concentration of wealth among the richest 1% in the United States was both economically unsustainable and inequitable, and needed to be changed. The protest then spread to other major cities, and the Occupy movement was born.

Why were people so upset? How much wealth is concentrated among the top 1% in our society? How did they acquire so much wealth? These are very real, very important questions in the United States now, and this chapter on poverty and economic inequality will help us address the causes behind this sentiment.

The labor markets that determine the pay that workers receive do not take into account how much income a family needs for food, shelter, clothing, and health care. Market forces do not worry about what happens to families when a major local employer goes out of business. Market forces do not take time to contemplate whether those who are earning higher incomes should pay an even higher share of taxes.

However, labor markets do create considerable income inequalities. In 2020, the median American household income was $67,521 (the median is the level where half of all families had more than that level and half had less). For family households, the median was $86,372; for non-family households, it was $40,464. The Census Bureau also reported that in 2020, there were 37.2 million people living in poverty, representing 11.4% of the population. Think about a family of three—perhaps a single mother with two children—attempting to pay for the basics of life on perhaps $17,916 per year. After paying for rent, healthcare, clothing, and transportation, such a family might have $6,000 to spend on food. Spread over 365 days, the food budget for the entire family would be about $17 per day. To put this in perspective, most cities have restaurants where $17 will buy you an appetizer for one.

This chapter explores how the U.S. government defines poverty, the balance between assisting the poor without discouraging work, and how federal antipoverty programs work. It also discusses income inequality—how economists measure inequality, why inequality has changed in recent decades, the range of possible government policies to reduce inequality, and the danger of a tradeoff that too great a reduction in inequality may reduce incentives for producing output.

## 15.1 Drawing the Poverty Line

**LEARNING OBJECTIVES**

By the end of this section, you will be able to:

- Explain economic inequality and how the poverty line is determined
- Analyze the U.S. poverty rate over time, noting its prevalence among different groups of citizens

Comparisons of high and low incomes raise two different issues: economic inequality and **poverty**. Poverty is measured by the number of people who fall below a certain level of income—called the **poverty line**—that defines the income one needs for a basic standard of living. **Income inequality** compares the share of the total income (or wealth) in society that different groups receive. For example, one of numerous ways to look at income inequality is to compare the share of income that the top 10% receive to the share of income that the bottom 10% receive.

In the United States, the official definition of the poverty line traces back to a single person: Mollie Orshansky. In 1963, Orshansky, who was working for the Social Security Administration, published an article called "Children of the Poor" in a highly useful and dry-as-dust publication called the *Social Security Bulletin*. Orshansky's idea was to define a poverty line based on the cost of a healthy diet.

Her previous job had been at the U.S. Department of Agriculture, where she had worked in an agency called the Bureau of Home Economics and Human Nutrition. One task of this bureau had been to calculate how much it would cost to feed a nutritionally adequate diet to a family. Orshansky found that the average family spent one-third of its income on food. She then proposed that the poverty line be the amount one requires to buy a nutritionally adequate diet, given the size of the family, multiplied by three.

The current U.S. poverty line is essentially the same as the Orshansky poverty line, although the government adjusts the dollar amounts to represent the same buying power over time. The U.S. poverty line in 2021 ranged from $12,880 for a single individual to $26,500 for a household of four people.

Figure 15.2 shows the U.S. **poverty rate** over time; that is, the percentage of the population below the poverty line in any given year. The poverty rate declined through the 1960s, rose in the early 1980s and early 1990s, but seems to have been slightly lower since the mid-1990s. However, in no year in the last six decades has the poverty rate been less than 10.5% of the U.S. population—that is, at best almost one American in nine is below the poverty line. In recent years, the poverty rate peaked at 15.1% in 2010, before dropping to 10.5% in 2019. Table 15.1 compares poverty rates for different groups in 2011. As you will see when we delve further into these numbers, poverty rates are relatively low for White people, for the elderly, for the well-educated, and for male-headed households. Poverty rates for females, Hispanic people, and African Americans are much higher than for White people. While Hispanic people and African Americans have a higher percentage of individuals living in poverty than others, most people in the United States living below the poverty line are White people.

## LINK IT UP

Visit this website (http://openstax.org/l/povertyprogram) for more information on U.S. poverty.

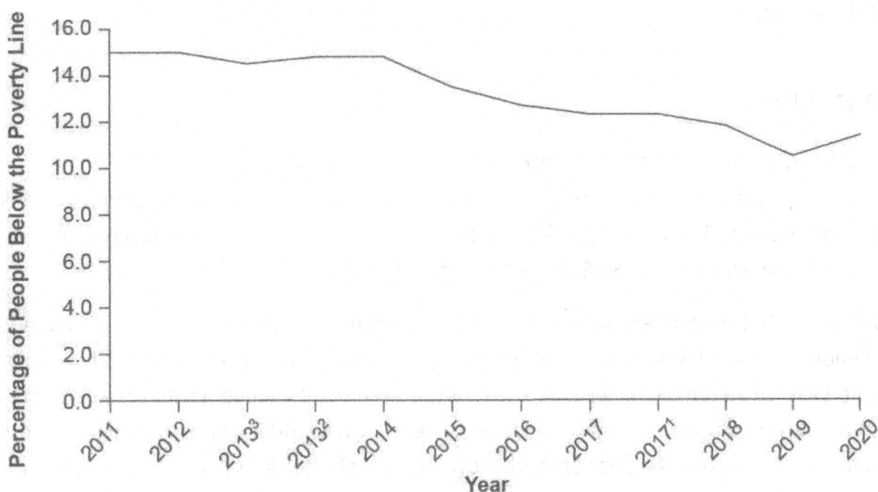


FIGURE 15.2 The U.S. Poverty Rate since 1960 The poverty rate fell dramatically during the 1960s, rose in the early 1980s and early 1990s, and, after declining in the 1990s through mid-2000s, rose to 15.1% in 2020, which is close to the 1960 levels. Between 2010 and 2019, the poverty rate declined to 10.5%, before rising to 11.4% in 2020 due to the onset of the COVID-19 pandemic in 2020. (Source: U.S. Census Bureau)

| Group | Poverty Rate |
|---|---|
| Females | 12.6% |
| Males | 10.2% |
| White (Non-Hispanic) | 8.2% |
| Black | 19.5% |
| Hispanic | 17.0% |
| Under age 18 | 16.1% |
| Ages 18–64 | 10.4% |
| Ages 65+ | 9.0% |

TABLE 15.1 Poverty Rates by Group, 2020

The concept of a poverty line raises many tricky questions. In a vast country like the United States, should there be a national poverty line? After all, according to the Federal Register, the median household income for a family of four was $109,113 in New Jersey and $59,701 in Mississippi in 2017, and prices of some basic goods like housing are quite different between states. The poverty line is based on cash income, which means it does not account for government programs that provide non-cash assistance such as Medicaid (health care for low-income individuals and families) and food aid. Also, low-income families can qualify for federal housing assistance. (We will discuss these and other government aid programs in detail later in this chapter.)

Should the government adjust the poverty line to account for the value of such programs? Many economists and policymakers wonder whether we should rethink the concept of what poverty means in the twenty-first century. The following Clear It Up feature explains the poverty lines set by the World Bank for low-income countries around the world.

 **CLEAR IT UP**

### How do economists measure poverty in low-income countries?

The World Bank sets two poverty lines for low-income countries around the world. One poverty line is set at an income of $1.90/day per person. The other is at $3.20/day. By comparison, the U.S. 2015 poverty line of $20,090 annually for a family of three works out to $18.35 per person per day.

Clearly, many people around the world are far poorer than Americans, as Table 15.2 shows. China and India both have more than a billion people; Nigeria is the most populous country in Africa; and Egypt is the most populous country in the Middle East. In all four of those countries, in the mid-2000s, a substantial share of the population subsisted on less than $2/day. About half the world lives on less than $2.50 a day, and 80 percent of the world lives on less than $10 per day. (Of course, the cost of food, clothing, and shelter in those countries can be very different from those costs in the United States, so the $2 and $2.50 figures may mean greater purchasing power than they would in the United States.)

| Country | Year | Percentage of Population with Income Less Than $1.90/Day/Person | Percentage of Population with Income Less Than $3.20/Day/Person |
|---|---|---|---|
| Brazil | 2019 | 4.6% | 9.1% |
| China | 2017 | 0.5% | 5.4% |
| Egypt | 2017 | 3.8% | 28.9% |
| India | 2011 | 22.5% | 61.7% |
| Mexico | 2018 | 1.7% | 6.5% |
| Nigeria | 2018 | 39.1% | 71.0% |

**TABLE 15.2 Poverty Lines for Low-Income Countries, mid-2000s** (Source: https://datatopics.worldbank.org/world-development-indicators/themes/poverty-and-inequality.html)

Any poverty line will be somewhat arbitrary, and it is useful to have a poverty line whose basic definition does not change much over time. If Congress voted every few years to redefine poverty, then it would be difficult to compare rates over time. After all, would a lower poverty rate change the definition, or is it the case that people were actually better off? Government statisticians at the U.S. Census Bureau have ongoing research programs to address questions like these.

## 15.2 The Poverty Trap

**LEARNING OBJECTIVES**

By the end of this section, you will be able to:
- Explain the poverty trap, noting how government programs impact it
- Identify potential issues in government programs that seek to reduce poverty
- Calculate a budget constraint line that represents the poverty trap

Can you give people too much help, or the wrong kind of help? When people are provided with food, shelter, healthcare, income, and other necessities, assistance may reduce their incentive to work, particularly if their work is likely to offer low wages and reduce government assistance. Consider a program to fight poverty that works in this reasonable-sounding manner: the government provides assistance to the those who need it, but as the recipients earn income to support themselves, the government reduces the level of assistance it provides. With such a program, every time a person earns $100, they lose $100 in government support. As a result, the person experiences no net gain for working. Economists call this problem the **poverty trap**.

Consider the situation a single-parent family faces. Figure 15.3 illustrates a single mother (earning $8 an hour) with two children. First, consider the labor-leisure budget constraint that this family faces in a situation without government assistance. On the horizontal axis is hours of leisure (or time spent with family responsibilities) increasing in quantity from left to right. Also on the horizontal axis is the number of hours at paid work, going from zero hours on the right to the maximum of 2,500 hours on the left. On the vertical axis is the amount of income per year rising from low to higher amounts of income. The budget constraint line shows that at zero hours of leisure and 2,500 hours of work, the maximum amount of income is $20,000 ($8 × 2,500 hours). At the other extreme of the budget constraint line, an individual would work zero hours, earn zero income, but enjoy 2,500 hours of leisure. At point A on the budget constraint line, by working 40 hours a week, 50 weeks a year, the utility-maximizing choice is to work a total of 2,000 hours per year and earn $16,000.

Now suppose that a government antipoverty program guarantees every family with a single mother and two children $18,000 in income. This is represented on the graph by a horizontal line at $18,000. With this program, each time the mother earns $1,000, the government will deduct $1,000 of its support. Table 15.3 shows what will happen at each combination of work and government support.

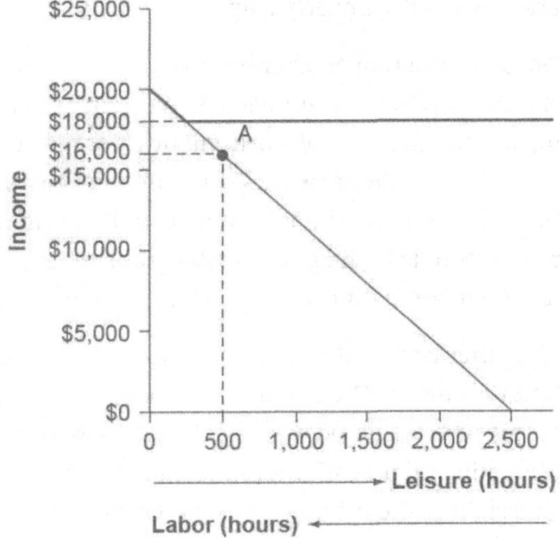


**FIGURE 15.3 The Poverty Trap in Action** The original choice is 500 hours of leisure, 2,000 hours of work at point A, and income of $16,000. With a guaranteed income of $18,000, this family would receive $18,000 whether it provides zero hours of work or 2,000 hours of work. Only if the family provides, say, 2,300 hours of work does its income rise above the guaranteed level of $18,000—and even then, the marginal gain to income from working many hours is small.

| Amount Worked (hours) | Total Earnings | Government Support | Total Income |
| --- | --- | --- | --- |
| 0 | 0 | $18,000 | $18,000 |
| 500 | $4,000 | $14,000 | $18,000 |
| 1,000 | $8,000 | $10,000 | $18,000 |
| 1,500 | $12,000 | $6,000 | $18,000 |
| 2,000 | $16,000 | $2,000 | $18,000 |
| 2,500 | $20,000 | 0 | $20,000 |

**TABLE 15.3** Total Income at Various Combinations of Work and Support

The new budget line, with the antipoverty program in place, is the horizontal and heavy line that is flat at $18,000. If the mother does not work at all, she receives $18,000, all from the government. If she works full time, giving up 40 hours per week with her children, she still ends up with $18,000 at the end of the year. Only if she works 2,300 hours in the year—which is an average of 44 hours per week for 50 weeks a year—does household income rise to $18,400. Even in this case, all of her year's work means that household income rises by only $400 over the income she would receive if she did not work at all. She would need to work 50 hours a week to reach $20,800.

The poverty trap is even stronger than this simplified example shows, because a working mother will have extra expenses like clothing, transportation, and child care that a nonworking mother will not face, making the economic gains from working even smaller. Moreover, those who do not work fail to build up job experience and contacts, which makes working in the future even less likely.

To reduce the poverty trap the government could design an antipoverty program so that, instead of reducing government payments by $1 for every $1 earned, the government would reduce payments by some smaller amount instead. Imposing requirements for work as a condition of receiving benefits and setting a time limit on benefits can also reduce the harshness of the poverty trap.

Figure 15.4 illustrates a government program that guarantees $18,000 in income, even for those who do not work at all, but then reduces this amount by 50 cents for each $1 earned. The new, higher budget line in Figure 15.4 shows that, with this program, additional hours of work will bring some economic gain. Because of the reduction in government income when an individual works, an individual earning $8.00 will really net only $4.00 per hour. The vertical intercept of this higher budget constraint line is at $28,000 ($18,000 + 2,500 hours × $4.00 = $28,000). The horizontal intercept is at the point on the graph where $18,000 and 2500 hours of leisure is set. Table 15.4 shows the total income differences with various choices of labor and leisure.

However, this type of program raises other issues. First, even if it does not eliminate the incentive to work by reducing government payments by $1 for every $1 earned, enacting such a program may still reduce the incentive to work. At least some people who would be working 2,000 hours each year without this program might decide to work fewer hours but still end up with more income—that is, their choice on the new budget line would be like S, above and to the right of the original choice P. Of course, others may choose a point like R, which involves the same amount of work as P, or even a point to the left of R that involves more work.

The second major issue is that when the government phases out its support payments more slowly, the antipoverty program costs more money. Still, it may be preferable in the long run to spend more money on a program that retains a greater incentive to work, rather than spending less money on a program that nearly eliminates any gains from working.

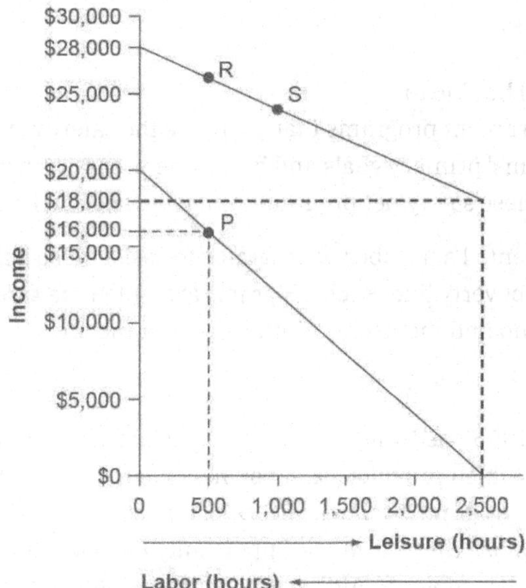


**FIGURE 15.4 Loosening the Poverty Trap: Reducing Government Assistance by 50 Cents for Every $1 Earned** On the original labor-leisure opportunity set, the lower, downward-sloping budget set, the preferred choice P is 500 hours of leisure and $16,000 of income. Then, the government created an antipoverty program that guarantees $18,000 in income even to those who work zero hours, shown by the hoizontal dashed line. In addition, every $1 earned means phasing out 50 cents of benefits at $18,000. This program leads to the higher budget set, which the diagram shows. The hope is that this program will provide incentives to work the same or more hours, despite receiving income assistance. However, it is possible that the recipients will choose a point on the new budget set like S, with less work, more leisure, and greater income, or a point like R, with the same work and greater income.

| Amount Worked (hours) | Total Earnings | Government Support | Total Income |
|---|---|---|---|
| 0 | 0 | $18,000 | $18,000 |
| 500 | $4,000 | $16,000 | $20,000 |
| 1,000 | $8,000 | $14,000 | $22,000 |
| 1,500 | $12,000 | $12,000 | $24,000 |
| 2,000 | $16,000 | $10,000 | $26,000 |
| 2,500 | $20,000 | $8,000 | $28,000 |

**TABLE 15.4 The Labor-Leisure Tradeoff with Assistance Reduced by 50 Cents for Every Dollar Earned**

The next module will consider a variety of government support programs focused specifically on people experiencing poverty, including welfare, SNAP (Supplemental Nutrition Assistance Program), Medicaid, and the earned income tax credit (EITC). Although these programs vary from state to state, it is generally a true statement that in many states from the 1960s into the 1980s, if poor people worked, their level of income barely rose—or did not rise at all—after factoring in the reduction in government support payments. The following Work It Out feature shows how this happens.

## 15.3 The Safety Net

**LEARNING OBJECTIVES**

By the end of this section, you will be able to:

- Identify the antipoverty government programs that comprise the safety net
- Explain the safety net programs' primary goals and how these programs have changed over time
- Discuss the complexities of these safety net programs and why they can be controversial

The U.S. government has implemented a number of programs to assist those below the poverty line and those who have incomes just above the poverty line. Such programs are called the **safety net**, to recognize that they offer some protection for those who find themselves without jobs or income.

### Temporary Assistance for Needy Families

From the Great Depression until 1996, the United States' most visible antipoverty program was Aid to Families with Dependent Children (AFDC), which provided cash payments to mothers with children who were below the poverty line. Many just called this program "welfare." In 1996, Congress passed and President Bill Clinton signed into law the Personal Responsibility and Work Opportunity Reconciliation Act, more commonly called the "welfare reform act." The new law replaced AFDC with Temporary Assistance for Needy Families (TANF).

### 🔗 LINK IT UP

Visit this website (http://openstax.org/l/Clinton_speech) to watch a video of President Bill Clinton's Welfare Reform speech.

---

TANF brought several dramatic changes in how welfare operated. Under the old AFDC program, states set the level of welfare benefits that they would pay to people experiencing poverty, and the federal government guaranteed it would chip in some of the money as well. The federal government's welfare spending would rise or fall depending on the number of people in need, and on how each state set its own welfare contribution.

Under TANF, however, the federal government gives a fixed amount of money to each state. The state can then use the money for almost any program with an antipoverty component: for example, the state might use the money to give funds to families with low income, or to reduce teenage pregnancy, or even to raise the high school graduation rate. However, the federal government imposed two key requirements. First, if states are to keep receiving the TANF grants, they must impose work requirements so that most of those receiving TANF benefits are working (or attending school). Second, no one can receive TANF benefits with federal money for more than a total of five years over their lifetime. The old AFDC program had no such work requirements or time limits.

TANF attempts to avoid the poverty trap by requiring that welfare recipients work and by limiting the length of time they can receive benefits. In its first few years, the program was quite successful. The number of families receiving payments in 1995, the last year of AFDC, was 4.8 million. November 2020, according to the Congressional Research Service, the number of families receiving payments under TANF was 1.0 million—a decline of nearly 80%.

TANF benefits to poor families vary considerably across states. For example, again according to the Congressional Research Service, in July 2020 the highest monthly payment in New Hampshire to a single mother with one child was $862, while in Mississippi the highest monthly payment to that family was $146. In part, these payments reflect differences in states' cost of living. As reported by the Department of Health and Human Services, in 1995 total spending on TANF was approximately $19 billion. Spending increased yearly through 2001, then it was roughly flat at approximately $26 billion until 2005, then it increased again through 2010, where it peaked at nearly $35 billion. It then decreased again to around $30 billion in 2020. When you take into account the effects of inflation, the decline is even greater. Moreover, there seemed little evidence that families were suffering a reduced standard of living as a result of TANF—although, on the other side, there was not much evidence that families had greatly improved their total levels of income, either.

## The Earned Income Tax Credit (EITC)

The **earned income tax credit (EITC)**, first passed in 1975, is a method of assisting the working poor through the tax system. The EITC is one of the largest assistance program for low-income groups, and as of December 2021, about 25 million eligible workers and families received about $60 billion in EITC. For the 2021 tax year, the earned income credit ranges from $1,502 to $6,728 depending on tax-filing status, income, and number of children. The average amount of EITC received nationwide was about $2,411. In 2021, for example, a single parent with two children would have received a tax credit of $5,980 up to a modest income level. The amount of the tax break increases with the amount of income earned, up to a point. The earned income tax credit has often been popular with both economists and the general public because of the way it effectively increases the payment received for work.

What about the danger of the poverty trap that every additional $1 earned will reduce government support payments by close to $1? To minimize this problem, the earned income tax credit is phased out slowly. For example, according to the Tax Policy Center, for a single-parent family with two children in 2013, the credit is not reduced at all (but neither is it increased) as earnings rise from $13,430 to $17,530. Then, for every $1 earned above $17,530, the amount received from the credit is reduced by 21.06 cents, until the credit phases out completely at an income level of $46,227.

Figure 15.5 illustrates that the earned income tax credits, child tax credits, and the TANF program all cost the federal government money—either in direct outlays or in loss of tax revenues. CTC stands for the government tax cuts for the child tax credit.

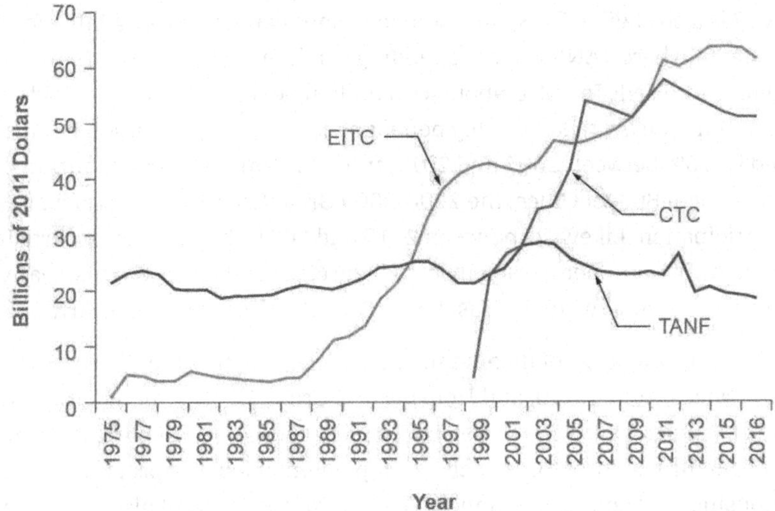


FIGURE 15.5 Real Federal Spending on CTC, EITC, and TANF, 1975–2016 EITC increased from under $10 billion in the late 1980s to almost $42 billion in 2000 and to over $61 billion in 2016, far exceeding estimated 2016 outlays in the CTC (Child Tax Credits) and TANF of over $25 billion and $18 billion, respectively. (Source: Office of Management and Budget)

In recent years, the EITC has become a hugely expensive government program for providing income assistance to people below or near the poverty line, costing about $60 billion in 2021. In that year, the EITC provided benefits to about 25 million families and individuals and, on average, is worth about $2,411 per family (with children), according to the Tax Policy Center. One reason that the TANF law worked as well as it did is that the government greatly expanded EITC in the late 1980s and again in the early 1990s, which increased the returns to work for low-income Americans.

## Supplemental Nutrition Assistance Program (SNAP)

Often called "food stamps," **Supplemental Nutrition Assistance Program (SNAP)** is a federally funded program, started in 1964, in which each month people receive a card like a debit card that they can use to buy food. The amount of food aid for which a household is eligible varies by income, number of children, and other factors but, in general, households are expected to spend about 30% of their own net income on food, and if 30% of their net income is not enough to purchase a nutritionally adequate diet, then those households are eligible for SNAP.

SNAP can contribute to the poverty trap. For every $100 earned, the government assumes that a family can spend $30 more for food, and thus reduces its eligibility for food aid by $30. This decreased benefit is not a complete disincentive to work—but combined with how other programs reduce benefits as income increases, it adds to the problem. SNAP, however, does try to address the poverty trap with its own set of work requirements and time limits.

Why give debit cards and not just cash? Part of the political support for SNAP comes from a belief that since recipients must spend the the cards on food, they cannot "waste" them on other forms of consumption. From an economic point of view, however, the belief that cards must increase spending on food seems wrong-headed. After all, say that a family is spending $2,500 per year on food, and then it starts receiving $1,000 per year in SNAP aid. The family might react by spending $3,500 per year on food (income plus aid), or it might react by continuing to spend $2,500 per year on food, but use the $1,000 in food aid to free up $1,000 that it can now spend on other goods. Thus, it is reasonable to think of SNAP cards as an alternative method, along with TANF and the earned income tax credit, of transferring income to those working but still experiencing poverty.

Anyone eligible for TANF is also eligible for SNAP, although states can expand eligibility for food aid if they wish to do so. In some states, where TANF welfare spending is relatively low, a poor family may receive more in support from SNAP than from TANF. In 2021, about 41.5 million people received food aid with total benefits of just over $108 billion, which is an average monthly benefit of about $287 per person per month. SNAP participation increased by 70% between 2007 and 2011, from 26.6 million participants to 45 million. According to the Congressional Budget Office, the 2008-2009 Great Recession and rising food prices caused this dramatic rise in participation. Likewise, between 2019 and 2021, the number of participants in SNAP increased by 5.8 million, the amount per person increased by 67%, and total benefits nearly doubled as a consequence of the sharp recession due to the onset of the COVID-19 pandemic in early 2020.

The federal government deploys a range of income security programs that it funds through departments such as Health and Human Services, Agriculture, and Housing and Urban Development (HUD) (see Figure 15.6). According to the Office of Management and Budget, collectively, these three departments provided an estimated $62 billion of aid through programs such as supplemental feeding programs for women and children, subsidized housing, and energy assistance. The federal government also transfers funds to individual states through special grant programs.

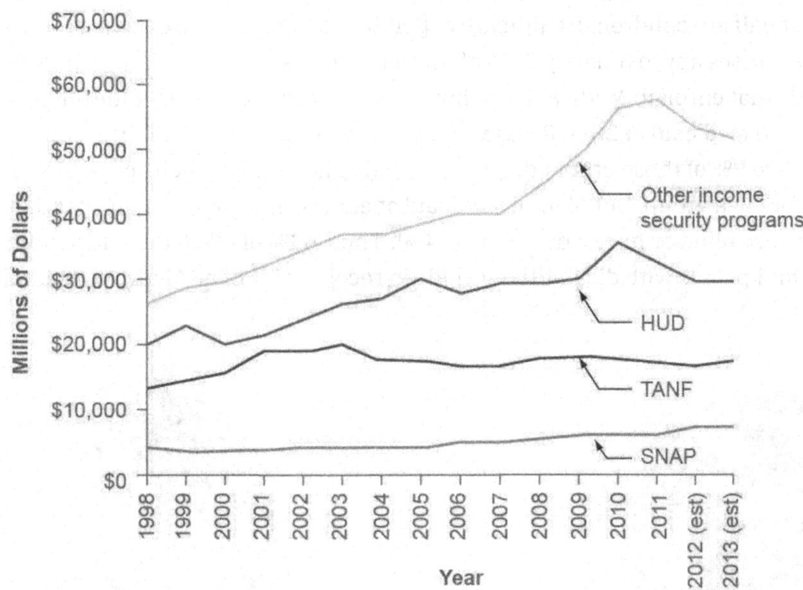


FIGURE 15.6 Expenditure Comparison of TANF, SNAP, HUD, and Other Income Security Programs, 1988–2013 (est.) Total expenditures on income security continued to rise between 1988 and 2010, while payments for TANF have increased from $13 billion in 1998 to an estimated $17.3 billion in 2013. SNAP has seen relatively small increments. These two programs comprise a relatively small portion of the estimated $106 billion dedicated to income security in 2013. Note that other programs and housing programs increased dramatically during the 2008 and 2010 time periods. (Source: Table 12.3 Section 600 Income Security, https://www.whitehouse.gov/sites/default/files/omb/budget/fy2013/assets/hist.pdf)

The safety net includes a number of other programs: government-subsidized school lunches and breakfasts for children from low-income families; the Special Supplemental Food Program for Women, Infants and Children (WIC), which provides food assistance for pregnant women and newborns; the Low Income Home Energy Assistance Program, which provides help with home heating bills; housing assistance, which helps pay the rent; and Supplemental Security Income, which provides cash support for people with disabilities and elderly people experiencing poverty.

## Medicaid

Congress created **Medicaid** in 1965. This is a joint health insurance program between both the states and the federal government. The federal government helps fund Medicaid, but each state is responsible for administering the program, determining the level of benefits, and determining eligibility. It provides medical insurance for certain people with low incomes, including those below the poverty line, with a focus on families with children, the elderly, and people with disabilities. About one-third of Medicaid spending is for low-income mothers with children. While an increasing share of the program funding in recent years has gone to pay for nursing home costs for older people who cannot afford to pay for housing. The program ensures that participants receive a basic level of benefits, but because each state sets eligibility requirements and provides varying levels of service, the program differs from state to state.

In the past, a common problem has been that many low-paying jobs pay enough to a breadwinner so that a family could lose its eligibility for Medicaid, yet the job does not offer health insurance benefits. A parent considering such a job might choose not to work rather than lose health insurance for their children. In this way, health insurance can become a part of the poverty trap. Many states recognized this problem in the 1980s and 1990s and expanded their Medicaid coverage to include people earning up to 135% or even 185% of the poverty line. Some states also guaranteed that children would not lose coverage if their parents worked.

These expanded guarantees cost the government money, of course, but they also helped to encourage those on welfare to enter the labor force. As of 2014, approximately 69.7 million people participated in Medicaid. Of those enrolled, almost half are children. Healthcare expenditures, however, are highest for the elderly population, which comprises approximately 25% of participants. As Figure 15.7 (a) indicates, the largest number of households that enroll in Medicaid are those with children. Lower-income adults are the next largest group enrolled in Medicaid at 28%. People who are blind or have a disability account for 16% of those enrolled, and seniors are 9% of those enrolled. Figure 15.7 (b) shows how much actual Medicaid dollars the government spends for each group. Out of total Medicaid spending, the government spends more on seniors (20%) and people who are blind or have a disability (44%). Thus, 64% of all Medicaid spending goes to seniors, those who are blind, and people with disabilities. Children receive 21% of all Medicaid spending, followed by adults at 15%.

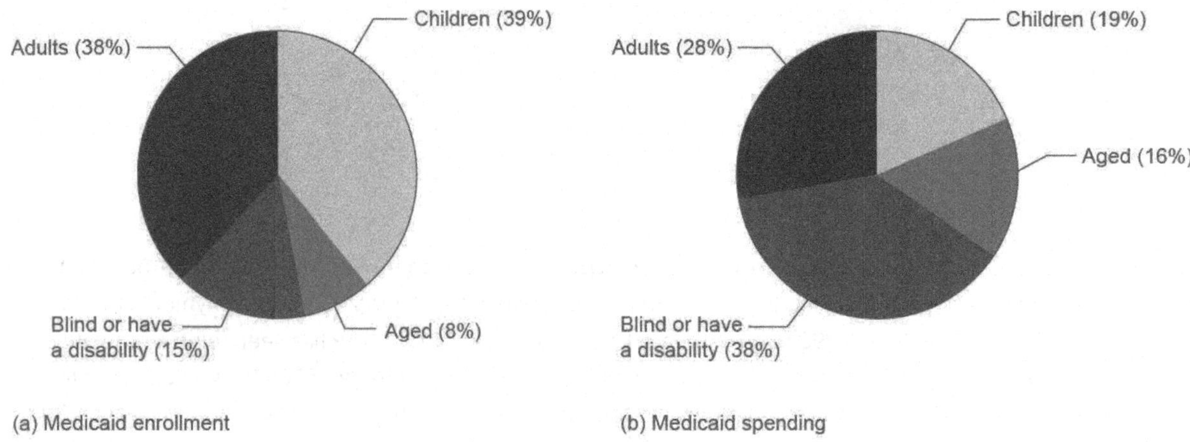


**FIGURE 15.7 Medicaid Enrollment and Spending** Part (a) shows the Medicaid enrollment by different populations, with children comprising the largest percentage at 47%, followed by adults at 28%, and those who are blind or have a disability at 16%. Part (b) shows that Medicaid spending is principally for those who are blind or have a disability, followed by the elderly. Although children are the largest population that Medicaid covers, expenditures on children are only at 19%.

## 15.4 Income Inequality: Measurement and Causes

### LEARNING OBJECTIVES

By the end of this section, you will be able to:

- Explain the distribution of income, and analyze the sources of income inequality in a market economy
- Measure income distribution in quintiles
- Calculate and graph a Lorenz curve
- Show income inequality through demand and supply diagrams

Poverty levels can be subjective based on the overall income levels of a country. Typically a government measures poverty based on a percentage of the median income. Income inequality, however, has to do with the distribution of that income, in terms of which group receives the most or the least income. Income inequality involves comparing those with high incomes, middle incomes, and low incomes—not just looking at those below or near the poverty line. In turn, measuring income inequality means dividing the population into various groups and then comparing the groups, a task that we can be carry out in several ways, as the next Clear It Up feature shows.

 **CLEAR IT UP**

### How do you separate poverty and income inequality?

Poverty can change even when inequality does not move at all. Imagine a situation in which income for everyone in the population declines by 10%. Poverty would rise, since a greater share of the population would now fall below the poverty line. However, inequality would be the same, because everyone suffered the same proportional loss. Conversely, a general rise in income levels over time would keep inequality the same, but reduce poverty.

It is also possible for income inequality to change without affecting the poverty rate. Imagine a situation in which a large number of people who already have high incomes increase their incomes by even more. Inequality would rise as a result—but the number of people below the poverty line would remain unchanged.

Why did inequality of household income increase in the United States in recent decades? A trend toward greater income inequality has occurred in many countries around the world, although the effect has been more powerful in the U.S. economy. Economists have focused their explanations for the increasing inequality on two factors that changed more or less continually from the 1970s into the 2000s. One set of explanations focuses on the changing shape of American households. The other focuses on greater inequality of wages, what some economists call "winner take all" labor markets. We will begin with how we measure inequality, and then consider the explanations for growing inequality in the United States.

## Measuring Income Distribution by Quintiles

One common way of measuring income inequality is to rank all households by income, from lowest to highest, and then to divide all households into five groups with equal numbers of people, known as **quintiles**. This calculation allows for measuring the distribution of income among the five groups compared to the total. The first quintile is the lowest fifth or 20%, the second quintile is the next lowest, and so on. We can measure income inequality by comparing what share of the total income each quintile earns.

U.S. income distribution by quintile appears in Table 15.5. In 2020, for example, the bottom quintile of the income distribution received 3.2% of income; the second quintile received 8.1%; the third quintile, 14.0%; the fourth quintile, 22.6%; and the top quintile, 52.2%. The final column of Table 15.5 shows what share of income went to households in the top 5% of the income distribution: 23.0% in 2020. Over time, from the late 1960s to the early 1980s, the top fifth of the income distribution typically received between about 43% to 44% of all income. The share of income that the top fifth received then begins to rise. Census Bureau researchers trace, much of this increase in the share of income going to the top fifth to an increase in the share of income going to the top 5%. The quintile measure shows how income inequality has increased in recent decades.

| Year | Lowest Quintile | Second Quintile | Third Quintile | Fourth Quintile | Highest Quintile | Top 5% |
|------|-----------------|-----------------|----------------|-----------------|------------------|--------|
| 1967 | 4.0 | 10.8 | 17.3 | 24.2 | 43.6 | 17.2 |
| 1970 | 4.1 | 10.8 | 17.4 | 24.5 | 43.3 | 16.6 |
| 1975 | 4.3 | 10.4 | 17.0 | 24.7 | 43.6 | 16.5 |
| 1980 | 4.2 | 10.2 | 16.8 | 24.7 | 44.1 | 16.5 |
| 1985 | 3.9 | 9.8 | 16.2 | 24.4 | 45.6 | 17.6 |
| 1990 | 3.8 | 9.6 | 15.9 | 24.0 | 46.6 | 18.5 |
| 1995 | 3.7 | 9.1 | 15.2 | 23.3 | 48.7 | 21.0 |
| 2000 | 3.6 | 8.9 | 14.8 | 23.0 | 49.8 | 22.1 |

**TABLE 15.5 Share of Aggregate Income Received by Each Fifth and Top 5% of Households, 1967–2020** (Source: U.S. Census Bureau, https://www.census.gov/data/tables/time-series/demo/income-poverty/historical-income-households.html, Table H-1, All Races.)

| Year | Lowest Quintile | Second Quintile | Third Quintile | Fourth Quintile | Highest Quintile | Top 5% |
|------|------|------|------|------|------|------|
| 2005 | 3.4 | 8.6 | 14.6 | 23.0 | 50.4 | 22.2 |
| 2010 | 3.3 | 8.5 | 14.6 | 23.4 | 50.3 | 21.3 |
| 2015 | 3.1 | 8.2 | 14.3 | 23.2 | 51.1 | 22.1 |
| 2020 | 3.0 | 8.1 | 14.0 | 22.6 | 52.2 | 23.0 |

**TABLE 15.5 Share of Aggregate Income Received by Each Fifth and Top 5% of Households, 1967–2020** (Source: U.S. Census Bureau, https://www.census.gov/data/tables/time-series/demo/income-poverty/historical-income-households.html, Table H-1, All Races.)

It can also be useful to divide the income distribution in ways other than quintiles; for example, into tenths or even into percentiles (that is, hundredths). A more detailed breakdown can provide additional insights. For example, the last column of Table 15.5 shows the income received by the top 5% of the income distribution. Between 1980 and 2020, the share of income going to the top 5% increased by 6.5 percentage points (from 16.5% in 1980 to 23.0% in 2020). From 1980 to 2020 the share of income going to the top quintile increased by 8.1 percentage points (from 44.1% in 1980 to 52.2% in 2013). Thus, the top 20% of householders (the fifth quintile) received over half (51%) of all the income in the United States in 2020.

## Lorenz Curve

We can present the data on income inequality in various ways. For example, you could draw a bar graph that showed the share of income going to each fifth of the income distribution. Figure 15.8 presents an alternative way of showing inequality data in a **Lorenz curve**. This curve shows the cumulative share of population on the horizontal axis and the cumulative percentage of total income received on the vertical axis.

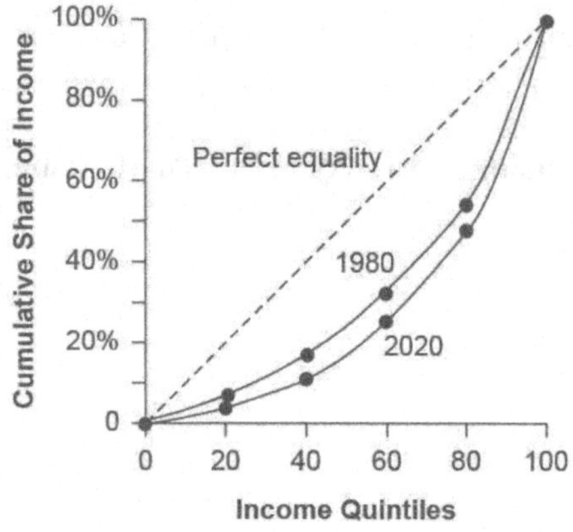


**FIGURE 15.8 The Lorenz Curve** A Lorenz curve graphs the cumulative shares of income received by everyone up to a certain quintile. The income distribution in 1980 was closer to the perfect equality line than the income distribution in 2020—that is, the U.S. income distribution became more unequal over time.

Every Lorenz curve diagram begins with a line sloping up at a 45-degree angle. We show it as a dashed line in Figure 15.8. The points along this line show what perfect equality of the income distribution looks like. It would mean, for example, that the bottom 20% of the income distribution receives 20% of the total income, the bottom 40% gets 40% of total income, and so on. The other lines reflect actual U.S. data on inequality for 1980 and 2020.

The trick in graphing a Lorenz curve is that you must change the shares of income for each specific quintile, which we show in the first and third columns of numbers in Table 15.6, into cumulative income, which we show in the second and fourth columns of numbers. For example, the bottom 40% of the cumulative income distribution will be the sum of the first and second quintiles; the bottom 60% of the cumulative income distribution will be the sum of the first, second, and third quintiles, and so on. The final entry in the cumulative income column needs to be 100%, because by definition, 100% of the population receives 100% of the income.

| Income Category | Share of Income in 1980 (%) | Cumulative Share of Income in 1980 (%) | Share of Income in 2020 (%) | Cumulative Share of Income in 2020 (%) |
|---|---|---|---|---|
| First quintile | 4.2 | 4.2 | 3.0 | 3.0 |
| Second quintile | 10.2 | 14.4 | 8.1 | 11.1 |
| Third quintile | 16.8 | 31.2 | 14.0 | 25.1 |
| Fourth quintile | 24.7 | 55.9 | 22.6 | 47.7 |
| Fifth quintile | 44.1 | 100.0 | 52.2 | 100.0 |

**TABLE 15.6 Calculating the Lorenz Curve**

In a Lorenz curve diagram, a more unequal distribution of income will loop farther down and away from the 45-degree line, while a more equal distribution of income will move the line closer to the 45-degree line. Figure 15.8 illustrates the greater inequality of the U.S. income distribution between 1980 and 2020 because the Lorenz curve for 2020 is farther from the 45-degree line than the Lorenz curve for 1980. The Lorenz curve is a useful way of presenting the quintile data that provides an image of all the quintile data at once. The next Clear It Up feature shows how income inequality differs in various countries compared to the United States.

 **CLEAR IT UP**

### How does economic inequality vary around the world?

The U.S. economy has a relatively high degree of income inequality by global standards. As Table 15.7 shows, based on a variety of national surveys for a selection of years in the second decade of this century, the U.S. economy has greater inequality than Germany (along with most Western European countries). The region of the world with the highest level of income inequality is Latin America, illustrated in the numbers for Brazil and Mexico. The level of inequality in the United States is higher than in some of the low-income countries of the world, like India and Nigeria, as well as in some middle-income countries, like China and Russia.

| Country | Survey Year | First Quintile | Second Quintile | Third Quintile | Fourth Quintile | Fifth Quintile |
|---|---|---|---|---|---|---|
| United States | 2020 | 3.0% | 8.1% | 14.0% | 22.6% | 52.2% |
| Germany | 2016 | 7.6% | 12.8% | 17.1% | 22.8% | 39.6% |

**TABLE 15.7 Income Distribution in Select Countries** (Source: U.S. data from U.S. Census Bureau Table H-1. Other data from The World Bank Poverty and Inequality Data Base, https://datatopics.worldbank.org/world-development-

| Country | Survey Year | First Quintile | Second Quintile | Third Quintile | Fourth Quintile | Fifth Quintile |
|---|---|---|---|---|---|---|
| Brazil | 2019 | 3.1% | 7.4% | 12.3% | 19.4% | 57.8% |
| Mexico | 2018 | 5.4% | 9.5% | 13.5% | 20.0% | 51.7% |
| China | 2016 | 6.5% | 10.7% | 15.3% | 22.2% | 45.3% |
| India | 2011 | 8.1% | 11.7% | 15.2% | 20.5% | 44.4% |
| Russia | 2018 | 7.1% | 11.2% | 15.2% | 21.4% | 45.1% |
| Nigeria | 2018 | 7.1% | 11.6% | 16.2% | 22.7% | 42.4% |

**TABLE 15.7 Income Distribution in Select Countries** (Source: U.S. data from U.S. Census Bureau Table H-1. Other data from The World Bank Poverty and Inequality Data Base, https://datatopics.worldbank.org/world-development-indicators/themes/poverty-and-inequality.html)

## ⊘ LINK IT UP

Visit this website (http://openstax.org/l/inequality/) to watch a video of wealth inequality across the world.

### Causes of Growing Inequality: The Changing Composition of American Households

In 1970, 41% of married women were in the labor force, but by 2019, according to the Bureau of Labor Statistics, 58.6% of married women were in the labor force. One result of this trend is that more households have two earners. Moreover, it has become more common for one high earner to marry another high earner. A few decades ago, the common pattern featured a man with relatively high earnings, such as an executive or a doctor, marrying a woman who did not earn as much, like a secretary or a nurse. Often, the woman would leave paid employment, at least for a few years, to raise a family. However, now doctors are marrying doctors and executives are marrying executives, and mothers with high-powered careers are often returning to work while their children are quite young. This pattern of households with two high earners tends to increase the proportion of high-earning households.

According to data in the National Journal, even as two-earner couples have increased, so have single-parent households. Of all U.S. families, in 2021, about 23% were headed by single mothers. The poverty rate among single-parent households tends to be relatively high.

These changes in family structure, including the growth of single-parent families who tend to be at the lower end of the income distribution, and the growth of two-career high-earner couples near the top end of the income distribution, account for roughly half of the rise in income inequality across households in recent decades.

## ⊘ LINK IT UP

Visit this website (http://openstax.org/l/US_wealth) to watch a video that illustrates the distribution of wealth in the United States.

### Causes of Growing Inequality: A Shift in the Distribution of Wages

Another factor behind the rise in U.S. income inequality is that earnings have become less equal since the late 1970s. In particular, the earnings of high-skilled labor relative to low-skilled labor have increased. Winner-take-all labor markets result from changes in technology, which have increased global demand for "stars,"—whether the best CEO, doctor, basketball player, or actor. This global demand pushes salaries far above productivity differences associated with educational differences. One way to measure this change is to take workers' earnings with at least a four-year college bachelor's degree (including those who went on and completed an advanced degree) and divide them by workers' earnings with only a high school degree. The result is that those in the 25–34 age bracket with college degrees earned about 1.85 times as much as high school graduates in 2020, up from 1.59 times in 1995, according to U.S. Census data. Winner-take-all labor market theory argues that the salary gap between the median and the top 1 percent is not due to educational differences.

Economists use the demand and supply model to reason through the most likely causes of this shift. According to the National Center for Education Statistics, in recent decades, the supply of U.S. workers with college degrees has increased substantially. For example, 840,000 four-year bachelor's degrees were conferred on Americans in 1970. In 2018–2019, 2.0 million such degrees were conferred—an increase of over 138%. In Figure 15.9, this shift in supply to the right, from $S_0$ to $S_1$, by itself should result in a lower equilibrium wage for high-skilled labor. Thus, we can explain the increase in the price of high-skilled labor by a greater demand, like the movement from $D_0$ to $D_1$. Evidently, combining both the increase in supply and in demand has resulted in a shift from $E_0$ to $E_1$, and a resulting higher wage.

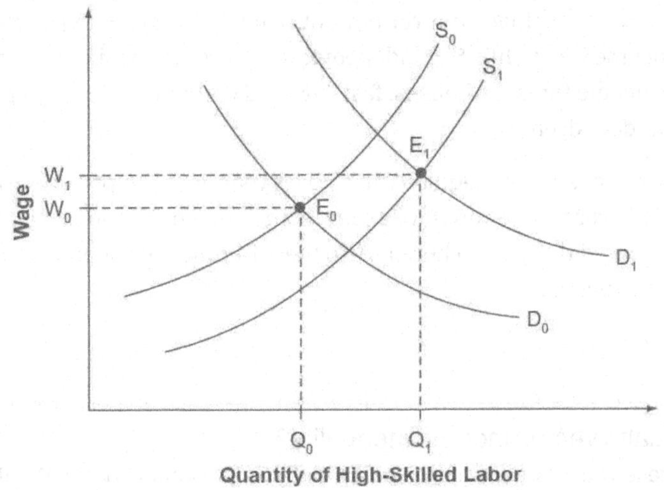


FIGURE 15.9 Why Would Wages Rise for High-Skilled Labor? The proportion of workers attending college has increased in recent decades, so the supply curve for high-skilled labor has shifted to the right, from $S_0$ to $S_1$. If the demand for high-skilled labor had remained at $D_0$, then this shift in supply would have led to lower wages for high-skilled labor. However, the wages for high-skilled labor, especially if there is a large global demand, have increased even with the shift in supply to the right. The explanation must lie in a shift to the right in demand for high-skilled labor, from $D_0$ to $D_1$. The figure shows how a combination of the shift in supply, from $S_0$ to $S_1$, and the shift in demand, from $D_0$ to $D_1$, led to both an increase in the quantity of high-skilled labor hired and also to a rise in the wage for such labor, from $W_0$ to $W_1$.

What factors would cause the demand for high-skilled labor to rise? The most plausible explanation is that while the explosion in new information and communications technologies over the last several decades has helped many workers to become more productive, the benefits have been especially great for high-skilled workers like top business managers, consultants, and design professionals. The new technologies have also helped to encourage globalization, the remarkable increase in international trade over the last few decades, by making it more possible to learn about and coordinate economic interactions all around the world. In turn, the rising impact of foreign trade in the U.S. economy has opened up greater opportunities for high-skilled workers to sell their services around the world, and lower-skilled workers have to compete with a larger supply of similarly skilled workers around the globe.

We can view the market for high-skilled labor as a race between forces of supply and demand. Additional education and on-the-job training will tend to increase the high-skilled labor supply and to hold down its relative wage. Conversely, new technology and other economic trends like globalization tend to increase the demand for high-skilled labor and push up its relative wage. We can view the greater inequality of wages as a sign that demand for skilled labor is increasing faster than supply. Alternatively, if the supply of lower skilled workers exceeds the demand, then average wages in the lower quintiles of the income distribution will decrease. The combination of forces in the high-skilled and low-skilled labor markets leads to increased income disparity.

## 15.5 Government Policies to Reduce Income Inequality

### LEARNING OBJECTIVES
By the end of this section, you will be able to:
- Explain the arguments for and against government intervention in a market economy
- Identify beneficial ways to reduce the economic inequality in a society
- Show the tradeoff between incentives and income equality

No society should expect or desire complete equality of income at a given point in time, for a number of reasons. First, most workers receive relatively low earnings in their first few jobs, higher earnings as they reach middle age, and then lower earnings after retirement. Thus, a society with people of varying ages will have a certain amount of income inequality. Second, people's preferences and desires differ. Some are willing to work long hours to have income for large houses, fast cars and computers, luxury vacations, and the ability to support children and grandchildren.

These factors all imply that a snapshot of inequality in a given year does not provide an accurate picture of how people's incomes rise and fall over time. Even if we expect some degree of economic inequality at any point in time, how much inequality should there be? There is also the difference between income and wealth, as the following Clear It Up feature explains.

 **CLEAR IT UP**

How do you measure wealth versus income inequality?
**Income** is a flow of money received, often measured on a monthly or an annual basis. **Wealth** is the sum of the value of all assets, including money in bank accounts, financial investments, a pension fund, and the value of a home. In calculating wealth, one must subtract all debts, such as debt owed on a home mortgage and on credit cards. A retired person, for example, may have relatively little income in a given year, other than a pension or Social Security. However, if that person has saved and invested over time, the person's accumulated wealth can be quite substantial.

In the United States, the wealth distribution is more unequal than the income distribution, because differences in income can accumulate over time to make even larger differences in wealth. However, we can measure the degree of inequality in the wealth distribution with the same tools we use to measure the inequality in the income distribution, like quintile measurements. Once every three years the Federal Reserve Bank publishes the *Survey of Consumer Finance* which reports a collection of data on wealth.

Even if they cannot answer the question of how much inequality is too much, economists can still play an important role in spelling out policy options and tradeoffs. If a society decides to reduce the level of economic inequality, it has three main sets of tools: redistribution from those with high incomes to those with low incomes; trying to assure that a ladder of opportunity is widely available; and a tax on inheritance.

### Redistribution

**Redistribution** means taking income from those with higher incomes and providing income to those with lower incomes. Earlier in this chapter, we considered some of the key government policies that provide support for people experiencing poverty: the welfare program TANF, the earned income tax credit, SNAP, and Medicaid. If a reduction in inequality is desired, these programs could receive additional funding.

The federal income tax, which is a **progressive tax system** designed in such a way that the rich pay a higher percent in income taxes than the poor, funds the programs. Data from household income tax returns in 2018 shows that the top 1% of households had an average income of $1,679,000 per year in pre-tax income and paid an average federal tax rate of 25.4%. The **effective income tax**, which is total taxes paid divided by total income (all sources of income such as wages, profits, interest, rental income, and government transfers such as veterans' benefits), was much lower. The effective tax paid by that top 1% of householders paid was 20.4%, while the bottom two quintiles actually paid negative effective income taxes, because of provisions like the earned income tax credit. News stories occasionally report on a high-income person who has managed to pay very little in taxes, but while such individual cases exist, according to the Congressional Budget Office, the typical pattern is that people with higher incomes pay a higher average share of their income in federal income taxes.

Of course, the fact that some degree of redistribution occurs now through the federal income tax and government antipoverty programs does not settle the questions of how much redistribution is appropriate, and whether more redistribution should occur.

## The Ladder of Opportunity

Economic inequality is perhaps most troubling when it is not the result of effort or talent, but instead is determined by the circumstances under which a child grows up. One child attends a well-run grade school and high school and heads on to college, while parents help out by supporting education and other interests, paying for college, a first car, and a first house, and offering work connections that lead to internships and jobs. Another child attends a poorly run grade school, barely makes it through a low-quality high school, does not go to college, and lacks family and peer support. These two children may be similar in their underlying talents and in the effort they put forth, but their economic outcomes are likely to be quite different.

Public policy can attempt to build a ladder of opportunities so that, even though all children will never come from identical families and attend identical schools, each child has a reasonable opportunity to attain an economic niche in society based on their interests, desires, talents, and efforts. Table 15.8 shows some of those initiatives.

| Children | College Level | Adults |
| --- | --- | --- |
| • Improved day care | • Widespread loans and grants for those in financial need | • Opportunities for retraining and acquiring new skills |
| • Enrichment programs for preschoolers | • Public support for a range of institutions from two-year community colleges to large research universities | • Prohibiting discrimination in job markets and housing on the basis of race, gender, age, and disability |
| • Improved public schools | - | - |

**TABLE 15.8 Public Policy Initiatives**

| Children | College Level | Adults |
|---|---|---|
| • After school and community activities | - | - |
| • Internships and apprenticeships | - | - |

**TABLE 15.8 Public Policy Initiatives**

Some have called the United States a land of opportunity. Although the general idea of a ladder of opportunity for all citizens continues to exert a powerful attraction, specifics are often quite controversial. Society can experiment with a wide variety of proposals for building a ladder of opportunity, especially for those who otherwise seem likely to start their lives in a disadvantaged position. The government needs to carry out such policy experiments in a spirit of open-mindedness, because some will succeed while others will not show positive results or will cost too much to enact on a widespread basis.

### Inheritance Taxes

There is always a debate about inheritance taxes. It goes like this: Why should people who have worked hard all their lives and saved up a substantial nest egg not be able to give their money and possessions to their children and grandchildren? In particular, it would seem un-American if children were unable to inherit a family business or a family home. Alternatively, many Americans are far more comfortable with inequality resulting from high-income people who earned their money by starting innovative new companies than they are with inequality resulting from high-income people who have inherited money from rich parents.

The United States does have an **estate tax**—that is, a tax imposed on the value of an inheritance—which suggests a willingness to limit how much wealth one can pass on as an inheritance. However, in 2022 the estate tax applied only to those leaving inheritances of more than $12.06 million and thus applies to only a tiny percentage of those with high levels of wealth.

### The Tradeoff between Incentives and Income Equality

Government policies to reduce poverty or to encourage economic equality, if carried to extremes, can injure incentives for economic output. The poverty trap, for example, defines a situation where guaranteeing a certain level of income can eliminate or reduce the incentive to work. An extremely high degree of redistribution, with very high taxes on the rich, would be likely to discourage work and entrepreneurship. Thus, it is common to draw the tradeoff between economic output and equality, as Figure 15.10 (a) shows. In this formulation, if society wishes a high level of economic output, like point A, it must also accept a high degree of inequality. Conversely, if society wants a high level of equality, like point B, it must accept a lower level of economic output because of reduced incentives for production.

This view of the tradeoff between economic output and equality may be too pessimistic, and Figure 15.10 (b) presents an alternate vision. Here, the tradeoff between economic output and equality first slopes up, in the vicinity of choice C, suggesting that certain programs might increase both output and economic equality. For example, the policy of providing free public education has an element of redistribution, since the value of the public schooling received by children of low-income families is clearly higher than what low-income families pay in taxes. A well-educated population, however, is also an enormously powerful factor in providing the skilled workers of tomorrow and helping the economy to grow and expand. In this case, equality and economic growth may complement each other.

Moreover, policies to diminish inequality and soften the hardship of poverty may sustain political support for a market economy. After all, if society does not make some effort toward reducing inequality and poverty, the alternative might be that people would rebel against market forces. Citizens might seek economic security by demanding that their legislators pass laws forbidding employers from ever laying off workers or reducing wages, or laws that would impose price floors and price ceilings and shut off international trade. From this viewpoint, policies to reduce inequality may help economic output by building social support for allowing markets to operate.

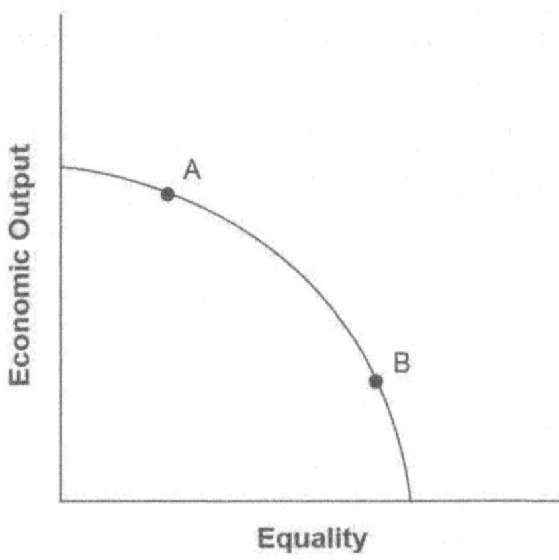


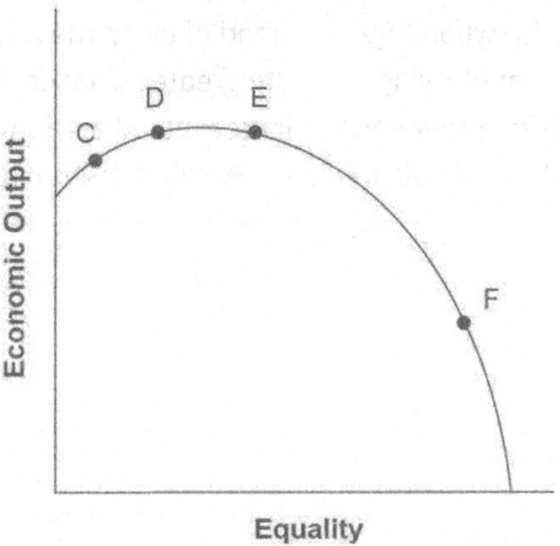


(a) Greater equality always reduces output

(b) Equality and output rise together but then face a tradeoff

**FIGURE 15.10 The Tradeoff between Incentives and Economic Equality** (a) Society faces a trade-off where any attempt to move toward greater equality, like moving from choice A to B, involves a reduction in economic output. (b) Situations can arise like point C, where it is possible both to increase equality and also to increase economic output, to a choice like D. It may also be possible to increase equality with little impact on economic output, like the movement from choice D to E. However, at some point, too aggressive a push for equality will tend to reduce economic output, as in the shift from E to F.

The tradeoff in Figure 15.10 (b) then flattens out in the area between points D and E, which reflects the pattern that a number of countries that provide similar levels of income to their citizens—the United States, Canada, European Union nations, Japan, and Australia—have different levels of inequality. The pattern suggests that countries in this range could choose a greater or a lesser degree of inequality without much impact on economic output. Only if these countries push for a much higher level of equality, like at point F, will they experience the diminished incentives that lead to lower levels of economic output. In this view, while a danger always exists that an agenda to reduce poverty or inequality can be poorly designed or pushed too far, it is also possible to discover and design policies that improve equality and do not injure incentives for economic output by very much—or even improve such incentives.

 **BRING IT HOME**

### Occupy Wall Street

The Occupy movement took on a life of its own over the last few months of 2011, bringing to light issues that many people faced on the lower end of the income distribution. The contents of this chapter indicate that there is a significant amount of income inequality in the United States. The question is: What should be done about it?

The 2008-2009 Great Recession caused unemployment to rise and incomes to fall. Many people attribute the recession to mismanagement of the financial system by bankers and financial managers—those in the 1% of the income distribution—but those in lower quintiles bore the greater burden of the recession through unemployment. This seemed to present the picture of inequality in a different light: the group that seemed responsible for the recession was not the group that seemed to bear the burden of the decline in output. A burden shared can bring a society closer together. A burden pushed off onto others can polarize it.

On one level, the problem with trying to reduce income inequality comes down to whether you still believe in the American Dream. If you believe that one day you will have your American Dream—a large income, large house, happy family, or whatever else you would like to have in life—then you do not necessarily want to prevent anyone else from living out their dream. You certainly would not want to run the risk that someone would want to take part of your dream away from you. Thus, there is some reluctance to engage in a redistributive policy to reduce inequality.

However, when those for whom the likelihood of living the American Dream is very small are considered, there are sound arguments in favor of trying to create greater balance. As the text indicated, a little more income equality, gained through long-term programs like increased education and job training, can increase overall economic output. Then everyone is made better off, and the 1% will not seem like such a small group any more.

## Key Terms

**earned income tax credit (EITC)** a method of assisting the working poor through the tax system
**effective income tax** percentage of total taxes paid divided by total income
**estate tax** a tax imposed on the value of an inheritance
**income** a flow of money received, often measured on a monthly or an annual basis
**income inequality** when one group receives a disproportionate share of total income or wealth than others
**Lorenz curve** a graph that compares the cumulative income actually received to a perfectly equal distribution of income; it shows the share of population on the horizontal axis and the cumulative percentage of total income received on the vertical axis
**Medicaid** a federal–state joint program enacted in 1965 that provides medical insurance for certain (not all) people with a low-income, including those near the poverty line as well as those below the poverty line, and focusing on low-income families with children, the low-income elderly, and people with disabilities
**poverty** the situation of being below a certain level of income one needs for a basic standard of living
**poverty line** the specific amount of income one requires for a basic standard of living
**poverty rate** percentage of the population living below the poverty line
**poverty trap** antipoverty programs set up so that government benefits decline substantially as people earn more income—as a result, working provides little financial gain
**progressive tax system** a tax system in which the rich pay a higher percentage of their income in taxes, rather than a higher absolute amount
**quintile** dividing a group into fifths, a method economists often use to look at distribution of income
**redistribution** taking income from those with higher incomes and providing income to those with lower incomes
**safety net** the group of government programs that provide assistance to people at or near the poverty line
**Supplemental Nutrition Assistance Program (SNAP)** a federally funded program, started in 1964, in which each month poor people receive SNAP cards they can use to buy food
**wealth** the sum of the value of all assets, including money in bank accounts, financial investments, a pension fund, and the value of a home

## Key Concepts and Summary

### 15.1 Drawing the Poverty Line

Wages are influenced by Supply and demand in labor markets influence wages. This can lead to very low incomes for some people and very high incomes for others. Poverty and income inequality are not the same thing. Poverty applies to the condition of people who cannot afford the necessities of life. Income inequality refers to the disparity between those with higher and lower incomes. The poverty rate is what percentage of the population lives below the poverty line, which the amount of income that it takes to purchase the necessities of life determines. Choosing a poverty line will always be somewhat controversial.

### 15.2 The Poverty Trap

A poverty trap occurs when government-support payments decline as the recipients earn more income. As a result, the recipients do not end up with much more income when they work, because the loss of government support largely or completely offsets any income that one earns by working. Phasing out government benefits more slowly, as well as imposing requirements for work as a condition of receiving benefits and a time limit on benefits can reduce the harshness of the poverty trap.

### 15.3 The Safety Net

We call the group of government programs that address poverty the safety net. In the United States, prominent safety net programs include Temporary Assistance to Needy Families (TANF), the Supplemental Nutrition Assistance Program (SNAP), the earned income tax credit (EITC), Medicaid, and the Special Supplemental Food Program for Women, Infants, and Children (WIC).

## 15.4 Income Inequality: Measurement and Causes

Measuring inequality involves making comparisons across the entire distribution of income. One way of doing this is to divide the population into groups, like quintiles, and then calculate what share of income each group receives. An alternative approach is to draw Lorenz curves, which compare the cumulative income actually received to a perfectly equal distribution of income. Income inequality in the United States increased substantially from the late 1970s and early 1980s into the 2000s. The two most common explanations that economists cite are changes in household structures that have led to more two-earner couples and single-parent families, and the effect of new information and communications technology on wages.

## 15.5 Government Policies to Reduce Income Inequality

Policies that can affect the level of economic inequality include redistribution between rich and poor, making it easier for people to climb the ladder of opportunity; and estate taxes, which are taxes on inheritances. Pushing too aggressively for economic equality can run the risk of decreasing economic incentives. However, a moderate push for economic equality can increase economic output, both through methods like improved education and by building a base of political support for market forces.

# Self-Check Questions

1. Describe how each of these changes is likely to affect poverty and inequality:
   a.  Incomes rise for low-income and high-income workers, but rise more for the high-income earners.
   b.  Incomes fall for low-income and high-income workers, but fall more for high-income earners.

2. Jonathon is a single father with one child. He can work as a server for $6 per hour for up to 1,500 hours per year. He is eligible for welfare, and so if he does not earn any income, he will receive a total of $10,000 per year. He can work and still receive government benefits, but for every $1 of income, his welfare stipend is $1 less. Create a table similar to Table 15.4 that shows Jonathan's options. Use four columns, the first showing number of hours to work, the second showing his earnings from work, the third showing the government benefits he will receive, and the fourth column showing his total income (earnings + government support). Sketch a labor-leisure diagram of Jonathan's opportunity set with and without government support.

3. Imagine that the government reworks the welfare policy that was affecting Jonathan in question 1, so that for each dollar someone like Jonathan earns at work, his government benefits diminish by only 30 cents. Reconstruct the table from question 1 to account for this change in policy. Draw Jonathan's labor-leisure opportunity sets, both for before this welfare program is enacted and after it is enacted.

4. We have discovered that the welfare system discourages recipients from working because the more income they earn, the less welfare benefits they receive. How does the earned income tax credit attempt to loosen the poverty trap?

5. How does the TANF attempt to loosen the poverty trap?

6. A group of 10 people have the following annual incomes: $24,000, $18,000, $50,000, $100,000, $12,000, $36,000, $80,000, $10,000, $24,000, $16,000. Calculate the share of total income that each quintile receives from this income distribution. Do the top and bottom quintiles in this distribution have a greater or larger share of total income than the top and bottom quintiles of the U.S. income distribution?

7. Table 15.9 shows the share of income going to each quintile of the income distribution for the United Kingdom in 1979 and 1991. Use this data to calculate what the points on a Lorenz curve would be, and sketch the Lorenz curve. How did inequality in the United Kingdom shift over this time period? How can you see the patterns in the quintiles in the Lorenz curves?

| Share of Income | 1979 | 1991 |
|---|---|---|
| Top quintile | 39.7% | 42.9% |
| Fourth quintile | 24.8% | 22.7% |
| Middle quintile | 17.0% | 16.3% |
| Second quintile | 11.5% | 11.5% |
| Bottom quintile | 7.0% | 6.6% |

**TABLE 15.9 Income Distribution in the United Kingdom, 1979 and 1991**

8. Using two demand and supply diagrams, one for the low-wage labor market and one for the high-wage labor market, explain how information technology can increase income inequality if it is a complement to high-income workers like salespeople and managers, but a substitute for low-income workers like file clerks and telephone receptionists.

9. Using two demand and supply diagrams, one for the low-wage labor market and one for the high-wage labor market, explain how a program that increased educational levels for a substantial number of low-skill workers could reduce income inequality.

10. Here is one hypothesis: A well-funded social safety net can increase economic equality but will reduce economic output. Explain why this might be so, and sketch a production possibility curve that shows this tradeoff.

11. Here is a second hypothesis: A well-funded social safety net may lead to less regulation of the market economy. Explain why this might be so, and sketch a production possibility curve that shows this tradeoff.

12. Which set of policies is more likely to cause a tradeoff between economic output and equality: policies of redistribution or policies aimed at the ladder of opportunity? Explain how the production possibility frontier tradeoff between economic equality and output might look in each case.

13. Why is there reluctance on the part of some in the United States to redistribute income so that greater equality can be achieved?

## Review Questions

14. How is the poverty rate calculated?

15. What is the poverty line?

16. What is the difference between poverty and income inequality?

17. How does the poverty trap discourage people from working?

18. How can the effect of the poverty trap be reduced?

19. How does the U.S. government specifically support elderly people experiencing poverty?

**20.** What is the safety net?

**21.** Briefly explain the differences between TANF, the earned income tax credit, SNAP, and Medicaid.

**22.** Who is included in the top income quintile?

**23.** What is measured on the two axes of a Lorenz curve?

**24.** If a country had perfect income equality what would the Lorenz curve look like?

**25.** How has the inequality of income changed in the U.S. economy since the late 1970s?

**26.** What are some reasons why a certain degree of inequality of income would be expected in a market economy?

**27.** What are the main reasons economists give for the increase in inequality of incomes?

**28.** Identify some public policies that can reduce the level of economic inequality.

**29.** Describe how a push for economic equality might reduce incentives to work and produce output. Then describe how a push for economic inequality might not have such effects.

## Critical Thinking Questions

**30.** What goods and services would you include in an estimate of the basic necessities for a family of four?

**31.** If a family of three earned $20,000, would they be able to make ends meet given the official poverty threshold?

**32.** Exercise 15.2 and Exercise 15.3 asked you to describe the labor-leisure tradeoff for Jonathon. Since, in the first example, there is no monetary incentive for Jonathon to work, explain why he may choose to work anyway. Explain what the opportunity costs of working and not working might be for Jonathon in each example. Using your tables and graphs from Exercise 15.2 and Exercise 15.3, analyze how the government welfare system affects Jonathan's incentive to work.

**33.** Explain how you would create a government program that would give an incentive for labor to increase hours and keep labor from falling into the poverty trap.

**34.** Many critics of government programs to help low-income individuals argue that these programs create a poverty trap. Explain how programs such as TANF, EITC, SNAP, and Medicaid will affect low-income individuals and whether or not you think these programs will benefit families and children.

**35.** Think about the business cycle: during a recession, unemployment increases; it decreases in an expansionary phase. Explain what happens to TANF, SNAP, and Medicaid programs at each phase of the business cycle (recession, trough, expansion, and peak).

**36.** Explain how a country may experience greater equality in the distribution of income, yet still experience high rates of poverty. *Hint*: Look at the Clear It Up "How do governments measure poverty in low-income countries?" and compare to Table 15.5.

**37.** The demand for skilled workers in the United States has been increasing. To increase the supply of skilled workers, many argue that immigration reform to allow more skilled labor into the United States is needed. Explain whether you agree or disagree.

**38.** Explain a situation using the supply and demand for skilled labor in which the increased number of college graduates leads to depressed wages. Given the rising cost of going to college, explain why a college education will or will not increase income inequality.

**39.** What do you think is more important to focus on when considering inequality: income inequality or wealth inequality?

40. To reduce income inequality, should the marginal tax rates on the top 1% be increased?

41. Redistribution of income occurs through the federal income tax and government antipoverty programs. Explain whether or not this level of redistribution is appropriate and whether more redistribution should occur.

42. How does a society or a country make the decision about the tradeoff between equality and economic output? *Hint*: Think about the political system.

43. Explain what the long- and short-term consequences are of not promoting equality or working to reduce poverty.

## Problems

44. In country A, the population is 300 million and 50 million people are living below the poverty line. What is the poverty rate?

45. In country B, the population is 900 million and 100 million people are living below the poverty line. What is the poverty rate?

46. Susan is a single mother with three children. She can earn $8 per hour and works up to 1,800 hours per year. However, if she does not earn any income at all, she will receive government benefits totaling $16,000 per year. For every $1 of income she earns, her level of government support will be reduced by $1. Create a table, patterned after this one. The first column should show Susan's choices of how many hours to work per year, up to 1,800 hours. The second column should show her earnings from work. The third column should show her level of government support, given her earnings. The final column should show her total income, combining earnings and government support. Based on the table you created, what are the likely impacts of this kind of assistance program on Susan's incentive to work? Are there additional opportunity costs that may reduce her incentive to work?

47. A group of 10 people have the following annual incomes: $55,000, $30,000, $15,000, $20,000, $35,000, $80,000, $40,000, $45,000, $30,000, $50,000. Calculate the share of total income each quintile of this income distribution received. Do the top and bottom quintiles in this distribution have a greater or larger share of total income than the top and bottom quintiles of the U.S. income distribution for 2005?

# Information, Risk, and Insurance 16

FIGURE 16.1 **Former President Obama's Health Care Reform** The Patient Protection and Affordable Care Act (PPACA), more commonly known as Obamacare, relates strongly to the topic of this chapter. While originally a controversial topic, it has gained majority approval at 55% as of March 2022. (Credit: "Obama at Healthcare rally at UMD" by Daniel Borman/Flickr Creative Commons, CC BY 2.0)

## CHAPTER OBJECTIVES

In this chapter, you will learn about:

- The Problem of Imperfect Information and Asymmetric Information
- Insurance and Imperfect Information

## Introduction to Information, Risk, and Insurance

 **BRING IT HOME**

### What's the Big Deal with Obamacare?

In August 2009, many members of the U.S. Congress used their summer recess to return to their home districts and hold town hall-style meetings to discuss President Obama's proposed changes to the U.S. healthcare system. This was officially known as the Patient Protection and Affordable Care Act (PPACA) or as the Affordable Care Act (ACA), but was more popularly known as Obamacare. The bill's opponents' claims ranged from the charge that the changes were unconstitutional and would add $750 billion to the deficit, to extreme claims about the inclusion of things like the implantation of microchips and so-called "death panels" that decide which critically-ill patients receive care and which do not.

Why did people react so strongly? After all, the intent of the law is to make healthcare insurance more affordable, to allow more people to obtain insurance, and to reduce the costs of healthcare. For each year from 2000 to 2011, these costs grew at least double the rate of inflation. In 2014, healthcare spending accounted for around 24% of all federal government spending. In the United States, we spend more for our healthcare than any other high-income nation, yet our health outcomes are worse than comparable high-income countries. In 2015, over 32 million people in the United States, about 12.8% of the non-elderly adult population, were without insurance. Even today, however, more than a decade after the Act was signed into law and after the Supreme Court mostly upheld it, a 2022 Kaiser Foundation poll found that 42% of likely voters viewed it unfavorably. Why is this?

The debate over the ACA and healthcare reform could take an entire textbook, but what this chapter will do is introduce the basics of insurance and the problems insurance companies face. It is these problems, and how insurance companies respond to them that, in part, explain the divided opinion about the ACA.

---

Every purchase is based on a belief about the satisfaction that the good or service will provide. In turn, these beliefs are based on the information that the buyer has available. For many products, the information available to the buyer or the seller is imperfect or unclear, which can either make buyers regret past purchases or avoid making future ones.

This chapter discusses how imperfect and asymmetric information affect markets. The first module of the chapter discusses how asymmetric information affects markets for goods, labor, and financial capital. When buyers have less information about the quality of the good (for example, a gemstone) than sellers do, sellers may be tempted to mislead buyers. If a buyer cannot have at least some confidence in the quality of what they are purchasing, then they will be reluctant or unwilling to purchase the products. Thus, we require mechanisms to bridge this information gap, so buyers and sellers can engage in a transaction.

The second module of the chapter discusses insurance markets, which also face similar problems of imperfect information. For example, a car insurance company would prefer to sell insurance only to those who are unlikely to have auto accidents—but it is hard for the firm to identify those perfectly safe drivers. Conversely, car insurance buyers would like to persuade the auto insurance company that they are safe drivers and should pay only a low price for coverage. If insurance markets cannot find ways to grapple with these problems of imperfect information, then even people who have low or average risks of making claims may not be able to purchase insurance. The chapter on financial markets (markets for stocks and bonds) will show that the problems of imperfect information can be especially poignant. We cannot eliminate imperfect information, but we can often manage it.

## 16.1 The Problem of Imperfect Information and Asymmetric Information

### LEARNING OBJECTIVES

By the end of this section, you will be able to:

- Analyze the impact of both imperfect information and asymmetric information
- Evaluate the role of advertisements in creating imperfect information
- Identify ways to reduce the risk of imperfect information
- Explain how imperfect information can affect price, quantity, and quality

Consider a purchase that many people make at important times in their lives: buying expensive jewelry. In May 1994, celebrity psychologist Doree Lynn bought an expensive ring from a jeweler in Washington, D.C., which included an emerald that cost $14,500. Several years later, the emerald fractured. Lynn took it to another jeweler who found that cracks in the emerald had been filled with an epoxy resin. Lynn sued the original jeweler in 1997 for selling her a treated emerald without telling her, and won. The case publicized a number of little-known facts about precious stones. Most emeralds have internal flaws, and so they are soaked in clear oil or an epoxy resin to hide the flaws and make the color more deep and clear. Clear oil can leak out over time, and epoxy resin can discolor with age or heat. However, using clear oil or epoxy to "fill" emeralds is completely legal, as long as it is disclosed.

After Doree Lynn's lawsuit, the NBC news show "Dateline" bought emeralds at four prominent jewelry stores in New York City in 1997. All the sales clerks at these stores, unaware that they were being recorded on a hidden camera, said the stones were untreated. When the emeralds were tested at a laboratory, however, technicians discovered they had all been treated with oil or epoxy. Emeralds are not the only gemstones that are treated. Diamonds, topaz, and tourmaline are also often irradiated to enhance colors. The general rule is that all treatments to gemstones should be revealed, but often sellers do not disclose this. As such, many buyers face a situation of **asymmetric information**, where two parties involved in an economic transaction have an unequal amount of information (one party knows much more than the other).

Many economic transactions occur in a situation of **imperfect information**, where either the buyer, the seller, or both, are less than 100% certain about the qualities of what they are buying and selling. Also, one may characterize the transaction as asymmetric information, in which one party has more information than the other regarding the economic transaction. Let's begin with some examples of how imperfect information complicates transactions in goods, labor, and financial capital markets. The presence of imperfect information can easily cause a decline in prices or quantities of products sold. However, buyers and sellers also have incentives to create mechanisms that will allow them to make mutually beneficial transactions even in the face of imperfect information.

If you are unclear about the difference between asymmetric information and imperfect information, read the following Clear It Up feature.

## CLEAR IT UP

### What is the difference between imperfect and asymmetric information?

For a market to reach equilibrium sellers and buyers must have full information about the product's price and quality. If there is limited information, then buyers and sellers may not be able to transact or will possibly make poor decisions.

Imperfect information refers to the situation where buyers and/or sellers do not have all of the necessary information to make an informed decision about the product's price or quality. The term imperfect information simply means that the buyers and/or sellers do not have all the information necessary to make an informed decision. Asymmetric information is the condition where one party, either the buyer or the seller, has more information about the product's quality or price than the other party. In either case (imperfect or asymmetric information) buyers or sellers need remedies to make more informed decisions.

---

### "Lemons" and Other Examples of Imperfect Information

Consider Marvin, who is trying to decide whether to buy a used car. Let's assume that Marvin is truly clueless about what happens inside a car's engine. He is willing to do some background research, like reading *Consumer Reports* or checking websites that offer information about used car makes and models and what they should cost. He might pay a mechanic to inspect the car. Even after devoting some money and time collecting information, however, Marvin still cannot be absolutely sure that he is buying a high-quality used car. He knows that he might buy the car, drive it home, and use it for a few weeks before discovering that car is a "lemon," which is slang for a defective product (especially a car).

Imagine that Marvin shops for a used car and finds two that look very similar in terms of mileage, exterior appearances, and age. One car costs $4,000, while the other car costs $4,600. Which car should Marvin buy?

If Marvin were choosing in a world of perfect information, the answer would be simple: he should buy the cheaper car. However, Marvin is operating in a world of imperfect information, where the sellers likely know more about the car's problems than he does, and have an incentive to hide the information. After all, the more problems the sellers disclose, the lower the car's selling price.

What should Marvin do? First, he needs to understand that even with imperfect information, prices still reflect information. Typically, used cars are more expensive on some dealer lots because the dealers have a trustworthy reputation to uphold. Those dealers try to fix problems that may not be obvious to their customers, in order to create good word of mouth about their vehicles' long term reliability. The short term benefits of selling their customers a "lemon" could cause a quick collapse in the dealer's reputation and a loss of long term profits. On other lots that are less well-established, one can find cheaper used cars, but the buyer takes on more risk when a dealer's reputation has little at stake. The cheapest cars of all often appear on Craigslist, where the individual seller has no reputation to defend. In sum, cheaper prices do carry more risk, so Marvin should balance his appetite for risk versus the potential headaches of many more unanticipated trips to the repair shop.

Similar problems with imperfect information arise in labor and financial capital markets. Consider Greta, who is applying for a job. Her potential employer, like the used car buyer, is concerned about ending up with a "lemon"—in this case a poor quality employee. The employer will collect information about Greta's academic and work history. In the end, however, a degree of uncertainty will inevitably remain regarding Greta's abilities, which are hard to demonstrate without actually observing her on the job. How can a potential employer screen for certain attributes, such as motivation, timeliness, and ability to get along with others? Employers often look to trade schools and colleges to pre-screen candidates. Employers may not even interview a candidate unless he has a degree and, sometimes, a degree from a particular school. Employers may also view awards, a high grade point average, and other accolades as a signal of hard work, perseverance, and ability. Employers may also seek references for insights into key attributes such as energy level and work ethic.

### How Imperfect Information Can Affect Equilibrium Price and Quantity

The presence of imperfect information can discourage both buyers and sellers from participating in the market. Buyers may become reluctant to participate because they cannot determine the product's quality. Sellers of high-quality or medium-quality goods may be reluctant to participate, because it is difficult to demonstrate the quality of their goods to buyers—and since buyers cannot determine which goods have higher quality, they are likely to be unwilling to pay a higher price for such goods.

Economists sometimes refer to a market with few buyers and few sellers as a thin market. By contrast, they call a market with many buyers and sellers a thick market. When imperfect information is severe and buyers and sellers are discouraged from participating, markets may become extremely thin as a relatively small number of buyer and sellers attempt to communicate enough information that they can agree on a price.

### When Price Mixes with Imperfect Information about Quality

A buyer confronted with imperfect information will often believe that the price reveals something about the product's quality. For example, a buyer may assume that a gemstone or a used car that costs more must be of higher quality, even though the buyer is not an expert on gemstones. Think of the expensive restaurant where the food must be good because it is so expensive or the shop where the clothes must be stylish because they cost so much, or the gallery where the art must be great, because the price tags are high. If you are hiring a lawyer, you might assume that a lawyer who charges $400 per hour must be better than a lawyer who charges $150 per hour. In these cases, price can act as a signal of quality.

When buyers use the market price to draw inferences about the products' quality, then markets may have trouble reaching an equilibrium price and quantity. Imagine a situation where a used car dealer has a lot full of used cars that do not seem to be selling, and so the dealer decides to cut the car prices to sell a greater quantity. In a market with imperfect information, many buyers may assume that the lower price implies low-quality cars. As a result, the lower price may not attract more customers. Conversely, a dealer who raises prices may find that customers assume that the higher price means that cars are of higher quality. As a result of raising prices, the dealer might sell more cars. (Whether or not consumers always behave rationally, as an economist would see it, is the subject of the following Clear It Up feature.)

The idea that higher prices might cause a greater quantity demanded and that lower prices might cause a lower quantity demanded runs exactly counter to the basic model of demand and supply (as we outlined in the Demand and Supply chapter). These contrary effects, however, will reach natural limits. At some point, if the price is high enough, the quantity demanded will decline. Conversely, when the price declines far enough, buyers will increasingly find value even if the quality is lower. In addition, information eventually becomes more widely known. An overpriced restaurant that charges more than the quality of its food is worth to many buyers will not last forever.

## CLEAR IT UP

### Is consumer behavior rational?

There is much human behavior that mainstream economists have tended to call "irrational" since it is consistently at odds with economists' utility maximizing models. The typical response is for economists to brush these behaviors aside and call them "anomalies" or unexplained quirks.

"If only you knew more economics, you would not be so irrational," is what many mainstream economists seem to be saying. A group known as behavioral economists has challenged this notion, because so much of this so-called "quirky" behavior is extremely common among us. For example, a conventional economist would say that if you lost a $10 bill today, and also received an extra $10 in your paycheck, you should feel perfectly neutral. After all, −$10 + $10 = $0. You are the same financially as you were before. However, behavioral economists have conducted research that shows many people will feel some negative emotion—anger or frustration—after those two things happen. We tend to focus more on the loss than the gain. Economists Daniel Kahneman and Amos Tversky in a famous 1979 *Econometrica* paper called this "loss aversion", where a $1 loss pains us 2.25 times more than a $1 gain helps us. This has implications for investing, as people tend to "overplay" the stock market by reacting more to losses than to gains.

Behavioral economics also tries to explain why people make seemingly irrational decisions in the presence of different situations, or how they "frame" the decision. We outline a popular example here: Imagine you have the opportunity to buy an alarm clock for $20 in Store A. Across the street, you learn, is the exact same clock at Store B for $10. You might say it is worth your time—a five-minute walk—to save $10. Now, take a different example: You are in Store A buying a $300 phone. Five minutes away, at Store B, the same phone is $290. You again save $10 by taking a five-minute walk. Do you do it?

Surprisingly, it is likely that you would not. Mainstream economists would say "$10 is $10" and that it would be irrational to make a five minute walk for $10 in one case and not the other. However, behavioral economists have pointed out that most of us evaluate outcomes relative to a reference point—here the cost of the product—and think of gains and losses as percentages rather than using actual savings.

Which view is right? Both have their advantages, but behavioral economists have at least shed a light on trying to describe and explain systematic behavior which some previously had dismissed as irrational. If most of us are engaged in some "irrational behavior," perhaps there are deeper underlying reasons for this behavior in the first place.

### Mechanisms to Reduce the Risk of Imperfect Information

If you were selling a good like emeralds or used cars where imperfect information is likely to be a problem, how could you reassure possible buyers? If you were buying a good where imperfect information is a problem, what would it take to reassure you? Buyers and sellers in the goods market rely on reputation as well as guarantees, warrantees, and service contracts to assure product quality. The labor market uses occupational licenses and certifications to assure competency, while the financial capital market uses cosigners and collateral as insurance against unforeseen, detrimental events.

In the goods market, the seller might offer a **money-back guarantee**, an agreement that functions as a promise of quality. This strategy may be especially important for a company that sells goods through mail-order catalogs or over the web, whose customers cannot see the actual products, because it encourages people to buy something even if they are not certain they want to keep it.

L.L. Bean started using money-back-guarantees in 1911, when the founder stitched waterproof shoe rubbers together with leather shoe tops, and sold them as hunting shoes. He guaranteed satisfaction. However, the stitching came apart and, out of the first batch of 100 pairs that were sold, customers returned 90 pairs. L.L. Bean took out a bank loan, repaired all of the shoes, and replaced them. The L.L. Bean reputation for customer satisfaction began to spread. Many firms today offer money-back-guarantees for a few weeks or months, but L.L. Bean offers a complete money-back guarantee. Customers can always return anything they have bought from L.L. Bean, no matter how many years later or what condition the product is in, for a full money-back guarantee.

L.L. Bean has very few stores. Instead, most of its sales are made by mail, telephone, or, now, through their website. For this kind of firm, imperfect information may be an especially difficult problem, because customers cannot see and touch what they are buying. A combination of a money-back guarantee and a reputation for quality can help for a mail-order firm to flourish.

Sellers may offer a **warranty**, which is a promise to fix or replace the good, at least for a certain time period. The seller may also offer a buyer a chance to buy a **service contract**, where the buyer pays an extra amount and the seller agrees to fix anything that goes wrong for a set time period. Service contracts are often an option for buyers of large purchases such as cars, appliances and even houses.

Guarantees, warranties, and service contracts are examples of explicit reassurance that sellers provide. In many cases, firms also offer unstated guarantees. For example, some movie theaters might refund the ticket cost to a customer who walks out complaining about the show. Likewise, while restaurants do not generally advertise a money-back guarantee or exchange policies, many restaurants allow customers to exchange one dish for another or reduce the price of the bill if the customer is not satisfied.

The rationale for these policies is that firms want repeat customers, who in turn will recommend the business to others. As such, establishing a good reputation is of paramount importance. When buyers know that a firm is concerned about its reputation, they are less likely to worry about receiving a poor-quality product. For example, a well-established grocery store with a good reputation can often charge a higher price than a temporary stand at a local farmer's market, where the buyer may never see the seller again.

Sellers of labor provide information through resumes, recommendations, school transcripts, and examples of their work. The labor market also uses **occupational licenses** to establish quality in the labor market. Occupational licenses, which government agencies typically issue, show that a worker has completed a certain type of education or passed a certain test. Some of the professionals who must hold a license are doctors, teachers, nurses, engineers, accountants, and lawyers. In addition, most states require a license to work as a barber, an embalmer, a dietitian, a massage therapist, a hearing aid dealer, a counselor, an insurance agent, and a real estate broker. Some other jobs require a license in only one state. Minnesota requires a state license to be a field archaeologist. North Dakota has a state license for bait retailers. In Louisiana, one needs a state license to be a "stress analyst" and California requires a state license to be a furniture upholsterer. According to a 2013 study from the University of Chicago, about 29% of U.S. workers have jobs that require occupational licenses.

Occupational licenses have their downside as well, as they represent a barrier to entry to certain industries. This makes it more difficult for new entrants to compete with incumbents, which can lead to higher prices and less consumer choice. In occupations that require licenses, the government has decided that the additional information provided by licenses outweighs the negative effect on competition.

## CLEAR IT UP

### Are advertisers allowed to benefit from imperfect information?

Many advertisements seem full of imperfect information—at least by what they imply. Driving a certain car, drinking a particular soda, or wearing a certain shoe are all unlikely to bring fashionable friends and fun automatically, if at all. The government rules on advertising, enforced by the Federal Trade Commission (FTC), allow advertising to contain a certain amount of exaggeration about the general delight of using a product. They, however, also demand that if one presents a claim as a fact, it must be true.

Legally, deceptive advertising dates back to the 1950s when Colgate-Palmolive created a television advertisement that seemed to show Rapid Shave shaving cream being spread on sandpaper and then the sand was shaved off the sandpaper. What the television advertisement actually showed was sand sprinkled on Plexiglas—without glue—and then scraped aside by the razor.

In the 1960s, in magazine advertisements for Campbell's vegetable soup, the company was having problems getting an appetizing soup picture, because the vegetables kept sinking. To remedy this, they filled a bowl with marbles and poured the soup over the top, so that the bowl appeared to be crammed with vegetables.

In the late 1980s, the Volvo Company filmed a television advertisement that showed a monster truck driving over cars, crunching their roofs—all except for the Volvo, which did not crush. However, the FTC found in 1991 that the Volvo's roof from the filming had been reinforced with an extra steel framework, while they cut the roof supports on the other car brands.

The Wonder Bread Company ran television advertisements featuring "Professor Wonder," who said that because Wonder Bread contained extra calcium, it would help children's minds work better and improve their memory. The FTC objected, and in 2002 the company agreed to stop running the advertisements.

As we can see in each of these cases, the Federal Trade Commission (FTC) often checks factual claims about the product's performance, at least to some extent. Language and images that are exaggerated or ambiguous, but not actually false, are allowed in advertising. Untrue "facts" are not permitted. In any case, an old Latin saying applies when watching advertisements: *Caveat emptor*—that is, "let the buyer beware."

On the buyer's side of the labor market, a standard precaution against hiring a "lemon" of an employee is to specify that the first few months of employment are officially a trial or probationary period, and that the employer can dismiss the worker for any reason or no reason during that time. Sometimes workers also receive lower pay during this trial period.

In the financial capital market, before a bank makes a loan, it requires a prospective borrower to fill out forms regarding incomes sources. In addition, the bank conducts a credit check on the individual's past borrowing. Another approach is to require a **cosigner** on a loan; that is, another person or firm who legally pledges to repay some or all of the money if the original borrower does not do so. Another approach is to require **collateral**, often property or equipment that the bank would have a right to seize and sell if borrower does not repay the loan.

Buyers of goods and services cannot possibly become experts in evaluating the quality of gemstones, used cars, lawyers, and everything else they buy. Employers and lenders cannot be perfectly omniscient about whether possible workers will turn out well or potential borrowers will repay loans on time. However, the mechanisms that we mentioned above can reduce the risks associated with imperfect information so that the buyer and seller are willing to proceed.

## 16.2 Insurance and Imperfect Information

**LEARNING OBJECTIVES**

By the end of this section, you will be able to:

- Explain how insurance works
- Identify and evaluate various forms of government and social insurance
- Discuss the problems caused by moral hazard and adverse selection
- Analyze the impact of government regulation of insurance

**Insurance** is a method that households and firms use to prevent any single event from having a significant detrimental financial effect. Generally, households or firms with insurance make regular payments, called **premiums**. The insurance company prices these premiums based on the probability of certain events occurring among a pool of people. Members of the group who then suffer a specified bad experience receive payments from this pool of money.

Many people have several kinds of insurance: health insurance that pays when they receive medical care; car insurance that pays if their car is in an automobile accident; house or renter's insurance that pays for stolen possessions or items damaged by fire; and life insurance, which pays for the family if the insured individual dies. Table 16.1 lists a set of insurance markets.

| Type of Insurance | Who Pays for It? | It Pays Out When . . . |
|---|---|---|
| Health insurance | Employers and individuals | Medical expenses are incurred |
| Life insurance | Employers and individuals | Policyholder dies |
| Automobile insurance | Individuals | Car is damaged, stolen, or causes damage to others |
| Property and homeowner's insurance | Homeowners and renters | Dwelling is damaged or burglarized |
| Liability insurance | Firms and individuals | An injury occurs for which you are partly responsible |
| Malpractice insurance | Doctors, lawyers, and other professionals | A poor quality of service is provided that causes harm to others |

**TABLE 16.1 Some Insurance Markets**

All insurance involves imperfect information in both an obvious way and in a deeper way. At an obvious level, we cannot predict future events with certainty. For example, we cannot know with certainty who will have a car accident, become ill, die, or have his home robbed in the next year. Imperfect information also applies to estimating the risk that something will happen to any individual. It is difficult for an insurance company to estimate the risk that, say, a particular 20-year-old male driver from New York City will have an accident, because even within that group, some drivers will drive more safely than others. Thus, adverse events occur out of a combination of people's characteristics and choices that make the risks higher or lower and then the good or bad luck of what actually happens.

### How Insurance Works

A simplified example of automobile insurance might work this way. Suppose we divide a group of 100 drivers into three groups. In a given year, 60 of those people have only a few door dings or chipped paint, which costs $100 each. Another 30 of the drivers have medium-sized accidents that cost an average of $1,000 in damages, and 10 of the drivers have large accidents that cost $15,000 in damages. For the moment, let's imagine that at the beginning of any year, there is no way of identifying the drivers who are low-risk, medium-risk, or high-risk. The total damage incurred by car accidents in this group of 100 drivers will be $186,000, that is:

$$\text{Total damage} = (60 \times \$100) + (30 \times \$1,000) + (10 \times \$15,000)$$
$$= \$6,000 + \$30,000 + \$150,000$$
$$= \$186,000$$

If each of the 100 drivers pays a $1,860 premium each year, the insurance company will collect the $186,000 that is needed to cover the costs of the accidents that occur.

Since insurance companies have such a large number of clients, they are able to negotiate with health care and other service providers for lower rates than the individual would be able to get, thus increasing the benefit to consumers of becoming insured and saving the insurance company itself money when it pays out claims.

Insurance companies receive income, as Figure 16.2 shows, from insurance premiums and investment income. The companies derive income from investing the funds that insurance companies received in the past but did not pay out as insurance claims in prior years. The insurance company receives a rate of return from investing these funds or reserves. The companies typically invest in fairly safe, liquid (easy to convert into cash) investments, as the insurance companies need to be able to readily access these funds when a major disaster strikes.

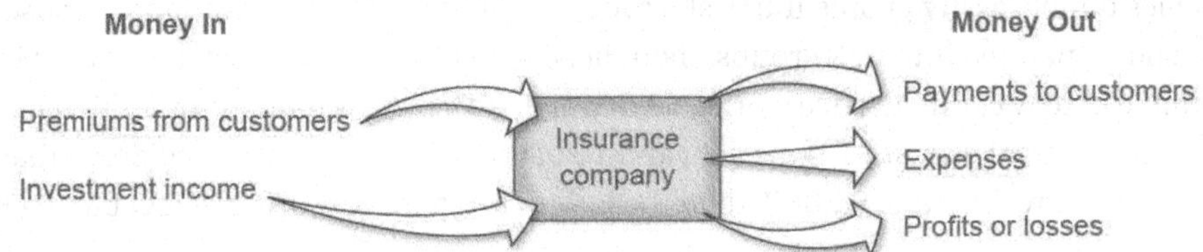


**FIGURE 16.2 An Insurance Company: What Comes In, What Goes Out** Money flows into an insurance company through premiums and investments and out through the payment of claims and operating expenses.

## Government and Social Insurance

Federal and state governments run a number of insurance programs. Some of the programs look much like private insurance, in the sense that the members of a group make steady payments into a fund, and those in the group who suffer an adverse experience receive payments. Other programs protect against risk, but without an explicit fund set up. Following are some examples.

- Unemployment insurance: Employers in every state pay a small amount for unemployment insurance, which goes into a fund to pay benefits to workers who lose their jobs and do not find new jobs, for a period of time, usually up to six months.
- Pension insurance: Employers that offer pensions to their retired employees are required by law to pay a small fraction of what they are setting aside for pensions to the Pension Benefit Guarantee Corporation, which pays at least some pension benefits to workers if a company goes bankrupt and cannot pay the pensions it has promised.
- Deposit insurance: Banks are required by law to pay a small fraction of their deposits to the Federal Deposit Insurance Corporation, which goes into a fund that pays depositors the value of their bank deposits up to $250,000 (the amount was raised from $100,000 to $250,000 in 2008) if the bank should go bankrupt.
- Workman's compensation insurance: Employers are required by law to pay a small percentage of the salaries that they pay into funds, typically run at the state level, that pay benefits to workers who suffer an injury on the job.
- Retirement insurance: All workers pay a percentage of their income into Social Security and into Medicare, which then provides income and health care benefits to the elderly. Social Security and Medicare are not

literally "insurance" in the sense that those currently contributing to the fund are not eligible for benefits. They function like insurance, however, in the sense that individuals make regular payments into the programs today in exchange for benefits they will receive in the case of a later event—either becoming old or becoming sick when old. A name for such programs is "social insurance."

The major additional costs to insurance companies, other than the payment of claims, are the costs of running a business: the administrative costs of hiring workers, administering accounts, and processing insurance claims. For most insurance companies, the insurance premiums coming in and the claims payments going out are much larger than the amounts earned by investing money or the administrative costs.

Thus, while factors like investment income earned on reserves, administrative costs, and groups with different risks complicate the overall picture, a fundamental law of insurance must hold true: The average person's payments into insurance over time must cover 1) the average person's claims, 2) the costs of running the company, and 3) leave room for the firm's profits.

## Risk Groups and Actuarial Fairness

Not all of those who purchase insurance face the same risks. Some people may be more likely, because of genetics or personal habits, to fall sick with certain diseases. Some people may live in an area where car theft or home robbery is more likely than in other areas. Some drivers are safer than others. A **risk group** can be defined as a group that shares roughly the same risks of an adverse event occurring.

Insurance companies often classify people into risk groups, and charge lower premiums to those with lower risks. If people are not separated into risk groups, then those with low risk must pay for those with high risks. In the simple example of how car insurance works, 60 drivers had very low damage of $100 each, 30 drivers had medium-sized accidents that cost $1,000 each, and 10 of the drivers had large accidents that cost $15,000. If all 100 of these drivers pay the same $1,860, then those with low damages are in effect paying for those with high damages.

If it is possible to classify drivers according to risk group, then the insurance company can charge each group according to its expected losses. For example, the insurance company might charge the 60 drivers who seem safest of all $100 apiece, which is the average value of the damages they cause. Then the intermediate group could pay $1,000 apiece and the high-cost group $15,000 each. When the level of insurance premiums that someone pays is equal to the amount that an average person in that risk group would collect in insurance payments, the level of insurance is said to be "actuarially fair."

Classifying people into risk groups can be controversial. For example, if someone had a major automobile accident last year, should the insurance company classify that person as a high-risk driver who is likely to have similar accidents in the future, or as a low-risk driver who was just extremely unlucky? The driver is likely to claim to be low-risk, and thus someone who should be in a risk group with those who pay low insurance premiums in the future. The insurance company is likely to believe that, on average, having a major accident is a signal of being a high-risk driver, and thus try to charge this driver higher insurance premiums. The next two sections discuss the two major problems of imperfect information in insurance markets—called moral hazard and adverse selection. Both problems arise from attempts to categorize those purchasing insurance into risk groups.

## The Moral Hazard Problem

**Moral hazard** refers to the case when people engage in riskier behavior with insurance than they would if they did not have insurance. For example, if you have health insurance that covers the cost of visiting the doctor, you may be less likely to take precautions against catching an illness that might require a doctor's visit. If you have car insurance, you will worry less about driving or parking your car in ways that make it more likely to get dented. In another example, a business without insurance might install absolute top-level security and fire sprinkler systems to guard against theft and fire. If it is insured, that same business might only install a minimum level of security and fire sprinkler systems.

We cannot eliminate moral hazard, but insurance companies have some ways of reducing its effect. Investigations to prevent insurance fraud are one way of reducing the extreme cases of moral hazard. Insurance companies can also monitor certain kinds of behavior. To return to the example from above, they might offer a business a lower rate on property insurance if the business installs a top-level security and fire sprinkler system and has those systems inspected once a year.

Another method to reduce moral hazard is to require the injured party to pay a share of the costs. For example, insurance policies often have **deductibles**, which is an amount that the insurance policyholder must pay out of their own pocket before the insurance coverage starts paying. For example, auto insurance might pay for all losses greater than $500. Health insurance policies often have a **copayment**, in which the policyholder must pay a small amount. For example, a person might have to pay $20 for each doctor visit, and the insurance company would cover the rest. Another method of cost sharing is **coinsurance**, which means that the insurance company covers a certain percentage of the cost. For example, insurance might pay for 80% of the costs of repairing a home after a fire, but the homeowner would pay the other 20%.

All of these forms of cost sharing discourage moral hazard, because people know that they will have to pay something out of their own pocket when they make an insurance claim. The effect can be powerful. One prominent study found that when people face moderate deductibles and copayments for their health insurance, they consume about one-third less in medical care than people who have complete insurance and do not pay anything out of pocket, presumably because deductibles and copayments reduce the level of moral hazard. However, those who consumed less health care did not seem to have any difference in health status.

A final way of reducing moral hazard, which is especially applicable to health care, is to focus on healthcare incentives of providers rather than consumers. Traditionally, most health care in the United States has been provided on a **fee-for-service** basis, which means that medical care providers are paid for the services they provide and are paid more if they provide additional services. However, in the last decade or so, the structure of healthcare provision has shifted to an emphasis on health maintenance organizations (HMOs). A **health maintenance organization (HMO)** provides healthcare that receives a fixed amount per person enrolled in the plan—regardless of how many services are provided. In this case, a patient with insurance has an incentive to demand more care, but the healthcare provider, which is receiving only a fixed payment, has an incentive to reduce the moral hazard problem by limiting the quantity of care provided—as long as it will not lead to worse health problems and higher costs later. Today, many doctors are paid with some combination of managed care and fee-for-service; that is, a flat amount per patient, but with additional payments for the treatment of certain health conditions.

Imperfect information is the cause of the moral hazard problem. If an insurance company had perfect information on risk, it could simply raise its premiums every time an insured party engages in riskier behavior. However, an insurance company cannot monitor all the risks that people take all the time and so, even with various checks and cost sharing, moral hazard will remain a problem.

## LINK IT UP

Visit this website (http://openstax.org/l/healtheconomics) to read about the relationship between health care and behavioral economics.

## The Adverse Selection Problem

**Adverse selection** refers to the problem in which insurance buyers have more information about whether they are high-risk or low-risk than the insurance company does. This creates an asymmetric information problem for the insurance company because buyers who are high-risk tend to want to buy more insurance, without letting the insurance company know about their higher risk. For example, someone purchasing health insurance or life insurance probably knows more about their family's health history than an insurer can reasonably find out even with a costly investigation. Someone purchasing car insurance may know that they are a high-risk driver who has not yet had a major accident—but it is hard for the insurance company to collect information about how people actually drive.

To understand how adverse selection can strangle an insurance market, recall the situation of 100 drivers who are buying automobile insurance, where 60 drivers had very low damages of $100 each, 30 drivers had medium-sized accidents that cost $1,000 each, and 10 of the drivers had large accidents that cost $15,000. That would equal $186,000 in total payouts by the insurance company. Imagine that, while the insurance company knows the overall size of the losses, it cannot identify the high-risk, medium-risk, and low-risk drivers. However, the drivers themselves know their risk groups. Since there is asymmetric information between the insurance company and the drivers, the insurance company would likely set the price of insurance at $1,860 per year, to cover the average loss (not including the cost of overhead and profit). The result is that those with low risks of only $100 will likely decide not to buy insurance; after all, it makes no sense for them to pay $1,860 per year when they are likely only to experience losses of $100. Those with medium risks of a $1,000 accident will not buy insurance either. Therefore, the insurance company ends up only selling insurance for $1,860 to high-risk drivers who will average $15,000 in claims apiece, and as a consequence, the insurance company ends up losing considerable money. If the insurance company tries to raise its premiums to cover the losses of those with high risks, then those with low or medium risks will be even more discouraged from buying insurance.

Rather than face such a situation of adverse selection, the insurance company may decide not to sell insurance in this market at all. If potential buyers are to receive insurance, then one of two things must happen. First, the insurance company might find some way of separating insurance buyers into risk groups with some degree of accuracy and charging them accordingly, which in practice often means that the insurance company tries not to sell insurance to those who may pose high risks. Another scenario is that those with low risks must buy insurance, even if they have to pay more than the actuarially fair amount for their risk group. The notion that people can be required to purchase insurance raises the issue of government laws and regulations that influence the insurance industry.

## U.S. Health Care in an International Context

The United States is the only high-income country in the world where private firms pay and provide for most health insurance. Greater government involvement in the provision of health insurance is one possible way of addressing moral hazard and adverse selection problems.

The moral hazard problem with health insurance is that when people have insurance, they will demand higher quantities of health care. In the United States, private healthcare insurance tends to encourage an ever-greater demand for healthcare services, which healthcare providers are happy to fulfill. Table 16.2 shows that on a per-person basis, U.S. healthcare spending towers above healthcare spending of other countries. Note that while healthcare expenditures in the United States are far higher than healthcare expenditures in other countries, the health outcomes in the United States, as measured by life expectancy and lower rates of childhood mortality, tend to be lower. Health outcomes, however, may not be significantly affected by healthcare expenditures. Many studies have shown that a country's health is more closely related to diet, exercise, and genetic factors than to healthcare expenditure. This fact further emphasizes that the United States is spending very large amounts on medical care with little obvious health gain.

In the U.S. health insurance market, the main way of solving this adverse selection problem is that health insurance is often sold through groups based on place of employment, or, under The Affordable Care Act, from a state government sponsored health exchange market. From an insurance company's point of view, selling insurance through an employer mixes together a group of people—some with high risks of future health problems and some with lower risks—and thus reduces the insurance firm's fear of attracting only those who have high risks. However, many small companies do not provide health insurance to their employees, and many lower-paying jobs do not include health insurance. Even after we take into account all U.S. government programs that provide health insurance for the elderly and people experiencing poverty, approximately 31 million Americans were without health insurance in 2020. While a government-controlled system can avoid the adverse selection problem entirely by providing at least basic health insurance for all, another option is to mandate that all Americans buy health insurance from some provider by preventing providers from denying individuals based on preexisting conditions. The Patient Protection and Affordable Care Act adopted this approach, which we will discuss later on in this chapter.

| Country | Health Care Spending per Person | Life Expectancy at Birth (Male) | Life Expectancy at Birth (Female) | Infant Mortality Rate (Male & Female), per 1,000 |
|---|---|---|---|---|
| United States | $10,948 | 75.5 | 80.2 | 5.7 |
| Germany | $6,731 | 79.0 | 83.7 | 3.2 |
| France | $5,564 | 79.2 | 85.3 | 3.5 |
| Canada | $5,370 | 80.0 | 84.2 | 4.4 |
| United Kingdom | $5,268 | 78.4 | 82.4 | 3.7 |

**TABLE 16.2 A Comparison of Health Care Spending per Person, Life Expectancy at Birth, and Infant Mortality, 2020** (Source: 2020 OECD study and World Fact Book)

At its best, the largely private U.S. system of health insurance and healthcare delivery provides an extraordinarily high quality of care, along with generating a seemingly endless parade of life-saving innovations. However, the system also struggles to control its high costs and to provide basic medical care to all. Compared to the United States, other countries have lower costs, more equal access, and better mortality outcomes, but they often struggle to provide rapid access to health care and to offer the near-miracles of the most up-to-date medical care. The challenge is a healthcare system that strikes the right balance between quality, access, and cost.

## Government Regulation of Insurance

The U.S. insurance industry is primarily regulated at the state level. Since 1871 there has been a National Association of Insurance Commissioners that brings together these state regulators to exchange information and strategies. The state insurance regulators typically attempt to accomplish two things: to keep the price of insurance low and to ensure that everyone has insurance. These goals, however, can conflict with each other and also become easily entangled in politics.

If insurance premiums are set at actuarially fair levels, so that people end up paying an amount that accurately reflects their risk group, certain people will end up paying considerable amounts. For example, if health insurance companies were trying to cover people who already have a chronic disease like AIDS, or who were elderly, they would charge these groups very high premiums for health insurance, because their expected health care costs are quite high. Women in the age bracket 18–44 consume, on average, about 65% more in health care spending than men. Young male drivers have more car accidents than young female drivers. Thus, actuarially fair insurance would tend to charge young men much more for car insurance than young women. Because people in high-risk groups would find themselves charged so heavily for insurance, they might choose not to buy insurance at all.

State insurance regulators have sometimes reacted by passing rules that attempt to set low premiums for insurance. Over time, however, the fundamental law of insurance must hold: the average amount individuals receive cannot exceed the average amount paid in premiums. When rules are passed to keep premiums low, insurance companies try to avoid insuring any high-risk or even medium-risk parties. If a state legislature passes strict rules requiring insurance companies to sell to everyone at low prices, the insurance companies always have the option of withdrawing from doing business in that state. For example, the insurance regulators in New Jersey are well-known for attempting to keep auto insurance premiums low, and more than 20 different insurance companies stopped doing business in the state in the late 1990s and early 2000s. Similarly, in 2009, State Farm announced that it was withdrawing from selling property insurance in Florida.

In short, government regulators cannot force companies to charge low prices and provide high levels of insurance coverage—and thus take losses—for a sustained period of time. If insurance premiums are set below the actuarially fair level for a certain group, some other group will have to make up the difference. There are two other groups who can make up the difference: taxpayers or other insurance buyers.

In some industries, the U.S. government has decided free markets will not provide insurance at an affordable price, and so the government pays for it directly. For example, private health insurance is too expensive for many people whose incomes are too low. To combat this, the U.S. government, together with the states, runs the Medicaid program, which provides health care to those with low incomes. Private health insurance also does not work well for the elderly, because their average health care costs can be very high. Thus, the U.S. government started the Medicare program, which provides health insurance to all those over age 65. Other government-funded health-care programs are aimed at military veterans, as an added benefit, and children in families with relatively low incomes.

Another common government intervention in insurance markets is to require that everyone buy certain kinds of insurance. For example, most states legally require car owners to buy auto insurance. Likewise, when a bank loans someone money to buy a home, the person is typically required to have homeowner's insurance, which protects against fire and other physical damage (like hailstorms) to the home. A legal requirement that everyone must buy insurance means that insurance companies do not need to worry that those with low risks will avoid buying insurance. Since insurance companies do not need to fear adverse selection, they can set their prices based on an average for the market, and those with lower risks will, to some extent, end up subsidizing those with higher risks. However, even when laws are passed requiring people to purchase insurance, insurance companies cannot be compelled to sell insurance to everyone who asks—at least not at low cost. Thus, insurance companies will still try to avoid selling insurance to those with high risks whenever possible.

The government cannot pass laws that make the problems of moral hazard and adverse selection disappear, but the government can make political decisions that certain groups should have insurance, even though the private market would not otherwise provide that insurance. Also, the government can impose the costs of that decision on taxpayers or on other buyers of insurance.

### The Patient Protection and Affordable Care Act

In March of 2010, President Obama signed into law the Patient Protection and Affordable Care Act (PPACA). The government started to phase in this highly contentious law over time starting in October of 2013. The goal of the act is to bring the United States closer to universal coverage. Some of the key features of the plan include:

- Individual mandate: All individuals, who do not receive health care through their employer or through a government program (for example, Medicare), were required to have health insurance or pay a fine. The individual mandate's goal was to reduce the adverse selection problem and keep prices down by requiring all consumers—even the healthiest ones—to have health insurance. Without the need to guard against adverse selection (whereby only the riskiest consumers buy insurance) by raising prices, health insurance companies could provide more reasonable plans to their customers. At the beginning of 2019, the fine for not having health insurance was eliminated.

- Each state is required to have health insurance exchanges, or utilize the federal exchange, whereby insurance companies compete for business. The goal of the exchanges is to improve competition in the market for health insurance.
- Employer mandate: All employers with more than 50 employees must offer health insurance to their employees.

The Affordable Care Act (ACA) is funded through additional taxes that include:

- Increasing the Medicare tax by 0.9 percent and adding a 3.8 percent tax on unearned income for high income taxpayers.
- Charging an annual fee on health insurance providers.
- Imposing other taxes such as a 2.3% tax on manufacturers and importers of certain medical devices.

Many people and politicians, including Donald Trump, have sought to overturn the bill. Those who oppose the bill believe it violates an individual's right to choose whether to have insurance or not. In 2012, a number of states challenged the law on the basis that the individual mandate provision is unconstitutional. In June 2012, the U.S. Supreme Court ruled in a 5–4 decision that the individual mandate is actually a tax, so it is constitutional as the federal government has the right to tax the populace. At the same time, some of the taxes that were implemented as part of the ACA have been eliminated.

 **BRING IT HOME**

## What's the Big Deal with Obamacare?

What is it that the Affordable Care Act (ACA) will actually do? To begin with, we should note that it is a massively complex law, with a large number of parts, some of which the Obama administration implemented immediately, and others that the government is supposed to phase in every year from 2013 through 2020. Three of these parts are coverage for the uninsured—those without health insurance, coverage for individuals with preexisting conditions, and the so-called employer and individual mandates, which require employers to offer and people to purchase health insurance. Under the Trump administration, several components of the ACA were repealed or overhauled, while under the Biden administration (and with the support of a majority of the population) the ACA has continued as a major element in provision of health care in the United States.

As we noted in the chapter, people face ever-increasing healthcare costs in the United States. Over the years, the ranks of the uninsured in the United States have grown as rising prices have pushed employers and individuals out of the market. Insurance companies have increasingly used pre-existing medical conditions to determine if someone is high risk, for whom insurance companies either charge higher prices, or they choose to deny insurance coverage to these individuals. Whatever the cause, we noted at the beginning of the chapter that prior to the ACA, more than 32 million Americans were uninsured. People who are uninsured tend to use emergency rooms for treatment—the most expensive form of healthcare, which has contributed significantly to rising costs.

The ACA introduced regulations designed to control increases in healthcare costs. One example is a cap on the amount healthcare providers can spend on administrative costs. Another is a requirement that healthcare providers switch to electronic medical records (EMRs), which will reduce administrative costs.

The ACA required that states establish health insurance exchanges, or markets, where people without health insurance, and businesses that do not provide it for their employees, can shop for different insurance plans. The purpose of these exchanges was to increase competition in insurance markets and thus reduce prices of policies.

Finally, the ACA mandated that people with preexisting conditions could no longer be denied health insurance. The U.S. Department of Health and Human Services estimates that the those without insurance in the US has fallen from 20.3% in 2012 to 11.5% in 2016. Accordingly, 20 million Americans gained coverage under the ACA. According to the Census, as of 2020, the share of the population without health insurance had fallen to 8.6%. So the ACA has resulted in a decline in the percentage of Americans without health insurance by almost 60%.

What was the cost of this increased coverage and how was it paid? An insurance policy works by insuring against the possibility of needing healthcare. If there are high risk individuals in the insurance pool, the pool must be expanded to include enough low risk individuals to keep average premiums affordable. To that end, the ACA imposed the individual mandate, requiring all individuals to purchase insurance (or pay a penalty) whether they were high risk or not. Many young adults would choose to skip health insurance since the likelihood of their needing significant healthcare is small. The individual mandate brought in a significant amount of money to pay for the ACA. However, despite the elimination of the penalty for not having insurance, ACA coverage has continued to increase. In addition, there were three other funding sources. The ACA took $716 billion which otherwise would have gone to Medicare spending. The ACA also increased the Medicare tax that wealthy Americans paid by an additional 0.9%. Despite these funding sources, the Congressional Budget Office estimates that the ACA will increase the federal debt by $137 billion over the next decade.

The impact of the Patient Protection and Affordable Care Act has been a rise in Americans with health insurance. However, due to the increased taxes to pay for the ACA and the increased deficit spending, the ACA faces continued opposition. The Trump administration vowed to repeal it on the campaign trail but no alternative bill has made its way before congress. Only time will tell if the Affordable Care Act will leave a legacy or will quickly be swept by the wayside, jeopardizing the 20 million newly insured Americans.

At the time of this writing, the final impact of the Patient Protection and Affordable Care Act is not clear. Millions of previously uninsured Americans now have coverage, but the increased taxes to pay for ACA and increased deficit spending have created significant political opposition. Whether or not that opposition eventually succeeds in overturning the ACA remains to be seen.

# Key Terms

**adverse selection** when groups with inherently higher risks than the average person seek out insurance, thus straining the insurance system

**asymmetric information** a situation where the seller or the buyer has more information than the other regarding the quality of the item for sale

**coinsurance** when an insurance policyholder pays a percentage of a loss, and the insurance company pays the remaining cost

**collateral** something valuable—often property or equipment—that a lender would have a right to seize and sell if the buyer does not repay the loan

**copayment** when an insurance policyholder must pay a small amount for each service, before insurance covers the rest

**cosigner** another person or firm who legally pledges to repay some or all of the money on a loan if the original borrower does not

**deductible** an amount that the insurance policyholders must pay out of their own pocket before the insurance coverage pays anything

**fee-for-service** when medical care providers are paid according to the services they provide

**health maintenance organization (HMO)** an organization that provides health care and is paid a fixed amount per person enrolled in the plan—regardless of how many services are provided

**imperfect information** a situation where either the buyer or the seller, or both, are uncertain about the qualities of what they are buying and selling

**insurance** method of protecting a person from financial loss, whereby policy holders make regular payments to an insurance entity; the insurance firm then remunerates a group member who suffers significant financial damage from an event covered by the policy

**money-back guarantee** a promise that the seller will refund the buyer's money under certain conditions

**moral hazard** when people have insurance against a certain event, they are less likely to guard against that event occurring

**occupational license** licenses issued by government agencies, which indicate that a worker has completed a certain type of education or passed a certain test

**premium** payment made to an insurance company

**risk group** a group that shares roughly the same risks of an adverse event occurring

**service contract** the buyer pays an extra amount and the seller agrees to fix anything specified in the contract that goes wrong for a set time period

**warranty** a promise to fix or replace the good for a certain period of time

## Key Concepts and Summary

### 16.1 The Problem of Imperfect Information and Asymmetric Information

Many make economic transactions in a situation of imperfect information, where either the buyer, the seller, or both are less than 100% certain about the qualities of what they are buying or selling. When information about the quality of products is highly imperfect, it may be difficult for a market to exist.

A "lemon" is a product that turns out, after the purchase, to have low quality. When the seller has more accurate information about the product's quality than the buyer, the buyer will be hesitant to buy, out of fear of purchasing a "lemon."

Markets have many ways to deal with imperfect information. In goods markets, buyers facing imperfect information about products may depend upon money-back guarantees, warranties, service contracts, and reputation. In labor markets, employers facing imperfect information about potential employees may turn to resumes, recommendations, occupational licenses for certain jobs, and employment for trial periods. In capital markets, lenders facing imperfect information about borrowers may require detailed loan applications and credit checks, cosigners, and collateral.

### 16.2 Insurance and Imperfect Information

Insurance is a way of sharing risk. People in a group pay premiums for insurance against some unpleasant event, and those in the group who actually experience the unpleasant event then receive some compensation. The fundamental law of insurance is that what the average person pays in over time cannot be less than what the average person gets out. In an actuarially fair insurance policy, the premiums that a person pays to the insurance company are the same as the average amount of benefits for a person in that risk group. Moral hazard arises in insurance markets because those who are insured against a risk will have less reason to take steps to avoid the costs from that risk.

Many insurance policies have deductibles, copayments, or coinsurance. A deductible is the maximum amount that the policyholder must pay out-of-pocket before the insurance company pays the rest of the bill. A copayment is a flat fee that an insurance policy-holder must pay before receiving services. Coinsurance requires the policyholder to pay a certain percentage of costs. Deductibles, copayments, and coinsurance reduce moral hazard by requiring the insured party to bear some of the costs before collecting insurance benefits.

In a fee-for-service health financing system, medical care providers receive reimbursement according to the cost of services they provide. An alternative method of organizing health care is through health maintenance organizations (HMOs), where medical care providers receive reimbursement according to the number of patients they handle, and it is up to the providers to allocate resources between patients who receive more or fewer health care services. Adverse selection arises in insurance markets when insurance buyers know more about the risks they face than does the insurance company. As a result, the insurance company runs the risk that low-risk parties will avoid its insurance because it is too costly for them, while high-risk parties will embrace it because it looks like a good deal to them.

## Self-Check Questions

1. For each of the following purchases, say whether you would expect the degree of imperfect information to be relatively high or relatively low:
   a. Buying apples at a roadside stand
   b. Buying dinner at the neighborhood restaurant around the corner
   c. Buying a used laptop computer at a garage sale
   d. Ordering flowers over the internet for your friend in a different city

2. Why is there asymmetric information in the labor market? What signals can an employer look for that might indicate the traits they are seeking in a new employee?

3. Why is it difficult to measure health outcomes?

## Review Questions

4. Why might it be difficult for a buyer and seller to agree on a price when imperfect information exists?

5. What do economists (and used-car dealers) mean by a "lemon"?

6. What are some ways a seller of goods might reassure a possible buyer who is faced with imperfect information?

7. What are some ways a seller of labor (that is, someone looking for a job) might reassure a possible employer who is faced with imperfect information?

8. What are some ways that someone looking for a loan might reassure a bank that is faced with imperfect information about whether the borrower will repay the loan?

9. What is an insurance premium?

10. In an insurance system, would you expect each person to receive in benefits pretty much what they pay in premiums or is it just that the average benefits paid will equal the average premiums paid?

11. What is an actuarially fair insurance policy?

12. What is the problem of moral hazard?

13. How can moral hazard lead to more costly insurance premiums than one was expected?

14. Define deductibles, copayments, and coinsurance.

15. How can deductibles, copayments, and coinsurance reduce moral hazard?

16. What is the key difference between a fee-for-service healthcare system and a system based on health maintenance organizations?

17. How might adverse selection make it difficult for an insurance market to operate?

18. What are some of the metrics economists use to measure health outcomes?

## Critical Thinking Questions

19. You are on the board of directors of a private high school, which is hiring new tenth-grade science teachers. As you think about hiring someone for a job, what are some mechanisms you might use to overcome the problem of imperfect information?

20. A website offers a place for people to buy and sell emeralds, but information about emeralds can be quite imperfect. The website then enacts a rule that all sellers in the market must pay for two independent examinations of their emerald, which are available to the customer for inspection.
    a.  How would you expect this improved information to affect demand for emeralds on this website?
    b.  How would you expect this improved information to affect the quantity of high-quality emeralds sold on the website?

21. How do you think the problem of moral hazard might have affected the safety of sports such as football and boxing when safety regulations started requiring that players wear more padding?

22. To what sorts of customers would an insurance company offer a policy with a high copay? What about a high premium with a lower copay?

## Problems

23. Using Exercise 16.20, sketch the effects in parts (a) and (b) on a single supply and demand diagram. What prediction would you make about how the improved information alters the equilibrium quantity and price?

24. Imagine that you can divide 50-year-old men into two groups: those who have a family history of cancer and those who do not. For the purposes of this example, say that 20% of a group of 1,000 men have a family history of cancer, and these men have one chance in 50 of dying in the next year, while the other 80% of men have one chance in 200 of dying in the next year. The insurance company is selling a policy that will pay $100,000 to the estate of anyone who dies in the next year.
    a.  If the insurance company were selling life insurance separately to each group, what would be the actuarially fair premium for each group?
    b.  If an insurance company were offering life insurance to the entire group, but could not find out about family cancer histories, what would be the actuarially fair premium for the group as a whole?
    c.  What will happen to the insurance company if it tries to charge the actuarially fair premium to the group as a whole rather than to each group separately?

FIGURE 17.1 **Building Home Equity** Many people choose to purchase their home rather than rent. This chapter explores how the global financial crisis has influenced home ownership. (Credit: "red sold sign" by Diana Parkhouse/ Flickr Creative Commons, CC BY 2.0)

## CHAPTER OBJECTIVES

In this chapter, you will learn about:

- How Businesses Raise Financial Capital
- How Households Supply Financial Capital
- How to Accumulate Personal Wealth

# Introduction to Financial Markets

 **BRING IT HOME**

### The Housing Bubble and the 2007 Financial Crisis

In 2006, housing equity in the United States peaked at $13 trillion. That means that the market prices of homes, less what was still owed on the loans they used to buy these houses, equaled $13 trillion. This was a very good number, since the equity represented the value of the financial asset most U.S. citizens owned.

However, by 2008 this number declined to $8.8 trillion, and it plummeted further still in 2009. Combined with the decline in value of other financial assets held by U.S. citizens, by 2010, U.S. homeowners' wealth had shrunk $14 trillion! This is a staggering result, and it affected millions of lives: people had to alter their retirement, housing, and other important consumption decisions. Just about every other large economy in the world suffered a decline in the market value of financial assets, as a result of the 2008-2009 global financial crisis.

This chapter will explain why people purchase houses (other than as a place to live), why they buy other types of financial assets, and why businesses sell those financial assets in the first place. The chapter will also give us insight into why financial markets and assets go through boom and bust cycles like the one we described here.

When a firm needs to buy new equipment or build a new facility, it often must go to the financial market to raise funds. Usually firms will add capacity during an economic expansion when profits are on the rise and consumer demand is high. Business investment is one of the critical ingredients needed to sustain economic growth. Even in the sluggish 2009 economy, U.S. firms invested $1.4 trillion in new equipment and structures, in the hope that these investments would generate profits in the years ahead.

Between the end of the recession in 2009 through the second quarter 2013, profits for the S&P 500 companies grew by 9.7% despite the weak economy, with cost cutting and reductions in input costs driving much of that amount, according to the *Wall Street Journal*. Figure 17.2 shows corporate profits after taxes (adjusted for inventory and capital consumption). Despite the steep decline in quarterly net profit in 2008, profits have recovered and surpassed pre-recession levels.

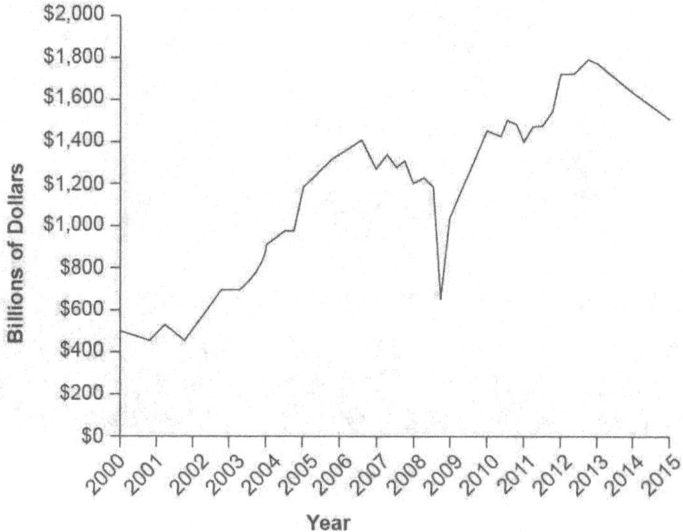


**FIGURE 17.2 Corporate Profits After Tax (Adjusted for Inventory and Capital Consumption)** Prior to 2008, corporate profits after tax more often than not increased each year. There was a significant drop in profits during 2008 and into 2009. The profit trend has since continued to increase each year, though at a less steady or consistent rate. (Source: Federal Reserve Economic Data (FRED) https://research.stlouisfed.org/fred2/series/CPATAX)

Many firms, from huge companies like General Motors to startup firms writing computer software, do not have the financial resources within the firm to make all the desired investments. These firms need financial capital from outside investors, and they are willing to pay interest for the opportunity to obtain a rate of return on the investment of that financial capital.

On the other side of the financial capital market, financial capital suppliers, like households, wish to use their savings in a way that will provide a return. Individuals cannot, however, take the few thousand dollars that they save in any given year, write a letter to General Motors or some other firm, and negotiate to invest their money with that firm. Financial capital markets bridge this gap: that is, they find ways to take the inflow of funds from many separate financial capital suppliers and transform it into the funds of financial capital demanders desire. Such financial markets include stocks, bonds, bank loans, and other financial investments.

Click to view content (https://openstax.org/books/principles-microeconomics-3e/pages/17-introduction-to-financial-markets)
Corporate Profits After Tax (Adjusted for Inventory and Capital Consumption)

## ⊚ LINK IT UP

Visit this website (http://openstax.org/l/marketoverview) to read more about financial markets.

---

Our perspective then shifts to consider how these financial investments appear to capital suppliers such as the households that are saving funds. Households have a range of investment options: bank accounts, certificates of deposit, money market mutual funds, bonds, stocks, stock and bond mutual funds, housing, and even tangible assets like gold. Finally, the chapter investigates two methods for becoming rich: a quick and easy method that does not work very well at all, and a slow, reliable method that can work very well over a lifetime.

# 17.1 How Businesses Raise Financial Capital

### LEARNING OBJECTIVES

By the end of this section, you will be able to:
- Describe financial capital and how it relates to profits
- Discuss the purpose and process of borrowing, bonds, and corporate stock
- Explain how firms choose between sources of financial capital

Firms often make decisions that involve spending money in the present and expecting to earn profits in the future. Examples include when a firm buys a machine that will last 10 years, or builds a new plant that will last for 30 years, or starts a research and development project. Firms can raise the financial capital they need to pay for such projects in four main ways: (1) from early-stage investors; (2) by reinvesting profits; (3) by borrowing through banks or bonds; and (4) by selling stock. When business owners choose financial capital sources, they also choose how to pay for them.

## Early-Stage Financial Capital

Firms that are just beginning often have an idea or a prototype for a product or service to sell, but few customers, or even no customers at all, and thus are not earning profits. Such firms face a difficult problem when it comes to raising financial capital: How can a firm that has not yet demonstrated any ability to earn profits pay a rate of return to financial investors?

For many small businesses, the original source of money is the business owner. Someone who decides to start a restaurant or a gas station, for instance, might cover the startup costs by dipping into their own bank account, or by borrowing money (perhaps using a home as collateral). Alternatively, many cities have a network of well-to-do individuals, known as "angel investors," who will put their own money into small new companies at an early development stage, in exchange for owning some portion of the firm.

**Venture capital** firms make financial investments in new companies that are still relatively small in size, but that have potential to grow substantially. These firms gather money from a variety of individual or institutional investors, including banks, institutions like college endowments, insurance companies that hold financial reserves, and corporate pension funds. Venture capital firms do more than just supply money to small startups. They also provide advice on potential products, customers, and key employees. Typically, a venture capital fund invests in a number of firms, and then investors in that fund receive returns according to how the fund as a whole performs.

The amount of money invested in venture capital fluctuates substantially from year to year: as one example, venture capital firms invested more than $48.3 billion in 2014, according to the National Venture Capital Association. All early-stage investors realize that the majority of small startup businesses will never hit it big; many of them will go out of business within a few months or years. They also know that getting in on the ground floor of a few huge successes like a Netflix or an Amazon.com can make up for multiple failures. Therefore, early-stage investors are willing to take large risks in order to position themselves to gain substantial returns on their investment.

## Profits as a Source of Financial Capital

If firms are earning profits (their revenues are greater than costs), they can choose to reinvest some of these profits in equipment, structures, and research and development. For many established companies, reinvesting their own profits is one primary source of financial capital. Companies and firms just getting started may have numerous attractive investment opportunities, but few current profits to invest. Even large firms can experience a year or two of earning low profits or even suffering losses, but unless the firm can find a steady and reliable financial capital source so that it can continue making real investments in tough times, the firm may not survive until better times arrive. Firms often need to find financial capital sources other than profits.

## Borrowing: Banks and Bonds

When a firm has a record of at least earning significant revenues, and better still of earning profits, the firm can make a credible promise to pay interest, and so it becomes possible for the firm to borrow money. Firms have two main borrowing methods: banks and bonds.

A bank loan for a firm works in much the same way as a loan for an individual who is buying a car or a house. The firm borrows an amount of money and then promises to repay it, including some rate of interest, over a predetermined period of time. If the firm fails to make its loan payments, the bank (or banks) can often take the firm to court and require it to sell its buildings or equipment to make the loan payments.

Another source of financial capital is a bond. A **bond** is a financial contract: a borrower agrees to repay the amount that it borrowed and also an interest rate over a period of time in the future. A **corporate bond** is issued by firms, but bonds are also issued by various levels of government. For example, a **municipal bond** is issued by cities, a state bond by U.S. states, and a **Treasury bond** by the federal government through the U.S. Department of the Treasury. A bond specifies an amount that one will borrow, the interest rate that one will pay, and the time until repayment.

A large company, for example, might issue bonds for $10 million. The firm promises to make interest payments at an annual rate of 8%, or $800,000 per year and then, after 10 years, will repay the $10 million it originally borrowed. When a firm issues bonds, it may choose to issue many bonds in smaller amounts that together reach the total amount it wishes to raise. A firm that seeks to borrow $50 million by issuing bonds, might actually issue 10,000 bonds of $5,000 each. In this way, an individual investor could, in effect, loan the firm $5,000, or any multiple of that amount. Anyone who owns a bond and receives the interest payments is called a **bondholder**. If a firm issues bonds and fails to make the promised interest payments, the bondholders can take the firm to court and require it to pay, even if the firm needs to raise the money by selling buildings or equipment. However, there is no guarantee the firm will have sufficient assets to pay off the bonds. The bondholders may recoup only a portion of what they loaned the firm.

Bank borrowing is more customized than issuing bonds, so it often works better for relatively small firms. The bank can get to know the firm extremely well—often because the bank can monitor sales and expenses quite accurately by looking at deposits and withdrawals. Relatively large and well-known firms often issue bonds instead. They use bonds to raise new financial capital that pays for investments, or to raise capital to pay off old bonds, or to buy other firms. However, the idea that firms or individuals use banks for relatively smaller loans and bonds for larger loans is not an ironclad rule: sometimes groups of banks make large loans and sometimes relatively small and lesser-known firms issue bonds.

## Corporate Stock and Public Firms

A **corporation** is a business that "incorporates"—that is owned by shareholders that have limited liability for the company's debt but share in its profits (and losses). Corporations may be private or public, and may or may not have publicly traded stock. They may raise funds to finance their operations or new investments by raising capital through selling stock or issuing bonds.

Those who buy the stock become the firm's owners, or **shareholders**. **Stock** represents firm ownership; that is, a person who owns 100% of a company's stock, by definition, owns the entire company. The company's stock is divided into **shares**. Corporate giants like IBM, AT&T, Ford, General Electric, Microsoft, Merck, and Exxon all have millions of stock shares. In most large and well-known firms, no individual owns a majority of the stock shares. Instead, large numbers of shareholders—even those who hold thousands of shares—each have only a small slice of the firm's overall ownership.

When a large number of shareholders own a company, there are three questions to ask:

1. How and when does the company obtain money from its sale of stock?
2. What rate of return does the company promise to pay when it sells stock?
3. Who makes decisions in a company owned by a large number of shareholders?

First, a firm receives money from the stock sale only when the company sells its own stock to the public (the public includes individuals, mutual funds, insurance companies, and pension funds). We call a firm's first stock sale to the public an **initial public offering (IPO)**. The IPO is important for two reasons. For one, the IPO, and any stock issued thereafter, such as stock held as treasury stock (shares that a company keeps in their own treasury) or new stock issued later as a secondary offering, provides the funds to repay the early-stage investors, like the angel investors and the venture capital firms. A venture capital firm may have a 40% ownership in the firm. When the firm sells stock, the venture capital firm sells its part ownership of the firm to the public. A second reason for the importance of the IPO is that it provides the established company with financial capital for substantially expanding its operations.

However, most of the time when one buys and sells corporate stock the firm receives no financial return at all. If you buy General Motors stock, you almost certainly buy it from the current share owner, and General Motors does not receive any of your money. This pattern should not seem particularly odd. After all, if you buy a house, the current owner receives your money, not the original house builder. Similarly, when you buy stock shares, you are buying a small slice of the firm's ownership from the existing owner—and the firm that originally issued the stock is not a part of this transaction.

Second, when a firm decides to issue stock, it must recognize that investors will expect to receive a rate of return. That rate of return can come in two forms. A firm can make a direct payment to its shareholders, called a **dividend**. Alternatively, a financial investor might buy a share of stock in Wal-Mart for $45 and then later sell it to someone else for $60, for $15 gain. We call the increase in the stock value (or of any asset) between when one buys and sells it a **capital gain**.

Third: Who makes the decisions about when a firm will issue stock, or pay dividends, or re-invest profits? To understand the answers to these questions, it is useful to separate firms into two groups: private and public.

A **private company** is frequently owned by the people who generally run it on a day-to-day basis. Individuals can run a private company. We call this a **sole proprietorship**. If a group runs it, we call it a **partnership**. A private company can also be a corporation, but with no publicly issued stock. A small law firm run by one person, even if it employs some other lawyers, would be a sole proprietorship. Partners may jointly own a larger law firm. Most private companies are relatively small, but there are some large private corporations, with tens of billions of dollars in annual sales, that do not have publicly issued stock, such as farm products dealer Cargill, the Mars candy company, and the Bechtel engineering and construction firm.

When a firm decides to sell stock, which financial investors can buy and sell, we call it a **public company**. Shareholders own a public company. Since the shareholders are a very broad group, often consisting of thousands or even millions of investors, the shareholders vote for a board of directors, who in turn hire top executives to run the firm on a day-to-day basis. The more stock a shareholder owns, the more votes that shareholder is entitled to cast for the company's board of directors.

In theory, the board of directors helps to ensure that the firm runs in the interests of the true owners—the shareholders. However, the top executives who run the firm have a strong voice in choosing the candidates who will serve on their board of directors. After all, few shareholders are knowledgeable enough or have enough personal incentive to spend energy and money nominating alternative board members.

## How Firms Choose between Financial Capital Sources

There are clear patterns in how businesses raise financial capital. We can explain these patterns in terms of imperfect information, which as we discussed in Information, Risk, and Insurance, is a situation where buyers and sellers in a market do not both have full and equal information. Those who are actually running a firm will almost always have more information about whether the firm is likely to earn profits in the future than outside investors who provide financial capital.

Any young startup firm is a risk. Some startup firms are only a little more than an idea on paper. The firm's founders inevitably have better information than anyone else about how hard they are willing to work, and whether the firm is likely to succeed. When the founders invested their own money into the firm, they demonstrate a belief in its prospects. At this early stage, angel investors and venture capitalists try to overcome the imperfect information, at least in part, by knowing the managers and their business plan personally and by giving them advice.

Accurate information is sometimes not available because **corporate governance**, the name economists give to the institutions that are supposed to watch over top executives, fails, as the following Clear It Up feature on Lehman Brothers shows.

 **CLEAR IT UP**

### How did lack of corporate governance lead to the Lehman Brothers failure?

In 2008, Lehman Brothers was the fourth largest U.S. investment bank, with 25,000 employees. The firm had been in business for 164 years. On September 15, 2008, Lehman Brothers filed for Chapter 11 bankruptcy protection. There are many causes of the Lehman Brothers failure. One area of apparent failure was the lack of oversight by the Board of Directors to keep managers from undertaking excessive risk. We can attribute part of the oversight failure, according to Tim Geithner's April 10, 2010, testimony to Congress, to the Executive Compensation Committee's emphasis on short-term gains without enough consideration of the risks. In addition, according to the court examiner's report, the Lehman Brother's Board of Directors paid too little attention to the details of the operations of Lehman Brothers and also had limited financial service experience.

The board of directors, elected by the shareholders, is supposed to be the first line of corporate governance and oversight for top executives. A second institution of corporate governance is the auditing firm the company hires to review the company's financial records and certify that everything looks reasonable. A third institution of corporate governance is outside investors, especially large shareholders like those who invest large mutual funds or pension funds. In the case of Lehman Brothers, corporate governance failed to provide investors with accurate financial information about the firm's operations.

As a firm becomes at least somewhat established and its strategy appears likely to lead to profits in the near future, knowing the individual managers and their business plans on a personal basis becomes less important, because information has become more widely available regarding the company's products, revenues, costs, and profits. As a result, other outside investors who do not know the managers personally, like bondholders and shareholders, are more willing to provide financial capital to the firm.

At this point, a firm must often choose how to access financial capital. It may choose to borrow from a bank, issue bonds, or issue stock. The great disadvantage of borrowing money from a bank or issuing bonds is that the firm commits to scheduled interest payments, whether or not it has sufficient income. The great advantage of borrowing money is that the firm maintains control of its operations and is not subject to shareholders. Issuing stock involves selling off company ownership to the public and becoming responsible to a board of directors and the shareholders.

The benefit of issuing stock is that a small and growing firm increases its visibility in the financial markets and can access large amounts of financial capital for expansion, without worrying about repaying this money. If the firm is successful and profitable, the board of directors will need to decide upon a dividend payout or how to reinvest profits to further grow the company. Issuing and placing stock is expensive, requires the expertise of investment bankers and attorneys, and entails compliance with reporting requirements to shareholders and government agencies, such as the federal Securities and Exchange Commission (SEC).

## 17.2 How Households Supply Financial Capital

### LEARNING OBJECTIVES

By the end of this section, you will be able to:

- Show the relationship between savers, banks, and borrowers
- Calculate bond yield
- Contrast bonds, stocks, mutual funds, and assets
- Explain the tradeoffs between return and risk

The ways in which firms would prefer to raise funds are only half the story of financial markets. The other half is what those households and individuals who supply funds desire, and how they perceive the available choices. The focus of our discussion now shifts from firms on the demand side of financial capital markets to households on the supply side of those markets. We can divide the mechanisms for savings available to households into several categories: deposits in bank accounts; bonds; stocks; money market mutual funds; stock and bond mutual funds; and housing and other tangible assets like owning gold. We need to analyze each of these investments in terms of three factors: (1) the expected rate of return it will pay; (2) the risk that the return will be much lower or higher than expected; and (3) the investment's **liquidity**, which refers to how easily one can exchange money or financial assets for a good or service. We will do this analysis as we discuss each of these investments in the sections below. First, however, we need to understand the difference between expected rate of return, risk, and actual rate of return.

### Expected Rate of Return, Risk, and Actual Rate of Return

The **expected rate of return** refers to how much a project or an investment is expected to return to the investor, either in future interest payments, capital gains, or increased profitability. It is usually the average return over a period of time, usually in years or even decades. We normally measure it as a percentage rate. **Risk** measures the uncertainty of that project's profitability. There are several types of risk, including default risk and interest rate risk. Default risk, as its name suggests, is the risk that the borrower fails to pay back the bond or loan. Interest rate risk is the danger that you might buy a long term bond at a 6% interest rate right before market rates suddenly rise, so had you waited, you could have received a similar bond that paid 9%. A high-risk investment is one for which a wide range of potential payoffs is reasonably probable. A low-risk investment may have actual returns that are fairly close to its expected rate of return year after year. A high-risk investment will have actual returns that are much higher than the expected rate of return in some months or years and much lower in other months or years. The **actual rate of return** refers to the total rate of return, including capital gains and interest paid on an investment at the end of a time period.

### Bank Accounts

An intermediary is one who stands between two other parties. For example, a person who arranges a blind date between two other people is one kind of intermediary. In financial capital markets, banks are an example of a **financial intermediary**—that is, an institution that operates between a saver who deposits funds in a bank and a borrower who receives a loan from that bank. When a bank serves as a financial intermediary, unlike the situation with a couple on a blind date, the saver and the borrower never meet. In fact, it is not even possible to make direct connections between those who deposit funds in banks and those who borrow from banks, because all deposited funds end up in one big pool, which the financial institution then lends out.

Figure 17.3 illustrates the position of banks as a financial intermediary, with a pattern of deposits flowing into a bank and loans flowing out, and then repayment of the loans flowing back to the bank, with interest payments for the original savers.

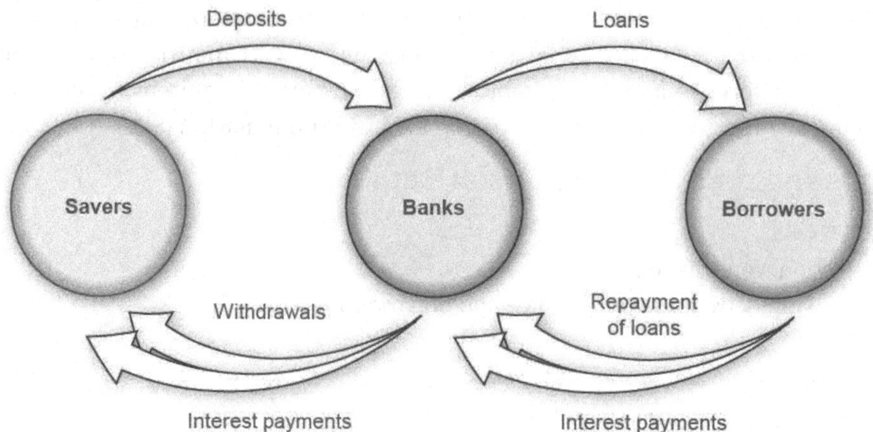


**FIGURE 17.3 Banks as Financial Intermediaries** Banks are a financial intermediary because they stand between savers and borrowers. Savers place deposits with banks, and then receive interest payments and withdraw money. Borrowers receive loans from banks, and repay the loans with interest.

Banks offer a range of accounts to serve different needs. A **checking account** typically pays little or no interest, but it facilitates transactions by giving you easy access to your money, either by writing a check or by using a **debit card** (that is, a card which works like a credit card, except that purchases are immediately deducted from your checking account rather than billed separately through a credit card company). A **savings account** typically pays some interest rate, but getting the money typically requires you to make a trip to the bank or an automatic teller machine (or you can access the funds electronically). The lines between checking and savings accounts have blurred in the last couple of decades, as many banks offer checking accounts that will pay an interest rate similar to a savings account if you keep a certain minimum amount in the account, or conversely, offer savings accounts that allow you to write at least a few checks per month.

Another way to deposit savings at a bank is to use a **certificate of deposit (CD)**. With a CD, you agree to deposit a certain amount of money, often measured in thousands of dollars, in the account for a stated period of time, typically ranging from a few months to several years. In exchange, the bank agrees to pay a higher interest rate than for a regular savings account. While you can withdraw the money before the allotted time, as the advertisements for CDs always warn, there is "a substantial penalty for early withdrawal."

Figure 17.4 shows the annual rate of interest paid on a six-month, one-year, and five-year CD since 1984, as reported by Bankrate.com. The interest rates that savings accounts pay are typically a little lower than the CD rate, because financial investors need to receive a slightly higher rate of interest as compensation for promising to leave deposits untouched for a period of time in a CD, and thus forfeiting some liquidity.

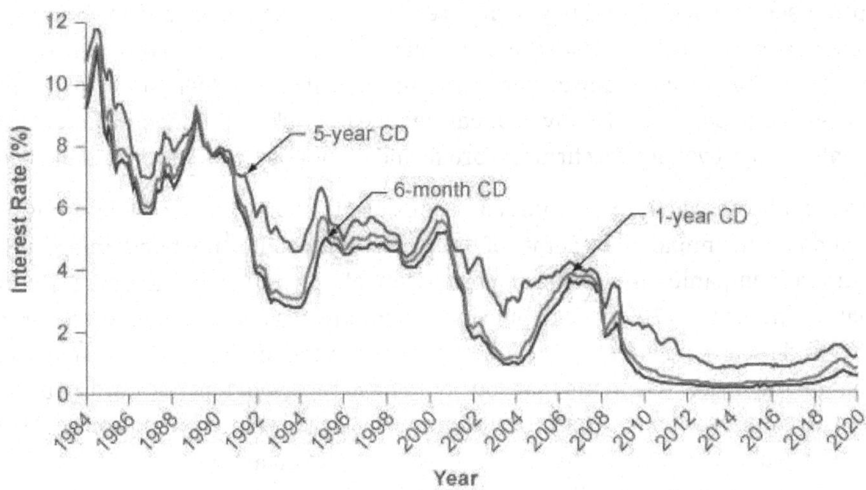


**FIGURE 17.4 Interest Rates on Six-Month, One-Year, and Five-Year Certificates of Deposit** The interest rates on certificates of deposit have fluctuated over time. The high interest rates of the early 1980s are indicative of the relatively high inflation rate in the United States at that time. Interest rates fluctuate with the business cycle, typically increasing during expansions and decreasing during a recession. Note the steep decline in CD rates since 2008, the beginning of the Great Recession.

The great advantages of bank accounts are that financial investors have very easy access to their money, and also money in bank accounts is extremely safe. In part, this safety arises because a bank account offers more security than keeping a few thousand dollars in the toe of a sock in your underwear drawer. In addition, the Federal Deposit Insurance Corporation (FDIC) protects the savings of the average person. Every bank is required by law to pay a fee to the FDIC, based on the size of its deposits. Then, if a bank should go bankrupt and not be able to repay depositors, the FDIC guarantees that all customers will receive their deposits back up to $250,000.

The bottom line on bank accounts looks like this: low risk means low rate of return but high liquidity.

## Bonds

An investor who buys a bond expects to receive a rate of return. However, bonds vary in the rates of return that they offer, according to the riskiness of the borrower. We always can divide an interest rate into three components (as we explained in Choice in a World of Scarcity): compensation for delaying consumption, an adjustment for an inflationary rise in the overall level of prices, and a risk premium that takes the borrower's riskiness into account.

The U.S. government is an extremely safe borrower, so when the U.S. government issues Treasury bonds, it can pay a relatively low interest rate. Firms that appear to be safe borrowers, perhaps because of their sheer size or because they have consistently earned profits over time, will pay a higher interest rate than the U.S. government. Firms that appear to be riskier borrowers, perhaps because they are still growing or their businesses appear shaky, will pay the highest interest rates when they issue bonds. We call bonds that offer high interest rates to compensate for their relatively high chance of default **high-yield bonds** or **junk bonds**. A number of today's well-known firms issued junk bonds in the 1980s when they were starting to grow, including Turner Broadcasting and Microsoft.

## ⊘ LINK IT UP

Visit this website (http://openstax.org/l/bondsecurities) to read about Treasury bonds.

---

A bond issued by the U.S. government or a large corporation may seem to be relatively low risk: after all, the bond issuer has promised to make certain payments over time, and except for rare bankruptcy cases, these payments will occur. If a corporate bond issuer fails to make the payments that it owes to its bondholders, the bondholders can require that the company declare bankruptcy, sell off its assets, and pay them as much as it can. Even in the case of junk bonds, a wise investor can reduce the risk by purchasing bonds from a wide range of different companies since, even if a few firms go broke and do not pay, they are not all likely to go bankrupt.

As we noted before, bonds carry an interest rate risk. For example, imagine you decide to buy a 10-year bond for $1,000 that would pay an annual interest rate of 8%. Soon after you buy the bond, interest rates on bonds rise, so that now similar companies are paying an annual rate of 12%. Anyone who buys a $1,000 bond now can receive annual payments of $120 per year, but since your bond was issued at an interest rate of 8%, you have tied up $1,000 and receive payments of only $80 per year. In the meaningful sense of opportunity cost, you are missing out on the higher payments that you could have received. Furthermore, you can calculate the amount you should be willing to pay now for future payments. To place a present discounted value on a future payment, decide what you would need in the present to equal a certain amount in the future. This calculation will require an interest rate. For example, if the interest rate is 25%, then a payment of $125 a year from now will have a present discounted value of $100—that is, you could take $100 in the present and have $125 in the future. (We discuss this further in the appendix on Present Discounted Value.)

In financial terms, a bond has several parts. A bond is basically an "I owe you" note that an investor receives in exchange for capital (money). The bond has a **face value**. This is the amount the borrower agrees to pay the investor at maturity. The bond has a **coupon rate** or interest rate, which is usually semi-annual, but can be paid at different times throughout the year. (Bonds used to be paper documents with coupons that investors clipped and turned in to the bank to receive interest.) The bond has a **maturity date** when the borrower will pay back its face value as well as its last interest payment. Combining the bond's face value, interest rate, and maturity date, and market interest rates, allows a buyer to compute a bond's **present value**, which is the most that a buyer would be willing to pay for a given bond. This may or may not be the same as the face value.

The **bond yield** measures the rate of return a bond is expected to pay over time. Investors can buy bonds when they are issued and they can buy and sell them during their lifetimes. When buying a bond that has been around for a few years, investors should know that the interest rate printed on a bond is often not the same as the bond yield, even on new bonds. Read the next Work It Out feature to see how this happens.

## WORK IT OUT

### Calculating the Bond Yield

You have bought a $1,000 bond whose coupon rate is 8%. To calculate your return or yield, follow these steps:

1. Assume the following:
   Face value of a bond: $1,000
   Coupon rate: 8 %
   Annual payment: $80 per year
2. Consider the risk of the bond. If this bond carries no risk, then it would be safe to assume that the bond will sell for $1,000 when it is issued and pay the purchaser $80 per year until its maturity, at which time the final interest payment will be made and the original $1,000 will be repaid. Now, assume that over time the interest rates prevailing in the economy rise to 12% and that there is now only one year left to this bond's maturity. This makes the bond an unattractive investment, since an investor can find another bond that perhaps pays 12%. To induce the investor to buy the 8% bond, the bond seller will lower its price below its face value of $1,000.
3. Calculate the bond's price when its interest rate is less than the market interest rate. The expected payments from the bond one year from now are $1,080, because in the bond's last year the bond's issuer will make the final interest payment and then also repay the original $1,000. Given that interest rates are

now 12%, you know that you could invest $964 in an alternative investment and receive $1,080 a year from now; that is, $964(1 + 0.12) = $1080. Therefore, you will not pay more than $964 for the original $1,000 bond.

4. Consider that the investor will receive the $1,000 face value, plus $80 for the last year's interest payment. The yield on the bond will be ($1080 − $964)/$964 = 12%. The yield, or total return, means interest payments, plus capital gains. Note that the interest or coupon rate of 8% did not change. When interest rates rise, bonds previously issued at lower interest rates will sell for less than face value. Conversely, when interest rates fall, bonds previously issued at higher interest rates will sell for more than face value.

Figure 17.5 shows bond yield for two kinds of bonds: 10-year Treasury bonds (which are officially called "notes") and corporate bonds issued by firms that have been given an AAA rating as relatively safe borrowers by Moody's, an independent firm that publishes such ratings. Even though corporate bonds pay a higher interest rate, because firms are riskier borrowers than the federal government, the rates tend to rise and fall together. Treasury bonds typically pay more than bank accounts, and corporate bonds typically pay a higher interest rate than Treasury bonds.

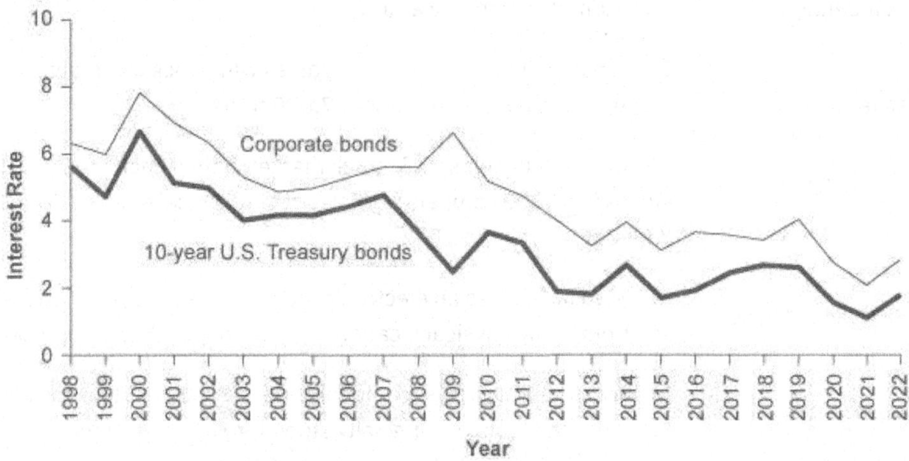


**FIGURE 17.5 Interest Rates for Corporate Bonds and Ten-Year U.S. Treasury Bonds** The interest rates for corporate bonds and U.S. Treasury bonds (officially "notes") rise and fall together, depending on conditions for borrowers and lenders in financial markets for borrowing. The corporate bonds always pay a higher interest rate, to make up for the higher risk they have of defaulting compared with the U.S. government.

The bottom line for bonds: rate of return—low to moderate, depending on the borrower's risk; risk—low to moderate, depending on whether interest rates in the economy change substantially after the bond is issued; liquidity—moderate, because the investor needs to sell the bond before the investor regains the cash.

## Stocks

As we stated earlier, the rate of return on a financial investment in a share of stock can come in two forms: as dividends paid by the firm and as a capital gain achieved by selling the stock for more than you paid. The range of possible returns from buying stock is mind-bending. Firms can decide to pay dividends or not. A stock price can rise to a multiple of its original price or sink all the way to zero. Even in short periods of time, well-established companies can see large movements in their stock prices. For example, on July 1, 2011, Netflix stock peaked at $295 per share; one year later, on July 30, 2012, it was at $53.91 per share; in 2022, it had recovered to $199. When Facebook went public, its shares of stock sold for around $40 per share, but in 2022, they were selling for slightly over $212.

We will discuss the reasons why stock prices fall and rise so abruptly below, but first you need to know how we measure stock market performance. There are a number of different ways to measure the overall performance of the stock market, based on averaging different subsets of companies' stock prices. Perhaps the best-known stock market measure is the Dow Jones Industrial Average, which is based on 30 large U.S. companies' stock prices. Another stock market performance gauge, the Standard & Poor's 500, follows the stock prices of the 500 largest U.S. companies. The Wilshire 5000 tracks the stock prices of essentially all U.S. companies that have stock the public can buy and sell.

Other stock market measures focus on where stocks are traded. For example, the New York Stock Exchange monitors the performance of stocks that are traded on that exchange in New York City. The Nasdaq stock market includes about 3,600 stocks, with a concentration of technology stocks. Table 17.1 lists some of the most commonly cited measures of U.S. and international stock markets.

| Measure of the Stock Market | Comments |
| --- | --- |
| Dow Jones Industrial Average (DJIA): https://www.spglobal.com/spdji/en/ | Based on 30 large companies from a diverse set of representative industries, chosen by analysts at Dow Jones and Company. The index was started in 1896. |
| Standard & Poor's 500: http://www.standardandpoors.com | Based on 500 large U.S. firms, chosen by analysts at Standard & Poor's to represent the economy as a whole. |
| Wilshire 5000: http://www.wilshire.com | Includes essentially all U.S. companies with stock ownership. Despite the name, this index includes about 7,000 firms. |
| New York Stock Exchange: http://www.nyse.com | The oldest and largest U.S. stock market, dating back to 1792. It trades stocks for 2,800 companies of all sizes. It is located at 18 Broad St. in New York City. |
| NASDAQ: http://www.nasdaq.com | Founded in 1971 as an electronic stock market, allowing people to buy or sell from many physical locations. It has about 3,600 companies. |
| FTSE: http://www.ftse.com | Includes the 100 largest companies on the London Stock Exchange. Pronounced "footsie." Originally stood for Financial Times Stock Exchange. |
| Nikkei: http://www.nikkei.co.jp/nikkeiinfo/en/ | Nikkei stands for *Nihon Keizai Shimbun*, which translates as the Japan Economic Journal, a major business newspaper in Japan. Index includes the 225 largest and most actively traded stocks on the Tokyo Stock Exchange. |
| DAX: http://www.exchange.de | Tracks 30 of the largest companies on the Frankfurt, Germany, stock exchange. DAX is an abbreviation for *Deutscher Aktien Index* (German Stock Index). |

**TABLE 17.1** Some Stock Market Measures

The trend in the stock market is generally up over time, but with some large dips along the way. Figure 17.6 shows the path of the Standard & Poor's 500 index (which is measured on the left-hand vertical axis) and the Dow Jones Index (which is measured on the right-hand vertical axis). Broad stock market measures, like the ones we list here, tend to move together. The S&P 500 Index is the weighted average market capitalization of the firms selected to be in the index. The Dow Jones Industrial Average is the price weighted average of 30 industrial stocks tracked on the New York Stock Exchange.

When the Dow Jones average rises from 5,000 to 10,000, you know that the average price of the stocks in that index has roughly doubled. Figure 17.6 shows that stock prices did not rise much in the 1970s, but then started a steady climb in the 1980s. From 2000 to 2013, stock prices bounced up and down, but ended up at about the same level.

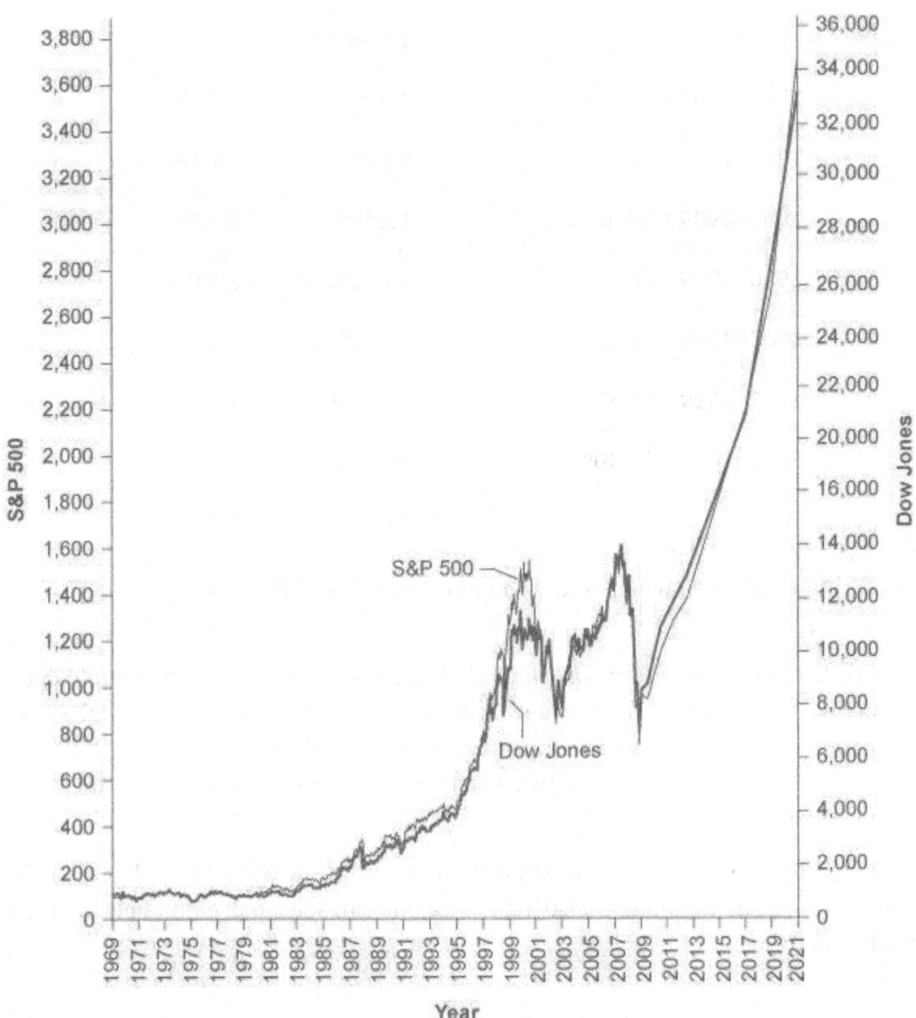


**FIGURE 17.6 The Dow Jones Industrial Index and the Standard & Poor's 500, 1965–2021** Stock prices rose dramatically from the 1980s up to about 2000. From 2000 to 2013, stock prices bounced up and down, but ended up at about the same level. Since 2009, both indexes have for the most part increased.

Table 17.2 shows the total annual rate of return an investor would have received from buying the stocks in the S&P 500 index over recent decades. The total return here includes both dividends paid by these companies and also capital gains arising from increases in the stock value. (For technical reasons related to how we calculate the numbers, the dividends and capital gains do not add exactly to the total return.) From the 1950s to the 1980s, the average firm paid annual dividends equal to about 4% of its stock value. Since the 1990s, dividends have dropped and now often provide a return closer to 1% to 2%. In the 1960s and 1970s, the gap between percent earned on capital gains and dividends was much closer than it has been since the 1980s. In the 1980s and 1990s, capital gains were far higher than dividends. In the 2000s, dividends remained low and, while stock prices fluctuated, they ended the decade roughly where they had started. In the 2010s, dividends remained low and stock prices increased, and this continued at the beginning of the 2020s.

| Period | Total Annual Return | Capital Gains | Dividends |
| --- | --- | --- | --- |
| 1950–1959 | 19.25% | 13.58% | 4.99% |
| 1960–1969 | 7.78% | 4.39% | 3.25% |
| 1970–1979 | 5.88% | 1.60% | 4.20% |
| 1980–1989 | 17.55% | 12.59% | 4.40% |
| 1990–1999 | 18.21% | 15.31% | 2.51% |
| 2000–2009 | –1.00% | –2.70% | 1.70% |
| 2010–2019 | 12.65% | 10.35% | 2.30% |
| 2020 | 18.40% | 16.26% | 2.14% |
| 2021 | 28.71% | 26.89% | 1.82% |

**TABLE 17.2** Annual Returns on S&P 500 Stocks, 1950–2021

The overall pattern is that stocks as a group have provided a high rate of return over extended periods of time, but this return comes with risks. The market value of individual companies can rise and fall substantially, both over short time periods and over the long run. During extended periods of time like the 1970s or the first decade of the 2000s, the overall stock market return can be quite modest. The stock market can sometimes fall sharply, as it did in 2008.

The bottom line on investing in stocks is that the rate of return over time will be high, but the risks are also high, especially in the short run. Liquidity is also high since one can sell stock in publicly held companies readily for spendable money.

## Mutual Funds

Buying stocks or bonds issued by a single company is always somewhat risky. An individual firm may find itself buffeted by unfavorable supply and demand conditions or hurt by unlucky or unwise managerial decisions. Thus, a standard recommendation from financial investors is **diversification**, which means buying stocks or bonds from a wide range of companies. A saver who diversifies is following the old proverb: "Don't put all your eggs in one basket." In any broad group of companies, some firms will do better than expected and some will do worse—but the diversification has a tendency to cancel out extreme increases and decreases in value.

Purchasing a diversified group of stocks or bonds has become easier in the internet age, but it remains something of a task. To simplify the process, companies offer **mutual funds**, which consist of a variety of stocks or bonds from different companies. The financial investor buys mutual fund shares, and then receives a return based on how the fund as a whole performs. In 2021, according to the Investment Company Factbook, just over 47% of U.S. households had a financial investment in a mutual fund—including many people who have their retirement savings or pension money invested in this way.

Mutual funds can focus in certain areas: one mutual fund might invest only in company stocks based in Indonesia, or only in bonds issued by large manufacturing companies, or only in biotechnology companies' stock. At the other end of the spectrum, a mutual fund might be quite broad. At the extreme, some mutual funds own a tiny share of every firm in the stock market, and thus the mutual fund's value will fluctuate with the overall stock market's average. We call a mutual fund that seeks only to mimic the market's overall performance an **index fund**.

Diversification can offset some of the risks of individual stocks rising or falling. Even investors who buy an indexed mutual fund designed to mimic some measure of the broad stock market, like the Standard & Poor's 500, had better prepare against some ups and downs, like those the stock market experienced in the first decade of the 2000s. In 2008 average U.S. stock funds declined 38%, reducing individual and household wealth. This steep drop in value hit hardest those who were close to retirement and were counting on their stock funds to supplement retirement income.

The bottom line on investing in mutual funds is that the rate of return over time will be high. The risks are also high, but the risks and returns for an individual mutual fund will be lower than those for an individual stock. As with stocks, liquidity is also high provided the mutual fund or stock index fund is readily traded.

## Housing and Other Tangible Assets

Households can also seek a rate of return by purchasing tangible assets, especially housing. About two-thirds of U.S. households own their own home. An owner's **equity** in a house is the monetary value the owner would have after selling the house and repaying any outstanding bank loans they used to buy the house. For example, imagine that you buy a house for $200,000, paying 10% of the price as a down payment and taking out a bank loan for the remaining $180,000. Over time, you pay off some of your bank loan, so that only $100,000 remains, and the house's value on the market rises to $250,000. At that point, your equity in the home is the value of the home minus the value of the loan outstanding, which is $150,000. For many middle-class Americans, home equity is their single greatest financial asset. The total value of all home equity held by U.S. households was $23.6 trillion as of the middle of 2021, according to Federal Reserve data.

Investment in a house is tangibly different from bank accounts, stocks, and bonds because a house offers both a financial and a nonfinancial return. If you buy a house to live in, part of the return on your investment occurs from your consumption of "housing services"—that is, having a place to live. (Of course, if you buy a home and rent it out, you receive rental payments for the housing services you provide, which would offer a financial return.) Buying a house to live in also offers the possibility of a capital gain from selling the house in the future for more than you paid for it. There can, however, be different outcomes, as the Clear It Up on the housing market shows.

Housing prices have usually risen steadily over time. For example, the median sales price for an existing one-family home was $122,900 in 1990, but 232,000 at the end of December 2016, according to FRED® Economic Data. Over these 24 years, home prices increased an average of 3.1% per year, which is an average financial return over this time. Figure 17.7 shows U.S. Census data for the average sales price of a new home in the United States from 1965 to 2021.

## ⊘ LINK IT UP

Go to this website (http://openstax.org/l/investopedia) to experiment with a compound annual growth rate calculator.

However, the possible capital gains from rising housing prices are riskier than these national price averages. Certain regions of the country or metropolitan areas have seen drops in housing prices over time. The median housing price for the United States as a whole fell almost 7% in 2008 and again in 2009, dropping the median price from $247,900 to $216,700. As of 2016, home values had recovered and even exceeded their pre-recession levels, and they have continued to increase into the early 2020s.

## ⊘ LINK IT UP

Visit this website (http://openstax.org/l/insidejob) to watch the trailer for *Inside Job*, a movie that explores the modern financial crisis.

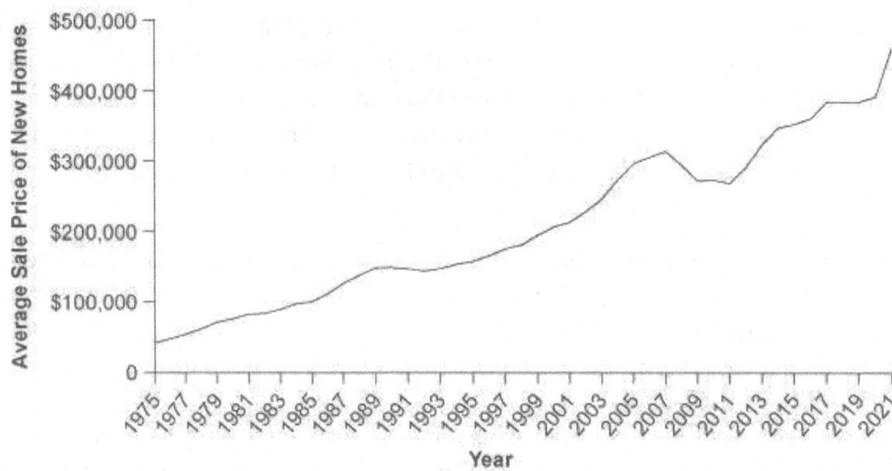

FIGURE 17.7 The Median Average Sales Price for New Single-Family Homes, 1990–2015 The median price is the price where half of sales prices are higher and half are lower. The median sales price for a new one-family home was $122,900 in 1990. It rose as high as $248,000 in 2007, before falling to $232,000 in 2008. In 2015, the median sales price was $294,000. Of course, this national figure conceals many local differences, like the areas where housing prices are higher or lower, or how housing prices have risen or fallen at certain times. (Source: U.S. Census)

Investors can also put money into other tangible assets such as gold, silver, and other precious metals, or in duller commodities like sugar, cocoa, coffee, orange juice, oil, and natural gas. The return on these investments derives from the saver's hope of buying low, selling high, and receiving a capital gain. Investing in, say, gold or coffee offers relatively little in the way of nonfinancial benefits to the user (unless the investor likes to caress gold or gaze upon a warehouse full of coffee). Typically, investors in these commodities never even see the physical good. Instead, they sign a contract that takes ownership of a certain quantity of these commodities, which are stored in a warehouse, and later they sell the ownership to someone else. As one example, from 1981 to 2005, the gold prices generally fluctuated between about $300 and $500 per ounce, but then rose sharply to over $1,100 per ounce by early 2010. In January 2017, prices were hovering around $1,191 per ounce, and they have since increased, reaching over $1,900 by early 2022.

A final area of tangible assets consists of "collectibles" like paintings, fine wine, jewelry, antiques, or even baseball cards. Most collectibles provide returns both in the form of services or of a potentially higher selling price in the future. You can use paintings by hanging them on the wall; jewelry by wearing it; baseball cards by displaying them. You can also hope to sell them someday for more than you paid for them. However, the evidence on prices of collectibles, while scanty, is that while they may go through periods where prices skyrocket for a time, you should not expect to make a higher-than-average rate of return over a sustained period of time from investing in this way.

The bottom line on investing in tangible assets: rate of return—moderate, especially if you can receive nonfinancial benefits from, for example, living in the house; risk—moderate for housing or high if you buy gold or baseball cards; liquidity—low, because it often takes considerable time and energy to sell a house or a piece of fine art and turn your capital gain into cash. The next Clear It Up feature explains the issues in the recent U.S. housing market crisis.

 **CLEAR IT UP**

### What was all the commotion in the recent U.S. housing market?

The cumulative average annual growth rate in housing prices from 1981 to 2000 was 5.1%. The price of an average U.S. home then took off from 2003 to 2005, rising more than 10% per year. No serious analyst believed this rate of growth was sustainable; after all, if housing prices grew at, say, 11% per year over time, the average price of a home would more than double every seven years. However, at the time many serious analysts saw no reason for deep concern. After all, housing prices often change in fits and starts, like all prices, and a price surge for a few years is often followed by prices that are flat or even declining a bit as local markets adjust.

The sharp rise in housing prices was driven by a high level of demand for housing. Interest rates were low, so financial institutions encouraged people to borrow money to buy a house. Banks became much more flexible in their lending, making what were called "subprime" loans. Banks loaned money with low, or sometimes no down payment. They offered loans with very low payments for the first two years, but then much higher payments after that. The idea was that housing prices would keep rising, so the borrower would just refinance the mortgage two years in the future, and thus would not ever have to make the higher payments. Some banks even offered so-called NINJA loans, which meant a financial institution issued a loan even though the borrower had no income, no job, nor assets.

In retrospect, these loans seem outlandish. Many borrowers figured, however, that as long as housing prices kept rising, it made sense to buy. Many lenders used a process called "securitizing," in which they sold their mortgages to financial companies, which put all the mortgages into a big pool, creating large financial securities, and then re-sold these mortgage-backed securities to investors. In this way, the lenders off-loaded the mortgage risks to investors. Investors were interested in mortgage-backed securities as they appeared to offer a steady stream of income, provided the borrowers repaid them. Investors relied on the ratings agencies to assess the credit risk associated with the mortgage-backed securities. In hindsight, it appears that the credit agencies were far too lenient in their ratings of many of the securitized loans. Bank and financial regulators watched the steady rise in the market for mortgage-backed securities, but saw no reason at the time to intervene.

When housing prices turned down, many households that had borrowed when prices were high found that what they owed the bank was more than what their home was worth. Many banks believed that they had diversified by selling their individual loans and instead buying securities based on mortgage loans from all over the country. After all, banks thought back in 2005, the average house price had not declined at any time since the Great Depression in the 1930s. These securities based on mortgage loans, however, turned out to be far riskier than expected. The bust in housing prices weakened both bank and household finances, and thus helped bring on the 2008–2009 Great Recession.

## The Tradeoffs between Return and Risk

The discussion of financial investments has emphasized the expected rate of return, the risk, and the liquidity of each investment. Table 17.3 summarizes these characteristics.

| Financial Investment | Return | Risk | Liquidity |
|---|---|---|---|
| Checking account | Very low | Very little | Very high |
| Savings account | Low | Very little | High |
| Certificate of deposit | Low to medium | Very little | Medium |
| Stocks | High | Medium to high | Medium |
| Bonds | Medium | Low to medium | Medium |
| Mutual funds | Medium to high | Medium to high | Medium to high |
| Housing | Medium | Medium | Low |

**TABLE 17.3 Key Characteristics of Financial Investments**

| Financial Investment | Return | Risk | Liquidity |
|---|---|---|---|
| Gold | Medium | High | Low |
| Collectibles | Low to medium | High | Low |

**TABLE 17.3 Key Characteristics of Financial Investments**

The household investment choices listed here display a tradeoff between the expected return and the degree of risk involved. Bank accounts have very low risk and very low returns; bonds have higher risk but higher returns; and stocks are riskiest of all but have the potential for still higher returns. In effect, the higher average return compensates for the higher degree of risk. If risky assets like stocks did not also offer a higher average return, then few investors would want them.

This tradeoff between return and risk complicates the task of any financial investor: Is it better to invest safely or to take a risk and go for the high return? Ultimately, choices about risk and return will be based on personal preferences. However, it is often useful to examine risk and return in the context of different time frames.

The high returns of stock market investments refer to a high average return that we can expect over a period of several years or decades. The high risk of such investments refers to the fact that in shorter time frames, from months to a few years, the rate of return may fluctuate a great deal. Thus, a person near retirement age, who already owns a house, may prefer reduced risk and certainty about retirement income. For young workers, just starting to make a reasonably profitable living, it may make sense to put most of their savings for retirement in mutual funds. Mutual funds are able to take advantage of their buying and selling size and thereby reduce transaction costs for investors. Stocks are risky in the short term, to be sure, but when the worker can look forward to several decades during which stock market ups and downs can even out, stocks will typically pay a much higher return over that extended period than will bonds or bank accounts. Thus, one must consider tradeoffs between risk and return in the context of where the investor is in life.

## 17.3 How to Accumulate Personal Wealth

**LEARNING OBJECTIVES**

By the end of this section, you will be able to:
- Explain the random walk theory
- Calculate simple and compound interest
- Evaluate how capital markets transform financial capital

Getting rich may seem straightforward enough. Figure out what companies are going to grow and earn high profits in the future, or figure out what companies are going to become popular for everyone else to buy. Those companies are the ones that will pay high dividends or whose stock price will climb in the future. Then, buy stock in those companies. Presto! Multiply your money!

Why is this path to riches not as easy as it sounds? This module first discusses the problems with picking stocks, and then discusses a more reliable but undeniably duller method of accumulating personal wealth.

### Why It Is Hard to Get Rich Quick: The Random Walk Theory

The chief problem with attempting to buy stock in companies that will have higher prices in the future is that many other financial investors are trying to do the same thing. Thus, in attempting to get rich in the stock market, it is no help to identify a company that is going to earn high profits if many other investors have already reached the same conclusion, because the stock price will already be high, based on the expected high level of future profits.

The idea that stock prices are based on expectations about the future has a powerful and unexpected implication. If expectations determine stock price, then shifts in expectations will determine shifts in the stock price. Thus, what matters for predicting whether the stock price of a company will do well is not whether the company will actually earn profits in the future. Instead, you must find a company that analysts widely believe at present to have poor prospects, but that will actually turn out to be a shining star. Brigades of stock market analysts and individual investors are carrying out such research 24 hours a day.

The fundamental problem with predicting future stock winners is that, by definition, no one can predict the future news that alters expectations about profits. Because stock prices will shift in response to unpredictable future news, these prices will tend to follow what mathematicians call a "random walk with a trend." The "random walk" part means that, on any given day, stock prices are just as likely to rise as to fall. "With a trend" means that over time, the upward steps tend to be larger than the downward steps, so stocks do gradually climb.

If stocks follow a random walk, then not even financial professionals will be able to choose those that will beat the average consistently. While some investment advisers are better than average in any given year, and some even succeed for a number of years in a row, the majority of financial investors do not outguess the market. If we look back over time, it is typically true that half or two-thirds of the mutual funds that attempted to pick stocks which would rise more than the market average actually ended up performing worse than the market average. For the average investor who reads the newspaper business pages over a cup of coffee in the morning, the odds of doing better than full-time professionals is not very good at all. Trying to pick the stocks that will gain a great deal in the future is a risky and unlikely way to become rich.

## Getting Rich the Slow, Boring Way

Many U.S. citizens can accumulate a large amount of wealth during their lifetimes, if they make two key choices. The first is to complete additional education and training. In 2020, the Bureau of Labor Statistics reported median weekly usual earnings for full-time wage and salary workers age 25 and over that corresponded to annual income of $40,612 for those with a high school diploma, $48,776 for those with a two-year associate degree, and $67,860 for those with a four-year bachelor's degree. Learning is not only good for you, but it pays off financially, too.

The second key choice is to start saving money early in life, and to give the power of compound interest a chance. Imagine that at age 25, you save $3,000 and place that money into an account that you do not touch. In the long run, it is not unreasonable to assume a 7% real annual rate of return (that is, 7% above the rate of inflation) on money invested in a well-diversified stock portfolio. After 40 years, using the formula for compound interest, the original $3,000 investment will have multiplied nearly fifteen fold:

$$3,000(1 + .07)^{40} = \$44,923$$

Having $45,000 does not make you a millionaire. Notice, however, that this tidy sum is the result of saving $3,000 exactly once. Saving that amount every year for several decades—or saving more as income rises—will multiply the total considerably. This type of wealth will not rival the riches of Microsoft CEO Bill Gates, but remember that only half of Americans have any money in mutual funds at all. Accumulating hundreds of thousands of dollars by retirement is a perfectly achievable goal for a well-educated person who starts saving early in life—and that amount of accumulated wealth will put you at or near the top 10% of all American households. The following Work It Out feature shows the difference between simple and compound interest, and the power of compound interest.

## WORK IT OUT

### Simple and Compound Interest

**Simple interest** is an interest rate calculation only on the principal amount.

Step 1. Learn the formula for simple interest:

$$\text{Principal} \times \text{Rate} \times \text{Time} = \text{Interest}$$

Step 2. Practice using the simple interest formula.

Example 1: $100 Deposit at a simple interest rate of 5% held for one year is:

$$\$100 \times 0.05 \times 1 = \$5$$

Simple interest in this example is $5.

Example 2: $100 Deposit at a simple interest rate of 5% held for three years is:

$$\$100 \times 0.05 \times 3 = \$15$$

Simple interest in this example is $15.

Step 3. Calculate the total future amount using this formula:

$$\text{Total future amount} = \text{principal} + \text{interest}$$

Step 4. Put the two simple interest formulas together.

$$\text{Total future amount (with simple interest)} = \text{Principal} + (\text{Principal} \times \text{Rate} \times \text{Time})$$

Step 5. Apply the simple interest formula to our three year example.

$$\text{Total future amount (with simple interest)} = \$100 + (\$100 \times 0.05 \times 3) = \$115$$

**Compound interest** is an interest rate calculation on the principal plus the accumulated interest.

Step 6. To find the compound interest, we determine the difference between the future value and the present value of the principal. This is accomplished as follows:

$$\text{Future Value} = \text{Principal} \times (1 + \text{interest rate})^{\text{time}}$$
$$\text{Compound interest} = \text{Future Value} - \text{Present Valve}$$

Step 7. Apply this formula to our three-year scenario. Follow the calculations in

Table 17.4

|  | Year 1 |
| --- | --- |
| Amount in Bank | $100 |
| Bank Interest Rate | 5% |
| Total | $105 |
|  | $100 + ($100 × 0.05) |
|  | **Year 2** |
| Amount in Bank | $105 |
| Bank Interest Rate | 5% |
| Total | $110.25 |

**TABLE 17.4**

|  | $105 + (\$105 \times .05)$ |
| --- | --- |
| **Year 3** |  |
| Amount in Bank | $110.25 |
| Bank Interest Rate | 5% |
| Total | $115.75 |
|  | $110.25 + (\$110.25 \times .05)$ |
| Compound interest | $115.76 − $100 = $15.76 |

**TABLE 17.4**

Step 8. Note that, after three years, the total is $115.76. Therefore the total compound interest is $15.76. This is $0.76 more than we obtained with simple interest. While this may not seem like much, keep in mind that we were only working with $100 and over a relatively short time period. Compound interest can make a huge difference with larger sums of money and over longer periods of time.

Obtaining additional education and saving money early in life obviously will not make you rich overnight. Additional education typically means deferring earning income and living as a student for more years. Saving money often requires choices like driving an older or less expensive car, living in a smaller apartment or buying a smaller house, and making other day-to-day sacrifices. For most people, the tradeoffs for achieving substantial personal wealth will require effort, patience, and sacrifice.

## How Capital Markets Transform Financial Flows

Financial capital markets have the power to repackage money as it moves from those who supply financial capital to those who demand it. Banks accept checking account deposits and turn them into long-term loans to companies. Individual firms sell shares of stock and issue bonds to raise capital. Firms make and sell an astonishing array of goods and services, but an investor can receive a return on the company's decisions by buying stock in that company. Financial investors sell and resell stocks and bonds to one another. Venture capitalists and angel investors search for promising small companies. Mutual funds combine the stocks and bonds—and thus, indirectly, the products and investments—of many different companies.

## 🔗 LINK IT UP

Visit this website (http://openstax.org/l/austerebaltic/) to read an article about how austerity can work. Then visit this website (http://openstax.org/l/counteraustere) for another perspective on austerity.

---

In this chapter, we discussed the basic mechanisms of financial markets. (A more advanced course in economics or finance will consider more sophisticated tools.) The fundamentals of those financial capital markets remain the same: Firms are trying to raise financial capital and households are looking for a desirable combination of rate of return, risk, and liquidity. Financial markets are society's mechanisms for bringing together these forces of demand and supply.

 **BRING IT HOME**

## The Housing Bubble and the Financial Crisis of 2007

The housing boom and bust in the United States, and the resulting multi-trillion-dollar decline in home equity, began with the fall of home prices starting in 2007. As home values dipped, many home prices fell below the amount the borrower owed on the mortgage and owners stopped paying and defaulted on their loan. Banks found that their assets (loans) became worthless. Many financial institutions around the world had invested in mortgage-backed securities, or had purchased insurance on mortgage-backed securities. When housing prices collapsed, the value of those financial assets collapsed as well. The asset side of the banks' balance sheets dropped, causing bank failures and bank runs. Around the globe, financial institutions were bankrupted or nearly so. The result was a large decrease in lending and borrowing, or a freezing up of available credit. When credit dries up, the economy is on its knees. The crisis was not limited to the United States. Iceland, Ireland, the United Kingdom, Spain, Portugal, and Greece all had similar housing boom and bust cycles, and similar credit freezes.

If businesses cannot access financial capital, they cannot make physical capital investments. Those investments ultimately lead to job creation. When credit dried up, businesses invested less, and they ultimately laid off millions of workers. This caused incomes to drop, which caused demand to drop. In turn businesses sold less, so they laid off more workers. Compounding these events, as economic conditions worsened, financial institutions were even less likely to make loans.

To make matters even worse, as businesses sold less, their expected future profit decreased, and this led to a drop in stock prices. Combining all these effects led to major decreases in incomes, demand, consumption, and employment, and to the Great Recession, which in the United States officially lasted from December 2007 to June 2009. During this time, the unemployment rate rose from 5% to a peak of 10.1%. Four years after the recession officially ended, unemployment was still stubbornly high, at 7.6%, and 11.8 million people were still unemployed.

As the world's leading consumer, if the United States goes into recession, it usually drags other countries down with it. The Great Recession was no exception. With few exceptions, U.S. trading partners also entered into recessions of their own, of varying lengths, or suffered slower economic growth. Like the United States, many European countries also gave direct financial assistance, so-called bailouts, to the institutions that make up their financial markets. There was good reason to do this. Financial markets bridge the gap between demanders and suppliers of financial capital. These institutions and markets need to function in order for an economy to invest in new financial capital.

However, much of this bailout money was borrowed, and this borrowed money contributed to another crisis in Europe. Because of the impact on their budgets of the financial crisis and the resulting bailouts, many countries found themselves with unsustainably high deficits. They chose to undertake austerity measures, large decreases in government spending and large tax increases, in order to reduce their deficits. Greece, Ireland, Spain, and Portugal all had to undertake relatively severe austerity measures. The ramifications of this crisis have spread. Economists even called into question the euro's viability.

## Key Terms

**actual rate of return** the total rate of return, including capital gains and interest paid on an investment at the end of a time period

**bond** a financial contract through which a borrower like a corporation, a city or state, or the federal government agrees to repay the amount that it borrowed and also a rate of interest over a period of time in the future

**bond yield** the rate of return a bond is expected to pay at the time of purchase

**bondholder** someone who owns bonds and receives the interest payments

**capital gain** a financial gain from buying an asset, like a share of stock or a house, and later selling it at a higher price

**certificate of deposit (CD)** a mechanism for a saver to deposit funds at a bank and promise to leave them at the bank for a time, in exchange for a higher interest rate

**checking account** a bank account that typically pays little or no interest, but that gives easy access to money, either by writing a check or by using a "debit card"

**compound interest** an interest rate calculation on the principal plus the accumulated interest

**corporate bond** a bond issued by firms that wish to borrow

**corporate governance** the name economists give to the institutions that are supposed to watch over top executives in companies that shareholders own

**corporation** a business owned by shareholders who have limited liability for the company's debt yet a share of the company's profits; may be private or public and may or may not have publicly-traded stock

**coupon rate** the interest rate paid on a bond; can be annual or semi-annual

**debit card** a card that lets the person make purchases, and the financial institution immediately deducts cost from that person's checking account

**diversification** investing in a wide range of companies to reduce the level of risk

**dividend** a direct payment from a firm to its shareholders

**equity** the monetary value a homeowner would have after selling the house and repaying any outstanding bank loans used to buy the house

**expected rate of return** how much a project or an investment is expected to return to the investor, either in future interest payments, capital gains, or increased profitability

**face value** the amount that the bond issuer or borrower agrees to pay the investor

**financial intermediary** an institution, like a bank, that receives money from savers and provides funds to borrowers

**high-yield bonds** bonds that offer relatively high interest rates to compensate for their relatively high chance of default

**index fund** a mutual fund that seeks only to mimic the market's overall performance

**initial public offering (IPO)** the first sale of shares of stock by a firm to outside investors

**junk bonds** see high-yield bonds

**liquidity** refers to how easily one can exchange money or financial assets for a good or service

**maturity date** the date that a borrower must repay a bond

**municipal bonds** a bond issued by cities that wish to borrow

**mutual funds** funds that buy a range of stocks or bonds from different companies, thus allowing an investor an easy way to diversify

**partnership** a company run by a group as opposed to an individual

**present value** a bond's current price at a given time

**private company** a firm frequently owned by the people who generally run it on a day-to-day basis

**public company** a firm that has sold stock to the public, which in turn investors then can buy and sell

**risk** a measure of the uncertainty of that project's profitability

**savings account** a bank account that pays an interest rate, but withdrawing money typically requires a trip to the bank or an automatic teller machine

**shareholders** people who own at least some shares of stock in a firm

**shares** a firm's stock, divided into individual portions

**simple interest** an interest rate calculation only on the principal amount

**sole proprietorship** a company run by an individual as opposed to a group

**stock** a specific firm's claim on partial ownership

**Treasury bond** a bond issued by the federal government through the U.S. Department of the Treasury

**venture capital** financial investments in new companies that are still relatively small in size, but that have potential to grow substantially

## Key Concepts and Summary

### 17.1 How Businesses Raise Financial Capital

Companies can raise early-stage financial capital in several ways: from their owners' or managers' personal savings, or credit cards and from private investors like angel investors and venture capital firms.

A bond is a financial contract through which a borrower agrees to repay the amount that it borrowed. A bond specifies an amount that one will borrow, the amounts that one will repay over time based on the interest rate when the bond is issued, and the time until repayment. Corporate bonds are issued by firms; municipal bonds are issued by cities, state bonds by U.S. states, and Treasury bonds by the federal government through the U.S. Department of the Treasury.

Stock represents firm ownership. A company's stock is divided into shares. A firm receives financial capital when it sells stock to the public. We call a company's first stock sale to the public the initial public offering (IPO). However, a firm does not receive any funds when one shareholder sells stock in the firm to another investor. One receives the rate of return on stock in two forms: dividends and capital gains.

A private company is usually owned by the people who run it on a day-to-day basis, although hired managers can run it. We call a private company owned and run by an individual a sole proprietorship, while a firm owned and run by a group is a partnership. When a firm decides to sell stock that financial investors can buy and sell, then the firm is owned by its shareholders—who in turn elect a board of directors to hire top day-to-day management. We call this a public company. Corporate governance is the name economists give to the institutions that are supposed to watch over top executives, though it does not always work.

### 17.2 How Households Supply Financial Capital

We can categorize all investments according to three key characteristics: average expected return, degree of risk, and liquidity. To obtain a higher rate of return, an investor must typically accept either more risk or less liquidity. Banks are an example of a financial intermediary, an institution that operates to coordinate supply and demand in the financial capital market. Banks offer a range of accounts, including checking accounts, savings accounts, and certificates of deposit. Under the Federal Deposit Insurance Corporation (FDIC), banks purchase insurance against the risk of a bank failure.

A typical bond promises the financial investor a series of payments over time, based on the interest rate at the time the financial institution issues the bond, and when the borrower repays it. Bonds that offer a high rate of return but also a relatively high chance of defaulting on the payments are called high-yield or junk bonds. The bond yield is the rate of return that a bond promises to pay at the time of purchase. Even when bonds make payments based on a fixed interest rate, they are somewhat risky, because if interest rates rise for the economy as a whole, an investor who owns bonds issued at lower interest rates is now locked into the low rate and suffers a loss.

Changes in the stock price depend on changes in expectations about future profits. Investing in any individual firm is somewhat risky, so investors are wise to practice diversification, which means investing in a range of companies. A mutual fund purchases an array of stocks and/or bonds. An investor in the mutual fund then receives a return depending on the fund's overall performance as a whole. A mutual fund that seeks to imitate the overall behavior of the stock market is called an index fund.

We can also regard housing and other tangible assets as forms of financial investment, which pay a rate of return in the form of capital gains. Housing can also offer a nonfinancial return—specifically, you can live in it.

### 17.3 How to Accumulate Personal Wealth

It is extremely difficult, even for financial professionals, to predict changes in future expectations and thus to choose the stocks whose price will rise in the future. Most Americans can accumulate considerable financial wealth if they follow two rules: complete significant additional education and training after graduating from high school and start saving money early in life.

## Self-Check Questions

1. Answer these three questions about early-stage corporate finance:
   a. Why do very small companies tend to raise money from private investors instead of through an IPO?
   b. Why do small, young companies often prefer an IPO to borrowing from a bank or issuing bonds?
   c. Who has better information about whether a small firm is likely to earn profits, a venture capitalist or a potential bondholder, and why?

2. From a firm's point of view, how is a bond similar to a bank loan? How are they different?

3. Calculate the equity each of these people has in their home:
   a. Eva just bought a house for $200,000 by putting 10% as a down payment and borrowing the rest from the bank.
   b. Freda bought a house for $150,000 in cash, but if she were to sell it now, it would sell for $250,000.
   c. Ben bought a house for $100,000. He put 20% down and borrowed the rest from the bank. However, the value of the house has now increased to $160,000 and he has paid off $20,000 of the bank loan.

4. Which has a higher average return over time: stocks, bonds, or a savings account? Explain your answer.

5. Investors sometimes fear that a high-risk investment is especially likely to have low returns. Is this fear true? Does a high risk mean the return must be low?

6. What is the total amount of interest from a $5,000 loan after three years with a simple interest rate of 6%?

7. If you receive $500 in simple interest on a loan that you made for $10,000 for five years, what was the interest rate you charged?

8. You open a 5-year CD for $1,000 that pays 2% interest, compounded annually. What is the value of that CD at the end of the five years?

## Review Questions

9. What are the most common ways for start-up firms to raise financial capital?

10. Why can firms not just use their own profits for financial capital, with no need for outside investors?

11. Why are banks more willing to lend to well-established firms?

12. What is a bond?

13. What does a share of stock represent?

14. When do firms receive money from a stock sale in their firm and when do they not receive money?

15. What is a dividend?

16. What is a capital gain?

17. What is the difference between a private company and a public company?

18. How do the shareholders who own a company choose the actual company managers?

19. Why are banks called "financial intermediaries"?

20. Name several different kinds of bank account. How are they different?

21. Why are bonds somewhat risky to buy, even though they make predetermined payments based on a fixed rate of interest?

22. Why should a financial investor care about diversification?

23. What is a mutual fund?

24. What is an index fund?

25. How is buying a house to live in a type of financial investment?

26. Why is it hard to forecast future movements in stock prices?

27. What are the two key choices U.S. citizens need to make that determines their relative wealth?

28. Is investing in housing always a very safe investment?

## Critical Thinking Questions

29. If you owned a small firm that had become somewhat established, but you needed a surge of financial capital to carry out a major expansion, would you prefer to raise the funds through borrowing or by issuing stock? Explain your choice.

30. Explain how a company can fail when the safeguards that should be in place fail.

31. What are some reasons why the investment strategy of a 30-year-old might differ from the investment strategy of a 65-year-old?

32. Explain why a financial investor in stocks cannot earn high capital gains simply by buying companies with a demonstrated record of high profits.

33. Explain what happens in an economy when the financial markets limit access to capital. How does this affect economic growth and employment?

34. You and your friend have opened an account on E-Trade and have each decided to select five similar companies in which to invest. You are diligent in monitoring your selections, tracking prices, current events, and actions the company has taken. Your friend chooses his companies randomly, pays no attention to the financial news, and spends his leisure time focused on everything besides his investments. Explain what might be the performance for each of your portfolios at the end of the year.

35. How do bank failures cause the economy to go into recession?

## Problems

36. The Darkroom Windowshade Company has 100,000 shares of stock outstanding. The investors in the firm own the following numbers of shares: investor 1 has 20,000 shares; investor 2 has 18,000 shares; investor 3 has 15,000 shares; investor 4 has 10,000 shares; investor 5 has 7,000 shares; and investors 6 through 11 have 5,000 shares each. What is the minimum number of investors it would take to vote to change the company's top management? If investors 1 and 2 agree to vote together, can they be certain of always getting their way in how the company will be run?

37. Imagine that a local water company issued $10,000 ten-year bond at an interest rate of 6%. You are thinking about buying this bond one year before the end of the ten years, but interest rates are now 9%.
    a. Given the change in interest rates, would you expect to pay more or less than $10,000 for the bond?
    b. Calculate what you would actually be willing to pay for this bond.

38. Suppose Ford Motor Company issues a five year bond with a face value of $5,000 that pays an annual coupon payment of $150.
    a. What is the interest rate Ford is paying on the borrowed funds?
    b. Suppose the market interest rate rises from 3% to 4% a year after Ford issues the bonds. Will the value of the bond increase or decrease?

39. How much money do you have to put into a bank account that pays 10% interest compounded annually to have $10,000 in ten years?

40. Many retirement funds charge an administrative fee each year equal to 0.25% on managed assets. Suppose that Alexx and Spenser each invest $5,000 in the same stock this year. Alexx invests directly and earns 5% a year. Spenser uses a retirement fund and earns 4.75%. After 30 years, how much more will Alexx have than Spenser?

# Public Economy

FIGURE 18.1 **Domestic Tires?** While these tires may all appear similar, some are made in the United States and others are not. Those that are not could be subject to a tariff that could cause the cost of all tires to be higher. (Credit: "Tires" by Jayme del Rosario/Flickr Creative Commons, CC BY 2.0)

**CHAPTER OBJECTIVES**

In this chapter, you will learn about:
- Voter Participation and Costs of Elections
- Special Interest Politics
- Flaws in the Democratic System of Government

## Introduction to Public Economy

 **BRING IT HOME**

### Chinese Tire Tariffs

Do you know where the tires on your car are made? If they were imported, they may be subject to a tariff (a tax on imported goods) that could raise the price of your car. What do you think about that tariff? Would you write to your representative or your senator about it? Would you start a Facebook or Twitter campaign?

Most people are unlikely to fight this kind of tax or even inform themselves about the issue in the first place. In *The Logic of Collective Action* (1965), economist Mancur Olson challenged the popular idea that, in a democracy, the majority view will prevail, and in doing so launched the modern study of public economy, sometimes referred to as public choice, a subtopic of microeconomics. In this chapter, we will look at the economics of government policy, why smaller, more organized groups have an incentive to work hard to enact certain policies, and why lawmakers ultimately make decisions that may result in bad economic policy.

---

As President Abraham Lincoln famously said in his 1863 *Gettysburg Address*, democratic governments are supposed to be "of the people, by the people, and for the people." Can we rely on democratic governments to enact sensible economic policies? After all, they react to voters, not to analyses of demand and supply curves. The main focus of an economics course is, naturally enough, to analyze the characteristics of markets and purely economic institutions. However, political institutions also play a role in allocating society's scarce resources, and economists have played an active role, along with other social scientists, in analyzing how such political institutions work.

Other chapters of this book discuss situations in which market forces can sometimes lead to undesirable results: monopoly, imperfect competition, and antitrust policy; negative and positive externalities; poverty and inequality of incomes; failures to provide insurance; and financial markets that may go from boom to bust. Many of these chapters suggest that the government's economic policies could address these issues.

However, just as markets can face issues and problems that lead to undesirable outcomes, a democratic system of government can also make mistakes, either by enacting policies that do not benefit society as a whole or by failing to enact policies that would have benefited society as a whole. This chapter discusses some practical difficulties of democracy from an economic point of view: we presume the actors in the political system follow their own self-interest, which is not necessarily the same as the public good. For example, many of those who are eligible to vote do not, which obviously raises questions about whether a democratic system will reflect everyone's interests. Benefits or costs of government action are sometimes concentrated on small groups, which in some cases may organize and have a disproportionately large impact on politics and in other cases may fail to organize and end up neglected. A legislator who worries about support from voters in their district may focus on spending projects specific to the district without sufficient concern for whether this spending is in the nation's interest.

When more than two choices exist, the principle that the majority of voters should decide may not always make logical sense, because situations can arise where it becomes literally impossible to decide what the "majority" prefers. Government may also be slower than private firms to correct its mistakes, because government agencies do not face competition or the threat of new entry.

## 18.1 Voter Participation and Costs of Elections

### LEARNING OBJECTIVES

By the end of this section, you will be able to:
- Explain the significance of rational ignorance
- Evaluate the impact of election expenses

In U.S. presidential elections over the last few decades, about 55% to 65% of voting-age citizens actually voted, according to the U.S. Census. In congressional elections when there is no presidential race, or in local elections, the turnout is typically lower, often less than half the eligible voters. In other countries, the share of adults who vote is often higher. For example, in national elections since the 1980s in Germany, Spain, and France, about 75% to 80% of those of voting age cast ballots. Even this total falls well short of 100%. Some countries have laws that require voting, among them Australia, Belgium, Italy, Greece, Turkey, Singapore, and most Latin American nations. At the time the United States was founded, voting was mandatory in Virginia, Maryland, Delaware, and Georgia. Even if the law can require people to vote, however, no law can require that each voter cast an informed or a thoughtful vote. Moreover, in the United States and in most countries around the world, the freedom to vote has also typically meant the freedom *not* to vote.

Why do people not vote? Perhaps they do not care too much about who wins, or they are uninformed about who is running, or they do not believe their vote will matter or change their lives in any way. These reasons are probably tied together, since people who do not believe their vote matters will not bother to become informed or care who wins. Economists have suggested why a utility-maximizing person might rationally decide not to vote or not to become informed about the election. While a single vote may decide a few elections in very small towns, in most elections of any size, the Board of Elections measures the margin of victory in hundreds, thousands, or even millions of votes. A rational voter will recognize that one vote is extremely unlikely to make a difference. This theory of **rational ignorance** holds that people will not vote if the costs of becoming informed and voting are too high, or they feel their vote will not be decisive in the election.

In a 1957 work, *An Economic Theory of Democracy*, the economist Anthony Downs stated the problem this way: "It seems probable that for a great many citizens in a democracy, rational behavior excludes any investment whatever in political information per se. No matter how significant a difference between parties is revealed to the rational citizen by his free information, or how uncertain he is about which party to support, he realizes that his vote has almost no chance of influencing the outcome... He will not even utilize all the free information available, since assimilating it takes time." In his classic 1948 novel *Walden Two*, the psychologist B. F. Skinner puts the issue even more succinctly via one of his characters, who states: "The chance that one man's vote will decide the issue in a national election...is less than the chance that he will be killed on his way to the polls." The following Clear It Up feature explores another aspect of the election process: spending.

## CLEAR IT UP

### How much is too much to spend on an election?

In the 2020 elections, it is estimated that spending for president, Congress, and state and local offices amounted to $14.4 billion, more than twice what had been spent in 2016. The money raised went to the campaigns, including advertising, fundraising, travel, and staff. Many people worry that politicians spend too much time raising money and end up entangled with special interest groups that make major donations. Critics would prefer a system that restricts what candidates can spend, perhaps in exchange for limited public campaign financing or free television advertising time.

How much spending on campaigns is too much? Five billion dollars will buy many potato chips, but in the U.S. economy, which was nearly $21 trillion in 2020, the $14.4 billion spent on political campaigns was about 1/15th of 1% of the overall economy. Here is another way to think about campaign spending. *Total* government spending programs in 2020, including federal and state governments, was about $8.8 trillion, so the cost of choosing the people who would determine how to spend this money was less than 2/10 of 1% of that. In the context of the enormous U.S. economy, $14.4 billion is not as much money as it sounds. U.S. consumers spend almost $2 billion per year on toothpaste and $7 billion on hair care products. In 2020, Proctor and Gamble spent almost $5 billion on advertising. It may seem peculiar that one company's spending on advertisements amounts to one third of what is spent on presidential and other elections.

Whatever we believe about whether candidates and their parties spend too much or too little on elections, the U.S. Supreme Court has placed limits on how government can limit campaign spending. In a 1976 decision, *Buckley v. Valeo*, the Supreme Court emphasized that the First Amendment to the U.S. Constitution specifies freedom of speech. The federal government and states can offer candidates a voluntary deal in which government makes some public financing available to candidates, but only if the candidates agree to abide by certain spending limits. Of course, candidates can also voluntarily agree to set certain spending limits if they wish. However, government cannot forbid people or organizations to raise and spend money above these limits if they choose.

In 2002, Congress passed and President George W. Bush signed into law the Bipartisan Campaign Reform Act (BCRA). The relatively noncontroversial portions of the act strengthen the rules requiring full and speedy disclosure of who contributes money to campaigns. However, some controversial portions of the Act limit the ability of individuals and groups to make certain kinds of political donations and they ban certain kinds of advertising in the months leading up to an election. Some called these bans into question after the release of two films: Michael Moore's *Fahrenheit 9/11* and Citizens United's *Hillary: The Movie*. At question was whether each film sought to discredit political candidates for office too close to an election, in violation of the BCRA. The lower courts found that Moore's film did not violate the Act, while Citizens United's did. The fight reached the Supreme Court, as *Citizens United v. Federal Election Commission*, saying that the First Amendment protects the rights of corporations as well as individuals to donate to political campaigns. The Court ruled, in a 5–4 decision, that the spending limits were unconstitutional. This controversial decision, which essentially allows unlimited contributions by corporations to political action committees, overruled several previous decisions and will likely be revisited in the future, due to the strength of the public reaction. For now, it has resulted in a sharp increase in election spending.

While many U.S. adults do not bother to vote in presidential elections, more than half do. What motivates them? Research on voting behavior has indicated that people who are more settled or more "connected" to society tend to vote more frequently. According to the *Washington Post*, more married people vote than single people. Those with a job vote more than the unemployed. Those who have lived longer in a neighborhood are more likely to vote than newcomers. Those who report that they know their neighbors and talk to them are more likely to vote than socially isolated people. Those with a higher income and level of education are also more likely to vote. These factors suggest that politicians are likely to focus more on the interests of married, employed, well-educated people with at least a middle-class level of income than on the interests of other groups. For example, those who vote may tend to be more supportive of financial assistance for the two-year and four-year colleges they expect their children to attend than they are of medical care or public school education aimed at families of unemployed people and those experiencing poverty.

## 🔗 LINK IT UP

Visit this website (http://openstax.org/l/votergroups) to see a breakdown of how different groups voted in 2020.

There have been many proposals to encourage greater voter turnout: making it easier to register to vote, keeping the polls open for more hours, or even moving Election Day to the weekend, when fewer people need to worry about jobs or school commitments. However, such changes do not seem to have caused a long-term upward trend in the number of people voting. After all, casting an informed vote will always impose some costs of time and energy. It is not clear how to strengthen people's feeling of connectedness to society in a way that will lead to a substantial increase in voter turnout. Without greater voter turnout, however, politicians elected by the votes of 60% or fewer of the population may not enact economic policy in the best interests of 100% of the population. Meanwhile, countering a long trend toward making voting easier, many states have recently enacted new voting laws that critics say are actually barriers to voting. States have passed laws reducing early voting, restricting groups who are organizing get-out-the-vote efforts, enacted strict photo ID laws, as well as laws that require showing proof of U.S. citizenship. The ACLU argues that while these laws profess to prevent voter fraud, they are in effect making it harder for individuals to cast their vote.

## 18.2 Special Interest Politics

### LEARNING OBJECTIVES

By the end of this section, you will be able to:
- Explain how special interest groups and lobbyists can influence campaigns and elections
- Describe pork-barrel spending and logrolling

Many political issues are of intense interest to a relatively small group, as we noted above. For example, many U.S. drivers do not much care where their car tires were made—they just want good quality as inexpensively as possible. In September 2009, President Obama and Congress enacted a tariff (taxes added on imported goods) on tires imported from China that would increase the price by 35 percent in its first year, 30 percent in its second year, and 25 percent in its third year. Interestingly, the U.S. companies that make tires did not favor this step, because most of them also import tires from China and other countries. (See Globalization and Protectionism for more on tariffs.) However, the United Steelworkers union, which had seen jobs in the tire industry fall by 5,000 over the previous five years, lobbied fiercely for the tariff. With this tariff, the cost of all tires increased significantly. (See the closing Bring It Home feature at the end of this chapter for more information on the tire tariff.)

**Special interest groups** are groups that are small in number relative to the nation, but quite well organized and focused on a specific issue. A special interest group can pressure legislators to enact public policies that do not benefit society as a whole. Imagine an environmental rule to reduce air pollution that will cost 10 large companies $8 million each, for a total cost of $80 million. The social benefits from enacting this rule provide an average benefit of $10 for every person in the United States, for a total of about $3 trillion. Even though the benefits are far higher than the costs for society as a whole, the 10 companies are likely to lobby much more fiercely to avoid $8 million in costs than the average person is to argue for $10 worth of benefits.

As this example suggests, we can relate the problem of special interests in politics to an issue we raised in Environmental Protection and Negative Externalities about economic policy with respect to negative externalities and pollution—the problem called regulatory capture (which we defined in Monopoly and Antitrust Policy). In legislative bodies and agencies that write laws and regulations about how much corporations will pay in taxes, or rules for safety in the workplace, or instructions on how to satisfy environmental regulations, you can be sure the specific industry affected has lobbyists who study every word and every comma. They talk with the legislators who are writing the legislation and suggest alternative wording. They contribute to the campaigns of legislators on the key committees—and may even offer those legislators high-paying jobs after they have left office. As a result, it often turns out that those regulated can exercise considerable influence over the regulators.

 **LINK IT UP**

Visit this website (http://openstax.org/l/lobbying) to read about lobbying.

---

In the early 2000s, about 40 million people in the United States were eligible for Medicare, a government program that provides health insurance for those 65 and older. On some issues, the elderly are a powerful interest group. They donate money and time to political campaigns, and in the 2020 presidential election, 76% of those ages 65–74 voted, while just 51% of those aged 18 to 24 cast a ballot, according to the U.S. Census.

In 2003, Congress passed and President George Bush signed into law a substantial expansion of Medicare that helped the elderly to pay for prescription drugs. The prescription drug benefit cost the federal government about $40 billion in 2006, and the Medicare system projected that the annual cost would rise to $121 billion by 2016. The political pressure to pass a prescription drug benefit for Medicare was apparently quite high, while the political pressure to assist the 40 million with no health insurance at all was considerably lower. One reason might be that the American Association for Retired People AARP, a well-funded and well-organized lobbying group represents senior citizens, while there is no umbrella organization to lobby for those without health insurance.

In the battle over passage of the 2010 Affordable Care Act (ACA), which became known as "Obamacare," there was heavy lobbying on all sides by insurance companies and pharmaceutical companies. However, labor unions and community groups financed a lobby group, Health Care for America Now (HCAN), to offset corporate lobbying. HCAN, spending $60 million dollars, was successful in helping pass legislation which added new regulations on insurance companies and a mandate that all individuals will obtain health insurance by 2014. The following Work It Out feature further explains voter incentives and lobbyist influence.

### Paying To Get Your Way

Suppose Congress proposes a tax on carbon emissions for certain factories in a small town of 10,000 people. Congress estimates the tax will reduce pollution to such an extent that it will benefit each resident by an equivalent of $300. The tax will also reduce profits to the town's two large factories by $1 million each. How much should the factory owners be willing to spend to fight the tax passage, and how much should the townspeople be willing to pay to support it? Why is society unlikely to achieve the optimal outcome?

Step 1. The two factory owners each stand to lose $1 million if the tax passes, so each should be willing to spend up to that amount to prevent the passage, a combined sum of $2 million. Of course, in the real world, there is no guarantee that lobbying efforts will be successful, so the factory owners may choose to invest an amount that is substantially lower.

Step 2. There are 10,000 townspeople, each standing to benefit by $300 if the tax passes. Theoretically, then, they should be willing to spend up to $3 million (10,000 × $300) to ensure passage. (Again, in the real world with no guarantees of success, they may choose to spend less.)

Step 3. It is costly and difficult for 10,000 people to coordinate in such a way as to influence public policy. Since each person stands to gain only $300, many may feel lobbying is not worth the effort.

Step 4. The two factory owners, however, find it very easy and profitable to coordinate their activities, so they have a greater incentive to do so.

Special interests may develop a close relationship with one political party, so their ability to influence legislation rises and falls as that party moves in or out of power. A special interest may even hurt a political party if it appears to a number of voters that the relationship is too cozy. In a close election, a small group that has been under-represented in the past may find that it can tip the election one way or another—so that group will suddenly receive considerable attention. Democratic institutions produce an ebb and flow of political parties and interests and thus offer both opportunities for special interests and ways of counterbalancing those interests over time.

### Identifiable Winners, Anonymous Losers

A number of economic policies produce gains whose beneficiaries are easily identifiable, but costs that are partly or entirely shared by a large number who remain anonymous. A democratic political system probably has a bias toward those who are identifiable.

For example, policies that impose price controls—like rent control—may look as if they benefit renters and impose costs only on landlords. However, when landlords then decide to reduce the number of rental units available in the area, a number of people who would have liked to rent an apartment end up living somewhere else because no units were available. These would-be renters have experienced a cost of rent control, but it is hard to identify who they are.

Similarly, policies that block imports will benefit the firms that would have competed with those imports—and workers at those firms—who are likely to be quite visible. Consumers who would have preferred to purchase the imported products, and who thus bear some costs of the protectionist policy, are much less visible.

Specific tax breaks and spending programs also have identifiable winners and impose costs on others who are hard to identify. Special interests are more likely to arise from a group that is easily identifiable, rather than from a group where some of those who suffer may not even recognize they are bearing costs.

## Pork Barrels and Logrolling

Politicians have an incentive to ensure that they spend government money in their home state or district, where it will benefit their constituents in a direct and obvious way. Thus, when legislators are negotiating over whether to support a piece of legislation, they commonly ask each other to include **pork-barrel spending**, legislation that benefits mainly a single political district. Pork-barrel spending is another case in which concentrated benefits and widely dispersed costs challenge democracy: the benefits of pork-barrel spending are obvious and direct to local voters, while the costs are spread over the entire country. Read the following Clear It Up feature for more information on pork-barrel spending.

### CLEAR IT UP

### How much impact can pork-barrel spending have?

Many observers widely regard U.S. Senator Robert C. Byrd of West Virginia, who was originally elected to the Senate in 1958 and served until 2010, as one of the masters of pork-barrel politics, directing a steady stream of federal funds to his home state. A journalist once compiled a list of structures in West Virginia at least partly government funded and named after Byrd: "the Robert C. Byrd Highway; the Robert C. Byrd Locks and Dam; the Robert C. Byrd Institute; the Robert C. Byrd Life Long Learning Center; the Robert C. Byrd Honors Scholarship Program; the Robert C. Byrd Green Bank Telescope; the Robert C. Byrd Institute for Advanced Flexible Manufacturing; the Robert C. Byrd Federal Courthouse; the Robert C. Byrd Health Sciences Center; the Robert C. Byrd Academic and Technology Center; the Robert C. Byrd United Technical Center; the Robert C. Byrd Federal Building; the Robert C. Byrd Drive; the Robert C. Byrd Hilltop Office Complex; the Robert C. Byrd Library; and the Robert C. Byrd Learning Resource Center; the Robert C. Byrd Rural Health Center." This list does not include government-funded projects in West Virginia that were not named after Byrd. Of course, we would have to analyze each of these expenditures in detail to figure out whether we should treat them as pork-barrel spending or whether they provide widespread benefits that reach beyond West Virginia. At least some of them, or a portion of them, certainly would fall into that category. Because there are currently no term limits for Congressional representatives, those who have been in office longer generally have more power to enact pork-barrel projects.

The amount that government spends on individual pork-barrel projects is small, but many small projects can add up to a substantial total. A nonprofit watchdog organization, called Citizens against Government Waste, produces an annual report, the *Pig Book* that attempts to quantify the amount of pork-barrel spending, focusing on items that only one member of Congress requested, that were passed into law without any public hearings, or that serve only a local purpose. Whether any specific item qualifies as pork can be controversial. The 2021 Congressional Pig Book identified 285 earmarks in FY 2021, with a cost of $16.8 billion. Recent growth in earmarks and their cost is apparent: in FY 2017, there were 163 earmarks at a cost of $6.8 billion. Hence, in only four years, there was a 75% increase in the number of earmarks and a 147% increase in the cost of those earmarks.

**Logrolling**, an action in which all members of a group of legislators agree to vote for a package of otherwise unrelated laws that they individually favor, can encourage pork barrel spending. For example, if one member of the U.S. Congress suggests building a new bridge or hospital in their own congressional district, the other members might oppose it. However, if 51% of the legislators come together, they can pass a bill that includes a bridge or hospital for every one of their districts.

As a reflection of this interest of legislators in their own districts, the U.S. government has typically spread out its spending on military bases and weapons programs to congressional districts all across the country. In part, the government does this to help create a situation that encourages members of Congress to vote in support of defense spending.

## 18.3 Flaws in the Democratic System of Government

**LEARNING OBJECTIVES**

By the end of this section, you will be able to:
- Assess the median voter theory
- Explain the voting cycle
- Analyze the interrelationship between markets and government

Most developed countries today have a democratic system of government: citizens express their opinions through votes and those votes affect the direction of the country. The advantage of democracy over other systems is that it allows everyone in a society an equal say and therefore may reduce the possibility of a small group of wealthy oligarchs oppressing the masses. There is no such thing as a perfect system, and democracy, for all its popularity, is not without its problems, a few of which we will examine here.

We sometimes sum up and oversimplify democracy in two words: "Majority rule." When voters face three or more choices, however, then voting may not always be a useful way of determining what the majority prefers.

As one example, consider an election in a state where 60% of the population is liberal and 40% is conservative. If there are only two candidates, one from each side, and if liberals and conservatives vote in the same 60–40 proportions in which they are represented in the population, then the liberal will win. What if the election ends up including two liberal candidates and one conservative? It is possible that the liberal vote will split and victory will go to the minority party. In this case, the outcome does not reflect the majority's preference.

Does the majority view prevail in the case of sugar quotas? Clearly there are more sugar consumers in the United States than sugar producers, but the U.S. domestic sugar lobby (www.sugarcane.org) has successfully argued for protection against imports since 1789. By law, therefore, U.S. cookie and candy makers must use 85% domestic sugar in their products. Meanwhile quotas on imported sugar restrict supply and keep the domestic sugar price up—raising prices for companies that use sugar in producing their goods and for consumers. The European Union allows sugar imports, and prices there are 40% lower than U.S. sugar prices. Sugar-producing countries in the Caribbean repeatedly protest the U.S. quotas at the World Trade Organization meetings, but each bite of cookie, at present, costs you more than if there were no sugar lobby. This case goes against the theory of the "median" voter in a democracy. The **median voter theory** argues that politicians will try to match policies to what pleases the median voter preferences. If we think of political positions along a spectrum from left to right, the median voter is in the middle of the spectrum. This theory argues that actual policy will reflect "middle of the road." In the case of sugar lobby politics, the *minority*, not the median, dominates policy.

Sometimes it is not even clear how to define the majority opinion. Step aside from politics for a moment and think about a choice facing three families (the Ortegas, the Schmidts, and the Alexanders) who are planning to celebrate New Year's Day together. They agree to vote on the menu, choosing from three entrees, and they agree that the majority vote wins. With three families, it seems reasonable that one producing choice will get a 2–1 majority. What if, however, their vote ends up looking like Table 18.1?

Clearly, the three families disagree on their first choice. However, the problem goes even deeper. Instead of looking at all three choices at once, compare them two at a time. (See Figure 18.2) In a vote of turkey versus beef, turkey wins by 2–1. In a vote of beef versus lasagna, beef wins 2–1. If turkey beats beef, and beef beats lasagna, then it might seem only logical that turkey must also beat lasagna. However, with the preferences, lasagna is preferred to turkey by a 2–1 vote, as well. If lasagna is preferred to turkey, and turkey beats beef, then surely it must be that lasagna also beats beef? Actually, no. Beef beats lasagna. In other words, the majority view may not win. Clearly, as any car salesperson will tell you, the way one presents choices to us influences our decisions.

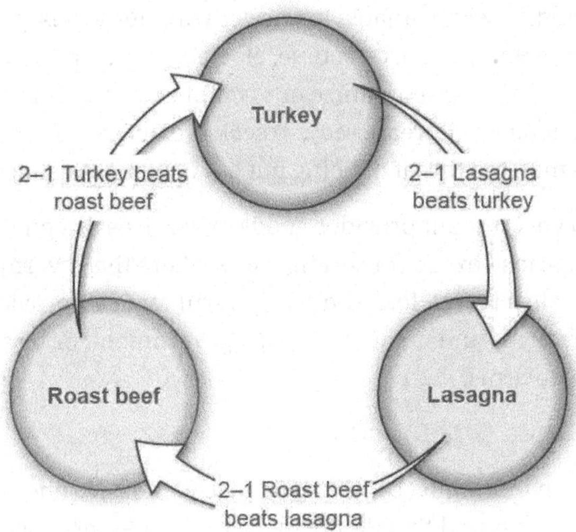


**FIGURE 18.2 A Voting Cycle** Given these choices, voting will struggle to produce a majority outcome. Turkey is favored over roast beef by 2–1 and roast beef is favored over lasagna by 2–1. If turkey beats roast beef and roast beef beats lasagna, then it might seem that turkey must beat lasagna, too. However, given these preferences, lasagna is favored over turkey by 2–1.

|  | The Ortega Family | The Schmidt Family | The Alexander Family |
|---|---|---|---|
| **First Choice** | Turkey | Roast beef | Lasagna |
| **Second Choice** | Roast beef | Lasagna | Turkey |
| **Third Choice** | Lasagna | Turkey | Roast beef |

**TABLE 18.1 Circular Preferences**

We call the situation in which Choice A is preferred by a majority over Choice B, Choice B is preferred by a majority over Choice C, and Choice C is preferred by a majority over Choice A a **voting cycle**. It is easy to imagine sets of government choices—say, perhaps the choice between increased defense spending, increased government spending on health care, and a tax cut—in which a voting cycle could occur. The result will be determined by the order in which interested parties present and vote on choices, not by majority rule, because every choice is both preferred to some alternative and also not preferred to another alternative.

## ⊘ LINK IT UP

Visit this website (http://www.fairvote.org/rcv#rcvbenefits) to read about ranked choice voting, a preferential voting system.

## Where Is Government's Self-Correcting Mechanism?

When a firm produces a product no one wants to buy or produces at a higher cost than its competitors, the firm is likely to suffer losses. If it cannot change its ways, it will go out of business. This self-correcting mechanism in the marketplace can have harsh effects on workers or on local economies, but it also puts pressure on firms for good performance.

Government agencies, however, do not sell their products in a market. They receive tax dollars instead. They are not challenged by competitors as are private-sector firms. If the U.S. Department of Education or the U.S. Department of Defense is performing poorly, citizens cannot purchase their services from another provider and drive the existing government agencies into bankruptcy. If you are upset that the Internal Revenue Service is slow in sending you a tax refund or seems unable to answer your questions, you cannot decide to pay your income taxes through a different organization. Of course, elected politicians can assign new leaders to government agencies and instruct them to reorganize or to emphasize a different mission. The pressure government faces, however, to change its bureaucracy, to seek greater efficiency, and to improve customer responsiveness is much milder than the threat of being put out of business altogether.

This insight suggests that when government provides goods or services directly, we might expect it to do so with less efficiency than private firms—except in certain cases where the government agency may compete directly with private firms. At the local level, for example, government can provide directly services like garbage collection, using private firms under contract to the government, or by a mix of government employees competing with private firms.

## A Balanced View of Markets and Government

The British statesman Sir Winston Churchill (1874–1965) once wrote: "No one pretends that democracy is perfect or all-wise. Indeed, it has been said that democracy is the worst form of government except for all of the other forms which have been tried from time to time." In that spirit, the theme of this discussion is certainly not that we should abandon democratic government. A practical student of public policy needs to recognize that in some cases, like the case of well-organized special interests or pork-barrel legislation, a democratic government may seek to enact economically unwise projects or programs. In other cases, by placing a low priority on the problems of those who are not well organized or who are less likely to vote, the government may fail to act when it could do some good. In these and other cases, there is no automatic reason to believe that government will necessarily make economically sensible choices.

"The true test of a first-rate mind is the ability to hold two contradictory ideas at the same time," wrote the American author F. Scott Fitzgerald (1896–1940). At this point in your study of microeconomics, you should be able to go one better than Fitzgerald and hold three somewhat contradictory ideas about the interrelationship between markets and government in your mind at the same time.

First, markets are extraordinarily useful and flexible institutions through which society can allocate its scarce resources. We introduced this idea with the subjects of international trade and demand and supply in other chapters and reinforced it in all the subsequent discussions of how households and firms make decisions.

Second, markets may sometimes produce unwanted results. A short list of the cases in which markets produce unwanted results includes monopoly and other cases of imperfect competition, pollution, poverty and inequality of incomes, discrimination, and failure to provide insurance.

Third, while government may play a useful role in addressing the problems of markets, government action is also imperfect and may not reflect majority views. Economists readily admit that, in settings like monopoly or negative externalities, a potential role exists for government intervention. However, in the real world, it is not enough to point out that government action might be a good idea. Instead, we must have some confidence that the government is likely to identify and carry out the appropriate public policy. To make sensible judgments about economic policy, we must see the strengths and weaknesses of both markets and government. We must not idealize or demonize either unregulated markets or government actions. Instead, consider the actual strengths and weaknesses of real-world markets and real-world governments.

These three insights seldom lead to simple or obvious political conclusions. As the famous British economist Joan Robinson wrote some decades ago: "[E]conomic theory, in itself, preaches no doctrines and cannot establish any universally valid laws. It is a method of ordering ideas and formulating questions." The study of economics is neither politically conservative, nor moderate, nor liberal. There are economists who are Democrats, Republicans, libertarians, socialists, and members of every other political group you can name. Of course, conservatives may tend to emphasize the virtues of markets and the limitations of government, while liberals may tend to emphasize the shortcomings of markets and the need for government programs. Such differences only illustrate that the language and terminology of economics is not limited to one set of political beliefs, but can be used by all.

 ## BRING IT HOME

### Chinese Tire Tariffs

In April 2009, the union representing U.S. tire manufacturing workers filed a request with the U.S. International Trade Commission (ITC), asking it to investigate tire imports from China. Under U.S. trade law, if imports from a country increase to the point that they cause market disruption in the United States, as determined by the ITC, then it can also recommend a remedy for this market disruption. In this case, the ITC determined that from 2004 to 2008, U.S. tire manufacturers suffered declines in production, financial health, and employment as a direct result of increases in tire imports from China. The ITC recommended placing an additional tax on tire imports from China. President Obama and Congress agreed with the ITC recommendation, and in June 2009 tariffs on Chinese tires increased from 4% to 39%. In addition, tariffs on Chinese tires increased further as part of President Trump's increases on a broad range of Chinese products.

Why would U.S. consumers buy imported tires from China in the first place? Most likely, because they are cheaper than tires produced domestically or in other countries. Therefore, this tariff increase should cause U.S. consumers to pay higher prices for tires, either because Chinese tires are now more expensive, or because U.S. consumers are pushed by the tariff to buy more expensive tires made by U.S. manufacturers or those from other countries. In the end, this tariff made U.S. consumers pay more for tires.

Was this tariff met with outrage expressed via social media, traditional media, or mass protests? Were there "Occupy Wall Street-type" demonstrations? The answer is a resounding "No". Most U.S. tire consumers were likely unaware of the tariff increase, although they may have noticed the price increase, which was between $4 and $13 depending on the type of tire. Tire consumers are also potential voters. Conceivably, a tax increase, even a small one, might make voters unhappy. However, voters probably realized that it was not worth their time to learn anything about this issue or cast a vote based on it. They probably thought their vote would not matter in determining the outcome of an election or changing this policy.

Estimates of the impact of this tariff show it costs U.S. consumers around $1.11 billion annually. Of this amount, roughly $817 million ends up in the pockets of foreign tire manufacturers other than in China, and the remaining $294 million goes to U.S. tire manufacturers. In other words, the tariff increase on Chinese tires may have saved 1,200 jobs in the domestic tire sector, but it cost 3,700 jobs in other sectors, as consumers had to reduce their spending because they were paying more for tires. People actually lost their jobs as a result of this tariff. Workers in U.S. tire manufacturing firms earned about $40,000 in 2010. Given the number of jobs saved and the total cost to U.S. consumers, the cost of saving one job amounted to $926,500!

This tariff caused a net decline in U.S. social surplus. (We discuss total surplus in the Demand and Supply chapter, and tariffs in the Introduction to International Trade chapter.) Instead of saving jobs, it cost jobs, and those jobs that it saved cost many times more than the people working in them could ever hope to earn. Why would the government do this?

The chapter answers this question by discussing the influence special interest groups have on economic policy. The steelworkers union, whose members make tires, saw increasingly more members lose their jobs as U.S. consumers consumed increasingly more cheap Chinese tires. By definition, this union is relatively small but well organized, especially compared to tire consumers. It stands to gain much for each of its members, compared to what each tire consumer may have to give up in terms of higher prices. Thus, the steelworkers union (joined by domestic tire manufacturers) has not only the means but the incentive to lobby economic policymakers and lawmakers. Given that U.S. tire consumers are a large and unorganized group, if they even are a group, it is unlikely they will lobby against higher tire tariffs. In the end, lawmakers tend to listen to those who lobby them, even though the results make for bad economic policy.

## Key Terms

**logrolling** the situation in which groups of legislators all agree to vote for a package of otherwise unrelated laws that they individually favor

**median voter theory** theory that politicians will try to match policies to what pleases the median voter preferences

**pork-barrel spending** spending that benefits mainly a single political district

**rational ignorance** the theory that rational people will not vote if the costs of becoming informed and voting are too high or because they know their vote will not be decisive in the election

**special interest groups** groups that are small in number relative to the nation, but well organized and thus exert a disproportionate effect on political outcomes

**voting cycle** the situation in which a majority prefers A over B, B over C, and C over A

## Key Concepts and Summary

### 18.1 Voter Participation and Costs of Elections

The theory of rational ignorance says voters will recognize that their single vote is extremely unlikely to influence the outcome of an election. As a consequence, they will choose to remain uninformed about issues and not vote. This theory helps explain why voter turnout is so low in the United States.

### 18.2 Special Interest Politics

Special interest politics arises when a relatively small group, called a special interest group, each of whose members has a large interest in a political outcome, devotes considerable time and energy to lobbying for the group's preferred choice. Meanwhile, the large majority, each of whose members has only a small interest in this issue, pays no attention.

We define pork--barrel spending as legislation whose benefits are concentrated on a single district while the costs are spread widely over the country. Logrolling refers to a situation in which two or more legislators agree to vote for each other's legislation, which can then encourage pork-barrel spending in many districts.

### 18.3 Flaws in the Democratic System of Government

Majority votes can run into difficulties when more than two choices exist. A voting cycle occurs when, in a situation with at least three choices, choice A is preferred by a majority vote to choice B, choice B is preferred by a majority vote to choice C, and choice C is preferred by a majority vote to choice A. In such a situation, it is impossible to identify what the majority prefers. Another difficulty arises when the vote is so divided that no choice receives a majority.

A practical approach to microeconomic policy will need to take a realistic view of the specific strengths and weaknesses of markets as well as government, rather than making the easy but wrong assumption that either the market or government is always beneficial or always harmful.

## Self-Check Questions

1. Based on the theory of rational ignorance, what should we expect to happen to voter turnout as the internet makes information easier to obtain?

2. What is the cost of voting in an election?

3. What is the main factor preventing a large community from influencing policy in the same way as a special interest group?

4. Why might legislators vote to impose a tariff on Egyptian cotton, when consumers in their districts would benefit from its availability?

5. True or false: Majority rule can fail to produce a single preferred outcome when there are more than two choices.

6. Anastasia, Emma, and Greta are deciding what to do on a weekend getaway. They each suggest a first, second, and third choice and then vote on the options. Table 18.2 shows their first, second, and third choice preferences . Explain why they will have a hard time reaching a decision. Does the group prefer mountain biking to canoeing? What about canoeing compared to the beach? What about the beach compared to the original choice of mountain biking?

|  | Anastasia | Emma | Greta |
|---|---|---|---|
| First Choice | Beach | Mountain biking | Canoeing |
| Second Choice | Mountain biking | Canoeing | Beach |
| Third Choice | Canoeing | Beach | Mountain biking |

**TABLE 18.2**

7. Suppose there is an election for Soft Drink Commissioner. The field consists of one candidate from the Pepsi party and four from the Coca-Cola party. This would seem to indicate a strong preference for Coca-Cola among the voting population, but the Pepsi candidate ends up winning in a landslide. Why does this happen?

## Review Questions

8. How does rational ignorance discourage voting?

9. How can a small special interest group win in a situation of majority voting when the benefits it seeks flow only to a small group?

10. How can pork-barrel spending occur in a situation of majority voting when it benefits only a small group?

11. Why do legislators vote for spending projects in districts that are not their own?

12. Why does a voting cycle make it impossible to decide on a majority-approved choice?

13. How does a government agency raise revenue differently from a private company, and how does that affect the way government makes decisions compared to business decisions?

## Critical Thinking Questions

14. What are some reasons people might find acquiring information about politics and voting rational, in contrast to rational ignorance theory?

15. What are some possible ways to encourage voter participation and overcome rational ignorance?

16. Given that rational ignorance discourages some people from becoming informed about elections, is it necessarily a good idea to encourage greater voter turnout? Why or why not?

17. When Microsoft was founded, the company devoted very few resources to lobbying activities. After a high-profile antitrust case against it, however, the company began to lobby heavily. Why does it make financial sense for companies to invest in lobbyists?

18. Representatives of competing firms often comprise special interest groups. Why are competitors sometimes willing to cooperate in order to form lobbying associations?

19. Special interests do not oppose regulations in all cases. The Marketplace Fairness Act of 2013 would require online merchants to collect sales taxes from their customers in other states. Why might a large online retailer like Amazon.com support such a measure?

20. To ensure safety and efficacy, the Food and Drug Administration regulates the medicines that pharmacies are allowed to sell in the United States. Sometimes this means a company must test a drug for years before it can reach the market. We can easily identify the winners in this system as those who are protected from unsafe drugs that might otherwise harm them. Who are the more anonymous losers who do not benefit from strict medical regulations?

21. How is it possible to bear a cost without realizing it? What are some examples of policies that affect people in ways of which they may not even be aware?

22. Is pork-barrel spending always a bad thing? Can you think of some examples of pork-barrel projects, perhaps from your own district, that have had positive results?

23. The United States currently uses a voting system called "first past the post" in elections, meaning that the candidate with the most votes wins. What are some of the problems with a "first past the post" system?

24. What are some alternatives to a "first past the post" system that might reduce the problem of voting cycles?

25. AT&T spent some $10 million dollars lobbying Congress to block entry of competitors into the telephone market in 1978. Why do you think it efforts failed?

26. Occupy Wall Street was a national (and later global) organized protest against the greed, bank profits, and financial corruption that led to the 2008–2009 recession. The group popularized slogans like "We are the 99%," meaning it represented the majority against the wealth of the top 1%. Does the fact that the protests had little to no effect on legislative changes support or contradict the chapter?

## Problems

27. Say that the government is considering a ban on smoking in restaurants in Tobaccoville. There are 1 million people living there, and each would benefit by $200 from this smoking ban. However, there are two large tobacco companies in Tobaccoville and the ban would cost them $5 million each. What are the proposed policy's total costs and benefits? Do you think it will pass?

FIGURE 19.1 **Apple or Samsung iPhone?** While the iPhone is readily recognized as an Apple product, many versions (including recently released offerings) have key components made by rival phone-maker, Samsung. In international trade, there are often "conflicts" like this as each country or company focuses on what it does best. (Credit: modification of "iPhone 4's Retina Display v.s. iPhone 3G" by Yutaka Tsutano/Flickr Creative Commons, CC BY 2.0)

## CHAPTER OBJECTIVES

In this chapter, you will learn about:

- Absolute and Comparative Advantage
- What Happens When a Country Has an Absolute Advantage in All Goods
- Intra-industry Trade between Similar Economies
- The Benefits of Reducing Barriers to International Trade

# Introduction to International Trade

 **BRING IT HOME**

### Just Whose iPhone Is It?

The iPhone is a global product. Apple does not manufacture the iPhone components, nor does it assemble them. The assembly is done by Foxconn Corporation, a Taiwanese company, at its factories in China and India. But, Samsung, the electronics firm and competitor to Apple, actually supplies many of the parts that make up an iPhone. In earlier models, Samsung parts made up as much as 26% of the total costs of production. And in more recent versions, Samsung manufactures the displays and cameras. In some ways, then, Samsung is both the biggest supplier and biggest competitor for Apple. Why do these two firms work together to produce the iPhone? To understand the economic logic behind international trade, you have to accept, as these firms do, that trade is about mutually beneficial exchange. Samsung is one of the world's largest electronics parts suppliers. Apple lets Samsung focus on making the best parts, which allows Apple to concentrate on its strength—designing elegant products that are easy to use. If each company (and by extension each country) focuses on what it does best, there will be gains for all through trade.

---

We live in a global marketplace. The food on your table might include fresh fruit from Chile, cheese from France, and bottled water from Scotland. Your wireless phone might have been made in Taiwan or Korea. The clothes you wear might be designed in Italy and manufactured in China. The toys you give to a child might have come from India. The car you drive might come from Japan, Germany, or Korea. The gasoline in the tank might be refined from crude oil from Saudi Arabia, Mexico, or Nigeria. As a worker, if your job is involved with farming, machinery, airplanes, cars, scientific instruments, or many other technology-related industries, the odds are good that a hearty proportion of the sales of your employer—and hence the money that pays your salary—comes from export sales. We are all linked by international trade, and the volume of that trade has grown dramatically in the last few decades.

The first wave of globalization started in the nineteenth century and lasted up to the beginning of World War I. Over that time, global exports as a share of global GDP rose from less than 1% of GDP in 1820 to 9% of GDP in 1913. As the Nobel Prize-winning economist Paul Krugman of Princeton University wrote in 1995:

> It is a late-twentieth-century conceit that we invented the global economy just yesterday. In fact, world markets achieved an impressive degree of integration during the second half of the nineteenth century. Indeed, if one wants a specific date for the beginning of a truly global economy, one might well choose 1869, the year in which both the Suez Canal and the Union Pacific railroad were completed. By the eve of the First World War steamships and railroads had created markets for standardized commodities, like wheat and wool, that were fully global in their reach. Even the global flow of information was better than modern observers, focused on electronic technology, tend to realize: the first submarine telegraph cable was laid under the Atlantic in 1858, and by 1900 all of the world's major economic regions could effectively communicate instantaneously.

This first wave of globalization crashed to a halt early in the twentieth century. World War I severed many economic connections. During the Great Depression of the 1930s, many nations misguidedly tried to fix their own economies by reducing foreign trade with others. World War II further hindered international trade. Global flows of goods and financial capital were rebuilt only slowly after World War II. It was not until the early 1980s that global economic forces again became as important, relative to the size of the world economy, as they were before World War I.

## 19.1 Absolute and Comparative Advantage

**LEARNING OBJECTIVES**

By the end of this section, you will be able to:

- Define absolute advantage, comparative advantage, and opportunity costs
- Explain the gains of trade created when a country specializes

The American statesman Benjamin Franklin (1706–1790) once wrote: "No nation was ever ruined by trade." Many economists would express their attitudes toward international trade in an even more positive manner. The evidence that international trade confers overall benefits on economies is pretty strong. Trade has accompanied economic growth in the United States and around the world. Many of the national economies that have shown the most rapid growth in the last several decades—for example, Japan, South Korea, China, and India—have done so by dramatically orienting their economies toward international trade. There is no modern example of a country that has shut itself off from world trade and yet prospered. To understand the benefits of trade, or why we trade in the first place, we need to understand the concepts of comparative and absolute advantage.

In 1817, David Ricardo, a businessman, economist, and member of the British Parliament, wrote a treatise called *On the Principles of Political Economy and Taxation*. In this treatise, Ricardo argued that specialization and free trade benefit all trading partners, even those that may be relatively inefficient. To see what he meant, we must be able to distinguish between absolute and comparative advantage.

A country has an **absolute advantage** over another country in producing a good if it uses fewer resources to produce that good. Absolute advantage can be the result of a country's natural endowment. For example, extracting oil in Saudi Arabia is pretty much just a matter of "drilling a hole." Producing oil in other countries can require considerable exploration and costly technologies for drilling and extraction—if they have any oil at all. The United States has some of the richest farmland in the world, making it easier to grow corn and wheat than in many other countries. Guatemala and Colombia have climates especially suited for growing coffee. Chile and Zambia have some of the world's richest copper mines. As some have argued, "geography is destiny." Chile will provide copper and Guatemala will produce coffee, and they will trade. When each country has a product others need and it can produce it with fewer resources in one country than in another, then it is easy to imagine all parties benefitting from trade. However, thinking about trade just in terms of geography and absolute advantage is incomplete. Trade really occurs because of comparative advantage.

Recall from the chapter Choice in a World of Scarcity that a country has a comparative advantage when it can produce a good at a lower cost in terms of other goods. The question each country or company should be asking when it trades is this: "What do we give up to produce this good?" It should be no surprise that the concept of comparative advantage is based on this idea of opportunity cost from Choice in a World of Scarcity. For example, if Zambia focuses its resources on producing copper, it cannot use its labor, land and financial resources to produce other goods such as corn. As a result, Zambia gives up the opportunity to produce corn. How do we quantify the cost in terms of other goods? Simplify the problem and assume that Zambia just needs labor to produce copper and corn. The companies that produce either copper or corn tell you that it takes two hours to mine a ton of copper and one hour to harvest a bushel of corn. This means the opportunity cost of producing a ton of copper is two bushels of corn. The next section develops absolute and comparative advantage in greater detail and relates them to trade.

## LINK IT UP

Visit this website (http://openstax.org/l/WTO) for a list of articles and podcasts pertaining to international trade topics.

## A Numerical Example of Absolute and Comparative Advantage

Consider a hypothetical world with two countries, Saudi Arabia and the United States, and two products, oil and corn. Further assume that consumers in both countries desire both these goods. These goods are homogeneous, meaning that consumers/producers cannot differentiate between corn or oil from either country. There is only one resource available in both countries, labor hours. Saudi Arabia can produce oil with fewer resources, while the United States can produce corn with fewer resources. Table 19.1 illustrates the advantages of the two countries, expressed in terms of how many hours it takes to produce one unit of each good.

| Country | Oil (hours per barrel) | Corn (hours per bushel) |
|---|---|---|
| Saudi Arabia | 1 | 4 |
| United States | 2 | 1 |

**TABLE 19.1** How Many Hours It Takes to Produce Oil and Corn

In Table 19.1, Saudi Arabia has an absolute advantage in producing oil because it only takes an hour to produce a barrel of oil compared to two hours in the United States. The United States has an absolute advantage in producing corn.

To simplify, let's say that Saudi Arabia and the United States each have 100 worker hours (see Table 19.2). Figure 19.2 illustrates what each country is capable of producing on its own using a production possibility frontier (PPF) graph. Recall from Choice in a World of Scarcity that the production possibilities frontier shows the maximum amount that each country can produce given its limited resources, in this case workers, and its level of technology.

| Country | Oil Production using 100 worker hours (barrels) | | Corn Production using 100 worker hours (bushels) |
|---|---|---|---|
| Saudi Arabia | 100 | or | 25 |
| United States | 50 | or | 100 |

**TABLE 19.2** Production Possibilities before Trade

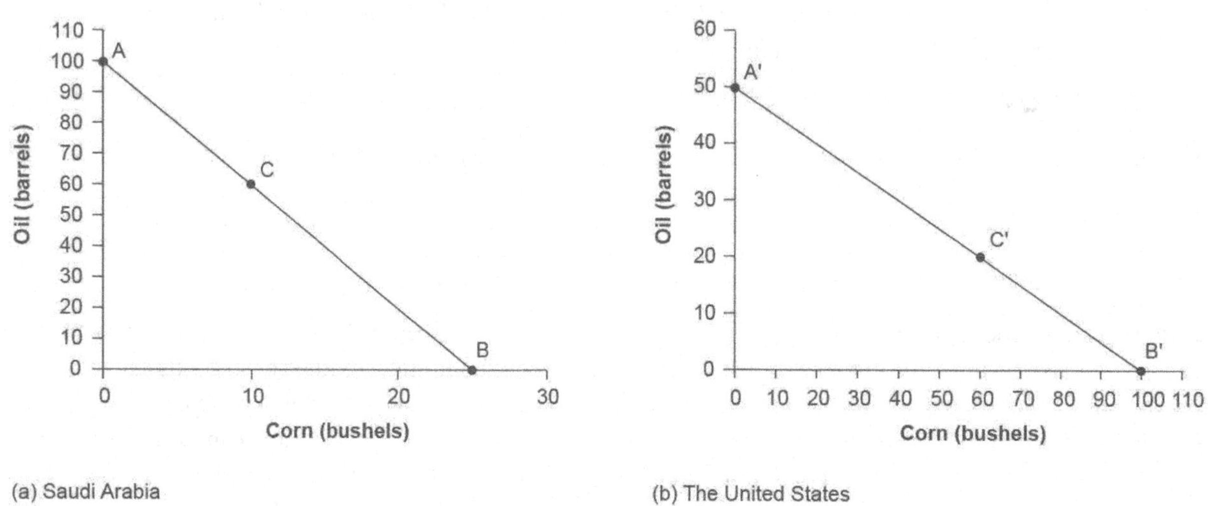


**FIGURE 19.2** Production Possibilities Frontiers (a) Saudi Arabia can produce 100 barrels of oil at maximum and zero corn (point A), or 25 bushels of corn and zero oil (point B). It can also produce other combinations of oil and corn if it wants to consume both goods, such as at point C. Here it chooses to produce/consume 60 barrels of oil, leaving 40 work hours that to allocate to produce 10 bushels of corn, using the data in Table 19.1. (b) If the United States produces only oil, it can produce, at maximum, 50 barrels and zero corn (point A'), or at the other extreme, it can produce a maximum of 100 bushels of corn and no oil (point B'). Other combinations of both oil and corn are possible, such as point C'. All points above the frontiers are impossible to produce given the current level of

resources and technology.

Arguably Saudi and U.S. consumers desire both oil and corn to live. Let's say that before trade occurs, both countries produce and consume at point C or C'. Thus, before trade, the Saudi Arabian economy will devote 60 worker hours to produce oil, as Table 19.3 shows. Given the information in Table 19.1, this choice implies that it produces/consumes 60 barrels of oil. With the remaining 40 worker hours, since it needs four hours to produce a bushel of corn, it can produce only 10 bushels. To be at point C', the U.S. economy devotes 40 worker hours to produce 20 barrels of oil and it can allocate the remaining worker hours to produce 60 bushels of corn.

| Country | Oil Production (barrels) | Corn Production (bushels) |
|---|---|---|
| Saudi Arabia (C) | 60 | 10 |
| United States (C') | 20 | 60 |
| **Total World Production** | **80** | **70** |

**TABLE 19.3** Production before Trade

The slope of the production possibility frontier illustrates the opportunity cost of producing oil in terms of corn. Using all its resources, the United States can produce 50 barrels of oil *or* 100 bushels of corn; therefore, the opportunity cost of one barrel of oil is two bushels of corn—or the slope is 1/2. Thus, in the U.S. production possibility frontier graph, every increase in oil production of one barrel implies a decrease of two bushels of corn. Saudi Arabia can produce 100 barrels of oil *or* 25 bushels of corn. The opportunity cost of producing one barrel of oil is the loss of 1/4 of a bushel of corn that Saudi workers could otherwise have produced. In terms of corn, notice that Saudi Arabia gives up the least to produce a barrel of oil. Table 19.4 summarizes these calculations.

| Country | Opportunity cost of one unit — Oil (in terms of corn) | Opportunity cost of one unit — Corn (in terms of oil) |
|---|---|---|
| Saudi Arabia | ¼ | 4 |
| United States | 2 | ½ |

**TABLE 19.4** Opportunity Cost and Comparative Advantage

Again recall that we defined comparative advantage as the opportunity cost of producing goods. Since Saudi Arabia gives up the least to produce a barrel of oil, ($\frac{1}{4} < 2$ in Table 19.4) it has a comparative advantage in oil production. The United States gives up the least to produce a bushel of corn, so it has a comparative advantage in corn production.

In this example, there is symmetry between absolute and comparative advantage. Saudi Arabia needs fewer worker hours to produce oil (absolute advantage, see Table 19.1), and also gives up the least in terms of other goods to produce oil (comparative advantage, see Table 19.4). Such symmetry is not always the case, as we will show after we have discussed gains from trade fully, but first, read the following Clear It Up feature to make sure you understand why the PPF line in the graphs is straight.

## CLEAR IT UP

### Can a production possibility frontier be straight?

When you first met the production possibility frontier (PPF) in the chapter on Choice in a World of Scarcity we drew it with an outward-bending shape. This shape illustrated that as we transferred inputs from producing one good to another—like from education to health services—there were increasing opportunity costs. In the examples in this chapter, we draw the PPFs as straight lines, which means that opportunity costs are constant. When we transfer a marginal unit of labor away from growing corn and toward producing oil, the decline in the quantity of corn and the increase in the quantity of oil is always the same. In reality this is possible only if the contribution of additional workers to output did not change as the scale of production changed. The linear production possibilities frontier is a less realistic model, but a straight line simplifies calculations. It also illustrates economic themes like absolute and comparative advantage just as clearly.

### Gains from Trade

Consider the trading positions of the United States and Saudi Arabia after they have specialized and traded. Before trade, Saudi Arabia produces/consumes 60 barrels of oil and 10 bushels of corn. The United States produces/consumes 20 barrels of oil and 60 bushels of corn. Given their current production levels, if the United States can trade an amount of corn fewer than 60 bushels and receive in exchange an amount of oil greater than 20 barrels, it will **gain from trade**. With trade, the United States can consume more of both goods than it did without specialization and trade. (Recall that the chapter Welcome to Economics! defined specialization as it applies to workers and firms. Economists also use specialization to describe the occurrence when a country shifts resources to focus on producing a good that offers comparative advantage.) Similarly, if Saudi Arabia can trade an amount of oil less than 60 barrels and receive in exchange an amount of corn greater than 10 bushels, it will have more of both goods than it did before specialization and trade. Table 19.5 illustrates the range of trades that would benefit both sides.

| The U.S. economy, after specialization, will benefit if it: | The Saudi Arabian economy, after specialization, will benefit if it: |
|---|---|
| Exports no more than 60 bushels of corn | Imports at least 10 bushels of corn |
| Imports at least 20 barrels of oil | Exports less than 60 barrels of oil |

**TABLE 19.5** The Range of Trades That Benefit Both the United States and Saudi Arabia

The underlying reason why trade benefits both sides is rooted in the concept of opportunity cost, as the following Clear It Up feature explains. If Saudi Arabia wishes to expand domestic production of corn in a world without international trade, then based on its opportunity costs it must give up four barrels of oil for every one additional bushel of corn. If Saudi Arabia could find a way to give up less than four barrels of oil for an additional bushel of corn (or equivalently, to receive more than one bushel of corn for four barrels of oil), it would be better off.

## CLEAR IT UP

### What are the opportunity costs and gains from trade?

The range of trades that will benefit each country is based on the country's opportunity cost of producing each good. The United States can produce 100 bushels of corn or 50 barrels of oil. For the United States, the opportunity cost of producing one barrel of oil is two bushels of corn. If we divide the numbers above by 50, we get the same ratio: one barrel of oil is equivalent to two bushels of corn, or (100/50 = 2 and 50/50 = 1). In a trade with Saudi Arabia, if the United States is going to give up 100 bushels of corn in exports, it must import at least 50 barrels of oil to be just as well off. Clearly, to gain from trade it needs to be able to gain more than a half barrel of oil for its bushel of corn—or why trade at all?

Recall that David Ricardo argued that if each country specializes in its comparative advantage, it will benefit from trade, and total global output will increase. How can we show gains from trade as a result of comparative advantage and specialization? Table 19.6 shows the output assuming that each country specializes in its comparative advantage and produces no other good. This is 100% specialization. Specialization leads to an increase in total world production. (Compare the total world production in Table 19.3 to that in Table 19.6.)

| Country | Quantity produced after 100% specialization — Oil (barrels) | Quantity produced after 100% specialization — Corn (bushels) |
|---|---|---|
| Saudi Arabia | 100 | 0 |
| United States | 0 | 100 |
| **Total World Production** | **100** | **100** |

**TABLE 19.6** How Specialization Expands Output

What if we did not have complete specialization, as in Table 19.6? Would there still be gains from trade? Consider another example, such as when the United States and Saudi Arabia start at C and C', respectively, as Figure 19.2 shows. Consider what occurs when trade is allowed and the United States exports 20 bushels of corn to Saudi Arabia in exchange for 20 barrels of oil.

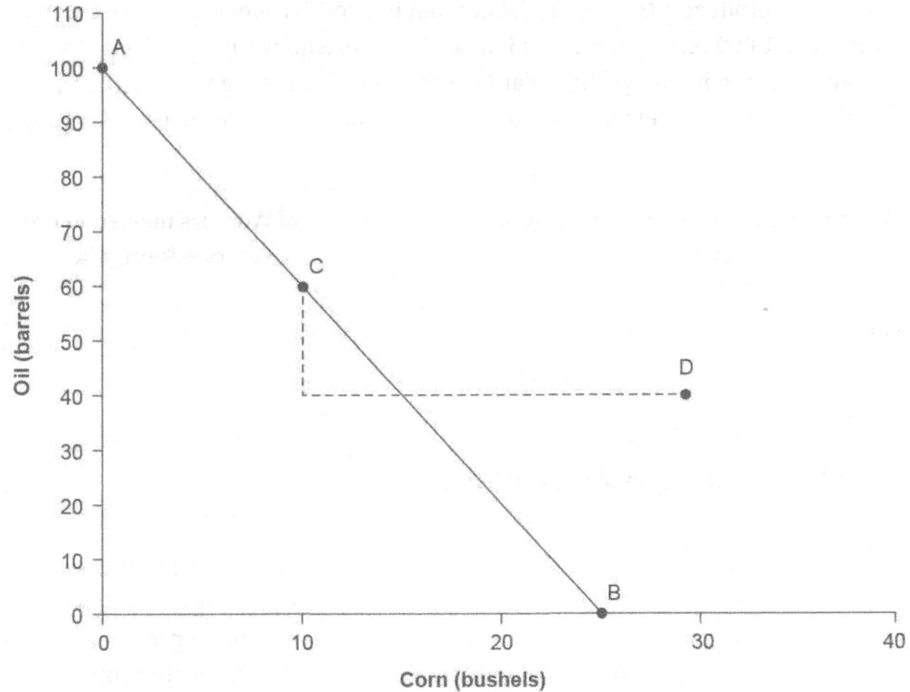


**FIGURE 19.3** Production Possibilities Frontier in Saudi Arabia Trade allows a country to go beyond its domestic production-possibility frontier

Starting at point C, which shows Saudi oil production of 60, reduce Saudi oil domestic oil consumption by 20, since 20 is exported to the United States and exchanged for 20 units of corn. This enables Saudi to reach point D, where oil consumption is now 40 barrels and corn consumption has increased to 30 (see Figure 19.3). Notice that even without 100% specialization, if the "trading price," in this case 20 barrels of oil for 20 bushels of corn, is greater than the country's opportunity cost, the Saudis will gain from trade. Since the post-trade consumption point D is beyond its production possibility frontier, Saudi Arabia has gained from trade.

## ⊘ LINK IT UP

Visit this website (http://wits.worldbank.org/trade-visualization.aspx) for trade-related data visualizations.

## 19.2 What Happens When a Country Has an Absolute Advantage in All Goods

### LEARNING OBJECTIVES

By the end of this section, you will be able to:
- Show the relationship between production costs and comparative advantage
- Identify situations of mutually beneficial trade
- Identify trade benefits by considering opportunity costs

What happens to the possibilities for trade if one country has an absolute advantage in everything? This is typical for high-income countries that often have well-educated workers, technologically advanced equipment, and the most up-to-date production processes. These high-income countries can produce all products with fewer resources than a low-income country. If the high-income country is more productive across the board, will there still be gains from trade? Good students of Ricardo understand that trade is about mutually beneficial exchange. Even when one country has an absolute advantage in all products, trade can still benefit both sides. This is because gains from trade come from specializing in one's comparative advantage.

### Production Possibilities and Comparative Advantage

Consider the example of trade between the United States and Mexico described in Table 19.7. In this example, it takes four U.S. workers to produce 1,000 pairs of shoes, but it takes five Mexican workers to do so. It takes one U.S. worker to produce 1,000 refrigerators, but it takes four Mexican workers to do so. The United States has an absolute advantage in productivity with regard to both shoes and refrigerators; that is, it takes fewer workers in the United States than in Mexico to produce both a given number of shoes and a given number of refrigerators.

| Country | Number of Workers needed to produce 1,000 units — Shoes | Number of Workers needed to produce 1,000 units — Refrigerators |
|---|---|---|
| United States | 4 workers | 1 worker |
| Mexico | 5 workers | 4 workers |

**TABLE 19.7** Resources Needed to Produce Shoes and Refrigerators

Absolute advantage simply compares the productivity of a worker between countries. It answers the question, "How many inputs do I need to produce shoes in Mexico?" Comparative advantage asks this same question slightly differently. Instead of comparing how many workers it takes to produce a good, it asks, "How much am I giving up to produce this good in this country?" Another way of looking at this is that comparative advantage identifies the good for which the producer's absolute advantage is relatively larger, or where the producer's absolute productivity disadvantage is relatively smaller. The United States can produce 1,000 shoes with four-fifths as many workers as Mexico (four versus five), but it can produce 1,000 refrigerators with only one-quarter as many workers (one versus four). So, the comparative advantage of the United States, where its absolute productivity advantage is relatively greatest, lies with refrigerators, and Mexico's comparative advantage, where its absolute productivity disadvantage is least, is in the production of shoes.

## Mutually Beneficial Trade with Comparative Advantage

When nations increase production in their area of comparative advantage and trade with each other, both countries can benefit. Again, the production possibility frontier is a useful tool to visualize this benefit.

Consider a situation where the United States and Mexico each have 40 workers. For example, as Table 19.8 shows, if the United States divides its labor so that 40 workers are making shoes, then, since it takes four workers in the United States to make 1,000 shoes, a total of 10,000 shoes will be produced. (If four workers can make 1,000 shoes, then 40 workers will make 10,000 shoes). If the 40 workers in the United States are making refrigerators, and each worker can produce 1,000 refrigerators, then a total of 40,000 refrigerators will be produced.

| Country | Shoe Production — using 40 workers | | Refrigerator Production — using 40 workers |
|---|---|---|---|
| United States | 10,000 shoes | or | 40,000 refrigerators |
| Mexico | 8,000 shoes | or | 10,000 refrigerators |

**TABLE 19.8 Production Possibilities before Trade with Complete Specialization**

As always, the slope of the production possibility frontier for each country is the opportunity cost of one refrigerator in terms of foregone shoe production–when labor is transferred from producing the latter to producing the former (see Figure 19.4).

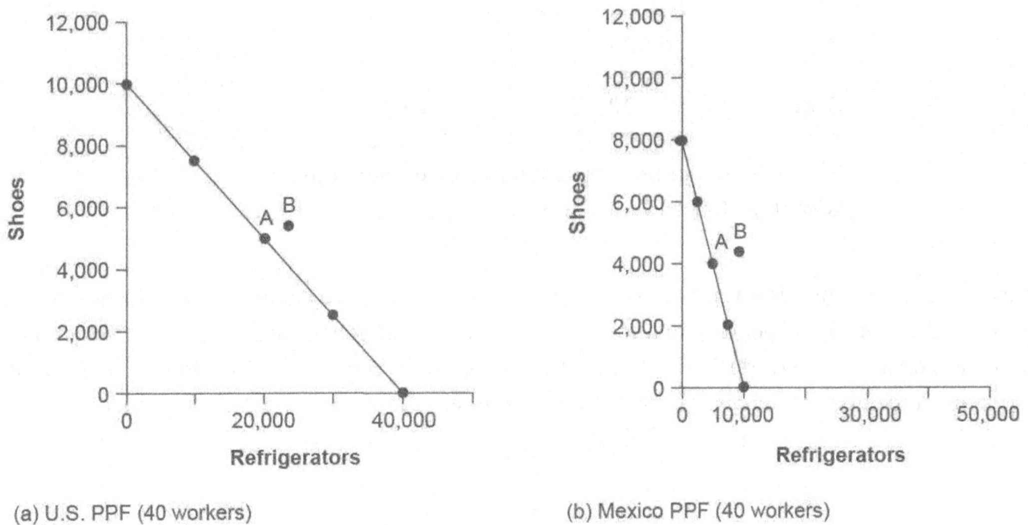


**FIGURE 19.4 Production Possibility Frontiers** (a) With 40 workers, the United States can produce either 10,000 shoes and zero refrigerators or 40,000 refrigerators and zero shoes. (b) With 40 workers, Mexico can produce a maximum of 8,000 shoes and zero refrigerators, or 10,000 refrigerators and zero shoes. All other points on the production possibility line are possible combinations of the two goods that can be produced given current resources. Point A on both graphs is where the countries start producing and consuming before trade. Point B is where they end up after trade.

Let's say that, in the situation before trade, each nation prefers to produce a combination of shoes and refrigerators that is shown at point A. Table 19.9 shows the output of each good for each country and the total output for the two countries.

| Country | Current Shoe Production | Current Refrigerator Production |
|---|---|---|
| United States | 5,000 | 20,000 |
| Mexico | 4,000 | 5,000 |
| **Total** | **9,000** | **25,000** |

**TABLE 19.9** Total Production at Point A before Trade

Continuing with this scenario, suppose that each country transfers some amount of labor toward its area of comparative advantage. For example, the United States transfers six workers away from shoes and toward producing refrigerators. As a result, U.S. production of shoes decreases by 1,500 units (6/4 × 1,000), while its production of refrigerators increases by 6,000 (that is, 6/1 × 1,000). Mexico also moves production toward its area of comparative advantage, transferring 10 workers away from refrigerators and toward production of shoes. As a result, production of refrigerators in Mexico falls by 2,500 (10/4 × 1,000), but production of shoes increases by 2,000 pairs (10/5 × 1,000). Notice that when both countries shift production toward each of their comparative advantages (what they are relatively better at), their combined production of both goods rises, as shown in Table 19.10. The reduction of shoe production by 1,500 pairs in the United States is more than offset by the gain of 2,000 pairs of shoes in Mexico, while the reduction of 2,500 refrigerators in Mexico is more than offset by the additional 6,000 refrigerators produced in the United States.

| Country | Shoe Production | Refrigerator Production |
|---|---|---|
| United States | 3,500 | 26,000 |
| Mexico | 6,000 | 2,500 |
| **Total** | **9,500** | **28,500** |

**TABLE 19.10** Shifting Production Toward Comparative Advantage Raises Total Output

This numerical example illustrates the remarkable insight of comparative advantage: even when one country has an absolute advantage in all goods and another country has an absolute disadvantage in all goods, both countries can still benefit from trade. Even though the United States has an absolute advantage in producing both refrigerators and shoes, it makes economic sense for it to specialize in the good for which it has a comparative advantage. The United States will export refrigerators and in return import shoes.

## How Opportunity Cost Sets the Boundaries of Trade

This example shows that both parties can benefit from specializing in their comparative advantages and trading. By using the opportunity costs in this example, it is possible to identify the range of possible trades that would benefit each country.

Mexico started out, before specialization and trade, producing 4,000 pairs of shoes and 5,000 refrigerators (see Figure 19.4 and Table 19.9). Then, in the numerical example given, Mexico shifted production toward its comparative advantage and produced 6,000 pairs of shoes but only 2,500 refrigerators. Thus, if Mexico can export no more than 2,000 pairs of shoes (giving up 2,000 pairs of shoes) in exchange for imports of at least 2,500 refrigerators (a gain of 2,500 refrigerators), it will be able to consume more of both goods than before trade. Mexico will be unambiguously better off. Conversely, the United States started off, before specialization and trade, producing 5,000 pairs of shoes and 20,000 refrigerators. In the example, it then shifted production toward its comparative advantage, producing only 3,500 shoes but 26,000 refrigerators. If the United States can export no more than 6,000 refrigerators in exchange for imports of at least 1,500 pairs of shoes, it will be able to consume more of both goods and will be unambiguously better off.

The range of trades that can benefit both nations is shown in Table 19.11. For example, a trade where the U.S. exports 4,000 refrigerators to Mexico in exchange for 1,800 pairs of shoes would benefit both sides, in the sense that both countries would be able to consume more of both goods than in a world without trade.

| The U.S. economy, after specialization, will benefit if it: | The Mexican economy, after specialization, will benefit if it: |
| --- | --- |
| *Exports* fewer than 6,000 refrigerators | *Imports* at least 2,500 refrigerators |
| *Imports* at least 1,500 pairs of shoes | *Exports* no more than 2,000 pairs of shoes |

TABLE 19.11 The Range of Trades That Benefit Both the United States and Mexico

Trade allows each country to take advantage of lower opportunity costs in the other country. If Mexico wants to produce more refrigerators without trade, it must face its domestic opportunity costs and reduce shoe production. If Mexico, instead, produces more shoes and then trades for refrigerators made in the United States, where the opportunity cost of producing refrigerators is lower, Mexico can in effect take advantage of the lower opportunity cost of refrigerators in the United States. Conversely, when the United States specializes in its comparative advantage of refrigerator production and trades for shoes produced in Mexico, international trade allows the United States to take advantage of the lower opportunity cost of shoe production in Mexico.

The theory of comparative advantage explains why countries trade: they have different comparative advantages. It shows that the gains from international trade result from pursuing comparative advantage and producing at a lower opportunity cost. The following Work It Out feature shows how to calculate absolute and comparative advantage and the way to apply them to a country's production.

## WORK IT OUT

### Calculating Absolute and Comparative Advantage

In Canada a worker can produce 20 barrels of oil or 40 tons of lumber. In Venezuela, a worker can produce 60 barrels of oil or 30 tons of lumber.

| Country | Oil (barrels) | | Lumber (tons) |
| --- | --- | --- | --- |
| Canada | 20 | or | 40 |
| Venezuela | 60 | or | 30 |

TABLE 19.12

a. Who has the absolute advantage in the production of oil or lumber? How can you tell?
b. Which country has a comparative advantage in the production of oil?
c. Which country has a comparative advantage in producing lumber?
d. In this example, is absolute advantage the same as comparative advantage, or not?
e. In what product should Canada specialize? In what product should Venezuela specialize?

Step 1. Make a table like Table 19.12.

Step 2. To calculate absolute advantage, look at the larger of the numbers for each product. One worker in Canada can produce more lumber (40 tons versus 30 tons), so Canada has the absolute advantage in lumber. One worker in Venezuela can produce 60 barrels of oil compared to a worker in Canada who can produce only 20.

Step 3. To calculate comparative advantage, find the opportunity cost of producing one barrel of oil in both countries. The country with the lowest opportunity cost has the comparative advantage. With the same labor time, Canada can produce either 20 barrels of oil or 40 tons of lumber. So in effect, 20 barrels of oil is equivalent to 40 tons of lumber: 20 oil = 40 lumber. Divide both sides of the equation by 20 to calculate the opportunity cost of one barrel of oil in Canada. 20/20 oil = 40/20 lumber. 1 oil = 2 lumber. To produce one additional barrel of oil in Canada has an opportunity cost of 2 lumber. Calculate the same way for Venezuela: 60 oil = 30 lumber. Divide both sides of the equation by 60. One oil in Venezuela has an opportunity cost of 1/2 lumber. Because 1/2 lumber < 2 lumber, Venezuela has the comparative advantage in producing oil.

Step 4. Calculate the opportunity cost of one lumber by reversing the numbers, with lumber on the left side of the equation. In Canada, 40 lumber is equivalent in labor time to 20 barrels of oil: 40 lumber = 20 oil. Divide each side of the equation by 40. The opportunity cost of one lumber is 1/2 oil. In Venezuela, the equivalent labor time will produce 30 lumber or 60 oil: 30 lumber = 60 oil. Divide each side by 30. One lumber has an opportunity cost of two oil. Canada has the lower opportunity cost in producing lumber.

Step 5. In this example, absolute advantage is the same as comparative advantage. Canada has the absolute and comparative advantage in lumber; Venezuela has the absolute and comparative advantage in oil.

Step 6. Canada should specialize in the commodity for which it has a relative lower opportunity cost, which is lumber, and Venezuela should specialize in oil. Canada will be exporting lumber and importing oil, and Venezuela will be exporting oil and importing lumber.

## Comparative Advantage Goes Camping

To build an intuitive understanding of how comparative advantage can benefit all parties, set aside examples that involve national economies for a moment and consider the situation of a group of friends who decide to go camping together. The six friends have a wide range of skills and experiences, but one person in particular, Jethro, has done lots of camping before and is also a great athlete. Jethro has an absolute advantage in all aspects of camping: he is faster at carrying a backpack, gathering firewood, paddling a canoe, setting up tents, making a meal, and washing up. So here is the question: Because Jethro has an absolute productivity advantage in everything, should he do all the work?

Of course not! Even if Jethro is willing to work like a mule while everyone else sits around, he, like all mortals, only has 24 hours in a day. If everyone sits around and waits for Jethro to do everything, not only will Jethro be an unhappy camper, but there will not be much output for his group of six friends to consume. The theory of comparative advantage suggests that everyone will benefit if they figure out their areas of comparative advantage—that is, the area of camping where their productivity disadvantage is least, compared to Jethro. For example, it may be that Jethro is 80% faster at building fires and cooking meals than anyone else, but only 20% faster at gathering firewood and 10% faster at setting up tents. In that case, Jethro should focus on building fires and making meals, and others should attend to the other tasks, each according to where their productivity disadvantage is smallest. If the campers coordinate their efforts according to comparative advantage, they can all gain.

# 19.3 Intra-industry Trade between Similar Economies

**LEARNING OBJECTIVES**

By the end of this section, you will be able to:
- Identify at least two advantages of intra-industry trading
- Explain the relationship between economies of scale and intra-industry trade

Absolute and comparative advantages explain a great deal about global trading patterns. For example, they help to explain the patterns that we noted at the start of this chapter, like why you may be eating fresh fruit from Chile or Mexico, or why lower productivity regions like Africa and Latin America are able to sell a substantial proportion of their exports to higher productivity regions like the European Union and North America. Comparative advantage, however, at least at first glance, does not seem especially well-suited to explain other common patterns of international trade.

## The Prevalence of Intra-Industry Trade between Similar Economies

The theory of comparative advantage suggests that trade should happen between economies with large differences in opportunity costs of production. Roughly half of all U.S. trade involves shipping goods between the fairly similar high-income economies of Japan, Canada, and the United States. Furthermore, the trade has an important geographic component—the biggest trading partners of the United States are Canada and Mexico (see Table 19.13).

| Country | U.S. Exports Go to ... | U.S. Imports Come from ... |
|---|---|---|
| China | 8.6% | 17.7% |
| Canada | 17.6% | 12.6% |
| Japan | 4.3% | 4.3% |
| Mexico | 15.8% | 13.6% |
| South Korea | 3.8% | 3.3% |

**TABLE 19.13 Top Trading Partners (November 2021)** (Source: https://www.census.gov/foreign-trade/statistics/highlights/toppartners.html)

Moreover, the theory of comparative advantage suggests that each economy should specialize to a degree in certain products, and then exchange those products. A high proportion of trade, however, is **intra-industry trade**—that is, trade of goods within the same industry from one country to another. For example, the United States produces and exports autos and imports autos. Table 19.14 shows some of the largest categories of U.S. exports and imports. In all of these categories, the United States is both a substantial exporter and a substantial importer of goods from the same industry. In 2021, according to the U.S. Census Bureau, the United States exported $131 billion worth of autos, and imported $317 billion worth of autos. About 60% of U.S. trade and 60% of European trade is intra-industry trade.

| Some U.S. Exports | Quantity of Exports ($ billions) | Quantity of Imports ($ billions) |
| --- | --- | --- |
| Autos | $131 | $317 |
| Food and beverages | $147 | $167 |
| Capital goods | $474 | $695 |
| Consumer goods | $201 | $699 |
| Industrial supplies | $578 | $589 |
| Other transportation | $63 | $113 |

**TABLE 19.14 Some Intra-Industry U.S. Exports and Imports in 2021** (Source: https://www.census.gov/foreign-trade/data/index.html)

Why do similar high-income economies engage in intra-industry trade? What can be the economic benefit of having workers of fairly similar skills making cars, computers, machinery and other products which are then shipped across the oceans to and from the United States, the European Union, and Japan? There are two reasons: (1) The division of labor leads to learning, innovation, and unique skills; and (2) economies of scale.

### Gains from Specialization and Learning

Consider the category of machinery, where the U.S. economy has considerable intra-industry trade. Machinery comes in many varieties, so the United States may be exporting machinery for manufacturing with wood, but importing machinery for photographic processing. The underlying reason why a country like the United States, Japan, or Germany produces one kind of machinery rather than another is usually not related to U.S., German, or Japanese firms and workers having generally higher or lower skills. It is just that, in working on very specific and particular products, firms in certain countries develop unique and different skills.

Specialization in the world economy can be very finely split. In fact, recent years have seen a trend in international trade, which economists call **splitting up the value chain**. The **value chain** describes how a good is produced in stages. As indicated in the beginning of the chapter, producing the iPhone involves designing and engineering the phone in the United States, supplying parts from Korea, assembling the parts in China, and advertising and marketing in the United States. Thanks in large part to improvements in communication technology, sharing information, and transportation, it has become easier to split up the value chain. Instead of production in a single large factory, different firms operating in various places and even different countries can divide the value chain. Because firms split up the value chain, international trade often does not involve nations trading whole finished products like automobiles or refrigerators. Instead, it involves shipping more specialized goods like, say, automobile dashboards or the shelving that fits inside refrigerators. Intra-industry trade between similar countries produces economic gains because it allows workers and firms to learn and innovate on particular products—and often to focus on very particular parts of the value chain.

### ⊘ LINK IT UP

Visit this website (http://openstax.org/l/iphoneassembly) for some interesting information about the assembly of the iPhone.

### Economies of Scale, Competition, Variety

A second broad reason that intra-industry trade between similar nations produces economic gains involves economies of scale. The concept of economies of scale, as we introduced in Production, Costs and Industry Structure, means that as the scale of output goes up, average costs of production decline—at least up to a point.

Figure 19.5 illustrates economies of scale for a plant producing toaster ovens. The horizontal axis of the figure shows the quantity of production by a certain firm or at a certain manufacturing plant. The vertical axis measures the average cost of production. Production plant S produces a small level of output at 30 units and has an average cost of production of $30 per toaster oven. Plant M produces at a medium level of output at 50 units, and has an average cost of production of $20 per toaster oven. Plant L produces 150 units of output with an average cost of production of only $10 per toaster oven. Although plant V can produce 200 units of output, it still has the same unit cost as Plant L.

In this example, a small or medium plant, like S or M, will not be able to compete in the market with a large or a very large plant like L or V, because the firm that operates L or V will be able to produce and sell its output at a lower price. In this example, economies of scale operate up to point L, but beyond point L to V, the additional scale of production does not continue to reduce average costs of production.

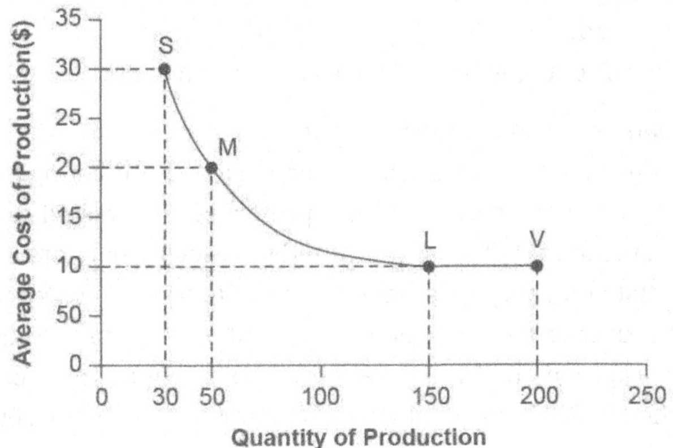


**FIGURE 19.5 Economies of Scale** Production Plant S, has an average cost of production of $30 per toaster oven. Production plant M has an average cost of production of $20 per toaster oven. Production plant L has an average cost of production of only $10 per toaster oven. Production plant V still has an average cost of production of $10 per toaster oven. Thus, production plant M can produce toaster ovens more cheaply than plant S because of economies of scale, and plants L or V can produce more cheaply than S or M because of economies of scale. However, the economies of scale end at an output level of 150. Plant V, despite being larger, cannot produce more cheaply on average than plant L.

The concept of economies of scale becomes especially relevant to international trade when it enables one or two large producers to supply the entire country. For example, a single large automobile factory could probably supply all the cars consumers purchase in a smaller economy like the United Kingdom or Belgium in a given year. However, if a country has only one or two large factories producing cars, and no international trade, then consumers in that country would have relatively little choice between kinds of cars (other than the color of the paint and other nonessential options). Little or no competition will exist between different car manufacturers.

International trade provides a way to combine the lower average production costs that come from economies of scale and still have competition and variety for consumers. Large automobile factories in different countries can make and sell their products around the world. If General Motors, Ford, and Chrysler were the only players in the U.S. automobile market, the level of competition and consumer choice would be considerably lower than when U.S. carmakers must face competition from Toyota, Honda, Suzuki, Fiat, Mitsubishi, Nissan, Volkswagen, Kia, Hyundai, BMW, Subaru, and others. Greater competition brings with it innovation and responsiveness to what consumers want. America's car producers make far better cars now than they did several decades ago, and much of the reason is competitive pressure, especially from East Asian and European carmakers.

## Dynamic Comparative Advantage

The sources of gains from intra-industry trade between similar economies—namely, the learning that comes from a high degree of specialization and splitting up the value chain and from economies of scale—do not contradict the earlier theory of comparative advantage. Instead, they help to broaden the concept.

In intra-industry trade, climate or geography do not determine the level of worker productivity. Even the general level of education or skill does not determine it. Instead, how firms engage in specific learning about specialized products, including taking advantage of economies of scale determine the level of worker productivity. In this vision, comparative advantage can be dynamic—that is, it can evolve and change over time as one develops new skills and as manufacturers split the value chain in new ways. This line of thinking also suggests that countries are not destined to have the same comparative advantage forever, but must instead be flexible in response to ongoing changes in comparative advantage.

## 19.4 The Benefits of Reducing Barriers to International Trade

**LEARNING OBJECTIVES**

By the end of this section, you will be able to:

- Explain tariffs as barriers to trade
- Identify at least two benefits of reducing barriers to international trade

**Tariffs** are taxes that governments place on imported goods for a variety of reasons. Some of these reasons include protecting sensitive industries, for humanitarian reasons, and protecting against dumping. Traditionally, tariffs were used simply as a political tool to protect certain vested economic, social, and cultural interests. The World Trade Organization (WTO) is committed to lowering barriers to trade. The world's nations meet through the WTO to negotiate how they can reduce barriers to trade, such as tariffs. WTO negotiations happen in "rounds," where all countries negotiate one agreement to encourage trade, take a year or two off, and then start negotiating a new agreement. The current round of negotiations is called the Doha Round because it was officially launched in Doha, the capital city of Qatar, in November 2001. In 2010, the WTO noted that the Doha Round's emphasis on market access and reforms of agricultural subsidies could add $121–$202 billion to the world economy.

In the context of a global economy that currently produces more than $80 trillion of goods and services each year, this amount is not large: it is an increase of less than 1%. But before dismissing the gains from trade too quickly, it is worth remembering two points.

- First, a gain of a few hundred billion dollars is enough money to deserve attention! Moreover, remember that this increase is not a one-time event; it would persist each year into the future.
- Second, the estimate of gains may be on the low side because some of the gains from trade are not measured especially well in economic statistics. For example, it is difficult to measure the potential advantages to consumers of having a variety of products available and a greater degree of competition among producers. Perhaps the most important unmeasured factor is that trade between countries, especially when firms are splitting up the value chain of production, often involves a transfer of knowledge that can involve skills in production, technology, management, finance, and law.

Low-income countries benefit more from trade than high-income countries do. In some ways, the giant U.S. economy has less need for international trade, because it can already take advantage of internal trade within its economy. However, many smaller national economies around the world, in regions like Latin America, Africa, the Middle East, and Asia, have much more limited possibilities for trade inside their countries or their immediate regions. Without international trade, they may have little ability to benefit from comparative advantage, slicing up the value chain, or economies of scale. Moreover, smaller economies often have fewer competitive firms making goods within their economy, and thus firms have less pressure from other firms to provide the goods and prices that consumers want.

The economic gains from expanding international trade are measured in hundreds of billions of dollars, and the gains from international trade as a whole probably reach well into the trillions of dollars. The potential for gains from trade may be especially high among the smaller and lower-income countries of the world.

 **LINK IT UP**

Visit this website (http://openstax.org/l/tradebenefits) for a list of some benefits of trade.

## From Interpersonal to International Trade

Most people find it easy to believe that they, personally, would not be better off if they tried to grow and process all of their own food, to make all of their own clothes, to build their own cars and houses from scratch, and so on. Instead, we all benefit from living in economies where people and firms can specialize and trade with each other.

The benefits of trade do not stop at national boundaries, either. Earlier we explained that the division of labor could increase output for three reasons: (1) workers with different characteristics can specialize in the types of production where they have a comparative advantage; (2) firms and workers who specialize in a certain product become more productive with learning and practice; and (3) economies of scale. These three reasons apply from the individual and community level right up to the international level. If it makes sense to you that interpersonal, intercommunity, and interstate trade offer economic gains, it should make sense that international trade offers gains, too.

International trade currently involves about $20 trillion worth of goods and services moving around the globe. Any economic force of that size, even if it confers overall benefits, is certain to cause disruption and controversy. This chapter has only made the case that trade brings economic benefits. Other chapters discuss, in detail, the public policy arguments over whether to restrict international trade.

 **BRING IT HOME**

### Just Whose iPhone Is It?

Apple Corporation uses a global platform to produce the iPhone. Now that you understand the concept of comparative advantage, you can see why the engineering and design of the iPhone is done in the United States. The United States has built up a comparative advantage over the years in designing and marketing products, and sacrifices fewer resources to design high-tech devices relative to other countries. China has a comparative advantage in assembling the phone due to its large skilled labor force. Korea has a comparative advantage in producing components. Korea focuses its production by increasing its scale, learning better ways to produce screens and computer chips, and uses innovation to lower average costs of production. Apple, in turn, benefits because it can purchase these quality products at lower prices. Put the global assembly line together and you have the device with which we are all so familiar.

## Key Terms

**absolute advantage** when one country can use fewer resources to produce a good compared to another country; when a country is more productive compared to another country

**gain from trade** a country that can consume more than it can produce as a result of specialization and trade

**intra-industry trade** international trade of goods within the same industry

**splitting up the value chain** many of the different stages of producing a good happen in different geographic locations

**tariffs** taxes that governments place on imported goods

**value chain** how a good is produced in stages

## Key Concepts and Summary

### 19.1 Absolute and Comparative Advantage

A country has an absolute advantage in those products in which it has a productivity edge over other countries; it takes fewer resources to produce a product. A country has a comparative advantage when it can produce a good at a lower cost in terms of other goods. Countries that specialize based on comparative advantage gain from trade.

### 19.2 What Happens When a Country Has an Absolute Advantage in All Goods

Even when a country has high levels of productivity in all goods, it can still benefit from trade. Gains from trade come about as a result of comparative advantage. By specializing in a good that it gives up the least to produce, a country can produce more and offer that additional output for sale. If other countries specialize in the area of their comparative advantage as well and trade, the highly productive country is able to benefit from a lower opportunity cost of production in other countries.

### 19.3 Intra-industry Trade between Similar Economies

A large share of global trade happens between high-income economies that are quite similar in having well-educated workers and advanced technology. These countries practice intra-industry trade, in which they import and export the same products at the same time, like cars, machinery, and computers. In the case of intra-industry trade between economies with similar income levels, the gains from trade come from specialized learning in very particular tasks and from economies of scale. Splitting up the value chain means that several stages of producing a good take place in different countries around the world.

### 19.4 The Benefits of Reducing Barriers to International Trade

Tariffs are placed on imported goods as a way of protecting sensitive industries, for humanitarian reasons, and for protection against dumping. Traditionally, tariffs were used as a political tool to protect certain vested economic, social, and cultural interests. The WTO has been, and continues to be, a way for nations to meet and negotiate in order to reduce barriers to trade. The gains of international trade are very large, especially for smaller countries, but are beneficial to all.

## Self-Check Questions

1. True or False: The source of comparative advantage must be natural elements like climate and mineral deposits. Explain.

2. Brazil can produce 100 pounds of beef or 10 autos. In contrast the United States can produce 40 pounds of beef or 30 autos. Which country has the absolute advantage in beef? Which country has the absolute advantage in producing autos? What is the opportunity cost of producing one pound of beef in Brazil? What is the opportunity cost of producing one pound of beef in the United States?

3. In France it takes one worker to produce one sweater, and one worker to produce one bottle of wine. In Tunisia it takes two workers to produce one sweater, and three workers to produce one bottle of wine. Who has the absolute advantage in production of sweaters? Who has the absolute advantage in the production of wine? How can you tell?

4. In Germany it takes three workers to make one television and four workers to make one video camera. In Poland it takes six workers to make one television and 12 workers to make one video camera.
   a. Who has the absolute advantage in the production of televisions? Who has the absolute advantage in the production of video cameras? How can you tell?
   b. Calculate the opportunity cost of producing one additional television set in Germany and in Poland. (Your calculation may involve fractions, which is fine.) Which country has a comparative advantage in the production of televisions?
   c. Calculate the opportunity cost of producing one video camera in Germany and in Poland. Which country has a comparative advantage in the production of video cameras?
   d. In this example, is absolute advantage the same as comparative advantage, or not?
   e. In what product should Germany specialize? In what product should Poland specialize?

5. How can there be any economic gains for a country from both importing and exporting the same good, like cars?

6. Table 19.15 shows how the average costs of production for semiconductors (the "chips" in computer memories) change as the quantity of semiconductors built at that factory increases.
   a. Based on these data, sketch a curve with quantity produced on the horizontal axis and average cost of production on the vertical axis. How does the curve illustrate economies of scale?
   b. If the equilibrium quantity of semiconductors demanded is 90,000, can this economy take full advantage of economies of scale? What about if quantity demanded is 70,000 semiconductors? 50,000 semiconductors? 30,000 semiconductors?
   c. Explain how international trade could make it possible for even a small economy to take full advantage of economies of scale, while also benefiting from competition and the variety offered by several producers.

| Quantity of Semiconductors | Average Total Cost |
| --- | --- |
| 10,000 | $8 each |
| 20,000 | $5 each |
| 30,000 | $3 each |
| 40,000 | $2 each |
| 100,000 | $2 each |

**TABLE 19.15**

7. If the removal of trade barriers is so beneficial to international economic growth, why would a nation continue to restrict trade on some imported or exported products?

## Review Questions

8. What is absolute advantage? What is comparative advantage?

9. Under what conditions does comparative advantage lead to gains from trade?

10. What factors does Paul Krugman identify that supported expanding international trade in the 1800s?

11. Is it possible to have a comparative advantage in the production of a good but not to have an absolute advantage? Explain.

12. How does comparative advantage lead to gains from trade?

13. What is intra-industry trade?

14. What are the two main sources of economic gains from intra-industry trade?

15. What is splitting up the value chain?

16. Are the gains from international trade more likely to be relatively more important to large or small countries?

## Critical Thinking Questions

17. Are differences in geography behind the differences in absolute advantages?

18. Why does the United States not have an absolute advantage in coffee?

19. Look at Exercise 19.2. Compute the opportunity costs of producing sweaters and wine in both France and Tunisia. Who has the lowest opportunity cost of producing sweaters and who has the lowest opportunity cost of producing wine? Explain what it means to have a lower opportunity cost.

20. You just overheard your friend say the following: "Poor countries like Malawi have no absolute advantages. They have poor soil, low investments in formal education and hence low-skill workers, no capital, and no natural resources to speak of. Because they have no advantage, they cannot benefit from trade." How would you respond?

21. Look at Table 19.9. Is there a range of trades for which there will be no gains?

22. You just got a job in Washington, D.C. You move into an apartment with some acquaintances. All your roommates, however, are slackers and do not clean up after themselves. You, on the other hand, can clean faster than each of them. You determine that you are 70% faster at dishes and 10% faster with vacuuming. All of these tasks have to be done daily. Which jobs should you assign to your roommates to get the most free time overall? Assume you have the same number of hours to devote to cleaning. Now, since you are faster, you seem to get done quicker than your roommate. What sorts of problems may this create? Can you imagine a trade-related analogy to this problem?

23. Does intra-industry trade contradict the theory of comparative advantage?

24. Do consumers benefit from intra-industry trade?

25. Why might intra-industry trade seem surprising from the point of view of comparative advantage?

26. In World Trade Organization meetings, what do you think low-income countries lobby for?

27. Why might a low-income country put up barriers to trade, such as tariffs on imports?

28. Can a nation's comparative advantage change over time? What factors would make it change?

# Problems

**29.** France and Tunisia both have Mediterranean climates that are excellent for producing/harvesting green beans and tomatoes. In France it takes two hours for each worker to harvest green beans and two hours to harvest a tomato. Tunisian workers need only one hour to harvest the tomatoes but four hours to harvest green beans. Assume there are only two workers, one in each country, and each works 40 hours a week.
   a. Draw a production possibilities frontier for each country. *Hint:* Remember the production possibility frontier is the maximum that all workers can produce at a unit of time which, in this problem, is a week.
   b. Identify which country has the absolute advantage in green beans and which country has the absolute advantage in tomatoes.
   c. Identify which country has the comparative advantage.
   d. How much would France have to give up in terms of tomatoes to gain from trade? How much would it have to give up in terms of green beans?

**30.** In Japan, one worker can make 5 tons of rubber or 80 radios. In Malaysia, one worker can make 10 tons of rubber or 40 radios.
   a. Who has the absolute advantage in the production of rubber or radios? How can you tell?
   b. Calculate the opportunity cost of producing 80 additional radios in Japan and in Malaysia. (Your calculation may involve fractions, which is fine.) Which country has a comparative advantage in the production of radios?
   c. Calculate the opportunity cost of producing 10 additional tons of rubber in Japan and in Malaysia. Which country has a comparative advantage in producing rubber?
   d. In this example, does each country have an absolute advantage and a comparative advantage in the same good?
   e. In what product should Japan specialize? In what product should Malaysia specialize?

**31.** Review the numbers for Canada and Venezuela from Table 19.12 which describes how many barrels of oil and tons of lumber the workers can produce. Use these numbers to answer the rest of this question.
   a. Draw a production possibilities frontier for each country. Assume there are 100 workers in each country. Canadians and Venezuelans desire both oil and lumber. Canadians want at least 2,000 tons of lumber. Mark a point on their production possibilities where they can get at least 3,000 tons.
   b. Assume that the Canadians specialize completely because they figured out they have a comparative advantage in lumber. They are willing to give up 1,000 tons of lumber. How much oil should they ask for in return for this lumber to be as well off as they were with no trade? How much should they ask for if they want to gain from trading with Venezuela? *Note:* We can think of this "ask" as the relative price or trade price of lumber.
   c. Is the Canadian "ask" you identified in (b) also beneficial for Venezuelans? Use the production possibilities frontier graph for Venezuela to show that Venezuelans can gain from trade.

**32.** In Exercise 19.31, is there an "ask" where Venezuelans may say "no thank you" to trading with Canada?

**33.** From earlier chapters you will recall that technological change shifts the average cost curves. Draw a graph showing how technological change could influence intra-industry trade.

**34.** Consider two countries: South Korea and Taiwan. Taiwan can produce one million mobile phones per day at the cost of $10 per phone and South Korea can produce 50 million mobile phones at $5 per phone. Assume these phones are the same type and quality and there is only one price. What is the minimum price at which both countries will engage in trade?

**35.** If trade increases world GDP by 1% per year, what is the global impact of this increase over 10 years? How does this increase compare to the annual GDP of a country like Sri Lanka? Discuss. *Hint:* To answer this question, here are steps you may want to consider. Go to the World Development Indicators (online) published by the World Bank. Find the current level of World GDP in constant international dollars. Also, find the GDP of Sri Lanka in constant international dollars. Once you have these two numbers, compute the amount the additional increase in global incomes due to trade and compare that number to Sri Lanka's GDP.

# Globalization and Protectionism 20

**FIGURE 20.1 Flat Screen Competition** The market for flat-panel displays in the United States is huge. The manufacturers of flat screens in the United States must compete against manufacturers from around the world. (Credit: modification of "IMG_4674" by "Jemimus"/Flickr Creative Commons, CC BY 2.0)

## CHAPTER OBJECTIVES

In this chapter, you will learn about:

- Protectionism: An Indirect Subsidy from Consumers to Producers
- International Trade and Its Effects on Jobs, Wages, and Working Conditions
- Arguments in Support of Restricting Imports
- How Trade Policy Is Enacted: Globally, Regionally, and Nationally
- The Tradeoffs of Trade Policy

## Introduction to Globalization and Protectionism

 **BRING IT HOME**

### What's the Downside of Protection?

Governments are motivated to limit and alter market outcomes for political or social ends. While governments can limit the rise in prices of some products, they cannot control how much people want to buy or how much firms are willing to sell. The laws of demand and supply still hold. Trade policy is an example where regulations can redirect economic forces, but it cannot stop them from manifesting themselves elsewhere.

Flat-panel displays, the displays for laptop computers, tablets, and flat screen televisions, are an example of such an enduring principle. In the early 1990s, the vast majority of flat-panel displays used in U.S.-manufactured laptops were imported, primarily from Japan. The small but politically powerful U.S. flat-panel-display industry filed a dumping complaint with the Commerce Department. They argued that Japanese firms were selling displays at "less than fair value," which made it difficult for U.S. firms to compete. This argument for trade protection is referred to as anti-dumping. Other arguments for protection in this complaint included national security. After a preliminary determination by the Commerce Department that the Japanese firms were dumping, the U.S. International Trade Commission imposed a 63% dumping margin (or tax) on the import of flat-panel displays. Was this a successful exercise of U.S. trade policy? See what you think after reading the chapter.

The world has become more connected on multiple levels, especially economically. In 1970, imports and exports made up 11% of U.S. GDP, while now they make up 32%. However, the United States, due to its size, is less internationally connected than most countries. For example, according to the World Bank, 97% of Botswana's economic activity is connected to trade. This chapter explores trade policy—the laws and strategies a country uses to regulate international trade. This topic is not without controversy.

As the world has become more globally connected, firms and workers in high-income countries like the United States, Japan, or the nations of the European Union, perceive a competitive threat from firms in medium-income countries like Mexico, China, or South Africa, that have lower costs of living and therefore pay lower wages. Firms and workers in low-income countries fear that they will suffer if they must compete against more productive workers and advanced technology in high-income countries.

On a different tack, some environmentalists worry that multinational firms may evade environmental protection laws by moving their production to countries with loose or nonexistent pollution standards, trading a clean environment for jobs. Some politicians worry that their country may become overly dependent on key imported products, like oil, which in a time of war could threaten national security. All of these fears influence governments to reach the same basic policy conclusion: to protect national interests, whether businesses, jobs, or security, imports of foreign products should be restricted. This chapter analyzes such arguments. First, however, it is essential to learn a few key concepts and understand how the demand and supply model applies to international trade.

## 20.1 Protectionism: An Indirect Subsidy from Consumers to Producers

### LEARNING OBJECTIVES

By the end of this section, you will be able to:

- Explain protectionism and its three main forms
- Analyze protectionism through concepts of demand and supply, noting its effects on equilibrium
- Calculate the effects of trade barriers

When a government legislates policies to reduce or block international trade it is engaging in **protectionism**. Protectionist policies often seek to shield domestic producers and domestic workers from foreign competition. Protectionism takes three main forms: tariffs, import quotas, and nontariff barriers.

Recall from International Trade that tariffs are taxes that governments impose on imported goods and services. This makes imports more expensive for consumers, discouraging imports. For example, in 2018, President Trump increased tariffs on Chinese-manufactured goods by 2–25%, including TVs, monitors, desktop PCs, smartwatches, and many other consumer goods. The intention behind the policy was to shelter U.S. manufacturers from competition, helping companies that operate domestically. China responded with tariffs on American goods, launching a trade war. President Biden retained these tariffs and considered additional ones, but as of August 2022, the administration was considering changes designed to reduce inflation.

Another way to control trade is through **import quotas**, which are numerical limitations on the quantity of products that a country can import. For instance, during the early 1980s, the Reagan Administration imposed a quota on the import of Japanese automobiles. In the 1970s, many developed countries, including the United States, found themselves with declining textile industries. Textile production does not require highly skilled workers, so producers were able to set up lower-cost factories in developing countries. In order to "manage" this loss of jobs and income, the developed countries established an international Multifiber Agreement that essentially divided the market for textile exports between importers and the remaining domestic producers. The agreement, which ran from 1974 to 2004, specified the exact quota of textile imports that each developed country would accept from each low-income country. A similar story exists for sugar imports into the United States, which are still governed by quotas.

**Nontariff barriers** are all the other ways that a nation can draw up rules, regulations, inspections, and paperwork to make it more costly or difficult to import products. A rule requiring certain safety standards can limit imports just as effectively as high tariffs or low import quotas, for instance. There are also nontariff barriers in the form of "rules-of-origin" regulations; these rules describe the "Made in Country X" label as the one in which the last substantial change in the product took place. A manufacturer wishing to evade import restrictions may try to change the production process so that the last big change in the product happens in their own country. For example, certain textiles are made in the United States, shipped to other countries, combined with textiles made in those other countries to make apparel—and then re-exported back to the United States for a final assembly, to escape paying tariffs or to obtain a "Made in the USA" label.

Despite import quotas, tariffs, and nontariff barriers, the share of apparel sold in the United States that is imported rose from about half in 1999 to about three-quarters today. According to the U.S. Bureau of Labor Statistics (BLS), estimated the number of U.S. jobs in textiles and apparel fell 44% from 2007 to 2014, and will fall by another 25% by 2024. Even more U.S. textile industry jobs would have been lost without tariffs. However, domestic jobs that are saved by import quotas come at a cost. Because textile and apparel protectionism adds to the costs of imports, consumers end up paying billions of dollars more for clothing each year.

When the United States eliminates trade barriers in one area, consumers spend the money they save on that product elsewhere in the economy. Thus, while eliminating trade barriers in one sector of the economy will likely result in some job loss in that sector, consumers will spend the resulting savings in other sectors of the economy and hence increase the number of jobs in those other sectors. Of course, workers in some of the poorest countries of the world who would otherwise have jobs producing textiles, would gain considerably if the United States reduced its barriers to trade in textiles. That said, there are good reasons to be wary about reducing barriers to trade. The 2012 and 2013 Bangladeshi fires in textile factories, which resulted in a horrific loss of life, present complications that our simplified analysis in the chapter will not capture.

Realizing the compromises between nations that come about due to trade policy, many countries came together in 1947 to form the General Agreement on Tariffs and Trade (GATT). (We'll cover the GATT in more detail later in the chapter.) This agreement has since been superseded by the **World Trade Organization (WTO)**, whose membership includes about 150 nations and most of the world's economies. It is the primary international mechanism through which nations negotiate their trade rules—including rules about tariffs, quotas, and nontariff barriers. The next section examines the results of such protectionism and develops a simple model to show the impact of trade policy.

## Demand and Supply Analysis of Protectionism

To the non-economist, restricting imports may appear to be nothing more than taking sales from foreign producers and giving them to domestic producers. Other factors are at work, however, because firms do not operate in a vacuum. Instead, firms sell their products either to consumers or to other firms (if they are business suppliers), who are also affected by the trade barriers. A demand and supply analysis of protectionism shows that it is not just a matter of domestic gains and foreign losses, but a policy that imposes substantial domestic costs as well.

Consider two countries, Brazil and the United States, who produce sugar. Each country has a domestic supply and demand for sugar, as Table 20.1 details and Figure 20.2 illustrates. In Brazil, without trade, the equilibrium price of sugar is 12 cents per pound and the equilibrium output is 30 tons. When there is no trade in the United States, the equilibrium price of sugar is 24 cents per pound and the equilibrium quantity is 80 tons. We label these equilibrium points as point E in each part of the figure.

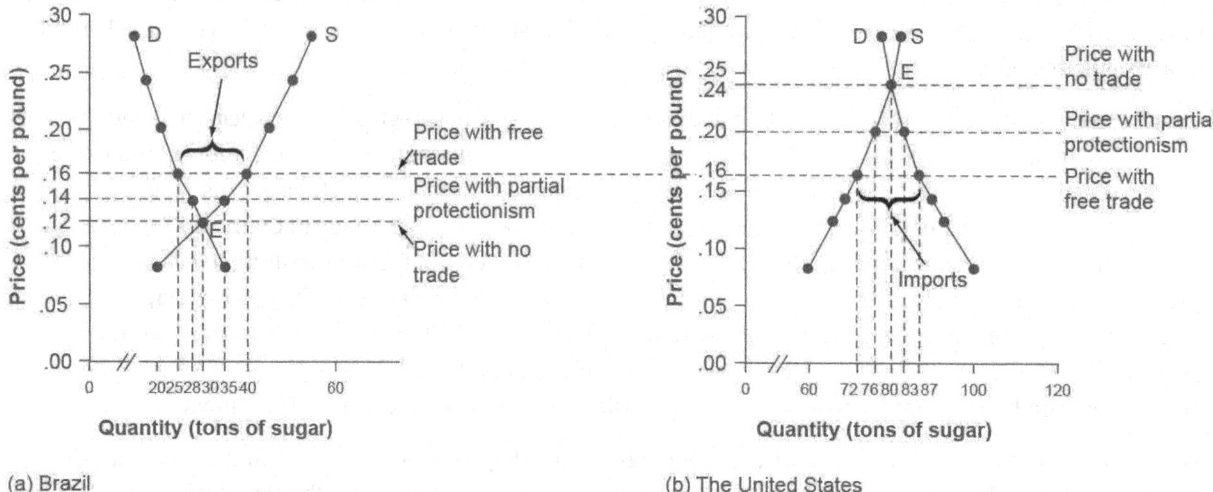


**FIGURE 20.2 The Sugar Trade between Brazil and the United States** Before trade, the equilibrium price of sugar in Brazil is 12 cents a pound and it is 24 cents per pound in the United States. When trade is allowed, businesses will buy cheap sugar in Brazil and sell it in the United States. This will result in higher prices in Brazil and lower prices in the United States. Ignoring transaction costs, prices should converge to 16 cents per pound, with Brazil exporting 15 tons of sugar and the United States importing 15 tons of sugar. If trade is only partly open between the countries, it will lead to an outcome between the free-trade and no-trade possibilities.

| Price | Brazil: Quantity Supplied (tons) | Brazil: Quantity Demanded (tons) | U.S.: Quantity Supplied (tons) | U.S.: Quantity Demanded (tons) |
|---|---|---|---|---|
| 8 cents | 20 | 35 | 60 | 100 |
| 12 cents | 30 | 30 | 66 | 93 |
| 14 cents | 35 | 28 | 69 | 90 |
| 16 cents | 40 | 25 | 72 | 87 |
| 20 cents | 45 | 21 | 76 | 83 |
| 24 cents | 50 | 18 | 80 | 80 |
| 28 cents | 55 | 15 | 82 | 78 |

**TABLE 20.1 The Sugar Trade between Brazil and the United States**

If international trade between Brazil and the United States now becomes possible, profit-seeking firms will spot an opportunity: buy sugar cheaply in Brazil, and sell it at a higher price in the United States. As sugar is shipped from Brazil to the United States, the quantity of sugar produced in Brazil will be greater than Brazilian consumption (with the extra production exported), and the amount produced in the United States will be less than the amount of U.S. consumption (with the extra consumption imported). Exports to the United States will reduce the sugar supply in Brazil, raising its price. Imports into the United States will increase the sugar supply, lowering its price. When the sugar price is the same in both countries, there is no incentive to trade further. As Figure 20.2 shows, the equilibrium with trade occurs at a price of 16 cents per pound. At that price, the sugar farmers of Brazil supply a quantity of 40 tons, while the consumers of Brazil buy only 25 tons.

The extra 15 tons of sugar production, shown by the horizontal gap between the demand curve and the supply curve in Brazil, is exported to the United States. In the United States, at a price of 16 cents, the farmers produce a quantity of 72 tons and consumers demand a quantity of 87 tons. The excess demand of 15 tons by American consumers, shown by the horizontal gap between demand and domestic supply at the price of 16 cents, is supplied by imported sugar. Free trade typically results in income distribution effects, but the key is to recognize the overall gains from trade, as Figure 20.3 shows. Building on the concepts that we outlined in Demand and Supply and Demand, Supply, and Efficiency in terms of consumer and producer surplus, Figure 20.3 (a) shows that producers in Brazil gain by selling more sugar at a higher price, while Figure 20.3 (b) shows consumers in the United States benefit from the lower price and greater availability of sugar. Consumers in Brazil are worse off (compare their no-trade consumer surplus with the free-trade consumer surplus) and U.S. producers of sugar are worse off. There are gains from trade—an increase in social surplus in each country. That is, both the United States and Brazil are better off than they would be without trade. The following Clear It Up feature explains how trade policy can influence low-income countries.

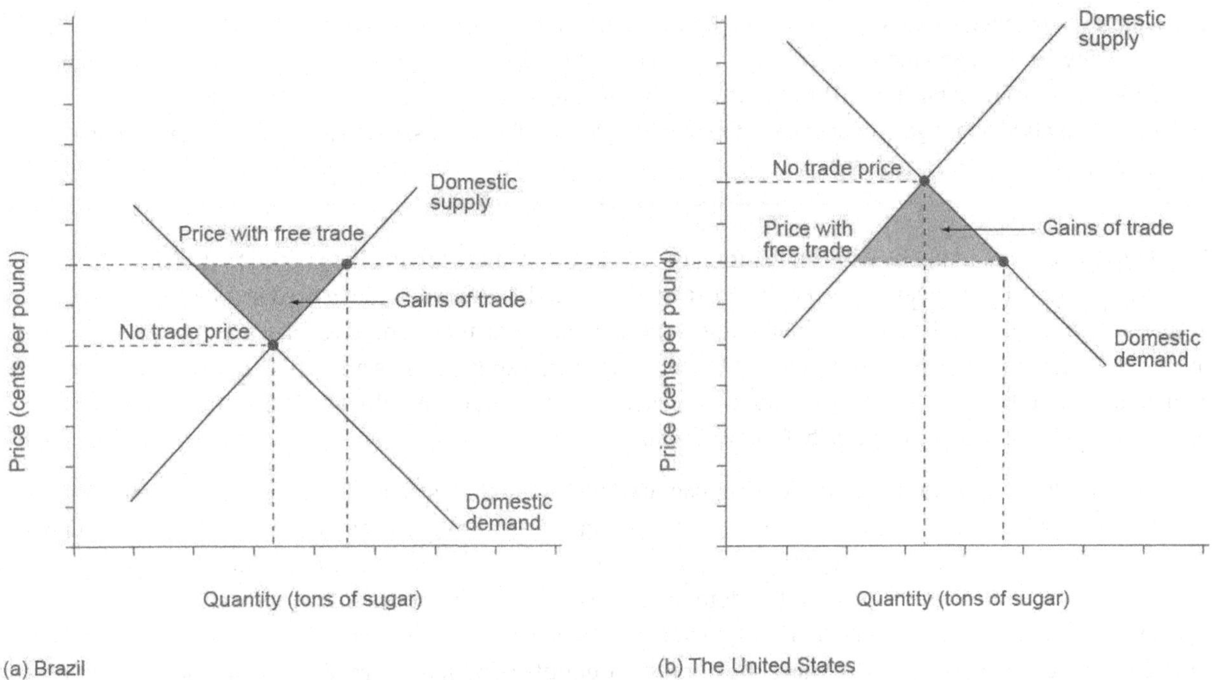


**FIGURE 20.3 Free Trade of Sugar** Free trade results in gains from trade. Total surplus increases in both countries, as the two blue-shaded areas show. However, there are clear income distribution effects. Producers gain in the exporting country, while consumers lose; and in the importing country, consumers gain and producers lose.

## ⊘ LINK IT UP

Visit this website (http://openstax.org/l/sugartrade) to read more about the global sugar trade.

   **CLEAR IT UP**

## Why are there low-income countries?

Why are the poor countries of the world poor? There are a number of reasons, but one of them will surprise you: the trade policies of the high-income countries. Following is a stark review of social priorities which the international aid organization, Oxfam International has widely publicized.

High-income countries of the world—primarily the United States, countries of the European Union, and Japan—subsidize their domestic farmers collectively by about $200 billion per year. Why does this matter?

It matters because the support of farmers in high-income countries is devastating to the livelihoods of farmers in low-income countries. Even when their climate and land are well-suited to products like cotton, rice, sugar, or milk, farmers in low-income countries find it difficult to compete. Farm subsidies in the high-income countries cause farmers in those countries to increase the amount they produce. This increase in supply drives down world prices of farm products below the costs of production. As Michael Gerson of the *Washington Post* describes it: "[T]he effects in the cotton-growing regions of West Africa are dramatic . . . keep[ing] millions of Africans on the edge of malnutrition. In some of the poorest countries on Earth, cotton farmers are some of the poorest people, earning about a dollar a day. . . . Who benefits from the current system of subsidies? About 20,000 American cotton producers, with an average annual income of more than $125,000."

As if subsidies were not enough, often, the high-income countries block agricultural exports from low-income countries. In some cases, the situation gets even worse when the governments of high-income countries, having bought and paid for an excess supply of farm products, give away those products in poor countries and drive local farmers out of business altogether.

For example, shipments of excess milk from the European Union to Jamaica have caused great hardship for Jamaican dairy farmers. Shipments of excess rice from the United States to Haiti drove thousands of low-income rice farmers in Haiti out of business. The opportunity costs of protectionism are not paid just by domestic consumers, but also by foreign producers—and for many agricultural products, those foreign producers are the world's poor.

---

Now, let's look at what happens with protectionism. U.S. sugar farmers are likely to argue that, if only they could be protected from sugar imported from Brazil, the United States would have higher domestic sugar production, more jobs in the sugar industry, and American sugar farmers would receive a higher price. If the United States government sets a high-enough tariff on imported sugar, or sets an import quota at zero, the result will be that the quantity of sugar traded between countries could be reduced to zero, and the prices in each country will return to the levels before trade was allowed.

Blocking only some trade is also possible. Suppose that the United States passed a sugar import quota of seven tons. The United States will import no more than seven tons of sugar, which means that Brazil can export no more than seven tons of sugar to the United States. As a result, the price of sugar in the United States will be 20 cents, which is the price where the quantity demanded is seven tons greater than the domestic quantity supplied. Conversely, if Brazil can export only seven tons of sugar, then the price of sugar in Brazil will be 14 cents per pound, which is the price where the domestic quantity supplied in Brazil is seven tons greater than domestic demand.

In general, when a country sets a low or medium tariff or import quota, the equilibrium price and quantity will be somewhere between those that prevail with no trade and those with completely free trade. The following Work It Out explores the impact of these trade barriers.

## Effects of Trade Barriers

Let's look carefully at the effects of tariffs or quotas. If the U.S. government imposes a tariff or quota sufficient to eliminate trade with Brazil, two things occur: U.S. consumers pay a higher price and therefore buy a smaller quantity of sugar. U.S. producers obtain a higher price and they sell a larger quantity of sugar. We can measure the effects of a tariff on producers and consumers in the United States using two concepts that we developed in Demand, Supply, and Efficiency: consumer surplus and producer surplus.

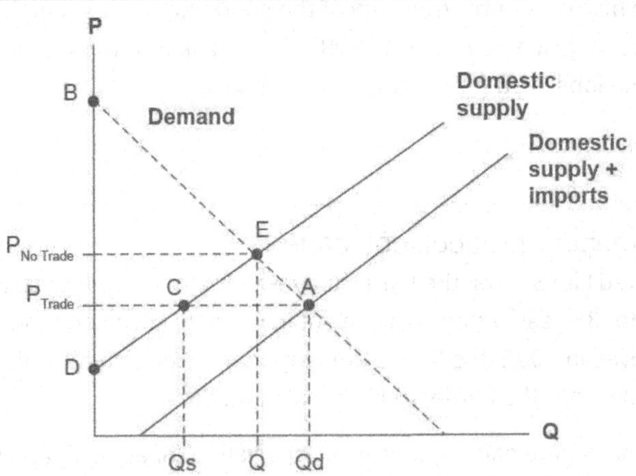


**FIGURE 20.4 U.S. Sugar Supply and Demand** When there is free trade, the equilibrium is at point A. When there is no trade, the equilibrium is at point E.

Step 1. Look at Figure 20.4, which shows a hypothetical version of the demand and supply of sugar in the United States.

Step 2. Note that when there is free trade the sugar market is in equilibrium at point A where Domestic Quantity Demanded (Qd) = Quantity Supplied (Domestic Qs + Imports from Brazil) at a price of $P_{Trade}$.

Step 3. Note, also, that imports are equal to the distance between points C and A.

Step 4. Recall that consumer surplus is the value that consumers get beyond what they paid for when they buy a product. Graphically, it is the area under a demand curve but above the price. In this case, the consumer surplus in the United States is the area of the triangle formed by the points $P_{Trade}$, A, and B.

Step 5. Recall, also, that producer surplus is another name for profit—it is the income producers get above the cost of production, which is shown by the supply curve here. In this case, the producer surplus with trade is the area of the triangle formed by the points $P_{trade}$, C, and D.

Step 6. Suppose that the barriers to trade are imposed, imports are excluded, and the price rises to $P_{NoTrade}$. Look what happens to producer surplus and consumer surplus. At the higher price, the domestic quantity supplied increases from Qs to Q at point E. Because producers are selling more quantity at a higher price, the producer surplus increases to the area of the triangle $P_{NoTrade}$, E, and D.

Step 7. Compare the areas of the two triangles and you will see the increase in the producer surplus.

Step 8. Examine the consumer surplus. Consumers are now paying a higher price to get a lower quantity (Q instead of Qd). Their consumer surplus shrinks to the area of the triangle $P_{NoTrade}$, E, and B.

Step 9. Determine the net effect. The producer surplus increases by the area $P_{trade}$, C, E, $P_{NoTrade}$. The loss of consumer surplus, however, is larger. It is the area $P_{trade}$, A, E, $P_{NoTrade}$. In other words, consumers lose more than producers gain as a result of the trade barriers and the United States has a lower social surplus.

## Who Benefits and Who Pays?

Using the demand and supply model, consider the impact of protectionism on producers and consumers in each of the two countries. For protected producers like U.S. sugar farmers, restricting imports is clearly positive. Without a need to face imported products, these producers are able to sell more, at a higher price. For consumers in the country with the protected good, in this case U.S. sugar consumers, restricting imports is clearly negative. They end up buying a lower quantity of the good and paying a higher price for what they do buy, compared to the equilibrium price and quantity with trade. The following Clear It Up feature considers why a country might outsource jobs even for a domestic product.

 **CLEAR IT UP**

### Why are Life Savers, an American product, not made in America?

In 1912, Clarence Crane invented Life Savers, the hard candy with the hole in the middle, in Cleveland, Ohio. Starting in the late 1960s and for 35 years afterward, a plant in Holland, Michigan produced 46 billion Life Savers a year, in 200 million rolls. However, in 2002, the Kraft Company announced that it would close the Michigan plant and move Life Saver production across the border to Montreal, Canada.

One reason is that Canadian workers are paid slightly less, especially in healthcare and insurance costs that are not linked to employment there. Another main reason is that the United States government keeps the sugar price high for the benefit of sugar farmers, with a combination of a government price floor program and strict quotas on imported sugar. In recent years, the price of U.S. sugar has been about double the price of sugar produced by the rest of the world. Life Saver production uses over 100 tons of sugar each day, because the candies are 95% sugar.

A number of other candy companies have also reduced U.S. production and expanded foreign production. Sugar-using industries have eliminated over 100,000 jobs over the last 20 years, more than seven times the total employment in sugar production. While the candy industry is especially affected by the cost of sugar, the costs are spread more broadly. U.S. consumers pay roughly $1 billion per year in higher food prices because of elevated sugar costs. Meanwhile, sugar producers in low-income countries are driven out of business. Because of the sugar subsidies to domestic producers and the quotas on imports, they cannot sell their output profitably, or at all, in the United States market.

The fact that protectionism pushes up prices for consumers in the country enacting such protectionism is not always acknowledged openly, but it is not disputed. After all, if protectionism did not benefit domestic producers, there would not be much point in enacting such policies in the first place. Protectionism is simply a method of requiring consumers to subsidize producers. The subsidy is indirect, since consumers pay for it through higher prices, rather than a direct government subsidy paid with money collected from taxpayers. However, protectionism works like a subsidy, nonetheless. The American satirist Ambrose Bierce defined "tariff" this way in his 1911 book, *The Devil's Dictionary*: "Tariff, n. A scale of taxes on imports, designed to protect the domestic producer against the greed of his consumer."

The effect of protectionism on producers and consumers in the foreign country is complex. When a government uses an import quota to impose partial protectionism, Brazilian sugar producers receive a lower price for the sugar they sell in Brazil—but a higher price for the sugar they are allowed to export to the United States. Notice that some of the burden of protectionism, paid by domestic consumers, ends up in the hands of foreign producers in this case. Brazilian sugar consumers seem to benefit from U.S. protectionism, because it reduces the price of sugar that they pay (compared to the free-trade situation). On the other hand, at least some of these Brazilian sugar consumers also work as sugar farmers, so protectionism reduces their incomes and jobs. Moreover, if trade between the countries vanishes, Brazilian consumers would miss out on better prices for imported goods—which do not appear in our single-market example of sugar protectionism.

The effects of protectionism on foreign countries notwithstanding, protectionism requires domestic consumers of a product (consumers may include either households or other firms) to pay higher prices to benefit domestic producers of that product. In addition, when a country enacts protectionism, it loses the economic gains it would have been able to achieve through a combination of comparative advantage, specialized learning, and economies of scale, concepts that we discuss in International Trade.

## 20.2 International Trade and Its Effects on Jobs, Wages, and Working Conditions

### LEARNING OBJECTIVES

By the end of this section, you will be able to:

- Discuss how international trade influences the job market
- Analyze the opportunity cost of protectionism
- Explain how international trade impacts wages, labor standards, and working conditions

In theory at least, imports might injure workers in several different ways: fewer jobs, lower wages, or poor working conditions. Let's consider these in turn.

### Fewer Jobs?

In the early 1990s, the United States was negotiating the North American Free Trade Agreement (NAFTA)[1] with Mexico, an agreement that reduced tariffs, import quotas, and nontariff barriers to trade between the United States, Mexico, and Canada. H. Ross Perot, a 1992 candidate for U.S. president, claimed, in prominent campaign arguments, that if the United States expanded trade with Mexico, there would be a "giant sucking sound" as U.S. employers relocated to Mexico to take advantage of lower wages. After all, average wages in Mexico were, at that time, about one-eighth of those in the United States. NAFTA passed Congress, President Bill Clinton signed it into law, and it took effect in 1995. For the next six years, the United States economy had some of the most rapid job growth and low unemployment in its history. Those who feared that open trade with Mexico would lead to a dramatic decrease in jobs were proven wrong.

This result was no surprise to economists. After all, the trend toward globalization has been going on for decades, not just since NAFTA. If trade reduced the number of available jobs, then the United States should have been seeing a steady loss of jobs for decades. While the United States economy does experience rises and falls in unemployment rates, the number of jobs is not falling over extended periods of time. The number of U.S. jobs rose from 71 million in 1970 to 150 million in 2021.

Protectionism certainly saves jobs in the specific industry being protected but, for two reasons, it costs jobs in other unprotected industries. First, if consumers are paying higher prices to the protected industry, they inevitably have less money to spend on goods from other industries, and so jobs are lost in those other industries. Second, if a firm sells the protected product to other firms, so that other firms must now pay a higher price for a key input, then those firms will lose sales to foreign producers who do not need to pay the higher price. Lost sales translate into lost jobs. The hidden opportunity cost of using protectionism to save jobs in one industry is jobs sacrificed in other industries. This is why the United States International Trade Commission, in its study of barriers to trade, predicts that reducing trade barriers would not lead to an overall loss of jobs. Protectionism reshuffles jobs from industries without import protections to industries that are protected from imports, but it does not create more jobs.

Moreover, the costs of saving jobs through protectionism can be very high. A number of different studies have attempted to estimate the cost to consumers in higher prices per job saved through protectionism. Table 20.2 shows a sample of results, compiled by economists at the Federal Reserve Bank of Dallas. Saving a job through

---

1   As of July 1, 2020, NAFTA was officially replaced with the United States-Mexico-Canada (USMCA) free trade agreement. It is broadly similar to the original NAFTA.

protectionism typically costs much more than the actual worker's salary. For example, a study published in 2002 compiled evidence that using protectionism to save an average job in the textile and apparel industry would cost $199,000 per job saved. In other words, those workers could have been paid $100,000 per year to be unemployed and the cost would only be half of what it is to keep them working in the textile and apparel industry. This result is not unique to textiles and apparel.

| Industry Protected with Import Tariffs or Quotas | Annual Cost per Job Saved |
| --- | --- |
| Sugar | $826,000 |
| Polyethylene resins | $812,000 |
| Dairy products | $685,000 |
| Frozen concentrated orange juice | $635,000 |
| Ball bearings | $603,000 |
| Machine tools | $479,000 |
| Women's handbags | $263,000 |
| Glassware | $247,000 |
| Apparel and textiles | $199,000 |
| Rubber footwear | $168,000 |
| Women's nonathletic footwear | $139,000 |

**TABLE 20.2** Cost to U.S. Consumers of Saving a Job through Protectionism
(Source: Federal Reserve Bank of Dallas)

Why does it cost so much to save jobs through protectionism? The basic reason is that not all of the extra money that consumers pay because of tariffs or quotas goes to save jobs. For example, if the government imposes tariffs on steel imports so that steel buyers pay a higher price, U.S. steel companies earn greater profits, buy more equipment, pay bigger bonuses to managers, give pay raises to existing employees—and also avoid firing some additional workers. Only part of the higher price of protected steel goes toward saving jobs. Also, when an industry is protected, the economy as a whole loses the benefits of playing to its comparative advantage—in other words, producing what it is best at. Therefore, part of the higher price that consumers pay for protected goods is lost economic efficiency, which we can measure as another deadweight loss, like what we discussed in Labor and Financial Markets.

There's a bumper sticker that speaks to the threat some U.S. workers feel from imported products: "Buy American—Save U.S. Jobs." If an economist were driving the car, the sticker might declare: "Block Imports—Save Jobs for Some Americans, Lose Jobs for Other Americans, and Also Pay High Prices."

## Trade and Wages

Even if trade does not reduce the number of jobs, it could affect wages. Here, it is important to separate issues about the average level of wages from issues about whether the wages of certain workers may be helped or hurt by trade.

Because trade raises the amount that an economy can produce by letting firms and workers play to their comparative advantage, trade will also cause the average level of wages in an economy to rise. Workers who can produce more will be more desirable to employers, which will shift the demand for their labor out to the right, and increase wages in the labor market. By contrast, barriers to trade will reduce the average level of wages in an economy.

However, even if trade increases the overall wage level, it will still benefit some workers and hurt others. Workers in industries that are confronted by competition from imported products may find that demand for their labor decreases and shifts back to the left, so that their wages decline with a rise in international trade. Conversely, workers in industries that benefit from selling in global markets may find that demand for their labor shifts out to the right, so that trade raises their wages.

## ⊘ LINK IT UP

View this website (http://openstax.org/l/fairtradecoffee) to read an article on the issues surrounding fair trade coffee.

---

One concern is that while globalization may be benefiting high-skilled, high-wage workers in the United States, it may also impose costs on low-skilled, low-wage workers. After all, high-skilled U.S. workers presumably benefit from increased sales of sophisticated products like computers, machinery, and pharmaceuticals in which the United States has a comparative advantage. Meanwhile, low-skilled U.S. workers must now compete against extremely low-wage workers worldwide for making simpler products like toys and clothing. As a result, the wages of low-skilled U.S. workers are likely to fall. There are, however, a number of reasons to believe that while globalization has helped some U.S. industries and hurt others, it has not focused its negative impact on the wages of low-skilled Americans. First, about half of U.S. trade is intra-industry trade. That means the U.S. trades similar goods with other high-wage economies like Canada, Japan, Germany, and the United Kingdom. For instance, in 2014 the U.S. exported over 2 million cars, from all the major automakers, and also imported several million cars from other countries.

Most U.S. workers in these industries have above-average skills and wages—and many of them do quite well in the world of globalization. Some evidence suggested that intra-industry trade between similar countries had a small impact on domestic workers but later evidence indicates that it all depends on how flexible the labor market is. In other words, the key is how flexible workers are in finding jobs in different industries. The effect of trade on low-wage workers depends considerably on the structure of labor markets and indirect effects felt in other parts of the economy. For example, in the United States and the United Kingdom, because labor market frictions are low, the impact of trade on low income workers is small.

Second, many low-skilled U.S. workers hold service jobs that imports from low-wage countries cannot replace. For example, we cannot import lawn care services or moving and hauling services or hotel maids from countries long distances away like China or Bangladesh. Competition from imported products is not the primary determinant of their wages.

Finally, while the focus of the discussion here is on wages, it is worth pointing out that low-wage U.S. workers suffer due to protectionism in all the industries—even those in which they do not work. For example, food and clothing are protected industries. These low-wage workers therefore pay higher prices for these basic necessities and as such their dollar stretches over fewer goods.

The benefits and costs of increased trade in terms of its effect on wages are not distributed evenly across the economy. However, the growth of international trade has helped to raise the productivity of U.S. workers as a whole—and thus helped to raise the average level of wages.

## Labor Standards and Working Conditions

Workers in many low-income countries around the world labor under conditions that would be illegal for a worker in the United States. Workers in countries like China, Thailand, Brazil, South Africa, and Poland are often paid less than the United States minimum wage. For example, in the United States, the national minimum wage is $7.25 per hour. A typical wage in many low-income countries might be more like $7.25 per day, or often much less. Moreover, working conditions in low-income countries may be extremely unpleasant, or even unsafe. In the worst cases, production may involve the child labor or even workers who are mistreated, abused, or entrapped in their jobs. These concerns over foreign labor standards do not affect most of U.S. trade, which is intra-industry and carried out with other high-income countries that have labor standards similar to the United States, but it is, nonetheless, morally and economically important.

In thinking about labor standards in other countries, it is important to draw some distinctions between what is truly unacceptable and what is painful to think about. Most people, economists included, have little difficulty with the idea that production by six-year-olds confined in factories, by people who are abused or mistreated, or by slave labor is morally unacceptable. They would support aggressive efforts to eliminate such practices—including shutting out imported products made with such labor. Many cases, however, are less clear-cut. An opinion article in the *New York Times* several years ago described the case of Ahmed Zia, a 14-year-old boy from Pakistan. He earned $2 per day working in a carpet factory. He dropped out of school in second grade. Should the United States and other countries refuse to purchase rugs made by Ahmed and his co-workers? If the carpet factories were to close, the likely alternative job for Ahmed is farm work, and as Ahmed says of his carpet-weaving job: "This makes much more money and is more comfortable."

Other workers may have even less attractive alternative jobs, perhaps scavenging garbage or prostitution. The real problem for Ahmed and many others in low-income countries is not that globalization has made their lives worse, but rather that they have so few good life alternatives. The United States went through similar situations during the nineteenth and early twentieth centuries.

In closing, there is some irony when the United States government or U.S. citizens take issue with labor standards in low-income countries, because the United States is not a world leader in government laws to protect employees. According to a recent study by the Organization for Economic Cooperation and Development (OECD), the U.S. is the only one of 41 countries that does not provide mandated paid leave for new parents, and among the 40 countries that do mandate paid leave, the minimum duration is about two months. Many European workers receive six weeks or more of paid vacation per year. In the United States, vacations are often one to three weeks per year. If European countries accused the United States of using unfair labor standards to make U.S. products cheaply, and announced that they would shut out all U.S. imports until the United States adopted paid parental leave, added more national holidays, and doubled vacation time, Americans would be outraged. Yet when U.S. protectionists start talking about restricting imports from poor countries because of low wage levels and poor working conditions, they are making a very similar argument. This is not to say that labor conditions in low-income countries are not an important issue. They are. However, linking labor conditions in low-income countries to trade deflects the emphasis from the real question to ask: "What are acceptable and enforceable minimum labor standards and protections to have the world over?"

## 20.3 Arguments in Support of Restricting Imports

### LEARNING OBJECTIVES

By the end of this section, you will be able to:
- Explain and analyze various arguments that are in support of restricting imports, including the infant industry argument, the anti-dumping argument, the environmental protection argument, the unsafe consumer products argument, and the national interest argument
- Explain dumping and race to the bottom
- Evaluate the significance of countries' perceptions on the benefits of growing trade

As we previously noted, protectionism requires domestic consumers of a product to pay higher prices to benefit domestic producers of that product. Countries that institute protectionist policies lose the economic gains achieved through a combination of comparative advantage, specialized learning, and economies of scale. With these overall costs in mind, let us now consider, one by one, a number of arguments that support restricting imports.

## The Infant Industry Argument

Imagine Bhutan wants to start its own computer industry, but it has no computer firms that can produce at a low enough price and high enough quality to compete in world markets. However, Bhutanese politicians, business leaders, and workers hope that if the local industry had a chance to get established, before it needed to face international competition, then a domestic company or group of companies could develop the skills, management, technology, and economies of scale that it needs to become a successful profit-earning domestic industry. Thus, the infant industry argument for protectionism is to block imports for a limited time, to give the infant industry time to mature, before it starts competing on equal terms in the global economy. (Revisit Macroeconomic Policy Around the World (http://openstax.org/books/principles-economics-3e/pages/32-introduction-to-macroeconomic-policy-around-the-world) for more information on the infant industry argument.)

The infant industry argument is theoretically possible, even sensible: give an industry a short-term indirect subsidy through protection, and then reap the long-term economic benefits of having a vibrant, healthy industry. Implementation, however, is tricky. In many countries, infant industries have gone from babyhood to senility and obsolescence without ever having reached the profitable maturity stage. Meanwhile, the protectionism that was supposed to be short-term often took a very long time to be repealed.

As one example, Brazil treated its computer industry as an infant industry from the late 1970s until about 1990. In an attempt to establish its computer industry in the global economy, Brazil largely barred imports of computer products for several decades. This policy guaranteed increased sales for Brazilian computers. However, by the mid-1980s, due to lack of international competition, Brazil had a backward and out-of-date industry, typically lagging behind world standards for price and performance by three to five years—a long time in this fast-moving industry. After more than a decade, during which Brazilian consumers and industries that would have benefited from up-to-date computers paid the costs and Brazil's computer industry never competed effectively on world markets, Brazil phased out its infant industry policy for the computer industry.

Protectionism for infant industries always imposes costs on domestic users of the product, and typically has provided little benefit in the form of stronger, competitive industries. However, several countries in East Asia offer an exception. Japan, Korea, Thailand, and other countries in this region have sometimes provided a package of indirect and direct subsidies targeted at certain industries, including protection from foreign competition and government loans at interest rates below the market equilibrium. In Japan and Korea, for example, subsidies helped get their domestic steel and auto industries up and running.

Why did the infant industry policy of protectionism and other subsidies work fairly well in East Asia? An early 1990 World Bank study offered three guidelines to countries thinking about infant industry protection:

1. Do not hand out protectionism and other subsidies to all industries, but focus on a few industries where your country has a realistic chance to be a world-class producer.
2. Be very hesitant about using protectionism in areas like computers, where many other industries rely on having the best products available, because it is not useful to help one industry by imposing high costs on many other industries.
3. Have clear guidelines for when the infant industry policy will end.

In Korea in the 1970s and 1980s, a common practice was to link protectionism and subsidies to export sales in global markets. If export sales rose, then the infant industry had succeeded and the government could phase out protectionism. If export sales did not rise, then the infant industry policy had failed and the government could phase out protectionism. Either way, the protectionism would be temporary.

Following these rules is easier said than done. Politics often intrudes, both in choosing which industries will receive the benefits of treatment as "infants" and when to phase out import restrictions and other subsidies. Also, if the country's government wishes to impose costs on its citizens so that it can provide subsidies to a few key industries, it has many tools for doing such as direct government payments, loans, targeted tax reductions, and government support of research and development of new technologies. In other words, protectionism is not the only or even the best way to support key industries.

## 🔗 LINK IT UP

Visit this website (http://openstax.org/l/integration) to view a presentation by Pankaj Ghemawat questioning how integrated the world really is.

---

## The Anti-Dumping Argument

**Dumping** refers to selling goods below their cost of production. **Anti-dumping laws** block imports that are sold below the cost of production by imposing tariffs that increase the price of these imports to reflect their cost of production. Since dumping is not allowed under World Trade Organization (WTO) rules, nations that believe they are on the receiving end of dumped goods can file a complaint with the WTO. According to the WTO, between 1995 and 2020, it oversaw 137 anti-dumping disputes. Note that dumping cases are countercyclical. During recessions, case filings increase. During economic booms, case filings go down. Individual countries have also frequently started their own anti-dumping investigations. The U.S. government has dozens of anti-dumping orders in place from past investigations. In 2022, for example, some U.S. imports that were under anti-dumping orders included olives from Spain, steel from South Korea, coated paper from Indonesia, light commercial vehicles from Germany and Italy, fish fillets from Vietnam, and cellulose pulp from Canada.

### Why Might Dumping Occur?

Why would foreign firms export a product at less than its cost of production—which presumably means taking a loss? This question has two possible answers, one innocent and one more sinister.

The innocent explanation is that demand and supply set market prices, not the cost of production. Perhaps demand for a product shifts back to the left or supply shifts out to the right, which drives the market price to low levels—even below the cost of production. When a local store has a going-out-of-business sale, for example, it may sell goods at below the cost of production. If international companies find that there is excess supply of steel or computer chips or machine tools that is driving the market price down below their cost of production—this may be the market in action.

The sinister explanation is that dumping is part of a long-term strategy. Foreign firms sell goods at prices below the cost of production for a short period of time, and when they have driven out the domestic U.S. competition, they then raise prices. Economists sometimes call this scenario predatory pricing, which we discuss in the Monopoly chapter.

### Should Anti-Dumping Cases Be Limited?

Anti-dumping cases pose two questions. How much sense do they make in economic theory? How much sense do they make as practical policy?

In terms of economic theory, the case for anti-dumping laws is weak. In a market governed by demand and supply, the government does not guarantee that firms will be able to make a profit. After all, low prices are difficult for producers, but benefit consumers. Moreover, although there are plenty of cases in which foreign producers have driven out domestic firms, there are zero documented cases in which the foreign producers then jacked up prices. Instead, foreign producers typically continue competing hard against each other and providing low prices to consumers. In short, it is difficult to find evidence of predatory pricing by foreign firms exporting to the United States.

Even if one could make a case that the government should sometimes enact anti-dumping rules in the short term, and then allow free trade to resume shortly thereafter, there is a growing concern that anti-dumping investigations often involve more politics than careful analysis. The U.S. Commerce Department is charged with calculating the appropriate "cost of production," which can be as much an art as a science.

For example, if a company built a new factory two years ago, should it count part of the factory's cost in this year's cost of production? When a company is in a country where the government controls prices, like China for example, how can one measure the true cost of production? When a domestic industry complains loudly enough, government regulators seem very likely to find that unfair dumping has occurred. A common pattern has arisen where a domestic industry files an anti-dumping complaint, the governments meet and negotiate a reduction in imports, and then the domestic producers drop the anti-dumping suit. In such cases, anti-dumping cases often appear to be little more than a cover story for imposing tariffs or import quotas.

In the 1980s, the United States, Canada, the European Union, Australia, and New Zealand implemented almost all the anti-dumping cases. By the 2000s, countries like Argentina, Brazil, South Korea, South Africa, Mexico, and India were filing the majority of the anti-dumping cases before the WTO. As the number of anti-dumping cases has increased, and as countries such as the United States and the European Union feel targeted by the anti-dumping actions of others, the WTO may well propose some additional guidelines to limit the reach of anti-dumping laws.

## The Environmental Protection Argument

The potential for global trade to affect the environment has become controversial. A president of the Sierra Club, an environmental lobbying organization, once wrote: "The consequences of globalization for the environment are not good. ... Globalization, if we are lucky, will raise average incomes enough to pay for cleaning up some of the mess that we have made. But before we get there, globalization could also destroy enough of the planet's basic biological and physical systems that prospects for life itself will be radically compromised."

If free trade meant the destruction of life itself, then even economists would convert to protectionism! While globalization—and economic activity of all kinds—can pose environmental dangers, it seems quite possible that, with the appropriate safeguards in place, we can minimize the environmental impacts of trade. In some cases, trade may even bring environmental benefits.

In general, high-income countries such as the United States, Canada, Japan, the United Kingdom, and the nations of the European Union have relatively strict environmental standards. In contrast, middle- and low-income countries like Brazil, Nigeria, India, and China have lower environmental standards. The general view of the governments of such countries is that environmental protection is a luxury: as soon as their people have enough to eat, decent healthcare, and longer life expectancies, then they will spend more money on items such as sewage treatment plants, scrubbers to reduce air pollution from factory smokestacks, and national parks to protect wildlife.

This gap in environmental standards between high-income and low-income countries raises two worrisome possibilities in a world of increasing global trade: the "race to the bottom" scenario and the question of how quickly environmental standards will improve in low-income countries.

### The Race to the Bottom Scenario

The **race to the bottom** scenario of global environmental degradation runs like this. Profit-seeking multinational companies shift their production from countries with strong environmental standards to countries with weak standards, thus reducing their costs and increasing their profits. Faced with such behavior, countries reduce their environmental standards to attract multinational firms, which, after all, provide jobs and economic clout. As a result, global production becomes concentrated in countries where firms can pollute the most and environmental laws everywhere "race to the bottom."

Although the race-to-the-bottom scenario sounds plausible, it does not appear to describe reality. In fact, the financial incentive for firms to shift production to poor countries to take advantage of their weaker environmental rules does not seem especially powerful. When firms decide where to locate a new factory, they look at many different factors: the costs of labor and financial capital; whether the location is close to a reliable suppliers of the inputs that they need; whether the location is close to customers; the quality of transportation, communications, and electrical power networks; the level of taxes; and the competence and honesty of the local government. The cost of environmental regulations is a factor, too, but typically environmental costs are no more than 1 to 2% of the costs that a large industrial plant faces. The other factors that determine location are much more important to these companies than trying to skimp on environmental protection costs.

When an international company does choose to build a plant in a low-income country with lax environmental laws, it typically builds a plant similar to those that it operates in high-income countries with stricter environmental standards. Part of the reason for this decision is that designing an industrial plant is a complex and costly task, and so if a plant works well in a high-income country, companies prefer to use the same design everywhere. Also, companies realize that if they create an environmental disaster in a low-income country, it is likely to cost them a substantial amount of money in paying for damages, lost trust, and reduced sales—by building up-to-date plants everywhere they minimize such risks. As a result of these factors, foreign-owned plants in low-income countries often have a better record of compliance with environmental laws than do locally-owned plants.

**Pressuring Low-Income Countries for Higher Environmental Standards**

In some cases, the issue is not so much whether globalization will pressure low-income countries to reduce their environmental standards, but instead whether the threat of blocking international trade can pressure these countries into adopting stronger standards. For example, restrictions on ivory imports in high-income countries, along with stronger government efforts to catch elephant poachers, have been credited with helping to reduce the illegal poaching of elephants in certain African countries.

However, it would be highly undemocratic for the well-fed citizens of high-income countries to attempt to dictate to the ill-fed citizens of low-income countries what domestic policies and priorities they must adopt, or how they should balance environmental goals against other priorities for their citizens. Furthermore, if high-income countries want stronger environmental standards in low-income countries, they have many options other than the threat of protectionism. For example, high-income countries could pay for anti-pollution equipment in low-income countries, or could help to pay for national parks. High-income countries could help pay for and carry out the scientific and economic studies that would help environmentalists in low-income countries to make a more persuasive case for the economic benefits of protecting the environment.

After all, environmental protection is vital to two industries of key importance in many low-income countries—agriculture and tourism. Environmental advocates can set up standards for labeling products, like "this tuna caught in a net that kept dolphins safe" or "this product made only with wood not taken from rainforests," so that consumer pressure can reinforce environmentalist values. The United Nations also reinforces these values, by sponsoring treaties to address issues such as climate change and global warming, the preservation of biodiversity, the spread of deserts, and the environmental health of the seabed. Countries that share a national border or are within a region often sign environmental agreements about air and water rights, too. The WTO is also becoming more aware of environmental issues and more careful about ensuring that increases in trade do not inflict environmental damage.

Finally, note that these concerns about the race to the bottom or pressuring low-income countries for more strict environmental standards do not apply very well to the roughly half of all U.S. trade that occurs with other high-income countries. Many European countries have stricter environmental standards in certain industries than the United States.

## The Unsafe Consumer Products Argument

One argument for shutting out certain imported products is that they are unsafe for consumers. Consumer rights groups have sometimes warned that the World Trade Organization would require nations to reduce their health and safety standards for imported products. However, the WTO explains its current agreement on the subject in this way: "It allows countries to set their own standards." It also says "regulations must be based on science. . . . And they should not arbitrarily or unjustifiably discriminate between countries where identical or similar conditions prevail." Thus, for example, under WTO rules it is perfectly legitimate for the United States to pass laws requiring that *all* food products or cars sold in the United States meet certain safety standards approved by the United States government, whether or not other countries choose to pass similar standards. However, such standards must have some scientific basis. It is improper to impose one set of health and safety standards for domestically produced goods but a different set of standards for imports, or one set of standards for imports from Europe and a different set of standards for imports from Latin America.

In 2007, Mattel recalled nearly two million toys imported from China due to concerns about high levels of lead in the paint, as well as some loose parts. It is unclear if other toys were subject to similar standards. In 2013, Japan blocked imports of U.S. wheat because of concerns that genetically modified (GMO) wheat might be included in the shipments. The science on the impact of GMOs on health is still developing.

## The National Interest Argument

Some argue that a nation should not depend too heavily on other countries for supplies of certain key products, such as oil, or for special materials or technologies that might have national security applications. On closer consideration, this argument for protectionism proves rather weak.

As an example, in the United States, oil provides about 36% of all the energy and 21% of the oil used in the United States economy is imported. Several times in the last few decades, when disruptions in the Middle East have shifted the supply curve of oil back to the left and sharply raised the price, the effects have been felt across the United States economy. This is not, however, a very convincing argument for restricting oil imports. If the United States needs to be protected from a possible cutoff of foreign oil, then a more reasonable strategy would be to import 100% of the petroleum supply now, and save U.S. domestic oil resources for when or if the foreign supply is cut off. It might also be useful to import extra oil and put it into a stockpile for use in an emergency, as the United States government did by starting a Strategic Petroleum Reserve in 1977. Moreover, it may be necessary to discourage people from using oil, and to start a high-powered program to seek out alternatives to oil. A straightforward way to do this would be to raise taxes on oil. Additionally, it makes no sense to argue that because oil is highly important to the United States economy, then the United States should shut out oil imports and use up its domestic supplies more quickly. U.S. domestic oil production is increasing. Shale oil is adding to domestic supply using fracking extraction techniques.

Whether or not to limit certain kinds of imports of key technologies or materials that might be important to national security and weapons systems is a slightly different issue. If weapons' builders are not confident that they can continue to obtain a key product in wartime, they might decide to avoid designing weapons that use this key product, or they can go ahead and design the weapons and stockpile enough of the key high-tech components or materials to last through an armed conflict. There is a U.S. Defense National Stockpile Center that has built up reserves of many materials, from aluminum oxides, antimony, and bauxite to tungsten, vegetable tannin extracts, and zinc (although many of these stockpiles have been reduced and sold in recent years). Think every country is pro-trade? How about the U.S.? The following Clear It Up might surprise you.

## CLEAR IT UP

### How does the United States really feel about expanding trade?

How do people around the world feel about expanding trade between nations? In summer 2007, the Pew Foundation surveyed 45,000 people in 47 countries. One of the questions asked about opinions on growing trade ties between countries. Table 20.3 shows the percentages who answered either "very good" or "somewhat good" for some of countries surveyed.

For those who think of the United States as the world's leading supporter of expanding trade, the survey results may be perplexing. When adding up the shares of those who say that growing trade ties between countries is "very good" or "somewhat good," Americans had the least favorable attitude toward increasing globalization, while the Chinese and South Africans ranked highest. In fact, among the 47 countries surveyed, the United States ranked by far the lowest on this measure, followed by Egypt, Italy, and Argentina.

| Country | Very Good | Somewhat Good | Total |
| --- | --- | --- | --- |
| China | 38% | 53% | 91% |
| South Africa | 42% | 43% | 87% |
| South Korea | 24% | 62% | 86% |
| Germany | 30% | 55% | 85% |
| Canada | 29% | 53% | 82% |
| United Kingdom | 28% | 50% | 78% |
| Mexico | 22% | 55% | 77% |
| Brazil | 13% | 59% | 72% |
| Japan | 17% | 55% | 72% |
| United States | 14% | 45% | 59% |

**TABLE 20.3 The Status of Growing Trade Ties between Countries** (Source: http://www.pewglobal.org/files/pdf/258.pdf)

One final reason why economists often treat the **national interest argument** skeptically is that lobbyists and politicians can tout almost any product as vital to national security. In 1954, the United States became worried that it was importing half of the wool required for military uniforms, so it declared wool and mohair to be "strategic materials" and began to give subsidies to wool and mohair farmers. Although the government removed wool from the official list of "strategic" materials in 1960, the subsidies for mohair continued for almost 40 years until the government repealed them in 1993, and then reinstated them in 2002. All too often, the national interest argument has become an excuse for handing out the indirect subsidy of protectionism to certain industries or companies. After all, politicians, not nonpartisan analysts make decisions about what constitutes a key strategic material.

## 20.4 How Governments Enact Trade Policy: Globally, Regionally, and Nationally

**LEARNING OBJECTIVES**

By the end of this section, you will be able to:

- Explain the origin and role of the World Trade Organization (WTO) and General Agreement on Tariffs and Trade (GATT)
- Discuss the significance and provide examples of regional trading agreements
- Analyze trade policy at the national level
- Evaluate long-term trends in barriers to trade

These public policy arguments about how nations should react to globalization and trade are fought out at several levels: at the global level through the World Trade Organization and through regional trade agreements between pairs or groups of countries.

## The World Trade Organization

The World Trade Organization (WTO) was officially born in 1995, but its history is much longer. In the years after the Great Depression and World War II, there was a worldwide push to build institutions that would tie the nations of the world together. The United Nations officially came into existence in 1945. The World Bank, which assists the poorest people in the world, and the International Monetary Fund, which addresses issues raised by international financial transactions, were both created in 1946. The third planned organization was to be an International Trade Organization, which would manage international trade. The United Nations was unable to agree to this. Instead, 27 nations signed the **General Agreement on Tariffs and Trade (GATT)** in Geneva, Switzerland on October 30, 1947 to provide a forum in which nations could come together to negotiate reductions in tariffs and other barriers to trade. In 1995, the GATT transformed into the WTO.

The GATT process was to negotiate an agreement to reduce barriers to trade, sign that agreement, pause for a while, and then start negotiating the next agreement. Table 20.4 shows rounds of talks in the GATT, and now the WTO. Notice that the early rounds of GATT talks took a relatively short time, included a small number of countries, and focused almost entirely on reducing tariffs. Since the mid-1960s, however, rounds of trade talks have taken years, included a large number of countries, and have included an ever-broadening range of issues.

| Year | Place or Name of Round | Main Subjects | Number of Countries Involved |
|---|---|---|---|
| 1947 | Geneva | Tariff reduction | 23 |
| 1949 | Annecy | Tariff reduction | 13 |
| 1951 | Torquay | Tariff reduction | 38 |
| 1956 | Geneva | Tariff reduction | 26 |
| 1960–61 | Dillon round | Tariff reduction | 26 |
| 1964–67 | Kennedy round | Tariffs, anti-dumping measures | 62 |
| 1973–79 | Tokyo round | Tariffs, nontariff barriers | 102 |
| 1986–94 | Uruguay round | Tariffs, nontariff barriers, services, intellectual property, dispute settlement, textiles, agriculture, creation of WTO | 123 |
| 2001– | Doha round | Agriculture, services, intellectual property, competition, investment, environment, dispute settlement | 147 |

**TABLE 20.4 The Negotiating Rounds of GATT and the World Trade Organization**

The sluggish pace of GATT negotiations led to an old joke that GATT really stood for Gentleman's Agreement to Talk and Talk. The slow pace of international trade talks, however, is understandable, even sensible. Having dozens of nations agree to any treaty is a lengthy process. GATT often set up separate trading rules for certain industries, like agriculture, and separate trading rules for certain countries, like the low-income countries. There were rules, exceptions to rules, opportunities to opt out of rules, and precise wording to be fought over in every case. Like the GATT before it, the WTO is not a world government, with power to impose its decisions on others. The total staff of the WTO Secretariat in 2021 is 625 people and its annual budget (as of 2020) is $197 million, which makes it smaller in size than many large universities.

## Regional Trading Agreements

There are different types of economic integration across the globe, ranging from **free trade agreements**, in which participants allow each other's imports without tariffs or quotas, to **common markets**, in which participants have a common external trade policy as well as free trade within the group, to full **economic unions**, in which, in addition to a common market, monetary and fiscal policies are coordinated. Many nations belong both to the World Trade Organization and to regional trading agreements.

The best known of these regional trading agreements is the European Union. In the years after World War II, leaders of several European nations reasoned that if they could tie their economies together more closely, they might be more likely to avoid another devastating war. Their efforts began with a free trade association, evolved into a common market, and then transformed into what is now a full economic union, known as the European Union. The EU, as it is often called, has a number of goals. For example, in the early 2000s it introduced a common currency for Europe, the euro, and phased out most of the former national forms of money like the German mark and the French franc, though a few have retained their own currency. Another key element of the union is to eliminate barriers to the mobility of goods, labor, and capital across Europe. In 2016, Britain voted to leave the European Union—a move that was completed in January 2020.

For the United States, perhaps the best-known regional trading agreement is the North American Free Trade Agreement (NAFTA). [2] The United States also participates in some less-prominent regional trading agreements, like the Caribbean Basin Initiative, which offers reduced tariffs for imports from these countries, and a free trade agreement with Israel.

The world has seen a flood of regional trading agreements in recent years. About 100 such agreements are now in place. Table 20.5 lists a few of the more prominent ones. Some are just agreements to continue talking. Others set specific goals for reducing tariffs, import quotas, and nontariff barriers. One economist described the current trade treaties as a "spaghetti bowl," which is what a map with lines connecting all the countries with trade treaties looks like.

There is concern among economists who favor free trade that some of these regional agreements may promise free trade, but actually act as a way for the countries within the regional agreement to try to limit trade from anywhere else. In some cases, the regional trade agreements may even conflict with the broader agreements of the World Trade Organization.

---

2   As of July 1, 2020, NAFTA was officially replaced with the United States-Mexico-Canada (USMCA) free trade agreement. It is broadly similar to the original NAFTA.

| Trade Agreements | Participating Countries |
|---|---|
| Asia Pacific Economic Cooperation (APEC) | Australia, Brunei, Canada, Chile, People's Republic of China, Hong Kong, China, Indonesia, Japan, Republic of Korea, Malaysia, Mexico, New Zealand, Papua New Guinea, Peru, Philippines, Russia, Singapore, Chinese Taipei, Thailand, United States, Vietnam |
| European Union (EU) | Austria, Belgium, Bulgaria, Cyprus, Czech Republic, Denmark, Estonia, Finland, France, Germany, Greece, Hungary, Ireland, Italy, Latvia, Lithuania, Luxembourg, Malta, Netherlands, Poland, Portugal, Romania, Slovakia, Slovenia, Spain, Sweden, United Kingdom* |
| North America Free Trade Agreement (NAFTA) | Canada, Mexico, United States |
| Latin American Integration Association (LAIA) | Argentina, Bolivia, Brazil, Chile, Columbia, Ecuador, Mexico, Paraguay, Peru, Uruguay, Venezuela, Panama |
| Association of Southeast Asian Nations (ASEAN) | Brunei, Cambodia, Indonesia, Laos, Malaysia, Myanmar, Philippines, Singapore, Thailand, Vietnam |
| Southern African Development Community (SADC) | Angola, Botswana, Comoros, Congo, Lesotho, Madagascar, Malawi, Mauritius, Mozambique, Namibia, Seychelles, South Africa, Swaziland, Tanzania, Zambia, Zimbabwe |

**TABLE 20.5 Some Regional Trade Agreements** * Following the 2016 referendum vote to leave the European Union, the UK government triggered the withdrawal process on March 29, 2017, setting the date for the UK to leave by April 2019. In January 2020, the withdrawal was complete and the United Kingdom is now no longer part of the EU trading bloc. Also, as of 2020, NAFTA has been replaced by the United States-Mexico-Canada (USMCA) free trade agreement.

## Trade Policy at the National Level

Yet another dimension of trade policy, along with international and regional trade agreements, happens at the national level. The United States, for example, imposes import quotas on sugar, because of a fear that such imports would drive down the price of sugar and thus injure domestic sugar producers. One of the jobs of the United States Department of Commerce is to determine if there is import dumping from other countries. The United States International Trade Commission—a government agency—determines whether the dumping has substantially injured domestic industries, and if so, the president can impose tariffs that are intended to offset the unfairly low price.

In the arena of trade policy, the battle often seems to be between national laws that increase protectionism and international agreements that try to reduce protectionism, like the WTO. Why would a country pass laws or negotiate agreements to shut out certain foreign products, like sugar or textiles, while simultaneously negotiating to reduce trade barriers in general? One plausible answer is that international trade agreements offer a method for countries to restrain their own special interests. A member of Congress can say to an industry lobbying for tariffs or quotas on imports: "Sure would like to help you, but that pesky WTO agreement just won't let me."

### ⌀ LINK IT UP

If consumers are the biggest losers from trade, why do they not fight back? The quick answer is because it is easier to organize a small group of people around a narrow interest (producers) versus a large group that has diffuse interests (consumers). This is a question about trade policy theory. Visit this website (http://openstax.org/l/tradepolicy) and read the article by Jonathan Rauch.

### Long-Term Trends in Barriers to Trade

In newspaper headlines, trade policy appears mostly as disputes and acrimony. Countries are almost constantly threatening to challenge other nations' "unfair" trading practices. Cases are brought to the dispute settlement procedures of the WTO, the European Union, NAFTA, and other regional trading agreements. Politicians in national legislatures, goaded on by lobbyists, often threaten to pass bills that will "establish a fair playing field" or "prevent unfair trade"—although most such bills seek to accomplish these high-sounding goals by placing more restrictions on trade. Protesters in the streets may object to specific trade rules or to the entire practice of international trade.

Through all the controversy, the general trend in the last 60 years is clearly toward lower barriers to trade. The average level of tariffs on imported products charged by industrialized countries was 40% in 1946. By 1990, after decades of GATT negotiations, it was down to less than 5%. One of the reasons that GATT negotiations shifted from focusing on tariff reduction in the early rounds to a broader agenda was that tariffs had been reduced so dramatically there was not much more to do in that area. U.S. tariffs have followed this general pattern: After rising sharply during the Great Depression, tariffs dropped off to less than 2% by the end of the century. Although measures of import quotas and nontariff barriers are less exact than those for tariffs, they generally appear to be at lower levels than they had been previously, too.

Thus, the last half-century has seen both a dramatic reduction in government-created barriers to trade, such as tariffs, import quotas, and nontariff barriers, and also a number of technological developments that have made international trade easier, like advances in transportation, communication, and information management. The result has been the powerful surge of international trade.

These trends were altered by two important events in 2016: the UK vote to leave the EU and the election of President Trump in the United States, whose administration pursued a policy of raising trade barriers. In 2018, tariffs on a broad range of imports from China were raised by around 25%. As of 2022, the UK has been out of the EU for two years, and it remains unclear if President Biden's administration will adjust or remove President Trump's trade barriers.

## 20.5 The Tradeoffs of Trade Policy

**LEARNING OBJECTIVES**

By the end of this section, you will be able to:

- Asses the complexity of international trade
- Discuss why a market-oriented economy is so affected by international trade
- Explain disruptive market change

Economists readily acknowledge that international trade is not all sunshine, roses, and happy endings. Over time, the average person gains from international trade, both as a worker who has greater productivity and higher wages because of the benefits of specialization and comparative advantage, and as a consumer who can benefit from shopping all over the world for a greater variety of quality products at attractive prices. The "average person," however, is hypothetical, not real—representing a mix of those who have done very well, those who have done all right, and those who have done poorly. It is a legitimate concern of public policy to focus not just on the average or on the success stories, but also on those who have not been so fortunate. Workers in other countries, the environment, and prospects for new industries and materials that might be of key importance to the national economy are also all legitimate issues.

The common belief among economists is that it is better to embrace the gains from trade, and then deal with the costs and tradeoffs with other policy tools, than it is to cut off trade to avoid the costs and tradeoffs.

To gain a better intuitive understanding for this argument, consider a hypothetical American company called Technotron. Technotron invents a new scientific technology that allows the firm to increase the output and quality of its goods with a smaller number of workers at a lower cost. As a result of this technology, other U.S. firms in this industry will lose money and will also have to lay off workers—and some of the competing firms will even go bankrupt. Should the United States government protect the existing firms and their employees by making it illegal for Technotron to use its new technology? Most people who live in market-oriented economies would oppose trying to block better products that lower the cost of services. Certainly, there is a case for society providing temporary support and assistance for those who find themselves without work. Many would argue for government support of programs that encourage retraining and acquiring additional skills. Government might also support research and development efforts, so that other firms may find ways of outdoing Technotron. Blocking the new technology altogether, however, seems like a mistake. After all, few people would advocate giving up electricity because it caused so much disruption to the kerosene and candle business. Few would suggest holding back on improvements in medical technology because they might cause companies selling leeches and snake oil to lose money. In short, most people view disruptions due to technological change as a necessary cost that is worth bearing.

Now, imagine that Technotron's new "technology" is as simple as this: the company imports what it sells from another country. In other words, think of foreign trade as a type of innovative technology. The objective situation is now exactly the same as before. Because of Technotron's new technology—which in this case is importing goods from another county—other firms in this industry will lose money and lay off workers. Just as it would have been inappropriate and ultimately foolish to respond to the disruptions of new scientific technology by trying to shut it down, it would be inappropriate and ultimately foolish to respond to the disruptions of international trade by trying to restrict trade.

Some workers and firms will suffer because of international trade. In a living, breathing market-oriented economy, some workers and firms will always be experiencing disruptions, for a wide variety of reasons. Corporate management can be better or worse. Workers for a certain firm can be more or less productive. Tough domestic competitors can create just as much disruption as tough foreign competitors. Sometimes a new product is a hit with consumers; sometimes it is a flop. Sometimes a company is blessed by a run of good luck or stricken with a run of bad luck. For some firms, international trade will offer great opportunities for expanding productivity and jobs; for other firms, trade will impose stress and pain. The disruption caused by international trade is not fundamentally different from all the other disruptions caused by the other workings of a market economy.

In other words, the economic analysis of free trade does not rely on a belief that foreign trade is not disruptive or does not pose tradeoffs; indeed, the story of Technotron begins with a particular **disruptive market change**—a new technology—that causes real tradeoffs. In thinking about the disruptions of foreign trade, or any of the other possible costs and tradeoffs of foreign trade discussed in this chapter, the best public policy solutions typically do not involve protectionism, but instead involve finding ways for public policy to address the particular issues resulting from these disruptions, costs, and tradeoffs, while still allowing the benefits of international trade to occur.

## BRING IT HOME

### What's the Downside of Protection?

The domestic flat-panel display industry employed many workers before the ITC imposed the dumping margin tax. Flat-panel displays make up a significant portion of the cost of producing laptop computers—as much as 50%. Therefore, the antidumping tax would substantially increase the cost, and thus the price, of U.S.-manufactured laptops. As a result of the ITC's decision, Apple moved its domestic manufacturing plant for Macintosh computers to Ireland (where it had an existing plant). Toshiba shut down its U.S. manufacturing plant for laptops. And IBM cancelled plans to open a laptop manufacturing plant in North Carolina, instead deciding to expand production at its plant in Japan. In this case, rather than having the desired effect of protecting U.S. interests and giving domestic manufacturing an advantage over items manufactured elsewhere, it had the unintended effect of driving the manufacturing completely out of the country. Many people lost their jobs and most flat-panel display production now occurs in countries other than the United States.

## Key Terms

**anti-dumping laws** laws that block imports sold below the cost of production and impose tariffs that would increase the price of these imports to reflect their cost of production

**common market** economic agreement between countries to allow free trade in goods, services, labor, and financial capital between members while having a common external trade policy

**disruptive market change** innovative new product or production technology which disrupts the status quo in a market, leading the innovators to earn more income and profits and the other firms to lose income and profits, unless they can come up with their own innovations

**dumping** selling internationally traded goods below their cost of production

**economic union** economic agreement between countries to allow free trade between members, a common external trade policy, and coordinated monetary and fiscal policies

**free trade agreement** economic agreement between countries to allow free trade between members

**General Agreement on Tariffs and Trade (GATT)** forum in which nations could come together to negotiate reductions in tariffs and other barriers to trade; the precursor to the World Trade Organization

**import quotas** numerical limits on the quantity of products that a country can import

**national interest argument** the argument that there are compelling national interests against depending on key imports from other nations

**nontariff barriers** ways a nation can draw up rules, regulations, inspections, and paperwork to make it more costly or difficult to import products

**protectionism** government policies to reduce or block imports

**race to the bottom** when production locates in countries with the lowest environmental (or other) standards, putting pressure on all countries to reduce their environmental standards

**World Trade Organization (WTO)** organization that seeks to negotiate reductions in barriers to trade and to adjudicate complaints about violations of international trade policy; successor to the General Agreement on Tariffs and Trade (GATT)

## Key Concepts and Summary

### 20.1 Protectionism: An Indirect Subsidy from Consumers to Producers

There are three tools for restricting the flow of trade: tariffs, import quotas, and nontariff barriers. When a country places limitations on imports from abroad, regardless of whether it uses tariffs, quotas, or nontariff barriers, it is said to be practicing protectionism. Protectionism will raise the price of the protected good in the domestic market, which causes domestic consumers to pay more, but domestic producers to earn more.

### 20.2 International Trade and Its Effects on Jobs, Wages, and Working Conditions

As international trade increases, it contributes to a shift in jobs away from industries where that economy does not have a comparative advantage and toward industries where it does have a comparative advantage. The degree to which trade affects labor markets has much to do with the structure of the labor market in that country and the adjustment process in other industries. Global trade should raise the average level of wages by increasing productivity. However, this increase in average wages may include both gains to workers in certain jobs and industries and losses to others.

In thinking about labor practices in low-income countries, it is useful to draw a line between what is unpleasant to think about and what is morally objectionable. For example, low wages and long working hours in poor countries are unpleasant to think about, but for people in low-income parts of the world, it may well be the best option open to them. Practices like child labor and forced labor are morally objectionable and many countries refuse to import products made using these practices.

### 20.3 Arguments in Support of Restricting Imports

There are a number of arguments that support restricting imports. These arguments are based around industry and competition, environmental concerns, and issues of safety and security.

The infant industry argument for protectionism is that small domestic industries need to be temporarily nurtured and protected from foreign competition for a time so that they can grow into strong competitors. In some cases, notably in East Asia, this approach has worked. Often, however, the infant industries never grow up. On the other hand, arguments against dumping (which is setting prices below the cost of production to drive competitors out of the market), often simply seem to be a convenient excuse for imposing protectionism.

Low-income countries typically have lower environmental standards than high-income countries because they are more worried about immediate basics such as food, education, and healthcare. However, except for a small number of extreme cases, shutting off trade seems unlikely to be an effective method of pursuing a cleaner environment.

Finally, there are arguments involving safety and security. Under the rules of the World Trade Organization, countries are allowed to set whatever standards for product safety they wish, but the standards must be the same for domestic products as for imported products and there must be a scientific basis for the standard. The national interest argument for protectionism holds that it is unwise to import certain key products because if the nation becomes dependent on key imported supplies, it could be vulnerable to a cutoff. However, it is often wiser to stockpile resources and to use foreign supplies when available, rather than preemptively restricting foreign supplies so as not to become dependent on them.

### 20.4 How Governments Enact Trade Policy: Globally, Regionally, and Nationally

Governments determine trade policy at many different levels: administrative agencies within government, laws passed by the legislature, regional negotiations between a small group of nations (sometimes just two), and global negotiations through the World Trade Organization. During the second half of the twentieth century, trade barriers have, in general, declined quite substantially in the United States economy and in the global economy. One reason why countries sign international trade agreements to commit themselves to free trade is to give themselves protection against their own special interests. When an industry lobbies for protection from foreign producers, politicians can point out that, because of the trade treaty, their hands are tied.

### 20.5 The Tradeoffs of Trade Policy

International trade certainly has income distribution effects. This is hardly surprising. All domestic or international competitive market forces are disruptive. They cause companies and industries to rise and fall. Government has a role to play in cushioning workers against the disruptions of the market. However, just as it would be unwise in the long term to clamp down on new technology and other causes of disruption in domestic markets, it would be unwise to clamp down on foreign trade. In both cases, the disruption brings with it economic benefits.

## Self-Check Questions

1.  Explain how a tariff reduction causes an increase in the equilibrium quantity of imports and a decrease in the equilibrium price. *Hint:* Consider the Work It Out "Effects of Trade Barriers."

2.  Explain how a subsidy on agricultural goods like sugar adversely affects the income of foreign producers of imported sugar.

3.  Explain how trade barriers save jobs in protected industries, but only by costing jobs in other industries.

4.  Explain how trade barriers raise wages in protected industries by reducing average wages economy-wide.

5.  How does international trade affect working conditions of low-income countries?

6.  Do the jobs for workers in low-income countries that involve making products for export to high-income countries typically pay these workers more or less than their next-best alternative?

7.  How do trade barriers affect the average income level in an economy?

8. How does the cost of "saving" jobs in protected industries compare to the workers' wages and salaries?

9. Explain how predatory pricing could be a motivation for dumping.

10. Why do low-income countries like Brazil, Egypt, or Vietnam have lower environmental standards than high-income countries like the Germany, Japan, or the United States?

11. Explain the logic behind the "race to the bottom" argument and the likely reason it has not occurred.

12. What are the conditions under which a country may use the unsafe products argument to block imports?

13. Why is the national security argument not convincing?

14. Assume a perfectly competitive market and the exporting country is small. Using a demand and supply diagram, show the impact of increasing standards on a low-income exporter of toys. Show the tariff's impact. Is the effect on toy prices the same or different? Why is a standards policy preferred to tariffs?

15. What is the difference between a free trade association, a common market, and an economic union?

16. Why would countries promote protectionist laws, while also negotiate for freer trade internationally?

17. What might account for the dramatic increase in international trade over the past 50 years?

18. How does competition, whether domestic or foreign, harm businesses?

19. What are the gains from competition?

## Review Questions

20. Who does protectionism protect? From what does it protect them?

21. Name and define three policy tools for enacting protectionism.

22. How does protectionism affect the price of the protected good in the domestic market?

23. Does international trade, taken as a whole, increase the total number of jobs, decrease the total number of jobs, or leave the total number of jobs about the same?

24. Is international trade likely to have roughly the same effect on the number of jobs in each individual industry?

25. How is international trade, taken as a whole, likely to affect the average level of wages?

26. Is international trade likely to have about the same effect on everyone's wages?

27. What are main reasons for protecting "infant industries"? Why is it difficult to stop protecting them?

28. What is dumping? Why does prohibiting it often work better in theory than in practice?

29. What is the "race to the bottom" scenario?

30. Do the rules of international trade require that all nations impose the same consumer safety standards?

31. What is the national interest argument for protectionism with regard to certain products?

32. Name several of the international treaties where countries negotiate with each other over trade policy.

33. What is the general trend of trade barriers over recent decades: higher, lower, or about the same?

34. If opening up to free trade would benefit a nation, then why do nations not just eliminate their trade barriers, and not bother with international trade negotiations?

35. Who gains and who loses from trade?

36. Why is trade a good thing if some people lose?

37.  What are some ways that governments can help people who lose from trade?

## Critical Thinking Questions

38.  Show graphically that for any tariff, there is an equivalent quota that would give the same result. What would be the difference, then, between the two types of trade barriers? *Hint*: It is not something you can see from the graph.

39.  From the Work It Out "Effects of Trade Barriers," you can see that a tariff raises the price of imports. What is interesting is that the price rises by less than the amount of the tariff. Who pays the rest of the tariff amount? Can you show this graphically?

40.  If trade barriers hurt the average worker in an economy (due to lower wages), why does government create trade barriers?

41.  Why do you think labor standards and working conditions are lower in the low-income countries of the world than in countries like the United States?

42.  How would direct subsidies to key industries be preferable to tariffs or quotas?

43.  How can governments identify good candidates for infant industry protection? Can you suggest some key characteristics of good candidates? Why are industries like computers not good candidates for infant industry protection?

44.  Microeconomic theory argues that it is economically rationale (and profitable) to sell additional output as long as the price covers the variable costs of production. How is this relevant to the determination of whether dumping has occurred?

45.  How do you think Americans would feel if other countries began to urge the United States to increase environmental standards?

46.  Is it legitimate to impose higher safety standards on imported goods that exist in the foreign country where the goods were produced?

47.  Why might the unsafe consumer products argument be a more effective strategy (from the perspective of the importing country) than using tariffs or quotas to restrict imports?

48.  Why might a tax on domestic consumption of resources critical for national security be a more efficient approach than barriers to imports?

49.  Why do you think that the GATT rounds and, more recently, WTO negotiations have become longer and more difficult to resolve?

50.  An economic union requires giving up some political autonomy to succeed. What are some examples of political power countries must give up to be members of an economic union?

51.  What are some examples of innovative products that have disrupted their industries for the better?

52.  In principle, the benefits of international trade to a country exceed the costs, no matter whether the country is importing or exporting. In practice, it is not always possible to compensate the losers in a country, for example, workers who lose their jobs due to foreign imports. In your opinion, does that mean that trade should be inhibited to prevent the losses?

53. Economists sometimes say that protectionism is the "second-best" choice for dealing with any particular problem. What they mean is that there is often a policy choice that is more direct or effective for dealing with the problem—a choice that would still allow the benefits of trade to occur. Explain why protectionism is a "second-best" choice for:
    a. helping workers as a group
    b. helping industries stay strong
    c. protecting the environment
    d. advancing national defense

54. Trade has income distribution effects. For example, suppose that because of a government-negotiated reduction in trade barriers, trade between Germany and the Czech Republic increases. Germany sells house paint to the Czech Republic. The Czech Republic sells alarm clocks to Germany. Would you expect this pattern of trade to increase or decrease jobs and wages in the paint industry in Germany? The alarm clock industry in Germany? The paint industry in Czech Republic? The alarm clock industry in Czech Republic? What has to happen for there to be no increase in total unemployment in both countries?

## Problems

55. Assume two countries, Thailand (T) and Japan (J), have one good: cameras. The demand (d) and supply (s) for cameras in Thailand and Japan is described by the following functions:

$$Qd^T = 60 - P$$

$$Qs^T = -5 + \tfrac{1}{4}P$$

$$Qd^J = 80 - P$$

$$Qs^J = -10 + \tfrac{1}{2}P$$

P is the price measured in a common currency used in both countries, such as the Thai Baht.
    a. Compute the equilibrium price (P) and quantities (Q) in each country without trade.
    b. Now assume that free trade occurs. The free-trade price goes to 56.36 Baht. Who exports and imports cameras and in what quantities?

56. You have just been put in charge of trade policy for Malawi. Coffee is a recent crop that is growing well and the Malawian export market is developing. As such, Malawi coffee is an infant industry. Malawi coffee producers come to you and ask for tariff protection from cheap Tanzanian coffee. What sorts of policies will you enact? Explain.

**57.** The country of Pepperland exports steel to the Land of Submarines. Information for the quantity demanded (Qd) and quantity supplied (Qs) in each country, in a world without trade, are given in Table 20.6 and Table 20.7.

| Price ($) | Qd | Qs |
|---|---|---|
| 60 | 230 | 180 |
| 70 | 200 | 200 |
| 80 | 170 | 220 |
| 90 | 150 | 240 |
| 100 | 140 | 250 |

**TABLE 20.6**
Pepperland

| Price ($) | Qd | Qs |
|---|---|---|
| 60 | 430 | 310 |
| 70 | 420 | 330 |
| 80 | 410 | 360 |
| 90 | 400 | 400 |
| 100 | 390 | 440 |

**TABLE 20.7** Land of
Submarines

a. What would be the equilibrium price and quantity in each country in a world without trade? How can you tell?
b. What would be the equilibrium price and quantity in each country if trade is allowed to occur? How can you tell?
c. Sketch two supply and demand diagrams, one for each country, in the situation before trade.
d. On those diagrams, show the equilibrium price and the levels of exports and imports in the world after trade.
e. If the Land of Submarines imposes an anti-dumping import quota of 30, explain in general terms whether it will benefit or injure consumers and producers in each country.
f. Does your general answer change if the Land of Submarines imposes an import quota of 70?

# APPENDIX A

## The Use of Mathematics in Principles of Economics

(This appendix should be consulted after first reading Welcome to Economics!) Economics is not math. There is no important concept in this course that cannot be explained without mathematics. That said, math is a tool that can be used to illustrate economic concepts. Remember the saying a picture is worth a thousand words? Instead of a picture, think of a graph. It is the same thing. Economists use models as the primary tool to derive insights about economic issues and problems. Math is one way of working with (or manipulating) economic models.

There are other ways of representing models, such as text or narrative. But why would you use your fist to bang a nail, if you had a hammer? Math has certain advantages over text. It disciplines your thinking by making you specify exactly what you mean. You can get away with fuzzy thinking in your head, but you cannot when you reduce a model to algebraic equations. At the same time, math also has disadvantages. Mathematical models are necessarily based on simplifying assumptions, so they are not likely to be perfectly realistic. Mathematical models also lack the nuances which can be found in narrative models. The point is that math is one tool, but it is not the only tool or even always the best tool economists can use. So what math will you need for this book? The answer is: little more than high school algebra and graphs. You will need to know:

- What a function is
- How to interpret the equation of a line (i.e., slope and intercept)
- How to manipulate a line (i.e., changing the slope or the intercept)
- How to compute and interpret a growth rate (i.e., percentage change)
- How to read and manipulate a graph

In this text, we will use the easiest math possible, and we will introduce it in this appendix. So if you find some math in the book that you cannot follow, come back to this appendix to review. Like most things, math has diminishing returns. A little math ability goes a long way; the more advanced math you bring in, the less additional knowledge that will get you. That said, if you are going to major in economics, you should consider learning a little calculus. It will be worth your while in terms of helping you learn advanced economics more quickly.

## Algebraic Models

Often economic models (or parts of models) are expressed in terms of mathematical functions. What is a function? A function describes a relationship. Sometimes the relationship is a definition. For example (using words), your professor is Adam Smith. This could be expressed as Professor = Adam Smith. Or Friends = Bob + Shawn + Margaret.

Often in economics, functions describe cause and effect. The variable on the left-hand side is what is being explained ("the effect"). On the right-hand side is what is doing the explaining ("the causes"). For example, suppose your GPA was determined as follows:

$$\text{GPA} = 0.25 \times \text{combined\_SAT} + 0.25 \times \text{class\_attendance} + 0.50 \times \text{hours\_spent\_studying}$$

This equation states that your GPA depends on three things: your combined SAT score, your class attendance, and the number of hours you spend studying. It also says that study time is twice as important (0.50) as either combined_SAT score (0.25) or class_attendance (0.25). If this relationship is true, how could you raise your GPA? By not skipping class and studying more. Note that you cannot do anything about your SAT score, since if you are in college, you have (presumably) already taken the SATs.

Of course, economic models express relationships using economic variables, like Budget =

money_spent_on_econ_books + money_spent_on_music, assuming that the only things you buy are economics books and music.

Most of the relationships we use in this course are expressed as linear equations of the form:

$$y = b + mx$$

**Expressing Equations Graphically**

Graphs are useful for two purposes. The first is to express equations visually, and the second is to display statistics or data. This section will discuss expressing equations visually.

To a mathematician or an economist, a variable is the name given to a quantity that may assume a range of values. In the equation of a line presented above, x and y are the variables, with x on the horizontal axis and y on the vertical axis, and b and m representing factors that determine the shape of the line. To see how this equation works, consider a numerical example:

$$y = 9 + 3x$$

In this equation for a specific line, the b term has been set equal to 9 and the m term has been set equal to 3. Table A1 shows the values of x and y for this given equation. Figure A1 shows this equation, and these values, in a graph. To construct the table, just plug in a series of different values for x, and then calculate what value of y results. In the figure, these points are plotted and a line is drawn through them.

| x | y |
|---|---|
| 0 | 9 |
| 1 | 12 |
| 2 | 15 |
| 3 | 18 |
| 4 | 21 |
| 5 | 24 |
| 6 | 27 |

**TABLE A1 Values for the Slope Intercept Equation**

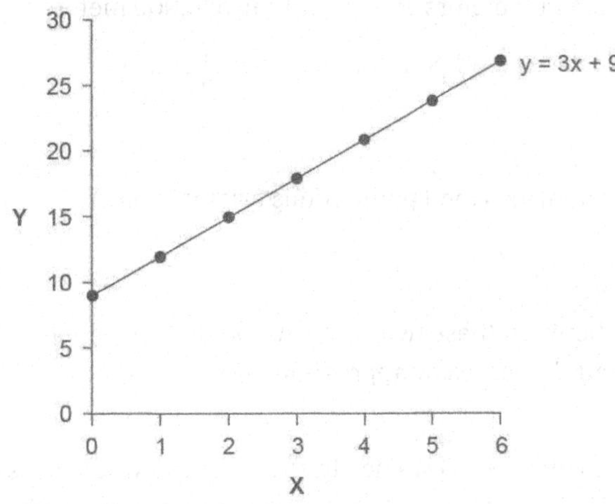


**FIGURE A1 Slope and the Algebra of Straight Lines** This line graph has *x* on the horizontal axis and y on the vertical axis. The y-intercept—that is, the point where the line intersects the y-axis—is 9. The slope of the line is 3; that is, there is a rise of 3 on the vertical axis for every increase of 1 on the horizontal axis. The slope is the same all along a straight line.

This example illustrates how the b and m terms in an equation for a straight line determine the shape of the line. The b term is called the y-intercept. The reason for this name is that, if x = 0, then the b term will reveal where the line intercepts, or crosses, the y-axis. In this example, the line hits the vertical axis at 9. The m term in the equation for the line is the slope. Remember that slope is defined as rise over run; more specifically, the slope of a line from one point to another is the change in the vertical axis divided by the change in the horizontal axis. In this example, each time the x term increases by one (the run), the y term rises by three. Thus, the slope of this line is three. Specifying a y-intercept and a slope—that is, specifying b and m in the equation for a line—will identify a specific line. Although it is rare for real-world data points to arrange themselves as an exact straight line, it often turns out that a straight line can offer a reasonable approximation of actual data.

### Interpreting the Slope

The concept of slope is very useful in economics, because it measures the relationship between two variables. A positive slope means that two variables are positively related; that is, when x increases, so does y, or when x decreases, y decreases also. Graphically, a positive slope means that as a line on the line graph moves from left to right, the line rises. The length-weight relationship, shown in Figure A3 later in this Appendix, has a positive slope. We will learn in other chapters that price and quantity supplied have a positive relationship; that is, firms will supply more when the price is higher.

A negative slope means that two variables are negatively related; that is, when x increases, y decreases, or when x decreases, y increases. Graphically, a negative slope means that, as the line on the line graph moves from left to right, the line falls. The altitude-air density relationship, shown in Figure A4 later in this appendix, has a negative slope. We will learn that price and quantity demanded have a negative relationship; that is, consumers will purchase less when the price is higher.

A slope of zero means that there is no relationship between x and y. Graphically, the line is flat; that is, zero rise over the run. Figure A5 of the unemployment rate, shown later in this appendix, illustrates a common pattern of many line graphs: some segments where the slope is positive, other segments where the slope is negative, and still other segments where the slope is close to zero.

The slope of a straight line between two points can be calculated in numerical terms. To calculate slope, begin by designating one point as the "starting point" and the other point as the "end point" and then calculating the rise over run between these two points. As an example, consider the slope of the air density graph between the points representing an altitude of 4,000 meters and an altitude of 6,000 meters:

Rise: Change in variable on vertical axis (end point minus original point)

$= 0.100 - 0.307$

$= -0.207$

Run: Change in variable on horizontal axis (end point minus original point)

$= 6,000 - 4,000$

$= 2,000$

Thus, the slope of a straight line between these two points would be that from the altitude of 4,000 meters up to 6,000 meters, the density of the air decreases by approximately 0.1 kilograms/cubic meter for each of the next 1,000 meters.

Suppose the slope of a line were to increase. Graphically, that means it would get steeper. Suppose the slope of a line were to decrease. Then it would get flatter. These conditions are true whether or not the slope was positive or negative to begin with. A higher positive slope means a steeper upward tilt to the line, while a smaller positive slope means a flatter upward tilt to the line. A negative slope that is larger in absolute value (that is, more negative) means a steeper downward tilt to the line. A slope of zero is a horizontal flat line. A vertical line has an infinite slope.

Suppose a line has a larger intercept. Graphically, that means it would shift out (or up) from the old origin, parallel to the old line. If a line has a smaller intercept, it would shift in (or down), parallel to the old line.

### Solving Models with Algebra

Economists often use models to answer a specific question, like: What will the unemployment rate be if the economy grows at 3% per year? Answering specific questions requires solving the "system" of equations that represent the model.

Suppose the demand for personal pizzas is given by the following equation:

$Qd = 16 - 2P$

where Qd is the amount of personal pizzas consumers want to buy (i.e., quantity demanded), and P is the price of pizzas. Suppose the supply of personal pizzas is:

$Qs = 2 + 5P$

where Qs is the amount of pizza producers will supply (i.e., quantity supplied).

Finally, suppose that the personal pizza market operates where supply equals demand, or

$Qd = Qs$

We now have a system of three equations and three unknowns (Qd, Qs, and P), which we can solve with algebra:

Since Qd = Qs, we can set the demand and supply equation equal to each other:

$$Qd = Qs$$

$$16 - 2P = 2 + 5P$$

Subtracting 2 from both sides and adding 2P to both sides yields:

$$16 - 2P - 2 = 2 + 5P - 2$$

$$14 - 2P = 5P$$

$$14 - 2P + 2P = 5P + 2P$$

$$14 = 7P$$

$$\frac{14}{7} = \frac{7P}{7}$$

$$2 = P$$

In other words, the price of each personal pizza will be $2. How much will consumers buy?

Taking the price of $2, and plugging it into the demand equation, we get:

$$Qd = 16 - 2P$$
$$= 16 - 2(2)$$
$$= 16 - 4$$
$$= 12$$

So if the price is $2 each, consumers will purchase 12. How much will producers supply? Taking the price of $2, and plugging it into the supply equation, we get:

$$Qs = 2 + 5P$$
$$= 2 + 5(2)$$
$$= 2 + 10$$
$$= 12$$

So if the price is $2 each, producers will supply 12 personal pizzas. This means we did our math correctly, since Qd = Qs.

### Solving Models with Graphs

If algebra is not your forte, you can get the same answer by using graphs. Take the equations for Qd and Qs and graph them on the same set of axes as shown in Figure A2. Since P is on the vertical axis, it is easiest if you solve each equation for P. The demand curve is then P = 8 – 0.5Qd and the supply curve is P = –0.4 + 0.2Qs. Note that the vertical intercepts are 8 and –0.4, and the slopes are –0.5 for demand and 0.2 for supply. If you draw the graphs carefully, you will see that where they cross (Qs = Qd), the price is $2 and the quantity is 12, just like the algebra predicted.

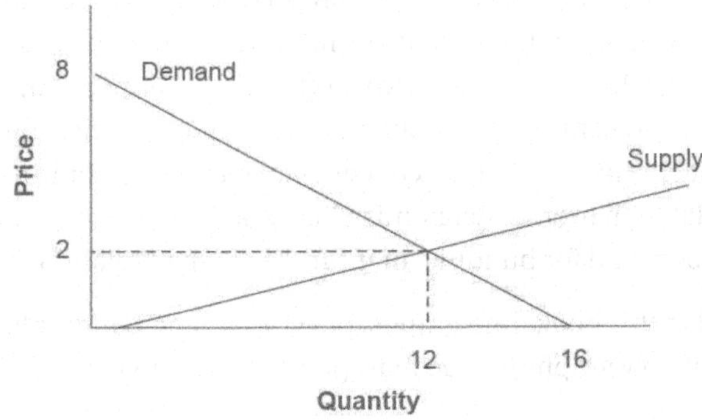


**FIGURE A2 Supply and Demand Graph** The equations for Qd and Qs are displayed graphically by the sloped lines.

We will use graphs more frequently in this book than algebra, but now you know the math behind the graphs.

## Growth Rates

Growth rates are frequently encountered in real world economics. A growth rate is simply the percentage change in some quantity. It could be your income. It could be a business's sales. It could be a nation's GDP. The formula for computing a growth rate is straightforward:

$$\text{Percentage change} = \frac{\text{Change in quantity}}{\text{Quantity}}$$

Suppose your job pays $10 per hour. Your boss, however, is so impressed with your work that he gives you a $2 per hour raise. The percentage change (or growth rate) in your pay is $2/$10 = 0.20 or 20%.

To compute the growth rate for data over an extended period of time, for example, the average annual growth in GDP over a decade or more, the denominator is commonly defined a little differently. In the previous example, we defined the quantity as the initial quantity—or the quantity when we started. This is fine for a one-time calculation, but when we compute the growth over and over, it makes more sense to define the quantity as the average quantity over the period in question, which is defined as the quantity halfway between the initial quantity and the next quantity. This is harder to explain in words than to show with an example. Suppose a nation's GDP was $1 trillion in 2005 and $1.03 trillion in 2006. The growth rate between 2005 and 2006 would be the change in GDP ($1.03 trillion – $1.00 trillion) divided by the average GDP between 2005 and 2006 ($1.03 trillion + $1.00 trillion)/2. In other words:

$$= \frac{\$1.03 \text{ trillion} - \$1.00 \text{ trillion}}{(\$1.03 \text{ trillion} + \$1.00 \text{ trillion}) / 2}$$

$$= \frac{0.03}{1.015}$$

$$= 0.0296$$

$$= 2.96\% \text{ growth}$$

Note that if we used the first method, the calculation would be ($1.03 trillion – $1.00 trillion) / $1.00 trillion = 3% growth, which is approximately the same as the second, more complicated method. If you need a rough approximation, use the first method. If you need accuracy, use the second method.

A few things to remember: A positive growth rate means the quantity is growing. A smaller growth rate means the quantity is growing more slowly. A larger growth rate means the quantity is growing more quickly. A negative growth rate means the quantity is decreasing.

The same change over times yields a smaller growth rate. If you got a $2 raise each year, in the first year the growth rate would be $2/$10 = 20%, as shown above. But in the second year, the growth rate would be $2/$12 = 0.167 or 16.7% growth. In the third year, the same $2 raise would correspond to a $2/$14 = 14.2%. The moral of the story is this: To keep the growth rate the same, the change must increase each period.

## Displaying Data Graphically and Interpreting the Graph

Graphs are also used to display data or evidence. Graphs are a method of presenting numerical patterns. They condense detailed numerical information into a visual form in which relationships and numerical patterns can be seen more easily. For example, which countries have larger or smaller populations? A careful reader could examine a long list of numbers representing the populations of many countries, but with over 200 nations in the world, searching through such a list would take concentration and time. Putting these same numbers on a graph can quickly reveal population patterns. Economists use graphs both for a compact and readable presentation of groups of numbers and for building an intuitive grasp of relationships and connections.

Three types of graphs are used in this book: line graphs, pie graphs, and bar graphs. Each is discussed below. We also provide warnings about how graphs can be manipulated to alter viewers' perceptions of the relationships in the data.

### Line Graphs

The graphs we have discussed so far are called line graphs, because they show a relationship between two variables: one measured on the horizontal axis and the other measured on the vertical axis.

Sometimes it is useful to show more than one set of data on the same axes. The data in Table A2 is displayed in Figure A3 which shows the relationship between two variables: length and median weight for American baby boys and girls during the first three years of life. (The median means that half of all babies weigh more than this and half weigh less.) The line graph measures length in inches on the horizontal axis and weight in pounds on the vertical axis. For example, point A on the figure shows that a boy who is 28 inches long will have a median weight of about 19 pounds. One line on the graph shows the length-weight relationship for boys and the other line shows the relationship for girls. This kind of graph is widely used by healthcare providers to check whether a child's physical development is roughly on track.

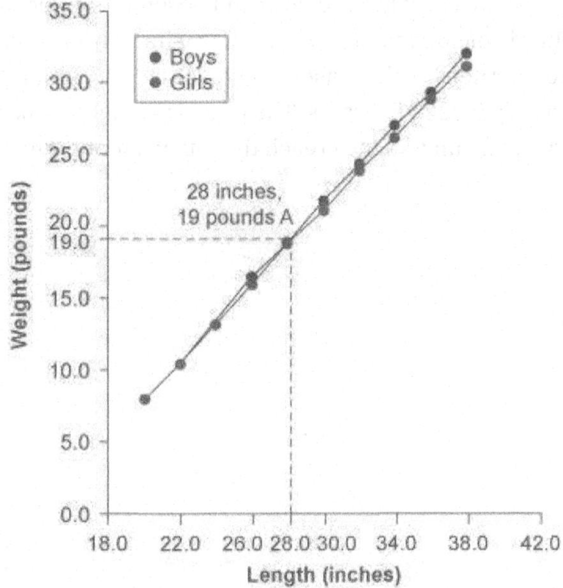



**FIGURE A3 The Length-Weight Relationship for American Boys and Girls** The line graph shows the relationship between height and weight for boys and girls from birth to 3 years. Point A, for example, shows that a boy of 28 inches in height (measured on the horizontal axis) is typically 19 pounds in weight (measured on the vertical axis). These data apply only to children in the first three years of life.

| Boys from Birth to 36 Months | | Girls from Birth to 36 Months | |
|---|---|---|---|
| Length (inches) | Weight (pounds) | Length (inches) | Weight (pounds) |
| 20.0 | 8.0 | 20.0 | 7.9 |
| 22.0 | 10.5 | 22.0 | 10.5 |
| 24.0 | 13.5 | 24.0 | 13.2 |
| 26.0 | 16.4 | 26.0 | 16.0 |
| 28.0 | 19.0 | 28.0 | 18.8 |
| 30.0 | 21.8 | 30.0 | 21.2 |
| 32.0 | 24.3 | 32.0 | 24.0 |
| 34.0 | 27.0 | 34.0 | 26.2 |
| 36.0 | 29.3 | 36.0 | 28.9 |
| 38.0 | 32.0 | 38.0 | 31.3 |

**TABLE A2 Length to Weight Relationship for American Boys and Girls**

Not all relationships in economics are linear. Sometimes they are curves. Figure A4 presents another example of a line graph, representing the data from Table A3. In this case, the line graph shows how thin the air becomes when you climb a mountain. The horizontal axis of the figure shows altitude, measured in meters above sea level. The vertical axis measures the density of the air at each altitude. Air density is measured by the weight of the air in a cubic meter of space (that is, a box measuring one meter in height, width, and depth).

As the graph shows, air pressure is heaviest at ground level and becomes lighter as you climb. Figure A4 shows that a cubic meter of air at an altitude of 500 meters weighs approximately one kilogram (about 2.2 pounds). However, as the altitude increases, air density decreases. A cubic meter of air at the top of Mount Everest, at about 8,828 meters, would weigh only 0.023 kilograms. The thin air at high altitudes explains why many mountain climbers need to use oxygen tanks as they reach the top of a mountain.

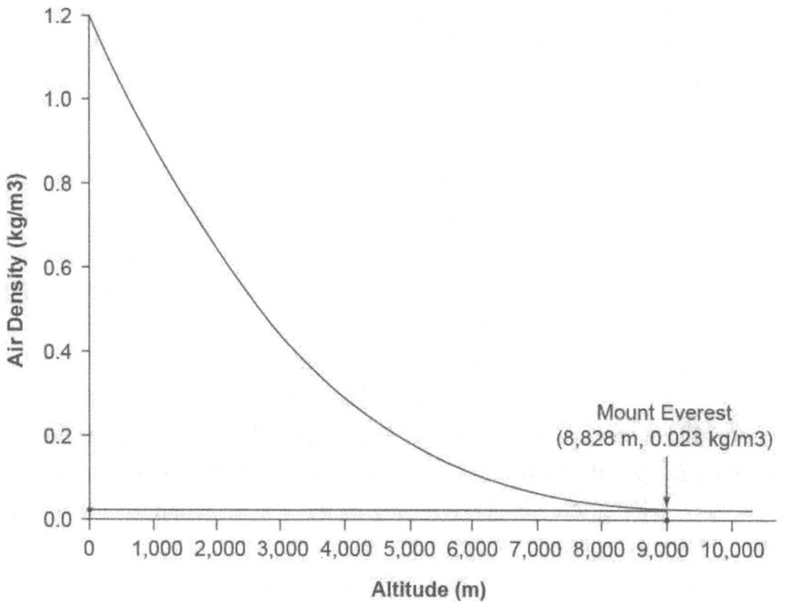


**FIGURE A4 Altitude-Air Density Relationship** This line graph shows the relationship between altitude, measured in meters above sea level, and air density, measured in kilograms of air per cubic meter. As altitude rises, air density declines. The point at the top of Mount Everest has an altitude of approximately 8,828 meters above sea level (the horizontal axis) and air density of 0.023 kilograms per cubic meter (the vertical axis).

| Altitude (meters) | Air Density (kg/cubic meters) |
| --- | --- |
| 0 | 1.200 |
| 500 | 1.093 |
| 1,000 | 0.831 |
| 1,500 | 0.678 |
| 2,000 | 0.569 |
| 2,500 | 0.484 |
| 3,000 | 0.415 |
| 3,500 | 0.357 |
| 4,000 | 0.307 |
| 4,500 | 0.231 |
| 5,000 | 0.182 |

**TABLE A3 Altitude to Air Density Relationship**

| Altitude (meters) | Air Density (kg/cubic meters) |
|---|---|
| 5,500 | 0.142 |
| 6,000 | 0.100 |
| 6,500 | 0.085 |
| 7,000 | 0.066 |
| 7,500 | 0.051 |
| 8,000 | 0.041 |
| 8,500 | 0.025 |
| 9,000 | 0.022 |
| 9,500 | 0.019 |
| 10,000 | 0.014 |

**TABLE A3** Altitude to Air Density Relationship

The length-weight relationship and the altitude-air density relationships in these two figures represent averages. If you were to collect actual data on air pressure at different altitudes, the same altitude in different geographic locations will have slightly different air density, depending on factors like how far you are from the equator, local weather conditions, and the humidity in the air. Similarly, in measuring the height and weight of children for the previous line graph, children of a particular height would have a range of different weights, some above average and some below. In the real world, this sort of variation in data is common. The task of a researcher is to organize that data in a way that helps to understand typical patterns. The study of statistics, especially when combined with computer statistics and spreadsheet programs, is a great help in organizing this kind of data, plotting line graphs, and looking for typical underlying relationships. For most economics and social science majors, a statistics course will be required at some point.

One common line graph is called a time series, in which the horizontal axis shows time and the vertical axis displays another variable. Thus, a time series graph shows how a variable changes over time. Figure A5 shows the unemployment rate in the United States since 1975, where unemployment is defined as the percentage of adults who want jobs and are looking for a job, but cannot find one. The points for the unemployment rate in each year are plotted on the graph, and a line then connects the points, showing how the unemployment rate has moved up and down since 1975. The line graph makes it easy to see, for example, that the highest unemployment rate during this time period was slightly less than 10% in the early 1980s and 2010, while the unemployment rate declined from the early 1990s to the end of the 1990s, before rising and then falling back in the early 2000s, and then rising sharply during the recession from 2008–2009.

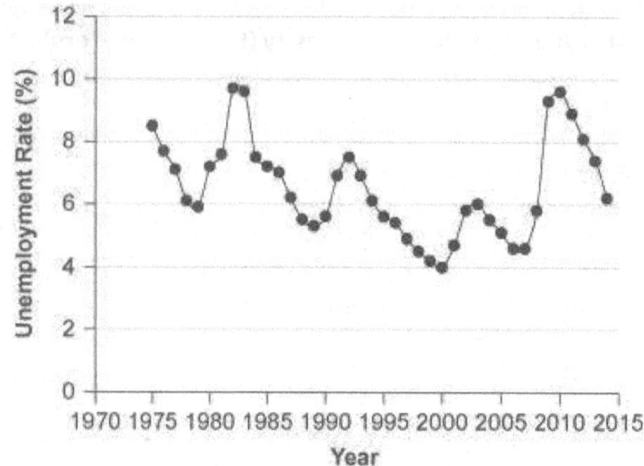


**FIGURE A5** U.S. Unemployment Rate, 1975–2014 This graph provides a quick visual summary of unemployment data. With a graph like this, it is easy to spot the times of high unemployment and of low unemployment.

**Pie Graphs**

A pie graph (sometimes called a pie chart) is used to show how an overall total is divided into parts. A circle represents a group as a whole. The slices of this circular "pie" show the relative sizes of subgroups.

Figure A6 shows how the U.S. population was divided among children, working age adults, and the elderly in 1970, 2000, and what is projected for 2030. The information is first conveyed with numbers in Table A4, and then in three pie charts. The first column of Table A4 shows the total U.S. population for each of the three years. Columns 2–4 categorize the total in terms of age groups—from birth to 18 years, from 19 to 64 years, and 65 years and above. In columns 2–4, the first number shows the actual number of people in each age category, while the number in parentheses shows the percentage of the total population comprised by that age group.

| Year | Total Population | 19 and Under | 20–64 years | Over 65 |
|---|---|---|---|---|
| 1970 | 205.0 million | 77.2 (37.6%) | 107.7 (52.5%) | 20.1 (9.8%) |
| 2000 | 275.4 million | 78.4 (28.5%) | 162.2 (58.9%) | 34.8 (12.6%) |
| 2030 | 351.1 million | 92.6 (26.4%) | 188.2 (53.6%) | 70.3 (20.0%) |

**TABLE A4** U.S. Age Distribution, 1970, 2000, and 2030 (projected)

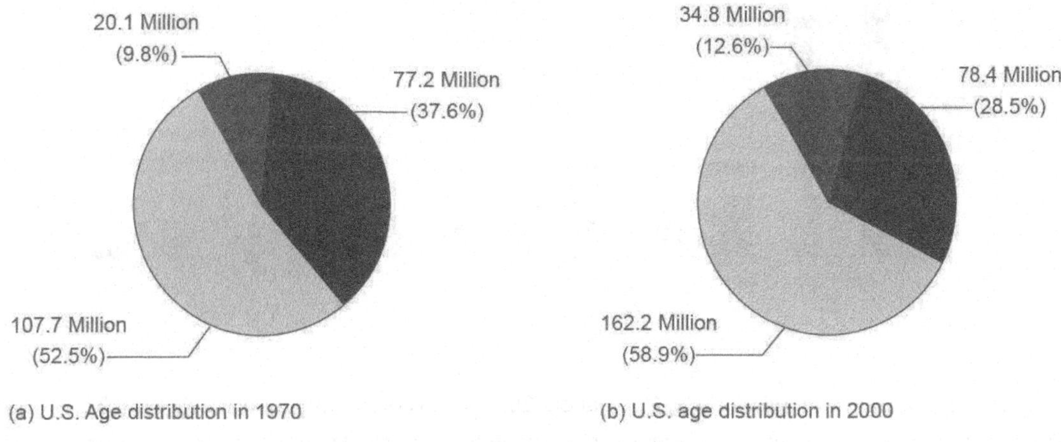


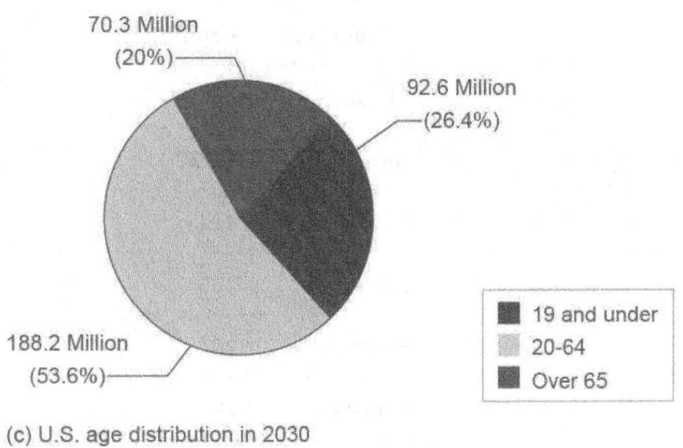


**FIGURE A6 Pie Graphs of the U.S. Age Distribution (numbers in millions)** The three pie graphs illustrate the division of total population into three age groups for the three different years.

In a pie graph, each slice of the pie represents a share of the total, or a percentage. For example, 50% would be half of the pie and 20% would be one-fifth of the pie. The three pie graphs in Figure A6 show that the share of the U.S. population 65 and over is growing. The pie graphs allow you to get a feel for the relative size of the different age groups from 1970 to 2000 to 2030, without requiring you to slog through the specific numbers and percentages in the table. Some common examples of how pie graphs are used include dividing the population into groups by age, income level, ethnicity, religion, occupation; dividing different firms into categories by size, industry, number of employees; and dividing up government spending or taxes into its main categories.

**Bar Graphs**

A bar graph uses the height of different bars to compare quantities. Table A5 lists the 12 most populous countries in the world. Figure A7 provides this same data in a bar graph. The height of the bars corresponds to the population of each country. Although you may know that China and India are the most populous countries in the world, seeing how the bars on the graph tower over the other countries helps illustrate the magnitude of the difference between the sizes of national populations.

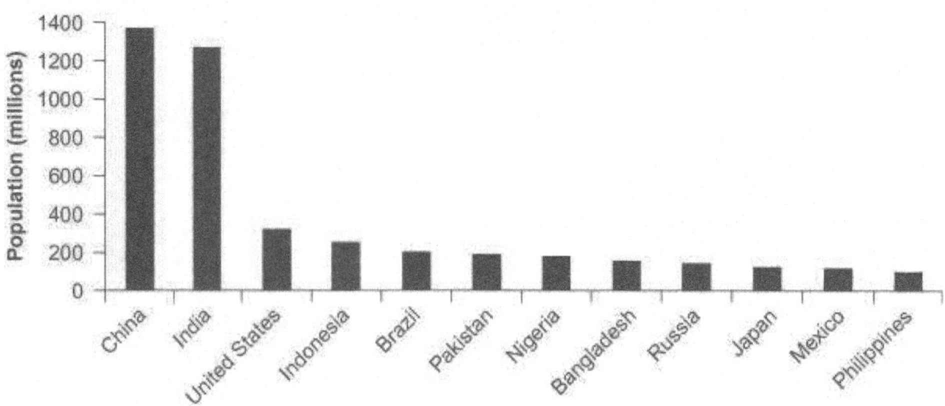


**FIGURE A7** Leading Countries of the World by Population, 2015 (in millions) The graph shows the 12 countries of the world with the largest populations. The height of the bars in the bar graph shows the size of the population for each country.

| Country | Population |
| --- | --- |
| China | 1,369 |
| India | 1,270 |
| United States | 321 |
| Indonesia | 255 |
| Brazil | 204 |
| Pakistan | 190 |
| Nigeria | 184 |
| Bangladesh | 158 |
| Russia | 146 |
| Japan | 127 |
| Mexico | 121 |
| Philippines | 101 |

**TABLE A5** Leading 12 Countries of the World by Population

Bar graphs can be subdivided in a way that reveals information similar to that we can get from pie charts. Figure A8 offers three bar graphs based on the information from Figure A6 about the U.S. age distribution in 1970, 2000, and 2030. Figure A8 (a) shows three bars for each year, representing the total number of persons in each age bracket for each year. Figure A8 (b) shows just one bar for each year, but the different age groups are now shaded inside the bar. In Figure A8 (c), still based on the same data, the vertical axis measures percentages rather than the number of persons. In this case, all three bar graphs are the same height, representing 100% of the population, with each bar divided according to the percentage of population in each age group. It is sometimes easier for a reader to run their eyes across several bar graphs, comparing the shaded areas, rather than trying to compare several pie graphs.

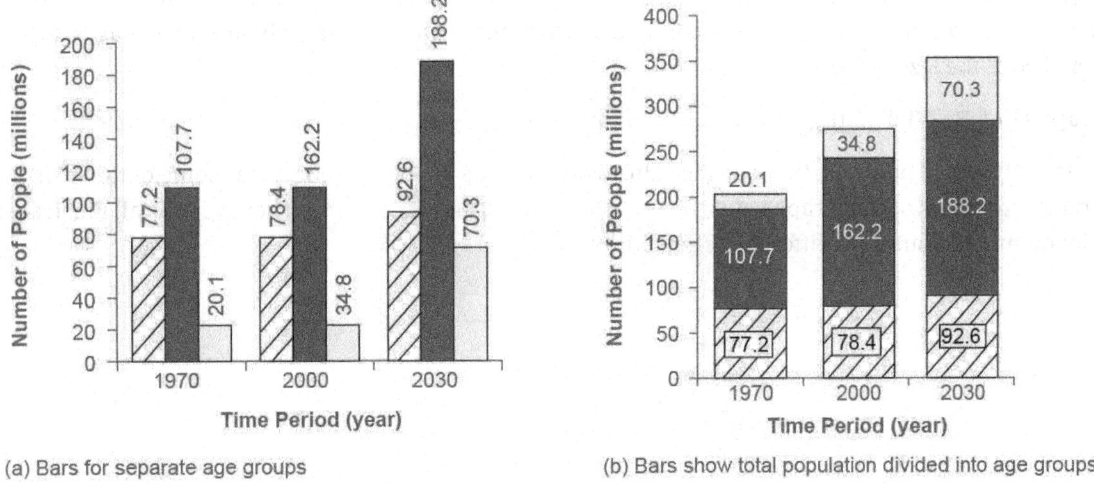

(a) Bars for separate age groups

(b) Bars show total population divided into age groups

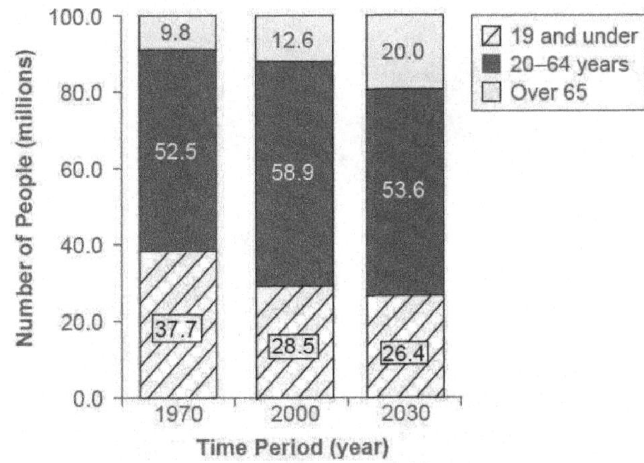

(c) Bars show total population divided into percentages

**FIGURE A8 U.S. Population with Bar Graphs** Population data can be represented in different ways. (a) Shows three bars for each year, representing the total number of persons in each age bracket for each year. (b) Shows just one bar for each year, but the different age groups are now shaded inside the bar. (c) Sets the vertical axis as a measure of percentages rather than the number of persons. All three bar graphs are the same height and each bar is divided according to the percentage of population in each age group.

Figure A7 and Figure A8 show how the bars can represent countries or years, and how the vertical axis can represent a numerical or a percentage value. Bar graphs can also compare size, quantity, rates, distances, and other quantitative categories.

## Comparing Line Graphs with Pie Charts and Bar Graphs

Now that you are familiar with pie graphs, bar graphs, and line graphs, how do you know which graph to use for your data? Pie graphs are often better than line graphs at showing how an overall group is divided. However, if a pie graph has too many slices, it can become difficult to interpret.

Bar graphs are especially useful when comparing quantities. For example, if you are studying the populations of different countries, as in Figure A7, bar graphs can show the relationships between the population sizes of multiple countries. Not only can it show these relationships, but it can also show breakdowns of different groups within the population.

A line graph is often the most effective format for illustrating a relationship between two variables that are both changing. For example, time series graphs can show patterns as time changes, like the unemployment rate over time. Line graphs are widely used in economics to present continuous data about prices, wages, quantities bought and sold, the size of the economy.

## How Graphs Can Be Misleading

Graphs not only reveal patterns; they can also alter how patterns are perceived. To see some of the ways this can be done, consider the line graphs of Figure A9, Figure A10, and Figure A11. These graphs all illustrate the unemployment rate—but from different perspectives.

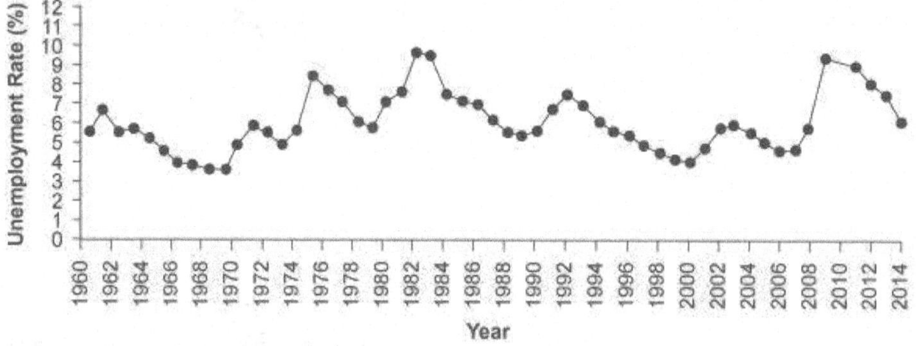

(a) Unemployment rate, wide and short

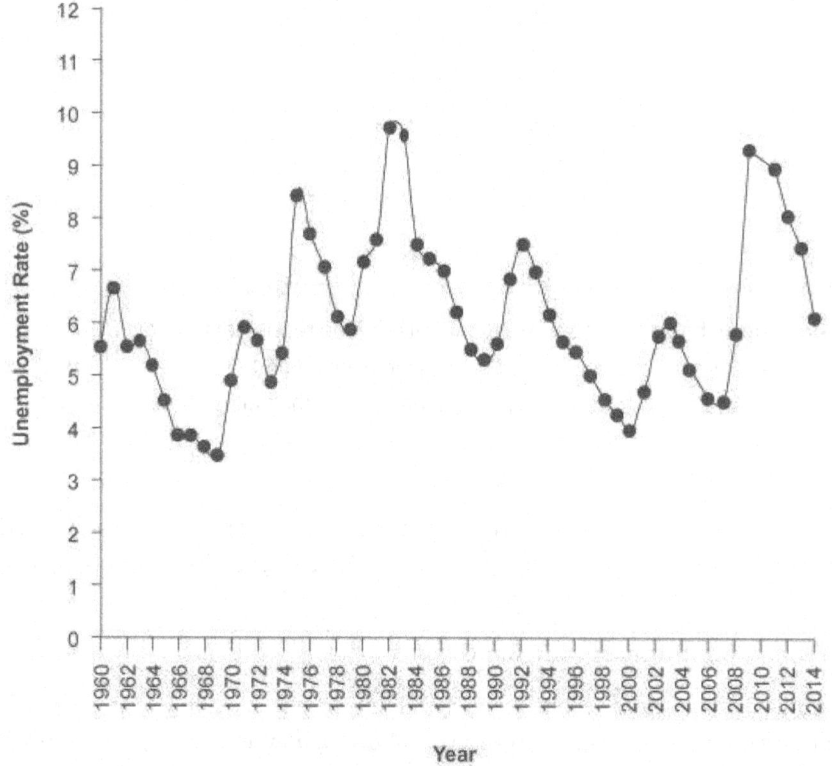

(b) Unemployment rate, narrow and tall

**FIGURE A9**

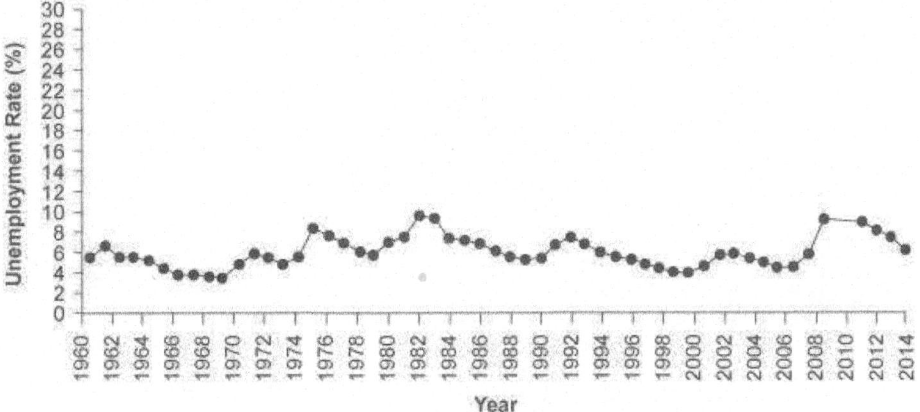


(c) Unemployment rate, with wider range of numbers on vertical axis

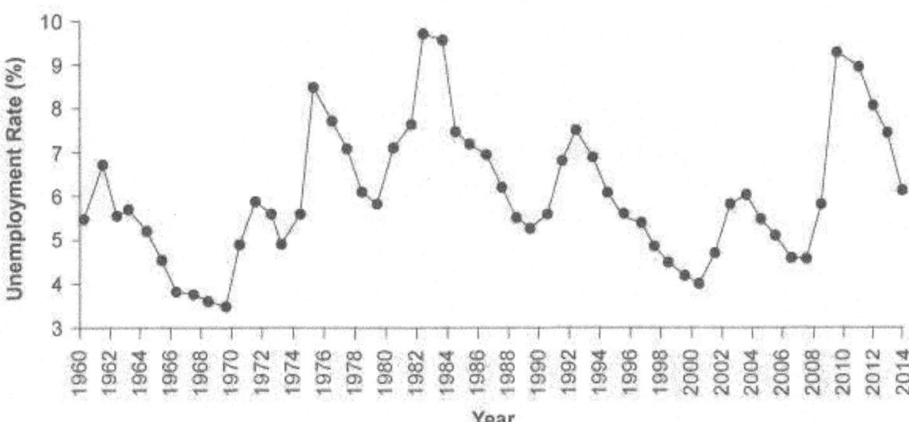


(d) Unemployment rate, with smaller range of numbers on vertical axis

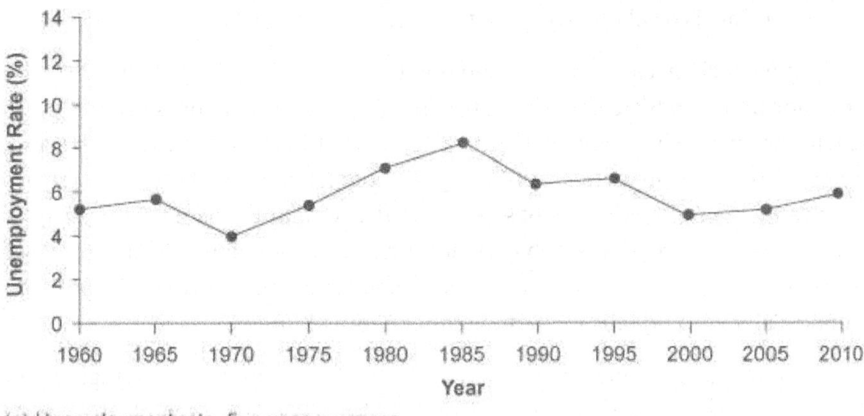


(e) Unemployment rate, five-year averages

**FIGURE A10 Presenting Unemployment Rates in Different Ways, All of Them Accurate** Simply changing the width and height of the area in which data is displayed can alter the perception of the data.

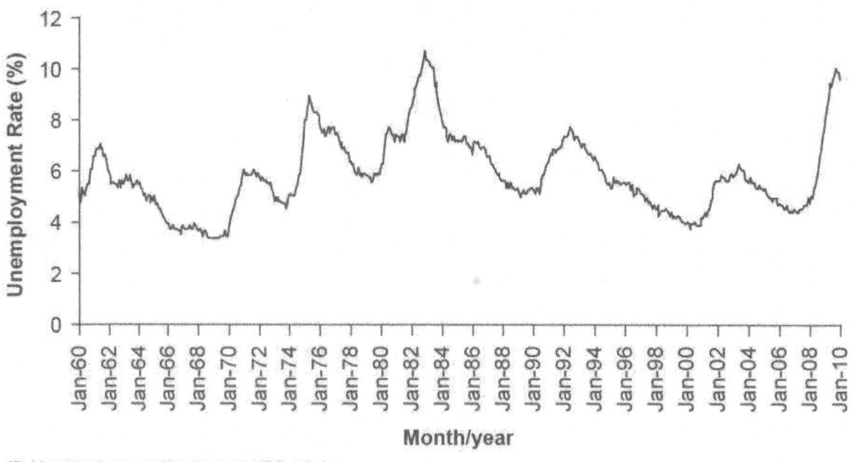

(f) Unemployment rate, monthly data

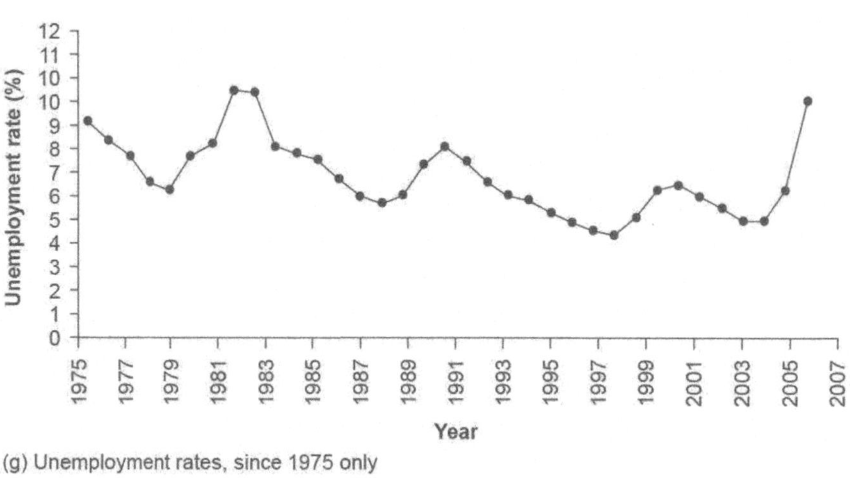

(g) Unemployment rates, since 1975 only

**FIGURE A11 Presenting Unemployment Rates in Different Ways, All of Them Accurate** Simply changing the width and height of the area in which data is displayed can alter the perception of the data.

Suppose you wanted a graph which gives the impression that the rise in unemployment in 2009 was not all that large, or all that extraordinary by historical standards. You might choose to present your data as in Figure A9 (a). Figure A9 (a) includes much of the same data presented earlier in Figure A5, but stretches the horizontal axis out longer relative to the vertical axis. By spreading the graph wide and flat, the visual appearance is that the rise in unemployment is not so large, and is similar to some past rises in unemployment. Now imagine you wanted to emphasize how unemployment spiked substantially higher in 2009. In this case, using the same data, you can stretch the vertical axis out relative to the horizontal axis, as in Figure A9 (b), which makes all rises and falls in unemployment appear larger.

A similar effect can be accomplished without changing the length of the axes, but by changing the scale on the vertical axis. In Figure A10 (c), the scale on the vertical axis runs from 0% to 30%, while in Figure A10 (d), the vertical axis runs from 3% to 10%. Compared to Figure A5, where the vertical scale runs from 0% to 12%, Figure A10 (c) makes the fluctuation in unemployment look smaller, while Figure A10 (d) makes it look larger.

Another way to alter the perception of the graph is to reduce the amount of variation by changing the number of points plotted on the graph. Figure A10 (e) shows the unemployment rate according to five-year averages. By averaging out some of the year-to-year changes, the line appears smoother and with fewer highs and lows. In reality, the unemployment rate is reported monthly, and Figure A11 (f) shows the monthly figures since 1960, which fluctuate more than the five-year average. Figure A11 (f) is also a vivid illustration of how graphs can compress lots of data. The graph includes monthly data since 1960, which over almost 50 years, works out to nearly 600 data points. Reading that list of 600 data points in numerical form would be hypnotic. You can, however, get a good intuitive sense of these 600 data points very quickly from the graph.

A final trick in manipulating the perception of graphical information is that, by choosing the starting and ending points carefully, you can influence the perception of whether the variable is rising or falling. The original data show a general pattern with unemployment low in the 1960s, but spiking up in the mid-1970s, early 1980s, early 1990s, early 2000s, and late 2000s. Figure A11 (g), however, shows a graph that goes back only to 1975, which gives an impression that unemployment was more-or-less gradually falling over time until the 2009 recession pushed it back up to its "original" level—which is a plausible interpretation if one starts at the high point around 1975.

These kinds of tricks—or shall we just call them "presentation choices"— are not limited to line graphs. In a pie chart with many small slices and one large slice, someone must decide what categories should be used to produce these slices in the first place, thus making some slices appear bigger than others. If you are making a bar graph, you can make the vertical axis either taller or shorter, which will tend to make variations in the height of the bars appear more or less.

Being able to read graphs is an essential skill, both in economics and in life. A graph is just one perspective or point of view, shaped by choices such as those discussed in this section. Do not always believe the first quick impression from a graph. View with caution.

## Key Concepts and Summary

Math is a tool for understanding economics and economic relationships can be expressed mathematically using algebra or graphs. The algebraic equation for a line is $y = b + mx$, where $x$ is the variable on the horizontal axis and $y$ is the variable on the vertical axis, the $b$ term is the y-intercept and the $m$ term is the slope. The slope of a line is the same at any point on the line and it indicates the relationship (positive, negative, or zero) between two economic variables.

Economic models can be solved algebraically or graphically. Graphs allow you to illustrate data visually. They can illustrate patterns, comparisons, trends, and apportionment by condensing the numerical data and providing an intuitive sense of relationships in the data. A line graph shows the relationship between two variables: one is shown on the horizontal axis and one on the vertical axis. A pie graph shows how something is allotted, such as a sum of money or a group of people. The size of each slice of the pie is drawn to represent the corresponding percentage of the whole. A bar graph uses the height of bars to show a relationship, where each bar represents a certain entity, like a country or a group of people. The bars on a bar graph can also be divided into segments to show subgroups.

Any graph is a single visual perspective on a subject. The impression it leaves will be based on many choices, such as what data or time frame is included, how data or groups are divided up, the relative size of vertical and horizontal axes, whether the scale used on a vertical starts at zero. Thus, any graph should be regarded somewhat skeptically, remembering that the underlying relationship can be open to different interpretations.

## Review Questions

Exercise A1
Name three kinds of graphs and briefly state when is most appropriate to use each type of graph.

Exercise A2
What is slope on a line graph?

Exercise A3
What do the slices of a pie chart represent?

Exercise A4

Why is a bar chart the best way to illustrate comparisons?

Exercise A5
How does the appearance of positive slope differ from negative slope and from zero slope?

# APPENDIX B

---

## Indifference Curves

Economists use a vocabulary of maximizing utility to describe people's preferences. In Consumer Choices, the level of utility that a person receives is described in numerical terms. This appendix presents an alternative approach to describing personal preferences, called indifference curves, which avoids any need for using numbers to measure utility. By setting aside the assumption of putting a numerical valuation on utility—an assumption that many students and economists find uncomfortably unrealistic—the indifference curve framework helps to clarify the logic of the underlying model.

### What Is an Indifference Curve?

People cannot really put a numerical value on their level of satisfaction. However, they can, and do, identify what choices would give them more, or less, or the same amount of satisfaction. An indifference curve shows combinations of goods that provide an equal level of utility or satisfaction. For example, Figure B1 presents three indifference curves that represent Lilly's preferences for the tradeoffs that she faces in her two main relaxation activities: eating doughnuts and reading paperback books. Each indifference curve (Ul, Um, and Uh) represents one level of utility. First we will explore the meaning of one particular indifference curve and then we will look at the indifference curves as a group.

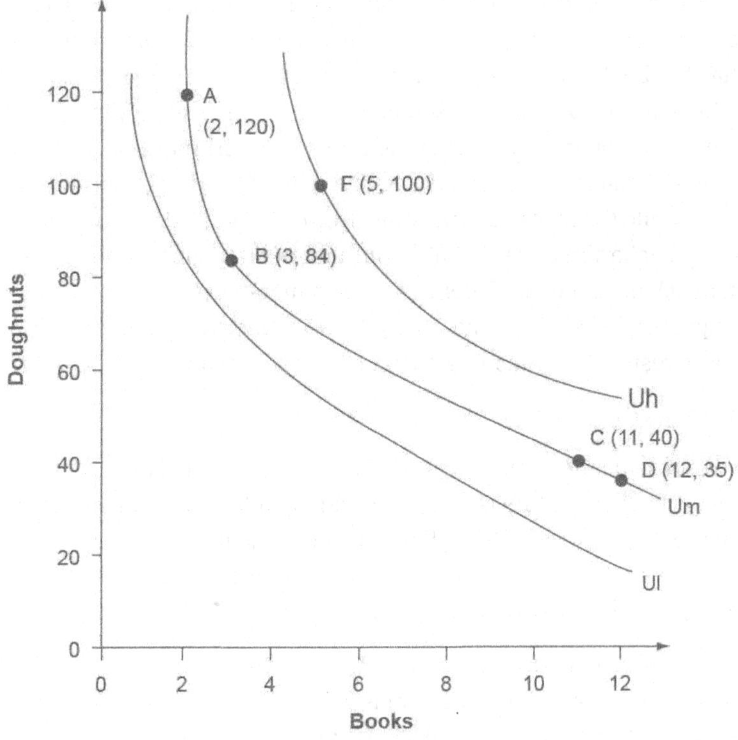


FIGURE B1 Lilly's Indifference Curves Lilly would receive equal utility from all points on a given indifference curve. Any points on the highest indifference curve Uh, like F, provide greater utility than any points like A, B, C, and D on the middle indifference curve Um. Similarly, any points on the middle indifference curve Um provide greater utility than any points on the lowest indifference curve Ul.

**The Shape of an Indifference Curve**

The indifference curve Um has four points labeled on it: A, B, C, and D. Since an indifference curve represents a set of choices that have the same level of utility, Lilly must receive an equal amount of utility, judged according to her personal preferences, from two books and 120 doughnuts (point A), from three books and 84 doughnuts (point B) from 11 books and 40 doughnuts (point C) or from 12 books and 35 doughnuts (point D). She would also receive the same utility from any of the unlabeled intermediate points along this indifference curve.

Indifference curves have a roughly similar shape in two ways: 1) they are downward sloping from left to right; 2) they are convex with respect to the origin. In other words, they are steeper on the left and flatter on the right. The downward slope of the indifference curve means that Lilly must trade off less of one good to get more of the other, while holding utility constant. For example, points A and B sit on the same indifference curve Um, which means that they provide Lilly with the same level of utility. Thus, the marginal utility that Lilly would gain from, say, increasing her consumption of books from two to three must be equal to the marginal utility that she would lose if her consumption of doughnuts was cut from 120 to 84—so that her overall utility remains unchanged between points A and B. Indeed, the slope along an indifference curve as the marginal rate of substitution, which is the rate at which a person is willing to trade one good for another so that utility will remain the same.

Indifference curves like Um are steeper on the left and flatter on the right. The reason behind this shape involves diminishing marginal utility—the notion that as a person consumes more of a good, the marginal utility from each additional unit becomes lower. Compare two different choices between points that all provide Lilly an equal amount of utility along the indifference curve Um: the choice between A and B, and between C and D. In both choices, Lilly consumes one more book, but between A and B her consumption of doughnuts falls by 36 (from 120 to 84) and between C and D it falls by only five (from 40 to 35). The reason for this difference is that points A and C are different starting points, and thus have different implications for marginal utility. At point A, Lilly has few books and many doughnuts. Thus, her marginal utility from an extra book will be relatively high while the marginal utility of additional doughnuts is relatively low—so on the margin, it will take a relatively large number of doughnuts to offset the utility from the marginal book. At point C, however, Lilly has many books and few doughnuts. From this starting point, her marginal utility gained from extra books will be relatively low, while the marginal utility lost from additional doughnuts would be relatively high—so on the margin, it will take a relatively smaller number of doughnuts to offset the change of one marginal book. In short, the slope of the indifference curve changes because the marginal rate of substitution—that is, the quantity of one good that would be traded for the other good to keep utility constant—also changes, as a result of diminishing marginal utility of both goods.

## The Field of Indifference Curves

Each indifference curve represents the choices that provide a single level of utility. Every level of utility will have its own indifference curve. Thus, Lilly's preferences will include an infinite number of indifference curves lying nestled together on the diagram—even though only three of the indifference curves, representing three levels of utility, appear on Figure B1. In other words, an infinite number of indifference curves are not drawn on this diagram—but you should remember that they exist.

Higher indifference curves represent a greater level of utility than lower ones. In Figure B1, indifference curve Ul can be thought of as a "low" level of utility, while Um is a "medium" level of utility and Uh is a "high" level of utility. All of the choices on indifference curve Uh are preferred to all of the choices on indifference curve Um, which in turn are preferred to all of the choices on Ul.

To understand why higher indifference curves are preferred to lower ones, compare point B on indifference curve Um to point F on indifference curve Uh. Point F has greater consumption of both books (five to three) and doughnuts (100 to 84), so point F is clearly preferable to point B. Given the definition of an indifference curve—that all the points on the curve have the same level of utility—if point F on indifference curve Uh is preferred to point B on indifference curve Um, then it must be true that all points on indifference curve Uh have a higher level of utility than all points on Um. More generally, for any point on a lower indifference curve, like Ul, you can identify a point on a higher indifference curve like Um or Uh that has a higher consumption of both goods. Since one point on the higher indifference curve is preferred to one point on the lower curve, and since all the points on a given indifference curve have the same level of utility, it must be true that all points on higher indifference curves have greater utility than all points on lower indifference curves.

These arguments about the shapes of indifference curves and about higher or lower levels of utility do not require any numerical estimates of utility, either by the individual or by anyone else. They are only based on the assumptions that when people have less of one good they need more of another good to make up for it, if they are keeping the same level of utility, and that as people have more of a good, the marginal utility they receive from additional units of that good will diminish. Given these gentle assumptions, a field of indifference curves can be mapped out to describe the preferences of any individual.

### The Individuality of Indifference Curves

Each person determines their own preferences and utility. Thus, while indifference curves have the same general shape—they slope down, and the slope is steeper on the left and flatter on the right—the specific shape of indifference curves can be different for every person. Figure B1, for example, applies only to Lilly's preferences. Indifference curves for other people would probably travel through different points.

## Utility-Maximizing with Indifference Curves

People seek the highest level of utility, which means that they wish to be on the highest possible indifference curve. However, people are limited by their budget constraints, which show what tradeoffs are actually possible.

### Maximizing Utility at the Highest Indifference Curve

Return to the situation of Lilly's choice between paperback books and doughnuts. Say that books cost $6, doughnuts are 50 cents each, and that Lilly has $60 to spend. This information provides the basis for the budget line shown in Figure B2. Along with the budget line are shown the three indifference curves from Figure B1. What is Lilly's utility-maximizing choice? Several possibilities are identified in the diagram.

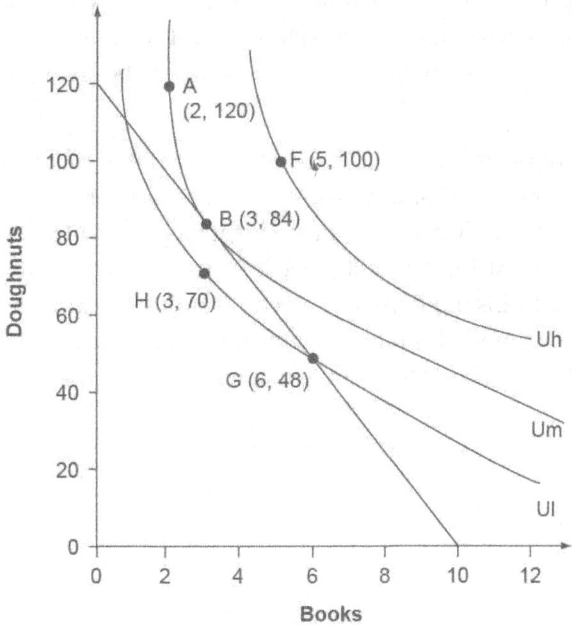


**FIGURE B2 Indifference Curves and a Budget Constraint** Lilly's preferences are shown by the indifference curves. Lilly's budget constraint, given the prices of books and doughnuts and her income, is shown by the straight line.

Lilly's optimal choice will be point B, where the budget line is tangent to the indifference curve Um. Lilly would have more utility at a point like F on the higher indifference curve Uh, but the budget line does not touch the higher indifference curve Uh at any point, so she cannot afford this choice. A choice like G is affordable to Lilly, but it lies on indifference curve Ul and thus provides less utility than choice B, which is on indifference curve Um.

The choice of F with five books and 100 doughnuts is highly desirable, since it is on the highest indifference curve Uh of those shown in the diagram. However, it is not affordable given Lilly's budget constraint. The choice of H with three books and 70 doughnuts on indifference curve Ul is a wasteful choice, since it is inside Lilly's budget set, and as a utility-maximizer, Lilly will always prefer a choice on the budget constraint itself. Choices B and G are both on the opportunity set. However, choice G of six books and 48 doughnuts is on lower indifference curve Ul than choice B of three books and 84 doughnuts, which is on the indifference curve Um. If Lilly were to start at choice G, and then thought about whether the marginal utility she was deriving from doughnuts and books, she would decide that some additional doughnuts and fewer books would make her happier—which would cause her to move toward her preferred choice B. Given the combination of Lilly's personal preferences, as identified by her indifference curves, and Lilly's opportunity set, which is determined by prices and income, B will be her utility-maximizing choice.

The highest achievable indifference curve touches the opportunity set at a single point of tangency. Since an infinite number of indifference curves exist, even if only a few of them are drawn on any given diagram, there will always exist one indifference curve that touches the budget line at a single point of tangency. All higher indifference curves, like Uh, will be completely above the budget line and, although the choices on that indifference curve would provide higher utility, they are not affordable given the budget set. All lower indifference curves, like Ul, will cross the budget line in two separate places. When one indifference curve crosses the budget line in two places, however, there will be another, higher, attainable indifference curve sitting above it that touches the budget line at only one point of tangency.

## Changes in Income

A rise in income causes the budget constraint to shift to the right. In graphical terms, the new budget constraint will now be tangent to a higher indifference curve, representing a higher level of utility. A reduction in income will cause the budget constraint to shift to the left, which will cause it to be tangent to a lower indifference curve, representing a reduced level of utility. If income rises by, for example, 50%, exactly how much will a person alter consumption of books and doughnuts? Will consumption of both goods rise by 50%, or will the quantity of one good rise substantially, while the quantity of the other good rises only a little, or even declines?

Since personal preferences and the shape of indifference curves are different for each individual, the response to changes in income will be different, too. For example, consider the preferences of Manuel and Natasha in Figure B3 (a) and Figure B3 (b). They each start with an identical income of $40, which they spend on yogurts that cost $1 and rental movies that cost $4. Thus, they face identical budget constraints. However, based on Manuel's preferences, as revealed by his indifference curves, his utility-maximizing choice on the original budget set occurs where his opportunity set is tangent to the highest possible indifference curve at W, with three movies and 28 yogurts, while Natasha's utility-maximizing choice on the original budget set at Y will be seven movies and 12 yogurts.

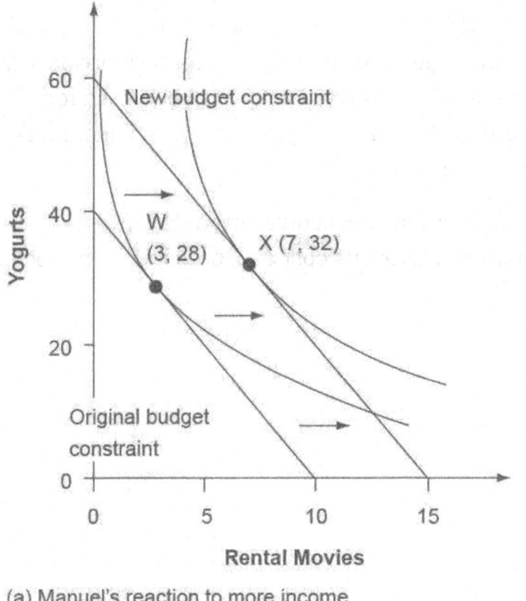



(a) Manuel's reaction to more income

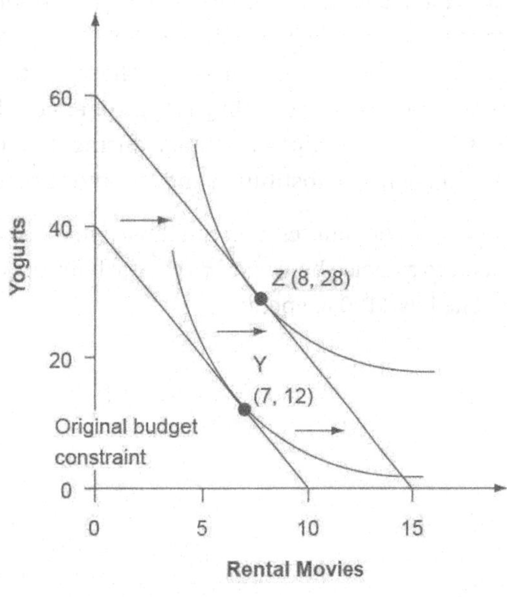



(b) Natasha's reaction to more income

**FIGURE B3 Manuel and Natasha's Indifference Curves** Manuel and Natasha originally face the same budget constraints; that is, same prices and same income. However, the indifference curves that illustrate their preferences are not the same. (a) Manuel's original choice at W involves more yogurt and more movies, and he reacts to the higher income by mainly increasing consumption of movies at X. (b) Conversely, Natasha's original choice (Y) involves relatively more movies, but she reacts to the higher income by choosing relatively more yogurts. Even when budget constraints are the same, personal preferences lead to different original choices and to different reactions in response to a change in income.

Now, say that income rises to $60 for both Manuel and Natasha, so their budget constraints shift to the right. As shown in Figure B3 (a), Manuel's new utility maximizing choice at X will be seven movies and 32 yogurts—that is, Manuel will choose to spend most of the extra income on movies. Natasha's new utility maximizing choice at Z will be eight movies and 28 yogurts—that is, she will choose to spend most of the extra income on yogurt. In this way, the indifference curve approach allows for a range of possible responses. However, if both goods are normal goods, then the typical response to a higher level of income will be to purchase more of them—although exactly how much more is a matter of personal preference. If one of the goods is an inferior good, the response to a higher level of income will be to purchase less of it.

## Responses to Price Changes: Substitution and Income Effects

A higher price for a good will cause the budget constraint to shift to the left, so that it is tangent to a lower indifference curve representing a reduced level of utility. Conversely, a lower price for a good will cause the opportunity set to shift to the right, so that it is tangent to a higher indifference curve representing an increased level of utility. Exactly how much a change in price will lead to the quantity demanded of each good will depend on personal preferences.

Anyone who faces a change in price will experience two interlinked motivations: a substitution effect and an income effect. The substitution effect is that when a good becomes more expensive, people seek out substitutes. If oranges become more expensive, fruit-lovers scale back on oranges and eat more apples, grapefruit, or raisins. Conversely, when a good becomes cheaper, people substitute toward consuming more. If oranges get cheaper, people fire up their juicing machines and ease off on other fruits and foods. The income effect refers to how a change in the price of a good alters the effective buying power of one's income. If the price of a good that you have been buying falls, then in effect your buying power has risen—you are able to purchase more goods. Conversely, if the price of a good that you have been buying rises, then the buying power of a given amount of income is diminished. (One common source of confusion is that the "income effect" does not refer to a change in actual income. Instead, it refers to the situation in which the price of a good changes, and thus the quantities of goods that can be purchased with a fixed amount of income change. It might be more accurate to call the "income effect" a "buying power effect," but the "income effect" terminology has been used for decades, and it is not going to change during this economics course.) Whenever a price changes, consumers feel the pull of both substitution and income effects at the same time.

Using indifference curves, you can illustrate the substitution and income effects on a graph. In Figure B4, Ogden faces a choice between two goods: haircuts or personal pizzas. Haircuts cost $20, personal pizzas cost $6, and he has $120 to spend.

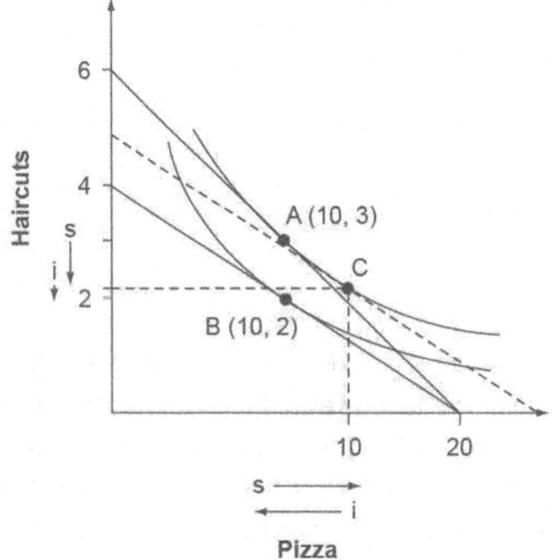


**FIGURE B4 Substitution and Income Effects** The original choice is A, the point of tangency between the original budget constraint and indifference curve. The new choice is B, the point of tangency between the new budget constraint and the lower indifference curve. Point C is the tangency between the dashed line, where the slope shows the new higher price of haircuts, and the original indifference curve. The substitution effect is the shift from A to C, which means getting fewer haircuts and more pizza. The income effect is the shift from C to B; that is, the reduction in buying power that causes a shift from the higher indifference curve to the lower indifference curve, with relative prices remaining unchanged. The income effect results in less consumed of both goods. Both substitution and income effects cause fewer haircuts to be consumed. For pizza, in this case, the substitution effect and income effect cancel out, leading to the same amount of pizza consumed.

The price of haircuts rises to $30. Ogden starts at choice A on the higher opportunity set and the higher indifference curve. After the price of haircuts increases, he chooses B on the lower opportunity set and the lower indifference curve. Point B with two haircuts and 10 personal pizzas is immediately below point A with three haircuts and 10 personal pizzas, showing that Ogden reacted to a higher price of haircuts by cutting back only on haircuts, while leaving his consumption of pizza unchanged.

The dashed line in the diagram, and point C, are used to separate the substitution effect and the income effect. To understand their function, start by thinking about the substitution effect with this question: How would Ogden change his consumption if the relative prices of the two goods changed, but this change in relative prices did not affect his utility? The slope of the budget constraint is determined by the relative price of the two goods; thus, the slope of the original budget line is determined by the original relative prices, while the slope of the new budget line is determined by the new relative prices. With this thought in mind, the dashed line is a graphical tool inserted in a specific way: It is inserted so that it is parallel with the new budget constraint, so it reflects the new relative prices, but it is tangent to the original indifference curve, so it reflects the original level of utility or buying power.

Thus, the movement from the original choice (A) to point C is a substitution effect; it shows the choice that

Ogden would make if relative prices shifted (as shown by the different slope between the original budget set and the dashed line) but if buying power did not shift (as shown by being tangent to the original indifference curve). The substitution effect will encourage people to shift away from the good which has become relatively more expensive—in Ogden's case, the haircuts on the vertical axis—and toward the good which has become relatively less expensive—in this case, the pizza on the vertical axis. The two arrows labeled with "s" for "substitution effect," one on each axis, show the direction of this movement.

The income effect is the movement from point C to B, which shows how Ogden reacts to a reduction in his buying power from the higher indifference curve to the lower indifference curve, but holding constant the relative prices (because the dashed line has the same slope as the new budget constraint). In this case, where the price of one good increases, buying power is reduced, so the income effect means that consumption of both goods should fall (if they are both normal goods, which it is reasonable to assume unless there is reason to believe otherwise). The two arrows labeled with "i" for "income effect," one on each axis, show the direction of this income effect movement.

Now, put the substitution and income effects together. When the price of pizza increased, Ogden consumed less of it, for two reasons shown in the exhibit: the substitution effect of the higher price led him to consume less and the income effect of the higher price also led him to consume less. However, when the price of pizza increased, Ogden consumed the same quantity of haircuts. The substitution effect of a higher price for pizza meant that haircuts became relatively less expensive (compared to pizza), and this factor, taken alone, would have encouraged Ogden to consume more haircuts. However, the income effect of a higher price for pizza meant that he wished to consume less of both goods, and this factor, taken alone, would have encouraged Ogden to consume fewer haircuts. As shown in Figure B4, in this particular example the substitution effect and income effect on Ogden's consumption of haircuts are offsetting—so he ends up consuming the same quantity of haircuts after the price increase for pizza as before.

The size of these income and substitution effects will differ from person to person, depending on individual preferences. For example, if Ogden's substitution effect away from pizza and toward haircuts is especially strong, and outweighs the income effect, then a higher price for pizza might lead to increased consumption of haircuts. This case would be drawn on the graph so that the point of tangency between the new budget constraint and the relevant indifference curve occurred below point B and to the right. Conversely, if the substitution effect away from pizza and toward haircuts is not as strong, and the income effect on is relatively stronger, then Ogden will be more likely to react to the higher price of pizza by consuming less of both goods. In this case, his optimal choice after the price change will be above and to the left of choice B on the new budget constraint.

Although the substitution and income effects are often discussed as a sequence of events, it should be remembered that they are twin components of a single cause—a change in price. Although you can analyze them separately, the two effects are always proceeding hand in hand, happening at the same time.

## Indifference Curves with Labor-Leisure and Intertemporal Choices

The concept of an indifference curve applies to tradeoffs in any household choice, including the labor-leisure choice or the intertemporal choice between present and future consumption. In the labor-leisure choice, each indifference curve shows the combinations of leisure and income that provide a certain level of utility. In an intertemporal choice, each indifference curve shows the combinations of present and future consumption that provide a certain level of utility. The general shapes of the indifference curves—downward sloping, steeper on the left and flatter on the right—also remain the same.

### A Labor-Leisure Example

Petunia is working at a job that pays $12 per hour but she gets a raise to $20 per hour. After family responsibilities and sleep, she has 80 hours per week available for work or leisure. As shown in Figure B5, the highest level of utility for Petunia, on her original budget constraint, is at choice A, where it is tangent to the lower indifference curve (Ul). Point A has 30 hours of leisure and thus 50 hours per week of work, with income of $600 per week (that is, 50 hours of work at $12 per hour). Petunia then gets a raise to $20 per hour, which shifts her budget constraint to the right. Her new utility-maximizing choice occurs where the new budget constraint is tangent to the higher indifference curve Uh. At B, Petunia has 40 hours of leisure per week and works 40 hours, with income of $800 per week (that is, 40 hours of work at $20 per hour).

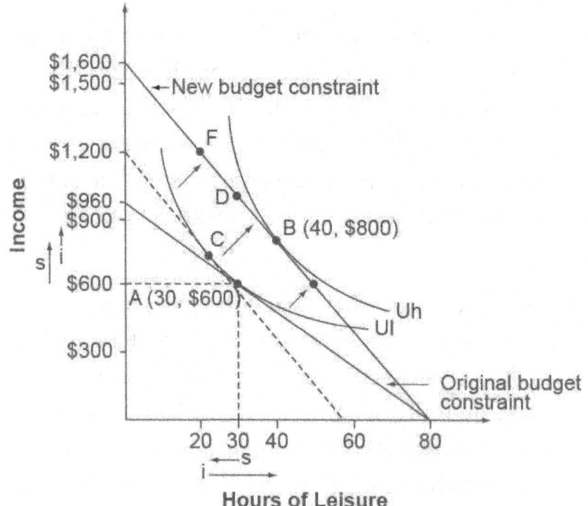


**FIGURE B5 Effects of a Change in Petunia's Wage** Petunia starts at choice A, the tangency between her original budget constraint and the lower indifference curve Ul. The wage increase shifts her budget constraint to the right, so that she can now choose B on indifference curve Uh. The substitution effect is the movement from A to C. In this case, the substitution effect would lead Petunia to choose less leisure, which is relatively more expensive, and more income, which is relatively cheaper to earn. The income effect is the movement from C to B. The income effect in this example leads to greater consumption of both goods. Overall, in this example, income rises because of both substitution and income effects. However, leisure declines because of the substitution effect but increases because of the income effect—leading, in Petunia's case, to an overall increase in the quantity of leisure consumed.

Substitution and income effects provide a vocabulary for discussing how Petunia reacts to a higher hourly wage. The dashed line serves as the tool for separating the two effects on the graph.

The substitution effect tells how Petunia would have changed her hours of work if her wage had risen, so that income was relatively cheaper to earn and leisure was relatively more expensive, but if she had remained at the same level of utility. The slope of the budget constraint in a labor-leisure diagram is determined by the wage rate. Thus, the dashed line is carefully inserted with the slope of the new opportunity set, reflecting the labor-leisure tradeoff of the new wage rate, but tangent to the original indifference curve, showing the same level of utility or "buying power." The shift from original choice A to point C, which is the point of tangency between the original indifference curve and the dashed line, shows that because of the higher wage, Petunia will want to consume less leisure and more income. The "s" arrows on the horizontal and vertical axes of Figure B5 show the substitution effect on leisure and on income.

The income effect is that the higher wage, by shifting the labor-leisure budget constraint to the right, makes it possible for Petunia to reach a higher level of utility. The income effect is the movement from point C to point B; that is, it shows how Petunia's behavior would change in response to a higher level of utility or "buying power," with the wage rate remaining the same (as shown by the dashed line being parallel to the new budget constraint). The income effect, encouraging Petunia to consume both more leisure and more income, is drawn with arrows on the horizontal and vertical axis of Figure B5.

Putting these effects together, Petunia responds to the higher wage by moving from choice A to choice B. This movement involves choosing more income, both because the substitution effect of higher wages has made income relatively cheaper or easier to earn, and because the income effect of higher wages has made it possible to have more income and more leisure. Her movement from A to B also involves choosing more leisure because, according to Petunia's preferences, the income effect that encourages choosing more leisure is stronger than the substitution effect that encourages choosing less leisure.

Figure B5 represents only Petunia's preferences. Other people might make other choices. For example, a person whose substitution and income effects on leisure exactly counterbalanced each other might react to a higher wage with a choice like D, exactly above the original choice A, which means taking all of the benefit of the higher wages in the form of income while working the same number of hours. Yet another person, whose substitution effect on leisure outweighed the income effect, might react to a higher wage by making a choice like F, where the response to higher wages is to work more hours and earn much more income. To represent these different preferences, you could easily draw the indifference curve Uh to be tangent to the new budget constraint at D or F, rather than at B.

## An Intertemporal Choice Example

Quentin has saved up $10,000. He is thinking about spending some or all of it on a vacation in the present, and then will save the rest for another big vacation five years from now. Over those five years, he expects to earn a total 80% rate of return. Figure B6 shows Quentin's budget constraint and his indifference curves between present consumption and future consumption. The highest level of utility that Quentin can achieve at his original intertemporal budget constraint occurs at point A, where he is consuming $6,000, saving $4,000 for the future, and expecting with the accumulated interest to have $7,200 for future consumption (that is, $4,000 in current financial savings plus the 80% rate of return).

However, Quentin has just realized that his expected rate of return was unrealistically high. A more realistic expectation is that over five years he can earn a total return of 30%. In effect, his intertemporal budget constraint has pivoted to the left, so that his original utility-maximizing choice is no longer available. Will Quentin react to the lower rate of return by saving more, or less, or the same amount? Again, the language of substitution and income effects provides a framework for thinking about the motivations behind various choices. The dashed line, which is a graphical tool to separate the substitution and income effect, is carefully inserted with the same slope as the new opportunity set, so that it reflects the changed rate of return, but it is tangent to the original indifference curve, so that it shows no change in utility or "buying power."

The substitution effect tells how Quentin would have altered his consumption because the lower rate of return makes future consumption relatively more expensive and present consumption relatively cheaper. The movement from the original choice A to point C shows how Quentin substitutes toward more present consumption and less future consumption in response to the lower interest rate, with no change in utility. The substitution arrows on the horizontal and vertical axes of Figure B6 show the direction of the substitution effect motivation. The substitution effect suggests that, because of the lower interest rate, Quentin should consume more in the present and less in the future.

Quentin also has an income effect motivation. The lower rate of return shifts the budget constraint to the left, which means that Quentin's utility or "buying power" is reduced. The income effect (assuming normal goods) encourages less of both present and future consumption. The impact of the income effect on reducing present and future consumption in this example is shown with "i" arrows on the horizontal and vertical axis of Figure B6.

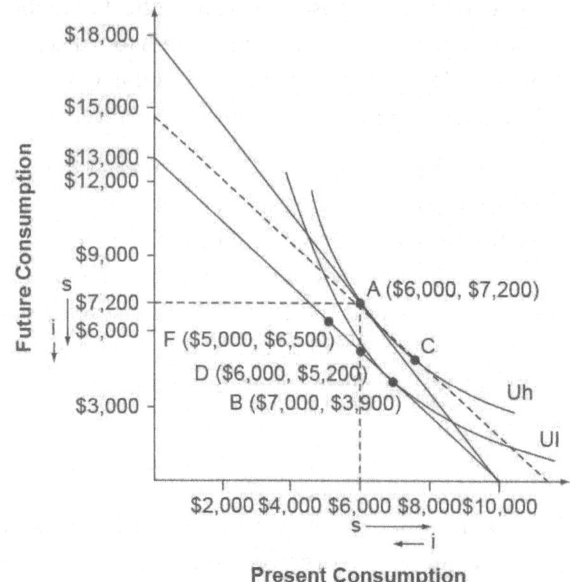


**FIGURE B6 Indifference Curve and an Intertemporal Budget Constraint** The original choice is A, at the tangency between the original budget constraint and the original indifference curve Uh. The dashed line is drawn parallel to the new budget set, so that its slope reflects the lower rate of return, but is tangent to the original indifference curve. The movement from A to C is the substitution effect: in this case, future consumption has become relatively more expensive, and present consumption has become relatively cheaper. The income effect is the shift from C to B; that is, the reduction in utility or "buying power" that causes a move to a lower indifference curve Ul, but with the relative price the same. It means less present and less future consumption. In the move from A to B, the substitution effect on present consumption is greater than the income effect, so the overall result is more present consumption. Notice that the lower indifference curve could have been drawn tangent to the lower budget constraint point D or point F, depending on personal preferences.

Taking both effects together, the substitution effect is encouraging Quentin toward more present and less future consumption, because present consumption is relatively cheaper, while the income effect is encouraging him to less present and less future consumption, because the lower interest rate is pushing him to a lower level of utility. For Quentin's personal preferences, the substitution effect is stronger so that, overall, he reacts to the lower rate of return with more present consumption and less savings at choice B. However, other people might have different preferences. They might react to a lower rate of return by choosing the same level of present consumption and savings at choice D, or by choosing less present consumption and more savings at a point like F. For these other sets of preferences, the income effect of a lower rate of return on present consumption would be relatively stronger, while the substitution effect would be relatively weaker.

## Sketching Substitution and Income Effects

Indifference curves provide an analytical tool for looking at all the choices that provide a single level of utility. They eliminate any need for placing numerical values on utility and help to illuminate the process of making utility-maximizing decisions. They also provide the basis for a more detailed investigation of the complementary motivations that arise in response to a change in a price, wage or rate of return—namely, the substitution and income effects.

If you are finding it a little tricky to sketch diagrams that show substitution and income effects so that the points of tangency all come out correctly, it may be useful to follow this procedure.

Step 1. Begin with a budget constraint showing the choice between two goods, which this example will call "candy" and "movies." Choose a point A which will be the optimal choice, where the indifference curve will be tangent—but it is often easier not to draw in the indifference curve just yet. See Figure B7.

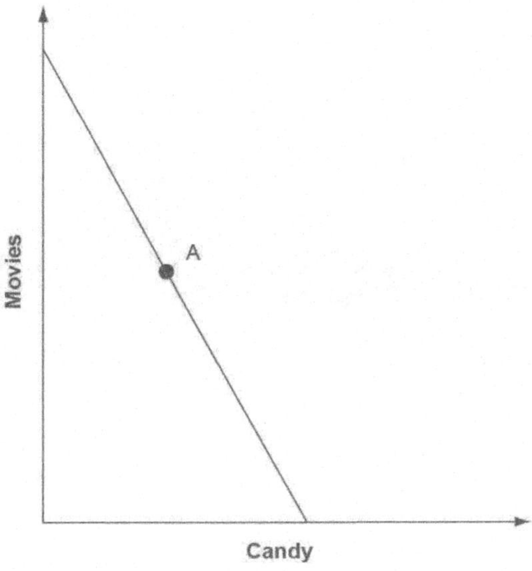



**FIGURE B7**

Step 2. Now the price of movies changes: let's say that it rises. That shifts the budget set inward. You know that the higher price will push the decision-maker down to a lower level of utility, represented by a lower indifference curve. But at this stage, draw only the new budget set. See Figure B8.

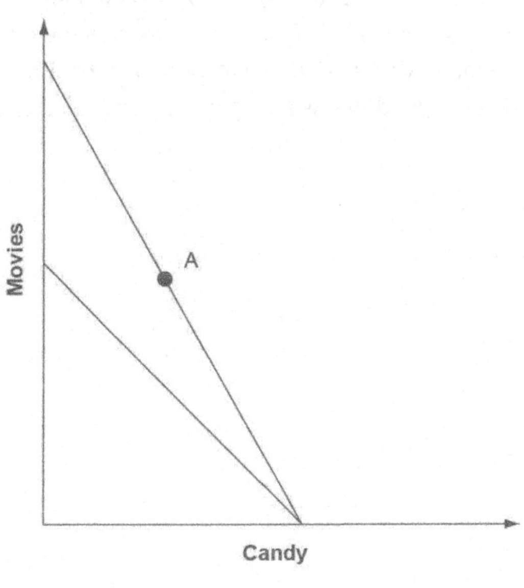



**FIGURE B8**

Step 3. The key tool in distinguishing between substitution and income effects is to insert a dashed line, parallel to the new budget line. This line is a graphical tool that allows you to distinguish between the two changes: (1) the effect on consumption of the two goods of the shift in prices—with the level of utility remaining unchanged—which is the substitution effect; and (2) the effect on consumption of the two goods of shifting from one indifference curve to the other—with relative prices staying unchanged—which is the income effect. The dashed line is inserted in this step. The trick is to have the dashed line travel close to the original choice A, but not directly through point A. See Figure B9.

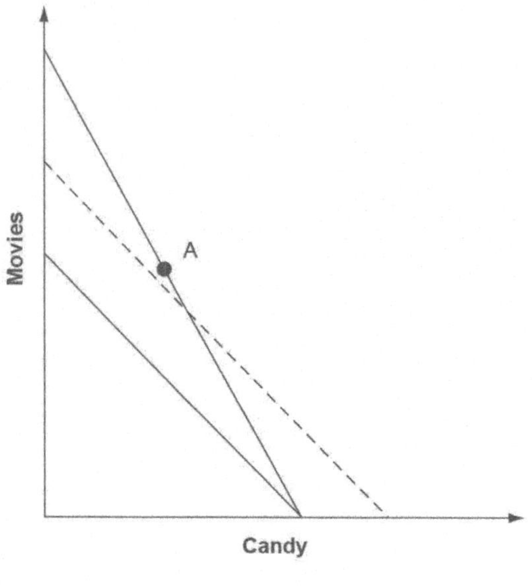



**FIGURE B9**

Step 4. Now, draw the original indifference curve, so that it is tangent to both point A on the original budget line and to a point C on the dashed line. Many students find it easiest to first select the tangency point C where the original indifference curve touches the dashed line, and then to draw the original indifference curve through A and C. The substitution effect is illustrated by the movement along the original indifference curve as prices change but the level of utility holds constant, from A to C. As expected, the substitution effect leads to less consumed of the good that is relatively more expensive, as shown by the "s" (substitution) arrow on the vertical axis, and more consumed of the good that is relatively less expensive, as shown by the "s" arrow on the horizontal axis. See Figure B10.

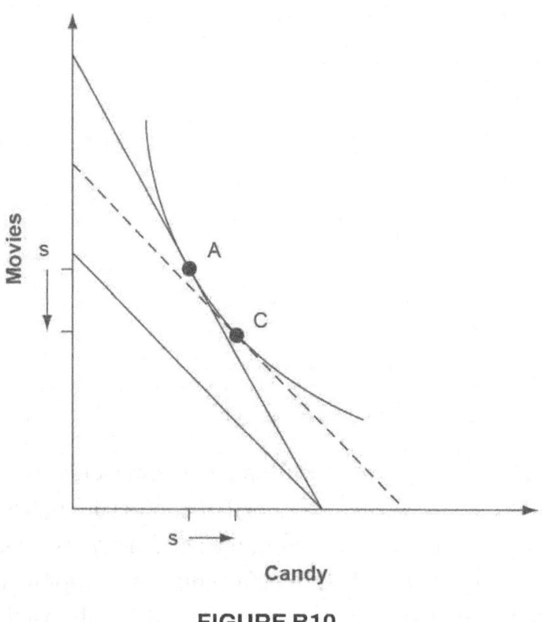



**FIGURE B10**

Step 5. With the substitution effect in place, now choose utility-maximizing point B on the new opportunity set. When you choose point B, think about whether you wish the substitution or the income effect to have a larger impact on the good (in this case, candy) on the horizontal axis. If you choose point B to be directly in a vertical line with point A (as is illustrated here), then the income effect will be exactly offsetting the substitution effect on the horizontal axis. If you insert point B so that it lies a little to right of the original point A, then the substitution effect will exceed the income effect. If you insert point B so that it lies a little to the left of point A, then the income effect will exceed the substitution effect. The income effect is the movement from C to B, showing how choices shifted as a result of the decline in buying power and the movement between two levels of utility, with relative prices remaining the same. With normal goods, the negative income effect means less consumed of each good, as shown by the direction of the "i" (income effect) arrows on the vertical and horizontal axes. See Figure B11.

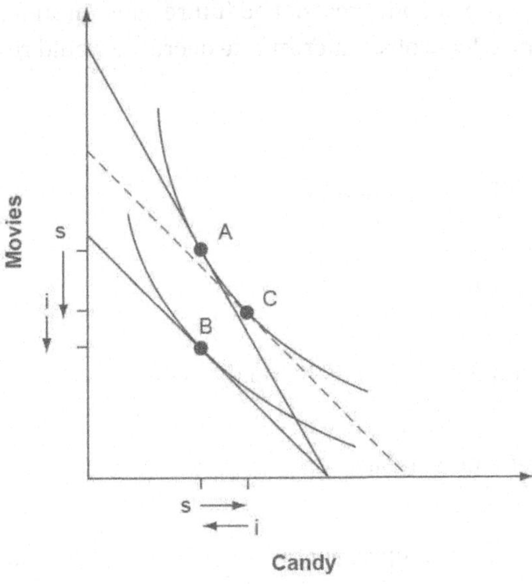

**FIGURE B11**

In sketching substitution and income effect diagrams, you may wish to practice some of the following variations: (1) Price falls instead of a rising; (2) The price change affects the good on either the vertical or the horizontal axis; (3) Sketch these diagrams so that the substitution effect exceeds the income effect; the income effect exceeds the substitution effect; and the two effects are equal.

One final note: The helpful dashed line can be drawn tangent to the new indifference curve, and parallel to the original budget line, rather than tangent to the original indifference curve and parallel to the new budget line. Some students find this approach more intuitively clear. The answers you get about the direction and relative sizes of the substitution and income effects, however, should be the same.

## Key Concepts and Summary

An indifference curve is drawn on a budget constraint diagram that shows the tradeoffs between two goods. All points along a single indifference curve provide the same level of utility. Higher indifference curves represent higher levels of utility. Indifference curves slope downward because, if utility is to remain the same at all points along the curve, a reduction in the quantity of the good on the vertical axis must be counterbalanced by an increase in the quantity of the good on the horizontal axis (or vice versa). Indifference curves are steeper on the far left and flatter on the far right, because of diminishing marginal utility.

The utility-maximizing choice along a budget constraint will be the point of tangency where the budget constraint touches an indifference curve at a single point. A change in the price of any good has two effects: a substitution effect and an income effect. The substitution effect motivation encourages a utility-maximizer to buy less of what is relatively more expensive and more of what is relatively cheaper. The income effect motivation encourages a utility-maximizer to buy more of both goods if utility rises or less of both goods if utility falls (if they are both normal goods).

In a labor-leisure choice, every wage change has a substitution and an income effect. The substitution effect of a wage increase is to choose more income, since it is cheaper to earn, and less leisure, since its opportunity cost has increased. The income effect of a wage increase is to choose more of leisure and income, since they are both normal goods. The substitution and income effects of a wage decrease would reverse these directions.

In an intertemporal consumption choice, every interest rate change has a substitution and an income effect. The substitution effect of an interest rate increase is to choose more future consumption, since it is now cheaper to earn future consumption and less present consumption (more savings), since the opportunity cost of present consumption in terms of what is being given up in the future has increased. The income effect of an interest rate increase is to choose more of both present and future consumption, since they are both normal goods. The substitution and income effects of an interest rate decrease would reverse these directions.

## Review Questions

Exercise B1
What point is preferred along an indifference curve?

Exercise B2
Why do indifference curves slope down?

Exercise B3
Why are indifference curves steep on the left and flatter on the right?

Exercise B4
How many indifference curves does a person have?

Exercise B5
How can you tell which indifference curves represent higher or lower levels of utility?

Exercise B6
What is a substitution effect?

Exercise B7
What is an income effect?

Exercise B8
Does the "income effect" involve a change in income? Explain.

Exercise B9
Does a change in price have both an income effect and a substitution effect? Does a change in income have both an income effect and a substitution effect?

Exercise B10
Would you expect, in some cases, to see only an income effect or only a substitution effect? Explain.

Exercise B11
Which is larger, the income effect or the substitution effect?

# APPENDIX C

## Present Discounted Value

As explained in Financial Markets, the prices of stocks and bonds depend on future events. The price of a bond depends on the future payments that the bond is expected to make, including both payments of interest and the repayment of the face value of the bond. The price of a stock depends on the expected future profits earned by the firm. The concept of a present discounted value (PDV), which is defined as the amount you should be willing to pay in the present for a stream of expected future payments, can be used to calculate appropriate prices for stocks and bonds. To place a present discounted value on a future payment, think about what amount of money you would need to have in the present to equal a certain amount in the future. This calculation will require an interest rate. For example, if the interest rate is 10%, then a payment of $110 a year from now will have a present discounted value of $100—that is, you could take $100 in the present and have $110 in the future. We will first shows how to apply the idea of present discounted value to a stock and then we will show how to apply it to a bond.

## Applying Present Discounted Value to a Stock

Consider the case of Babble, Inc., a company that offers speaking lessons. For the sake of simplicity, say that the founder of Babble is 63 years old and plans to retire in two years, at which point the company will be disbanded. The company is selling 200 shares of stock and profits are expected to be $15 million right away, in the present, $20 million one year from now, and $25 million two years from now. All profits will be paid out as dividends to shareholders as they occur. Given this information, what will an investor pay for a share of stock in this company?

A financial investor, thinking about what future payments are worth in the present, will need to choose an interest rate. This interest rate will reflect the rate of return on other available financial investment opportunities, which is the opportunity cost of investing financial capital, and also a risk premium (that is, using a higher interest rate than the rates available elsewhere if this investment appears especially risky). In this example, say that the financial investor decides that appropriate interest rate to value these future payments is 15%.

Table C1 shows how to calculate the present discounted value of the future profits. For each time period, when a benefit is going to be received, apply the formula:

$$\text{Present discounted value} = \frac{\text{Future value received years in the future}}{(1 + \text{Interest rate})^{\text{numbers of years } t}}$$

| Payments from Firm | Present Value |
| --- | --- |
| $15 million in present | $15 million |
| $20 million in one year | $20 million/$(1 + 0.15)^1$ = $17.4 million |
| $25 million in two years | $25 million/$(1 + 0.15)^2$ = $18.9 million |
| Total | *$51.3 million* |

**TABLE C1** Calculating Present Discounted Value of a Stock

Next, add up all the present values for the different time periods to get a final answer. The present value calculations ask what the amount in the future is worth in the present, given the 15% interest rate. Notice that a different PDV calculation needs to be done separately for amounts received at different times. Then, divide the PDV of total profits by the number of shares, 200 in this case: 51.3 million/200 = 0.2565 million. The price per share should be about $256,500 per share.

Of course, in the real world expected profits are a best guess, not a hard piece of data. Deciding which interest rate to apply for discounting to the present can be tricky. One needs to take into account both potential capital gains from the future sale of the stock and also dividends that might be paid. Differences of opinion on these issues are exactly why some financial investors want to buy a stock that other people want to sell: they are more optimistic about its future prospects. Conceptually, however, it all comes down to what you are willing to pay in the present for a stream of benefits to be received in the future.

## Applying Present Discounted Value to a Bond

A similar calculation works in the case of bonds. Financial Markets explains that if the interest rate falls after a bond is issued, so that the investor has locked in a higher rate, then that bond will sell for more than its face value. Conversely, if the interest rate rises after a bond is issued, then the investor is locked into a lower rate, and the bond will sell for less than its face value. The present value calculation sharpens this intuition.

Think about a simple two-year bond. It was issued for $3,000 at an interest rate of 8%. Thus, after the first year, the bond pays interest of 240 (which is 3,000 × 8%). At the end of the second year, the bond pays $240 in interest, plus the $3,000 in principle. Calculate how much this bond is worth in the present if the discount rate is 8%. Then, recalculate if interest rates rise and the applicable discount rate is 11%. To carry out these calculations, look at the stream of payments being received from the bond in the future and figure out what they are worth in present discounted value terms. The calculations applying the present value formula are shown in Table C2.

| Stream of Payments (for the 8% interest rate) | Present Value (for the 8% interest rate) | Stream of Payments (for the 11% interest rate) | Present Value (for the 11% interest rate) |
| --- | --- | --- | --- |
| $240 payment after one year | $240/(1 + 0.08)^1 = $222.20 | $240 payment after one year | $240/(1 + 0.11)^1 = $216.20 |
| $3,240 payment after second year | $3,240/(1 + 0.08)^2 = $2,777.80 | $3,240 payment after second year | $3,240/(1 + 0.11)^2 = $2,629.60 |
| Total | $3,000 | Total | $2,845.80 |

**TABLE C2** Computing the Present Discounted Value of a Bond

The first calculation shows that the present value of a $3,000 bond, issued at 8%, is just $3,000. After all, that is how much money the borrower is receiving. The calculation confirms that the present value is the same for the lender. The bond is moving money around in time, from those willing to save in the present to those who want to borrow in the present, but the present value of what is received by the borrower is identical to the present value of what will be repaid to the lender.

The second calculation shows what happens if the interest rate rises from 8% to 11%. The actual dollar payments in the first column, as determined by the 8% interest rate, do not change. However, the present value of those payments, now discounted at a higher interest rate, is lower. Even though the future dollar payments that the bond is receiving have not changed, a person who tries to sell the bond will find that the investment's value has fallen.

Again, real-world calculations are often more complex, in part because, not only the interest rate prevailing in the market, but also the riskiness of whether the borrower will repay the loan, will change. In any case, the price of a bond is always the present value of a stream of future expected payments.

## Other Applications

Present discounted value is a widely used analytical tool outside the world of finance. Every time a business thinks about making a physical capital investment, it must compare a set of present costs of making that investment to the present discounted value of future benefits. When government thinks about a proposal to, for example, add safety features to a highway, it must compare costs incurred in the present to benefits received in the future. Some academic disputes over environmental policies, like how much to reduce carbon dioxide emissions because of the risk that they will lead to a warming of global temperatures several decades in the future, turn on how one compares present costs of pollution control with long-run future benefits. Someone who wins the lottery and is scheduled to receive a string of payments over 30 years might be interested in knowing what the present discounted value is of those payments. Whenever a string of costs and benefits stretches from the present into different times in the future, present discounted value becomes an indispensable tool of analysis.

# ANSWER KEY

---

## Chapter 1

1. Scarcity means human wants for goods and services exceed the available supply. Supply is limited because resources are limited. Demand, however, is virtually unlimited. Whatever the supply, it seems human nature to want more.
2. 100 people / 10 people per ham = a maximum of 10 hams per month if all residents produce ham. Since consumption is limited by production, the maximum number of hams residents could consume per month is 10.
3. She is very productive at her consulting job, but not very productive growing vegetables. Time spent consulting would produce far more income than it what she could save growing her vegetables using the same amount of time. So on purely economic grounds, it makes more sense for her to maximize her income by applying her labor to what she does best (i.e. specialization of labor).
4. The engineer is better at computer science than at painting. Thus, his time is better spent working for pay at his job and paying a painter to paint his house. Of course, this assumes he does not paint his house for fun!
5. There are many physical systems that would work, for example, the study of planets (micro) in the solar system (macro), or solar systems (micro) in the galaxy (macro).
6. Draw a box outside the original circular flow to represent the foreign country. Draw an arrow from the foreign country to firms, to represents imports. Draw an arrow in the reverse direction representing payments for imports. Draw an arrow from firms to the foreign country to represent exports. Draw an arrow in the reverse direction to represent payments for imports.
7. There are many such problems. Consider the AIDS epidemic. Why are so few AIDS patients in Africa and Southeast Asia treated with the same drugs that are effective in the United States and Europe? It is because neither those patients nor the countries in which they live have the resources to purchase the same drugs.
8. Public enterprise means the factors of production (resources and businesses) are owned and operated by the government.
9. The United States is a large country economically speaking, so it has less need to trade internationally than the other countries mentioned. (This is the same reason that France and Italy have lower ratios than Belgium or Sweden.) One additional reason is that each of the other countries is a member of the European Union, where trade between members occurs without barriers to trade, like tariffs and quotas.

## Chapter 2

1. The opportunity cost of bus tickets is the number of burgers that must be given up to obtain one more bus ticket. Originally, when the price of bus tickets was 50 cents per trip, this opportunity cost was 0.50/2 = .25 burgers. The reason for this is that at the original prices, one burger ($2) costs the same as four bus tickets ($0.50), so the opportunity cost of a burger is four bus tickets, and the opportunity cost of a bus ticket is .25 burgers (the inverse of the opportunity cost of a burger). With the new, higher price of bus tickets, the opportunity cost rises to $1/$2 or 0.50 burgers. You can see this graphically since the slope of the new budget constraint is steeper than the original one. If Alphonso spends all of his budget on burgers, the higher price of bus tickets has no impact so the vertical intercept of the budget constraint is the same. If he spends his entire budget on bus tickets, he can now afford only half as many, so the horizontal intercept is half as much. In short, the budget constraint rotates clockwise around the vertical intercept, steepening as it goes and the opportunity cost of bus tickets increases.

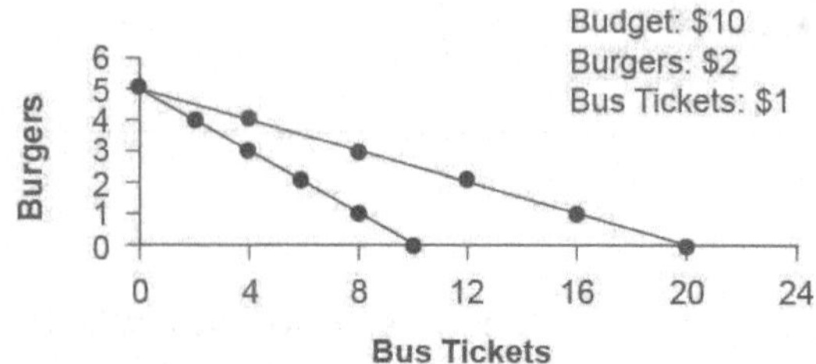


2. Because of the improvement in technology, the vertical intercept of the PPF would be at a higher level of healthcare. In other words, the PPF would rotate clockwise around the horizontal intercept. This would make the PPF steeper, corresponding to an increase in the opportunity cost of education, since resources devoted to education would now mean forgoing a greater quantity of healthcare.
3. No. Allocative efficiency requires productive efficiency, because it pertains to choices along the production possibilities frontier.
4. Both the budget constraint and the PPF show the constraint that each operates under. Both show a tradeoff between having more of one good but less of the other. Both show the opportunity cost graphically as the slope of the constraint (budget or PPF).
5. When individuals compare cost per unit in the grocery store, or characteristics of one product versus another, they are behaving approximately like the model describes.
6. Since an op-ed makes a case for what should be, it is considered normative.
7. Assuming that the study is not taking an explicit position about whether soft drink consumption is good or bad, but just reporting the science, it would be considered positive.

## Chapter 3

1. Since $1.60 per gallon is above the equilibrium price, the quantity demanded would be lower at 550 gallons and the quantity supplied would be higher at 640 gallons. (These results are due to the laws of demand and supply, respectively.) The outcome of lower Qd and higher Qs would be a surplus in the gasoline market of 640 − 550 = 90 gallons.
2. To make it easier to analyze complex problems. *Ceteris paribus* allows you to look at the effect of one factor at a time on what it is you are trying to analyze. When you have analyzed all the factors individually, you add the results together to get the final answer.
3. a. An improvement in technology that reduces the cost of production will cause an increase in supply. Alternatively, you can think of this as a reduction in price necessary for firms to supply any quantity. Either way, this can be shown as a rightward (or downward) shift in the supply curve.
   b. An improvement in product quality is treated as an increase in tastes or preferences, meaning consumers demand more paint at any price level, so demand increases or shifts to the right. If this seems counterintuitive, note that demand in the future for the longer-lasting paint will fall, since consumers are essentially shifting demand from the future to the present.
   c. An increase in need causes an increase in demand or a rightward shift in the demand curve.
   d. Factory damage means that firms are unable to supply as much in the present. Technically, this is an increase in the cost of production. Either way you look at it, the supply curve shifts to the left.

4. a. More fuel-efficient cars means there is less need for gasoline. This causes a leftward shift in the demand for gasoline and thus oil. Since the demand curve is shifting down the supply curve, the equilibrium price and quantity both fall.
   b. Cold weather increases the need for heating oil. This causes a rightward shift in the demand for heating oil and thus oil. Since the demand curve is shifting up the supply curve, the equilibrium price and quantity both rise.
   c. A discovery of new oil will make oil more abundant. This can be shown as a rightward shift in the

supply curve, which will cause a decrease in the equilibrium price along with an increase in the equilibrium quantity. (The supply curve shifts down the demand curve so price and quantity follow the law of demand. If price goes down, then the quantity goes up.)

d. When an economy slows down, it produces less output and demands less input, including energy, which is used in the production of virtually everything. A decrease in demand for energy will be reflected as a decrease in the demand for oil, or a leftward shift in demand for oil. Since the demand curve is shifting down the supply curve, both the equilibrium price and quantity of oil will fall.

e. Disruption of oil pumping will reduce the supply of oil. This leftward shift in the supply curve will show a movement up the demand curve, resulting in an increase in the equilibrium price of oil and a decrease in the equilibrium quantity.

f. Increased insulation will decrease the demand for heating. This leftward shift in the demand for oil causes a movement down the supply curve, resulting in a decrease in the equilibrium price and quantity of oil.

g. Solar energy is a substitute for oil-based energy. So if solar energy becomes cheaper, the demand for oil will decrease as consumers switch from oil to solar. The decrease in demand for oil will be shown as a leftward shift in the demand curve. As the demand curve shifts down the supply curve, both equilibrium price and quantity for oil will fall.

h. A new, popular kind of plastic will increase the demand for oil. The increase in demand will be shown as a rightward shift in demand, raising the equilibrium price and quantity of oil.

5. Step 1. Draw the graph with the initial supply and demand curves. Label the initial equilibrium price and quantity.
Step 2. Did the economic event affect supply or demand? Jet fuel is a cost of producing air travel, so an increase in jet fuel price affects supply.
Step 3. An increase in the price of jet fuel caused an increase in the cost of air travel. We show this as an upward or leftward shift in supply.
Step 4. A leftward shift in supply causes a movement up the demand curve, increasing the equilibrium price of air travel and decreasing the equilibrium quantity.

6. Step 1. Draw the graph with the initial supply and demand curves. Label the initial equilibrium price and quantity.
Step 2. Did the economic event affect supply or demand? A tariff is treated like a cost of production, so this affects supply.
Step 3. A tariff reduction is equivalent to a decrease in the cost of production, which we can show as a rightward (or downward) shift in supply.
Step 4. A rightward shift in supply causes a movement down the demand curve, lowering the equilibrium price and raising the equilibrium quantity.

7. A price ceiling (which is below the equilibrium price) will cause the quantity demanded to rise and the quantity supplied to fall. This is why a price ceiling creates a shortage.

8. A price ceiling is just a legal restriction. Equilibrium is an economic condition. People may or may not obey the price ceiling, so the actual price may be at or above the price ceiling, but the price ceiling does not change the equilibrium price.

9. A price ceiling is a legal maximum price, but a price floor is a legal minimum price and, consequently, it would leave room for the price to rise to its equilibrium level. In other words, a price floor below equilibrium will not be binding and will have no effect.

10. Assuming that people obey the price ceiling, the market price will be below equilibrium, which means that Qd will be more than Qs. Buyers can only buy what is offered for sale, so the number of transactions will fall to Qs. This is easy to see graphically. By analogous reasoning, with a price floor the market price will be above the equilibrium price, so Qd will be less than Qs. Since the limit on transactions here is demand, the number of transactions will fall to Qd. Note that because both price floors and price ceilings reduce the number of transactions, social surplus is less.

11. Because the losses to consumers are greater than the benefits to producers, so the net effect is negative. Since the lost consumer surplus is greater than the additional producer surplus, social surplus falls.

## Chapter 4

1. Changes in the wage rate (the price of labor) cause a movement along the demand curve. A change in anything else that affects demand for labor (e.g., changes in output, changes in the production process that use more or less labor, government regulation) causes a shift in the demand curve.
2. Changes in the wage rate (the price of labor) cause a movement along the supply curve. A change in anything else that affects supply of labor (e.g., changes in how desirable the job is perceived to be, government policy to promote training in the field) causes a shift in the supply curve.
3. Since a living wage is a suggested minimum wage, it acts like a price floor (assuming, of course, that it is followed). If the living wage is binding, it will cause an excess supply of labor at that wage rate.
4. Changes in the interest rate (i.e., the price of financial capital) cause a movement along the demand curve. A change in anything else (non-price variable) that affects demand for financial capital (e.g., changes in confidence about the future, changes in needs for borrowing) would shift the demand curve.
5. Changes in the interest rate (i.e., the price of financial capital) cause a movement along the supply curve. A change in anything else that affects the supply of financial capital (a non-price variable) such as income or future needs would shift the supply curve.
6. If market interest rates stay in their normal range, an interest rate limit of 35% would not be binding. If the equilibrium interest rate rose above 35%, the interest rate would be capped at that rate, and the quantity of loans would be lower than the equilibrium quantity, causing a shortage of loans.
7. b and c will lead to a fall in interest rates. At a lower demand, lenders will not be able to charge as much, and with more available lenders, competition for borrowers will drive rates down.
8. a and c will increase the quantity of loans. More people who want to borrow will result in more loans being given, as will more people who want to lend.
9. A price floor prevents a price from falling below a certain level, but has no effect on prices above that level. It will have its biggest effect in creating excess supply (as measured by the entire area inside the dotted lines on the graph, from D to S) if it is substantially above the equilibrium price. This is illustrated in the following figure.

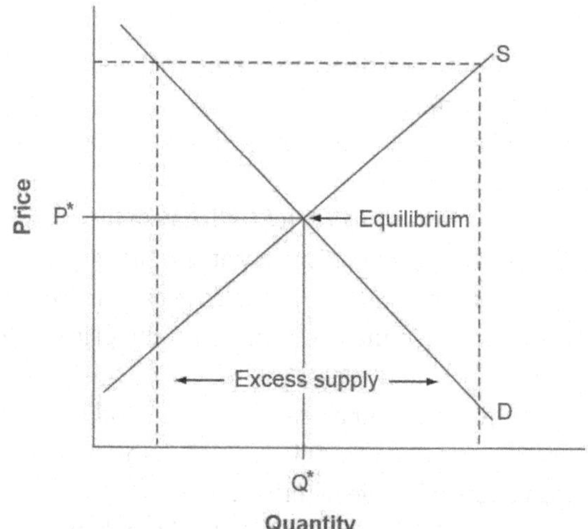


It will have a lesser effect if it is slightly above the equilibrium price. This is illustrated in the next figure.

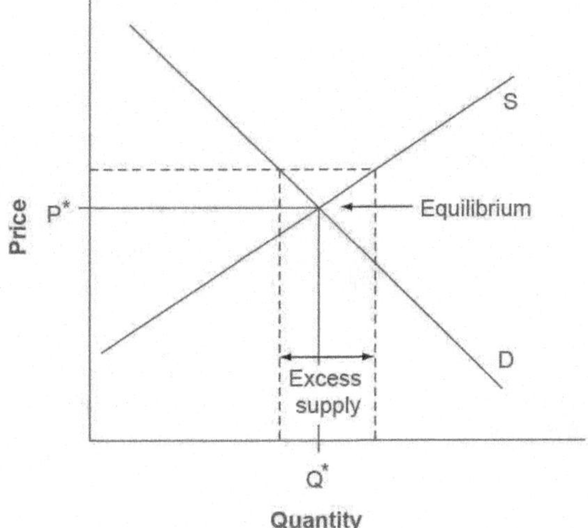



It will have no effect if it is set either slightly or substantially below the equilibrium price, since an equilibrium price above a price floor will not be affected by that price floor. The following figure illustrates these situations.

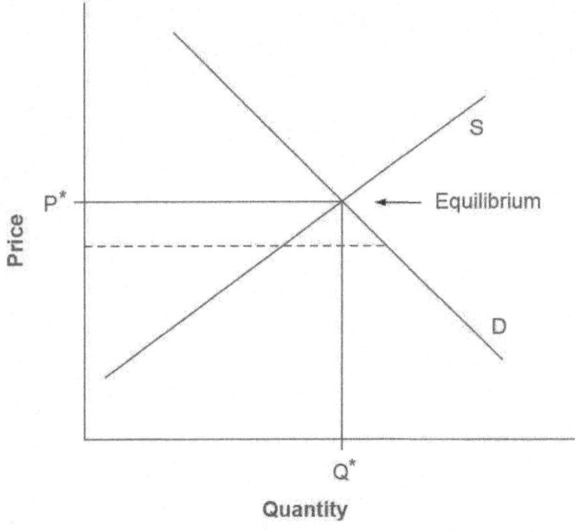



(a) Price floor slightly below equilibrium price

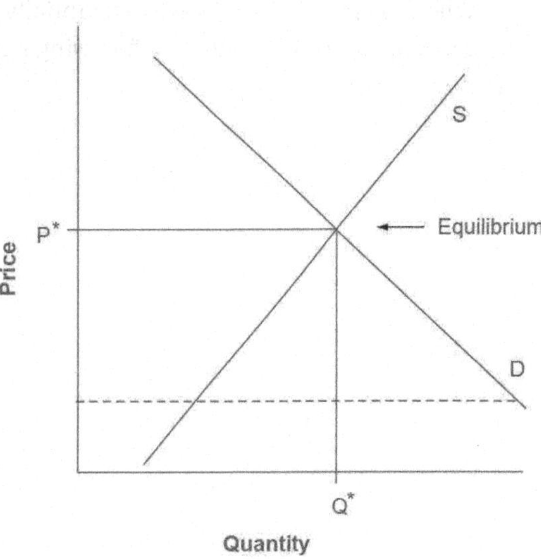



(b) Price floor substantially below equilibrium price

10. A price ceiling prevents a price from rising above a certain level, but has no effect on prices below that level. It will have its biggest effect in creating excess demand if it is substantially below the equilibrium price. The following figure illustrates these situations.

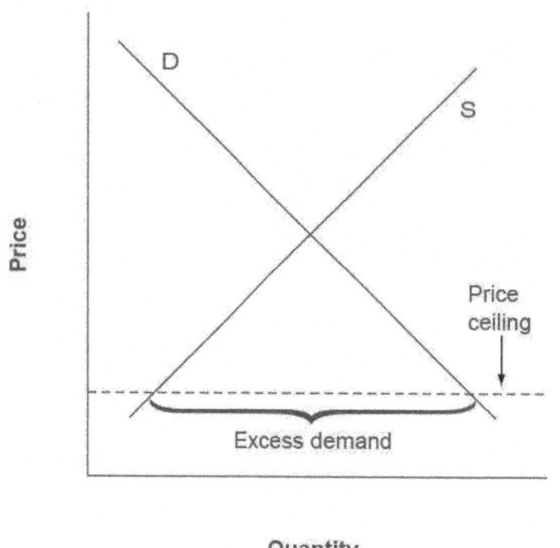

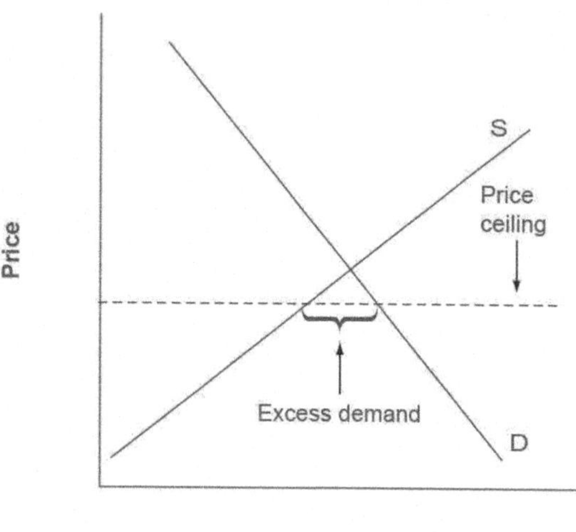

(a) Price ceiling substantially below equilibrium price

(b) Price ceiling slightly below equilibrium price

When the price ceiling is set substantially or slightly above the equilibrium price, it will have no effect on creating excess demand. The following figure illustrates these situations.

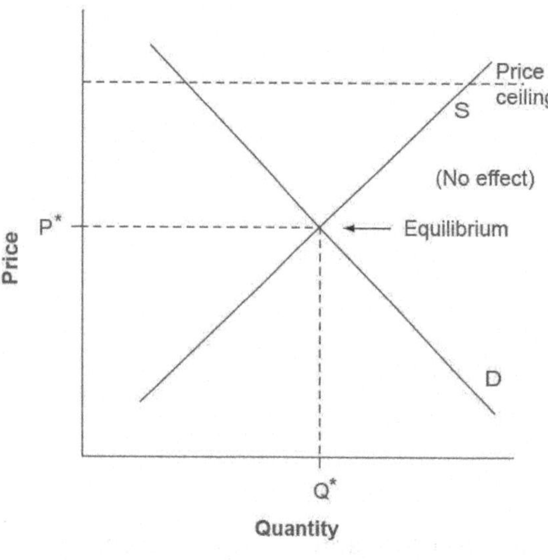

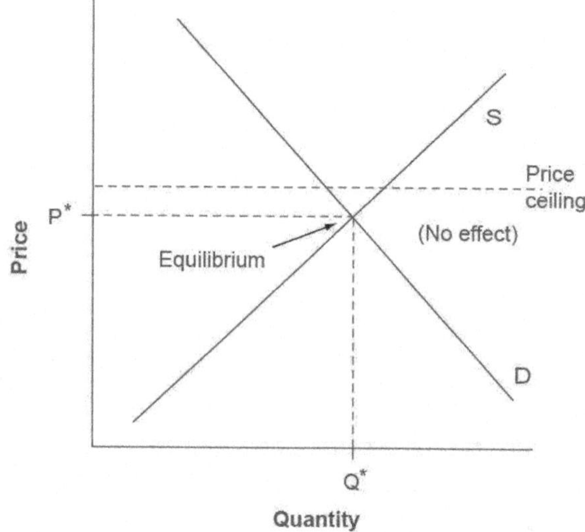

(a) Price ceiling substantially above equilibrium price

(b) Price ceiling slightly above equilibrium price

11. Neither. A shift in demand or supply means that at every price, either a greater or a lower quantity is demanded or supplied. A price floor does not shift a demand curve or a supply curve. However, if the price floor is set above the equilibrium, it will cause the quantity supplied on the supply curve to be greater than the quantity demanded on the demand curve, leading to excess supply.

12. Neither. A shift in demand or supply means that at every price, either a greater or a lower quantity is demanded or supplied. A price ceiling does not shift a demand curve or a supply curve. However, if the price ceiling is set below the equilibrium, it will cause the quantity demanded on the demand curve to be greater than the quantity supplied on the supply curve, leading to excess demand.

## Chapter 5

1. From point B to point C, price rises from $70 to $80, and Qd decreases from 2,800 to 2,600. So:

$$\% \text{ change in quantity} = \frac{2600-2800}{(2600+2800)\div 2} \times 100$$

$$= \frac{-200}{2700} \times 100$$

$$= -7.41$$

$$\% \text{ change in price} = \frac{80-70}{(80+70)\div 2} \times 100$$

$$= \frac{10}{75} \times 100$$

$$= 13.33$$

$$\text{Elasticity of Demand} = \frac{-7.41\%}{13.33\%}$$

$$= 0.56$$

The demand curve is inelastic in this area; that is, its elasticity value is less than one.

Answer from Point D to point E:

$$\% \text{ change in quantity} = \frac{2200-2400}{(2200+2400)\div 2} \times 100$$

$$= \frac{-200}{2300} \times 100$$

$$= -8.7$$

$$\% \text{ change in price} = \frac{100-90}{(100+90)\div 2} \times 100$$

$$= \frac{10}{95} \times 100$$

$$= 10.53$$

$$\text{Elasticity of Demand} = \frac{-8.7\%}{10.53\%}$$

$$= 0.83$$

The demand curve is inelastic in this area; that is, its elasticity value is less than one.

Answer from Point G to point H:

$$\% \text{ change in quantity} = \frac{1600-1800}{1700} \times 100$$

$$= \frac{-200}{1700} \times 100$$

$$= -11.76$$

$$\% \text{ change in price} = \frac{130-120}{125} \times 100$$

$$= \frac{10}{125} \times 100$$

$$= 8.00$$

$$\text{Elasticity of Demand} = \frac{-11.76\%}{8.00\%}$$

$$= -1.47$$

The demand curve is elastic in this interval.

2. From point J to point K, price rises from \$8 to \$9, and quantity rises from 50 to 70. So:

$$\% \text{ change in quantity} = \frac{70-50}{(70+50)\div 2} \times 100$$

$$= \frac{20}{60} \times 100$$

$$= 33.33$$

$$\% \text{ change in price} = \frac{\$9-\$8}{(\$9+\$8)\div 2} \times 100$$

$$= \frac{1}{8.5} \times 100$$

$$= 11.76$$

$$\text{Elasticity of Supply} = \frac{33.33\%}{11.76\%}$$

$$= 2.83$$

The supply curve is elastic in this area; that is, its elasticity value is greater than one.

From point L to point M, the price rises from \$10 to \$11, while the Qs rises from 80 to 88:

$$\% \text{ change in quantity} = \frac{88-80}{(88+80)\div 2} \times 100$$

$$= \frac{8}{84} \times 100$$

$$= 9.52$$

$$\% \text{change in price} = \frac{\$11-\$10}{(\$11+\$10)\div 2} \times 100$$

$$= \frac{1}{10.5} \times 100$$

$$= 9.52$$

$$\text{Elasticity of Demand} = \frac{9.52\%}{9.52\%}$$

$$= 1.0$$

The supply curve has unitary elasticity in this area.

From point N to point P, the price rises from \$12 to \$13, and Qs rises from 95 to 100:

$$\% \text{ change in quantity} = \frac{100-95}{(100+95)\div 2} \times 100$$

$$= \frac{5}{97.5} \times 100$$

$$= 5.13$$

$$\% \text{ change in price} = \frac{\$13-\$12}{(\$13+\$12)\div 2} \times 100$$

$$= \frac{1}{12.5} \times 100$$

$$= 8.0$$

$$\text{Elasticity of Supply} = \frac{5.13\%}{8.0\%}$$

$$= 0.64$$

The supply curve is inelastic in this region of the supply curve.

3. The demand curve with constant unitary elasticity is concave because the absolute value of declines in price are not identical. The left side of the curve starts with high prices, and then price falls by smaller amounts as it goes down toward the right side. This results in a slope of demand that is steeper on the left but flatter on the right, creating a curved, concave shape.

4. The constant unitary elasticity is a straight line because the curve slopes upward and both price and quantity are increasing proportionally.

5. Carmakers can pass this cost along to consumers if the demand for these cars is inelastic. If the demand for these cars is elastic, then the manufacturer must pay for the equipment.

6. If the elasticity is 1.4 at current prices, you would advise the company to lower its price on the product, since a decrease in price will be offset by the increase in the amount of the drug sold. If the elasticity were 0.6, then you would advise the company to increase its price. Increases in price will offset the decrease in number of units sold, but increase your total revenue. If elasticity is 1, the total revenue is already maximized, and you would advise that the company maintain its current price level.

7. The percentage change in quantity supplied as a result of a given percentage change in the price of gasoline.

$$\text{Percentage change in quantity demanded} = [(\text{change in quantity})/(\text{original quantity})] \times 100$$

$$= [22 - 30]/[(22 + 30)/2] \times 100$$

$$= -8/26 \times 100$$

$$= -30.77$$

8.

$$\text{Percentage change in income} = [(\text{change in income})/(\text{original income})] \times 100$$

$$= [38,000 - 25,000]/[(38,000 + 25,000)/2] \times 100$$

$$= 13/31.5 \times 100$$

$$= 41.27$$

In this example, bread is an inferior good because its consumption falls as income rises.

9. The formula for cross-price elasticity is % change in Qd for apples / % change in P of oranges. Multiplying

both sides by % change in P of oranges yields:

% change in Qd for apples = cross-price elasticity X% change in P of oranges

= 0.4 × (−3%) = −1.2%, or a 1.2 % decrease in demand for apples.

## Chapter 6

1. The rows of the table in the problem do not represent the actual choices available on the budget set; that is, the combinations of round trips and phone minutes that Jeremy can afford with his budget. One of the choices listed in the problem, the six round trips, is not even available on the budget set. If Jeremy has only $10 to spend and a round trip costs $2 and phone calls cost $0.05 per minute, he could spend his entire budget on five round trips but no phone calls or 200 minutes of phone calls, but no round trips or any combination of the two in between. It is easy to see all of his budget options with a little algebra. The equation for a budget line is:

$$Budget = P_{RT} \times Q_{RT} + P_{PC} \times Q_{PC}$$

where P and Q are price and quantity of round trips ($_{RT}$) and phone calls ($_{PC}$) (per minute). In Jeremy's case the equation for the budget line is:

$$\$10 = \$2 \times Q_{RT} + \$.05 \times Q_{PC}$$

$$\frac{\$10}{\$.05} = \frac{\$2Q_{RT} + \$.05Q_{PC}}{\$.05}$$

$$200 = 40Q_{RT} + Q_{PC}$$

$$Q_{PC} = 200 - 40Q_{RT}$$

If we choose zero through five round trips (column 1), the table below shows how many phone minutes can be afforded with the budget (column 3). The total utility figures are given in the table below.

| Round Trips | Total Utility for Trips | Phone Minutes | Total Utility for Minutes | Total Utility |
|---|---|---|---|---|
| 0 | 0 | 200 | 1100 | 1100 |
| 1 | 80 | 160 | 1040 | 1120 |
| 2 | 150 | 120 | 900 | 1050 |
| 3 | 210 | 80 | 680 | 890 |
| 4 | 260 | 40 | 380 | 640 |
| 5 | 300 | 0 | 0 | 300 |

Adding up total utility for round trips and phone minutes at different points on the budget line gives total utility at each point on the budget line. The highest possible utility is at the combination of one trip and 160 minutes of phone time, with a total utility of 1120.

2. The first step is to use the total utility figures, shown in the table below, to calculate marginal utility, remembering that marginal utility is equal to the change in total utility divided by the change in trips or minutes.

| Round Trips | Total Utility | Marginal Utility (per trip) | Phone Minutes | Total Utility | Marginal Utility (per minute) |
|---|---|---|---|---|---|
| 0 | 0 | - | 200 | 1100 | - |
| 1 | 80 | 80 | 160 | 1040 | 60/40 = 1.5 |

| Round Trips | Total Utility | Marginal Utility (per trip) | Phone Minutes | Total Utility | Marginal Utility (per minute) |
|---|---|---|---|---|---|
| 2 | 150 | 70 | 120 | 900 | 140/40 = 3.5 |
| 3 | 210 | 60 | 80 | 680 | 220/40 = 5.5 |
| 4 | 260 | 50 | 40 | 380 | 300/40 = 7.5 |
| 5 | 300 | 40 | 0 | 0 | 380/40 = 9.5 |

Note that we cannot directly compare marginal utilities, since the units are trips versus phone minutes. We need a common denominator for comparison, which is price. Dividing MU by the price, yields columns 4 and 8 in the table below.

| Round Trips | Total Utility | Marginal Utility (per trip) | MU/P | Phone Minutes | Total Utility | Marginal utility (per minute) | MU/P |
|---|---|---|---|---|---|---|---|
| 0 | 0 | - | - | 200 | 1100 | 60/40 = 1.5 | 1.5/$0.05 = 30 |
| 1 | 80 | 80 | 80/$2 = 40 | 160 | 1040 | 140/40 = 3.5 | 3.5/$0.05 = 70 |
| 2 | 150 | 70 | 70/$2 = 35 | 120 | 900 | 220/40 = 5.5 | 5.5/$0.05 = 110 |
| 3 | 210 | 60 | 60/$2 = 30 | 80 | 680 | 300/40 =7.5 | 7.5/$0.05 = 150 |
| 4 | 260 | 50 | 50/$2 = 25 | 40 | 380 | 380/40 = 9.5 | 9.5/$0.05 = 190 |
| 5 | 300 | 40 | 40/$2 = 20 | 0 | 0 | - | - |

Start at the bottom of the table where the combination of round trips and phone minutes is (5, 0). This starting point is arbitrary, but the numbers in this example work best starting from the bottom. Suppose we consider moving to the next point up. At (4, 40), the marginal utility per dollar spent on a round trip is 25. The marginal utility per dollar spent on phone minutes is 190.

Since 25 < 190, we are getting much more utility per dollar spent on phone minutes, so let's choose more of those. At (3, 80), $MU/P_{RT}$ is 30 < 150 (the $MU/_{PM}$), but notice that the difference is narrowing. We keep trading round trips for phone minutes until we get to (1, 160), which is the best we can do. The MU/P comparison is as close as it is going to get (40 vs. 70). Often in the real world, it is not possible to get MU/P exactly equal for both products, so you get as close as you can.

3. This is the opposite of the example explained in the text. A decrease in price has a substitution effect and an income effect. The substitution effect says that because the product is cheaper relative to other things the consumer purchases, the consumer will tend to buy more of the product (and less of the other things). The income effect says that after the price decline, the consumer could purchase the same goods as before, and still have money left over to purchase more. For both reasons, a decrease in price causes an increase in quantity demanded.

4. This is a negative income effect. Because your parents' check failed to arrive, your monthly income is less than normal and your budget constraint shifts in toward the origin. If you only buy normal goods, the decrease in your income means you will buy less of every product.

## Chapter 7

1. Accounting profit = total revenues minus explicit costs = $1,000,000 – ($600,000 + $150,000 + $200,000) = $50,000.
2. Economic profit = accounting profit minus implicit cost = $50,000 – $30,000 = $20,000.
3.

| Quantity | Variable Cost | Fixed Cost | Total Cost | Average Variable Cost | Average Total Cost | Marginal Cost |
|---|---|---|---|---|---|---|
| 0 | 0 | $30 | $30 | - | - | |
| 1 | $10 | $30 | $40 | $10.00 | $40.00 | $10 |
| 2 | $25 | $30 | $55 | $12.50 | $27.50 | $15 |
| 3 | $45 | $30 | $75 | $15.00 | $25.00 | $20 |
| 4 | $70 | $30 | $100 | $17.50 | $25.00 | $25 |
| 5 | $100 | $30 | $130 | $20.00 | $26.00 | $30 |
| 6 | $135 | $30 | $165 | $22.50 | $27.50 | $35 |

4. a. Total revenues in this example will be a quantity of five units multiplied by the price of $25/unit, which equals $125. Total costs when producing five units are $130. Thus, at this level of quantity and output the firm experiences losses (or negative profits) of $5.
   b. If price is less than average cost, the firm is not making a profit. At an output of five units, the average cost is $26/unit. Thus, at a glance you can see the firm is making losses. At a second glance, you can see that it must be losing $1 for each unit produced (that is, average cost of $26/unit minus the price of $25/unit). With five units produced, this observation implies total losses of $5.
   c. When producing five units, marginal costs are $30/unit. Price is $25/unit. Thus, the marginal unit is not adding to profits, but is actually subtracting from profits, which suggests that the firm should reduce its quantity produced.

5. The marginal product of the third painter is 75 square feet.
   marginal product  =  change in total product/change in variable output
   
   change in total product = 275 square feet – 200 square feet
   
   change in total product = 75 square feet
   
   marginal product  =  75 square feet/1 worker
   
   marginal product  =  75
6. The new table should look like this:

|  | Labor Cost | Machine Cost | Total Cost |
|---|---|---|---|
| Cost of technology 1 | 10 × $40 = $400 | 2 × $50 = $100 | $500 |
| Cost of technology 2 | 7 × $40 = $280 | 4 × $50 = $200 | $480 |
| Cost of technology 3 | 3 × $40 = $120 | 7 × $50 = $350 | $470 |

The firm should choose production technology 3 since it has the lowest total cost. This makes sense since, with cheaper machine hours, one would expect a shift in the direction of more machines and less labor.

7.

|  | Labor Cost | Machine Cost | Total Cost |
|---|---|---|---|
| Cost of technology 1 | 10 × $40 = $400 | 2 × $55 = $110 | $510 |
| Cost of technology 2 | 7 × $40 = $280 | 4 × $55 = $220 | $500 |
| Cost of technology 3 | 3 × $40 = $120 | 7 × $55 = $385 | $505 |

The firm should choose production technology 2 since it has the lowest total cost. Because the cost of machines increased (relative to the previous question), you would expect a shift toward less capital and more labor.

8. This is the situation that existed in the United States in the 1970s. Since there is only demand enough for 2.5 firms to reach the bottom of the average cost curve, you would expect one firm will not be around in the long run, and at least one firm will be struggling.

# Chapter 8

1. No, you would not raise the price. Your product is exactly the same as the product of the many other firms in the market. If your price is greater than that of your competitors, then your customers would switch to them and stop buying from you. You would lose all your sales.
2. Possibly. Independent truckers are by definition small and numerous. All that is required to get into the business is a truck (not an inexpensive asset, though) and a commercial driver's license. To exit, one need only sell the truck. All trucks are essentially the same, providing transportation from point A to point B. (We're assuming we not talking about specialized trucks.) Independent truckers must take the going rate for their service, so independent trucking does seem to have most of the characteristics of perfect competition.
3. Holding total cost constant, profits at every output level would increase.
4. When the market price increases, marginal revenue increases. The firm would then increase production up to the point where the new price equals marginal cost, at a quantity of 90.
5. If marginal costs exceeds marginal revenue, then the firm will reduce its profits for every additional unit of output it produces. Profit would be greatest if it reduces output to where MR = MC.
6. The firm will be willing to supply fewer units at every price level. In other words, the firm's individual supply curve decreases and shifts to the left.
7. With a technological improvement that brings about a reduction in costs of production, an adjustment process will take place in the market. The technological improvement will result in an increase in supply curves, by individual firms and at the market level. The existing firms will experience higher profits for a while, which will attract other firms into the market. This entry process will stop whenever the market supply increases enough (both by existing and new firms) so profits are driven back to zero.
8. When wages increase, costs of production increase. Some firms would now be making economic losses and would shut down. The supply curve then starts shifting to the left, pushing the market price up. This

process ends when all firms remaining in the market earn zero economic profits. The result is a contraction in the output produced in the market.

9. Perfect competition is considered to be "perfect" because both allocative and productive efficiency are met at the same time in a long-run equilibrium. If a market structure results in long-run equilibrium that does not minimize average total costs and/or does not charge a price equal to marginal cost, then either allocative or productive (or both) efficiencies are not met, and therefore the market cannot be labeled "perfect."

10. Think of the market price as representing the gain to society from a purchase, since it represents what someone is willing to pay. Think of the marginal cost as representing the cost to society from making the last unit of a good. If P > MC, then the benefits from producing more of a good exceed the costs, and society would gain from producing more of the good. If P < MC, then the social costs of producing the marginal good exceed the social benefits, and society should produce less of the good. Only if P = MC, the rule applied by a profit-maximizing perfectly competitive firm, will society's costs and benefits be in balance. This choice will be the option that brings the greatest overall benefit to society.

## Chapter 9

1. a. A patent is a government-enforced barrier to entry.
   b. This is not a barrier to entry.
   c. This is not a barrier to entry.
   d. This is a barrier to entry, but it is not government-enforced.
   e. This is a barrier to entry, but it is not directly government enforced.

2. a. This is a government-enforced barrier to entry.
   b. This is an example of a government law, but perhaps it is not much of a barrier to entry if most people can pass the safety test and get insurance.
   c. Trademarks are enforced by government, and therefore are a barrier to entry.
   d. This is probably not a barrier to entry, since there are a number of different ways of getting pure water.
   e. This is a barrier to entry, but it is not government-enforced.

3. Because of economies of scale, each firm would produce at a higher average cost than before. (They would each have to build their own power lines.) As a result, they would each have to raise prices to cover their higher costs. The policy would fail.

4. Shorter patent protection would make innovation less lucrative, so the amount of research and development would likely decline.

5. If price falls below AVC, the firm will not be able to earn enough revenues even to cover its variable costs. In such a case, it will suffer a smaller loss if it shuts down and produces no output. By contrast, if it stayed in operation and produced the level of output where MR = MC, it would lose all of its fixed costs plus some variable costs. If it shuts down, it only loses its fixed costs.

6. This scenario is called "perfect price discrimination." The result would be that the monopolist would produce more output, the same amount in fact as would be produced by a perfectly competitive industry. However, there would be no consumer surplus since each buyer is paying exactly what they think the product is worth. Therefore, the monopolist would be earning the maximum possible profits.

## Chapter 10

1. An increase in demand will manifest itself as a rightward shift in the demand curve, and a rightward shift in marginal revenue. The shift in marginal revenue will cause a movement up the marginal cost curve to the new intersection between MR and MC at a higher level of output. The new price can be read by drawing a line up from the new output level to the new demand curve, and then over to the vertical axis. The new price should be higher. The increase in quantity will cause a movement along the average cost curve to a possibly higher level of average cost. The price, though, will increase more, causing an increase in total

profits.

2. As long as the original firm is earning positive economic profits, other firms will respond in ways that take away the original firm's profits. This will manifest itself as a decrease in demand for the original firm's product, a decrease in the firm's profit-maximizing price and a decrease in the firm's profit-maximizing level of output, essentially unwinding the process described in the answer to question 1. In the long-run equilibrium, all firms in monopolistically competitive markets will earn zero economic profits.

3. a. If the firms form a cartel, they will act like a monopoly, choosing the quantity of output where MR = MC. Drawing a line from the monopoly quantity up to the demand curve shows the monopoly price. Assuming that fixed costs are zero, and with an understanding of cost and profit, we can infer that when the marginal cost curve is horizontal, average cost is the same as marginal cost. Thus, the cartel will earn positive economic profits equal to the area of the rectangle, with a base equal to the monopoly quantity and a height equal to the difference between price (on the demand above the monopoly quantity) and average cost, as shown in the following figure.

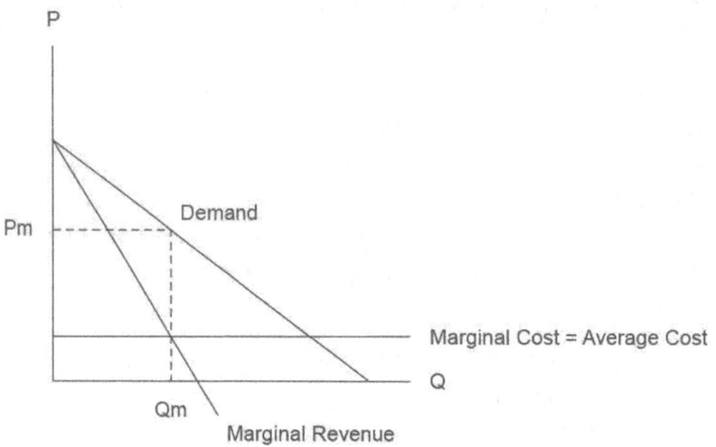


b. The firms will expand output and cut price as long as there are profits remaining. The long-run equilibrium will occur at the point where average cost equals demand. As a result, the oligopoly will earn zero economic profits due to "cutthroat competition," as shown in the next figure.

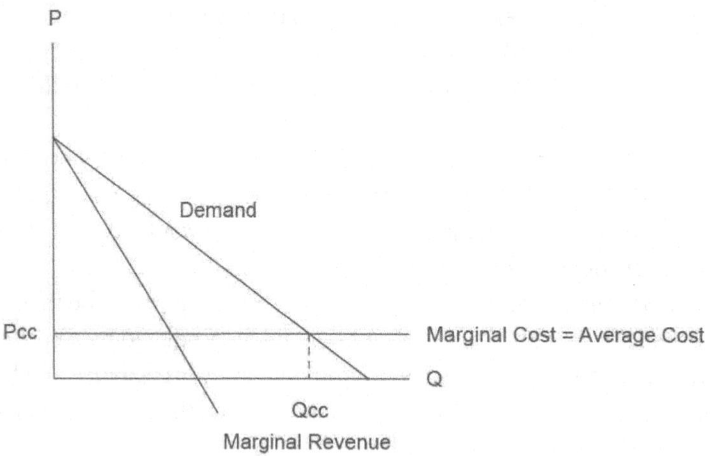


c. Pc > Pcc. Qc < Qcc. Profit for the cartel is positive and large. Profit for cutthroat competition is zero.

4. Firm B reasons that if it cheats and Firm A does not notice, it will double its money. Since Firm A's profits will decline substantially, however, it is likely that Firm A will notice and if so, Firm A will cheat also, with the result that Firm B will lose 90% of what it gained by cheating. Firm A will reason that Firm B is unlikely to risk cheating. If neither firm cheats, Firm A earns $1000. If Firm A cheats, assuming Firm B does not cheat, A can boost its profits only a little, since Firm B is so small. If both firms cheat, then Firm A loses at least 50% of what it could have earned. The possibility of a small gain ($50) is probably not enough to

induce Firm A to cheat, so in this case it is likely that both firms will collude.

## Chapter 11

1. Yes, it is true. The HHI example is easy enough: since the market shares of all firms are included in the HHI calculation, a merger between two of the firms will change the HHI. For the four-firm concentration ratio, it is quite possible that a merger between, say, the fifth and sixth largest firms in the market could create a new firm that is then ranked in the top four in the market. In this case, a merger of two firms, neither in the top four, would still change the four-firm concentration ratio.

2. No, it is not true. The HHI includes the market shares of all firms in its calculation, but the squaring of the market shares has the effect of making the impact of the largest firms relatively bigger than in the 4-firm or 8-firm ratio.

3. The bus companies wanted the broader market definition (i.e., the second definition). If the narrow definition had been used, the combined bus companies would have had a near-monopoly on the market for intercity bus service. But they had only a sliver of the market for intercity transportation when everything else was included. The merger was allowed.

4. The common expectation is that the definition of markets will become broader because of greater competition from faraway places. However, this broadening doesn't necessarily mean that antitrust authorities can relax. There is also a fear that companies with a local or national monopoly may use the new opportunities to extend their reach across national borders, and that it will be difficult for national authorities to respond.

5. Because outright collusion to raise profits is illegal and because existing regulations include gray areas which firms may be able to exploit.

6. Yes, all curves have normal shapes.

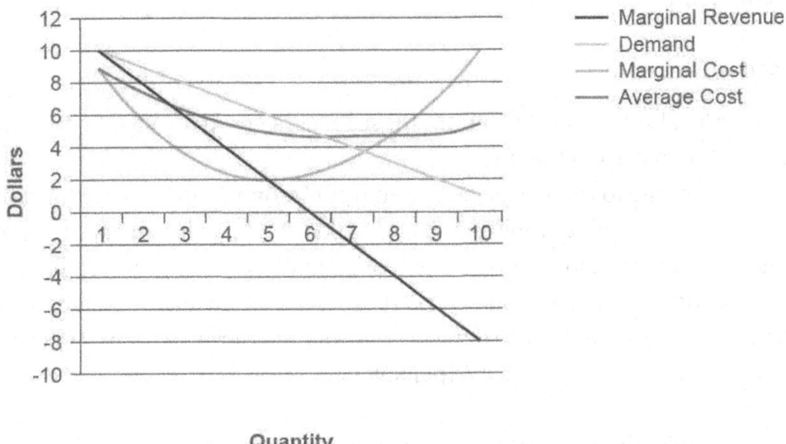


7. Yes it is a natural monopoly because average costs decline over the range that satisfies the market demand. For example, at the point where the demand curve and the average cost curve meet, there are economies of scale.

8. Improvements in technology that allowed phone calls to be made via microwave transmission, communications satellites, and other wireless technologies.

9. More consumer choice. Cheaper phone calls, especially long distance. Better-quality phone service in many cases. Cheaper, faster, and better-quality data transmission. Spin-off technologies like free Internet-based calling and video calling.

10. More choice can sometimes make for difficult decisions—not knowing if you got the best plan for your situation, for example. Some phone service providers are less reliable than AT&T used to be.

## Chapter 12

1.  a.  positive externality
    b.  negative externality
    c.  positive externality
    d.  negative externality
    e.  negative externality

2.  a.  supply shifts left
    b.  supply shifts left
    c.  supply stays the same
    d.  supply shifts left

3.  a.  price will rise
    b.  price will rise
    c.  price stays the same
    d.  price will rise.

4. The original equilibrium (before the external social cost of pollution is taken into account) is where the private supply curve crosses the demand curve. This original equilibrium is at a price of $15 and a quantity of 440. After taking into account the additional external cost of pollution, the production becomes more costly, and the supply curve shifts up. The new equilibrium will be at a price of $30 and a quantity of 410.

5. The first policy is command-and-control because it is a requirement that applies to all producers.

6.  a.  market-based
    b.  command-and-control
    c.  command-and-control
    d.  market-based
    e.  market-based

7. Even though state or local governments impose these taxes, a company has the flexibility to adopt technologies that will help it avoid the tax.

8. First, if each firm is required to reduce its garbage output by one-fourth, then Elm will reduce five tons at a cost of $5,500; Maple will reduce 10 tons at a cost of $13,500; Oak will reduce three tons at a cost of $22,500; and Cherry will reduce four tons at a cost of $18,000. Total cost of this approach: $59,500. If the system of marketable permits is put in place, and those permits shrink the weight of allowable garbage by one-quarter, then pollution must still be reduced by the same overall amount. However, now the reduction in pollution will take place where it is least expensive.

| Reductions in Garbage | Who does the reducing? | At what cost? |
| --- | --- | --- |
| First 5 tons | Cherry | $3,000 |
| Second 5 tons | Cherry | $4,000 |
| Third 5 tons | Cherry | $5,000 |
| Fourth 5 tons | Elm | $5,500 |
| Fifth and sixth 5 tons | Elm and Cherry | $6,000 each |
| Seventh 5 tons | Maple | $6,300 |

| Reductions in Garbage | Who does the reducing? | At what cost? |
|---|---|---|
| Eighth 5 tons | Elm | $6,500 |
| Ninth and tenth 5 tons | Elm and Cherry | $7,000 each |

Thus, the overall pattern of reductions here will be that Elm reduces garbage by 20 tons and has 15 tons of permits to sell. Maple reduces by five tons and needs to buy five tons of permits. Oak does not reduce garbage at all, and needs to buy 15 tons of permits. Cherry reduces garbage by 25 tons, which leaves it with five tons of permits to sell. The total cost of these reductions would be $56,300, a definite reduction in costs from the $59,500 cost of the command-and-control option.

9.

| | Incentives to Go Beyond | Flexibility about Where and How Pollution Will Be Reduced | Political Process Creates Loopholes and Exceptions |
|---|---|---|---|
| **Pollution Charges** | If you keep reducing pollution you reduce your charge | Reducing pollution by any method is fine | If charge applies to all emissions of pollution then no loopholes |
| **Marketable Permits** | If you reduce your pollution you can sell your extra pollution permits | Reductions of pollution will happen at firms where it is cheapest to do so, by the least expensive methods | If all polluters are required to have permits then there are no loopholes |
| **Property Rights** | The party that has to pay for the pollution has incentive to do so in a cost effect way | Reducing pollution by any method is fine | If the property rights are clearly defined, then it is not legally possible to avoid cleanup |

10.  a.  See the answers in the following table. The marginal cost is calculated as the change in total cost divided by the change in quantity.

| | Total Cost (in thousands of dollars) [marginal cost] | Total Benefits (in thousands of dollars) [marginal benefit] |
|---|---|---|
| 16 million gallons | Current situation | Current situation |
| 12 million gallons | 50  [50] | 800  [800] |
| 8 million gallons | 150  [100] | 1,300  [500] |
| 4 million gallons | 500  [350] | 1,850  [350] |
| 0 gallons | 1,200  [700] | 2,000  [150] |

b.  The "optimal" level of pollution is where the marginal benefits of reducing it are equal to the marginal cost. This is at four million gallons.

c. Marginal analysis tells us if the marginal costs of cleanup are greater than the marginal benefit, society could use those resources more efficiently elsewhere in the economy.

**11.** a. See the next table for the answers, which were calculated using the traditional calculation of marginal cost equal to change in total cost divided by change in quantity.

| Land Restored (in acres) | Total Cost [marginal cost] | Total Benefit [marginal benefit] |
|---|---|---|
| 0 | $0 | $0 |
| 100 | $20 [0.2] | $140 [1.4] |
| 200 | $80 [0.6] | $240 [1] |
| 300 | $160 [0.8] | $320 [0.8] |
| 400 | $280 [1.2] | $480 [0.6] |

b. The optimal amount of restored land is 300 acres. Beyond this quantity the marginal costs are greater than the marginal benefits.

**12.**

| | | Country B | |
|---|---|---|---|
| | | Protect | Not Protect |
| Country A | Protect | Both A and B have a cost of 10 and a benefit of 16; each country has net = 6 | A has a cost of 10 and a benefit of 8 (net = −2); B has a cost of 0 and a benefit of 8 (net = 8) |
| | Not Protect | A has a cost of 0 and a benefit of 8 (net = 8); B has a cost of 10 and a benefit of 8 (net = −2) | Both A and B have a zero cost and a zero benefit; each country has net = 0 |

Country B will reason this way: If A protects the environment, then we will have benefits of 6 if we act to protect the environment, but 8 if we do not, so we will not protect it. If A is not protecting the environment, we will have losses of 2 if we protect, but have zero if we do not protect, so again, we will not protect it. Country A will reason in a similar manner. The result is that both countries choose to not protect, even though they will achieve the largest social benefits—a combined benefit of 12 for the two countries—if they both choose to protect. Environmental treaties can be viewed as a way for countries to try to extricate themselves from this situation.

**13.** a.

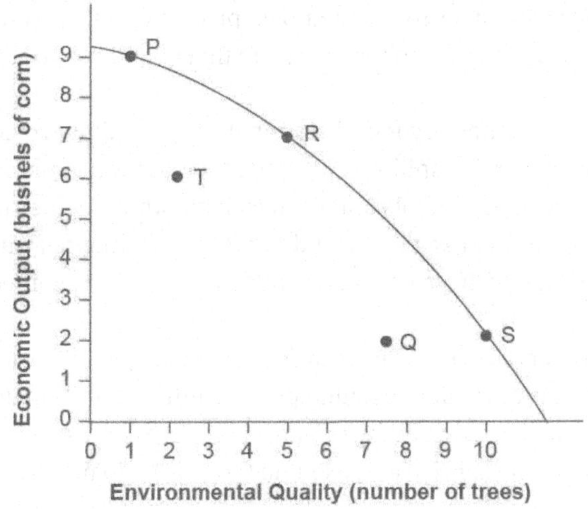

b. Of the choices provided, P, R, and S demonstrate productive efficiency. These are the choices on the production possibility frontier.

c. Allocative efficiency is determined by the preferences—in this case by the preferences of society as expressed through government and other social institutions. Because you do not have information about these preferences, you really cannot say much about allocative efficiency.

d. In the choice between T and R, R should clearly be preferred, because it has both more corn and more trees. This answer illustrates why productive efficiency is beneficial. Compared with choices inside the PPF, it means more of one or both goods.

e. In the choice between T and S, it is not possible to say which choice is better. True, S is on the PPF and T is not—but that only addresses the issue of productive efficiency. If a society has a strong preference for economic output and places a lower value on trees, then allocative efficiency may lead to a choice of T over S. Of course, the reverse could also be true, leading to a choice of S. Without information on society's preferences to judge allocative efficiency, this question cannot be answered.

f. Compared with command-and-control policies, market-oriented policies allow either more output with the same environmental protection or more environmental protection with the same level of output—or more of both environmental protection and output. Thus, a choice like Q inside the PPF is more likely to represent a command-and-control policy demand than a choice like S on the frontier of the PPF.

# Chapter 13

**1.** No. A market demand curve reflects only the private benefits of those who are consuming the product. Positive externalities are benefits that spill over to third parties, so they create social benefits, and are not captured by a market (or private benefit) demand curve.

**2.** Clearly Samsung is benefiting from the investment, so the 20% increase in profits is a private benefit. If Samsung is unable to capture all of the benefit, perhaps because other companies quickly copy and produce close substitutes, then Samsung's investment will produce social benefits.

**3.** a. $102 million.

   b. If the interest rate is 9%, the cost of financial capital, and the firm can capture the 5% return to society, the firm would invest as if its effective rate of return is 4%, so it will invest $183 million.

**4.** When the Junkbuyers Company purchases something for resale, presumably both the buyer and the seller benefit—otherwise, they would not need to make the transaction. However, the company also reduces the amount of garbage produced, which saves money for households and/or for the city that disposes of garbage. So the social benefits are larger than the private benefits.

5. Government programs that either pay for neighborhood clean-up directly or that provide reduced tax payments for those who clean up or fix up their own property could be enacted. It is also easy to imagine how a city might allow its businesses to form a group that would pay for and manage neighborhood cleanup.

6. Government programs that either pay for education directly or that provide loans or reduced tax payments for education could create positive spillovers. A city might allow its businesses to form a group that would coordinate business efforts with schools and local colleges and universities—allowing students to obtain real-world experience in their chosen fields and providing businesses with enthusiastic, trained workers.

7.  a. Once citizens are protected from crime, it is difficult to exclude someone from this protection, so it is nonexcludable.
    b. Some satellite radio services, such as SiriusXM, are sold by subscription fee, so it is excludable.
    c. Once a road is built it is difficult to exclude people, although toll roads can exclude non-payers.
    d. Primary education can be provided by private companies and so it is excludable.
    e. Companies sell cell phone service and exclude those who do not pay.

8.  a. Two people cannot enjoy the same slice of pizza at the same time, so private goods, such as a slice of pizza, are rivalrous.
    b. Two people cannot use one laptop at the same time, so they are rivalrous in consumption.
    c. Public radio can be heard by anyone with a radio, so many people can listen at the same time—the good is nonrivalrous.
    d. It is difficult for two people to simultaneously eat an ice cream cone, so it is rivalrous in consumption.

## Chapter 14

1.  a. For a firm operating in a perfectly competitive output market, the value of the marginal product is the marginal product of labor multiplied by the firm's output price.
    b. In a perfectly competitive labor market where the going market wage is $12, a profit-maximizing firm will hire workers up to the point where the market wage equals the marginal revenue product. In this case, the market wage equals the marginal revenue product when the labor is 5 because at that level, the marginal revenue product is $12.

2.  a. For firms with some market power in their output market, like a monopoly, the value of additional output sold is the firm's marginal revenue, not the price. This is because they face a downward sloping demand curve for output, which means that in order to sell additional output, the firm must lower its price. The marginal revenue product equals the marginal product of labor multiplied by the marginal revenue.
    b. A profit-maximizing firm will hire workers up to the point where the market wage equals the marginal revenue product. If the going market wage is $20, in this scenario, the profit-maximizing level of employment is 4 because at that point, the marginal revenue product is $20.

3.  a. With no union, the equilibrium wage rate would be $18 per hour and there would be 8,000 bus drivers.
    b. If the union has enough negotiating power to raise the wage to $4 per hour higher than under the original equilibrium, the new wage would be $22 per hour. At this wage, 4,000 workers would be demanded while 10,000 would be supplied, leading to an excess supply of 6,000 workers.

4. Unions have sometimes opposed new technology out of a fear of losing jobs, but in other cases unions have helped to facilitate the introduction of new technology because unionized workers felt that the union was looking after their interests or that their higher skills meant that their jobs were essentially protected. And the new technologies meant increased productivity.

5. In a few other countries (such as France and Spain), the percentage of workers belonging to a union is similar to that in the United States. Union membership rates, however, are generally lower in the United States. When the share of workers whose wages are determined by union negotiations is considered, the

United States ranks by far the lowest (because in countries like France and Spain, union negotiations often determine pay even for nonunion employees).

6. No. While some unions may cause firms to go bankrupt, other unions help firms to become more competitive. No overall pattern exists.

7. From a social point of view, the benefits of unions and the costs seem to counterbalance. There is no evidence that in countries with a higher percentage of unionized workers, the economies grow more or less slowly.

8. a. The marginal cost of labor is the cost to the firm of hiring one more worker. To find the marginal cost of labor, one must divide the change in wage by the change in labor.

    b. Because the monopsonist is the sole employer in the labor market, it can offer any wage that it wishes. However, the marginal cost of labor will be greater than the wage for any number of workers more than one because hiring more than one worker requires paying a higher wage rate for both the new worker and all previous hires. A monopsony will hire workers up to the point where its demand for labor equals the marginal cost of additional labor.

9. a. Firms have a profit incentive to sell to everyone, regardless of race, ethnicity, religion, or gender.

    b. A business that needs to hire workers to expand may also find that if it draws only from its accustomed pool of workers—say, White men—it lacks the workers it needs to expand production. Such a business would have an incentive to hire more women and minorities.

    c. A discriminatory business that is underpaying its workers may find those workers leaving for jobs with another employer who offers better pay. This market pressure could cause the discriminatory business to behave better.

10. No. The earnings gap does not prove discrimination because it does not compare the wages of men and women in the same job who have the same amounts of education, experience, and productivity.

11. If a large share of immigrants have relatively low skills, then reducing the number of immigrants would shift the supply curve of low-skill labor back to the left, which would tend to raise the equilibrium wage for low-skill labor.

## Chapter 15

1. a. Poverty falls, inequality rises.
    b. Poverty rises, inequality falls.

2. Jonathon's options for working and total income are shown in the following table. His labor-leisure diagram is shown in the figure following the table.

| Number of Work Hours | Earnings from Work | Government Benefits | Total Income |
| --- | --- | --- | --- |
| 1,500 | $9,000 | $1,000 | $10,000 |
| 1,200 | $7,200 | $2,800 | $10,000 |
| 900 | $5,400 | $4,600 | $10,000 |
| 600 | $3,600 | $6,400 | $10,000 |
| 300 | $1,800 | $8,200 | $10,000 |
| 0 | $0 | $10,000 | $10,000 |

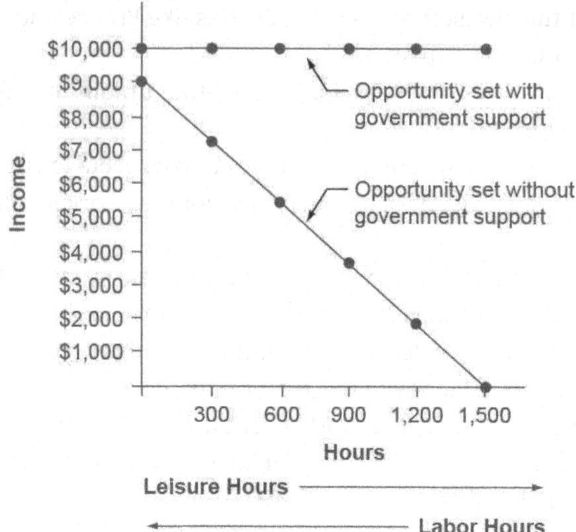


3. The following table shows a policy where only 30 cents in government support is pulled right back for every $1 of income earned. Jonathon's labor-leisure diagram is shown in the figure following the table. "Opportunity set after program" extends from (0, $16,300) to (1,500, $10,000). "Opportunity set before program" slopes downward from (0, $9,000) to (1,500, $0).

| Number of Work Hours | Earnings from Work | Government Benefits | Total Income |
| --- | --- | --- | --- |
| 1,500 | $9,000 | $7,300 | $16,300 |
| 1,200 | $7,200 | $7,840 | $15,040 |
| 900 | $5,400 | $8,380 | $13,780 |
| 600 | $3,600 | $8,920 | $12,520 |
| 300 | $1,800 | $9,460 | $22,260 |
| 0 | $0 | $10,000 | $10,000 |

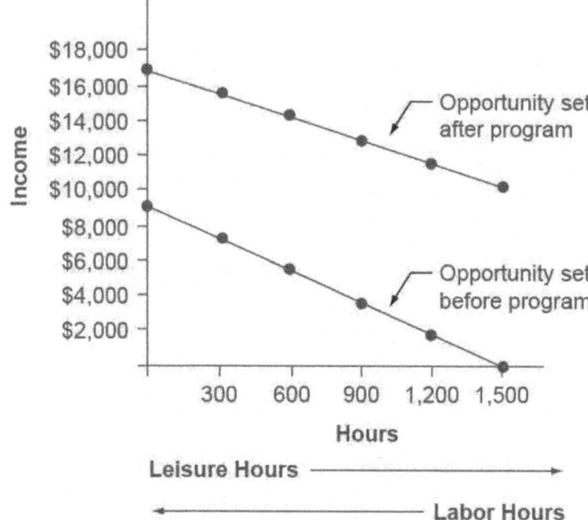


4. The earned income tax credit works like this: a family receives a tax break that increases according to how much they work. Families that work more get more. In that sense it loosens the poverty trap by encouraging work. As families earn above the poverty level, the earned income tax credit is gradually reduced. For those near-poor families, the earned income tax credit is a partial disincentive to work.

5. TANF attempts to loosen the poverty trap by providing incentives to work in other ways. Specifically, it requires that people work (or complete their education) as a condition of receiving TANF benefits, and it places a time limit on benefits.

6. A useful first step is to rank the households by income, from lowest to highest. Then, since there are 10 households total, the bottom quintile will be the bottom two households, the second quintile will be the third and fourth households, and so on up to the top quintile. The quintiles and percentage of total income for the data provided are shown in the following table. Comparing this distribution to the U.S. income distribution for 2005, the top quintile in the example has a smaller share of total income than in the U.S. distribution and the bottom quintile has a larger share. This pattern usually means that the income distribution in the example is more equal than the U.S. distribution.

| Income | Quintile | % of Total Income |
|---|---|---|
| $10,000<br>$12,000 | Total first quintile income: $22,000 | 6.0% |
| $16,000<br>$18,000 | Total second quintile income: $34,000 | 9.2% |
| $24,000<br>$24,000 | Total third quintile income: $48,000 | 13.0% |
| $36,000<br>$50,000 | Total fourth quintile income: $86,000 | 23.2% |
| $80,000<br>$100,000 | Total top quintile income: $180,000 | 48.6% |
| **$370,000** | **Total Income** | |

7. Just from glancing at the quintile information, it is fairly obvious that income inequality increased in the United Kingdom over this time: The top quintile is getting a lot more, and the lowest quintile is getting a bit less. Converting this information into a Lorenz curve, however, is a little trickier, because the Lorenz curve graphs the cumulative distribution, not the amount received by individual quintiles. Thus, as explained in the text, you have to add up the individual quintile data to convert the data to this form. The following table shows the actual calculations for the share of income in 1979 versus 1991. The figure following the table shows the perfect equality line and the Lorenz curves for 1979 and 1991. As shown, the income distribution in 1979 was closer to the perfect equality line than the income distribution in 1991—that is, the United Kingdom income distribution became more unequal over time.

| Share of income received | 1979 | 1991 |
|---|---|---|
| Bottom 20% | 7.0% | 6.6% |
| Bottom 40% | 18.5% | 18.1% |
| Bottom 60% | 35.5% | 34.4% |
| Bottom 80% | 60.3% | 57.1% |
| All 100% | 100.0% | 100.0% |

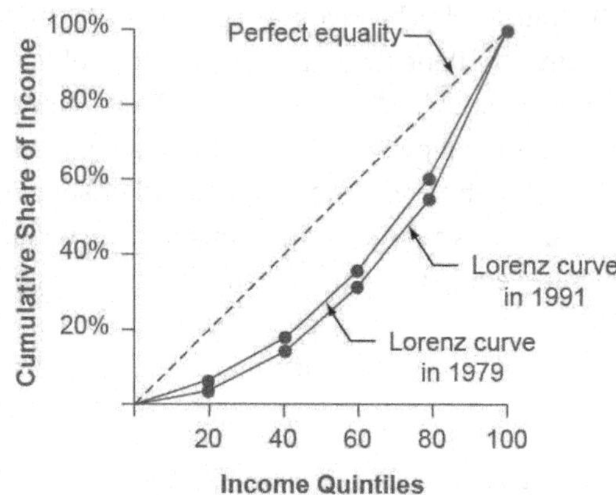



8. In the market for low-wage labor, information technology shifts the demand for low-wage labor to the left. One reason is that technology can often substitute for low-wage labor in certain kinds of telephone or bookkeeping jobs. In addition, information technology makes it easier for companies to manage connections with low-wage workers in other countries, thus reducing the demand for low-wage workers in the United States. In the market for high-wage labor, information technology shifts the demand for high-wage labor to the right. By using the new information and communications technologies, high-wage labor can become more productive and can oversee more tasks than before. The following figure illustrates these two labor markets. The combination of lower wages for low-wage labor and higher wages for high-wage labor means greater inequality.

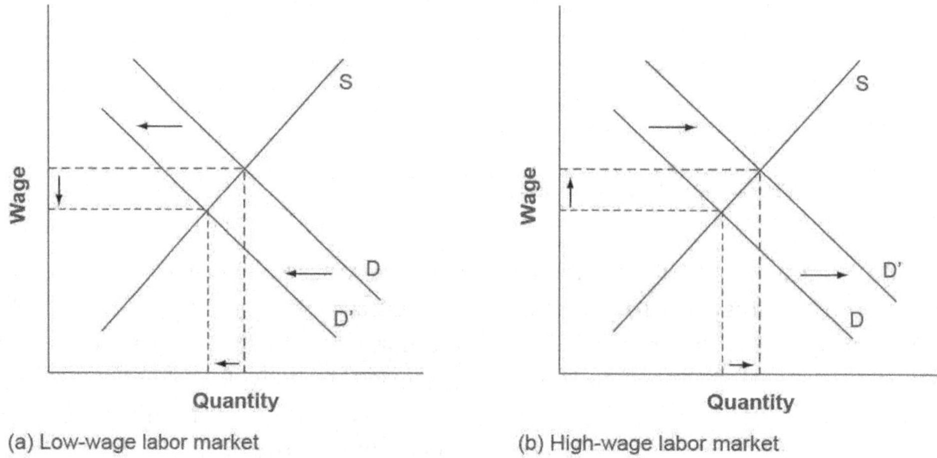



(a) Low-wage labor market     (b) High-wage labor market

9. In the market for low-wage labor, a skills program will shift supply to the left, which will tend to drive up wages for the remaining low-skill workers. In the market for high-wage labor, a skills program will shift supply to the right (because after the training program there are now more high-skilled workers at every wage), which will tend to drive down wages for high-skill workers. The combination of these two programs will result in a lesser degree of inequality. The following figure illustrates these two labor markets. In the market for high-wage labor, a skills program will shift supply to the right, which will tend to drive down wages for high-skill workers.

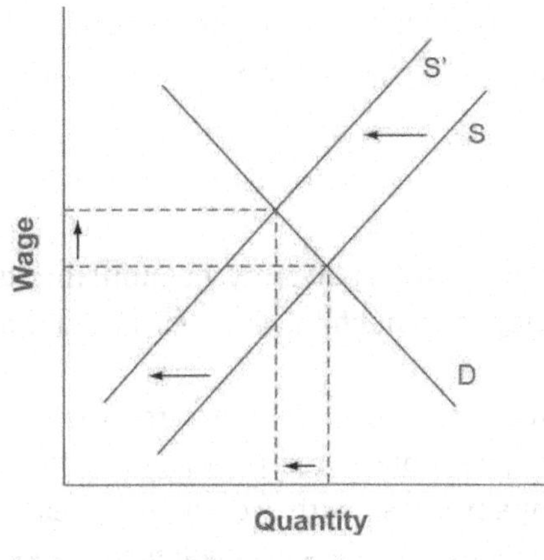



(a) Low-wage labor market

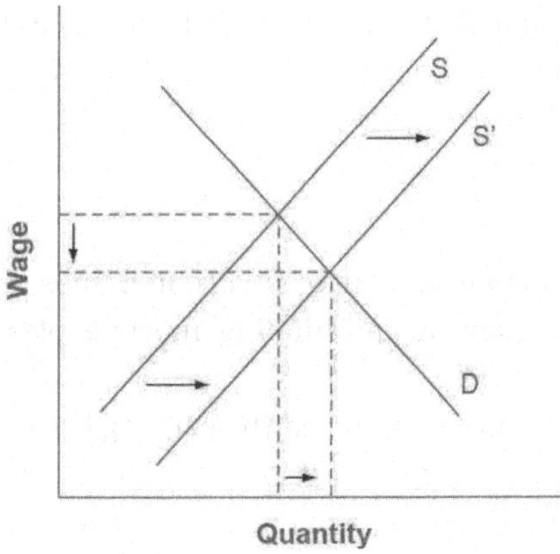



(b) High-wage labor market

10. A very strong push for economic equality might include extremely high taxes on high-wage earners to pay for extremely large government social payments for people with much lower incomes. Such a policy could limit incentives for the high-wage workers, lock the poor into a poverty trap, and thus reduce output. The PPF in this case will have the standard appearance: it will be downward sloping.

11. For the second hypothesis, a well-funded social safety net might make people feel that even if their company goes bankrupt or they need to change jobs or industries, they will have some degree of protection. As a result, people may be more willing to allow markets to work without interference, and not to lobby as hard for rules that would prevent layoffs, set price controls, or block foreign trade. In this case, safety net programs that increase equality could also allow the market to work more freely in a way that could increase output. In this case, at least some portion of the PPF between equality and economic output would slope up.

12. Pure redistribution is more likely to cause a sharp tradeoff between economic output and equality than policies aimed at the ladder of opportunity. A production possibility frontier showing a strict tradeoff between economic output and equality will be downward sloping. A PPF showing that it is possible to increase equality, at least to some extent, while either increasing output or at least not diminishing it would have a PPF that first rises, perhaps has a flat area, and then falls.

13. Many view the redistribution of income to achieve greater equality as taking away from the rich to pay the poor, or as a "zero sum" game. By taking taxes from one group of people and redistributing them to another, the tax system is robbing some of the American Dream.

## Chapter 16

1. a. Imperfect information is relatively low; after all, you can see the apples.
   b. Imperfect information is relatively low. The neighborhood restaurant probably has a certain local reputation.
   c. Imperfect information is relatively high. How can you tell whether the computer is really in good working order? Why are they selling it?
   d. Imperfect information is relatively high. What do those flowers really look like?

2. Asymmetric information often exists in the labor market because employers cannot observe many key employee attributes until after the person is hired. Employees, however, know whether they are energetic or detailed-oriented. Employers, therefore, often seek schools to pre-screen candidates. Employers may not even interview a candidate unless he has a degree and often a degree from a particular school. Employers may also view awards, a high grade point average, and other accolades as a signal of hard work, perseverance, and ability. Finally, employers seek references for insights into key attributes such as energy level, work ethic, and so on.

3. It is almost impossible to distinguish whether a health outcome such as life expectancy was the result of personal preferences that might affect health and longevity, such as diet, exercise, certain risky behavior, and consumption of certain items like tobacco, or the result of expenditures on health care (for example, annual check-ups).

## Chapter 17

1. a. The management of small companies might rather do an IPO right away, but until they get the company up and running, most people would not pay very much for the stock because of the risks involved.
   b. A small company may be earning few or zero profits, and its owners want to reinvest their earnings in the future growth of the company. If this company issues bonds or borrows money, it is obligated to make interest payments, which can eat up the company's cash. If the company issues stock, it is not obligated to make payments to anyone (although it may choose to pay dividends).
   c. Venture capitalists are private investors who can keep close tabs on the management and strategy of the company—and thus reduce the problems of imperfect information about whether the firm is being well run. Venture capitalists often own a substantial portion of the firm and have much better information than a typical shareholder would.

2. From a firm's point of view, a bond is very similar to a bank loan. Both are ways of borrowing money. Both require paying interest. The major difference is who must be persuaded to lend money: a bank loan requires persuading the bank, while issuing bonds requires persuading a number of separate bondholders. Since a bank often knows a great deal about a firm (especially if the firm has its accounts with that bank), bank loans are more common where imperfect information would otherwise be a problem.

3. a. Remember, equity is the market value of the house minus what is still owed to the bank. Thus: the value of the house is $200,000, Fred owes $180,000 to the bank, and his equity is $20,000.
   b. The value of Freda's house is $250,000. It does not matter what price she bought it for. She owes zero to the bank, so her equity is the whole $250,000.
   c. The value of Frank's house is $160,000. He owes $60,000 to the bank (the original $80,000 minus the $20,000 he has paid off the loan). His equity is $100,000.

4. Over a sustained period of time, stocks have an average return higher than bonds, and bonds have an average return higher than a savings account. This is because in any given year the value of a savings account changes very little. In contrast, stock values can grow or decline by a very large amount (for example, the S&P 500 increased 26% in 2009 after declining 37% in 2008. The value of a bond, which depends largely on interest rate fluctuations, varies far less than a stock, but more than a savings account.

5. When people believe that a high-risk investment must have a low return, they are getting confused between what risk and return mean. Yes, a high-risk investment might have a low return, but it might also have a high return. Risk refers to the fact that a wide range of outcomes is possible. However, a high-risk investment must, on average, expect a relatively high return or else no one would be willing to take the risk. Thus, it is quite possible—even likely—for an investment to have high risk and high return. Indeed, the reason that an investment has a high expected return is that it also has a high risk.

6. Principal + (principal × rate × time)
   $5,000 + ($5,000 × 0.06 × 3) = $5,900

7. Principal + (principal × rate × time); Interest = Principal × rate × time; $500 = $10,000 × rate × 5 years; $500 = $50,000 × rate; $500/$50,000 = rate; Rate = 1%

8. Principal(1 + interest rate)$^{time}$ = $1,000(1+0.02)^5$ =$1,104.08

## Chapter 18

1. All other things being equal, voter turnout should increase as the cost of casting an informed vote

decreases.

2. The cost in time of voting, transportation costs to and from the polling place, and any additional time and effort spent becoming informed about the candidates.

3. The costs of organization and the small benefit to the individual.

4. Domestic cotton producers would lobby heavily to protect themselves from the competition, whereas the consumers have little incentive to organize.

5. True. This is exactly what occurs in a voting cycle. That is, the majority can prefer policy A to policy B, policy B to policy C, but also prefer policy C to policy A. Then, the majority will never reach a conclusive outcome.

6. The problem is an example of a voting cycle. The group will vote for mountain biking over canoeing by 2–1. It will vote for canoeing over the beach by 2–1. If mountain biking is preferred to canoeing and canoeing is preferred to the beach, it might seem that it must be true that mountain biking is the favorite. But in a vote of the beach versus mountain biking, the beach wins by a 2–1 vote. When a voting cycle occurs, choosing a single favorite that is always preferred by a majority becomes impossible.

7. The four Coca-Cola candidates compete with each other for Coca-Cola voters, whereas everyone who prefers Pepsi had only one candidate to vote for. Thus the will of the majority is not satisfied.

## Chapter 19

1. False. Anything that leads to different levels of productivity between two economies can be a source of comparative advantage. For example, the education of workers, the knowledge base of engineers and scientists in a country, the part of a split-up value chain where they have their specialized learning, economies of scale, and other factors can all determine comparative advantage.

2. Brazil has the absolute advantage in producing beef and the United States has the absolute advantage in autos. The opportunity cost of producing one pound of beef is 1/10 of an auto; in the United States it is 3/4 of an auto.

3. In answering questions like these, it is often helpful to begin by organizing the information in a table, such as in the following table. Notice that, in this case, the productivity of the countries is expressed in terms of how many workers it takes to produce a unit of a product.

| Country | One Sweater | One Bottle of wine |
| --- | --- | --- |
| France | 1 worker | 1 worker |
| Tunisia | 2 workers | 3 workers |

In this example, France has an absolute advantage in the production of both sweaters and wine. You can tell because it takes France less labor to produce a unit of the good.

4. a. In Germany, it takes fewer workers to make either a television or a video camera. Germany has an absolute advantage in the production of both goods.

   b. Producing an additional television in Germany requires three workers. Shifting those three German workers will reduce video camera production by 3/4 of a camera. Producing an additional television set in Poland requires six workers, and shifting those workers from the other good reduces output of video cameras by 6/12 of a camera, or 1/2. Thus, the opportunity cost of producing televisions is lower in Poland, so Poland has the comparative advantage in the production of televisions. *Note*: Do not let the fractions like 3/4 of a camera or 1/2 of a video camera bother you. If either country was to expand television production by a significant amount—that is, lots more than one unit—then we will be talking about whole cameras and not fractional ones. You can also spot this conclusion by noticing that Poland's absolute disadvantage is relatively lower in televisions, because Poland needs twice as many workers to produce a television but three times as many to produce a video camera, so the product with the relatively lower absolute disadvantage is Poland's comparative advantage.

c. Producing a video camera in Germany requires four workers, and shifting those four workers away from television production has an opportunity cost of 4/3 television sets. Producing a video camera in Poland requires 12 workers, and shifting those 12 workers away from television production has an opportunity cost of two television sets. Thus, the opportunity cost of producing video cameras is lower in Germany, and video cameras will be Germany's comparative advantage.

d. In this example, absolute advantage differs from comparative advantage. Germany has the absolute advantage in the production of both goods, but Poland has a comparative advantage in the production of televisions.

e. Germany should specialize, at least to some extent, in the production of video cameras, export video cameras, and import televisions. Conversely, Poland should specialize, at least to some extent, in the production of televisions, export televisions, and import video cameras.

5. There are a number of possible advantages of intra-industry trade. Both nations can take advantage of extreme specialization and learning in certain kinds of cars with certain traits, like gas-efficient cars, luxury cars, sport-utility vehicles, higher- and lower-quality cars, and so on. Moreover, nations can take advantage of economies of scale, so that large companies will compete against each other across international borders, providing the benefits of competition and variety to customers. This same argument applies to trade between U.S. states, where people often buy products made by people of other states, even though a similar product is made within the boundaries of their own state. All states—and all countries—can benefit from this kind of competition and trade.

6. a. Start by plotting the points on a sketch diagram and then drawing a line through them. The following figure illustrates the average costs of production of semiconductors.

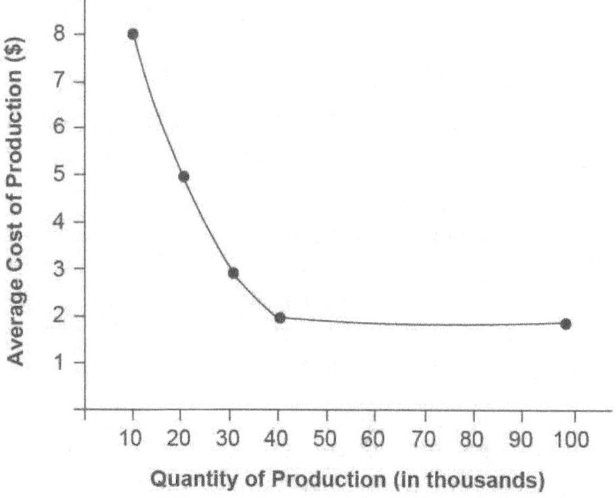


The curve illustrates economies of scale by showing that as the scale increases—that is, as production at this particular factory goes up—the average cost of production declines. The economies of scale exist up to an output of 40,000 semiconductors; at higher outputs, the average cost of production does not seem to decline any further.

b. At any quantity demanded above 40,000, this economy can take full advantage of economies of scale; that is, it can produce at the lowest cost per unit. Indeed, if the quantity demanded was quite high, like 500,000, then there could be a number of different factories all taking full advantage of economies of scale and competing with each other. If the quantity demanded falls below 40,000, then the economy by itself, without foreign trade, cannot take full advantage of economies of scale.

c. The simplest answer to this question is that the small country could have a large enough factory to take full advantage of economies of scale, but then export most of the output. For semiconductors, countries like Taiwan and Korea have recently fit this description. Moreover, this country could also import semiconductors from other countries which also have large factories, thus getting the benefits of competition and variety. A slightly more complex answer is that the country can get these benefits of economies of scale without producing semiconductors, but simply by buying semiconductors made at low cost around the world. An economy, especially a smaller country, may well end up specializing and producing a few items on a large scale, but then trading those items for other items produced on a large scale, and thus gaining the benefits of economies of scale by trade, as well as by direct production.

7. A nation might restrict trade on imported products to protect an industry that is important for national security. For example, nation X and nation Y may be geopolitical rivals, each with ambitions of increased political and economic strength. Even if nation Y has comparative advantage in the production of missile defense systems, it is unlikely that nation Y would seek to export those goods to nation X. It is also the case that, for some nations, the production of a particular good is a key component of national identity. In Japan, the production of rice is culturally very important. It may be difficult for Japan to import rice from a nation like Vietnam, even if Vietnam has a comparative advantage in rice production.

## Chapter 20

1. This is the opposite case of the Work It Out feature. A reduced tariff is like a decrease in the cost of production, which is shown by a downward (or rightward) shift in the supply curve.
2. A subsidy is like a reduction in cost. This shifts the supply curve down (or to the right), driving the price of sugar down. If the subsidy is large enough, the price of sugar can fall below the cost of production faced by foreign producers, which means they will lose money on any sugar they produce and sell.
3. Trade barriers raise the price of goods in protected industries. If those products are inputs in other industries, it raises their production costs and then prices, so sales fall in those other industries. Lower sales lead to lower employment. Additionally, if the protected industries are consumer goods, their customers pay higher prices, which reduce demand for other consumer products and thus employment in those industries.
4. Trade based on comparative advantage raises the average wage rate economy-wide, though it can reduce the incomes of import-substituting industries. By moving away from a country's comparative advantage, trade barriers do the opposite: they give workers in protected industries an advantage, while reducing the average wage economy-wide.
5. By raising incomes, trade tends to raise working conditions also, even though those conditions may not (yet) be equivalent to those in high-income countries.
6. They typically pay more than the next-best alternative. If a Nike firm did not pay workers at least as much as they would earn, for example, in a subsistence rural lifestyle, they many never come to work for Nike.
7. Since trade barriers raise prices, real incomes fall. The average worker would also earn less.
8. Workers working in other sectors and the protected sector see a decrease in their real wage.
9. If imports can be sold at extremely low prices, domestic firms would have to match those prices to be competitive. By definition, matching prices would imply selling under cost and, therefore, losing money. Firms cannot sustain losses forever. When they leave the industry, importers can "take over," raising prices to monopoly levels to cover their short-term losses and earn long-term profits.
10. Because low-income countries need to provide necessities—food, clothing, and shelter—to their people. In other words, they consider environmental quality a luxury.
11. Low-income countries can compete for jobs by reducing their environmental standards to attract business to their countries. This could lead to a competitive reduction in regulations, which would lead to greater environmental damage. While pollution management is a cost for businesses, it is tiny relative to other costs, like labor and adequate infrastructure. It is also costly for firms to locate far away from their customers, which many low-income countries are.
12. The decision should not be arbitrary or unnecessarily discriminatory. It should treat foreign companies

the same way as domestic companies. It should be based on science.

13. Restricting imports today does not solve the problem. If anything, it makes it worse since it implies using up domestic sources of the products faster than if they are imported. Also, the national security argument can be used to support protection of nearly any product, not just things critical to our national security.

14. The effect of increasing standards may increase costs to the small exporting country. The supply curve of toys will shift to the left. Exports will decrease and toy prices will rise. Tariffs also raise prices. So the effect on the price of toys is the same. A tariff is a "second best" policy and also affects other sectors. However, a common standard across countries is a "first best" policy that attacks the problem at its root.

15. A free trade association offers free trade between its members, but each country can determine its own trade policy outside the association. A common market requires a common external trade policy in addition to free trade within the group. An economic union is a common market with coordinated fiscal and monetary policy.

16. International agreements can serve as a political counterweight to domestic special interests, thereby preventing stronger protectionist measures.

17. Reductions in tariffs, quotas, and other trade barriers, improved transportation, and communication media have made people more aware of what is available in the rest of the world.

18. Competition from firms with better or cheaper products can reduce a business's profits, and may drive it out of business. Workers would similarly lose income or even their jobs.

19. Consumers get better or less expensive products. Businesses with the better or cheaper products increase their profits. Employees of those businesses earn more income. On balance, the gains outweigh the losses to a nation.

# REFERENCES


## Welcome to Economics!

Bureau of Labor Statistics, U.S. Department of Labor. 2015. "The Employment Situation—February 2015." Accessed March 27, 2015. http://www.bls.gov/news.release/pdf/empsit.pdf.

Williamson, Lisa. "US Labor Market in 2012." *Bureau of Labor Statistics*. Accessed December 1, 2013. http://www.bls.gov/opub/mlr/2013/03/art1full.pdf.

The Heritage Foundation. 2015. "2015 Index of Economic Freedom." Accessed March 11, 2015. http://www.heritage.org/index/ranking.

Garling, Caleb. "S.F. plane crash: Reporting, emotions on social media," *The San Francisco Chronicle*. July 7, 2013. http://www.sfgate.com/news/article/S-F-plane-crash-Reporting-emotions-on-social-4651639.php.

Irvine, Jessica. "Social Networking Sites are Factories of Modern Ideas." *The Sydney Morning Herald*. November 25, 2011.http://www.smh.com.au/federal-politics/society-and-culture/social-networking-sites-are-factories-of-modern-ideas-20111124-1nwy3.html#ixzz2YZhPYeME.

Pew Research Center. 2015. "Social Networking Fact Sheet." Accessed March 11, 2015. http://www.pewinternet.org/fact-sheets/social-networking-fact-sheet/.

Royal Swedish Academy of Sciences. 2019. "Research to Help the World's Poor." https://www.nobelprize.org/uploads/2019/10/popular-economicsciencesprize2019.pdf.

The World Bank Group. 2015. "World Data Bank." Accessed March 30, 2014. http://databank.worldbank.org/data/.

## Choice in a World of Scarcity

Bureau of Labor Statistics, U.S. Department of Labor. 2015. "Median Weekly Earnings by Educational Attainment in 2014." Accessed March 27, 2015. http://www.bls.gov/opub/ted/2015/median-weekly-earnings-by-education-gender-race-and-ethnicity-in-2014.htm.

Robbins, Lionel. *An Essay on the Nature and Significance of Economic Science*. London: Macmillan. 1932.

United States Department of Transportation. "Total Passengers on U.S Airlines and Foreign Airlines U.S. Flights Increased 1.3% in 2012 from 2011." Accessed October 2013. http://www.rita.dot.gov/bts/press_releases/bts016_13

Smith, Adam. "Of Restraints upon the Importation from Foreign Countries." In *The Wealth of Nations*. London: Methuen & Co., 1904, first pub 1776), I.V. 2.9.

Smith, Adam. "Of the Propriety of Action." In *The Theory of Moral Sentiments*. London: A. Millar, 1759, 1.

## Demand and Supply

Costanza, Robert, and Lisa Wainger. "No Accounting For Nature: How Conventional Economics Distorts the Value of Things." *The Washington Post*. September 2, 1990.

European Commission: Agriculture and Rural Development. 2013. "Overview of the CAP Reform: 2014-2024." Accessed April 13, 205. http://ec.europa.eu/agriculture/cap-post-2013/.

Radford, R. A. "The Economic Organisation of a P.O.W. Camp." *Economica*. no. 48 (1945): 189-201. http://www.jstor.org/stable/2550133.

Landsburg, Steven E. *The Armchair Economist: Economics and Everyday Life*. New York: The Free Press. 2012. specifically Section IV: How Markets Work.

National Chicken Council. 2015. "Per Capita Consumption of Poultry and Livestock, 1965 to Estimated 2015, in Pounds." Accessed April 13, 2015. https://www.nationalchickencouncil.org/about-the-industry/statistics/per-capita-consumption-of-poultry-and-livestock-1965-to-estimated-2012-in-pounds/.

Wessel, David. "Saudi Arabia Fears $40-a-Barrel Oil, Too." *The Wall Street Journal*. May 27, 2004, p. 42. https://online.wsj.com/news/articles/SB108561000087822300.

Pew Research Center. "Pew Research: Center for the People & the Press." http://www.people-press.org/.


## Labor and Financial Markets


American Community Survey. 2012. "School Enrollment and Work Status: 2011." Accessed April 13, 2015. http://www.census.gov/prod/2013pubs/acsbr11-14.pdf.

National Center for Educational Statistics. "Digest of Education Statistics." (2008 and 2010). Accessed December 11, 2013. nces.ed.gov.

CreditCards.com. 2013. http://www.creditcards.com/credit-card-news/credit-card-industry-facts-personal-debt-statistics-1276.php.

Williams, Walter E. 2017. "Mimimum Wage and Discrimination." Distributed by Creators Syndicate. Accessed 2022. https://www.lubbockonline.com/story/opinion/columns/2017/02/13/walter-williams-minimum-wage-and-discrimination/14874014007.


## Elasticity


Abkowitz, A. "How Netflix got started: Netflix founder and CEO Reed Hastings tells Fortune how he got the idea for the DVD-by-mail service that now has more than eight million customers." *CNN Money*. Last Modified January 28, 2009. http://archive.fortune.com/2009/01/27/news/newsmakers/hastings_netflix.fortune/index.htm.

Associated Press (a). "Analyst: Coinstar gains from Netflix pricing moves." *Boston Globe Media Partners, LLC*. Accessed June 24, 2013. http://www.boston.com/business/articles/2011/10/12/analyst_coinstar_gains_from_netflix_pricing_moves/.

Associated Press (b). "Netflix loses 800,000 US subscribers in tough 3Q." *ABC Inc*. Accessed June 24, 2013. http://abclocal.go.com/wpvi/story?section=news/business&id=8403368

Baumgardner, James. 2014. "Presentation on Raising the Excise Tax on Cigarettes: Effects on Health and the Federal Budget." Congressional Budget Office. Accessed March 27, 2015. http://www.cbo.gov/sites/default/files/45214-ICA_Presentation.pdf.

Funding Universe. 2015. "Netflix, Inc. History." Accessed March 11, 2015. http://www.fundinguniverse.com/company-histories/netflix-inc-history/.

Laporte, Nicole. "A tale of two Netflix." *Fast Company* 177 (July 2013) 31-32. Accessed December 3 2013. http://www.fastcompany-digital.com/fastcompany/20130708?pg=33#pg33

Liedtke, Michael, The Associated Press. "Investors bash Netflix stock after slower growth forecast - fee hikes expected to take toll on subscribers most likely to shun costly bundled Net, DVD service." *The Seattle Times*. Accessed June 24, 2013 from NewsBank on-line database (Access World News).

Netflix, Inc. 2013. "A Quick Update On Our Streaming Plans And Prices." Netflix (blog). Accessed March 11, 2015. http://blog.netflix.com/2014/05/a-quick-update-on-our-streaming-plans.html.

Organization for Economic Co-Operation and Development (OECC). n.d. "Average annual hours actually worked per worker." Accessed March 11, 2015. https://stats.oecd.org/Index.aspx?DataSetCode=ANHRS.

Savitz, Eric. "Netflix Warns DVD Subs Eroding; Q4 View Weak; Losses Ahead; Shrs Plunge." *Forbes.com*, 2011. Accessed December 3, 2013. http://www.forbes.com/sites/ericsavitz/2011/10/24/netflix-q3-top-ests-but-shares-hit-by-weak-q4-outlook/.

Statistica.com. 2014. "Coffee Export Volumes Worldwide in November 2014, by Leading Countries (in 60-kilo sacks)." Accessed March 27, 2015. http://www.statista.com/statistics/268135/ranking-of-coffee-exporting-countries/.

Stone, Marcie. "Netflix responds to customers angry with price hike; Netflix stock falls 9%." *News & Politics Examiner*, 2011. Clarity Digital Group. Accessed June 24, 2013. http://www.examiner.com/article/netflix-responds-to-customers-angry-with-price-hike-netflix-stock-falls-9.

Weinman, J. (2012). Die hard, hardly dying. Maclean's, 125(18), 44.

The World Bank Group. 2015. "Gross Savings (% of GDP)." Accessed March 11, 2015. http://data.worldbank.org/indicator/NY.GNS.ICTR.ZS.

Yahoo Finance. Retrieved from http://finance.yahoo.com/q?s=NFLX

## Consumer Choices

U.S. Bureau of Labor Statistics. 2015. "Consumer Expenditures in 2013." Accessed March 11, 2015. http://www.bls.gov/cex/csxann13.pdf.

U.S. Bureau of Labor Statistics. 2015. "Employer Costs for Employee Compensation—December 2014." Accessed March 11, 2015. http://www.bls.gov/news.release/pdf/ecec.pdf.

U.S. Bureau of Labor Statistics. 2015. "Labor Force Statistics from the Current Population Survey." Accessed March 11, 2015. http://www.bls.gov/cps/cpsaat22.htm.

Holden, Sarah, and Daniel Schrass. 2012. "The rose of IRAs in U.S Households' Saving for Retirement, 2012." *ICI Research Perspective* 18.8 (2012). http://www.ici.org/pdf/per18-08.pdf.

Kahneman, Daniel and Amos Tversky. "Prospect Theory: An Analysis of Decision under Risk." *Econometrica* 47.2 (March 1979) 263-291.

Thaler, Richard H. "Shifting Our Retirement Savings into Automatic." *The New York Times*, April 6, 2013. http://www.nytimes.com/2013/04/07/business/an-automatic-solution-for-the-retirement-savings-problem.html?pagewanted=all.

UNESCO Institute for Statistics. "Statistics in Brief / Profiles" Accessed August 2013. http://stats.uis.unesco.org/unesco/TableViewer/document.aspx?ReportId=121 &IF_Language=en&BR_Country=5580.

## Production, Costs, and Industry Structure

2010 U.S. Census. www.census.gov.

## Perfect Competition

Index Mundi. n.d. "Wheat Monthly Price—U.S. Dollars per Metric Ton." Accessed March 11, 2015. http://www.indexmundi.com/commodities/?commodity=wheat.

Knutson, J. "Wheat on the Defensive in the Northern Plains." *Agweek, Associated Press State Wire: North Dakota (ND)*. April 14, 2013.

SBA Office of Advocacy. 2014. "Frequently Asked Questions: Advocacy: the voice of small business in government." Accessed March 11, 2015. https://www.sba.gov/sites/default/files/advocacy/FAQ_March_2014_0.pdf.

## Monopoly

Aboukhadijeh, Feross. "Chapter 20: Girding for War - The North and the South, 1861-1865." *StudyNotes, Inc.* Accessed July 7, 2013. http://www.apstudynotes.org/us-history/outlines/chapter-20-girding-for-war-the-north-and-the-south-1861-1865/.

British Parliament. "(28 August 1833). Slavery Abolition Act 1833; Section LXIV." Accessed July 2013. http://www.pdavis.nl/Legis_07.htm.

Dattel, E. (nd). "Cotton and the Civil War." *Mississippi Historical Society.* Accessed July 2013. http://mshistorynow.mdah.state.ms.us/articles/291/cotton-and-the-civil-war.

Gartner. 2015. "Gartner Says Tablet Sales Continue to Be Slow in 2015." Accessed March 12, 2015. http://www.gartner.com/newsroom/id/2954317.

Grogan, David. 2015. "Federal Judge Finds AmEx's Anti-Steering Rule Violates Antitrust Law." American Booksellers Association. Accessed March 12, 2015. http://www.bookweb.org/news/federal-judge-finds-amex%E2%80%99s-anti-steering-rule-violates-antitrust-law.

Massachusetts Historical Society. "The Coming of the American Revolution 1764-1776: The Boston Tea Party." Retrieved from http://www.masshist.org/revolution/teaparty.php.

Massachusetts Historical Society. "Whereas our Nation." *The Massachusetts Gazette*, p. 2. Accessed July 2013 http://www.masshist.org/revolution/image-viewer.php?old=1&item_id=457&img_step=1&nmask=1&mode=large.

Pelegrin, William. 2015. "Judge Overrules Antitrust Case Against Google , Says Setting Default Search Engines Is Fair." Digital Trends. Accessed March 12, 2015. http://www.digitaltrends.com/mobile/judge-tosses-out-google-antitrust-lawsuit/.

## Monopolistic Competition and Oligopoly

Kantar Media. "Our Insights: Infographic—U.S. Advertising Year End Trends Report 2012." Accessed October 17, 2013. http://kantarmedia.us/insight-center/reports/infographic-us-advertising-year-end-trends-report-2012.

Statistica.com. 2015. "Number of Restaurants in the United States from 2011 to 2014." Accessed March 27, 2015. http://www.statista.com/statistics/244616/number-of-qsr-fsr-chain-independent-restaurants-in-the-us/.

The United States Department of Justice. "Antitrust Division." Accessed October 17, 2013. http://www.justice.gov/atr/.

eMarketer.com. 2014. "Total US Ad Spending to See Largest Increase Since 2004: Mobile advertising leads growth; will surpass radio, magazines and newspapers this year. Accessed March 12, 2015. http://www.emarketer.com/Article/Total-US-Ad-Spending-See-Largest-Increase-Since-2004/1010982.

Federal Trade Commission. "About the Federal Trade Commission." Accessed October 17, 2013. http://www.ftc.gov/ftc/about.shtm.

## Monopoly and Antitrust Policy

Bishop, Todd. 2014. "Microsoft Exec Admits New Reality: Market Share No Longer 90% — It's 14%."GeekWire. Accessed March 27, 2015. http://www.geekwire.com/2014/microsoft-exec-admits-new-reality-market-share-longer-90-14/.

Catan, T., & Dezember, R. "Kinder-El Paso Merger to Face Antitrust Scrutiny," *Wall Street Journal.* October 19, 2011.

Collins, A. "Tallgrass Energy to Acquire Kinder Morgan Assets for $1.8B." *The Middle Market*, Accessed August 2013. http://www.themiddlemarket.com/news/tallgrass-energy-to-acquire-kinder-morgan-assets-for-1-point-8-billion-232862-1.html.

Conoco Phillips. "Why Natural Gas." Accessed August 2013. http://www.powerincooperation.com/en/pages/useful.html?gclid=COXg7rH3hrgCFWlp7AodtkgA3g.

De la Merced, M. (2012, August 20). "Kinder Morgan to Sell Assets to Tallgrass for $1.8 Billion." *The New York Times*. August 20, 2012.

The Federal Trade Commission. n.d. "The Federal Trade Commission's (FTC) Mission." Accessed March 27, 2015. https://www.ftc.gov/system/files/documents/reports/2014-one-page-ftc-performance-snapshot/150218fy14snapshot.pdf.

Kahn, C. "Kinder Morgan to Buy El Paso Corp. for $20.7B." *USA Today*. October 17, 2011.

Kinder Morgan. (2013). "Investor Information." Accessed August 2013. http://www.kindermorgan.com/investor/.

Rogowsky, Mark. 2014. "There'd Be No Wireless Wars Without The Blocked T-Mobile Merger, So Where Does That Leave Comcast-TWC?" Forbes.com. Accessed March 12, 2015. http://www.forbes.com/sites/markrogowsky/2014/08/27/t-mobile-and-sprint-continue-to-battle-thanks-to-the-government/.

U.S. Energy Information Administration (a). "Natural Gas Consumption by End User." Accessed May 31, 2013. http://www.eia.gov/dnav/ng/ng_cons_sum_dcu_nus_a.htm.

U.S. Energy Information Administration (b). "Natural Gas Prices." Accessed June 28, 2013. http://www.eia.gov/dnav/ng/ng_pri_sum_dcu_nus_a.htm.

The Wall Street Journal. 2015. "Auto Sales." Accessed April 10, 2015. http://online.wsj.com/mdc/public/page/2_3022-autosales.html.

## Environmental Protection and Negative Externalities

Johnson, Oscar William. "Back on Track: Earth Day Success Story; The Chattanooga Choo-Choo No Longer Spews Foul Air." *Sports Illustrated*. April 30, 1990. http://www.si.com/vault/1990/04/30/121923/back-on-track-earth-day-success-story-the-chattanooga-choo-choo-no-longer-spews-foul-air.

U.S. Energy Information Administration. "Total Energy: Monthly Energy Review." *U.S. Department of Energy*. Accessed December 19, 2013. http://www.eia.gov/totalenergy/data/monthly/.

Environmental Protection Agency. "2006 Pay-As-You-Throw Programs." Accessed December 20, 2013. http://www.epa.gov/epawaste/conserve/tools/payt/states/06comm.htm.

European Union. "Durban Conference Delivers Breakthrough for Climate." Press release. December 11, 2012. Accessed December 19, 2013. http://europa.eu/rapid/press-release_MEMO-11-895_en.htm?locale=en.

## Positive Externalities and Public Goods

Arias, Omar and Walter W. McMahon. "Dynamic Rates of Return to Education in the U.S." *Economics of Education Review*. 20, 2001. 121–138.

Biography.com. 2015. "Alan Turing." Accessed April 1, 2015. http://www.biography.com/people/alan-turing-9512017.

Canty Media. 2015. "The World: Life Expectancy (2015) - Top 100+." Accessed April 1, 2015. http://www.geoba.se/population.php?pc=world&type=15.

Hyclak, Thomas, Geraint Johnes, and Robert Thornton. *Fundamentals of Labor Economics*. Boston: Houghton Mifflin Company, 2005.

McMahon, Walter. *Education and Development: Measuring the Social Benefits.* Oxford: Oxford University Press, 2000.

McTigue, Kathleen. 2019. "Economic Benefits of the Global Position System to the Private Sector." *National Institute of Standards and Technology.* https://www.nist.gov/news-events/news/2019/10/economic-benefits-global-positioning-system-us-private-sector-study.

Mazzucato, Mariana and Carlota Perez. 2014. "Innovation as Growth Policy: The Challenge for Europe." *Science Policy Research Unit.* https://www.sussex.ac.uk/webteam/gateway/file.php?name=2014-13-swps-mazzucato-perez.pdf&site=25.

Mazzucato, Mariana. *The Entreprenurial State: Debunking Public vs. Private Sector Myths.* Public Affairs, 2015.

National Institute of Health. 2015. "Global Competitiveness—The Importance of U.S. Leadership in Science and Innovation for the Future of Our Economy and Our Health." Accessed April 1, 2015. http://www.nih.gov/about/impact/impact_global.pdf.

National Science Foundation. 2013. "U.S. R&D Spending Resumes Growth in 2010 and 2011 but Still Lags Behind the Pace of Expansion of the National Economy." Accessed April 1, 2015. http://www.nsf.gov/statistics/infbrief/nsf13313/.

Ostrom, Elinor. *Governing the Commons: The Evolution of Institutions for Collective Action.* Cambrige University Press, 1990.

Perez, Carlota. 2009. "Long Run Economic Transformation: After the Crisis." OME Annual Report 2009–2010.

Psacharopoulos, George. "Returns to Investment in Education: A Global Update." *World Development* 22, 1994. 1325–1343.

Salientes-Narisma, Corrie. "Samsung Shift to Innovative Devices Pay Off." *Inquirer Technology.* Accessed May 15, 2013. http://technology.inquirer.net/23831/samsungs-shift-to-innovative-devices-pays-off.

United States Department of the Treasury. "Research and Experimentation Tax Credit." Accessed November 2013. http://www.treasury.gov/press-center/news/Pages/investing-in-us-competitiveness.aspx.

U.S. Patent and Trademark Office. 2015. "U.S. Patent Statistics: Calendar Years 1963–2014." Accessed April 10, 2015. http://www.uspto.gov/web/offices/ac/ido/oeip/taf/us_stat.pdf.

United for Medical Research. "Profiles of Prosperity: How NIH-Supported Research Is Fueling Private Sector Growth and Innovation." Introduction. Accessed January 2014. http://www.unitedformedicalresearch.com/wp-content/uploads/2013/07/UMR_ProsperityReport_071913a.pdf.

Cowen, Tyler. *Average Is Over: Powering America Beyond the Age of the Great Stagnation.* Dutton Adult, 2013.

Hardin, Garret. "The Tragedy of the Commons." *Science* 162 (3859): 1243–48 (1968).

## Labor Markets and Income

AFL-CIO. "Training and Apprenticeships." http://www.aflcio.org/Learn-About-Unions/Training-and-Apprenticeships.

Cook, Lisa D. 2020. "Policies To Broaden Participation in the Innovation Process." *The Hamilton Project.* https://www.hamiltonproject.org/assets/files/Cook_PP_LO_8.13.pdf.

Darity Jr., William A. 1998. "Evidence of Discrimination in Employment: Codes of Color, Codes of Gender." *Journal of Economic Perspectives* 12 (2): 63–90.

Central Intelligence Agency. "The World Factbook." https://www.cia.gov/library/publications/the-world-factbook/index.html.

Clark, John Bates. *Essentials of Economic Theory: As Applied to Modern Problems of Industry and Public Policy*. New York: A. M. Kelley, 1907, 501.

United Auto Workers (UAW). "About: Who We Are." http://www.uaw.org/page/who-we-are.

United States Department of Labor: Bureau of Labor Statistics. "Economic News Release: Union Members Summary." Last modified January 23, 2013. http://www.bls.gov/news.release/union2.nr0.htm.

United States Department of Labor, Bureau of Labor Statistics. 2015. "Economic News; Union Members Summary." Accessed April 13, 2015. http://www.bls.gov/news.release/union2.nr0.htm.

Clune, Michael S. "The Fiscal Impacts of Immigrants: A California Case Study." In *The Immigration Debate: Studies on the Economic, Demographic, and Fiscal Effects of Immigration*, edited by James P. Smith and Barry Edmonston. Washington, DC: National Academy Press, 1998, 120–182. http://www.nap.edu/openbook.php?record_id=5985&page=120.

Smith, James P. "Immigration Reform." *Rand Corporation: Rand Review*. http://www.rand.org/pubs/periodicals/rand-review/issues/2012/fall/leadership/immigration-reform.html.

U.S. Department of Homeland Security: Office of Immigration Statistics. "2011 Yearbook of Immigration Statistics." September 2012. http://www.dhs.gov/sites/default/files/publications/immigration-statistics/yearbook/2011/ois_yb_2011.pdf.

Anderson, Deborah J., Melissa Binder, and Kate Krause. "The Motherhood Wage Penalty Revisited: Experience, Heterogeneity, Work Effort, and Work-Schedule Flexibility." *Industrial and Labor Relations Review*. no. 2 (2003): 273–294. http://www2.econ.iastate.edu/classes/econ321/orazem/anderson_motherhood-penalty.pdf.

Turner, Margery Austin, Rob Santos, Diane K. Levy, Doug Wissoker, Claudia Aranda, Rob Pitingolo, and The Urban Institute. "Housing Discrimination Against Racial and Ethnic Minorities 2012." *U.S. Department of Housing and Urban Development*. Last modified June 2013. http://www.huduser.org/Publications/pdf/HUD-514_HDS2012.pdf.

Austin, Algernon. "The Unfinished March: An Overview." *Economic Policy Institute*. Last modified June 18, 2013. http://www.epi.org/publication/unfinished-march-overview/.

Bertrand, Marianne, and Sendhil Mullainathan. "Are Emily and Greg More Employable Than Lakisha and Jamal? A Field Experiment on Labor Market Discrimination." *American Economic Review*. no. 4 (2004): 991-1013. https://www.aeaweb.org/articles.php?doi=10.1257/0002828042002561&fnd=s.

Blau, Francine D., and Laurence M. Kahn. "The Gender Pay Gap: Have Women Gone as Far as They Can?" *Academy of Management Perspectives*. no. 1 (2007): 7–23. 10.5465/AMP.2007.24286161.

Card, David, and Alan B. Kruger. "Trends in Relative Black–White Earnings Revisited (Working Paper #310)." *Princeton University and the National Bureau of Economic Research*. December 1992. http://harris.princeton.edu/pubs/pdfs/310.pdf.

Donovan, Theresa. Jurist. "Federal Judge Rejects Class Status in Wal-Mart Discrimination Suit." Last modified August 5, 2013. http://jurist.org/paperchase/2013/08/federal-judge-rejects-class-status-in-wal-mart-discrimination-suit.php.

Harris, Elizabeth A. "Labor Panel Finds Illegal Punishments at Walmart." *The New York Times*, November 18, 2013. http://www.nytimes.com/2013/11/19/business/labor-panel-finds-illegal-punishments-at-walmart.html?_r=1&.

Kolesnikova, Natalia A., and Yang Liu. Federal Reserve Bank of St. Louis: The Regional Economist. "Gender Wage Gap May Be Much Smaller Than Most Think." Last modified October 2011. http://www.stlouisfed.org/publications/re/articles/?id=2160.

Podmolik, Mary Ellen. "HUD Finds Housing Discrimination 'Hidden' But Prevalent." *Chicago Tribune: Business*, June 12, 2013. http://articles.chicagotribune.com/2013-06-12/business/ct-biz-0612-housing-discrimination-20130612_1_renters-testers-chicago-area.

Spreen, Thomas Luke. United States Department of Labor: Bureau of Labor Statistics. "Recent College Graduates in the U.S. Labor Force: Data from the Current Population Survey." *Monthly Labor Review* (February, 2013). http://www.bls.gov/opub/mlr/2013/02/art1full.pdf .

U.S. Bureau of Labor Statistics: BLS Reports. 2014. "Women in the Labor Force: A Databook (Report 1052)." Accessed April 13, 2015. http://www.bls.gov/opub/reports/cps/women-in-the-labor-force-a-databook-2014.pdf.

U.S. Equal Employment Opportunity Commission, "Walmart to Pay More than $11.7 Million to Settle EEOC Sex Discrimination Suit." Last modified March 1, 2010. http://www.eeoc.gov/eeoc/newsroom/release/3-1-10.cfm.

United States Census Bureau. 2014. "Table 1. Educational Attainment of the Population 18 Years and Over, by Age, Sex, Race, and Hispanic Origin: 2014." Accessed April 13, 2015. http://www.census.gov/hhes/socdemo/education/data/cps/2014/tables.html.

United States Department of Labor: Bureau of Labor Statistics. "News Release: Usual Weekly Earnings of Wage and Salary Workers (Third Quarter 2013)." November 1, 2013. http://www.bls.gov/news.release/pdf/wkyeng.pdf.

Warner, Judith. 2014. "Fact Sheet: The Women's Leadership Gap: Women's Leadership by the Numbers." Center for American Progress. Accessed March 16, 2015. https://www.americanprogress.org/issues/women/report/2014/03/07/85457/fact-sheet-the-womens-leadership-gap/.

Weinberger, Catherine J., and Lois Joy. "The Relative Earnings of Black College Graduates, 1980–2001." In *Race and Economic Opportunity in the 21st Century*, edited by Marlene Kim. New York: Routledge, 2007. http://www.econ.ucsb.edu/~weinberg/grads.pdf.

## Poverty and Economic Inequality

Ebeling, Ashlea. 2014. "IRS Announces 2015 Estate And Gift Tax Limits." Forbes. Accessed March 16, 2015. http://www.forbes.com/sites/ashleaebeling/2014/10/30/irs-announces-2015-estate-and-gift-tax-limits/.

Federal Register: The Daily Journal of the United States Government. "State Median Income Estimates for a Four-Person Household: Notice of the Federal Fiscal Year (FFY) 2013 State Median Income Estimates for Use Under the Low Income Home Energy Assistance Program (LIHEAP)." Last modified March 15, 2012. https://www.federalregister.gov/articles/2012/03/15/2012-6220/state-median-income-estimates-for-a-four-person-household-notice-of-the-federal-fiscal-year-ffy-2013#t-1.

Luhby, Tami. 2014. "Income is on the rise . . . finally!" Accessed April 10, 2015. http://money.cnn.com/2014/08/20/news/economy/median-income/.

Meyer, Ali. 2015. "56,023,000: Record Number of Women Not in Labor Force." CNSNews.com. Accessed March 16, 2015. http://cnsnews.com/news/article/ali-meyer/56023000-record-number-women-not-labor-force.

Orshansky, Mollie. "Children of the Poor." *Social Security Bulletin*. 26 no. 7 (1963): 3–13. http://www.ssa.gov/policy/docs/ssb/v26n7/v26n7p3.pdf.

The World Bank. "Data: Poverty Headcount Ratio at $1.25 a Day (PPP) (% of Population)." http://data.worldbank.org/indicator/SI.POV.DDAY.

U.S. Department of Commerce: United States Census Bureau. "American FactFinder." http://factfinder2.census.gov/faces/nav/jsf/pages/index.xhtml.

U.S. Department of Commerce: United States Census Bureau. "Current Population Survey (CPS): CPS Table Creator." http://www.census.gov/cps/data/cpstablecreator.html.

U.S. Department of Commerce: United States Census Bureau. "Income: Table F-6. Regions—Families (All Races) by Median and Mean Income." http://www.census.gov/hhes/www/income/data/historical/families/.

U.S. Department of Commerce: United States Census Bureau. "Poverty: Poverty Thresholds." Last modified 2012. http://www.census.gov/hhes/www/poverty/data/threshld/.

U.S. Department of Health & Human Services. 2015. "2015 Poverty Guidelines." Accessed April 10, 2015. http://www.medicaid.gov/medicaid-chip-program-information/by-topics/eligibility/downloads/2015-federal-poverty-level-charts.pdf.

U.S. Department of Health & Human Services. 2015. "Information on Poverty and Income Statistics: A Summary of 2014 Current Population Survey Data." Accessed April 13, 2015. http://aspe.hhs.gov/hsp/14/povertyandincomeest/ib_poverty2014.pdf.

Congressional Budget Office. 2015. "The Effects of Potential Cuts in SNAP Spending on Households With Different Amounts of Income." Accessed April 13, 2015. https://www.cbo.gov/publication/49978.

Falk, Gene. Congressional Research Service. "The Temporary Assistance for Needy Families (TANF) Block Grant: Responses to Frequently Asked Questions." Last modified October 17, 2013. http://www.fas.org/sgp/crs/misc/RL32760.pdf.

Library of Congress. "Congressional Research Service." http://www.loc.gov/crsinfo/about/.

Office of Management and Budget. "Fiscal Year 2013 Historical Tables: Budget of the U.S. Government." http://www.whitehouse.gov/sites/default/files/omb/budget/fy2013/assets/hist.pdf.

Tax Policy Center: Urban Institute and Brookings Institution. "The Tax Policy Briefing Book: Taxation and the Family: What is the Earned Income Tax Credit?" http://www.taxpolicycenter.org/briefing-book/key-elements/family/eitc.cfm.

Frank, Robert H., and Philip J. Cook. *The Winner-Take-All Society*. New York: Martin Kessler Books at The Free Press, 1995.

Institute of Education Sciences: National Center for Education Statistics. "Fast Facts: Degrees Conferred by Sex and Race." http://nces.ed.gov/fastfacts/display.asp?id=72.

Nhan, Doris. "Census: More in U.S. Report Nontraditional Households." *National Journal*. Last modified May 1, 2012. http://www.nationaljournal.com/thenextamerica/demographics/census-more-in-u-s-report-nontraditional-households-20120430.

U.S. Bureau of Labor Statistics: BLS Reports. "Report 1040: Women in the Labor Force: A Databook." Last modified March 26, 2013. http://www.bls.gov/cps/wlf-databook-2012.pdf.

U.S. Department of Commerce: United States Census Bureau. "Income: Table H-2. Share of Aggregate Income Received by Each Fifth and Top 5 Percent of Households." http://www.census.gov/hhes/www/income/data/historical/household/.

United States Census Bureau. 2014. "2013 Highlights." Accessed April 13, 2015. http://www.census.gov/hhes/www/poverty/about/overview/.

United States Census Bureau. 2014. "Historical Income Tables: Households: Table H-2 Share of Aggregate Income Received by Each Fifth and Top 5% of Income. All Races." Accessed April 13, 2015. http://www.census.gov/hhes/www/income/data/historical/household/.

Board of Governors of the Federal Reserve System. "Research Resources: Survey of Consumer Finances." Last modified December 13, 2013. http://www.federalreserve.gov/econresdata/scf/scfindex.htm.

Congressional Budget Office. "The Distribution of Household Income and Federal Taxes, 2008 and 2009." Last modified July 10, 2012. http://www.cbo.gov/publication/43373.

Huang, Chye-Ching, and Nathaniel Frentz. "Myths and Realities About the Estate Tax." *Center on Budget and Policy Priorities*. Last modified August 29, 2013. http://www.cbpp.org/files/estatetaxmyths.pdf.

## Information, Risk, and Insurance

Center on Budget and Policy Priorities. 2015. "Policy Basics: Where Do Our Federal Tax Dollars Go?" Accessed April 1, 2015. http://www.cbpp.org/cms/?fa=view&id=1258.

Consumer Reports. "Consumer Reports.org." http://www.consumerreports.org/cro/index.htm.

Federal Trade Commission. "About the Federal Trade Commission." Last modified October 17, 2013. http://www.ftc.gov/ftc/about.shtm.

Huffington Post. 2015. "HUFFPOLLSTER: Poll Shows Uptick In Obamacare Favorable Rating." Accessed April 1, 2015. http://www.huffingtonpost.com/2015/03/19/affordable-care-act-fav_n_6900938.html.

Kahneman, Daniel, and Amos Tversky. "Prospect Theory: An Analysis of Decision under Risk." *Econometrica*. 47, no. 2 (1979): 263-291. http://www.princeton.edu/~kahneman/docs/Publications/prospect_theory.pdf.

Rasmussen Reports, LLC. "Rasmussen Reports." http://www.rasmussenreports.com/.

Central Intelligence Agency. "The World Factbook." https://www.cia.gov/library/publications/the-world-factbook/index.html.

National Association of Insurance Commissioners. "National Association of Insurance Commissioners & The Center for Insurance Policy and Research." http://www.naic.org/.

OECD. "The Organisation for Economic Co-operation and Development (OECD)." http://www.oecd.org/about/.

USA Today. 2015. "Uninsured Rates Drop Dramatically under Obamacare." Accessed April 1, 2015. http://www.usatoday.com/story/news/nation/2015/03/16/uninsured-rates-drop-sharply-under-obamacare/24852325/.

Thaler, Richard H., and Sendhil Mullainathan. "The Concise Encyclopedia of Economics: Behavioral Economics." *Library of Economics and Liberty*. http://www.econlib.org/library/Enc/BehavioralEconomics.html.

Henry J. Kaiser Family Foundation, The. "Health Reform: Summary of the Affordable care Act." Last modified April 25, 2013. http://kff.org/health-reform/fact-sheet/summary-of-new-health-reform-law/.

## Financial Markets

National Venture Capital Association. "Recent Stats & Studies." http://www.nvca.org/index.php?option=com_content&view=article&id=344&Itemid=103Update.

Freddie Mac. 2015. "Freddie Mac Update: March 2015." Accessed April 13, 2015. http://www.freddiemac.com/investors/pdffiles/investor-presentation.pdf.

Former, Jamie D. "Should Your Small Business Go Public? Consider the Benefits and Risks of Becoming a Publicly Traded Company." *U.S. Small Business Administration: Community Blog (blog)*. Publication date March 23, 2010. http://www.sba.gov/community/blogs/community-blogs/business-law-advisor/should-your-small-business-go-public-consider-0.

Howley, Kathleen M. Bloomberg. "Home Value Highest Since '07 as U.S. Houses Make Cash." Last modified March 26, 2013. http://www.bloomberg.com/news/2013-03-26/home-value-highest-since-07-as-u-s-houses-make-cash-mortgages.html.

NASDAQ.com. 2015. "Facebook, Inc. Historical Stock Prices." Accessed March 28, 2015. http://www.nasdaq.com/symbol/fb/historical.

National Association of Realtors. 2015. "Existing-Home Sales: Latest News." Accessed April 1, 2015. http://www.realtor.org/topics/existing-home-sales/data.

PricewaterhouseCoopers LLP. 2015. "Annual Venture Capital Investment Tops $48 Billion in 2014, Reaching Hightest Level in Over a Decade, According to the Moneytree Report." Accessed April 1, 2015. http://www.pwc.com/us/en/press-releases/2015/annual-venture-capital-investment-tops-48-billion.jhtml.

Rooney, Ben. "Trading Program Sparked May 'Flash Crash'." *CNN Money*. Last modified October 1, 2010. http://money.cnn.com/2010/10/01/markets/SEC_CFTC_flash_crash/index.htm.

Investment Company Institute. "2013 Investment Company Fact Book, Chapter 6: Characteristics of Mutual Fund Owners." http://icifactbook.org/fb_ch6.html.

U.S. Department of Commerce: United States Census Bureau. "Income: Table H-13. Educational Attainment of Householder—Households with Householder 25 Years Old and Over by Median and Mean Income." http://www.census.gov/hhes/www/income/data/historical/household/.

United States Department of Labor. Bureau of Labor Statistics. 2015. "Table 9. Quartiles and Selected Deciles of Usual Weekly Earnings of Full-Time Wage and Salary Workers by Selected Characteristics, 2014 Annual Averages." Accessed April 1, 2015. http://www.bls.gov/news.release/wkyeng.t09.htm.

## Public Economy

Olson, Mancur. *The Logic of Collective Action: Public Goods and the Theory of Groups*, (Boston: Harvard University Press, 1965).

Downs, Anthony. *An Economic Theory of Democracy*. New York: Harper, 1957.

Skinner, B.F. *Walden Two*. Indianapolis: Hackett Publishing Company, Inc., 1948.

American Civil Liberties Union (ACLU). "Voting Rights." https://www.aclu.org/voting-rights.

The New York Times. "The 2012 Money Race: Compare the Candidates." http://elections.nytimes.com/2012/campaign-finance.

The Washington Post. "Exit Polls 2012: Where Americans Stood this Election." Last modified November 7, 2012. http://www.washingtonpost.com/wp-srv/special/politics/2012-exit-polls/national-breakdown/.

Cornell University Law School: Legal Information Institute. "Citizens United v. Federal Election Committee (No. 08-205)." Last modified January 21, 2010. http://www.law.cornell.edu/supct/html/08-205.ZS.html.

U.S. Department of Commerce: United States Census Bureau. "Voting and Registration: Historical Time Series Tables; Table A-9: Reported Voting Rates in Presidential Election Years, by Selected Characteristics: November 1964 to 2012." http://www.census.gov/hhes/www/socdemo/voting/publications/historical/index.html

Roper Center Public Opinion Archives. "A Brief History of Public Opinion on the Government's Role in Providing Health Care." Last modified September 23, 2013.

U.S. Department of Commerce: United States Census Bureau. "Voting and Registration: Historical Time Series Tables; Table A-10: Reported Registration Rates in Presidential Election Years, by Selected Characteristics: November 1968 to 2012." http://www.census.gov/hhes/www/socdemo/voting/publications/historical/index.html

Nixon, Ron. "American Candy Makers. Pinched by Inflated Sugar Prices. Look Abroad." *The New York Times*. Last modified October 30, 2013. http://www.nytimes.com/2013/10/31/us/american-candy-makers-pinched-by-inflated-sugar-prices-look-abroad.html?_r=0.

Hufbauer, Gary Clyde, and Sean Lowry. "U.S. Tire Tariffs: Saving Few Jobs at High Cost (Policy Brief 12-9)." *Peterson Institute for International Economics.* Last modified April 2012.

## International Trade

Krugman, Paul R. *Pop Internationalism.* The MIT Press, Cambridge. 1996.

Krugman, Paul R. "What Do Undergrads Need to Know about Trade?" *American Economic Review* 83, no. 2. 1993. 23-26.

Ricardo, David. *On the Principles of Political Economy and Taxation.* London: John Murray, 1817.

Ricardo, David. "On the Principles of Political Economy and Taxation." *Library of Economics and Liberty.* http://www.econlib.org/library/Ricardo/ricP.html.

Bernstein, William J. *A Splendid Exchange: How Trade Shaped the World.* Atlantic Monthly Press. New York. 2008.

U.S. Census Bureau. 2015. "U.S. International Trade in Goods and Services: December 2014." Accessed April 13, 2015. http://www.bea.gov/newsreleases/international/trade/2015/pdf/trad1214.pdf.

U.S. Census Bureau. U.S. Bureau of Economic Analysis. 2015. "U.S. International Trade in Goods and Services February 2015." Accessed April 10, 2015. https://www.census.gov/foreign-trade/Press-Release/current_press_release/ft900.pdf.

Vernengo, Matias. "What Do Undergraduates Really Need to Know About Trade and Finance?" in *Political Economy and Contemporary Capitalism: Radical Perspectives on Economic Theory and Policy*, ed. Ron Baiman, Heather Boushey, and Dawn Saunders. M. E. Sharpe Inc, 2000. Armonk. 177-183.

World Trade Organization. "The Doha Round." Accessed October 2013. http://www.wto.org/english/tratop_e/dda_e/dda_e.htm.

The World Bank. "Data: World Development Indicators." Accessed October 2013. http://data.worldbank.org/data-catalog/world-development-indicators.

## Globalization and Protectionism

Bureau of Labor Statistics. "Industries at a Glance." Accessed December 31, 2013. http://www.bls.gov/iag/.

Oxfam International. Accessed January 6, 2014. http://www.oxfam.org/.

Bureau of Labor Statistics. "Data Retrieval: Employment, Hours, and Earnings (CES)." Last modified February 1, 2013. http://www.bls.gov/webapps/legacy/cesbtab1.htm.

Dhillon, Kiran. 2015. "Why Are U.S. Oil Imports Falling?" Time.com. Accessed April 1, 2015. http://time.com/67163/why-are-u-s-oil-imports-falling/.

Kristof, Nicholas. "Let Them Sweat." *The New York Times*, June 25, 2002. http://www.nytimes.com/2002/06/25/opinion/let-them-sweat.html.

Kohut, Andrew, Richard Wike, and Juliana Horowitz. "The Pew Global Attitudes Project." *Pew Research Center.* Last modified October 4, 2007. http://www.pewglobal.org/files/pdf/258.pdf.

Lutz, Hannah. 2015. "U.S. Auto Exports Hit Record in 2014." Automotive News. Accessed April 1, 2015. http://www.autonews.com/article/20150206/OEM01/150209875/u.s.-auto-exports-hit-record-in-2014.

United States Department of Labor. Bureau of Labor Statistics. 2015. "Employment Situation Summary." Accessed April 1, 2015. http://www.bls.gov/news.release/empsit.nr0.htm.

United States Department of Commerce. "About the Department of Commerce." Accessed January 6, 2014. http://www.commerce.gov/about-department-commerce.

United States International Trade Commission. "About the USITC." Accessed January 6, 2014. http://www.usitc.gov/press_room/about_usitc.htm.

E. Helpman, and O. Itskhoki, "Labour Market Rigidities, Trade and Unemployment," *The Review of Economic Studies*, 77. 3 (2010): 1100-1137.

M.J. Melitz, and D. Trefler. "Gains from Trade when Firms Matter." *The Journal of Economic Perspectives*, 26.2 (2012): 91-118.

Rauch, J. "Was Mancur Olson Wrong?" *The American*, February 15, 2013. http://www.american.com/archive/2013/february/was-mancur-olson-wrong.

Office of the United States Trade Representative. "U.S. Trade Representative Froman Announces FY 2014 WTO Tariff-Rate Quota Allocations for Raw Cane Sugar, Refined and Specialty Sugar and Sugar-Containing Products."Accessed January 6, 2014. http://www.ustr.gov/about-us/press-office/press-releases/2013/september/WTO-trq-for-sugar.

The World Bank. "Merchandise trade (% of GDP)." Accessed January 4, 2014. http://data.worldbank.org/indicator/TG.VAL.TOTL.GD.ZS.

World Trade Organization. 2014. "Annual Report 2014." Accessed April 1, 2015. https://www.wto.org/english/res_e/booksp_e/anrep_e/anrep14_chap10_e.pdf.

# INDEX